THE CROSS OF ST PATRICK

The Catholic Unionist Tradition in Ireland

JOHN BIGGS-DAVISON
and
GEORGE CHOWDHARAY-BEST

THE KENSAL PRESS

British Library in Publication Data.
Biggs-Davison, John
The Cross of Saint Patrick: the Catholic Unionist tradition in Ireland.
Ulster Unionist Party—History 2. Catholics—Northern Ireland—History 3. Christianity and politics
1. Title II. Chowdharay-Best, George

305.6'2'0416   BR115.P7

ISBN 0-946041-26-1

Published by The Kensal Press
Kensal House, Abbotsbrook, Bourne End, Buckinghamshire.

Printed and bound in Great Britain by
Butler & Tanner Ltd., Frome & London

Typeset by Tek, England

PREFACE

This book is needed and traverses new ground. Told that it was being prepared, a highly educated politician, who shall be nameless, replied: 'But were there any Catholic Unionists?' He reminds one of us of the Member of Parliament (unfortunately untypical) who was being briefed on the Royal Ulster Constabulary by an Assistant Chief Constable, who happened to be a Roman Catholic, and asked him whether there were any Catholics in the police.

This book is dedicated to those many Catholics who wrote and spoke and who fought and died in foreign wars and Irish troubles, faithful to the crown and loyal to the Union. Theirs was a noble, and living, cause, and the title of this book symbolizes both cause and sacrifice.

The earliest Irish (as distinct from Norman-Irish or Anglo-Irish) device known is the red hand of the O'Neills, which one of us chose as the emblem of his earlier book, *The Hand is Red*. But the red saltire of St Patrick, too, is of a respectable antiquity. It appears in the arms of the FitzGeralds of Kildare from at least the fifteenth century, and G.A. Hayes-McCoy in his posthumously-published and definitive *History of Irish Flags* (1979) has pointed to evidence of its use as an Irish national flag at least as early as 1612. In 1783 it was included in the badge of the Knights of St Patrick, the Irish counterpart of the Order of the Garter in England and of the Thistle in Scotland. The FitzGeralds of Kildare became Dukes of Leinster after 1766; a FitzGerald remains premier Duke of Ireland; and the Republic's *Oireachtas* or Parliament occupies Leinster House, the former ducal residence in Dublin, today. Even more germane to our story is the fact that it was one of the FitzGeralds who gave his name to the first major Unionist document in the strict sense, the Leinster Declaration of 1830, which was drawn up by a Catholic solicitor and signed by many of his co-religionists as well as by Protestants.

When the Union between Great Britain and Ireland was formally ratified in 1801, the cross saltire of St Patrick was incorporated in the Union Flag, where it has remained to this day. The justification of that continued inclusion lies in the fact of Northern Ireland's still being an integral element in that Union. The breakaway of the south has led to much bloodshed, and, in the long perspective of centuries, may come to be seen as merely an episode in an association sometimes violent, sometimes peaceful. At any rate the events of the last century and more have failed to destroy friendships and mutual esteem, which in individual cases have grown rather than diminished. Long may that friendship survive.

We acknowledge our debt to the following individuals and institutions, and if any through inadvertence have been missed out we ask their forgiveness — but any mistakes are ours alone: the late Major Eric Beaumont, Dr Mary Belton, Mr Louis Boyle, The British Library, Mr Robin Chichester-Clarke, Mr Alistair B. Cooke, the late 12th Earl of Fingall, Mr Adrian FitzGerald, Dr Roy Foster, Sir James Henry, Bt., The Library of the House of Commons, The London Library, Dr A.P. Malcomson, Dr H. Montgomery Hyde, The National Library of Ireland (Dublin), His Grace the Duke of Norfolk, K.G. and His Grace's Librarian and Assistant Librarian, Mr Bill O'Hara, Sir John Pope-Hennessy, Public Record Office (London), Public Record Office of Northern Ireland (Belfast), Professor Robert Shackleton, F.B.A.

We also thank Miss Fay Stockwell and Miss Virginia Utley and, above all, our wives Pamela and Elspeth for their encouragement and forbearance.

Contents

Illustrations

The tenth Earl of Ormonde's instructions for a parley with O'Neill. (1599)

Father James Healy of Little Bray.

Sir John Ross-of-Bladensburg.

Dr. John Healy, Catholic Archbishop of Tuam.

Henry, 15th Duke of Norfolk as Lord Mayor of Sheffield by E. Moore.
Arundel Castle. By permission of His Grace the Duke of Norfolk.

Sir Denis Henry, Bt by permission of Sir James Henry, Bt.

Edmund, 1st Viscount FitzAlan of Derwent by Oswald Birley.
Arundel Castle. By permission of His Grace the Duke of Norfolk.

C. E. McGloughlin 1866–1932 taken in 1930.

PART I

The Union and its Aftermath

CHAPTER ONE

Introduction

The just interest of the crown of England is only preserved in
Ireland by maintaining in a high state the true conquerors of
that kingdom, who by their blood annexed the Irish crown to
the English diadem, for which the Kings of England stand for
ever indebted unto their bravery. Those victors, being Catholicks,
landed from England in Ireland, under the happy Fortune of
Henry the second . . . Their posterity have continued in the like
gallantry and loyalty even to this day, propping the true kings
of England, at the hazard of their lives and fortunes, while the
upstart Protestants have of late years endeavoured to cast down
those crowned heads, and actually prevailed.
A Jacobite Narrative of the War in Ireland 1688-91, ed.
J.J. Gilbert (Dublin, 1892), p.5.

'Where does Irish history begin?' Eoin McNeill asked at University
College, Dublin, in 1904.[1] For most nationalists it began with the Gael.
The history of the United States of America began with the Thirteen
Colonies. In North America the Redskin, in Ireland, the Cruthin or
Picts, have only the rights of the vanquished and the massacred.

The Geraldines and the Gaelic chieftains of the sixteenth century
warred with the English crown; but, as the Young Irelander John
Mitchel remarked in his *Life of Hugh O'Neill,* published in 1846,

There was in the 16th century, no Irish nation . . . Save the tie
of a common language, the chieftain of Clan-Conal O'Donnell
had no more connexion with the Lord of Clan-Carrha Cork
than either had with the English Pale. The Anglo-Norman
colony was regarded rather as one of the independent tribes of
the island.[2]

It was not for any Irish nation in the modern sense that Hugh
O'Neill fought and won the battle of the Yellow Ford.

Many of those reckoned as early champions of national independence were Anglo-Norman or Old English.[3] The Confederation of Kilkenny was pledged to loyalty to the Stuarts. The Old Englishman St Oliver Plunket, fell victim to the 'Popish Plot' against the monarchy to which he was devoted.

By contrast, the separatist republicans of French Revolutionary inspiration were, in the main, Protestants or Presbyterians, free-thinkers, quasi-Jacobins. Neither Wolfe Tone nor Lord Edward FitzGerald nor Robert Emmet was of Gaelic stock or Catholic faith. At its inception the parliamentary Union was a cause for Catholics. It was contested by Orangemen. Whatever Stormont was or was not, theirs in Dublin was assuredly a Protestant parliament for a Protestant people. Charles Stewart Parnell was not of the Gael. Isaac Butt and Joseph Gillis Biggar of the Irish Republican Brotherhood were Protestants. The latter, an Ulster Presbyterian, eventually became a Catholic. Yet the catacomb mentality instilled by the memory of Penal days and a sense of Catholic and Gaelic identity were tributaries to the stream of Irish nationalism.

The separatist struggles were made up of religious, racial and class ingredients. For a peasant population the land mattered more than almost everything. Absenteeism, evictions, boycotts, famine, emigration dimmed the lustre of the Union. But land purchase by the occupier, subsidized by Government, went far towards the killing of Home Rule by kindness. George Wyndham, the Tory Chief Secretary, who enacted the great Land Purchase measure, ended thus his chapter contributed in 1912 to the symposium, *Against Home Rule: The Case for Union:* 'The Unionist policy of Land Purchase vindicates the Union . . . and . . . the treatment it has received demonstrates the futility, and the tragedy, of granting Home Rule'.[4]

Not that land purchase made every peasant a Unionist. The Gaelic League and the Gaelic Athletic Association nourished a sentiment that was divisive both of the Union and of Ireland. In Ulster, the province of 'tenant right', land purchase strengthened the Union and lent popular and loyal support to the natural and Unionist leadership exercised by a squirearchy of military service and tradition.

Ulster had always been different. Ulster is fourteen miles from the British mainland. Scotland is visible from Antrim. Sir William Petty, who made that Cromwellian Domesday Book, the Down Survey, may well have thought of attaching Ulster to Scotland. The notion was revived at the time of the third Home Rule Bill. Rathlin Island, north of Antrim, scene of Bruce's encounter with the spider, has been a Tom

Tiddler's ground for Irishman and Scot.[5] Ulster was cut off from the rest of Ireland by forests, bogs, and loughs.

Ulster's distinct identity is older than partition, older than the plantations (which were of Catholics as well as Protestants), older even than the Gaelic conquerors who built a Great Wall of Ulster, the Black Pigs' Dyke, from Carlingford Lough to Donegal Bay. Ulster, always different, was the last of the old provinces to be forced into England's united Ireland. In the north of Ireland, as in the north of England, old allegiances and old faith persisted and resisted longest, whether against de Courcy's English knights who carried Norman banners to the Giant's Causeway or under the great O'Neill who led the last stand of the northern chiefs in Gaelic reaction against Tudor modernity.

The north of Ireland, like the north of England, fought longest for the old Catholic order but was first to undergo the industrial revolution. Burke, Nassau Senior, Macaulay, W.F. Monypenny, identified two countries, peoples, nations in Ireland.[6] Ulster capitalist and Ulster workers came to value the Union as the gateway to British, imperial and world markets. Clyde and Mersey were more real than Shannon and Liffey. Carson pronounced it intolerable for industrial Ulster, whose economic fortunes were so closely tied to those of Great Britain, to be placed 'at the mercy of and governed by . . . some three or four hundred thousand small farmers, with the labourers attached, in the south and west of Ireland'.[7]

The movement he inspired was not of class but of the masses. Parnell and Gladstone achieved what Eoin McNeill, a historian and inaugurator of the Irish Volunteers, described in 1913 as a 'wonderful state of things' in Ulster: the coming together against Home Rule of 'the Orange industrial workers, mainly Church of Ireland Protestants; the Presbyterian rural community; and the remnant of the feudal aristocracy.'[8]

As Lord Dunsany's son, Horace Plunkett, Unionist and Irish patriot, put it:

> The question which the Nationalists had to answer in 1886 and 1893 [the years of the first two Home Rule Bills], and which they have to answer today, is this:— In the Ireland of their conception is the Unionist part of Ulster to be coerced or persuaded to come under the new regime? To those who adopt the former alternative my reply is simply that, if England is to do the coercion, the idea is politically absurd. If we were left to fight it out among ourselves, it is physically absurd. The task of

the Empire in South Africa was light compared with that which the Nationalist would have on their hands. I am aware that, at the time when we were all talking at concert pitch on the Irish Question, a good deal was said about dying in the last ditch by men who at the threat of any real trouble would be found more discreetly perched on the first fence. But those who know the temper and fighting qualities of the working-men opponents of Home Rule in the North are under no illusion as to the account they would give of themselves if called upon to defend the cause of Protestantism, liberty, and imperial unity as they understand it.[9]

At the turn of the century Ireland and not merely Ulster was prosperous. The Fenian nightmare had faded. "Physical force" to achieve the political end was in abeyance. The centenary of '98 caused small stir and in 1899 the Irish regiments were in South Africa as "Soldiers of the Queen", although on embarking, some of them cheered for Kruger! That there were also Irish with the Boers was part of the pattern of their history.

When a greater war broke out the rival political armies, nationalist and Unionist, entered the king's service. They had a prosperous land to defend. Speaking in Dublin on 1st July 1915, John Redmond could say that:

Today the people, broadly speaking, own the soil . . . the labourers live in decent habitations . . . there is absolute freedom in local government and taxation . . . we have the widest Parliamentary and municipal franchise . . . the congested districts[10] have been transformed . . . farms have been enlarged, decent dwellings have been provided.[11]

In 1920 Carson, denouncing as 'mad' the giving up of Irish representation in the imperial parliament, recalled that 'Every injustice and every harm committed on Ireland . . . were inflicted before the Union and not since the Union.'[12] At Easter 1916 Kilmainham Gaol was emptier than the nigh-vacant Bastille in 1789.[13]

As in India, so in Ireland, partition was the price of self-determination. In order to quit, the British had to split. The transfer of power both at Dublin Castle and at New Delhi ended an imperial unity. In the south of Ireland those most clamorous for the unity of the island did most to smash symbols cherished in the north and to break down the bridges. The Dominion Home Rule advocated by Plunkett and others and accepted by many southern Irish Unionists proved but a springboard from which the separatist republic could be gained. This Carson and Leo Amery and others had predicted. Others have argued that if only the Six Counties had not opted out the balance would have been tilted against the neutral republic and in favour of the crown and commonwealth. But it is useless to talk in terms of compromise, which was so alien to Ireland, or of democratic majorities and combinations. Too much of Ireland's story is written in blood by armed bands.

That story has been distorted by myth and propaganda. The great myth, the big lie, is the equation of 'Catholic' with 'nationalist' or 'republican'. For this there is no warrant in theology. We show in these pages that there is no warrant in history either.

CHAPTER TWO

Before 1700

In the mists of ancient history Ireland was seen as a threat to Britain. Even in Gaul, according to one semi-legendary source, they trembled at Irish galleys.[1] For good or for ill — many think for ill — Ireland was occupied neither by the Caesars nor by the Norman Conqueror of England, though there is a record of temporary invasion by Egfrid, King of Northumberland, in 684 and by Edgar at a later date. Through centuries of tribal rule there were several kingdoms and sometimes a high king. A deposed king, Dermot (Diarmait) Mac Murchada, fled to England and to Aquitaine to seek help from the Angevin king of England, Henry II. With ecclesiastical and exchequer backing he returned to Ireland, came to terms with his enemies and brought a Fitzstephen and a FitzGerald to form a vanguard for the invasion by the motley forces of a feudal 'European Community' that stretched from Scotland to Spain. Henry aspired to be emperor, although G.H. Orpen's view of the expedition to Ireland as an expression of Henrician ambition has been criticized by W.L. Warren, who points out that it rests on very fragile evidence, and that the papal bull *Laudabiliter* reads to him 'more like an attempt to encourage a hesitant King'.[2]

The Pope, Adrian IV, was the Englishman Nicholas Breakspear, and the Anglo-Norman conquest was in a sense a Catholic enterprise. The 'English' came to Ireland as Catholics with the papal commission to take order with the Irish Church, and while Sir James O'Connor may have exaggerated when he said that 'it is to the English we owe Roman Catholicism'[3], it is nevertheless a fact that the episcopal system adopted under St Patrick and his successors was far different from what it afterwards became. In 1171 the second 'Strongbow' Earl of Pembroke became King of Leinster and Henry landed at Waterford where a bevy of Irish chieftains made their submission. The synod of Cashel accepted the supremacy, under Rome, of Armagh and 'the usage of the Church of England' for the divine offices.

The Pope had made the express condition that the English crown should uphold the rights of the Irish Church and people. In 1310 an Irish parliament enacted that 'no mere Irishman *(nullus merus hibernicus)* shall be received into a religious order among the English in the land of peace.'[4]

The 'land of peace' (subsequently known as 'the Pale', because it was regarded as, figuratively speaking, 'fenced off') consisted of shires distinguished both from the march lands held by feudal Lords and from the 'land of war' beyond England's sway, whilst 'mere Irishmen' were Gaels of the independent races, not subject to the settlers. It was the English Archbishop of Armagh, Walter Jorz (Joyce) who appealed successfully to Edward II for the repeal of the Act, which was revoked almost at once, though it continued to work mischief for a little while due to unawareness, in those distant days of poor communications, of its abrogation. In 1317 Donal O'Neill and other chiefs made remonstrance to the Avignon Pope John XXII (who had embraced Edward II's cause against the Bruces) concerning the oppressive violation of Adrian IV's grant, particularly that part of it safeguarding the Church. They alleged slavery: 'The English of Ireland . . . lay and cleric assert that it is no more sin to kill an Irishman than it is to kill a dog'.

There were thus Irish parliaments early on, and Irish parliaments that could be as oppressive as they were unrepresentative. Richardson and Sayles date the holding of them in Ireland back to an assembly at Castledermot in mid-June 1264; elected representatives are present from 1297.[5] Irish business also came before the English parliament at this time, especially between 1290 and 1310, and Edward I summoned barons, prelates and citizens to serve in England for this purpose. There was also such Irish representation under Edward III, for in July 1376 the Justiciars of Ireland and the Archbishop of Dublin were required to issue writs to the commons of several counties, cities and boroughs for 'reasonable expenses' of travel and maintenance for 'the men of Ireland last coming to the council in England'.[6] Such references are, however, few, for by this time the practice of sending parliamentary representatives to England was falling into disuse. Danger, difficulty, and distance — thus William Molyneux, member of parliament for Dublin University in both of the Irish parliaments of William III — militated in favour of Irish parliaments.

According to the chroniclers Roger of Hoveden and Benedict of Peterborough, Henry II was received 'for King and Lord of Ireland' ('receperunt eum in regem et dominum Hyberniae').[7] However, the title 'King' in relation to Ireland very soon fell into disuse, particularly when Henry appointed his son John to the lordship. When John succeeded his father, the lordship was re-united with the crown, but again in 1254 Edward, eldest son of Henry III, was appointed separately to that office by his father. This created problems with the king's officials, and the experiment was not repeated; but there was nevertheless a vague idea, disputed by some, that the King of England held Ireland not as sovereign, but as mesne lord to His Holiness the Pope. Hence the persistence of the title until in Henry VIII's reign it was firmly asserted that 'the Kings highnesse, his heyres and successours, Kings of England, be alwayes Kings of this land of Ireland'.[8] Indeed, Con O'Neill submitted to King Henry as 'the Supreme Head on Earth, immediately under Christ, of the Church of England and Ireland'.[9]

Ireland shared at least the forms of English constitutional development. Her parliaments were bicameral. Unlike the colonies, she had a House of Lords and was ruled by 'King, Lords and Commons in Parliament assembled'. But, as a consequence of Lambert Simnel's impostorship, that parliament's legislative function was, from 1495, restricted to consenting to, or rejecting, Bills which had been previously approved by the English privy council, although an explanatory statute passed under Philip and Mary made it plain that if something unforeseen occurred during the course of an Irish parliament, that too could be made the subject of an Irish Bill, provided that the consent of England was duly obtained under the Great Seal. In 1782 the Act was further modified.[10]

Philip and Mary are also notable in Irish history for having given their names to Philipstown and Maryborough (formerly Dengan) and to the King's and Queen's Counties (formerly Leix and Offaly together with other places) in which they were situated.[11] In the same year (1556) provision was made for the 'disposition' (i.e. plantation) of those counties by 'English or Irish, borne within this realme, or within the realme of England'.[12] There were indeed Catholic before there were Protestant planters in Ireland, and even so early we find reference in an Irish statute to 'Scottes [having] of late inhabited in the northe partes of this realme in severall places' and having 'oute thereof expulsed the verrie inheritours of the same'.[13] James I and VI, a Scotsman himself, repealed, as might be expected, this particular Act, but not all of his planters, even in Ulster, were Protestants.[14]

Parliaments might sit within the Pale. Beyond the Pale, Brehon law, rather than the king's writ, ran. To the centralizing Tudor monarchy the interposition of mesne lords between the crown and common subject was repugnant. To the Irish way of thinking, though no doubt a few regarded it as a compliment, to convert an O'Neill and other patriarchal chiefs into peers was an affront. Nevertheless it is interesting to note how far, amidst all the turbulence of the sixteenth century, Irish loyalty to the crown remained unshaken. 'One of the most striking incidents in Irish history', stated Eleanor Hull, was 'the stern rebuke delivered in Armagh Cathedral by Richard Creagh ("the Pope's Primate") to Shane O'Neill who, with his army of 600 men, attended the sermon in the expectation that his new Archbishop, recently arrived with his papal commission, would encourage his men to fight against his enemies'. Creagh 'sharply called on him to forsake his disloyal courses and return to his allegiance'.[15] This was in the early part of Gloriana's reign: no less striking was the submission of the Irish Church to the king rather than the Pope when on the death of the Primate of All Ireland, George Cromer, in 1543, Henry appointed George Dowdall, a man whom the Pope refused to confirm. Indeed His Holiness responded by nominating Robert Wauchope or Waucop to the primacy; but although Wauchope sat in the Council of Trent, he was never acknowledged in Ireland, and was passed over even in Queen Mary's time when the primatial see again became vacant.[16]

At this time the Church of Ireland continued undivided and, in form, Catholic. In 1521 Sir Thomas More had complained that, in King Henry's book against Luther, the Pope's authority was too 'highly advanced and with strong arguments mightily defended'; and although in his later years the king's views changed, it was only under Edward VI that the English liturgy was introduced and Irish bishops favourable to reform gradually appointed. The Primate of All Ireland, Archbishop Dowdall, is reported as contemptuously saying of the proposed new liturgy that then 'shall every illiterate fellow read Mass',[17] but after further exchanges he was forced to concede defeat: Archbishop Browne of Dublin was made Primate of All Ireland in his place. Dowdall left (or, as some say, was banished), and Goodacre, an Englishman, was appointed to his see in 1553, another Englishman, Bale, being consecrated Bishop of Ossory. Bale particularly favoured the use of revised services, insisting on one for his own ordination and attempting to impose the new Prayer Book on reluctant parishes. In this he was unsuccessful; and with Mary's accession was forced to retire to the continent. Dowdall was recalled and again became Primate of All Ireland. Browne and other bishops were deprived of their sees, but there were no burnings as in England. Archbishop Curwen, who succeeded Browne at Dublin, was an Englishman who combined a taste for Roman theological doctrines with a willingness to acknowledge the Royal Supremacy.

But if there was loyalty, there was also disaffection. Young Hugh O'Neill, Baron of Dungannon in Ulster, was groomed in 'English civility' for royal service in the Irish parliament, at the Court of Gloriana and in her servant Leicester's household. Like that of Harrow and Sandhurst in the decline of the British Empire, the schooling had an unintended effect. Full of the new learning of the renaissance, O'Neill took the lead of the old Catholic and Gaelic order, whose learning was of bards and brehons. He served with an English troop in the suppression of rebellion in Munster, was granted permission to keep soldiers in the queen's pay, and attired them in red coats. Then he turned his own.

O'Neill was not, however, supported by all Catholics. Many priests and friars asserted that it was lawful not only to assist the queen but also to resist the rebel party. In 1599 the tenth Earl of Ormonde issued instructions for a parley with O'Neill. He was to be acquainted that he had no title within the Pale. Further,

> You are to tell him (if he pretend he doth the same for the advancement of the Catholic religion, as he commonly giveth out) that all the inhabitants of the English Pale, for the more part, and specially myself, are Catholics, and were so when he was not thought to be one, and many of us, having heard and read more than he did, could never find in Scripture, General Council, by the Fathers, or any other authenticall authority, that subjects ought to carry arms against their anointed Christian princes . . . this gross and inexcusable ignorance is not sufficient for him to seek our destruction, who must regard our duty unto our native and gracious Prince [Queen Elizabeth I] more than what life or living he can deprive us of.[18]

O'Neill, on being presented with these terms, denied that he wished to enjoy any of the Pale for himself; he only wished to establish the Catholic religion. However, he was obliged to admit that the 'English Palemen' were a 'kind of Catholic' and his criticism of them centred on the point that such as the Lord of Delvin 'would not hazard the loss of a foot of land, or forego his good meat, drink or lodging, to advance the Catholic religion'.

It has been argued, for example by Charles Stuart Parnell's grandfather, William Parnell, that rebellions in Ireland were just as frequent when the government was Catholic as when it became

Protestant. Nevertheless the Oath of Supremacy did constitute a difficulty for many Catholics, comprising as it did a declaration that

> the Quenes Hignes is thonelye supreme Governour of this Realme . . . and that no forreine Prince Person Prelate State or Potentate hathe or oughte to have any Jurisdiccon Power Superioritee Preheminence or Authoritee Ecclesiasticall or Spiritual within this Realme.[19]

Henry VIII had however found a modicum of Irish bishops to take his own even more uncompromising oath and make him pseudo-Pope; indeed there is evidence that the Act of 1542 was greatly welcomed in Ireland, where Popes had never been universally popular. What was disturbing was the attempt to impose the English liturgy, the destruction of holy relics, and the loot of abbey lands. Where would England and Europe have been without Irish monks and missionaries? In Dublin Archbishop Browne had the *Baculum Jesu,* believed to be the staff of Christ and St Patrick's crozier, burned in public.[20] As in England, the mass continued under Henry, who clung to every Catholic doctrine compatible with his divorce, his finances, and his public policy. But the dissolution of religious houses inflicted a grievous wound in both islands but more especially in Ireland, which was poorer in towns, villages and manor houses and the cultural benefits they afforded.

Ulster, ever different and distinct in folklore and fact from the 'kingdoms of the south' against which Cu Chulainn[21] warred, held out longest for the old faith and the old ways. The northern chiefs combined for the last stand of the Gaelic reaction in the fastnesses west of Lough Neagh. The Elizabethan army in Ireland was never large. It was mainly Irish and Catholic. Many of the common people, unlike the Lords of insurrection, preferred the Tudor to Tyrone. The rebels, however, had their successes; and Essex, compelled to a truce with O'Neill, was recalled. He ended on the scaffold at Tower Hill. His successor, Sir Charles Blount, Lord Mountjoy, did better. He shut O'Neill up in Ulster , cutting him off from any allies in the south. Spain, which Mountjoy said, could 'make the War of England . . . in Ireland', lost her Armada. Only in Ulster did the castaways of the galleons find succour. Between 1587 and 1590 Archbishop Magauran of Armagh sought help from the Pope and Philip of Spain. O'Neill pursued Fabian tactics. There was a long guerilla war. In 1601 the rebels and their Spanish allies were forced to give battle and were routed at Kinsale.

The viceroy had detected 'Spanish and Papist hearts' even among the Old English of the Pale, the Old English being those of predominantly English descent who clung to the religion of their forbears whilst tending to be more loyal to the crown than their co-religionists outside.[22] We shall see more of them later. But, as on other occasions, those who put subversive inclination to the test of armed uprising were few; and Irish lords from within as well as without the Pale rode with Mountjoy at Kinsale. Thomas Stafford, in the preface to the second volume of his *Pacata Hibernica* tells of 'the loyal fidelity of the greater part of the Irish nation to their lawful prince' during the later Desmond rebellions.

These were earlier than the Tyrone rebellion and are worth further examination.

Thomas Roe FitzGerald was by birth heir apparent, according to English law, of the fourteenth Earl of Desmond, being the son of his father's first wife; but when his father died in 1558 his half-brother Gerald was chosen to succeed him. The new queen confirmed Gerald in the title.[23] But Thomas Roe was a 'much-enduring man'. Gerald quarrelled with the Earl of Ormonde and was summoned to England to make amends. He did not return until 1564, when he was involved in another quarrel, in which Ormonde was supported by Sir Maurice FitzGerald. At Affane in Waterford he had his thigh broken by Ormonde's brother and was taken prisoner. He was again summoned to London to explain his conduct, and on this occasion was, for a time, imprisoned in the Tower.[24]

Thomas, as the acting head of the family, now represented the Earl in Munster; but the Earl attempted to supersede him as his deputy by James FitzMaurice. Again there was a conflict;[25] and both were, for a time, detained, apparently on the orders of the Countess of Desmond. The government, finding that FitzMaurice was supported both by the Earl and by his Countess, backed him against Thomas. But he soon became a rebel, whilst Thomas took the side of government and was knighted on 2 September 1569. Unsuccessful attempts were made to tamper with his allegiance and he aided the government against the Butlers, who had invaded Desmond territory.

The Earl had been allowed to leave England in 1566, but on his arrival in Dublin was detained for debt. He was again arrested in 1567 and removed to London where he remained until 1573. During this period Sir Thomas remained active in support of the government, and with the president of Munster, Sir John Perrot, pursued James FitzMaurice into Tipperary, for which he received the thanks of the queen.[26]

The Earl's return was the signal for a fresh outbreak. With the help of Rory McShane McCraghe, a 'craftie and blouddie rebell', he drove Sir Thomas away from his castle at Conna and seized his wife Elice and son James. Walsh wrote to Burghley that all this was done upon a pretended challenge of right, 'yet Sir Thomas writeth all this was done because he would not combine with him against the Prince, which if he had done, all chalendge should have been cessed'.

Sir Thomas was one of the most prompt to attend upon Sir Henry Sidney when he returned to Ireland as Lord Deputy in 1575. He waited upon the deputy again, in 1576, 1579, 1580 and 1581. Ormonde, it is true, thought he was insufficiently active in the king's service, but there is no real doubt of his loyalty; nor is there any clear evidence of his ever having supported rebels against the crown.

James FitzMaurice now raised the banner of revolt, this time with the assistance of Spain. Eight hundred Spaniards and Italians landed at Smerwick, on the coast of Kerry, in 1579. They advanced in procession with a banner followed by two Jesuits and the bishop of Killaloe in full canonicals. The Earl himself held aloof, but his brother John went forward with a detachment against the forces of government.

The deputy was now Lord Grey de Wilton. He had the poet Spenser for his secretary and Ralegh came to serve under him. Grey marched south against the invaders, who parleyed, asking for terms. The deputy replied that as neither Spain nor Italy was at war with England, the rebels had no proper commission or authority; neither could they be treated as prisoners of war. Ralegh and the others under his command were ordered to give them no quarter. FitzMaurice was attacked and pursued by the Burkes (another Catholic family) and was mortally wounded.[27] Then the Earl of Desmond joined the rebels, and by November 1579 all the Geraldines were confederate, 'except Sir Thomas and his son James, Sir James of the Decies and Mr John FitzGerald, of Cloyne'. But the Earl's brother John was soon surrounded in a wood near Castle Lyons.

Sir Thomas's eldest son, known as James FitzThomas FitzGerald, repaired to London and petitioned the queen, pointing out that the Earl was not the rightful heir, concluding his petition with the words 'and he shall perpetually praye for your Majesties reigne, and sarve your gracious Highnes with all fidelitie duringe liffe'.

The queen responded by granting him a pension of a mark (66 pence) a day, and said his case would be looked into. The pension was not bad pay, for the president of Munster himself only received £130 a year. FitzThomas returned home saying that the queen had promised 'to do him justice on the death of his uncle', But after that uncle's death he was, as 'Sugan' ('wisp of straw') Earl of Desmond, to fall into rebellion, and he died in the Tower in about 1608. Sir Thomas, significantly, took no part in these proceedings, though he may have advised behind the scenes. If so, his counsel may have been for caution and quiescence, but young men are hot-blooded.

The fifteenth Earl was defeated by Captain Zouch and escaped to the Atherlow woods in Tipperary, with barely his shirt. He spent Christmas in a wood near Kilmallock, where he was surprised by some soldiers; and to avoid being seen he and his Countess had to stand up to their necks in water. The following year (1583) he was traced to a glen in Kerry. Five or six of his followers fled, and he himself was slain by one Kelly, who ignoring his cries that he was the Earl of Desmond, cut off his head and sent it to Lord Ormonde, who had it pickled. It ultimately found its way to a spike on London Bridge. The killing was unauthorized and the murderer was subsequently executed.

Thus fell the fifteenth Earl of Desmond. Thousands more perished. There was famine everywhere. The Earl's half million or more acres were split up into allotments of 12,000 acres each; Ralegh was allotted 42,000, Spenser 3,000. As for Sir Thomas, he died peacefully at Conna Castle on 18th January 1595. An active life had been devoted to queen and government, and though he felt wronged, Sir Thomas never made unreasonable demands. We never hear of his exacting revenge, imprisoning or executing anyone, nor did he plot. 'Had he been made earl', wrote the Reverend A.G. L'Estrange (*Conna & Desmond,* 1902) 'how much misery would Munster have escaped'.[28]

On the day Queen Elizabeth fell mortally sick, certain priests presented a protestation of allegiance to her English council. They declared that even if the Pope should 'excommunicate every one born within Her Majesty's dominions', they would not 'forsake the defence of Her Majesty and realms, and take part with such conspirators and invaders; in these and all other such like cases, we do think ourselves and all the lay Catholics . . . bound in conscience not to obey this or any such censure, but will defend our Prince and country, accounting it our duty to do so'.[29]

The 'shiring' of Ireland had been a long drawn-out process. At the death of Edward I the area governed by royal officials was very great. In south-east Ireland only Wexford, Kilkenny and Trim were still 'liberties'. The existence of a liberty did not, moreover, exclude the king's writ, only his sheriffs; and even the liberty of Ulster was governed by the king's officials for considerable periods in the thirteenth century. The north-western corner of Ireland was outside the sphere of shire or liberty altogether, as were a few other wild or mountainous enclaves; but elsewhere outside Ulster the king's justiciars visited in person the most distant shires, as did the itinerant justices.[30]

In the fourteenth century the area of strictly English authority became contracted, not so much because of the incursions of the Gael (Gaelic Irish) but because of the increase in power, relative to the crown, of Gaelic or gaelicized Anglo-Norman peers who held without a grant from the monarch and in many cases in defiance of a title given by feudal law. These were the so-called 'degenerate English'.[31] The position in about 1485 was that the Pale consisted of the counties of Dublin, Louth, Meath (including Westmeath) and Kildare. Within a second ring (Kilkenny, Tipperary, Carlow, Wexford, Waterford, Cork, Kerry and Limerick) the royal administration was supreme in law but in practice had only limited effectiveness. In a third group of counties (Galway, Down and Antrim) there was even less ability to enforce the king's writ; and in a fourth area (the remaining sixteen modern counties) the native Irish kingships retained their power, though there were subsidy treaties with such as the MacMurroughs, Kings of Leinster (Wicklow), the O'Connors, Kings of Offaly, and the O'Briens, Kings of Thomond (Clare).

Butler and FitzGerald alternated in power at Dublin. When there was an English lieutenant or deputy they retired to their principalities and English power diminished accordingly. As late as 1517 it was possible for Chiericati, papal nuncio at the court of Henry VIII, to write of a visit he had paid to Ireland, that the king owned 'only the third part of it, that is the places on the sea-coast', and that the rest was in the hands of 'divers lords, who . . . say that the Pope is their King. And accordingly the other lords place upon their coins the keys and the three Papal crowns'.[32]

What altered the balance was the existence, after 1534, of a standing army financed from England which made it possible for a Dublin government to intervene forcibly in local affairs outside the Pale. The impetus to do so no doubt derived in part from Henry's conflict with the Pope, but also, as has been pointed out by Brendan Bradshaw, from what he calls 'the gentry and gentry-associated professions of the Pale community, who saw their livelihoods threatened' by the magnate power outside the Pale. The development of a more vocal professional class may itself be seen as the product of renaissance and reformation, but that is another story. What we need to note here is that although, as Parnell's grandfather correctly pointed out, rebellions and feuds had been persistent during the period of the English lordship and indeed before, now for the first time there was the power and the impetus available to unify the country, perhaps for the first time, and this was ultimately achieved, though at the cost of considerable bloodshed.[33]

By the early seventeenth century, Ireland was fully shired and strategically planted. Unlike Catholicism in England and Wales, that of Ireland could not present the causes of forty martyrs in Rome. Yet Bishop O'Devaney of Connor and Down suffered for the faith in 1612; and Sir Arthur Chichester, who succeeded Mountjoy, proceeded to 'strong measure' against the papists and their priests. It would be misleading to suggest that the English government then had no enlightened policy of *'parcere subiectis et debellare superbos'*. Sincere attempts were made to reach an accommodation with Catholics. After the Gunpowder Plot, an oath of allegiance was devised which, in the words of King James, was intended

> to make a separation between so many of my subjects who although they were otherwise Popishly affected, yet retained in their hearts the print of their natural duty to their sovereign

and others who, like the 'Powder traitors', 'thought diversity of religion a safe pretext for all kinds of treasons and rebellions against their sovereign'.[34] Unlike the Oath of Supremacy, which was however retained for certain purposes,[35] it did not deny the Pope's spiritual authority over Catholics:

> For as the Oath of Supremacie was devised for putting a difference betweene Papists, and them of our profession; so was this Oath . . . ordained for making difference betweene the civilly obedient Papists and the peruerse disciples of the Powder-Treason.[36]

It confined itself, therefore, to requiring Catholics to abjure the claim of the Pope to depose the king, and to absolve his subjects from their natural obedience. Nevertheless, it raised a storm of controversy throughout Europe, to which King James's pamphlet, issued in Latin and English, was intended to reply, and papal briefs were issued three years in succession, with a fourth in 1626, condemning it. Loyal Catholics were thrown into some perplexity, and did not know which way to turn. In Ireland it was not required by any statute, but was frequently tendered to persons whose loyalty was doubtful.[37]

Another feature of the 'New Deal' was the remodelling of the Irish parliament, which has been stated to be 'more representative of the Catholic Irish and Anglo-Irish' than any previously. Sir John Davies, Attorney-General for Ireland, enlarged it from less than 100 to 232 members. A hundred of those returned in 1613 were Catholics. There were unpleasant scenes on the first day when the members were asked to choose a Speaker. Sir John Everard, a former Justice of the King's Bench who had resigned in 1607 rather than take the Oath of Supremacy, was put up, as, in effect, the Catholic candidate.[38] It was then the custom, when a vote was taken, for the ayes only to leave the chamber, the symbolism of this procedure, in the days before division lobbies, probably lying in the fact that they only were in favour of the Bill being 'carried' up to the Lords. Davies's supporters did this, whereupon the Catholic nominee, Everard, occupied the chair and refused to budge when the ayes, in a majority of about thirty, returned. Davies was then, it is said, bodily lifted into Everard's lap, and Everard forcibly removed. Ninety-eight Roman Catholics then left the House and did not return that session. Eleven Catholic peers also withdrew.

The parliament was prorogued; and after inquiring into their grievances, the king rebuked their representatives in London in a characteristic speech (12th April 1614). Professor Hugh Kearney has explained that what he calls the 'Catholic gentry of the country party', led in the Lords by Gormanston, Slane, Trimleston, Louth and Dunsany, and in the Commons by Everard, were in truth in agreement with the 'court party' on some major issues such as the attainder of O'Neill and O'Donnell. On other questions they would resemble a modern 'loyal' opposition. The main point of conflict centred on alleged seat-rigging.[39] Amity was restored when the parliament met again, thanks being returned by both Houses for the 'many blessings and benefits poured upon this realm' in the shape of an Act of Oblivion and special charters of pardon to many thousands, also for the king's care in the plantation of Ulster. Sir John Davies wrote

> The Speaker at several times invited the principal gentlemen and merchants of the recusant party to his house . . . and they accepted his entertainment cheerful and friendly. So now their

disjointed body is joined so well together that the public service proceeds without impediment, and, if they could agree as well in the Church as they did in the Parliament House, the peace of Ireland were established for ever.[40]

There was a unanimous vote for the attainder of Tyrone, Tyrconnell, and the other Ulster chiefs who had risen in the late rebellions, and for the confiscation of their estates. Parliament was dissolved in October 1615. Tyrone died in Spanish exile the following year. His adherents gave up hope of restoration and sought their patents from the Stuart crown.

Charles I evoked sentiments of loyalty among Irish Catholics, both in the parliament of 1634-35, and in that of 1640, in which they predominated. A preamble was inserted to the latter's Act of Supply, thanking the king for the 'wise and beneficient administration' of Thomas Wentworth, Earl of Strafford:

For this your tender care over us, showed by the deputing and supporting so good a Governor, we . . . acknowledge ourselves more bound than we can with tongue or pen express.[41]

On 23rd March the Commons promised to assist the King with 'their lives, fortunes and estates' if the occasion should require,[42] and assured his majesty, as did the Lords concurring, that 'the kingdom hath the happiness to be governed by the best of Kings'.[43]

The concurrence of substantial numbers of Catholics in these Acts and declarations should not be seen as the servile abasements of a subjugated people. In 1613 they were as unruly as when the Irish parliamentary party provoked the introduction by Gladstone of closure and 'guillotine'. Nor were Catholics oppressed at this time. True, they could not hold office without taking the Oath of Supremacy; but attempts had been made to introduce a less exacting oath of allegiance for less important purposes, and the Oath of Supremacy itself had been interpreted, notably by Queen Elizabeth herself in her Injunctions, as not implying spiritual authority for the monarch. Not since the time of Queen Mary have English sovereigns claimed to be 'Head' of the Church of England: our present queen is 'Supreme Governor', not 'Head', the only Head acknowledged being Our Lord himself, as is made explicit in the case of the relevant Scottish Act.[44] The Oath of Supremacy, moreover, was rarely required after the scare produced by the Gunpowder Plot had passed away; and in 1628, a new and less objectionable oath, similar to the oath of allegiance operative in England, was appointed to be administered to lawyers and those suing out livery of their lands on the death of their father.[45] 'Graces' such as these did much to bind important Catholics to the crown.

The Irish Act of Uniformity imposed a fine on those who failed to attend their parish church. But this statute too was rarely enforced; Strafford in particular would not hear of it, and even before his time, in 1613, it was stated officially that it had been executed only in Dublin, and that a mere £15 had been levied during the preceding year.[46] By 1640 Catholics were, as we have seen, predominant in parliament. There were also Catholic sheriffs of cities and counties, justices of the peace and mayors and aldermen of corporations. Catholics practised at the Bar; held commissions in the army; were judges in the supreme court, recorders of towns, governors of counties; and in 1650 a Catholic who had been for many years president of the town and county of Galway, became Lord Deputy of the Kingdom.[47] The Roman Catholic Archdeacon of Tuam, who was forced to flee to France on the surrender of Galway to the parliamentary army in 1652, tells us that 'the Bishops exercised their episcopal functions, the priests their parochial duties. Almost every city and town in Ireland had religious communities, which lodged in houses hired for the purpose, and were not prohibited to perform all the duties of their orders'.[48]

In these circumstances the rising of 1641 is difficult to understand unless we bear in mind that there was another side to the picture. Strafford's ten-year régime was seen by some as imperious and autocratic, and he had made enemies. Those enemies rejoiced at his fall, and very nearly succeeded in seizing Dublin. It very often happens that on the downfall of a strong and powerful administrator all kinds of grievances, hitherto unexpressed or fully answered, come to the boil. This is what happened then. The Catholics of the Pale were, to begin with, unmoved, and offered their support to King Charles. But such was the feeling of revulsion produced by the attempt to seize Dublin Castle that their offers were repulsed and they began to be treated as traitors. They were seen as all tarred with the same brush, and to be feared just as much as the most disloyal of the rebels. Frustrated in their attempts to rally round the forces of law and order, some felt obliged to make terms with the rebels, whilst continuing to protest their loyalty.

In May 1642 the Catholic bishops of Ulster declared the rebellion to be justified; and in an all-Ireland synod at Kilkenny, a confederation was formed which again protested loyalty to the king but in effect, with an assembly and supreme council of its own, took on the character of a parallel government.[49] Not all the Catholics of the Pale were prepared to join the confederation; some no doubt preferred a quiet life above all else, and there was an important minority of ultra-loyalists, who felt that to take up arms, even indirectly, against the king's lieutenant, was tantamount to treachery, however hardly they had been used in the past and expected to be in the future. The Catholic Earl of Westmeath, who had had a distinguished, if somewhat chequered career as representative of his co-religionists at the court of King Charles, was one such. Ormonde, by then lieutenant, ordered Sir Richard Grenville to send him a party of forty horse as a convoy for his escape to Dublin, but on his way the rebels robbed him, stripped his wife and her attendant, and so maltreated him that he died shortly afterwards. His house and property too were destroyed.[50] John FitzGerald, Knight of Kerry, was excommunicated by his bishop for refusing to join, and Thomas Dease, Bishop of Meath, was rebuked by the Synod of Kells in March 1642 for having allegedly said that the war was groundless and unjust. Sir Thomas Sherlock, for refusing to join or to lend money to buy ammunition from France was stripped of everything and turned out of his castle at Butlerstown 'in his slippers, without stockings, leaving him only a red cap and green mantle'.[51]

It is true that both FitzGerald and Sherlock were commended under the Commonwealth, the former for his 'affection to the English and Protestants, and the protecting of them from the rage and cruelty of the rebels',[52] but it is probably too simple and anglocentric to regard them as Parliamentarians *pur sang*. The truth is that the Ireland of this time, as at many other epochs, displays a confused jumble of motives. Passive obedience to duly constituted authority, to the 'powers that be' is easy enough in quiet times, but at this period there was an abundance, if not an excess, of such authorities. There was the Confederation of Kilkenny with its resounding motto, *Pro Deo, Rege et Patria Hibernia unanimis;* there was the kings' lieutenant, the great Duke of Ormonde as he afterwards became;[53] there was the Parliament in Dublin; there were the Lord Justices who spoke there for the revolutionary English parliament; and there was the papal nuncio, urging his demands on the purportedly loyal confederation and sometimes succeeding, sometimes failing. The attitude of the loyal Catholic at that time recalls the words of John Byrom in the next century as he surveyed the troubled scene;

God bless the King, I mean the Faith's defender;
God bless — no harm in blessing — the Pretender;
But who Pretender is, or who is King,
God bless us all — that's quite another thing.

When the confederacy, in 1646, concluded a peace with Ormonde,
the nuncio at once denounced it in a convocation of Irish clergy at
Waterford, and deposed the supreme council of the confederates. Again
in 1648 a truce was made by the confederacy, this time with Murrough
O'Brien, first Earl of Inchiquin, who had become master of the south of
Ireland, and had declared for King Charles. Whereupon the nuncio,
Rinuccini, pronounced a sentence of excommunication against all who
were accomplices in it, and an interdict on all places where it should be
recognised.[54]

The nuncio was however ultimately forced to flee. Ormonde
concluded a peace with the confederates in January 1649. This included
very favourable terms for the Catholics. But he was soon to be replaced
by the Cromwellians. Meanwhile the nunciists had resumed their
activities. Certain of the bishops were won over. A synod set up on
10th August 1650 sent a letter to Ormonde requiring him to leave the
kingdom. This he did in December, the Cromwellians having earlier on
gained Dublin; and his successor, Clanricarde, though a Roman Catholic,
received no more support from the bishops than he had. Indeed they
excommunicated him; sent envoys to the Duke of Lorraine so as to
frustrate his applications to that prince for assistance; and to add insult to
injury his own commissioners accredited to the duke turned traitor and
signed a treaty conferring on the latter the sovereignty of Ireland[55].
Clanricarde of course repudiated his representatives, but it was too late:
the Cromwellians were gaining ground in Ireland, and when Galway
capitulated in May 1652 the fate of the country was sealed.

'Hell or Connaught' was the doom pronounced on the leading
Roman Catholic proprietors; those who had not fled abroad were
transplanted to Connaught, where they received portions equal to one-
third or two-thirds of the estates formerly enjoyed by them, according
as they had, or had not, borne arms during the troubles. Despite their
professed loyalty, the activities of the confederation had in fact made
Roman Catholics unpopular both with parliamentarians and with
royalists. Notwithstanding its motto, it was not always *unanimis,* and, as
we have seen, at least in its early days, treated dissentients harshly.

One result of Cromwell's victory was the incorporation of Ireland with the rest of the empire. Under the Commonwealth she sent thirty representatives to the Protectorate parliaments of 1654 and 1656. The new Great Seal ordered by the Long Parliament and used by the Lord Protector bore on one side the arms of England and Ireland, with the inscription 'The Great Seal of England'; and, on the reverse, the House of Commons, then the sole chamber of parliament, sitting within the motto, 'In the first year of freedom by God's blessing restored'. Regimes that speak often of freedom are often those that destroy it.

When the monarchy was restored there was no restoration of Catholic lands confiscated by Cromwell, except to the limited extent envisaged by the Act of Settlement (not to be confused with the Act of Settlement of the Crown in the early part of the eighteenth century). Provision was made for Catholics innocent of rebellion, but not at the expense of adventurers and soldiers settled by Cromwell. An Explanatory Act of 1665 somewhat enlarged provision for Catholics, giving them in effect one-fifth of Ireland, compared with the three-fifths which they had held before.[56] Full restoration of the estates was asked for in 1670; but although the king and his brother, afterwards James II, were in favour, the English House of Commons imposed its veto.

Consideration of what had already begun to be called the Penal Laws (although they bore less hardly than those enacted later) began early in the reign. A Catholic remonstrance was drawn up in 1660 by Richard Belling, formerly secretary to the Kilkenny Confederation, who made use of an English petition presented to parliament in 1641 which contained a full and explicit renunciation of the deposing and absolving powers of the Pope. This remonstrance made it clear that 'we do hold it impious and against the word of God, to maintain that any private Subject may kill or murther the Anointed of God, his Prince, though of a different belief and Religion from his'.[57] Ninety-seven Irish noblemen and gentlemen signed it and presented it to the king, and a considerable amelioration of the position of Irish Catholics in regard to the exercise of their religion is said to have ensued.[58]

Papal agents, such as the nuncio at Brussels, who had charge of the Irish priesthood, were however outraged, and Cardinal Barberini wrote to the noblemen of Ireland condemning the remonstrance as a violation of Catholic faith. The English government were in a quandary, and no such electoral test as today's 'referendum' being available to them, decided to allow a national synod of Catholics to be convened in Dublin. Special passports were issued to enable expatriate prelates to attend. Again the cardinal and the nuncio wrote denouncing the remonstrance and even the synod itself. This body, which sat from 11th to 16th June 1666, drew up a remonstrance of its own, containing no explicit denial of the Pope's deposing power, nor even a mention of his name. Ormonde was dissatisfied with it, and the synod was dissolved. Nevertheless, loyalty was expressed in the solemn protestation 'before God and His Holy Angels that we own and acknowledge your Majesty to be our true and lawful King . . . that the petitioners were bound in conscience to be obedient to your Majesty in all civil and temporal affairs' and they 'undertook to discover rebellion and conspiracy'.[59]

Certain Irish Catholic hopes were raised by the accession of James II in 1685, especially when Talbot, who in that year was created Earl of Tyrconnell and who had for many years represented the Catholic Irish party at court, was appointed viceroy. By his orders an attempt was made to disarm the Protestants of Ireland, and when in 1686 Henry Hyde, second Earl of Clarendon, came over as lieutenant, Tyrconnell was given command of the forces, which he promptly proceeded to purge in the Catholic interest. The Lord Lieutenant protested to the king in vain; the Protestants were alarmed, and a mass exodus began. In 1687 Clarendon was formally superseded by Tyrconnell, who became Lord Deputy.[60]

The more moderate Catholics of England opposed his appointment, because he was dedicated to a repeal of the Acts of Settlement and Explanation, which at least had the effect of binding Ireland to England. They may well also have feared a terrible reaction and reckoning to come. The judges were replaced, and dispensed from taking the Oath of Supremacy. In 1687 the corporations were deprived of their charters, and the new ones issued to them required in general that two-thirds of the members should be Catholics. Catholics were also sworn members of the Privy Council of Ireland.

Crowned by the established Church of England with special splendour on St George's day 1685, James by 1688 had dissipated the enthusiastic loyalty of the Tories[61] and Anglicans who had sustained him against over-mighty Whig grandees and resentful republicans. The Prince of Orange was sent for. King James, disheartened and dismayed, dropped the Great Seal in the Thames, wandered about in Kent, was persuaded by his supporters to return to London, and ultimately, on his final departure from the capital, was glad to accept the escort of the Prince's Blue Guards, themselves, ironically enough, of his own persuasion. Harris relates that when the king asked them how they could serve in an expedition designed to destroy their own religion, one of them replied that his soul was God's, but his sword belonged to the Prince of Orange.[62]

Meanwhile in Ireland Tyrconnell was prepared. He had, as we have seen, replaced Protestants by Catholics in all key positions, and when the deposed king arrived in March 1689, what purported to be a parliament was summoned. Tyrconnell had still not secured the repeal of the Acts of Settlement and Explanation, and there was to be a further hitch, for at its opening James, who was not the bigot of Whig propaganda, declared himself 'against invading any man's property', although at Chester, when still King of England, he had agreed upon repeal with Tyrconnell. But the parliament was adamant, and Acts of Attainder of Protestants and of repeal of the Acts of Settlement were passed.[63] It went further: an Act was passed declaring the independence of the Irish legislature, and that the English parliament possessed no authority over it. Charles I had indeed offered the repeal of Poynings' Law in 1641; but this was going somewhat further. The Attainder Act condemned to death over 2,400 Protestants; their names were kept secret until the period of a possible pardon from James was past. With somewhat more colour of justice, tithes payable by Roman Catholics to Protestant clergy were abolished; but another Act went further, and abolished Church rates in corporate towns largely inhabited by Protestants. Thus was an attempt made to turn the wheel full circle, and substitute oppressive laws against one denomination for those against another.

The Prince of Orange, now William III of England, had landed at Torbay on 5th November 1688, the anniversary of the Gunpowder Plot. By 1690 he had won a decisive victory over James's forces at the Boyne. But the Protestant hero's polyglot army was not all Protestant. His loyal Blue Guards were, as we have seen, Catholic, and although some Frenchmen defected, there is little truth in the sectarian myths about the Williamite war. No matter that the victory of Boyne water was acclaimed in an illuminated Vatican and that *Te Deum* was offered in most Catholic Vienna. For the eclipse of *Rí Shamus* by Boyne side and in 'Aughrim's great disaster' was check to the continental ambitions of that gallicizing *Roi Soleil,* Louis XIV. These battlefields were indeed but part of the board on which the game of Europe was played. The Irish struggles of the sixteenth and seventeenth centuries were side shows to the drama of reformation and counter-reformation and of English Civil Wars.

The Treaty of Limerick of 1691 sealed William's triumph. James had foreseen that his Irish parliament's repeal of the Acts of Settlement and Explanation would have the effect of dispossessing many loyal Catholics who had benefited under them. Describing the surrender of Galway which immediately preceded the second siege of Limerick, Colonel O'Kelly says that it was the predominance of those who desired the re-establishment of the Acts that led to the abrupt surrender of the town to the Williamite forces under Godert de Ginkell, afterwards first Earl of Athlone.[64]

CHAPTER THREE

The Penal Laws

The Penal Laws against Catholics, though in many cases unenforceable, remained on the statute book and were now revived in full force by the Treaty of Limerick. Under an Act of Queen Elizabeth's reign, it was forbidden for a priest to say Mass, and even, on one interpretation of the same statute, for any Roman Catholic to hear mass.[1] Roman Catholics who failed to attend a Protestant church were liable to a fine. No Roman Catholic priest could remain in Ireland lawfully without taking the Oath of Supremacy and renouncing the Pope's civil authority.[2] Roman Catholics were bound to inform against such priests, and were forbidden to send their children to be educated abroad without special licence of the privy council.

Further restrictions were introduced in the reign of Charles II. Thus under one Act, no Roman Catholic could act as a schoolmaster or private tutor without taking the Oath of Supremacy and renouncing the Pope's authority, and such steps also had to be taken before a Catholic could sit in parliament.[3] At least up to 1780, Catholic peers who were prepared merely to take the Oath of Allegiance were regularly refused leave to sit.[4] Under authority of another Act, rules were made by the Lord Lieutenant and council disabling Catholics from becoming justices of the peace, mayors, recorders, aldermen or burgesses of any corporation. In the reign of William III and his successors, these restrictions were amplified and tightened. Under an Act of 1695, Catholics could not sell arms and ammunition, and another of 1703-4 forbade them to hold leases for more than thirty-one years. They could not buy land, nor could they possess a horse valued at more than five pounds, build churches or schools, or endow charities of a purely Catholic nature.

Nevertheless, even in the early eighteenth century what in the preceding century and a half had been but loosely enforced was often flexibly applied. Moreover, in respect of voting rights and seats in parliament, there is evidence to show that Catholics were treated more harshly in England than in Ireland at this period.

After an attempt to assassinate William III an English Act of 1696 empowered magistrates to require voters to take an oath denying the Pope's deposing power. The Irish House of Commons prepared a similar Bill which was approved by the English privy council under Poynings' Law procedure. But it was rejected by the Irish House of Lords despite protests by fourteen peers headed by Archbishop Narcissus Marsh. Other Protestants, notably William King, then bishop of Derry, were opposed, and stood out for the rights of Catholics. Similarly in 1721 enough bishops voted against a Popery Bill to defeat it.[5]

In 1703 a clause was added to a Bill providing that Catholics must take an Oath of Abjuration of the Pretender as well as the Oath of Allegiance provided for by Article 9 of the Treaty of Limerick. Unlike the oath against the Pope's deposing power, this did not contravene any specific Catholic doctrine and was in fact taken by a number of Catholics, though many others refused it. In 1709 an Act was passed empowering magistrates to require both the oaths from any person over 16, and also from priests, who from 1704 were legally allowed to remain in Ireland after registering.[6] Out of 1,080 priests on the register, however, fewer than 40 took it, and their brethren condemned them.[7] Nevertheless the oath continued to be taken by Catholics; thus in 1712 William Brabazon of Lough Mask, repudiating an alleged recantation, declared that he had deliberately taken the Oath of Abjuration and thought there was nothing wrong in doing so.[8] According to the *Dublin Intelligence* of 30th August 1715 'a good number of the Chief Papists' took the Oath of Abjuration at Santry.

Again in 1709 the Irish Commons discussed the question of voting. It was argued successfully in debate that it was unreasonable that so large a population should be bound by laws that were not made by their representatives, and that religion should be taken into account only insofar as it endangered the State. The prohibitory clause was, accordingly, omitted. The situation remained uncertain until 1728, when an Act 'for the better preventing Papists from voting in elections' provided that 'no Papist . . . shall be intitled or admitted to vote at the election of any member to serve in Parliament as Knight, citizen, or burgess, or at the election of any magistrate for any city or other town-corporate; any law, statute, or usage, to the contrary notwithstanding'.[9] This Act immediately followed upon an Address of congratulation presented by Lord Delvin and others on behalf of the Catholics to King George II on his accession; to which no official answer was condescended, though an Address from the Roman Catholics of Maryland was graciously received and printed in the *London Gazette*.[10] In 1733 the Penal

Code was extended by an Act further preventing Catholics from practising as solicitors. Another Act disabled even converts from Catholicism from acting as justices of the peace, if their wives had failed to conform or their children were being brought up as Catholics. Resolutions of the Irish House of Commons having similar effect had been passed in 1725, extending to virtually all offices, including membership of the House itself.[11]

All this contrasted markedly with the treatment accorded to Protestant Dissenters and to Quakers, who for a trial period (made indefinite by an Act of 1735) were allowed to affirm instead of swearing oaths. Their Address of congratulation and condolence was duly printed in the *London Gazette* of 11th-15th July 1727.[12] Although still obliged to pay tithes, Dissenters had been excused from attending church by an Act of 1719; the necessary Oaths of Allegiance, Supremacy, and Abjuration of the Pretender, and the Declaration against transubstantiation presented them with no difficulty.[13]

We have already referred to the comparatively tolerant attitude of the Irish House of Lords on the subject of voting. Irish peers who refused to take any more than the Oath of Allegiance, or 'Oath of Fidelity', as it was sometimes called in the seventeenth century, were excluded from the House as early as 1692.[14] This however did not prevent them from being heard before the House or its committees. Thus in 1704 when a Bill was under consideration which, as passed, prevented Catholics from holding leases for more than thirty-one years, a petition was considered from Lords Kingsland and Bellew and other gentlemen described as 'Popish', who were represented by counsel.[15] Lord Kingsland, Sir Stephen Rice and other Catholics with counsel were heard against the Popery Bill of 1709, Rice appearing in person; and in 1719 a petition was heard from Festus Burk, George Aylmer, Richard Blake and Michael Nugent, 'setting forth, that they and several other *Roman Catholics,* would be greatly prejudiced if a Clause in the Bill . . . in relation to the reversionary Leases, should pass'.[16] Counsel for the petitioners were heard on 30th October and the opinion of the judges was asked on certain points. On 2nd November the Bill was rejected.[17]

Contrary to what is generally supposed, therefore, Catholics were not totally without a voice in political matters during the early eighteenth century; and indeed it may be argued that but for fears of Jacobite invasion many more laws directed against them would have been withdrawn or withheld. In September 1723 the Lord Lieutenant, in his speech opening the new session, alluded to the need to 'prevent more effectually the eluding of those "laws" in being, against *Popish* Priests'.[18] As we have seen, such priests (though not the higher clergy) had been able, since 1704, to register provided they took the Oath of Allegiance, and since 1709 they could also be asked to take the Oath of Abjuration of the Pretender. This latter provision was not, however, universally enforced, and it was still possible for a priest who did not comply lawfully to say mass. A Bill was introduced into the Irish House of Commons to make it high treason for a priest to decline the Oath of Abjuration as well as the Oath of Allegiance.[19] Cornelius Nary, parish priest of St Michan's, in Dublin wrote a pamphlet on the subject. Educated at Naas and at the Irish College in Paris, in 1696 he became tutor, in London, to Lord Antrim, an Irish Catholic peer. In 1702 he was arrested in Dublin. Having registered under the Acts of 1703-4, however, he was allowed to exercise his ministry unmolested, and remained at St Michan's until his death in 1738.[20]

His pamphlet, entitled *The Case of the Roman Catholics in Ireland,* is not known to have been definitively published until 1754, though it must have been clandestinely available.[21] Father Nary argued that the Oath of Allegiance alone was sufficient, since it bound all who took it to discover plots and conspiracies. It could be taken 'with a safe Conscience to any Prince who conquers me, and the Country of which I am a Member, tho' he be never so great a Tyrant or Usurper, even to the *Zar of Muscovy,* or the Grand *Turk'*. The Oath of Abjuration was different, however. First, a Catholic could not in good conscience swear that 'the late King *James* or the *Pretender'* had no right or title to the Crown of England, and secondly because to swear to maintain the succession in the Protestant line might mean that if George I turned Catholic he would be obliged to desert him. Henry of Navarre had done so, as had the Duke of Saxony in more recent times when he became king of Poland. King William III, Father Nary contended, would not have insisted on such an oath.

> For in the 3d year of his Reign when an Act of Parliament passed in *England,* intituled an Act for the abrogating the Oath of Supremacy, and appointing other Oaths, requiring all Officers, Magistrates, Lawyers, &c in *Ireland* to take the same, there was a saving for such Roman Catholicks as were intituled to the Benefit of the Articles of *Limerick*; and it was expressly provided by the said Act that they should be obliged to take the Oath of Allegiance and no other.

The Bill provided that no Catholic priest who had not taken the Oath of Abjuration should say mass on pain of high treason, and there was a £100 reward for informers. But of the 1,100 priests registered under the 1703 Act, only thirty-three or less had ever taken this oath, and half of these were now dead. To treat the Catholic priesthood 'as the French King did the *Hugonets [sic]*', i.e. banish them, 'wou'd be much more tolerable'. The Bill was moreover 'unpolitick', firstly because it would make it more difficult for the government to 'get a toleration for Protestants from Roman Catholic Princes abroad', and secondly because it would cause emigration, even of 'estated' Catholics. Those who could afford to leave, would; the remainder would become thieves and robbers. Thirdly, as the Catholics then in Ireland were largely 'Hewers of Wood, and Drawers of Water', Protestants would have to be brought in to replace those who might emigrate. Religious hatred was not so deeply ingrained that Protestants would necessarily welcome this. Fourthly, the revenue of the kingdom would suffer, since Catholic merchants and dealers, who paid more customs and duty for imported goods than Protestants, might be forced out.

Catholics generally were being charged with the accusation, first, that 'their Heart and Affections are not for the Government' and, secondly, 'that there are a great many Priests come of late from Foreign Countries into this Kingdom'. To the first charge, Nary replied in the words of the General of the Veientines who, when asked by the Roman Consul how long peace would last between his people and the Romans, replied, 'so long as you use us well'. And to the second count, if native priests were driven out, the influx of foreigners would be likely to increase, not diminish. The Irish House of Lords seems to have accepted the strength of the latter argument when on 3rd December 1725 it resolved that 'the most probable way of restraining of *Popish* Priests and Regulars coming into this Kingdom, will be to allow a competent Number of Secular Priests to exercise their Functions, under such Rules and Limitations, as may be for the Security of the Civil State'.[22]

Nary's pamphlet was not wholly critical; and it concluded with an expression of thankfulness that no further Penal Laws had been introduced since the accession of George I. We do not know for certain that it was read by those in authority, either in Dublin or in England. What we do know is that on 12th December 1723 the Speaker of the Irish House of Commons reported that the Lord Lieutenant had been attended upon at the Castle with a view to the Bill's being transmitted to England, and that His Grace replied somewhat delphically that 'I have so much at heart a matter, which I recommended to the consideration of Parliament, at the beginning of this Session, that the House of Commons may depend upon a due regard, on my part, to what is desired'.[23] The Journals recorded no more of the matter, neither is there any evidence that it was brought before the Irish House of Lords. It was suggested by Lecky that the Bill was duly transmitted to England under Poynings' Law, but not returned. 'It is probable', he wrote, 'that the humane feelings of Walpole were revolted by a law that was worthy of Alva or Torquemada'.[24]

Here then were two successes due at least in part to the political activities of Catholics in the early part of the century. The tone of the Irish House of Lords was invariably much less hostile to them than that of the Commons; and in 1733 Lords Mountgarrett and Cahir, together with Michael Nugent, William Purcell and John Reilly, were allowed to petition the House 'on behalf of themselves and the rest of the Roman Catholics of Ireland' against a Bill to annul marriages celebrated by *'Popish* priests or Friars', and to illegitimize their issue. On 20th December it was ruled that they could be heard by counsel. Counsel were duly heard two days later, and consideration of the Bill was adjourned for a week. No more of it is recorded in the House of Lords Journals, and there is no evidence that it passed into law.

In the following year four of the five petitioners (the commoners being described as 'esquires') engaged in further petition, this time against the Solicitors' Bill. They were joined by 'Francis Lynch and Augustine Clark, of the City of *Dublin,* Merchants', evidence that the banning of Catholic solicitors from practice impinged harshly on the business community, and also that Catholic merchants were of growing importance in the life of Dublin and other places.[25] The petition was unsuccessful; and indeed the Act itself was merely intended to confirm and strengthen existing legislation. On 17th December 1725 the Irish House of Lords had ordered the Attorney-General forthwith to prosecute one *'Joseph Nagle, a Papist,* for acting as a Solicitor, Agent or Manager of Causes, in several of His Majesty's Courts, contrary to the several Acts of Parliament, made in this Kingdom, to prevent *Papists* being Solicitors'.[26]

Catholics do not seem to have been active in the early days in promoting the idea of a Union between Great Britain and Ireland. There is, however, little doubt that business considerations played an important part; indeed it was the Irish Council of Trade who in 1676 reported to the Lord Lieutenant in favour of an incorporate union with England resembling that between England and Wales. Sir William Petty, economic adviser to both Commonwealth and Restoration governments, is celebrated for the 'Domesday Book' for Ireland, known as the Down Survey because it measured 'down' on the ground. The map which he constructed for the purpose superseded the old method of merely listing lands with their extent and value.[27] He too believed in such a Union. For

> if both kingdoms were under one legislature, power and Parliament, the members whereof should be proportionable in power and wealth of each nation, there would be no danger such a Parliament should do anything to the prejudice of the English interest in Ireland, nor could the Irish ever complain of partiality when they shall be freely and proportionably represented in all Parliaments.[28]

Only by Union, Petty believed, could the Irish Catholics, if admitted to power, be prevented from persecuting the Protestants. This enlightened advocate of religious freedom wanted to enlist the Roman Catholic interest in England against Protestant bigotry. James Bonnell wrote to Robert Harley from Dublin in November 1691 favouring the re-establishment of a Cromwellian-type Union or a special committee of the English parliament to hear Irish grievances. The Irish parliament, he claimed, had 'bred jealousy of England towards us, and made us seem to have separate interests'. William Molyneux argued that

> If . . . it be concluded that the Parliament of *England* may bind Ireland; it must also be allowed that the People of *Ireland* ought to have their *Representatives* in the Parliament of England.[29]

Which is what would be said almost a century later in revolutionary America.

The chairman of one of the committees that addressed Queen Anne on the question of Union, Mr (afterwards Lord) Molesworth, quoted the advantages to the 'rich and opulent country', England, of her union with Wales.

But Ireland, like the American colonies, was concerned for her own trade and taxes. In 1703, upon learning that Union between England and Scotland was afoot, the Irish parliament made a bid for incorporate, or legislative Union with England. In an Address to Queen Anne the Irish House of Commons declared that far from seeking independence for Ireland, it was their entire conviction that their welfare depended on the English connexion. On 25th October the House of Lords in Dublin resolved that:

> Upon due Consideration of the present Constitution of this Kingdom that such an humble Representation be made to the Queen of the State and Condition thereof, as may best incline Her Majesty, by such proper means as to her Majesty seem fit, to promote such an Union with *England* as may qualify the States of this Kingdom, to be represented in the Parliament there.[30]

In 1707 the Commons returned to the charge. They congratulated Anne on the Union with Scotland and renewed their request of 1703:

> May God long preserve that life on which your people's happiness so much depends. May he put in your royal heart to add greater strength and lustre to your crown by a yet more comprehensive union.[31]

The Lords added their felicitations; but the Queen and her Ministers were unmoved.

The Irish Catholics had little or no part in this for, as we have seen, they had in effect been deprived of the right to sit in the parliament of Ireland and they were shortly to be completely disfranchised. Pressure for a Union came largely from Protestants who, in the words of the 1703 Commons resolution, felt that Ireland's foreign trade was 'under such restrictions and discouragements, as to be now become in a manner unprofitable, although this Kingdom hath of late, by its Blood and Treasure, contributed to secure the Plantation Trade to the People of England'.[32] This, no doubt, was a reference to an agreement to suppress the Irish woollen trade made in 1698 at the request of the English Lords and Commons. That the agreement failed in its effects is shown by the statistics, which indicate that the value of wool exports from Ireland had, by 1745, risen to seven times the 1697 level, and that after 1740 Irish domestic consumption grew so as to absorb the entire production.[33] Moreover the agreement of 1698, whilst it may have had some deleterious effect on the woollen trade, was of enormous advantage to Ireland in encouraging the manufacture and export of linen goods, which were not only admitted into England free of duty, but benefited by a bounty on their subsequent re-export. By the end of the eighteenth century more than thirty times as much linen was being exported from Ireland as had been at its beginning.[34]

Indeed, it can be argued that if the Irish parliament had been less solicitous for the welfare of its sheep and more for that of its people, many of the troubles of the eighteenth century might have been averted. For a man may exist, even contentedly exist, without education, the right to vote for members of parliament, to keep a horse, own land, or carry a sword or pistol; but he cannot exist without eating. Pasture abounded in Ireland, but tillage was almost non-existent. A man might travel ten or fifteen miles without seeing a house or a cornfield, whilst the peasants, mainly Catholics, were driven into bogs or mountainous territory to eke out a humble existence by growing potatoes. It has indeed been estimated that only one-fortieth of Ireland was under tillage in 1730, and that the number of cultivated acres had decreased by 100,000 since the time of Petty. A statute of 1727 aimed at slowing this process down; but then in 1735 the conversion of tillage to pasture was accelerated by the abolition of the tithe of agistment which even harmed the Protestant Church of Ireland clergy by depriving them of this tax on pasturage land. In other words, the humble holder of tillage was discriminated against in favour of the rich grazier; and whilst the causes of rebellions are never simple, there is little doubt that this policy of the Irish parliament was in some measure directly responsible for the Whiteboy insurrections of the 1760s, and the later events in Munster in 1785-7, a cruel feature of which was the houghing (hamstringing) of cattle.[35]

Loyalties were also confused by the papal recognition of the Old Pretender, Prince James Edward Stuart, as King James III. The Irish Catholics languished under the Penal Laws. These included provision that a Protestant might compulsorily purchase for anything above a statutory five pounds the noblest hunter or carriage horse belonging to a Catholic.[36] In 1733, a Catholic as eminent as Lord Gormanston was among those apprehended and indicted for wearing swords when on his way to pay his respects to the gentlemen of the county and to the judges at Meath Assizes. Yet no Catholic resident in Ireland could be proved to have been in any way involved in the Stuart rebellion, and when in 1745 the Young Pretender was engaged on his march to invade England, Faulkner's *Dublin Journal*, 'at the request of several Roman Catholic gentlemen' drew attention to the way in which the Catholic clergy of the city for some weeks past had

> earnestly recommended to their people to behave themselves peaceably and quietly like good subjects, to avoid like true Christians all riots, mobs, drunkenness or late hours, to give no offence either in their words or actions to their neighbours, but to behave themselves so in every respect, as to be worthy of the favours and liberties they now enjoy.

The author of a *Tour Through Ireland* (1748) was informed that 'his Majesty has a large number of loyal subjects among the Roman Catholicks'.[37]

Until the Old Pretender's death in 1766 successive Popes would usually accept his nominations to Irish bishoprics; and although such 'titular' bishops were not, in theory, allowed to be in the country at all, an Act of 1709 having required all Catholic superior clergy, including deans and vicars-general, to leave the country on pain of high treason, with a reward of £50 for their discovery, they were often permitted to carry out their functions more or less unmolested. A letter from Bryan O'Gara, titular Archbishop of Tuam, to Lord Athenry, dated 6th June 1726, expressed agreement to his Lordship's nomination of a priest to the parish of Dunmore. The letter fell into the hands of the authorities, and the Irish House of Lords resolved that both O'Gara and the priest should be immediately taken into custody. But they could not be found, and O'Gara is believed to have continued to administer his diocese until his death in 1740. Dominicans and Franciscans were Jacobite; and in 1727 the latter's Provincial, Francis Stuart, opposed the proposal of Christopher Nugent, Lord Delvin, for a loyal Address from the Irish Catholics to George II on his accession.

Nonetheless, an Address was presented which, after referring to the 'goodness and lenity' of the 'government' of George I, went on to 'crave leave to assure your majesty of our steady allegiance and most humble duty to your majesty's person and government'. This duty and allegiance proceeded 'not only from our inclination and the sincerity of our hearts: but also from a firm belief of its being a religious duty, which no power on earth can dispense with'.

The Lord Lieutenant, Carteret, in a 'letter to a noble peer in Ireland' had, according to the *Dublin Journal* of 2nd September 1727, stated that the king had received the Address 'very graciously' and had 'commanded him to assure his lordship that his majesty desired nothing more than to make all his subjects easy and happy under his government'. But, as Hugh Boulter, Protestant Primate of All Ireland wrote to Carteret on 20th July, 'the address yesterday presented by some Roman Catholics, occasions great heat and divisions among those of that religion here'.[38]

The securing of the Hanoverian line took much of the heart out of Jacobitism. The land settlement took on a permanency. An Irish Brigade stood and died on the Jacobite side at Culloden; but the Protestant-Anglican ascendancy was firmly established in Ireland and it was left to bards and poets and the hedge schoolmasters to cherish the Gaelic lore and language as the despised heirlooms of a Catholic peasantry which, as a result of confiscation and impoverishment, had absorbed many a noble name. As Boyce has written in his *Nationalism in Ireland* (1982), the myth of James II's brief reign 'was a powerful and enduring one; and the verse of the contemporary Gaelic poet, David O Bruadair, reflected the impression that the confederate watchwords of God, King and country had wrought upon Gaelic political ideas. In his *Summary of the purgatory of the men of Ireland,* O Bruadair execrated the 'gang who betrayed King Charles'. And in his long eulogy on the *Triumph of James I*, composed in October 1687, he avowed:

> That it is not Elizabeth I magnify,
> But the Stuart King James, bright star of royalty,
> That hath risen under God to succour us.

Throughout most of the eighteenth century the old faith, which might have consecrated, and later did consecrate, a natural alliance of Throne and Altar, was practised in holes and corners.

In time the Penal Code, always somewhat erratic in its application, became softened. Lord Chief Baron Forster told Arthur Young in July 1776 that Popery laws were by then 'rarely executed'[39]; and although the English Army was barred to Catholics, they were recruited as Marines during the Seven Years' War, which was appropriate enough since the Corps of Marines started as the Catholic James Duke of York and Albany's Maritime Regiment of Foot. During the 1760s, stated Lecky, 'the army became gradually a resource for impoverished and adventurous Catholics'.[40] Catholics and Protestant Dissenters did moreover take their fair share and more of the trade of the kingdom. Archbishop King was writing of this to the Archbishop of Canterbury as early as 1718; and even in Limerick and Galway, where they were placed under special restrictions from early in the century[41]; the corporations petitioned parliament complaining that they controlled most of the trade and wealth of the city. Merchants were prominent in the Catholic Committee of Dublin, set up in the 1750s to advance Catholic interests, and commercial questions played a large part in their deliberations, more especially the question of 'quarterage', exacted by the guilds, who held a monopoly of certain trades, and would not admit Catholics as full members. 'Quarterage' — so-called because it was payable quarterly — went to set up a fund payable to sick or unfortunate members, but as Catholics did not count as members, or 'free brothers', they were in effect subsidizing Protestants by being obliged to subscribe as so-called 'quarter-brothers' for the privilege of exercising their trade. They were also subject to an impost called 'intrusion money'. Catholic resistance to these exactions came to a head in November 1758 and was fortified by a court judgement; but they did not finally cease until the 1780s.[42]

Economics was also paramount, as we have seen, in the arguments for and against Union with Great Britain. Not only did ecclesiastics such as the philosopher Bishop George Berkeley of Cloyne see the hurtfulness of mutual jealousy and 'the true interest of both Nations to become one People',[43] but in 1744 Sir Matthew Decker [44] called for legislative union and the abolition of trade restrictions between England and Ireland: 'By an Union with Ireland . . . no discontent could arise, but a general improvement, spread over the three Kingdoms without prejudice to each other.' Having quoted these, Professor T. Dunbar Ingram, to whom every student of the Act of Union is indebted, comes to what he calls the *'clarum et venerabile nomen* of Adam Smith', who found that by Union Ireland would gain not only 'freedom of trade' but other much more important advantages. These

would much more than compensate any increase of taxes that might acompany that union. By the union with England, the middling and inferior ranks of people in Scotland gained a complete deliverance from the power of an aristocracy, which had always before oppressed them. By an union with Great Britain, the greater part of the people of all ranks in Ireland would gain an equally complete deliverance from a much more oppressive aristocracy; an aristocracy not founded, like that of Scotland, in the natural and respectable distinctions of birth and fortune, but in the most odious of all distinctions, those of religious and political prejudices . . . Without an union with

Great Britain, the inhabitants of Ireland are not likely, for many ages, to consider themselves as one people.[45]

During the year 1759 the French, during the Seven Years' War, laid plans for a descent upon Great Britain. But in November the naval force of invasion was defeated by Lord Hawke at the great battle of Quiberon Bay, in Brittany. Loud were the rejoicings, and the Catholics of Ireland were prominent in their expressions of loyalty. Those of Dublin took advantage of the occasion to couple such expressions with hope for an amelioration of their plight. After conveying 'hearty Congratulations on those glorious Successes, by Sea and Land, which have attended His Majesty's Arms, in the Prosecution of this just and necessary War', their Address to the Lord Lieutenant went on to assert that 'our Allegiance . . . is confirmed by Affection and Gratitude; our Religion commands it, and it shall be our invariable Rule firmly and inviolably to adhere to it'. In conclusion, a hope was expressed for means to be found 'to render so numerous a Body more useful Members to the Community, and more strengthening Friends to the State, than they could possibly have hitherto been, under the Restraint of the many Penal Laws against them'.[46] Over 300 signatures were appended, and the Address was presented, in the first instance, to the Speaker of the Irish House of Commons, John Ponsonby, for onward transmission.[47]

The Address was duly answered, though with no reference to the concluding representations which it contained, and printed in the *Dublin Gazette*, which also published two other, quite separate, Addresses from the 'Roman Catholicks of the City of Limerick' and from 'the Roman Catholicks of the town of Galway' respectively. Each of these was signed by some ninety people, and the first was presented by Charles Smyth and Richard Maunsell, M.P.s for the city of Limerick. Neither made any mention of the Penal Laws, and were confined to expressions of attachment and loyalty. There is evidence of Catholic Addresses having been presented from Cork and Waterford, as well as Dublin, Limerick and Galway.[48]

Thus we see two strands of Catholic loyalism persisting from the previous century. There were those who were prepared to be loyal at all costs, and passively to obey a government which might be seen by others as actively unjust and yet deserving of obedience and respect within limits. Nicholas, Viscount Taafe, was expressing the first point of view when he wrote in his *Observations on Affairs in Ireland,* published in 1766, that the British and Irish Catholics should continue steady in that loyalty, that subserviency to the ruling powers, which their religion prescribes; grateful to the sovereign who protects them; patient and resigned under the laws which punish them. Let their civil conduct, like their civil principles be such, as every government must approve, and which our own legislature may (possibly) one day reward. Should it however be deemed expedient, to continue the burthens they lie under, let them consider their sufferings as remedies, not as evils; as the preventives of crime on the one hand, and as the punishment of their sins on the other — in a state of suffering, Christians often fill their proper post, and of that post self-denial is the outgard. A state of prosperity, is the state of danger, often as fatal, as it is flattering. Let us not, therefore, lose the merit of the sacrifice we make . . . Sincerity, insulted and punished sincerity, is a source of comfort in the world we inhabit.

Of similar mind were the Cork priests who, according to Samuel Derrick, 'declaimed publicly from their altars, with all the vehemence of the Presbytery, against French politics; nor could the more orthodox son of the Church of England more zealously recommend submission to the government, and fidelity to the house of Hanover'.

Derrick was writing in September 1760; and shortly thereafter Addresses of congratulation and condolence were presented to King George III (via the Lord Lieutenant) on His Majesty's accession. On this occasion the principal Address, instead of being from 'the Roman Catholick Gentlemen, Merchants, and Citizens, of the City of Dublin' purported to be the 'humble Address of the Roman Catholicks of the Kingdom of Ireland'. More tart than its predecessor, and with a touch of irony, it stated that

Ever since the Accession of Your Majesty's Royal House to the Throne of these Realms, we have, in a particular Manner, experienced the Paternal Interposition of your Illustrious Predecessors. We, Most Gracious Sovereign, who are so unfortunately distinguished from the rest of our Fellow-Subjects, cannot subsist without a Continuance of the Royal Favour and Protection.

The Address went on to

> assure your Majesty of our grateful and constant Return of
> Affection and Loyalty; a Loyalty, which our Conduct has
> proved, and our Religion enforces; happy! might it intitle us to
> express a Wish, that of all your Majesty's dutiful Subjects of
> this Kingdom, we alone may not be left incapable of promoting
> the general Welfare and Prosperity of it.[49]

The 'Humble Address of the Roman Catholick Noblemen and
Gentlemen of the counties of Meath and Westmeath in the Kingdom of
Ireland' took quite a different line:

> We come, Sir, to your Feet with Hearts full of Loyalty, Duty,
> warm Wishes and Affection, and offer you all that Persons, in
> our Situation, can, faithful Hearts and Hands, unarmed indeed
> but ready, earnest and desirous to exert themselves strenuously
> and faithfully, whenever your Majesty shall think them worthy
> to be employed in your and their Country's Cause.[50]

The Address, which was dated Trim, County Meath, 5th January
1761, concluded, quite without sarcasm or irony, with the hope that 'the
Happiness of your Loyal Christian Subjects, without Distinction, may
be the wish and envy of all other People'. Both the Addresses were
recorded as having been received 'very graciously'.[51]

The times were not, however, propitious for the redress of Catholic
grievances. The Whiteboy insurrection enraged many Protestants,
notwithstanding that it was a Catholic priest, Father Cahill, who at
Ballyragget, Co. Kilkenny, organized the first successful resistance to
the insurgents.[52] The Catholic Association was dissolved because of
differences amongst its members, and even the efforts of Edmund
Burke, who drew up an Address and petition to the king setting out the
Roman Catholics' most serious grievances, could not avail; the Address
was not presented, and in 1761-2 and 1763-4 Bills enabling Catholics to
take mortgages as security when they lent money to Protestants were
rejected.[53]

The Seven Years' War of 1756-63 was both a continental and a
colonial and maritime struggle. During it and afterwards ministers were
in search of a rational structure for the empire. Not only the colonies

but Ireland had, by and large, been going their separate ways. 'What matters it to us who are ministers in England? Let us stick to our own circle and manage our own little game as well as we can.' That is what the Earl of Bessborough's younger son, John Ponsonby, wrote to Anthony Foster.[54] Ireland was prosperous in the years following the war. The Irish Treasury housed a surplus and there was disagreement between the king and his ministers, on the one hand, and, on the other, the parliament in Dublin about the manner in which that surplus should be distributed. On the eve of a revolutionary epoch Ireland, more than once a place of lodgement for pretenders to, and enemies of, the crown, approached an incoherence perilous to the survival of the empire itself.

It was not however the Irish Catholics who threatened the State. The death of the Old Pretender in 1766 and the withholding of papal recognition of the Young Pretender, the 'Bonnie' Prince Charles Edward Stuart, as Charles III enabled Catholics to come to terms with the House of Hanover. The landowners and merchants of the now re-formed Catholic Committee desired the Irish parliament to enact an oath of political allegiance which they could take. This was done;[55] but the form included phrases derogatory to the Pope. A number of leading laymen and some bishops took the oath; other bishops refused. Rome disapproved the oath without condemning it. The Catholic Committee was deeply divided on the question, 'but by 1778 virtually all opposition to the oath was abandoned'.[56]

In October 1775 the Speech from the Throne at the opening of the Irish parliament mentioned the rebellion in America. A loyal Address was at once drawn up expressing 'abhorrence' and 'indignation' against the rebels (in whose ranks Scotch-Irish from Ulster became prominent). The Address was passed by a comfortable majority; but it was violently opposed in a chamber half full. Irish sympathy with the American rebels was not confined to Ulster, though there most pronounced. Indeed the revolution across the Atlantic set radicalism afire in the Protestant north.

The Catholic population remained steady and loyal. An Address was presented through Sir John de Blaquière,

> justly abhorring the unnatural rebellion which had lately broken out among some of his American subjects against his most sacred person and government. We hardly presume to lay at his feet two millions of loyal, faithful, and affectionate hearts and hands.

The claim was made that 'our dispositions and sentiments we well know to be those also of all our fellow Roman Catholic Irish subjects'. Archbishop Butler of Cashel issued a Pastoral to the clergy of Cashel and Emly in October 1775 denouncing any who countenanced rioters. The Irish government's rapport with the Catholic Archbishop was close. Even closer was its relationship with Lord Kenmare, who had taken a leading part in the revival of the Catholic Committee. In the early summer he had offered to raise 1,100 men for American service from Kerry and Cork. Although his efforts were not entirely successful, Kenmare had, in the words of R.E. Burns,

> nonetheless tried to contribute to British military preparations for war in America. His lordship's demonstrated loyalty during the grim and uncertain days after Bunker Hill persuaded other Irish Catholic gentlemen and merchants to emulate him.[57]

During the summer, a number of other well-known Catholics, headed by Lords Fingall and Trimleston and by John Curry, the historian, formed a committee to raise funds for 'encouraging recruits to enlist for His Majesty's service'. Protestant fears of arming Catholics however led Blaquière (the Chief Secretary) to thank Fingall's groups for their intentions but to indicate that their efforts were unnecessary; and on 30th September Fingall and the others sent a letter to him regretting the government's decision but assuring him of their sincere and grateful loyalty to the king.[58]

The Lord Lieutenant, Harcourt, was then replaced, and his successor, Buckinghamshire, was faced, on the day before parliament opened in October 1777, with a petition for Catholic Relief signed by Kenmare, other Catholic peers, and more than 300 gentlemen. This was modelled on the Address which had been prepared by Edmund Burke thirteen years earlier, but never submitted, and was principally concerned with the acquisition and transmission of landed property. The Earl of Buckinghamshire agreed to transmit the petition to the king, but was reluctant to endorse it favourably. When it finally arrived in England, two months later, English ministers were dismayed by the Lieutenant's timidity. They were anxious to recruit Catholics for the Army, and to this end Lord Weymouth, the new Secretary of State for the Southern Department, asked Buckinghamshire for a statement on what could be done. The fear of some Protestants was, expressed bluntly, that 2,000 disciplined Catholics would return from America and train perhaps five times that number of their co-religionists to murder Protestants. Nevertheless, the campaign continued, and early in 1778 Catholic leaders began to press the Irish government for support of a Relief Bill. A Mr. Talbot, described by the Earl as a 'Roman Catholick gentleman of considerable fortune', brought the Chief Secretary a draft for the Lord Lieutenant's consideration. It aimed too high, pressing as it did for the opening of virtually all positions to Catholics subscribing the oath of 1774. There was a reaction; and on 12th March 1778 a Bill introduced by James FitzGerald enabling Catholics to take long leases and to build in towns and villages was withdrawn.

The situation was transformed by the outbreak of hostilities against France. On 23rd March Hussey Burgh, prime sergeant and principal Government spokesman in the House of Commons, was at pains to assure the House that the attachment and loyalty of Irish Catholics had been demonstrated, and an Act was passed, and took effect in August, empowering Catholics to hold long leases provided that they subscribed the special oath of allegiance and declaration of 1774, which had been devised in order to provide for their testifying before the courts.

When France, Spain and Holland joined the war against England, volunteer corps were raised in Ireland. Intended to oppose invasion, they constituted in effect a military arm of the Patriot Party, giving formidable expression to discontent. Lord North enacted measures to free Irish trade; but the Patriot demand was also for legislative independence.

Catholics were, at the outset, prominent in expressing support for the volunteers, as has been pointed out by James O'Donovan (*Journal of the Cork Historical and Archeological Society*, (lxxxvii, 1982). When in June 1779 a French fleet was reportedly sighted in Bantry Bay, a 'great number' of Catholics at once offered to join with their Protestant fellow-citizens in the ranks of the 'True Blues' who kept the peace in Cork on the departure of the regular troops for Bantry. According to the *Hibernian Chronicle* (3rd June 1779) they were 'well received'. At Fethard on 4th June Sir Richard FitzGerald and other Catholics waited upon the Chief Magistrate and presented a loyal Address which began:

> We his majesty's loyal subjects, the Roman Catholics of the town and neighbourhood of Fethard . . . beg leave to offer . . . their service at this time of public alarm, for the protection of the Kingdom against foreign invasion or domestic disturbance.

One volunteer body, the Passage Union, returned 'their sincere thanks to their Roman Catholic neighbours who so loyally and spiritedly offered to join them . . . on the alarm of our perfidious enemies the French having landed at Bantry Bay'; and other associations passed similar resolutions. It has been claimed that it was the Catholics who kept the City of Cork quiet while the volunteers marched to Bantry; and whilst in February 1780 Maurice O'Connell refused the Knight of Kerry's request to help in the formation of a corps at Iveragh, on the grounds that Catholics were forbidden to carry arms, the Dingle Volunteers from August 1779 issued an 'open invitation' to Catholics, upon which a 'Roman Catholic gentleman' in Dublin advised the Catholics there 'to associate and like their loyal and spirited brethren of the town of Dingle, reciprocally unite with their friends and countrymen in the common cause against their avowed enemies the French and Spaniards'. (*Freeman's Journal*, 11th September 1779, quoted by O'Donovan).

A Dundalk correspondent, writing in the *Hibernian Magazine* for August 1780, referring to the parade by the Volunteers of that town in honour of the king's birthday, remarked that the corps was partly composed of Catholics, and so was the First Regiment of the 'Irish Brigade' embodied in Dublin in October of 1781. In February 1782 reference was made in the House of Commons to the Kilkenny Volunteers containing within their ranks 'some very respectable gentlemen' of the Roman Catholic religion 'whose zeal got the better of the restrictions of the law' (*Parliamentary Register,* p.294). In the same month, delegates of 143 Volunteer corps attended a convention at Dungannon in County Tyrone. Those present included Henry Flood, brilliant radical son of a chief justice, and a uniformed Henry Grattan, The Earl of Charlemont, Commander-in-chief of the Volunteers and Governor of Armagh, presided. Unbeknown to Charlemont and Flood, Grattan drew up a resolution which affirmed 'the right of private judgement, in matters of religion', and rejoiced 'in the relaxation of the PENAL LAWS against our ROMAN CATHOLIC FELLOW-SUBJECTS' as conducive 'to the unity and prosperity of the inhabitants of Ireland'.[59] The motion was passed with but two dissentients. Another of the resolutions passed at Dungannon disputed the powers of the two privy councils under Poynings' Law.

Beset by foreign foes, the government made concessions to the Irish. In 1782 legislative independence was won. Under Yelverton's Act, Poynings' Law was modified to provide that the Acts of the Irish parliament were to be transmitted without alteration by the Lord

Lieutenant and the Irish privy council. Although some relaxation of the Penal Laws had already taken place, and in 1793 they were to be largely repealed, it remains true that independence had at this stage been won by the Protestants[60] to be enjoyed by what Flood called the Protestant nation. Neither he nor Charlemont agreed with Grattan that the Roman Catholics should be accorded full civil liberties. At the same time, some radicals in both Belfast and Dublin wanted the Volunteers, who were being disbanded with the end of hostilities, to stay embodied and to insist on Catholic Relief.

On 21st June 1784, an 'aggregate meeting of the citizens of Dublin' agreed upon a petition to the king. This included a section condemning 'that remnant of the penal code of laws which still oppresses our Roman Catholic Fellow-subjects — laws which tend to prohibit education and liberality, restrain certain privileges, and to proscribe industry, love of liberty and patriotism'.[61] On the anniversary of the Battle of the Boyne, three weeks later, a pro-Catholic petition was presented to Lord Charlemont by the Belfast Volunteers, paraded in the Catholic chapel. Although it was still illegal for Catholics to bear arms, it was proposed to allow them to enlist in this force; and nearly 200 were enrolled in Dublin.

Four years later, at the centenary commemoration of the raising of the siege of Derry, the Roman Catholic bishop and his clergy took their part in a public procession of all the citizens of Derry to the Cathedral. At the concluding dinner of nearly a thousand persons,

> religious dissensions in particular seemed to be buried in oblivion, and Roman Catholics vied with Protestants in expressing, by every possible mark, their sense of the blessings, secured to them by our happy constitution, and the cordial part they took in the celebration of this joyful day
> (*Ordnance Survey of Ireland 1837: The Anti-Protestantism of the Irish Executive Government Exposed*, 1850, p.8).

On 4th November every year, until the ceremony was given up by the Duke of Bedford in 1806, the Lord Lieutenant held a court in honour of King William's birthday, and headed a procession around the statue in College Green. Loyal Roman Catholics made no scruple to attend, and ladies would appear at the drawing room in orange ribbons. Lord Chesterfield, more famous for his letter-writing, but viceroy in

Ireland from 1745-6, is reputed to have said to one such:

Say, pretty traitor, where's the jest
Of wearing orange on your breast,
Whilst that breast, upheaving, shows
The whiteness of the rebel rose?

The verse, if uttered, was no doubt intended as a compliment, but is revealing as indicative of a natural tendency by Englishmen, even at that date, to assume that Catholic loyalism could not possibly be natural and spontaneous.

In 1785 the two kingdoms entered into commercial and financial negotiations, but failed to place trade between Great Britain and Ireland on a satisfactory basis. This was a factor in convincing the younger Pitt that Union was necessary. Ministers of the crown also compared the inequitable treatment of Irish Catholics so near home with that given to the predominantly Catholic population of conquered Canada under the Treaty of Paris of 1763. Catholics were admitted to the colonial Council of Grenada. The enlargement of toleration provided for in the Catholic Relief Act of 1793 owed much to enlightened colonial practice overseas.

From 1783, the Catholic Committee in Dublin had been virtually dormant, but in 1790 it again sprang to life. An attempt was made to present a petition to parliament asking that the case of the Catholics should be taken into consideration. No member of the Irish House of Commons could be found to support it; and later in the same year an Address to the Lord Lieutenant, Westmorland, was returned because it presumed to express the hope that a further relaxation of the Penal Laws might take place.[62] The Catholic Committee then began to split up. On one side were those of its members, notably Lord Kenmare, who favoured a cautious, moderate approach; on the other stood the hotheads like John Keogh, a Dublin merchant. These, in the eyes of the prelates, peers and gentry who had hitherto formed the backbone of the movement, represented all that was bourgeois and brash. Lord Kenmare and his associates, some sixty in all, seceded, after proposing unsuccessfully at a meeting of the committee on 17th December 1791 that 'any circumstances of the times, or any consideration of the general welfare of the Empire, could render a repeal of the Penal Laws imprudent or inexpedient'.[63]

There followed an exchange of Addresses and counter-Addresses, which at moments became acrimonious. Thus the Catholics of Drumana

(Leitrim) resolved at a meeting on 28th December that 'the Address now promoted by a Southern Lord' [Kenmare] 'and his Associate, appears to us calculated to disturb the peace of the Catholics, and thereby frustrate (if possible) their honest hope of relief'. The meeting went further and asserted that

> the said Lord is an object of contempt for his weakness and vanity, in assuming himself a right to dictate to the Roman Catholics of Ireland, whom he has with shameless effrontery opposed and counteracted in all their dutiful applications for redress, since the time that they detected his views and had the presumption to declare that they were not satisfied to wear their chains for his L(or)d(shi)p's aggrandisement.[64]

Such choice pieces of invective were not universally approved, especially in Kilkenny, where a resolution of at least some Catholics declared that 'grateful for former concessions, we do not presume to point out the measure or extent to which such repeal should be carried, but leave the same to the wisdom and discretion of the legislature'.[65] This was followed by a formal statement by the bulk of the Committee on 4th February 1792 denying that it was pressing for 'total emancipation'. Its aims were limited, it asserted, to obtaining for Catholics admission to the profession and practice of the law, including the capacity to serve as magistrates and sit on juries; and its applications in regard to the franchise was confined, so it stated, to the right to vote in counties only, for Protestant candidates. To qualify as a voter, it was proposed that a Catholic should cultivate a farm worth £20 a year in addition to his forty-shilling freehold.[66] Violent, menacing, and intimidating motives were disclaimed; and in an *Address to our Protestant Fellow-subjects* the Committee went on to explain that:

> Dark and cruel surmises have been dispersed abroad. The ears of men have been filled with imputations of sedition and turbulence . . . A division, in the Catholic body, has been artfully imagined, and strongly insisted upon; of which one part is honoured, with the appellation of the *real* Catholics; the men of *birth, property, education, character, morals and understanding.* The other part is represented as a *base, unlettered, mechanical, poor and vulgar herd;* the obscure tenants of the counting-house, and the rude tillers of the soil.

However, 'no such division has yet been effected among the Roman Catholics. It is true, indeed, that a *division* (if the defection of so small a number can be called a division) has been fomented, and yet subsists, which however . . . is not of the nature above described.' The two parties were, first, those who 'have been induced to put their hands to the address of the 17th of December; for which act Lord Kenmare has been declared unworthy of our confidence' and the other consisted of the Committee and those who had come forward in its support. 'We solicit relief not for the sake of the rich, but for the sake of the poor', the Committee added. Lord Kenmare and his 'addressers' were represented as constituting the landed interest, yet the Committee in fact held more property than they.

The remainder of the pamphlet is concerned to refute the proposition that the Committee was 'turbulent and seditious, that we have formed regular *plans* for the *intimidation* of Parliament, and that instead of making applications for *favours,* we assert claims of *right,* of *speculative right* unknown to the constitution and subversive of society'. Appended is an 'Oath of the Roman Catholics of Ireland', which explicitly denies any right to 'Charles III' and abjures papal civil authority. Also included are answers to three questions which had been put to continental faculties of theology and sent to Pitt by the English Catholics. Paris, Douai, Louvain, Alcalá, Salamanca and Valladolid had all denied that the Pope had any civil authority; that His Holiness could dispense any subject from his allegiance; or that there was any authority for not keeping faith with heretics. Louvain indeed went so far as to express astonishment that such questions should be put 'at the end of this eighteenth century'.

Lecky acquits Pitt and most of the other ministers of 'every vestige of religious intolerance', adding that 'the events of the French revolution had thrown them into close alliance with the Catholics of Europe'.[67] English anti-Popery indeed lost much of its virulence when priests and nuns crossed the Channel to escape the atheistical republic that despoiled and persecuted the Gallican Church and also threatened to overturn the continental balance of power.

The 1793 Relief Act falls to be discussed in a later chapter. We must here note, however, that the Lord Lieutenant, Westmorland, shared the fears and objections of the Protestant Ascendancy, and that it took pressure from Pitt and from Henry Dundas, the Secretary of State then responsible for Ireland, to induce Dublin Castle to back the moderate Catholic Relief Bill introduced in 1792 by Sir Hercules Langrishe.

Dundas observed that the Catholics would 'take the first favourable moment to extort by force what is denied to them as a matter of grace'. Justice and policy alike decreed that their 'fair claims' be met.

> The Roman Catholics form the great body of the inhabitants of the kingdom of Ireland, and as such are entitled to the communication of all such advantages as can be given to them without danger to the existing establishment and to the general interests of the Empire.[68]

It has been noted that earlier in the century Edmund Burke, himself married to a Catholic, had helped to draft an Address for Roman Catholic Relief; and he had in addition written tracts upon the Popery Laws.[69] His part in securing the passage of the Roman Catholic Relief Bill of 1778 had been discussed by A.P. Lovack, who points out that not only his wife, but his mother, and his sister Juliana were devout Catholics, and that from his sixth to eleventh years he lived with his mother's Catholic brothers in County Cork, where he attended a 'Hedge' school (so-called because Catholics were, in general, not allowed to open schools, and hence were forced to teach under hedges and similar places).[70] After graduating from Trinity College in 1748 and spending more than ten years in England, he returned to Dublin in 1761 as private secretary to W.G. Hamilton, the chief secretary; and although his spell in Ireland was comparatively brief, he retained his interest. For his part in the passage of the 1778 Bill the Catholic Association of Dublin voted him 500 guineas, and Lord Kenmare, in a letter of 11th August of that year, expressed his appreciation of his services.[71]

In 1790 Burke was an English M.P., who had become famous for his support of the American colonists and for the part he played in the impeachment of Warren Hastings. His *Reflections on the Revolution in France* placed this philosopher of British conservatism at the zenith of his achievement. What more natural, therefore, than that the Catholic Committee should turn to his son Richard? A practising barrister, he was appointed as their paid adviser in August 1790, before the departure of Lord Kenmare and the seceders; and although his efforts were at first purely literary, from the close of 1791 he took a more active part. He seems however to have aroused more antagonism than support, and in September 1792 the Committee finally broke with him.[72] Wolfe Tone then appeared upon the scene.

Tone was a Protestant lawyer who in October 1791 had founded the first Society of United Irishmen in Belfast. One of the first acts of this body was to order the re-printing of *An Argument on behalf of the Catholics of Ireland,* which he had written earlier in the year under the pseudonym 'Northern Whig'. In it he denounced the insufficiency of the 1782 'revolution' as he called it. When it came to oaths, he pointed out that Protestants could not have it both ways; if they asserted that it was Catholic belief that no faith was to be kept with heretics, then why did Catholics so generally refuse to take them? To the argument that Catholics were not prepared for liberty he replied: 'Is liberty a disease for which we are to be prepared as for inoculation?' As for the Supreme Pontiff:

> I do believe that the Pope has now more power in Ireland than in some Catholic countries, or than he perhaps ought to have . . . [But] Persecution will keep alive the foolish bigotry and superstition of any sect . . . Persecution bound the Irish Catholic to this Priest, and the Priest to the Pope: the bond of union is drawn tighter by oppression; relaxation will undo it. The emancipated and liberal Irishman, like the emancipated and liberal Frenchman, may go to mass, and tell his beads; but neither the one nor the other will attend to the rusty and extinguished thunderbolts of the Vatican, or the idle anathemas, which indeed his Holiness is now-a-days too prudent and cautious to issue.

In reply to the argument that if Catholics were able to sit in the Irish House of Commons, they would swamp it, he pointed out that in 1790, 'when the majority of the electors of the Kingdom are Protestant Dissenters, they do not return above *three* of their own persuasion to Parliament'. He proposed a lower property qualification for electors than that advocated by the Catholic Committee.

The Society of United Irishmen, formed for the ostensible purpose of uniting Irishmen of different religious persuasions so as to secure a measure of parliamentary reform, had from the outset a republican and revolutionary trend. Witty, musical and free-thinking, Tone despised Poor Pat and his priests, and when the Pope was dethroned and exiled he rejoiced. Yet they recite the rosary for him at Bodenstown. His espousal of the revolution, a cause to which, paradoxically, he sought to harness that of Catholic rights, owed at least something to his having been snubbed by Pitt, after which rebuff he toyed with the idea of entering the East India Company's service. When, as secretary of the United Irishmen of Dublin, he sent a deputation to the Catholic Committee to assure them of the Society's support, the deputation was side-tracked. Yet the secession of Kenmare and his supporters, who included Lords Fingall and Gormanston, and Archbishop Troy, opened the door to a more militant element. At least five of the remaining members of the Catholic Committee, including Keogh, have been identified as United Irishmen. Nonetheless, they were not all extremists. Theobald MacKenna, a Dublin physician and lawyer, drew up their declaration under the title 'Society for Promoting Unanimity among Irishmen and Removing Religious Prejudices', subsequently altered, after much criticism, to 'Catholic Society of Dublin', and in July 1792 he proceeded to Belfast with the others to attend a meeting of the United Irishmen. On the 14th, a day of revolutionary import, there was a meeting of the United Irish leaders, including Tone, at which MacKenna was present. So was Napper Tandy. MacKenna supported the idea of more moderate resolutions to be proposed in the Linen Hall that afternoon than those favoured by Tone. The Catholics were still very timid, and a repulse would be fatal to any alliance between them and the Dissenters. Tone was furious and attacked MacKenna as cowardly.

In the afternoon, at the Linen Hall meeting, an Address in favour of the French Revolutionists was passed with enthusiasm. But the second, in favour of immediate and unqualified Catholic Emancipation, was not so favoured. After a long debate, the moderates were defeated by only five votes. It may be surmised that MacKenna thereupon took his departure from the Catholic Committee together with Richard Burke; we do know for certain that Tone stepped in to become agent and secretary to the sub-committee which looked after the affairs of the Committee in the intervals between its meetings.[73]

An Act introduced by Langrishe in the early part of 1792 removed a number of disabilities, enabling Catholics to become lawyers (though not Kings's Counsel or judges), to open schools without the licence of the bishop, and to intermarry lawfully with Protestants.[74] What it did not do was grant them the elective franchise. A petition for this purpose was drawn up by the Catholic Committee, but this was rejected without debate partly on the ground that it was signed by citizens only with no signatures from the counties. The Committee determined to meet this implied disavowal of its representative character, and at Tone's instigation letters were dispatched to every parish priest, asking for Catholics to be elected in every parish by primary and secondary assemblies to a national convention in Dublin. They were to press for the elective franchise, and for 'an equal participation in the benefits of Trial by Jury'. Keogh, in a speech on 31st October, was at pains to elicit from his audience a clear disavowal that either he or the Catholics generally wished to alter 'the present Constitution of King, Lords and Commons'; rather, their prayer was to be allowed to vote for 'Protestant representatives, and to strengthen and defend the constitution against any innovation'.

On these terms, the seceders began to return to the fold, and when in December 1792 the convention was duly held in Tailor's Hall, Back Lane, Dublin (whence it was commonly known as the Back-Lane Parliament), John Troy, now Roman Catholic Archbishop of Dublin, took a leading part in drafting its petition. He and the bishop of Cork, Moylan, signed 'for ourselves and the Roman Catholic prelates and clergy of Ireland'. Lay signatures were very numerous, and five members were deputed to take the petition over to the mainland for submission to the king. It was received very graciously, and the stage was thus set for the concession of the elective franchise in the following year.[75]

Even after that, however, parliament in Dublin remained what Craigavon would call the Stormont parliament: 'a Protestant Parliament for a Protestant people'. Corporations and grand juries resounded with resolutions expressing fears for the Ascendancy. According to Cavour, 'During the whole of the last century the whole business of the Irish Parliament was to keep the Catholic masses in check, without a single thought of improving their condition.'[76]

But how stood those Catholic masses and their spiritual leaders? Like that of 1916, the rising of 1798 was a blood sacrifice without sanction of Holy Church or Catholic doctrine on the right to rise up and make war. Pearse wrote: 'God spoke to Ireland through Tone'. Both Tone and Pearse were men of hate. But one of the many differences between the two rebellions was that whereas in 1797 Belfast was a disaffected city, Cork was a loyalist town.

Catholics were late arrivals among the United Irishmen. Their basis was Presbyterian, their birthplace Belfast. Ulster was notorious for its levelling republicans, although there were many Royalist Presbyterians too. In Counties Armagh and Londonderry, and all parts which had suffered Catholic massacre in 1641, the feeling was more conservative. The northern strength of the Society of United Irishmen was in Antrim and Down. After 1795 they joined forces with the Defenders, a secret society for the defence of the peasantry against the landlords. This alliance brought many Catholics into the ranks. The physicians, lawyers and rhetoricians of Dublin and Belfast who hardly knew the sight or smell of a peasant unleashed a Jacquerie. Yet in County Monaghan the cause of the crown was sustained by Catholic militiamen while in Wexford the suppression of republican 'croppies' incited fears and spread rumours of Orange terror and brought the Catholic peasantry out in revolt. Reports of Catholic atrocities aroused the Presbyterian radical of Counties Down and Antrim.

An Irish republic was proclaimed in May and June of what its promoters styled 'the first year of liberty'. Green flags fluttered. Phrygian caps were sported. But two expeditions mounted by the Jacobin patrons of the Irish republic miscarried. One may note that Hoche, who commanded the first, and Humbert, who took part in the second expedition had been distinguished hammers of the Catholic peasantry in La Vendée. Bonaparte, whom Tone had importuned when frequenting the ante-rooms of the regicides, had followed his star to Egypt. It was fitting that Tone should be captured aboard the French flagship in Lough Swilly. The failure of the French and the degeneration of the revolutionary movement into anti-Orange sectarianism ended an insurrection inspired by principles that were as un-Catholic as those that imbue the nominal Catholics of the modern movement of physical force republicanism.

When Louis XVI was guillotined in the same aura of Christian martyrdom as that which surrounded King Charles I, the 'wild geese', those old royalists of the Irish Brigade who went over to the continent on the abdication of James II and later, flew home from France to fight for King George III,[77] while new republicans joined the Irish Legion to fight for revolutionary France. Jacobite did not accord with Jacobin or Catholic transcendentalism with the sacred principles of 1789. Castlereagh was essentially mistaken in describing the rebellion of the United men as a 'religious frenzy'.

Leading Catholics, laymen and prelates, opposed it. Its alien ideology worked upon the grievances of rent and tithe. On 10th March 1798, Dr. Lanigan, Archbishop of Ossory, wrote to the Archbishop of Dublin, Dr. Troy:

> The priests told me, and I believe them, that the fear of assassination prevents them from speaking as much as they wished against United Irishmen. This did not deter me from exposing, at the altar, in the neighbourhood of the Queen's County, their horrid principles.[78]

Whereas some of the younger clergy, then as in later times, were republican, the hierarchy's loyalty to the crown was typically expressed in the bishop of Kilmacduagh and Kilfenora, Dr. Dillon's, pastoral of 6th April 1798:

> Let me conjure you to reject, with horror, all clandestine oaths which may be proposed to you. As for my part, it will be the pride of my life, and the greatest consolation which I can enjoy here below, should I be, in any degree, instrumental in preserving you from the machinations of dangerous and designing men.[79]

England had become a champion against those who had 'reviled and calumniated', and stripped of his property, 'The Supreme Pastor of their Church'.

On 27th May Dr. Troy adjured the clergy of the diocese of Dublin to call upon anyone seduced into a combination against the State to withdraw free from it and to surrender his arms. The insurrection had 'the most horrid effects'. 'Assassinations, murder, atrocities of every kind have been committed.'[80] In January 1799 the Roman hierarchy resolved that in the appointment of prelates to the Roman Catholic religion to vacant sees within the kingdom, such interference of government 'as may enable it to be satisfied with the loyalty of the person appointed is just and ought to be agreed to'. The signatories were the two Primates, Archbishops O'Reilly of Armagh and Troy of Dublin; Archbishops Dillon of Tuam and Bray of Cashel; Bishops Plunket of Meath, Moylan of Cork, Delany of Kildare, French of Elphin, Caulfield of Ferns and Cruise of Ardagh. The Bishops also 'admitted that a provision through the Government for the Roman Catholic clergy of this kingdom, competent and secured, ought to be thankfully accepted'[81], and in 1800 prescribed a form of catechism in which obedience to the constituted authority was indicated.

When the rebellion was over, the Masters of Maynooth College, which had been opened in 1795 by the Lord Lieutenant, Lord Camden, took pride in the part that the seminary had played in its suppression. The students had been sent home lest they be forced by United Irishmen to join their treason. Some of them were expelled for sedition, a crime condemned by the Pope in a letter circulated to the Irish bishops by his secretary of state in 1793. 'You may signify emphatically how much you condemn the conduct of those misled Catholics', he wrote.[82]

The Prefect of the College of Maynooth joined the bishops and professors of divinity in supporting the declaration of 6th May 1798 calling for a return of rebels to their allegiance. This was signed by such leading Catholic laymen as Lords Fingall, Gormanston, Southwell and Kenmare, and by Sir Edward Bellew. It gave warning against seduction 'by a set of desperate and profligate men, availing themselves of the want of education and experience in those whom they seek to use as instruments for gratifying their own wicked and interested views'.[83]

Presbyterians and Papists both suffered disabilities and persecution from the legislation of English and Irish parliaments and from the Church establishment. But in this period of peril the Catholic Church in general shone in loyalty to the crown. In the period ahead the bulk of Irish Catholics would be a force for Unionism.

CHAPTER FOUR

Enfranchisement

A session of the Irish parliament opened early in 1793. The Speech from the Throne, delivered on 10th January, asked the Houses to consider 'the situation of his Majesty's Catholic subjects'. This was the first time since the reign of James II that the expression 'Catholic' was used in an official pronouncement in Ireland, though 'Roman Catholic' had replaced 'Papist' the previous year.[1]

On 4th February, the chief secretary, Hobart, introduced a Bill into the House of Commons which granted Catholics the franchise in town and country on the same terms as Protestants; permitted them to sit on all juries, to endow colleges, universities and schools, to obtain degrees at Dublin University, to become magistrates, to hold commissions in the Army and Navy, and all civil offices, with certain exceptions. After five weeks of debate the Bill passed into law virtually unaltered in its main provisions; Catholic enfranchisement was carried by 144 votes to 72. Lord Fitzgibbon, the Irish Lord Chancellor, distinguished himself by voting in favour of the measure whilst expressing opinions strongly opposed to it. In Lecky's view the 1793 Act was far more important for Catholics than that of 1829; for just as they could, previously, often find Protestant nominees to hold property on their behalf, so 'Catholic constituencies have never found any difficulty in obtaining Protestants to act as their instruments'.[2]

At the same time Lecky, following George Ponsonby,[3] held the effect of the Act to be potentially mischievous in that whilst it placed the mass of the Catholics on the same footing in regard to the franchise as their Protestant counterparts, the Catholic gentry continued to be in an inferior position. For they were excluded from parliament. Grattan had always foreseen the danger of the Catholic masses becoming detached from the gentry by such a measure. Sir Lawrence Parsons opposed the granting of the franchise to forty-shilling freeholders. The government, he said, were alarmed at the levelling principles advocated in the North, and at the proposed alliance between Catholics and Dissenters, and thought they could conciliate the Catholics by this means. But further reforms would be pressed for. The measure 'courts the Catholic rabble and insults the Catholic gentry. It gives power to those who are ignorant . . . and withholds it from those who are enlightened'.[4]

The difficulty for the government was that in Ireland the forty-shilling Protestant freeholder was already enfranchised, as was the case in a few, but only a few, boroughs in England before the Reform Bill of 1832. To raise the franchise qualification in the Bill for Catholics would therefore be to create an invidious distinction, and this the government was not prepared to do. Nevertheless, some such distinctions remained. Catholics could still not sit in either House of parliament, and were excluded from most government and judicial positions, including the Privy Council, Fellowships of Trinity College and the offices of King's Counsel, sheriffs or sub-sheriffs and generals of the staff.

The year 1793 also saw the enactment of a militia Bill to raise 16,000 men over four years, and a Bill to increase the military establishment from 15,000 to 20,000. Catholics were not excluded, as such, from the militia, although an amendment was unsuccessfully moved at a late stage in the Irish House of Lords requiring the Oath of Supremacy from commissioned officers. Fitzgibbon, the Lord Chancellor, was inclined to support it, but other speakers, such as the Bishop of Cork[5], were 'not afraid of the fidelity or the gallantry of the Roman Catholics which had been proved in every quarter of the globe.'[6] Moreover in many counties Protestant officers might be hard to find. Volunteer meetings in Dublin, and later in the North, were 'proclaimed', that is to say forbidden, and the militia was to be conscripted.

In April the Catholic Convention dissolved itself, passing a resolution in favour of further parliamentary reform. It recommended Catholics to co-operate in 'all loyal and constitutional means'. Although £1,500 and a gold medal was voted to Wolfe Tone, £2,000 was given for a statue of the king. Catholic prelates expressed their gratitude; the United Irishmen congratulated the Catholics, and pressed for further reform.

The immediate effect of the Roman Catholic Relief Act was to enlarge the electorate by about 30,000. A Convention Act was passed in order to prevent the United Irishmen setting up an Assembly in Athlone similar to that which the Catholics had held at Dublin.[7]

Ireland was now beset by open dissension. Such men as Wolfe Tone and Hamilton Rowan looked upon the French revolution with favour; but Grattan, as leader of the parliamentary opposition, unlike his English counterpart Fox, refused to denounce the war against revolutionary France. Open murmurs against him were few; but the Ulster Presbyterian synod expressed its opposition to the war, and the ballot for the militia was strongly resisted. Volunteers rapidly took the place of reluctant conscripts, but riots and conspiracies multiplied. Most of the trouble was caused by the United Irishmen and their sympathizers, who were predominantly Presbyterians or Episcopalian Protestants of the Church of Ireland; but many were indifferent to religious influence. As Lecky states:

> Almost the whole guiding influence of the seditious movement in 1793 was Protestant or Deistical, while the Catholic gentry, the Catholic prelates, and as far as can . . . be judged the bulk of the Catholic priesthood were strongly opposed to it.[8]

It was in these circumstances that Theobald MacKenna, just before the passage of the Roman Catholic Relief Bill, published his *Essay on Parliamentary Reform*. MacKenna was a Catholic who before 1791 had been secretary to the Catholic Committee. He seceded with Kenmare when the influence of Wolfe Tone was brought to bear, and became the most prominent literary representative of Catholic loyalism in the remaining years before the Union.

MacKenna's pamphlet favoured a moderate measure of reform, and was particularly concerned to point out that not only were Catholics excluded from political power, but so also were merchants. He reserved his principal fire, however, for Wolfe Tone and his supporters. Ireland, he claimed, was not on the whole an ill-governed country. Its taxes, even compared with its means, were lower than those of any other and they fell moreover

> on the superfluities, not on the necessaries of life, and a reduction of them would not augment the poor man's comfort . . . If the connection were dissolved, or if we adhered so loosely to England that she should learn to consider us a separate nation, the expense of a distinct Government would amount to much more than our present revenue.

In the twentieth century we have seen this happen, and some other quotations from the pamphlet seem equally apt for the present day:

> Severe to those below, refractory to those above him, the public spirit of the Republican is not infrequently animated by envy. His desire of Equality seldom reaches lower than his own

rank . . . It is the first of privileges to enjoy the advantages of order. Liberty is valuable as it arises, not as it recedes from it. A mode of government may be bad, but an alteration, designed to improve, may be still worse!

Archdeacon Paley was quoted on the point that 'political innovations commonly produce many effects, besides those that are intended . . . Incidental, remote, or unthought-of evils frequently exceed the good that is designed, or the evils that are foreseen'. The neglect of this precept had transformed Tom Paine from a 'good political writer into an incendiary'. Although 'we are members of a commercial country . . . commerce or manufacture cannot run, if the entire people be kept star-gazing, on political phenomena'. The people's influence ought to be enlarged, but a limited monarchy 'exactly poised, as is that of England', ought to be maintained.[9]

Theobald MacKenna was thus a Catholic Conservative of considerable learning and eloquence. He appears to have been a lawyer by training, though the title page of the pamphlet describes him as 'Doctor'. In later years he became someone to reckon with when the question of Union was under active discussion.

Meanwhile the United Irishmen's Lisburn Committee had become openly seditious. Catholics were duly appointed to juries, but corporations failed to elect them, that of Dublin in particular remaining virulently anti-Catholic, though a few of its constituent bodies, such as the Guild of St Luke and the Corporation of Apothecaries, were prepared to admit them as Freemen.[10] Nevertheless the Catholic prelates, in an Address to the Lord Lieutenant, expressed 'unbounded loyalty and unqualified gratitude'.[11]

Disturbances between Defenders and Peep o'Day Boys had first arisen in Armagh in 1784-5. The latter, first recorded in 1780, were a mainly Protestant group who went about in the early morning (hence the name) searching for arms. As their maraudings were mainly directed against Catholics, the latter responded by forming themselves into groups known as Defenders. These latter gradually turned into a new Whiteboy movement, aiming at the abolition of tithes and the redress of agrarian grievances. The Militia Bill did not help, as rumours were spread that compulsory enlistment of Catholics might result in their dispatch to Botany Bay as convicts. In May 1794 about seventy people were killed in a clash between Defenders and Peep o'Day Boys at Ballina.

Nevertheless 1794 was in general a quiet year apart from the secession in July of a number of prominent Whigs to Pitt's administration. The Duke of Portland, principal seceder, became Home Secretary and, as such, responsible for Ireland; some said, indeed, that he had made this a condition of forming the coalition. Portland was known to favour Catholic Emancipation; he had been Lord Lieutenant in 1782 when the independence of the Irish parliament was conceded; and Catholic expectations were inevitably aroused. Lord Fitzwilliam, another Whig, after a brief period as Lord President of the Council, replaced Westmorland as Lord Lieutenant.

Pitt, however, seemed lukewarm, saying that Ireland 'has already got much'; and when he found that the Lord Lieutenant designate was planning the removal of Fitzgibbon, the Lord Chancellor, and that a change in the system was to be made, he began to have second thoughts. He was already committed to the idea of a Union and in November 1792 had written to Westmorland that 'the idea of the present fermentation gradually bringing both parties to think of an union with this country has long been in my mind . . . The admission of Catholics to a share of suffrage could not then be dangerous'.[12] On condition that Fitzgibbon remained Lord Chancellor of Ireland, and Lord Westmorland would be made Master of the Horse, Fitzwilliam's appointment was confirmed: he was directed neither to bring forward Catholic Emancipation nor to oppose it outright.

In January 1795 Fitzwilliam arrived in Ireland and was immediately presented with an Address by the Catholic Committee calling for total repeal of penal and restrictive laws. Other Catholic Addresses from Dublin and elsewhere expressed a more uncomplicated loyalty, and Fitzwilliam played for time. Lords Kenmare and Fingall had been sounded. They wanted remaining disabilities to be removed but at the same time were anxious to avoid embarrassing the government. Fingall in particular felt that whilst it was true that the great mass of Catholics already had equal rights, and might be expected to be loyal,

> The reason of the thing did not decide the multitude . . . they did know that something remained undone for those of their persuasion, and that if there was disaffection to be found among that class . . . he conceived this to be the ground of it.[13]

Fitzwilliam speedily concluded that all remaining disabilities should be removed at once. Sackville Hamilton, the Under-Secretary, and Cooke, the Irish Secretary for War, were dismissed, as were the Attorney-and Solicitor-General, and John Beresford, First Commissioner of the Revenue, who with his dependants and connexions occupied a key position, and was nicknamed 'King of Ireland'.[14] The bishop of Cloyne wrote to Westmorland that the Ponsonbys had now become powerful in his place, and that Fitzwilliam was laying 'the crown' at the feet of Ned Byrne of the Catholic Committee.

French successes on the continent fed fears of an invasion of the British Isles. The parliament of Ireland increased the combined force of militia and regulars to 40,000 men and carried a special vote of £200,000 for the Navy moved by Grattan. Kenmare and the other seceders from the Catholic Committee were again consulted, and expressed their known support for Emancipation. 'Not even the seals nor the bench' were to be excluded from the scope of Catholic ambition. Over half a million signatures were said to have been appended to petitions for Emancipation, worded in an eminently respectful tone.

Pitt and Portland procrastinated. Fitzwilliam replied to objections to Beresford's dismissal by accusing him of corruption. Portland feared the overthrow of the Protestant establishment. Fitzwilliam concluded that English ministers wished to delay further Emancipation until Union had been accomplished; but he feared that the rebellion which he foresaw would jeopardize the chances of Union with Great Britain and would lead instead to union with the French Republic. Portland complained that the English Cabinet should have been consulted before a Bill was allowed to be presented to the Irish parliament; but Pitt, in a letter of 21st February 1795, placed most emphasis upon the dismissal of Beresford as the reason for Fitzwilliam's recall. For his part the king was known to oppose further Emancipation,[15] certainly within a purely Irish context, as tending to a complete separation of the two kingdoms; and Fitzgibbon maintained that by assenting to such a measure His Majesty would violate his coronation oath. It was also argued that as the Act of Union with Scotland had purportedly preserved for all time the Act of Uniformity and other Acts maintaining the Protestant establishment, any admission of Catholics to parliament was precluded by the existing Union itself.

When Fitzwilliam's recall was announced, the Catholic Bishop of Waterford and Lismore, Dr. Hussey, who had in the previous year been employed by the government to check disaffection among Catholics in the public service,[16] wrote to Burke that 'Ireland is now on the brink of Civil War'. The Catholic Committee petitioned the king for his retention, but to no avail; and on the return of their representatives from London a meeting was held at which resolutions were passed in favour of Irish independence and against 'even our own emancipation, if proposed to be conceded upon the ignominious terms of an acquiescence in the fatal measure of an union with the sister kingdom'.[17] Fitzwilliam had been indiscreet and had released confidential correspondence for publication. He left, on 25th March. All the shops in Dublin were shut, and his coach was drawn to the waterside by a small army of his Irish supporters. Catholic opinion, and not merely that of the Catholic Committee, now turned against the government of the new Viceroy, Lord Camden.

Camden's instructions were to prevent further Emancipation at almost any cost, but also to conciliate the Catholics. Seminaries were to be established, and there was even a proposal for a grant-in-aid for the parochial priesthood. The Union was not mentioned at the opening of parliament and a Bill introduced by Grattan to secure further Emancipation was rejected by 155 votes to 84.[18] Fitzgibbon became Earl of Clare.

The year 1795 saw the founding both of the Catholic seminary at Maynooth and of the Orange Society. The first of these, a concrete result of the new policy, arose from the initiative of the Catholic bishops, who had pointed out to Lord Westmorland that the 400 students being educated abroad could no longer continue because of the French revolution, and had asked for a royal licence to endow ecclesiastical seminaries in Ireland under Catholic auspices. Burke and Grattan both favoured the scheme, as, paradoxically, did Wolfe Tone, but for different reasons. Whereas the two statesmen feared that education abroad might expose candidates for the priesthood to atheism and Jacobin principles, Tone felt that in their home territory they would become more, not less, radical. Events proved him right, though the precise influence of Maynooth itself upon the politics of its alumni remains debatable.

The Orange Society came into existence on 22nd September 1795, after the Catholic rout in the battle of the Diamond in Armagh. Bound to support the Protestant Ascendancy and to commemorate the Battle of the Boyne on 12th July, the Society by its very formation seemed to presage a terrible onslaught against Catholics in Armagh, which might be bloodily spread to Tyrone, Down, Antrim and Derry. The Governor of Armagh, Lord Gosford, and the principal magistrates, almost all Protestants, determined to put down the disturbances and secure the safety of the Catholics. Both Protestants and Catholics sat on the juries,

and two Defenders and two Orangemen were convicted of murder.
Many Catholics obtained compensation.

Like certain loyalist firebrands in more recent times, the Orange
Society drove many Catholics into the arms of the republicans. Leonard
McNally, a government informer who had penetrated the ranks of the
United Irishmen, wrote in 1796 that the Catholic Committee had now
made 'total separation from Great Britain' their grand object.[19] Addressing
the Irish parliament in the autumn on the subject of Emancipation,
Grattan asserted:

> Do you imagine there is any man that would prefer the wild
> schemes of republicanism to the sober blessings of the English
> constitution, if he enjoyed them? What is the tree of liberty? It
> is sprinkled with the blood of kings and nobles . . . If you force
> your fellow-subjects you will leave them . . . to repose under
> the shade of the dreadful tree.[20]

The North continued troublesome, and disputes between Protestant
and Catholic extended even into the militia. Some Catholic priests
helped the government by acting as informers. A volunteer force of
Yeomanry, first styled 'armed associations', was set up, mainly as a
protection against United Irishmen and Defenders.[21] This 'Home Guard'
would doubtless have been used against an enemy invading in strength;
but in Ireland the Yeomanry Corps of Napoleonic times also became on
occasion a *gendarmerie* for the suppression of disorder. At the beginning
of 1797 it consisted of 440 corps or about 24,000 men; by June 1798
there were 540 corps with about 40,000 men. It was predominantly
Protestant, but there were Catholic commanders of corps; Fingall,
Kenmare and Sir Edward Bellew were among them. In Cork there was
the Loyal Cork Legion, joined by a number of Catholics, as well as the
Protestant Cork Volunteers; and Lord Downshire in County Down
wrote in November 1796 that he was happy to say that 'there are some
respectable and loyal papists' in the Newry corps, but that the infantry,
chiefly Orangemen, had refused to enrol them. The Catholic Committee
disliked their enlisting, but in the south of Ireland there was no reluctance
either to enrol or to be enrolled, and, according to Lecky, even Lord
Clare, then the arch-opponent of Emancipation, 'has borne an emphatic
testimony to the loyalty then shown by the Catholic peasantry in the
southern and midland districts'. The Catholics of Ulster, Lecky added:

seem to have been both more political and more anti-English than those of other parts, and the United Irish leaders, who were chiefly Protestant, and whose . . . knowledge of the Catholic mind was chiefly derived from Ulster, appear to me to have . . . greatly exaggerated both the intensity and the amount of Catholic disaffection. With the exception of a few traders in the chief towns . . . their uniform conduct during many troubled years, certainly betrays nothing of the rooted antipathy to British rule, which Tone and Emmet ascribed to them.[22]

Nevertheless, in 1796 many 'Defenders' joined the United Irishmen, which in turn took on a military character.

Vanquished at sea, French arms prospered on land. Lord Malmesbury sued in vain for peace with the Directory, finding the way to Paris a long one, Burke said, because 'he went the whole way on his knees'. Soon afterwards a French fleet was discovered to have anchored at Bantry Bay. This Irish expedition was organised largely on the basis of information supplied by Wolfe Tone, who had forsaken an uncongenial American Republic for that of Jacobinical France. He was as anti-papal as ever, even suggesting that the defeated Pope should be influenced to put pressure on the priests in favour of French plans in Ireland.

The Irish Brigade did not take part in the expedition. Many of its leaders were still men of Irish Catholic descent who had ranged themselves against atheistical revolution, and by a strange irony, found themselves returning to fight for Britain, just as the new republicans were going out to the Irish legion to fight for France.[23] In September 1794 the Duke of Portland invited the Duke of Fitzjames into the English service, 'with the regiment of the Marshal de Berwick, and with the Irish Brigade, on the same footing as it had been in the service of his Christian Majesty' (i.e. the late King of France). Portland added that it was the government's intention to add a fourth regiment to the Irish Brigade, and place it under the command of Daniel O'Connell's uncle, who had been one of the most distinguished officers in the old French Army. These offers were accepted, and a recruiting mission was organized. Grattan expressed surprise that the government should think that the presence of twenty or thirty Catholic gentlemen in the Irish parliament endangered the Constitution, whilst they were prepared to arm a brigade of 6,000 Catholics under Catholic and French officers.[24] But the United Irishmen and the Catholic Committee repudiated and insulted the recruiters, as Tone informed his French friends.[25] There were insufficient volunteers for six regiments, and superfluous officers had to be reduced to half pay. Nevertheless the new regiments served in the West Indies, in North America and in Egypt, though the identity of the Brigade was not kept up.

The French expedition sailed from Brest on 15th December 1796. It included seventeen ships-of-the-line and thirteen frigates: forty-three sail all told. About 15,000 soldiers were embarked. Wolfe Tone, as 'Adjutant-General Smith' was on board the *Indomptable.* Despite various accidents, the bulk of the fleet cast anchor off Bere Island on the 22nd. Dalrymple, commanding at Cork, heard the news the same night, perhaps partly through the agency of another of O'Connell's uncles, 'Hunting Cap', whose family property at Darrynane was quite near the point of anchor.[26] Troops were concentrated, and the Yeomanry were called together, but no more than 8,000 men could be mustered immediately for the defence of Cork. But the weather favoured the crown. A strong easterly gale blew up and snow fell. The French fleet was dispersed for a fourth time. Only the fifteen ships already anchored, with six to seven thousand men aboard, could be used to effect a landing. Fog succeeded wind and snow; the French general's orders to beat a retreat went unheard in the *Indomptable*; the Admiral demurred; but in the early days of 1797 the entire squadron withdrew to Brest.

Dalrymple wrote from Bandon that the 'goodwill, zeal and activity' of the local people, mainly Catholics, 'exceed all description' and General Smith reported from Limerick that 'the country is reported to me to be infinitely more attached to Government, than common report ever allowed of . . . the cabins of every town are reported to me to be boiling their potatoes for the soldiers'.[27] Dr. Moylan, the Catholic Bishop of Cork, produced a loyal Address, Lord Kenmare exerted loyal influence and the chief bankers and traders came forward with offers of money. In a word, Catholic Cork, Galway and Limerick vied with each other to show loyalty whilst Belfast, centre of Irish Protestantism, was so disaffected that Yeomen could not be enlisted without great difficulty.

Arthur O'Leary was a Catholic priest who in 1771 had settled in Cork after having been for a time a Franciscan friar at St Malo, where he ministered to Catholic British soldiers taken prisoner during the Seven Years' War. When asked by the French authorities to tamper with their allegiance, he steadfastly refused to do so. In his pamphlet *Loyalty Asserted* (1777) he questioned the right of the Stuarts to continue to claim the loyalty of Irish Catholics. The right of succession was not indefeasible; Edward the Confessor was chosen king in the lifetime of the lawful heir.

The crown is hereditary in the wearer, but the king and both Houses of parliament can defeat this hereditary right. A son born after his father was deposed, as was the Young Pretender, can, on the authority of Grotius, be deprived of his right with the consent of the people.[28] Moreover, 'Whose is this image and superscription?' The Hanoverians were in control; the coins of the realm were theirs and had been for nearly a hundred years. And, if long possession fails to cure a defective title, what of the claim of William the Conqueror's descendants, even of the ancient Saxons, who plundered and dispossessed the Britons?

When in 1779 the French and Spanish fleets rode menacing and unopposed in the Channel and Ireland's armies had been drained by the needs of America, O'Leary's *Address to the Common People* inculcated and explained the obligation and duties of undivided allegiance. In this Address he referred to the 'unshaken loyalty of the Catholics of Cork and Kerry', adding that 'it would not be with a view to feed an hungry Irishman, that a number of French dragoons would make excursions from their camp: it would be with a design to carry off his calf or pig, and to kill himself if he resisted'. The French (then still royalist) would not be landing 'with a design to promote the Catholic cause!' They had failed to help the English Catholics when Cromwell banished them, and even sided with him against Spain.[29] Moreover, if 30,000 men, under the denomination of French troops, landed, half would be Protestants. There were even Protestant generals in the French Army. 'Let none then say', he went on,

> we will have a Catholic 'King'. Subjects are little concerned in the religion of governors. Thousands of Catholics lose their souls in France and Italy, after leading a loose and dissolute life; thousands of them work their salvation in the Protestant states of Holland and Germany. It is then equal to man, what religion his neighbour or King be of, provided his own conscience be pure, and his life upright.

'Let religion', he concluded, 'which by patience has triumphed over the Caesars, and displayed the cross in the banners of Kings, without sowing disorders in their realms, support itself without the accursed aid of insurrections and crimes'.

O'Leary was not a mere uncritical supporter of the government. In 1780 he wrote against John Wesley's attacks on Catholicism.[30] and in 1781 published his *Essay on Toleration,* directed against persecution, in all its forms, on grounds of religion. The Quakers, and William Penn in particular, are praised; neither is Lord Baltimore, the Catholic founder of Maryland, omitted. The dissertation rises to considerable heights of eloquence, and makes no attempt to excuse the rescripts of certain Popes. In 1781 O'Leary was invited to become a member of the Order of the Monks of St Patrick, which had been founded in 1779 to promote the legislative independence of Ireland and which included Flood, Grattan and Yelverton among its members. On 11th November 1783 he was in Dublin at the 'National Convention'. A message supposed to be from Lord Kenmare was read out stating that the Catholics were satisfied, and desired no more.[31]

But not all the Catholics were agreed, and on 26th September 1784 Sydney wrote to the Duke of Rutland, Lord Lieutenant, from Frognall about the 'dangerous spirit' of those who had promoted a meeting at Tholsel. He had had two conversations with the Primate on the subject of Ireland. The latter was clear that 'the Papists' 'meant a separation of the two kingdoms and a Popish King'. The Primate had mentioned

> a Popish Committee, with Sir Patrick Bellew at their head, who disavowed Lord Kenmare's declaration, and asserted that they were the real heads of the Roman Catholics, 'and declared that nothing less than a general participation, of the rights of citizens would satisfy them'.

He likewise thought that Bellew spoke the sense of the 'bulk of the Roman Catholics of Ireland'. O'Leary was mentioned as a 'dangerous man . . . He may be a tolerably good spy, he says, but you may be certain that if he is an equal one between both partys "sic" it is as much as you are to expect.' He thought he might be used, 'but with some other spy upon him perhaps'.

Rutland replied from Phoenix Park on 7th October. The Primate, he said, was a pessimist; 'his prejudices against the Roman Catholics' increased his apprehensions. 'Though some of them may meditate the most dangerous designs, I can hardly persuade myself that the larger and better proportion of them do not abhor the dangerous plans meditated by some'. As for Sir Patrick Bellew, he was an extremist who 'carries his ideas of mischief as far as any Catholick in Ireland'.[32]

Rutland may have been an optimist, but he had his own evidence of Catholic support and loyalty. On 9th September 1784 Kenmare had written from Killarney:

I regret that, having been detained in Dublin by these disgraceful riots, you are unable to visit this district, where I think your tour would convince you that this spirit of faction and insolence is confined to the walls of the metropolis.[33]

Lawlessness, indeed, was as much directed against Catholics as against Protestants. The Whiteboys, who had begun their activities in Munster, began in 1775 to harass both priest and parson. At Ballyraggett, two hundred of them attacked a house belonging to the Catholic Archbishop of Cashel's brother. In King's County, they attacked the house of the Catholic bishop coadjutor of Meath for preaching against them. Bishop Geoghegan fired from above the stairs and killed one of the principal malefactors.[34]

In 1785 there was trouble in Cork and Kerry. Although it was at first thought that it was being stirred up by itinerant monks, by December it had become clear that Catholic priests were themselves under attack, for although the agitation of the Whiteboys and the Rightboys (led by a self-styled Captain Right) was partly against tithes paid to support the Protestant Church of Ireland, it was also directed against 'the exactions, as they assert of the Romish clergy'.[35]

O'Leary was asked to intervene on similar lines to 1779, and published three *Addresses to the People of Ireland, Particularly Such of them as are called Whiteboys*, accordingly.[36] He accompanied the magistrates to various places and persuaded many people to return to their allegiance. He was attacked for his pains by Dr. Duigenan, writing under the pseudonym *Theophilus*, and by Dr. Richard Woodward, Protestant Bishop of Cloyne. Lord Kenmare spoke up on his behalf, and O'Leary himself published a reply to his critics, who seem to have fastened upon one of his Addresses in which he had referred to the people having grievances. But the 'grievances' referred to in the Addresses were as much those which the people might have against their priests as against the government, and such Protestant sniping not only missed the target but proved, in the modern phrase, counter-productive. In May 1786 Cork priests were insulted in their chapels. One was knocked off his horse when facing a mob. At Bantry on 29th June the Catholic priest of Creagh and Tullagh was 'brought out naked in the midst of wind and rain' and made to swear. This did not stop him preaching against the Whiteboys and warning his congregation against taking unlawful oaths, and on 2nd July he destroyed the Whiteboys' 'swearing book'. As a result he was forced to fly to Archdeacon Tisdall's house which was properly munitioned and barricaded.[37]

At the end of June the Catholic Archbishop of Cashel and all the Munster bishops assembled in 'rebel Cork' to see what could be done. The Whiteboys, like the modern IRA, were issuing their own regulations limiting assistance to Catholic clergymen both pecuniarily and in kind. So unpopular were the clergy with these terrorists that men and women were beaten merely for inviting them to dinner.

The prelates decided to play it cool. Fees, even when due, were not to be pressed for from those not 'well able to pay'. These principles were implemented by the Bishops of Kerry (Francis Moylan) and of Cloyne and Ross (Matthew McKenna) but despite their efforts and those of Lord Kenmare, the county was not pacified until September 1786 when Luttrell arrived with 2,000 troops. McKenna found that some of his flock were deserting to the established Church. Indeed, the Catholic Bishop of Cork himself, Dr. Butler, now Lord Dunboyne, married in May 1787 and in August conformed.[38]

Luttrell received firm support from John Troy, then Catholic Bishop of Ossory. Troy locked up all the chapels in Kilkenny City and urged the people to obedience and good order. Luttrell's march through the affected districts was a success; but the Catholic landlords of the South complained that they had lost influence with their tenants; priests said the same of their parishioners. The Duke of Rutland, in a draft letter to Sydney, paid tribute to a number of people whose efforts had been especially helpful. 'Their exertions in their several counties seem calculated to establish and preserve tranquility. I must also mention Lord Kenmare in terms of the most pointed and honourable eulogium'.[39] But O'Leary, smarting and saddened by Protestant bigotry, went to London in 1789, becoming one of the chaplains to the Spanish Embassy. Later he founded his own chapel on the site of what is now St Patrick's, Soho Square, where there is a plaque to this memory. He continued to keep in touch with Irish affairs, and in January 1797 wrote to a supporter of the government that

> Ireland owes its present security to the inconstant elements, and to the constant loyalty of the majority of the people, a loyalty which, I am sorry to find, a blind, blundering, and tyrannical policy is constantly endeavouring to shake, if not entirely to annihilate.[40]

CHAPTER FIVE

The Rebellion of 1798

The North, as we have seen, was comparatively disaffected at the time of the Bantry Bay expedition. Even there, however, William Hamilton, an active magistrate in Donegal, was able to write at the beginning of 1797 that he had 'rallied the entire body of Protestants, and detached almost the whole of the Romans from the Dissenters . . . from the moment the French appeared on the coast . . . One hundred and twenty Protestants and a hundred and ten Romans have in two days taken the oath of allegiance before me'.[1]

Nevertheless the situation steadily worsened. The United Irishmen now clearly aimed at an independent Republic of Ireland, and their ranks had been swollen by Whiteboys Defenders and, like the modern IRA, by a gallimaufry of criminal and quasi-criminal elements. 'May the skins of all Kings make drumheads for United Irishmen' was their toast; 'to take the livings from the gentlemen, and every man to have equal riches' was their oath. And their catechism ran:

Question: What have you got in your hand?
Answer: A green bough.
Question: Where did it first grow?
Answer: In America.
Question: Where did it bud?
Answer: In France.
Question: Where are you going to plant it?
Answer: In the crown of Great Britain.[2]

Dr. Hamilton himself was murdered at the house of a clergyman friend. Soldiers near Derry had to deposit their arms every night in the court-house, to prevent them being taken by force. General Lake was empowered to place virtually the whole of Ulster under martial law. The legality of this was questioned in both the English and Irish parliaments, and the government replied that their actions were justified by that overriding law — *salus populi suprema lex*.[3]

A large deputation to the most moderate and respectable Irish Catholic peers went to the castle to ask for some measure of relief. They were 'curtly and decisively' refused.[4] General Loftus, in Munster, was certain that the Catholics there were 'loyal, and attached to good order and government'. Parliamentary reform as such did not interest them, but they did expect total Emancipation. 'Give it to them, and they will, in my opinion, be your firm friends'[5] Camden, however, was adamant, and Portland supported him, adding that 'His Majesty, under his own hand, commands me "to express to you most positively his approbation of your conduct . . . and authorise me to assure you that his sentiments are those of the year 1795" '.

The military forces in Ireland were, for the time, considerable, consisting as they did of some 15,000 regular soldiers, 18,000 militia and 30,000 Yeomanry, of whom 18,000 were cavalry. But so were the dangers. Lake was convinced that his forces in Ulster were inadequate; and although the United Irishmen had been unable to prevent the enlistment of a substantial body of Yeomanry (who numbered some 50,000 at the height of the rebellion), the quality of some of them left much to be desired.

In the disarming of places under suspicion some atrocities were committed; and the fact that the Defenders had largely joined the United Irishmen made the Orangemen natural supporters of the government. They were joined by some Protestant country gentlemen, and many enlisted in the Yeomanry. A book of rules and regulations was drawn up; the Orangeman was to be loyal to king and country, and was to abstain from cursing, swearing or intemperance. General Knox, who commanded at Dungannon, observed in May 1797 that whilst the Orangemen 'were originally a bigoted set of men, who were ready to destroy the Roman Catholics . . . they now form a political party, and are the only barrier we have against the United Irishmen'.[6]

As a long-term solution Knox advocated a Union of the legislatures.

The first step is by a strong military coercion to subdue the people; and while Ireland is yet full of British or foreign troops, to offer the people parliamentary reform; emancipation of Catholics; abolition of sinecure places &c. &c. on condition of their acceding to an Union; thereby subduing the aristocracy with the assistance of the people.

Emancipation alone, however, was not enough, for the mass of Catholics of Ireland 'feel little interest' in it.

> When the question was started, and Catholic Emancipation supported by the Presbyterians of the North, it failed of the effect of rousing the lower order of Roman Catholics, and the Republicans were therefore obliged to throw in the bait of abolition of tithes and reduction of rents. This has completely answered the purpose, and the whole mass of the Catholics of Ulster are United Irishmen. . . . The interest of the aristocracy and of the city of Dublin alone oppose an Union. The former are now of no weight, and the latter deserves punishment. I look upon it that Ireland must soon stand in respect to England in one of these three situations — united with her, the Legislatures being joined; separated from her, and forming a republic, or as an half-subdued province.

In a footnote to this letter Lecky observed that nationalist agitation in his own day having 'signally failed to rouse the farming classes', the nationalists had adopted, and with success, the plan of connecting it with an attack on rents.

In May 1797 Catholic Emancipation was again raised in the Irish parliament. The government replied by moving the adjournment, arguing that the time was inopportune; but Grattan would not be silenced. 'There are two periods, it seems, in which reform should not be agitated; one is the period of War, and the other is that of peace.'[7] The government asserted that the aim of the United Irishmen was not reform, but an independent republic, and that reform, in consequence, would not pacify them. Grattan thought otherwise; rather would it reconcile the bulk of the nation, and if the leaders of the conspiracy remained unsatisfied, they would at least have lost their proselytes. Having failed to prevent an adjournment, Grattan retired from the Irish parliament, as had Fox from the parliament at Westminster; and appeared no more upon the scene until the debates on the Union.

Meanwhile sedition had affected both Yeomanry and militia. Even the Orangemen were believed to be harbouring traitors. Archbishop Troy, a Dominican, was likewise suspected, as were other priests, mainly regulars. Francis Higgins ('the Sham Squire'), a prominent convert from Catholicism and proprietor of the *Freeman's Journal* (at that time a pro-government paper), stated in May that there were not more than twenty loyal priests in Dublin, and Leonard MacNally, a Dublin barrister who had mingled with the United Irishmen, warned the government that the lower clergy were among the most active organizers of sedition. Not for the last time in the history of Irish discontents, it was boasted that there were traitors in the castle.

By the summer, the situation in the North had slightly improved, but it was felt that a stronger military commander was required. Lord Cornwallis was offered the Commandership-in-Chief and, if required, the Viceroyalty. He replied that whilst he would come over if invasion were actual or imminent, he strongly favoured concessions to the Catholics in order to detach them from the Dissenters. Since this was not the view of the government, the proposed appointment was abandoned.

The militia were mainly Catholics, and were widely distributed in the North. On the 12th of July, the Kerry Militia clashed with the Dragoons and Yeomen at Stewartstown in Tyrone. The affray followed an earlier incident when the Yeomanry had torn off green ribbons and handkerchiefs. Many Catholics felt, as in 1641, that they were being marked out for massacre. It was widely asserted that Orangemen swore a secret oath to the effect that 'I will be true to the King and Government, and I will exterminate, as far as I am able, the Catholics of Ireland'.

The rebellion began to spread. At first it took the form of 'Defender' outrages, and fed on the suppressed, and largely imaginary, 'Orange' threat. In June Macneven[8], a Catholic physician, was sent by the United Irishmen as an envoy to the French Directory. He drew up for them an elaborate memorandum which described the Catholic priests in Ireland as largely disaffected and 'good republicans'. It alleged that the Prince of Wales had sent an emissary to an unresponsive parliamentary opposition in the hope of creating a movement to make him Lord Lieutenant, pledged to support Emancipation and parliamentary reform.

On 9th July Burke died at Beaconsfield. In his last months he had been much preoccupied with Irish affairs. 'Great Britain', he wrote, 'would be ruined by the separation of Ireland; but as there are degrees even in ruin, it would fall the most heavily on Ireland . . . Little do many people in Ireland consider how much of its prosperity has been owing to, and still depends upon, its intimate connection with this Kingdom'.[9]

Burke's death coincided with the last dissolution of parliament in Ireland before the Union. Lord Kenmare's ancestor, Sir Valentine

Browne, had been ennobled by James II immediately after his abdication. His title had therefore never been recognized by subsequent governments, though he was universally accorded it by courtesy. Camden renewed an application, first made in 1795, for him to be raised to the peerage; and this time the king acceded to his request, though Kenmare could not of course sit in the Irish House of Lords because of the oaths he would be required to take. At the same time it was proposed to ennoble another Catholic, Sir Thomas Ffrench of Galway, who had exerted influence favourable to the government upon the Catholic Committee, but it was decided instead to confer the peerage upon his Protestant mother, with the right of ultimate descent to Sir Thomas.[10] So it was done in February 1798. The king was also persuaded to create Kenmare a Viscount.

The general election passed off quietly, and the new Catholic voters aroused little attention. Grattan refused to stand, complaining of corruption and a failure to carry out further reform.

> Democracy, a gigantic form, walks the earth, smiting crowns with a hundred hands, and opening for the seduction of their subjects a hundred arms. . . We implored ministers against such an enemy to ally and identify the King with all his people, without distinction of religion.[11]

But the real reason for his secession was that he and his friends 'did not approve of the conduct of the United Men, and we could not approve of the conduct of the Government. We were afraid of encouraging the former by making speeches against the latter'.[12] In after years he admitted that his *Letter to the Citizens of Dublin* was imprudent: 'it was true, it was well written, but it tended to inflame'.[13]

In November 1797 Carhampton was replaced as Commander-in-chief by Sir Ralph Abercromby. This able soldier had served in Ireland before, but he could not get on with Lake in the North, and Dalrymple in the South had expected promotion. Abercromby believed that regular troops should be concentrated at a few points, and that the maintenance of internal order should be chiefly entrusted to the Yeomanry. His general orders of 26th February 1798 enjoining moderation and strict discipline and the avoidance of excessive use of force aroused controversy. The loyalists were seen, even in London, as having been abandoned to ruin. Despite qualified support from Camden he resigned his command. Scarcely any other event, wrote Camden to Portland, could have been so calculated to 'shake his Majesty's interest in Ireland' and it was now 'absolutely essential that an officer of the most approved ability and experience should be sent to this kingdom'.[14] The military were now ordered to act without waiting for instruction from the civil magistrates, when dispersing tumultuous assemblies; and on 30th March martial law was proclaimed throughout Ireland.

Abercromby was replaced by Lake and Catholic conciliation was firmly abandoned, despite the warnings of 'Sham Squire' Higgins, who asserted that at a meeting of the United Irishmen great alarm had been expressed that at the opening of the new parliament the Speech from the Throne might give some hope to the Catholics. The government were urged to enlist the services of Father O'Leary, whose writings and preachings had prevented the Whiteboys and insurgents of the South from joining the rabble of Cork, and rising *en masse* 'at a period when the combined fleets of Spain, France, &c. were in the English Channel'.[15]

The situation worsened. On 10th April Beresford wrote to Auckland that 'the Irish Directory have now so organised every part of the Kingdom, that they can make them rise when they please. In Munster, Leinster, and Connaught, it is a Popish plot; in Ulster, a Presbyterian plot; but in each case the end is the same — a separation from Great Britain, and a republican government'.[16] Beresford was no doubt exaggerating; but he was nearer the mark than Abercromby, who had thought Camden ill advised to declare the kingdom to be in rebellion. In London, Portland opposed further Emancipation, but favoured a generally conciliatory policy towards the Catholics. He noted that of the four provinces, Protestant Ulster was the most disaffected; that five-sixths of the leaders of the United Irishmen were Protestants; that Munster, though by then disturbed, had been loyal during the Bantry Bay expedition of 1796; and that Connaught, the most purely Catholic province, was still tranquil. 'He believed with good reason', wrote Lecky, 'that the genius of the Catholic Church was essentially opposed to the revolutionary spirit, and that the higher clergy, at least, were sincere in their hostility to it, and he probably hoped that the influence of the Papacy might contribute something to the peace of Ireland'.[17]

In October 1793 Burke had advocated some form of diplomatic representation at the Vatican. This already existed quasi-officially in the person of John Hippisley[18], technically attached to the Embassy at Naples. Hippisley had already secured an assurance that no friar would in future be appointed to the Irish Episcopacy, and in 1793 the Pope sent over, at his suggestion, Monsignor Erskine, grandson of an Earl of Kellie, to be his unofficial resident emissary in England. Erskine remained in London until 1801, when he was made a Cardinal, and had many interviews both with Pitt and King George III. Catholic chaplains were appointed to the now loyal Irish Brigade with royal approval; and at Hippisley's suggestion the Catholic catechism as used in Ireland was re-inforced with clauses enjoining obedience to the civil power. Despite his strong views on Catholic Emancipation, the king was wise and generous enough to pension the Cardinal of York, the last direct heir of the Stuarts, who had been plundered by the French. In Canada the State virtually held the nomination of the Catholic bishops. Portland himself in March 1798, felt that some State provision of a financial nature should be made for the Catholic clergy in Ireland. Leonard McNally had already drawn up a scheme, but found that whilst the secular clergy were favourable, the regulars were strongly opposed to a government endowment.[19]

The United Irishmen were now ready to rise. Some 280,000 were under arms, 111,000 in Ulster, 101,000 in Munster, and 68,000 in Leinster. No returns were available for Connaught. Two members of the executive of five were Catholic; William Macneven and Richard McCormick. The latter had once been secretary to the Catholic Committee. His dislike and fear of violence caused him to flee Ireland in March. Nacneven and eighteen others were arrested on 12th March after a Catholic silk merchant, Thomas Reynolds, a brother-in-law of Wolfe Tone and a prominent United Irishman in Leinster, turned informer. Lord Edward Fitzgerald, a distant connexion and neighbour of Reynolds, eluded arrest.

On 30th March martial law and free quarters for troops were proclaimed. In many districts any house in which a single weapon was found was immediately set ablaze, and it was announced on occasion that whole districts would be burned if arms were not brought to an appointed place within a given period. 'Croppies' — those who cut their hair short in the manner of republicans in France — were particularly marked down as suspects and sometimes put to the torture. On 6th May the leading Catholic clergy and gentry, including the professors of the recently-established College of Maynooth, issued an appeal to their co-religionists to return to their allegiances. For their part, the signatories declared their firm determination 'to stand or fall with the present existing Constitution' and they predicted that if the rebellion succeeded it would end in the downfall of the clergy as well as of 'the ancient families and respectable commercial men of the Roman Catholic religion'.[20]

On 19th May, mainly thanks to another Catholic informer, Francis Magan, and 'Sham Squire' Higgins, Fitzgerald was arrested in Dublin. On the 23rd a plot to rescue him from prison was discovered through the help of a Catholic priest. By then all the important revolutionary leaders had been arrested. Nevertheless the rebellion could not be prevented from breaking out. Mail coaches from Dublin to Belfast and other cities were stopped, and on 24th May an attempt was made on the town of Naas in Co. Kildare. The attack was repulsed, but in Prosperous, near Clane, twenty of the Ancient Britons, a Welsh regiment, were virtually annihilated. Though at least one Catholic traitor, Dr. Esmonde, appeared upon the scene, elsewhere Catholic loyalists displayed conspicuous gallantry. Lord Fingall took a prominent and energetic part, at the head of Yeomanry mainly of his own persuasion;[21] an Address of loyalty was presented to the Lord Lieutenant by many Dublin Catholics, and Archbishop Troy instructed that an exhortation to this effect be read at every Mass. After the Emmet rebellion he was obliged to fight a lawsuit to clear his name from the imputation that the exhortation was drawn up in advance of the event and that he had failed to communicate information to the authorities![22]

The plan of the rebels to capture the castle and the principal officials of Ireland was foiled by the arrest of the ringleaders. Nevertheless there were many isolated outbreaks. At Rathangan in Kildare the City of Cork Militia, mainly Catholic, put the rebels to flight with a loss of some sixty of their number.[23] The largely Catholic militia, contrary to rebel expectations, had remained loyal, but in Wicklow some priests had favoured the conspiracy and the 'Ancient Britons', quartered there, aroused a peculiar hatred. In Wexford the Yeomanry officers found that a number of Catholics in their ranks had been seduced from their allegiance, and a great part had to be disbanded. Respectable Catholics at Gorey offered a reward of a hundred guineas for the detection of those who had spread a rumour that on 29th April all churches were to be attacked, and that this would be followed by a general massacre of Protestants. Even those who had recently come forward in their chapels, and in the presence of their priest, to take the Oath of Allegiance, were found to be manufacturing pikes. The magistrates thereupon decided that surrender of arms was necessary in order to prove loyalty, and some innocent persons are said to have been so terrified that they tried to obtain arms in order to hand them in.

On 26th May Father John Murphy, curate of Boulavogue, between Wexford and Gorey, raised the standard of revolt. A number of Catholic

Yeomen deserted to him, but some of the rebels were dispersed by 250 Yeomanry on Killthomas Hill. The main body, however, under Father John, killed nearly 110 of the North Cork Militia on Oulart Hill. This desecration of the sabbath (for it was Whitsunday) was followed up by the capture of Enniscorthy on 28th May. The rebels took their stand on Vinegar Hill. Two Catholics, who had been arrested on supicion, were released from Wexford gaol and sent to negotiate with the rebels, but to no avail. The Donegal Militia with a six-pounder arrived from Duncannon Fort on the 29th. Father John, crucifix in hand, led his men to a place called Three Rocks. There they killed over seventy regulars who were advancing from Duncannon under General Fawcett, and captured two cannon. The Wexford garrison, ignorant of their fate, advanced upon the rebels, numbering at least 16,000, and retired in their turn, leaving a colonel dead. Wexford was captured by the rebels on the 30th.

Henry Alexander, a northern magistrate then employed in Dublin, wrote to Pelham, the chief secretary[24], on 3rd June that the Wicklow rebels had been defeated and driven into the mountains by Lord Roden and a party of the 5th Dragoons. Lord Fingall had shown 'great personal gallantry' at the battle of Tara Hill, where the ancient kings of Ireland are said to have had their seat and held their assemblies up to A.D. 563; and the King's County Militia 'who behaved so well under L'Estrange' were almost all Catholics. Alexander believed that the 'great mass' of them was 'decidedly against' the government, but was forced to admit that 'the bishops, and some of their noblemen and gentry, are coming forward with loyal addresses'.

Fingall family tradition relates that on the night of the Tara Hill engagement his lordship was seeing home his cousin, Lord Dunsany, after dinner when they saw a light on the hill. They called out the Yeomanry and galloped up. Fingall cleared a wall on the way but Dunsany, not so well-mounted, took a more circuitous route and was later in arriving. The king's troops, consisting of 210 Rea Fencibles, joined them, and 400 of the three or four thousand rebels were killed or wounded. The strength of the rebel position consisted in the fact that the hill was very steep and there were three circular Danish forts with ramparts and fosses, with a churchyard and high wall at the summit.[25]

Although the Wicklow rising was important, Vinegar Hill in Wexford was the centre of the rebellion. The rebels remained there for nearly a month, and murdered several hundred Protestants. The priests were equivocal; their fierce sermons aroused fanaticism; but they intervened to save some Protestants from death. Gorey was successfully attacked, and during the assault on New Ross Lord Mountjoy, formerly as Luke Gardiner, a firm supporter of the Catholics and an early advocate of their Emancipation, was killed commanding the Dublin County Regiment.[26] The streets of Ross, according to General Johnson, were strewn with rebel carcasses. Camden wrote to England complaining that not a soldier had been sent, though the rebellion had lasted a fortnight; the Lord Lieutenant ought to be a military man, and it ought to be Cornwallis. The loyalists had won at New Ross, but it was something of a Pyrrhic victory.

Castlereagh now became acting chief secretary because of Pelham's illness. It was encouraging that Connaught was quiet, likewise the Catholic counties of the South. In Ulster, firm measures had been taken early, and Orangeism, bloody but loyal, was beginning to attract more Presbyterians than did United Irishism. The equivocal attitude of the priests in Wexford alienated non-Catholics. The French had failed to arrive; and what was known of their terror and dominance in the Republics of Genoa and Switzerland was not reassuring. The Ulster Presbyterians, moreover, had strong ties with New England; and the commercial treaty negotiated between England and the United States between 1794 and 1795 had antagonized the French. Bishop Percy wrote that Ulster republicans had turned monarchist because of the 'scurvy treatment which the French have shown to the United States of America'.[27] Small outbreaks in Antrim and Down were suppressed in a few days. At Ballinahinch the majority of the rebels were Protestant, while the Monaghan Militia, almost exclusively Catholic, were prominent among the loyalists.

Meanwhile in Wexford the chief command had been taken over by a priest called Philip Roche, variously described as having 'a generous, humane heart'[28] and as 'an inhuman savage'.[29] It is certain that he was a man of gigantic stature and strength, and he may well have prevented a recurrence of the murders which had taken place at the previous camp on Vinegar Hill.

On 9th June a mass of rebels, up to 20,000 strong, advanced from Gorey towards Arklow. The Durham Fencibles, heavily outnumbered, beat them off, and Father Michael Murphy, the rebel leader, supposed to be invulnerable, was killed. The rebellion now rapidly declined. Nevertheless next day Lady Camden and her children and others were sent over to England for safety. McNally wrote that 'among Roman Catholics of property and education I find strong principles, not only of aristocracy, but monarchy'.[30] Many of the 'middling' Catholics, however, despised the Pope and his misfortune at French hands, and rumours spread that the government intended to revive the Penal Laws. On the 16th five English regiments landed at Waterford, and later in June English militia began to arrive. The rebels were gradually forced to retreat to Vinegar Hill, where they were surrounded and defeated on 21st June. Enniscorthy and Wexford were retaken, and Father Roche hanged on Wexford Bridge, together with his Protestant associate, Matthew Keugh.

Meanwhile Lord Cornwallis had arrived in Ireland to take over from Camden. Not all the Catholic priests, even in the affected areas, had sided with the rebels; 'Sham Squire' Higgins assured ministers that they would find no means of obtaining arms so efficacious as a promise of pardon from Catholic altars; he pointed out that when the rebellion was raging, the parish priest of Clontarf, Father Ryan, had in five days prevailed upon his flock to surrender nine cartloads of weapons. Other priests, potentially loyal, were intimidated by the rebels; they were threatened with being denied the casual collections and charitable donations upon which they relied for their subsistence, and were forced to comply.

As often in Ireland, informers infested rebellion. Higgins records that it was through the priest who officiated at the 'Adam and Eve chapel' that he was able to inform the government of the plot to begin the rebellion by releasing prisoners from Dublin gaols.[31] The same priest had warned of an intended desertion to the rebels of a corps of yeomen at Rathfarnham. Only about fifteen priests had actually appeared with the rebels on the battlefield. Of these Father John Murphy of Boulavogue, who had begun the Wexford rebellion, alone remained with five or six thousand men on the Three Rocks mountain. Deciding that attack was the best form of defence, he proceeded into Carlow and captured Castlecomer in Kilkenny, then an important mining town. But the miners on whom he had relied to join him speedily deserted, and the rebels found Queen's County equally unhelpful. On Kilcomney Hill, on 26th June, Father Murphy was defeated by Sir Charles Asgill, with the assistance of the Queen's County Militia. The reverend rebel is said to have been executed at Tullow, but his fate is not certain. Other engagements followed, but by the end of June the rebellion was largely over.

Cornwallis wrote with indignation of the practice of 'substituting the word *Catholicism* instead of Jacobinism, as the foundation of the present rebellion'[32] and by 1st July was already referring to 'the great object of consolidating the British Empire'. An Act of Amnesty was speedily passed absolving all the rebels who surrendered their arms, deserted their leaders, and took the Oath of Allegiance.

Meanwhile the French had not been inactive, though Bonaparte himself had been diverted by his Egyptian expedition. 'Small expeditions' was the *mot d'ordre* of the Directory, and one such set sail for Aix on 6th August, under the command of Humbert, with three frigates and 1,000 soldiers. On the 22nd it anchored near Killala, flying British flags. The castle was taken, and the Protestant bishop imprisoned. The many local recruits were disappointed to discover that the French republicans were less devout Catholics than themselves. The invaders pushed on towards Castlebar, but were disillusioned at finding no signs of a general rising. Castlebar was taken with ease, and Lake's beaten army fled to Tuam, thirty miles off. Humbert proclaimed a provisional government in Connaught, and some Catholic priests supported him. Some of Lake's militia, also Catholic, deserted, but most of them afterwards deserted the rebel cause as well.

Cornwallis countered in strength by rapid marches. The French proceeded to Sligo, and were attacked at Colooney by a small force under Colonel Vereker. They beat it off. Humbert made towards Granard, where there were insurgents, but was intercepted by Cornwallis and Lake at Ballinamuck, and surrendered on 8th September. In the subsequent capture of Killala, the Kerry Militia, almost wholly Catholic, distinguished themselves.

Two other 'small expeditions' were mounted. In one of these Napper Tandy, whom the French had made a general, sailed for the North from Dunkirk on board the *Anacreon*. On 16th September it landed at Rutland in Donegal. The population fled into the mountains, and Napper Tandy contented himself with examining newspapers and letters in the post office. Having learned of Humbert's failure, he decided to withdraw, but not without a glass or two for stirrup cup; one of Castlereagh's correspondents described him as so drunk that he had to be carried on board.[33]

The third expedition sailed from Brest on 14th September. Wolfe Tone took passage in the ship-of-the-line, the *Hoche*. In October she was surrounded near Lough Swilly and surrendered. Three frigates were also captured. Wolfe Tone cut his throat with a penknife on the eve of the day appointed for his execution. Napper Tandy was ultimately extradited from Hamburg, imprisoned until his trial in 1801, sentenced to death, reprieved and allowed to retire to France. Cornwallis thought him 'a fellow of so contemptible a character, that no person in this country seems to care in the smallest degree about him', yet he has passed into legend in Ulster as the very type of republican traitor, and on the other side as the hero of 'The Wearing of the Green'.[34]

Thus ended the rebellion. Catholics had been active on both sides, but, as the authorities acknowledge, loyalty had been uppermost.

Not all Protestants, however, were convinced. Sir Richard Musgrave published a history of the rebellion which contained a scathing indictment of the Catholic part in it. He especially singled out for condemnation the Catholic Bishop of Ferns, Dr. Caulfield, and his clergy of the County of Wexford, thinking it scarcely credible that Caulfield should remain 'unarraigned and unindicted'. Caulfield's reply, published in 1801, began by pointing out that there was no stage at which the insurrectionary spirit was not opposed by Roman Catholics. Between Bray and Wexford, a distance of nearly fifty miles, almost every Roman Catholic place of worship was reduced to ashes. The government, especially Cornwallis, had been able to perceive that some Catholics were loyal, but there was no convincing such as Sir Richard Musgrave. Caulfield had been accused of having prior knowledge of the rebellion, but he had heard about it only in that year. He had returned from Dublin a day before it broke out; at Oulart men were giving up their pikes to magistrates and swearing allegiance. He had spent about an hour there 'advising and exhorting the people to peace, good order and allegiance'.

At Wexford he set about writing to Catholic pastors to the same effect, but the rebellion was by then beginning to break out. When he had

> endeavoured to prevail on a party of rebels, who were plundering the house of my next door neighbour, Mr Matt. Kavanagh, to desist and come away, they told me in a most insulting and menacing tone, that they had information against my house, they rushed into it and searched for what they called Orangemen, bad men &c . . . Pray is this kneeling to crave or receive Doctor Caulfield's benediction? Was this revering their bishop and parish priest as men, or adoring them as Gods? Not one of them had even the civility to bow or to take off his hat. Shame then on the mischievous effrontery, that dared to invent and publish such malicious falsehood.

The few 'renegade, abandoned reprobate Priests' who had joined or headed the rebellion, might have had an influence on the mob; but this was not so of the majority of peaceable, law-abiding ones.[35]

Musgrave published a rejoinder, but it is unconvincing. He used the familiar tactic of trying to turn his enemy's good actions into evidence for his own side. Thus he asked why Caulfield needed to write to his parish priests if he were sure of their loyalty. The obvious answer is that in the dangerous circumstances then prevailing it was a matter of common prudence to draw their attention to the danger of encouraging rebellion, perhaps by inadvertence. It is precisely a bishop's duty to keep in touch with his clergy at times like this, whether they be loyal or otherwise. Other bishops addressed their people directly. Thus Dr. Coppinger addressed a *Remonstrance . . . to the lower Orders of Roman Catholics in the Diocese of Cloyne and Ross* beginning 'My Dear Deluded People!' and Dr. Francis Moylan's *Pastoral Instruction to the Roman Catholics of the Diocese of Cork,* dated 28th April 1798 was similarly addressed to 'the lower Order'. 'Associate not', wrote Moylan, 'with those Atheistical Incendiaries, who would extinguish that horror, which every *human* breast must feel against the execrable crimes of robbery and murder, by which the national character has of late been attempted to be stained'.[36]

In more recent times, Dr. Charles Dickson[37] has also questioned Musgrave's assertion that the rebellion in Wexford was a 'Popish plot'. He states that the Catholic hierarchy and its parish priests must be acquitted of any charge of complicity, although at least eleven Catholic curates took part, of whom three were executed, one was killed at Arklow, and one died of wounds. Fr John Redmond of Camolin was also hanged, 'although almost certainly his only participation was an attempt to prevent looting at the house of his friend Lord Mount Norris'. Dickson adds that in the Counties of Antrim and Down, eighteen Presbyterian ministers were implicated, of whom two were hanged, six transported, three 'proclaimed' and two imprisoned. Indeed Myles Byrne in his memoirs[38] denounced the Catholic clergy, not for having participated in the war in Wexford, but for not having done so, and declared that the 'priests saved the infamous English Government in Ireland from destruction'.

CHAPTER SIX

The Union

In 1798 luck favoured England. But, as Napoleon said to Las Cases at St Helena, "If, instead of the expedition to Egypt, I had made that of Ireland . . . what would England have been today?"[1]

The strategy of survival concentrated minds on both sides of St George's Channel and the Irish Sea on the idea of full Union. Many minds were changed. Dean Warburton, for example, wrote that

> Very many gentlemen, who formerly flew out at the bare mention of Union are now earnestly wishing for it. The late events have revived and establish'd religious animosity so much that moderate men are of opinion it will be necessary to remove from this Kingdom the object of political contention, and they think if we have no parliament, we may have peace and security.[2]

The title to nearly every estate in Ireland was derived from confiscation and settlement under Tudor or Stuart or Cromwell or Orange. These confiscations and settlements had been reversed and revived by successive parliaments. How then could the landowners feel secure if there were a Catholic majority in an Irish parliament? Canning referred in the House of Commons to Duigenan's opinion that, failing Union, the Protestant Ascendancy might have to be fortified by a renewal of the Penal Laws.[3] To Lord Clare it seemed obvious that nothing short of a Union with Great Britain could save Ireland. Otherwise, it would be "utterly impossible to preserve this country to the British Crown".[4] But, as Cornwallis pointed out in September, Clare would not hear of Roman Catholics sitting in the United Parliament. He for his part was convinced that, "until the Catholics are admitted into a general participation of rights (which when incorporated with the British Government they cannot abuse), there will be no peace or safety in Ireland".[5]

William Eden, Lord Auckland, a member of Pitt's administration who had Irish experience, was more concerned about "the whole system of needy and illiterate, and disaffected Papist priests". A respectable priesthood should, he thought, be endowed from the public purse, and Catholics should be relieved from having to support Protestant clergy by paying tithes, but a legislative Union would be difficult to arrange and execute, and "precarious in its consequences". Carlisle, who had been Lord Lieutenant in 1782 was, somewhat hesitantly, in favour of Union. "Ireland in its present state . . . is a ship on fire, and must either be cast off or extinguished".[6]

Clare, the Irish Lord Chancellor, and a firm opponent, as we have seen, of Catholic emancipation, sailed to England to confer with Pitt. Cornwallis acquiesced, but wrote that "if it is in contemplation ever to extend the privileges of the Union to the Roman Catholics, the present appears to be the only opportunity which the British Ministry can have of obtaining any credit from the boon".

Pitt was convinced by Clare and others that further Emancipation was impracticable.[7] He inclined to Auckland's view that tithes and the clergy should be attended to.[8] Various persons of note in Ireland were sounded, and only the Speaker of the Irish House of Commons, Foster, was found to be strongly against. Cooke, the Under-Secretary, said of the people generally, that "I do not think the idea of Union popular with the Protestants. There is some inclination to it among the Catholics".[9] Cornwallis took a similar view. The Under-Secretary was instructed to write a pamphlet giving arguments in favour of a Union, and this was duly published under the title *Arguments for and Against an Union between Great Britain and Ireland*. With regard to the Catholics, it was made clear that "it may be advisable to connect with an Union a proper support for their clergy, and some system of regulation for their Church not inconsistent with their ecclesiastical principles"; but no promises were made except that "all privileges they had obtained from the Irish Parliament would be secured by the Union"; and that "an opening may be left in any plan of Union for future admission of Catholics to additional privileges". There was no pledge of further emancipation.

This pamphlet was followed by a spate of others; at least twenty-four, some of them opposed to Union, had appeared by the end of 1798. At a meeting of the Dublin Bar on 9th December an anti-Unionist resolution was carried by 166 votes to 32. Bankers and merchants of Dublin, and the Corporation, denounced the idea of Union. Ulster, however, was more favourable.

Englishmen like William Elliot, Under-Secretary to the Lord Lieutenant for the Military Department, thought that the Government were profoundly mistaken in failing to drive the horses of Union and Emancipation in double harness; but leading loyalist Catholics took a different view. Lords Fingall and Kenmare, the Archbishop Troy, considered that "it would be injurious to the Catholic claims to have them discussed in the present temper of the Irish Parliament" and that it would be "much more in their interest that the question should rest till it could be submitted in quieter times to the unprejudiced decision of the United Parliament, relying on their receiving hereafter every indulgence which could be extended to them without endangering the Protestant establishment". Kenmare and Fingall favoured the Auckland idea of a State endowment of priests, "which would make them less dependent on the most ignorant and turbulent classes".[10] Castlereagh however felt "it would particularly increase the jealousy of the Protestants, and render them less inclined to the question".

Outside the charmed circle of leading Catholic prelates, peers and gentry, opinion was at first less certain. Theobald Mackenna, whom we have encountered as a leading Catholic opponent of the republican views of Wolfe Tone, and who had followed Kenmare in his famous secession from the Catholic Committee, was commissioned by Castlereagh to write a pamphlet in favour of the Union. This was published in 1799 under the title *Memoirs on Some Questions Respecting the Projected Union of Great Britain and Ireland*. Mackenna was a man of independent, if conservative views, and no mere hack. The advantages of a Union were clearly described:

> The people of Ireland will then have an undivided interest. Foreign capital may be induced to visit us; the property of natives will stagnate in the country, and be formed into masses sufficient to give employment to our people. It is from hence I expect the augmentation of our trade, the increase of export and of home consumption.[11]

He was, however, careful to add that "unless the servants of the Crown mean, among other internal regulations, to include a settlement under the head of religious difference completely coextensive with the grievance, then will an incorporation of the Legislatures be found a measure bad for Ireland, but, if possible, worse for Britain".

Mackenna's pamphlet sitrred up a hornet's nest of criticism. The British Library contains at least five pamphlets by different authors, some anonymous, attacking his arguments, but it is noteworthy that Mackenna himself is invariably spoken of with respect. Thus C. Molyneux's *Reply to the Memoire of Theobald Mackenna Esq* (1799) begins by expressing disappointment that "one who had so ably, and so successfully distinguished himself in the proud career, of supporting three-fourths of the people of Ireland, against penal laws, now sallies forth to overthrow the liberties of *all* the people of Ireland, and becomes suddenly the champion of a junto, he had so ably and honourably opposed". Far from the Union "simplifying" the Irish Constitution it would, stated Molyneux, have the effect of "annihilating" it for ever. It would not tranquillize Ireland but irritate all her people.

Another pamphleteer, John Hamilton, in his *Letter to Theobald Mackenna* took a more moderate line. Though not an out-and-out anti-Unionist, he asserted that "Independence is preferable to dependence — independence can secure us all we desire, and therefore must be retained". He was worried about the prospects for trade under the Union. Before 1782, "Great Britain, I may say, legislated for us, and before that time our personal liberty was well secured, but our trade was not". The merchants of Dublin had, he asserted, attributed their recent prosperity to the existence of an independent Irish Parliament.

Mackenna replied to Hamilton's pamphlet by another entitled *Constitutional Objections to the Government of Ireland by a Separate Legislature*. Conceding that some time back he too would have opposed a legislative union, he went on to point out that Hamilton's argument was fallacious in that as an alternative to Union he had nothing to advocate save "patience and forbearance". "If Ireland really does maintain the port and figure of an independent state, nothing less than irremediable abuse in the conduct of public affairs, can justify the sacrifice of national dignity". But Ireland did not: "the public law of Europe recognizes no such state as independent Ireland". The United Irishmen, indeed, had proposed "to introduce this island into the world, in the new character of a substantive government. I reject and reprobate their design", but on Hamilton's principles "without the dignity of being a separate state, we have all the inconvenience of being a separated people". From a learned review of Irish constitutional history[12] he concluded that there was "no paramount or pre-eminent token of consideration, reserved to Ireland, except the *droit de potence*.[13] The Penal Laws were strongly to be condemned, but they

> never found an advocate out of Ireland; they were discredited in appeals to Westminster. Lord Camden and Lord Mansfield were the first who cried shame upon the system. Lenity came from

abroad, whilst harshness was the immediate and natural propensity of our own government; no unfavourable omen for the meditated change, no light inducement to prefer the usual composition of the British Legislature, to the native rule, recommended by volumes of coercive laws, and a century of inauspicious interference.[14]

Here were powerful arguments to appeal to moderate Catholic opinion, coming as they did from a man whom even his opponents were constrained to admire for his excellent private character as well as his abilities.[15] But, at the end of 1798, the Dublin Catholics at least still hesitated; two important meetings were held at Lord Fingall's, but no resolution was arrived at.[16]

In January 1799 there was an important meeting of the Catholic bishops in Dublin. They agreed "thankfully to accept a provision for the Catholic clergy and were also agreeable to a Government veto on the appointment of Catholic bishops provided that the original, and any subsequent, names which might have to be suggested were brought forward by the priests and Bishops themselves. These proposals which were brought to Castlereagh by Archbishop Troy and Bishop Moylan of Cork, went no further, indeed in some respects considerably less far, than was the practice on the Continent. In Russia and Prussia Catholic bishops had to be expressly nominated by the non-Catholic sovereign, not merely sanctioned; and even within the British Empire, in Canada, no Catholic bishop could be appointed without the Civil Governor's approval.[17] As to a subsidy, the "Regium *Donum*" bestowed upon the Presbyterian ministers of Ireland, originally by King Charles II, provided an analogy. In Scotland some such assistance was already being given to Catholic priests, whose property had been confiscated in France. In England too, there was talk of such provision being made, but English ministers were kept in ignorance of the Irish government's plans.[18]

On 22nd January, the Irish Parliament met, and the subject of a Union was at once introduced. After a long debate, the Address was carried in the lower House by only 107 to 105, but the Lords gave the Government a substantial majority. When the Address came to be reported to the Commons, however, an amendment to omit the clause relating to the Union was carried by 111 votes to 106.[19] Mr Speaker Foster was accused of having influenced the House to reject the clause, and was drawn to his house in triumph by the mob. Lord Clare had his windows broken.

The adverse vote made no difference to the determination of British Ministers. Pitt brought the question before the English Parliament on 31st January in a notable speech, in which he spoke of a "united legislative body" promising "a more effectual remedy" for Catholic grievances "than could be likely to result from any local arrangements". Sheridan and a few others opposed him, but the Resolutions, at that time deemed a necessary preliminary to important legislation, were duly carried.[20]

Leading Catholics, notably Moylan, Bishop of Cork, regretted the rejection of the Union by the Irish House of Commons. On 9th March Moylan wrote to Pelham that "it is impossible to extinguish the feuds and animosities which disgrace this kingdom . . . without an Union with Great Britain . . . The earlier it is accomplished, the better".[21] Dr Bodkin, agent of the majority of secular prelates at Rome, wrote from Galway that the Union was "the only means left to save from ruin and destruction that poor, infatuated Ireland". Opinion polls had not then been invented, but when Isaac Corry accepted office as Irish Chancellor of the Exchequer, and had in consequence to seek re-election at Newry, it was the Catholics, according to a Newry priest, who "stuck together like a Macedonian phalanx" and turned the scales in his favour.[22]

Lecky was a moderate Liberal who afterwards became a Unionist. He published his *History of Ireland in the Eighteenth Century* between 1878 and 1890 as part of his *History of England*. In 1892 it was reissued separately. Lecky thought that Cornwallis was probably justified when he spoke of "a large proportion of the Catholics" being in favour of the Union. An Irishman by birth, Lecky did not, at least when he was writing his great history, approve of the means whereby the Union was brought about. His testimony on this score must therefore carry particular weight. There is indeed abundant evidence of Catholic support for the Union later in 1799, and in 1800. In April 1799 both Houses of the English Parliament presented Addresses to the Crown on the Union but on 1st June the Irish Parliamentary Session was closed without the Union having proceeded any further.

Subsequent events left Cornwallis open to the charge of "bribery". It is true that sixteen new peerages were given; but nine were unconnected with the Union. Lord Kenmare was promoted to an Earldom, but as he could not sit in either House of Lords, bribery seems too strong a word to describe his promotion. There were a few cases where borough-owners like Lord Ely were won over by such expectations, but on the whole, and judging by the standards of the day, a remarkable degree of rectitude was observed. As for monetary compensation to borough-owners, this was a feature of the English Reform Bill of 1785, and even so late as 1832, Lord Eldon maintained that proprietary boroughs were strictly property.[23] £15,000 was the approximate price of each, and eighty such boroughs, returning 160 Members, were purchased. Opponents of the Union, such as Lord Downshire, benefitted equally with supporters; they received about a third of the money.

The Irish Parliament was not dissolved, but 63 seats became vacant, through the death or resignation of Members. Much has been made of this, and it is said that the majority of these resignations was due to the conversion of borough patrons and to the unwritten gentleman's agreement which made it incumbent upon borough members to resign their seats if the patron changed his opinion; but in so far as a change did take place, it is by no means clear that it was caused by bribery. Influence was no doubt exerted, as was the custom of the day; but bribery has never been proved, and O'Connell's assertion that as much as £8,000 was given for a vote in favour of the Union will not bear examination. Mr Gladstone's later attempt to revive these accusations in a review of Ingram's book on the Union in the pages of the *Nineteenth Century* was conclusively refuted by Ingram; and although Mr Gladstone was allowed to have the last word, he failed to substantiate his charges, nor did he add anything to what was by then known of these transactions.[24] Such as is known, indeed, rather tends to the conclusion that it was the opposition that was guilty of bribery and that the pot was calling the kettle black; and it is undoubtedly absurd to think that the comparatively small sums in secret service money sent over from England during this period could have been applied to such a purpose. Ingram replied thus to Lecky's accusations:

> Though he knew that Lord Cornwallis had declared that his Government had neither the means to bribe, nor the wish to resort to such vile measures, he gravely quotes a passage . . . in which Cornwallis expressed his hatred of jobbing, as a proof of his own numerous and individual acts of bribery. The only other proof of the corruption which he termed vast, flagrant, and shameful is even more ridiculous, namely, 'one supporter of the Government in the House of Commons appears to have been excused a debt of £3,000'. We know nothing of the details of this matter, nor does Mr Lecky. It may have been a perfectly innocent transaction.[25]

Even if the means alleged by opponents had been used, they cannot have been very successful, for in the last days of 1799 Cornwallis was writing that "we have a lukewarm, and in some instances, an unwilling majority; the enemy have a bold and deeply interested minority which will, I am afraid, even after our friends are reckoned, run us much nearer than most people expect". Lord Glandore stated categorically in a private letter to Maurice FitzGerald (28 March 1801) that far from having been bribed or rewarded for his support of the Union, he was worse off than previously.[26]

Nevertheless the tour which Cornwallis had begun in July for the purpose of winning over of anti-Unionist opinion proved more successful than he had expected. Amongst the many Addresses in favour of the Union which he then received not a few were from Catholics, for example that of 31 July from the "Catholic inhabitants of Tipperary and Caher, and their vicinity", which was signed by 89 inhabitants[27]; and that of 9th July from the Roman Catholics of Kilkenny, with the Bishop of Ossory as a principal signatory.[28] The Catholics of New Ross and Wexford, scenes of the late rebellion, were not behindhand in expression of loyalty. At Wexford more than 3,000 signed an Address presented by Lord Ely. This referred to the desirability of "the happy completion of the great and useful measure of a legislative Union between Great Britain and Ireland"[29] and at New Ross the Roman Catholic inhabitants asserted that "an Union between Great Britain and Ireland would be attended with the most beneficial effects to both kingdoms, by increasing their wealth, resources and security, by destroying religious animosity, and giving permanent success to both countries, to effectually oppose the attempts of foreign or domestic enemies".[30]

Similar Addresses were presented from the Catholics of Dundalk[31], from those of County Longford, where the Bishop of Ardagh and Clonmacnoise, Dr Cruise, took the chair[32], from the Baronies of Tyrawly and Tyerargh (signed by Dr Bellew, Bishop of Killala)[33], from the City of Waterford[34] (signed by 163 Roman Catholics), and from the Roman Catholic clergy of the diocese of Elphin and County Roscommon.[35] This last concluded with the words:

> Should anything still prove wanting to perpetuate the renewed loyalty of Ireland, and fully re-establish public confidence, so fatally disturbed by the late disgraceful Events, which tarnished the Fame of Ireland, and wasted so much of her Blood; it will,

we presume, be amply supplied by a Legislative Union of this Country with Great Britain.[36]

In a survey of all the Irish dioceses at this period, T. A. Burke found that only one Roman Catholic Bishop (Young of Limerick) is known to have opposed the Union, and of priests and curates whose opinion is recorded, eighty-eight favoured the Union and only twenty were opposed.[37]

Addresses in favour of the Union signed exclusively by Roman Catholics were of course far outnumbered by general Declarations and Addresses signed by persons of all denominations, including Catholics. Thus the declaration of County Meath in favour of the Union was signed, amongst others, by Lord Gormanston and at least two parish priests. A number of parish clergy also signed the County Westmeath declaration.[38]

"The Union", Cornwallis wrote in November 1799, "is, I trust, making progress. The great body of the people in general, and of the Catholics in particular, are decidedly for it".[39] Mackenna was active in pamphleteering, as we have seen, and was recommended as an agent for superintending Unionist literature.[40] He later wrote, in a memorial sent to Abbot, by then Chief Secretary, that

> the four Administrations which successively ruled Ireland, from 1793 to 1800, have each, unsolicited by me, called for that little aid to the cause of civil society and good government which I was able to contribute . . . but the affair of the Union constitutes that ground on which my claim, at least to a certain extent, is beyond all question irresistible. You know that, in consequence of application made to me, I gave up my time and trouble to the cultivation of that question. If contributing nearly as much as any other person to render that transaction palatable to the public, and to extend the credit of it, as a service to Government, that service I must say I rendered.[41]

Among the supporters of the Union was Father Arthur O'Leary, whom we have already mentioned. Lecky describes him as "the most brilliant writer of the Irish Catholics".[42] O'Leary believed that Union would put an end to all religious disqualifications and national jealousies.[43]

Another Unionist was Maurice ("Hunting Cap") O'Connell, Daniel O'Connell's uncle. His was one of the few Catholic families that survived into the late eighteenth century still in possession of some of their ancestral property.[44] He was made a Justice of the Peace on the passing of the Relief Act in 1793, and in 1796 demonstrated his loyalty when he was one of the first to report the arrival of a French fleet at Bantry Bay, a few miles to the south of his house at Darrynane.

Though opposed to the Penal Laws, Maurice O'Connell was of the opinion that it was the duty of Catholics

> to confine themselves to that line of conduct marked out for
> them by the Legislature, and with humility and resignation wait
> for a further relaxation of the laws, which a more enlightened
> and liberal way of thinking, added to the clearer and more
> deliberate attention to the real interests and prosperity of the
> country, will, I hope, soon bring about.[45]

That was written in 1780; and during the nineties O'Connell disapproved of the activities of the Catholic Committee, and in particular of Wolfe Tone's takeover. In a letter to his nephew written in January 1800 he declared that he had for some years disapproved of the "unwise and intemperate" conduct of the Catholics, "whether they assumed the character of the Catholic convention or of the aggregate or select meeting of the Catholics of Dublin". They disregarded their debt for such favours as they had received, not to the Irish Parliament in Dublin, for which he had scant respect, but to the Government in London. It was to that Government to which Catholics must look for future favours, a point which Mackenna, as we have seen, had also made. Such ingrates had, in his view,

> all along been the dupes of designing and insidious men, who
> under a mask of fellowfeeling and liberal friendship were slyly
> and assiduously and treacherously urging them on to their ruin,
> subtly depreciating the favours they received, and artfully
> holding out objects, not attainable at the moment, to excite
> their impatience and involve them in ill-timed and intemperate
> measures and demands.[46]

"Hunting Cap"[47] was a Catholic of independent mind. In some respects his views resembled those of Lord Kenmare, but he did not at first come out in favour of the Union. Lord Glandore, a landlord in North Kerry and Governor of the County, wrote to Castlereagh in

August 1799 that he was "a very sensible man, of considerable property both landed and personal and of great influence amongst the Roman Catholics, by whom he is considered as the head of the independent part of their communion — I mean such as do not derive immediately under my lord Kenmare". Glandore added that Hunting Cap attributed his conversion to the cause of the Union to the arguments he had adduced. Hunting Cap had adopted his nephew, Daniel, as his heir, and was distinctly displeased when the latter spoke to anti–Union resolutions at a Catholic meeting held in Dublin in January 1800. Maurice FitzGerald, Knight of Kerry, who first entered the Irish Parliament in 1795, recalled in a letter to Peel how, having accepted office as a supporter of the Union, he

> went into two elections pending the measure, and was returned without opposition in a county where Roman Catholic interest greatly preponderated, and a Declaration almost unanimous in favour of the Union proceeded from the county of Kerry . . .
> One of my most strenuous supporters in bringing forward that Declaration was Mr Maurice O'Connell, a gentleman of wealth, respectability, and decided loyalty, uncle of Mr Daniel O'Connell.[48]

Some Catholics, as we have seen, were opposed to the Union, though we have found no authority for Lecky's assertion that there were specifically Catholic Addresses against it, and Ingram, in his reply to Gladstone's review in the *Nineteenth Century*, disputed the Grand Old Man's claim that there were substantial bodies of Catholics petitioning against it. The *Anti-Union*, begun in December 1799, mentions three local declarations by Catholics against the Union, but they presented no petition.[49] Moreover Lecky's assertion that "the Catholics looked mainly, in their approval of the Union, to Catholic objects, or were actuated by very natural feelings of resentment or panic" rests on very little evidence.[50] Their pro-Union Addresses make no mention of Emancipation as such; and although the '98 rebellion is widely referred to, "resentment and panic" seem unsuitable words to describe their feelings. They certainly looked forward, under the Union, to a period of greater peace and stability, and one bringing with it greater opportunity; but these could not be secured without the former.

Nevertheless Lord Cornwallis and many other Englishmen, were disappointed that Union and further emancipation could not be run in tandem. With hindsight, it is possible to see that if the Government had been bolder and called a general election in Ireland, the Union would have acquired more legitimacy than it has subsequently seemed sometimes to possess. For although the accusations of bribery were, as we have shown them to be, very largely groundless, the fact remains that they were made, and made by persons holding powerful political positions both in Ireland and Great Britain. Even readers of this account may be tempted to remark that "there's no smoke without a fire"; and although, as we have tried to show, this smokescreen very largely consisted of lies to hide the nefarious antics of the Union's opponents, Mr Gladstone and others later in the nineteenth century were very successful in convincing gullible people that there was something in them. It seems more than possible that a successful "appeal to the country" (the phrase had not then been invented) in Ireland would have enabled the Union to rest on surer foundations. For if we compare and contrast the Union of the three kingdoms, it is fairly easy to see that the Union with Scotland was much more a union between equals than were those made with Ireland and Wales. Contemporaries, however, seem to have been concerned very little with these issues.

On 15th January 1800, the last Session of the Irish Parliament opened. The Speech from the Throne contained no reference to the Union, but Sir Lawrence Parsons moved a fiercely-debated amendment to the Address, insisting that the subject be discussed. He accused the Government of packing the Irish House of Commons in order to force it through. If indeed this was happening (and there is good reason to think that it was not) it was wholly unsuccessful in the case of Grattan, who after a protracted nervous illness was elected for Wicklow on the very day the House assembled, and took his seat on the following morning. Grattan's speech lasted for two hours; but despite all his eloquence and that of others, the anti-Unionist amendment was lost by 138 votes to 96.[51]

The Opposition, disturbed by the support for the Union which had been forthcoming from all parts of the country and which had, in large part, been spontaneous, sent out a letter asking for anti-Union petitions. £100,000 was subscribed, three seats were bought, and other measures of what Lecky himself describes as "a more than dubious kind" were taken. "One venal member — a brother-in-law of Lord Clare — who had voted for the Union in 1799, was unquestionably bribed by a sum of £4,000 to vote against it in 1800, and it is stated by Grattan's biographer that another vote was lost only because the money was not forthcoming for another bribe."[52]

On 5th February 1800, a message from the Lord Lieutenant was delivered to both Houses, recommending the Union in the strongest possible terms. Castlereagh expounded the project, including its financial provisions. These were that the debt charge of Ireland, being so much lower than that of Great Britain, should be kept completely separate. Revenue should be raised by each of the former kingdoms in the proportion of two parts for Ireland to Great Britain's fifteen, this to be reviewable after twenty years. Any surplus from the revenues of Ireland would be applied for purely Irish purposes. All articles were to be exported duty free between the two countries; but in order to encourage and protect Irish industries, import duties at ten per cent were imposed for a limited period on exports of manufactures into Ireland. In the Upper House of the united parliament, Ireland was to be represented by four spiritual peers sitting by rotation, and twenty-eight temporal peers elected for life. In the lower House she was to have sixty-four county Members and thirty-six borough Members, including the University of Dublin.

The debate was long, and included an all-night sitting. At the end of it the Government had a majority of forty-three. Eight members stayed away. In the Lords there was a larger majority, and the speeches of the Opposition were curiously muted. Lord Downshire, after denying the existence of a fund to bribe anti-Unionists, went so far as to assert that he had been no admirer of the Constitution of 1782, and that if a Union had been proposed in that year or at the time of the Regency, he might have supported it.[53]

The Opposition in both Houses were reduced to delaying tactics, but these too were unsuccessful, and towards the end only the commercial clauses were seriously disputed. Some protectionist duties were to be reduced by the Union; nevertheless, divisions on the matter were comfortably carried. By 28th March the Articles had passed both Houses. The Irish Parliament then adjourned for six weeks in order to enable the British Legislature to proceed with the measure. Opposition in London was, as in the previous year, inconsiderable, and the Resolutions were returned with a favourable reply on 12th May. On 21st May a Bill based upon them was introduced and duly passed through both the Irish Houses with little further opposition. A new flag, combining the three crosses of St George, St Andrew, and St Patrick was hoisted in London,

Edinburgh and Dublin, and changes were introduced into the Royal Style and Title, the opportunity being taken to drop the claim to the Kingdom of France, whose cause England had espoused against the Revolution.

CHAPTER SEVEN

Emancipation

The Union was not a piece of sharp practice: rather it was an unintended deception of the Catholics of Ireland. In all the official arguments in favour of the Union in the autumn of 1799, stress had been laid upon the fact that it would make an extension of Catholic emancipation possible without endangering the Church of Ireland; and although no specific pledge was made, there was a strong understanding to the effect that emancipation would follow Union as night followed day.[1] Up to a hundred Catholic members of a *United* Parliament could not be a danger: only in Ireland would difficulty be apprehended. So Cooke had contended in his pamphlet, *Arguments for and Against an Union between Great Britain and Ireland Considered* (1798); and although Pitt, in his January 1799 speech had been vaguer, Castlereagh was given the impression, from conversations with British Ministers in the autumn of that year, that although no pledge was given to the Catholics, yet it was their firm intention to introduce the measure as soon as might be after Union were accomplished.[2]

These however were but informal conversations; and when in September 1800 the Catholic question was formally brought before the Cabinet in London, the Lord Chancellor, Loughborough, convinced of the implacable opposition of the King, with whom he had been staying in Weymouth, objected to anything being granted to the Catholics except a commutation of tithes.

Loughborough indeed had been against modifying the oaths for Members of Parliament as long ago as 1795; and he now enlisted the aid of the Archbishops of Canterbury and of Armagh, and of the Bishop of London, to bring pressure upon His Majesty. The cat had thus been let out of the bag too early for Pitt, who had probably planned that a united Cabinet should present a unanimously agreed measure to the monarch, thus making a Royal veto difficult; as it was, King George was heard to say at a levée on 28 January 1801 that Lord Castlereagh's proposal was "the most Jacobinical thing" he had ever heard of, and that he would consider any man his "personal enemy" who proposed such a measure. He even wrote to Mr Speaker Addington, urging him to persuade Pitt not even to mention the subject.[3]

Knowledge of the King's views at once created a party in the cabinet opposed to the measure; and when Pitt wrote to His Majesty on 31 January he was able to state merely that the majority of the cabinet supported his scheme for the admission of Catholics and Dissenters to public offices, and of Catholics to Parliament, for which Dissenters were already eligible. Pitt's proposals included State regulation and partial endowment of the Catholic clergy, and superintendence both of Catholic and Dissenting preachers. If his policy was unacceptable, he intimated that he might feel obliged to resign. The King was obdurate, replying that his support for the Union "was principally founded on a trust that uniting the Established Churches of the two Kingdoms would for ever shut the door to any further measures with respect to the Roman Catholics"; and he advised Pitt to drop the subject.[4] As has been pointed out in John Brooke's biography of the King, to which a very illuminating preface was contributed by the present Prince of Wales, His Majesty took a simple, soldierlike view of his Coronation Oath, which made no allowance for changed circumstances.[5]

Nevertheless the King might have been forced into a corner and overborne, as he had been over the acknowledgement of American independence. After all, there was no serious alternative to Pitt as "First Minister"[6], and the Opposition, headed by Fox and Grey, were decidedly in favour of Emancipation. But Pitt decided to resign, and Addington took his place: "Pitt is to Addington, As London is to Paddington", the witticism went, Paddington then being a small village outside the metropolis.[7] The bulk of the Ministry remained in office, and the Opposition described the change as a mere juggle.

Cornwallis, for his part, thought that the Union would do little or no good unless it were speedily followed by a Relief Bill. However, he was too percipient to be entirely convinced, even so early as October 1800, that the Cabinet were disposed to agree to Emancipation. "These things which if now liberally granted might make the Irish a loyal people, will be of little avail when they are extorted on a future day".[8] Hearing the news of the rejection of the measure, he confined himself to addressing two papers to leading Catholics in which he asserted first that Mr Pitt was on their side, and second that any agitation on their part would be counter-productive.

Pitt's conduct can only be explained by his devotion to the King. In February 1801 the monarch had a recurrence of his old malady (now diagnosed as porphyria or some other metabolic condition rather than insanity[9]); on his recovery he attributed his indisposition to Pitt's badgering him about Catholic Relief. The latter assured His Majesty that while he reigned he would never again raise the matter. Cornwallis was replaced by Lord Hardwicke, and Clare, who died in 1802, to the last a bitter opponent of emancipation, was succeeded as Lord Chancellor of Ireland by Sir John Mitford, created Lord Redesdale. He too followed Clare's policy, though less strenuously. Lady Hardwicke wrote to Mrs Abbot that her husband's was the only Administration that had never invited the leaders of the Catholic clergy to Dublin Castle.[10] When Lord Fingall was appointed a magistrate for the County of Meath, Redesdale alluded in notable correspondence to "Your Lordship's distinguished loyalty at all times, and on all occasions". Redesdale went on to point out that some of his co-religionists had seemed less loyal; and he appealed to Fingall to exercise his influence:

> True allegiance is an active duty, requiring every man not only to suppress rebellion, when it shall show itself in violence, but to disclose to that Government, under which he lives . . . every thing which can raise ground for such suspicion of disloyalty in others.[11] I can consider no man, whatever his professions of loyalty may be, as truly the loyal subject of a King, whom he thus holds up to his people as an object of disaffection, nay of hatred, because that King holds a different opinion in matters of religion from those who adhere to the See of Rome.

Fingall replied (19th August 1803) that he was "much obliged to you for appointing me a Magistrate of the County of Meath, at a time when the task is so arduous". He agreed entirely with Redesdale on the subject of "active loyalty". On the subject of religion, he entered very reluctantly. He had

> never heard a Catholic wish for the overthrow of the Protestant Establishment, and setting up in its place one of its own religion. This was not the object of the promoters of the rebellion in 1798; nor do I believe it was that of the ruffians and murderers who disgraced this country on a late occasion.[12] The Catholic is ready at this moment to sacrifice his life, his property, every thing dear to him, in support of the present Constitution; in defence of that beloved Sovereign to whom

your Lordship does not seem to think we look up, with that veneration, gratitude, and attachment, which I assure you we do. The Catholic wishes no other Family on the Throne; no other Constitution . . . Catholic loyalty and allegiance, I need not tell your Lordship, would oblige every one of that persuasion to resist and repel, even the head of the See of Rome, were it possible to suppose that the usurper[13] who now disturbs the peace of the world, could send him here with his invading armies.

Fingall then referred to the "doctrine of allegiance" being "unceasingly preached" by the Catholic clergy. "In the year 1796, when Hoche's fleet was in Bantry Bay, the Rev. Dr Moylan published an address to his people, for which, had the French landed, he would undoubtedly have lost his head".

Redesdale replied that "many parts of your Lordship's letter have given me much pain". He himself might well be charitable, but others treated Protestants as heathen. Dr Troy's Pastoral on the duties of Christian citizens (1793) was quoted as holding up high "the exclusive doctrine" and Dr Hussey's Pastoral letter was asserted to be still stronger. "Very little regard can be paid to addresses of the nature to which your Lordship refers me. They are given to the winds, as long as the priests of the See of Rome shall think fit to hold up to their flocks, that all who do not yield obedience to that See are guilty of rebellion against it". Fingall replied that he could not "attempt to vindicate all those who have at different times addressed the Catholics; but the late exhortations . . . are intended and calculated to inspire sentiments of loyalty, obedience, and Christian Charity: and they will, I trust, have that effect".

Redesdale continued the correspondence by replying that he felt the Catholics must change their attitude, otherwise peace could not be secured. Fingall had not convinced him that it was *not* Catholic teaching that those not in spiritual obedience to the Pope were regarded as pagans or rebels. Fingall in reply (4 September 1803) played for time, asking leave to submit Redesdale's points to "our superior clergy"; but as to the Emmet rebellion:

I cannot attribute the unfortunate situation of this country to any thing connected with matters of religious faith; Jacobinism

and French principles and politics, the want of morality, and
the depraved state of the human mind

were the source of its misfortunes, though religion may have been made
a tool by "wicked and designing people".[14]

Hardwicke's Administration was mild and, on the whole, popular.
Catholic chapels were rebuilt at Government expense, and efforts were
made to end corruption. At the general election of 1802 not a single
candidate who had supported the Union was defeated; and Robert
Emmet's conspiracy of 1803, to which Fingall's correspondence with
Redesdale refers, was but a fantastic flicker from the ashes of 1798.

Emmet's brother, Thomas Addis, had been a United Irishman. Like
Wolfe Tone, Robert sought to place his revolt under the patronage of
the French Revolution. Like Tone, he was received by Bonaparte, now
First Consul, who promised aid. Article One of the rebel proclamation
provided for the confiscation of church property. Another rising leagued
with France thus revealed itself anti-clerical as well as anti-British. Yet
Emmet's picture adorns many an Irish cottage wall in company with the
Sacred Heart and other pieties. He is portrayed resplendent in uniform
of green and white. It was perhaps magnificent; but it was not
revolution. The Government were forewarned, but took little action.
Emmet nearly abandoned his men, who killed without mercy: the Lord
Chief Justice of Ireland, Kilwarden, was dragged from his carriage and
stabbed to death with pikes.[15] Approaching the marshalsea or prison,
which was but lightly guarded, they shot the corporal, and then fled.
The rebels' stores were seized, and they soon dispersed. Before eleven
o'clock on that night of 23rd July, Dublin was quiet.[16]

On the 28th, Parliament in London suspended Habeas Corpus and
imposed Martial Law. In Dublin on 4 August, the Earl of Fingall,
Viscount Gormanston, and the titular Bishops of Armagh and Dublin,
waited upon Lord Hardwicke with an Address signed by Catholics in
and around the capital expressing the utmost horror and detestation of
the insurrection. After customary expressions of loyalty, it went on to
assert that "however ardent their wish might be to participate in the full
enjoyment" of the benefits of the Constitution to which they had
professed themselves attached, "they never should be brought to seek
for such participation through any other medium, than that of the free
unbiassed determination of the legislature".[17]

Hardwicke's reply was, as might be expected, gracious and
conciliatory, but ignored the reference to emancipation. He had received

two other Addresses from Waterford and Kilkenny respectively, which omitted all reference to the subject.[18] Pastoral exhortations to loyalty, calling upon people to inform against conspirators, were read in all Roman Catholic chapels. After a month, Emmet was captured and tried. The twenty-four year old son of an eminent Cork physician, and a member of the Protestant Established Church, he was executed together with most of his associates.

In the Imperial Parliament, it was argued whether the Irish Act of 1793 which amongst other things enabled Catholics to serve in the militia, applied to Irish Catholics serving on the mainland, where the English Catholics were still excluded. Plowden, writing in 1811, recalled that when the 1793 provisions were going through the Irish Parliament, the Lord Chancellor, Clare, had asserted that it would soon be necessary for the English Parliament to pass a similar Act, so as to remove any inconsistency. But this had not been done, and in 1811 the Test Act operated precisely as it did when James II granted a commission in his guards to Sir Edward Hales, a Catholic. A famous case ensued concerning the "Dispensing Power", i.e. the supposed power of the monarch to dispense with the operation of statues. It was formally abolished under William and Mary. In 1803 the Government argued that it was perfectly legal for Catholics to serve in any part of the King's dominions.

Few Catholics then held commissions in the militia, and those who did often felt that they were discriminated against in promotions. Anti-Papist prejudice was sometimes self-defeating. Thus a Mr Bulstrode was refused the Paymastership in the Nottinghamshire militia by the Duke of Portland, a distant relative, on the grounds of his religion; but the King granted him a commission in the infantry, despite the fact that he remained a Catholic. And the son of a Mr Taaffe, of Smarmore Castle, Louth, having been refused a commission in the dragoon regiment of his choice, was allowed to join the infantry. Plowden himself drafted a clarifying bill, but it was refused.[19] It was not until 1817 that the matter was cleared up.

In May 1804 Addington resigned and Pitt again became First Minister. The King was ill, and French invasion threatened. Nevertheless, some Catholic hopes were raised; frequent meetings were held in Dublin, one of which at least was attended by the young Daniel O'Connell. Kenmare wrote to Maurice FitzGerald (13 February 1805) that in November 1804 Fingall learnt that there was to be a meeting at Mr Ryan's, Marlborough Street, to get up a petition. Fingall found that the meeting was "moderate and well-disposed" and agreed to join it with all

The tenth Earl of Ormonde's instructions for a parley with O'Neill. (1599)

Father James Healy of Little Bray.

Sir John Ross-of-Bladensburg.

Dr. John Healy, Catholic Archbishop of Tuam.

his friends, of whom Kenmare was one. After two or three meetings, a committee of "very respectable and good men" was set up to draw up a petition to Parliament, and the general meeting then adjourned to 2nd February 1805. On that day it emerged that there was a "cautious" party among the Catholics, no doubt produced in part by the pressure which had been brought to bear by the Administration on such as Lord Fingall. Counsellor Bellew, a member of this party, succeeded in adjourning the meeting for a fortnight. Kenmare wrote on 13th February that "Lord Fingall and all of us who act together do not consider *this* a proper time to bring forward this business". Pitt's view was not in doubt, but difficulties remained from a "high and respectable" quarter. The Prince of Wales and His Majesty's Opposition might be in favour, but "what is the use of a petition, when the result of it is beyond doubt in the present state of things?" Nevertheless, the question remained: what should be the attitude of the "cautious" party should the majority of the Catholic body support a petition? Kenmare preferred to leave Lord Fingall to decide that question, but he inclined to the view that the cautious faction should sign rather than not sign.[20]

On 16th February 1805, at a large meeting of Catholics in Dublin, the petition was ordered to be presented to Pitt by Fingall, Sir Thomas Ffrench, Sir Edward Bellew, Denys Scully and Mr Ryan, with the addition of Lords Gormanston and Southwell. This strong deputation was instructed to add that should Mr Pitt "feel himself precluded by strong reasons from supporting the petition at that moment . . . they would not press for the immediate adoption of the measure prayed for". Kenmare wrote to FitzGerald on 24 February to say that Fingall had decided not to divide the Catholic body. After a long discussion the Committee had decided on a compromise whereby Pitt would be left quite free and at liberty to act in whatever way he saw fit after receipt of the petition. As for Kenmare himself, whilst he "felt the liberality of the leaders of the old and new opposition towards us", it remained his wish that the Government, "to whom alone in fact *we* owe all we have obtained" should continue to handle the issue. Moreover, he had his "personal obligations to his majesty for all he has done for me, though a Catholic".[21]

Hardwicke tried to prevent counter-petitions. However, at the Easter Assembly of the Corporation of Dublin a Mr John Giffard proposed three resolutions against the petition, all of which were carried with large majorities. He was immediately dismissed by Lord Hardwicke.[22]

On 12th March 1805 Pitt received the Catholic delegation in London. The Earl of Shrewsbury and Lord Trimleston were also included. Pitt expressed himself as favourable, but thought the move ill-timed. He hinted at the fundamental difficulty, namely the hostility of the monarch. However, he congratulated the delegation on bringing their petition forward "in a manner most peaceable moderate and laudable . . . but at that time it was impossible for him to present their petition". Scully recorded Kenmare as stating to Pitt that the Catholics "looked to him as their patron, and 'were determined to cling to him and His Majesty's government as long as they possibly could'."[23] The deputation replied that Pitt might perhaps encourage at least a declaratory vote or resolution of the two Houses of Parliament, which would in no way entrench formally upon the Royal prerogative. But Pitt was unwilling even to do this, or to present the petition with the rider that immediate adoption of the measure was not pressed for. He drily observed that if, as the delegation had mentioned, they would if he rejected it take the petition to another Member, he would prefer that, as less embarrassing.

So they applied to Grenville, who with Lord Spencer and William Windham had left office with Pitt in 1801, and to Fox, who was leader of the Opposition. These two presented the petition in both Houses on 25th March 1805; it was debated in May, but rejected by both Lords and Commons.

In the same year Dr Troy, Catholic Archbishop of Dublin, won a case in the English Courts against the *Anti-Jacobin Review*, which had accused him of disloyalty on the grounds that as exhortations to loyalty were read out in many Catholic chapels in his diocese on the very morrow of Emmet's rebellion (24 July 1803), the prelate must have known of it in advance. It was similarly alleged that a Roman Catholic Address of loyalty had been prepared before the 1798 Rebellion which broke out on 23rd May. In the one case it was shown that the Archbishop had written his exhortation on the morning of the 24 July. In the other instance, the response also followed rather than preceded the event.[24]

On 23rd January 1806 Pitt died, and Grenville became First Lord of the Treasury. Fox was now a member of the Government, but refused to consider repeal of the Union, which was to be urged in 1808 by several of the constituent corporations of Dublin.[25] Hardwicke was recalled, and the Lord Chancellor of Ireland, Redesdale, went with him.

The suspension of Habeas Corpus was allowed to expire and the sixth Duke of Bedford became Lord Lieutenant.

After the failure of the petition of 1805, the Catholics dissolved their Committee and elected a new one, with James Ryan, representing the mercantile interest, as secretary. When in London for purposes connected with the petition Ryan had got to know Fox, now become, in effect, "Minister for Ireland". When he applied to Fox for a post, his fellow Catholics in Dublin disapproved of what they felt to be an abuse of his position. Fox promised his good offices, but deprecated another immediate petition. He was hopeful about tithes and about the right to serve in the Army; but added that if the petition were presented, he would himself certainly support it, but could not answer for the survival of the Ministry.[26]

On 1st March a meeting was held in Ryan's house in Marlborough Street to consider the letter. Lord Southwell expressed himself against the presentation of a petition. "He would oppose the agitation of any question, that could tend to create ferments, alarms, or disunion amongst his Majesty's subjects; he was a friend to the present administration; every Catholic in the land, who had a principle of gratitude in his heart, should be friendly to it". When called upon to preside over the meeting, he refused at first to do so, and only agreed after some tumult. Ryan was vehemently denounced for presuming to correspond with Fox, and about twenty dissidents, including Lord Ffrench, left the meeting. A new committee was, nevertheless, appointed in their absence. This agreed that a petition would be inexpedient and drew up an Address of loyalty to the Lord Lieutenant.

On 29th April, an agreed Address was presented to Bedford by Lords Gormanston and Southwell, Sir Edward Bellew and ten others, and signed by more than 1,000 Catholics from different parts of Ireland. After customary expressions of loyalty, it alluded obliquely to "sentiments, in which all Irish Catholics can have but one voice . . . should the wise generosity of our lawgivers vouchsafe to crown that hope, which their justice inspires, it would be no longer our duty alone, but our pride, to appear foremost against approaching danger". Bedford in his reply assured his Addressers that his first object was to secure "the advantages of a mild and beneficent administration of the law".

Other Catholic gatherings were held, and other Addresses presented. On 3rd April, at one such meeting presided over by James Nangle, "the Catholic noblemen and principal gentlemen of Ireland" were invited to join an association to forward emancipation.

Fox died before the year was out, and in Ireland a fresh set of troublemakers, the *Threshers*, made their appearance. Their mischief was directed primarily against tithe proctors, i.e. collectors of tithes and their underlings. Letters were sent, over the signature of *Captain Thresher*, warning growers of flax and oats to leave their tithes in kind in the fields, and to pay no money to rectors and vicars or their agents, the proctors. The Threshers would then destroy whatever tithe corn fell in their way. They were not however rated enough of a menace to justify Martial Law or the suspension of Habeas Corpus.

At the general election of 1805 Grattan was elected to the United Parliament for a Dublin constituency. In May C. L. Dundas had been induced to make way for him at Malton, so that he could participate in the debate on the Catholic petition. The Catholics of Dublin, in an Address to Grattan, complained that not one of their number could vote as a freeman of the Dublin Corporation: they offered Grattan his election expenses, which he declined. The following year saw little Catholic activity of note, but in January 1807 there were several meetings, and in February others, presided over by Lord Fingall, which led to the drafting of a petition. Lord Ffrench, John Keogh and John Burke were also active.

Then in March 1807 a debate took place in the House of Commons on the proposal to increase the grant to Maynooth college. This was duly passed, but Lord Howick's Catholic Officers Bill caused great dissension. It was intended to open all ranks in the Army and Navy to Catholics, in whatever part of the world they might happen to serve; and although this was, as we have seen, already becoming common practice, its enshrinement in legislation was seen as a threat to the Protestant Establishment. Petitions of protest flowed in; there were speeches in the House; and the Coalition Government "Of all the Talents", as it was afterwards called, threatened to break up. Lord Howick withdrew his Bill, but this was insufficient, and the Grenville Administration was dismissed. The Duke of Portland, too infirm even to travel to Windsor for an audience, was asked through Lords Eldon and Hawkesbury to form a new Administration, which he succeeded in doing. Lord Grenville afterwards asserted in the House of Lords that retiring Ministers had been asked, after agreeing to drop the Catholic Officers Bill, to give "a written pledge, that no further concessions to the Catholics should be proposed".[27] The new Government replied that dismissed Ministers had unconstitutionally attempted to drag the Sovereign to the Bar of the House of Commons, to which the Whigs rejoined that the pledge attempted to be exacted was contrary to the Privy Counsellor's oath "faithfully and truly to declare his mind and opinion to his heart and conscience". It was thus the pledge itself, they asserted, that was unconstitutional, not its revelation. "Such an innovation . . . would be in practice to convert the mature negative . . . into an abortive *Veto*, by enabling the King to strangle the *foetus* on its first conception in the House of Commons".[28] But the new Ministers had a majority in both Houses. Thus only a few years after the Union, Irish affairs, and the Irish Catholics, were seen to play a crucial role in Imperial politics.

Meanwhile in Dublin on 18th April the Catholics held yet another meeting with Lord Fingall in the chair. Grattan had been invited to present their petition, but had replied that in his opinion it would have injurious results. Keogh proposed moderation; the petition should be "consigned to the care of the Earl of Fingal" that is to say, neither put forward nor withdrawn. O'Connell was, on this occasion as on many others, intensely respectful of the Throne. However favourable the previous Administration had been to Catholic claims, "he could not tolerate those calumniators of the good old King".[29] However unworthy present Ministers were, "they stand within the shadow of his throne, and . . . it behoves the grateful loyalty of the Irish Catholics to concede the temporary suspension of their just claims". when Hussey persisted in demanding that a definite time should be fixed for presenting the petition, Lord Fingall said that if that were insisted upon by the meeting, he would feel obliged to withdraw. Kenmare, like Fingall, thought that "useless attempts are likely to do more harm than good". The former, indeed, went so far as to say, in a private letter to Maurice FitzGerald, that he would almost prefer an exchange or modification of tithes to Catholic emancipation, though both would be desirable.[30]

During an interlude in his military career, Wellington (then Sir Arthur Wellesley) had become an M.P., and was now chief Secretary for Ireland. The Liverpool papers at the British Library record a conversation between him and Lord Fingall on 26th April 1807. Fingall began by saying that the City of Dublin in particular had suffered considerably from the Union, but that he himself had always been friendly to it, even long before it was publicly agitated, "and that he thought Ireland had derived some advantage from that measure". The subject of emancipation was then discussed. Wellington stated that the Cabinet were indifferent as to whether the question were brought forward or not. "All they felt any anxiety about was the tranquillity of Ireland" a subject upon which

Fingall assured him that he and the Catholic gentlemen were "greatly anxious". Fingall said that he was not always able to act in such matters as he wanted, or as he thought most appropriate for the public, or even for the cause of emancipation itself.

> But he had explained to Mr Pitt that he had placed himself at the Head of the Catholics of Ireland in order to prevent them from passing into the hands of more violent men; but that he was not always able to guide them; & in order to retain any influence over them he was frequently obliged to adopt means which were imprudent, & of which he disapproved.

The subject of the Militia Bill was then alluded to. Wellington claimed that Catholics could already serve the King in any part of the world and that "it was notorious that no officer of the Army or Navy had been required for many years to take any oath". Lord Fingall replied that he thought Wellington mistaken; at the behest of the Duke of York he had brought his own brother over for foreign service, only to have him refused. Lord Kenmare was similarly unhappy about the situation. In a letter to Maurice FitzGerald about Kenmare's brother-in-law, Captain Aylmer, who was visiting Kerry to recruit for the line from the militia, he wrote that the service was

> not very encouraging for Catholics. I must first know for certain whether any objection will be made to the signing of a commission for a son of mine, *well known to be what he is*. Persons who are not as generally known as we are meet with no difficulty, but I am determined that any son of mine who enters the service should do so openly and without any disguise.[31]

There followed at Westminster what Plowden called a "No Popery" Parliament. An Act had been passed by the Irish Parliament in 1796 which gave the Lord Lieutenant power to "proclaim" any county where disturbances existed. In a "proclaimed" county, curfew was imposed, and anyone breaking it might be impressed for the Navy. This measure was now to be re-enacted. Grattan supported, Sheridan opposed, the Bill. An Arms Bill was also passed, and another relating to the Irish militia. According to Plowden, writing at the end of the decade, some two-thirds of the militiamen were Catholics, but commissioned officers were mainly Protestant, except in five or six regiments. Under the Act, those enlisting from the militia into the line were required merely to swear a straightforward Oath of Allegiance. But even this did not completely resolve the problems of Catholics serving in regiments of the line or in the Navy. Some ten years later, Captain Whyte, a Catholic of Loughbrickland, after being promoted from First Lieutenant in the Navy, was denied pay because he refused to take the Declaration against Transubstantiation. He appealed to the Prince Regent and was given a new commission in March 1817. An Act was passed which in effect opened the higher commissions in the Army and Navy to Catholics.[32]

The dangers of French intervention in Ireland and of internal commotion gave point to the legislation of 1807. The Threshers in Connaught had been largely suppressed under existing law, but new factions had appeared, called *Shanavests* (because they wore old waistcoats) and *Caravats*. They were mutually opposed, but both were capable of causing trouble.

On 19th January 1808 the Catholic body again met in Dublin, Lord Fingall presiding. It was resolved that he should present their petition to Parliament at the earliest possible moment. Rumours were afloat that the Pope had issued a Bull to the Catholics of Ireland inciting them to support Napoleon, and much was made of this by the anti-Catholic party. Lord Fingall meanwhile followed the same procedure as had been adopted in 1805, when Pitt was Premier, and first of all tried to present the petition through the King's First Minister, Portland. Grenville and Grattan were then approached, and they undertook to present the petition to their respective Houses, and to support it vigorously, though they were sure that it would be rejected. At this point, perhaps prompted by the rumours of Papal intervention, Fingall discussed with the petition's sponsors and with George Ponsonby, Leader of the Opposition, the possibility of the Crown exercising some influence upon the appointment or nomination of the Catholic prelacy. This subject had already been broached late in the previous century, and it will be recalled that the Catholic bishops had then agreed in principle to some kind of veto. Now, despite the offer of a veto, the petition was rejected in both Houses of Parliament, to the consternation of much of Catholic Ireland. Dr John Milner, the accredited agent of the bishops, repudiated his agreement to a veto. A national synod condemned it, but three bishops supported the veto against twenty-six. The petition of 1809 avoided all mention of the subject; and in 1810 the bishops again pronounced against it.

Lord Kenmare had, in 1810, no very decided view on the subject. The Catholic bishops had, he believed, acted according to conscience and to the best of their judgement. On the other hand, Protestants could not be blamed for wanting a veto. In the present crisis, it should only be a secondary consideration. The existing oaths of the Catholic clergy as well as laity disavowing "all foreign influence of the Pope in temporal concerns" was sufficient. If the securities already given "by their and our oaths", he wrote to Maurice FitzGerald, "are not regarded as valid, nothing else that can be proposed can make them so". The veto might be acceptable if it were in the hands of the monarch, as was the case in those European States most often cited as precedents. But for a Government which changed "oftener than we change our clothes", to have such a power would be "alarming and inconvenient". In a later letter to FitzGerald (26th May 1810) he added that the great cry of the Catholics was that they had no wish to see their Bishops appointed by the credit and influence of powerful men "like so many excisemen and gaugers. I firmly believe also", he added, no doubt referring to such as Daniel O'Connell, "that there are many of the great agitators who perhaps carry their views beyond *catholic emancipation*, who would be almost sorry that there was not some difficulty or other to throw in the way of it, for the sake of keeping up their consequence". Government could head off such agitation if it could "bring itself to despatch what relates to the great body, and leave the ecclesiastical part of the business ad referendum".[33]

On 13th February 1811, Wellesley-Pole, who had succeeded his brother as Chief Secretary for Ireland in 1809, signed a circular letter to the sheriffs and chief magistrates calling for the arrest of anyone involved in publishing notices regarding proposed nominations to "an unlawful assembly sitting in Dublin, and calling itself the Catholic Committee".

As the Earl of Rosse said in the House of Lords, the Catholic Committee had prepared the usual petitions to both Houses and resolved to send a deputation of ten from every Irish county to a kind of Convention. Added to the thirty-eight of the Dublin committee, this would form a representative body of 358. Pole informed the Commons that the Committee of 1810, unlike that of 1809, took upon itself the power to manage, not merely the Catholic petition, but Catholic affairs. A Committee of grievances was appointed. It met weekly, and modelled itself upon the House of Commons. Fingall for one, felt this was going too far. He and his associates took alarm and put through a motion, afterwards rescinded, that the proposal to delegate ten members from each county was *ultra vires*. According to Pole, the petition having been transmitted to England, Lord Ffrench exclaimed: "Your Commission is at an end; you have exceeded your powers; do you mean to erect yourselves into a perpetual parliament!" Lord Fingall was publicly attacked at a meeting for his moderation.[35]

As a result of Pole's letter, two magistrates repaired to the customary meeting-place of the Catholic Committee on 23rd February. Lord Ffrench was called to the chair, and made the excuse that this was not a meeting of the Catholic *Committee*, but merely one of Catholic *gentlemen*, for the purpose of signing and forwarding a petition to Parliament.

On 19th October a new committee, nearly 300 strong, assembled at the theatre in Fishamble Street, watched by a throng of spectators. Lord Fingall presided and spoke; Lord Netterville offered a petition which was unanimously approved; but after seventeen minutes and at the close of business the magistrates appeared. Councillor Hare, their principal, was assured that none among the Catholics meant to show disrespect; but "were all determined to join heart and hand with their fellow-subjects of every religious persuasion, in the defence of their country, to the last drop of their blood". Nevertheless five Catholics were arrested for allegedly breaching the Convention Act by arranging for delegates to be appointed on 9th July. At the trial of one of these, Dr Sheridan, the jury, all Protestants, brought in a verdict of not guilty against the charge of the Chief Justice. The Attorney-General then abandoned the other prosecutions.

The General Catholic Committee met again on 23rd December in Fishamble Street. This time the magistrates arrived punctually and Hare was in his place next to the chair shortly before Lord Fingall came to occupy it. Lord Netterville opened the proceedings, which were tumultuous. It was only through the intervention of Fingall and O'Connell that Hare was allowed to intervene. Addressing himself to the chairman, he asked: were they the Catholic Committee? Fingall replied: "This is a meeting for the sole purpose of legally and constitutionally petitioning Parliament for the redress of grievances".[36] Hare claimed that this was not an answer and asked whether this was a meeting of the General Committee of the Catholics of Ireland, consisting of the Roman Catholic peers, and their eldest sons, the Catholic baronets, the prelates of the Catholic Church, and of certain persons appointed by the counties of Ireland, and by the parishes of Dublin, for the purpose of preparing a petition to the legislature on the part of the Roman Catholics of Ireland. After certain further exchanges, and disorderly interruptions,

O'Connell was instrumental in allowing Hare to speak again. This time he said: "this is an unlawful Assembly, and, as such, I . . . request it to disperse forthwith". Fingall replied that he had

> the honour of being Chairman of this meeting, and it is not my intention to do any thing in violation of the law of the land. I am ready to submit to any legal authority, or to the *assumption* of legal authority; however, I am determined not to quit this chair, unless there shall be such means used as will enable me to bring an action, and to obtain legal redress.

Hare then took his Lordship by the arm and removed him from the Chair. He did the same to Netterville who was asked to take his place. Efforts were made to replace Netterville in turn with Lord Ffrench and Mr Barnewall, but ultimately, on the recommendation of Sir Edward Bellew, the meeting dispersed, or rather adjourned to a tavern, where a requisition for an aggregate meeting of Catholics was signed by over 300 people. The tavern meeting was also interrupted by Hare; but upon being assured that this was merely "a meeting of individual gentlemen", he withdrew. Protestants were present at both meetings, among them Lord Lismore and Hamilton Rowan.

On 26th December the Aggregate meeting was duly held in Fishamble Street, Lord Fingall once more in the chair. In one of the more fulsome tributes, he was described as "Father of the Catholics of Ireland", and indeed his conduct had been a model of courtesy and correctness. Lord Moira wrote from London:

> allow me to offer my sincere compliments on the dignified and admirably temperate conduct which you have so recently displayed. The firmness was necessary to bring to issue a question of incalculable importance to the community, and the moderation must command the most favourable [? presumption] for your cause.[37]

Strong resolutions were passed against submitting to what was described as a perversion of law and abuse of power. It was resolved to send a humble and dutiful Address to the Prince Regent, and a General Committee of Catholics in Ireland was asked to assemble on 28th February 1812. The preparation of the Address was entrusted to a Board.

In January 1812 a Mr Kirwan was given only a nominal fine for acting as a delegate for one of the parishes of Dublin and on 28th February the aggregate meeting of Catholics was duly held and unanimously voted the petition to the Prince Regent. "Our object", it said in part, "extends to an equal participation of the civil rights of the constitution of our country . . . it extends no further". The petition to Parliament however sustained a third defeat; "nor did it appear", stated the *Annual Register*, "that the accession of the Prince Regent to the full authority of the Crown had made any difference as to the sentiments and conduct of his ministers on this important occasion".[38] Nevertheless His Royal Highness the Duke of Sussex spoke in the Lords in its favour, and in June a motion by Canning to consider the laws relating to the Catholics "early in the next Session" was passed by a decisive majority in the Commons, though rejected by the Lords.[39] O'Connell's uncle, "Hunting Cap" wrote in May that "the only consolation left to the Catholics is what I have frequently known beaten armies to assume and set up, which is that they had made strenuous and vigorous efforts and a firm, resolute and determined stand".[40]

Protestants were by now active in the cause of emancipation; but so were petitioners against it. It was against considerable odds that Grattan rose in February 1813 to present his motion for a Committee. All the old arguments were rehearsed; the motion for a committee was carried by a small majority, and Grattan's consequential Bill, although it obtained a second reading, ran into the sands after Mr Speaker Abbot himself spoke in favour of the words "to sit and vote in either House of Parliament" being left out of the Bill.

The Bill had earlier been amended in Committee so as to reserve the power of veto over the appointment of Catholic prelates to the civil power: it envisaged Boards of Commissioners with both Catholic and non-Catholic members for Great Britain and for Ireland as preliminary "vetters". The Irish Catholic bishops disapproved of these provisions; and in a pastoral Address dated 26 May 1813 stated that they would "willingly swear, if required by the legislature, that we will never concur in the appointment or consecration of any Bishop whom we do not conscientiously believe to be of unimpeachable loyalty and peaceable conduct".[41]

Peel, who had become Chief Secretary in 1812, wrote on 21 October 1813 to Sidmouth that the Catholics of Ireland were divided into four classes — "the clergy, the lower order of the people, the moderate and respectable part of the Catholics, and the violent party, with O'Connell and Scully at their head".[42]

Michael Burke, a Protestant, was used by Peel in his efforts to detach moderate Catholics from extremists. On 19th March 1814 he wrote to Peel that in Galway one of the most intelligent of the Catholics had told him that he "had not thought it possible that any body of Catholics could become so unpopular among the Catholic gentry as the Board are". Some members of this Catholic Board, as the Committee had now come to be known, seceded on the subject of the veto.[43] Professor Norman Gash[44] has established that though the county correspondence over the whole period of Peel's Secretaryship (1812–18) contained a good deal of generalized assertion of the disaffection of the Roman Catholic clergy, it also furnished some specific instances of their loyalty, their co-operation with the civil authorities, and their attempts to discourage lawlessness.[45]

Exceptional saintliness of character could sometimes bridge sectarian differences. John Jebb (1775–1833), Protestant Bishop of Limerick from 1822 to 1833, was a noted opponent of Catholic emancipation; yet in 1824 his Catholic counterpart, Dr Tuohy, said that a pastoral of his "breathed the true spirit of Christian charity, brotherly love, and conciliation", and when Jebb's Vicar-General died the Catholic clergy, led by their Bishop, walked in the funeral as far as the door of the cathedral. When Jebb himself was seriously ill, prayers were offered for his recovery.[46]

In May 1814 a letter from Quarantotti, President of the Sacred Missions at Rome, was made public. With a few exceptions, the veto provisions of the Catholic Emancipation Bill were given papal approval. O'Connell, at a meeting of the Catholic Board on 7th May, denounced the interference of the "slaves at Rome"; he would rather not have emancipation at all, he said, if the veto were to be made a condition of it.[47] The Catholic priests of Dublin and many provincial clergy also came out against the Quarantotti rescript; and the Bishops, at a general meeting at Maynooth on 25th May declared the rescript non-mandatory and deputed two persons to wait upon His Holiness.

On 3rd June the Catholic Board was declared unlawful. O'Connell's response was an "aggregate meeting" of Dublin Catholics at which a resolution was passed denying this commination. Subjects, it was asserted, had a right to petition, and this right had been especially saved by the Convention Act. General Count O'Connell, Hunting-Cap's brother, wrote to his nephew from Paris:

I cannot refrain myself from congratulating you on the fair opportunity the late proclamation affords you of bidding farewell to the late Catholic council, or committee of Dublin, as well as to all your political pursuits, and to confine yourself in future solely to the practice of your profession in which you are sure to reap both honour and profit . . . all past and future measures, in the manner and course followed till now, will tend to no useful purpose nor will ever lead towards the accomplishment of the great object.[48]

The only effective way to attain emancipation, he added, was a "prudent, peaceable and loyal deportment . . . tumultuous assemblies or meetings . . . intemperate speeches and hasty resolutions are better calculated to defeat than to promote that object". Some Catholics, especially in Cork, where a meeting was held on 24th August 1814, deeply resented what was seen as an abandonment of their cause by Grattan and Donoughmore; but O'Connell advocated again entrusting them with petitions.[49]

Towards the end of the year there were signs of some closing of the Catholic ranks; on 13th December 1814 a meeting was held at the house of Lord Fingall. Some who had formerly seceded were present, and it was agreed that future activities should be confined strictly to petitioning.[50] Grattan advised the Catholics to adopt conciliatory tactics, and not to press for unconditional Emancipation; but on 17th January 1815, at another meeting with the seceders, O'Connell declared himself ready to perpetuate the division rather than agree to anything less than unqualified emancipation. In an eloquent speech, Fingall took the view that the question could not be carried through Parliament without "some understanding between the see of Rome and the Crown, on the subject of appointment of Bishops". But the bulk of the meeting was against him; and a Mr Eneas MacDonnell suggested that the speech had been his "farewell address to the Catholic body". Fingall denied this; but the *Dublin Evening Post* (19th January 1815) declared that "the Vetoists, with Lord Fingall at their head, have been routed". On 24th January Fingall felt constrained to decline the chair at an aggregate meeting, declaring that faith had been broken with him respecting the Veto. Perhaps for the first time, he found himself to be unpopular with a substantial section of his co-religionists, and "retired in a torrent of hisses".[51] Resolutions for unqualified emancipation were then moved and carried. The other seceders did not attend. The Irish bishops, too, were in militant mood.

In an Address to the Prince Regent, after congratulations on the victory at Waterloo and expressions of gratitude for benefits already conferred, they complained that any form of veto "would only substitute for one mode of servitude, another still more galling and oppressive". Dr Murray had visited Rome on their behalf, and the Quarantotti rescript had been recalled.[52] On 17th February, Peel wrote to Sidmouth that "the schism which has long existed between the Catholic aristocracy and the 'Catholic leaders', as they call themselves, is openly avowed . . . I think you will find that the mob, and the priesthood, and the prelacy, will adhere to the 'leaders' ".[53]

The Catholic Board was now re-formed under the name of "Catholic Association" (not to be confused with the better-known Association of the same name formed in 1823). Its ostensible purpose was to petition Parliament and its first reported meeting was on 4th February 1815. Grattan was not prepared to present a petition from the meeting held on 24th January 1815 and the new Association, having drawn a blank with the Knight of Kerry, prevailed upon Sir Henry Parnell to officiate. The latter failed in the House, and later in the year the Association presented the Pope with a remonstrance, purportedly from the "Catholic laity of Ireland" praying His Holiness not to countenance State interference in the appointment of bishops. This failed in its effect, and their envoy, Richard Hayes, was ultimately deported from the Papal States in July 1817.[54]

Meanwhile the seceders were not inactive. At a meeting at Lord Trimleston's house on 13th February 1816 a petition was drafted which declared that the Catholics of Ireland were prepared to accept a qualified emancipation. Lord Southwell was in the chair, and William Bellew (Sir Edward's brother) was appointed to manage the details. This petition was circulated for signature throughout Ireland, as was a rival petition from the Catholic Association. Vetoists squabbled with anti-vetoists, for example in the chapel at Skibbereen.[55] Grattan agreed on 23rd February to present the vetoist petition, and in the absence of Lord Southwell and Sir Edward Bellew, it was presented to him by Lord Trimleston and others. But it was rejected in the House of Commons by thirty-one votes. Sir Henry Parnell presented the anti-Vetoist petition, signed by twenty-three prelates and 1,052 priests; it too was rejected, as were both petitions in the Lords, presented impartially by Lord Donoughmore.[56]

On 17th December 1816 a further attempt was made to bridge the gap between the Association and the seceders, at a meeting held at the Clarendon Street Chapel under the chairmanship of Sir Thomas Esmonde.

It was agreed that the petition of 1812, signed by Fingall and the others before the Veto controversy arose, should be re-adopted; and a resolution was passed favouring nomination of Catholic bishops in Ireland by Dean and Chapter.

But a further meeting of the seceders was held on 4th February 1817, "confined to those persons who signed the Petition entrusted to Mr Grattan last year". According to the *Dublin Evening Post*, "a foot-boy of Sir Edward Bellew was stationed in the hall of the house . . . to prevent the entry of any but the vetoists". Despite this, O'Connell and others succeeded in entering, and a Mr Mahon declared that he was determined to remain. Lord Southwell asked the anti-Vetoists to withdraw, for they had not been invited. O'Connell said he would not withdraw. Bellew and his brother, who was a lawyer, then consulted, and after Southwell had taken the chair, Sir Edward moved the adjournment on the grounds that there were persons present who had not been summoned. O'Connell opposed the motion, it is said with such eloquence that Bellew's brother agreed to withdraw the motion of adjournment.

Two resolutions were then moved, the first calling on Grattan to present again his petition of the previous year, and the other expressly recognizing the legislature's right to make laws governing the doctrine and discipline of Catholics but asking it not to interfere in either. Mahon and O'Connell both spoke, the latter saying that he was prepared to accept any concession which would procure unanimity except "express or implied assent to any Vetoistical measure". He proposed a joint committee, two from each side, in order to secure unanimity. An adjournment for four days was moved by James Connolly, one of the Vetoists, but it was rejected by fourteen votes to seven, those of O'Connell and Mahon not being counted. Lord Southwell from the chair said that there could be no unanimity unless Vetoist arrangements were accepted. After the count, O'Connell rose and said that he had made every effort to promote unanimity but he had failed; "he would announce to them the undoubted truth, that their puny efforts for a Veto were poor and impotent, and would be blasted by the voice of the Catholic clergy and People of Ireland". He and his friends then withdrew, and the resolution was adopted, and transmitted to Grattan, who promised to move upon their petition. The Vetoists were supported by the English Catholic Board.[57]

Sir Thomas Esmonde was still chairman of the Association, and in a circular letter he again pressed "domestic nomination" as an alternative which might unite all parties. But the seceders remained firm, and during a visit to England in June 1817 O'Connell wrote to his wife that he had waited on Fingall as well as on the English Catholic Board but: "as a *great secret*, I mention to you that I do *not* think he will come back to the Catholics".[58] On his return to Ireland O'Connell descended to smear tactics. "Division does exist among the Catholics", he asserted on 3rd July, and the leader of the secession was "the pensioner of the Castle — the stipendiary of the enemies of Catholic freedom and Catholic right . . . Mr William Bellew". Bellew, a brother of Sir Edward and a Counsellor, as barristers were called in Ireland had, claimed O'Connell, had two pensions of £300 a year from the Castle. In 1813 he had, he asserted, come to the Catholic board, tried to make it censure the Bishops, and after having divided it in the proportion of eighteen to sixty, "trained off the seceders, separated them from the Catholic people, and that day fortnight obtained an additional pension of £150 a year from the persecuting Duke of Richmond" (a polite reference to the fourth Duke, who was Lord Lieutenant of Ireland from 1807–13). The Duke had then, he added, quickly issued a proclamation against the Board. O'Connell ended with a plea to the Earl of Fingall to "return and resume his proper station at the head of the Catholic people".

On 12th July 1817 the Catholic Board was reconstituted in Dublin. The news had come through from Rome that this issue of domestic nomination of prelates (that is to say, by Dean and Chapter in Ireland instead of by the Holy See) had been taken out of the hands of Propaganda (the branch of the Roman Curia dealing with Irish affairs) and remitted to higher authority. The anti-Vetoists' emissary, Hayes, had, it was learnt, been banished from the Papal States. All this was blamed by an anonymous correspondent in the *Dublin Evening Post* (10 July 1817) on the activities of the Vetoists in London, acting it was said through the English Consul-General and the Hanoverian Ambassador. The sole object of the appointment of Baron Ompteda to the latter post seemed to the anti-Vetoists to be to interfere in the affairs of Ireland.

The Catholic Board prepared a letter which was sent to all Irish bishops protesting amongst other things at the fact that "Catholic discipline in Ireland has been submitted to the Propaganda, as if this were a mere missionary country without a national Church". Domestic nomination ought, it said, to receive the "active approbation" of Catholic prelates. The Board could then submit it with more confidence to Rome.

Dr Troy, Archbishop of Dublin, and Murray, his coadjutor, replied on 18th July 1817 to the effect that the bishops did not need the Board to tell them their business; but that they would "be ever ready to pursue with a firm and steady step the path of duty which their consciences shall point out". Other bishops were more favourable to the Board's view. O'Connell complained on 27th July that "the. pliant Trojan" (meaning Dr Troy) had persuaded Murray to support the veto. This was galling, as Murray had, according to O'Connell, formerly compared the vetoists to Judas.[59]

By August 1818 the re-constituted Board was being referred to as the "little Parliament". Towards the end of that year negotiations were again resumed with Lord Fingall and his associates, but O'Connell eventually concluded that they must do without him, although "in truth, I am sincerely sorry for it because he is an excellent gentleman and personally as pure as gold . . . We must not arraign his motives".[60] Thomas Wyse, too, had a very high opinion of his Lordship. "From his placid lips", he wrote, "there never burst an unworthy complaint; he boasted and promised little; but neither what he promised, did he fail to perform". His countenance:

> full of benignity, was a fit expression of the interior man: he was mild and modest: but there was also in him the firmness and honour of a true gentleman, the spirit and perseverance of a true patriot . . . He screened by his individual character, pure even from the breath of calumny, the errors and offences of an easily-excited people . . . Conciliating to all; bearing all in patience; sacrificing in nothing and to none his principle; after a series of the most contrasted events, exhibiting the most opposite principles, he fully succeeded in producing a spirit of unanimity until then unknown in the Catholic community.[61]

In this spirit, he was still prepared to co-operate with O'Connell for certain purposes, and in a letter of 10 January 1819 wrote that he would "ever feel most grateful for the kindness and partiality of those who wish my interference though convinced they much overrate any services I could render". And, with characteristic modesty: "I was for a long time, when better fitted to take a part, a very unsuccessful participant in our political proceedings".

Fingall lived on until 1836; but in his later years, particularly after he was made a peer of the United Kingdom and had to spend long periods in London, his son and heir, Lord Killeen, largely assumed his mantle. In 1819 numerous petitions were presented for and against Emancipation. Grattan introduced no fewer than eight Catholic, and five Protestant, petitions. His motion was rejected by a small majority. In the Lords the petitions were defeated, but the Bishops were not unanimous in their rejection. Lord Grey later attempted to move a bill to relieve Catholics of the need to take the Declaration against Transubstantiation and against the Invocation of Saints. This however was rejected on second reading.

1820 saw the death both of George III and of Grattan. In his dying hour, the latter exhorted the Catholics "never to make common cause with the abettors of radical reform". In 1819, he had said of the Union, which had earlier opposed, that "the marriage having taken place it is now the duty, as it ought to be the inclination, of every individual to render it as fruitful, as profitable, and as advantageous as possible".

On 30th May 1820 all was sweetness and light at a meeting of Catholic gentlemen held at the D'Arcy Tavern, Essex Street, with John O'Connell in the chair. Dr Troy, Archbishop of Dublin, agreed that the Liffey Street Chapel be used for the next aggregate meeting, and Stephen Woulfe read a petition prepared by Daniel O'Connell. The possibility of an Address to the new King was also mooted and Sir Edward Bellew was mentioned as among those who would go to England if called upon to present it. Bellew took the chair at an adjourned meeting on 2 June, for which Lawless had prepared a draft Address. After paying tribute to Lord Fingall, Bellew opined that "we have little to apprehend in this benigner age from the malignant aspersions of former times, and not more from the obsolete calumnies of controversial strife . . . We do not come as jealous and suspicious rivals to gavel the constitution, but with fraternal minds to participate in the great incorporeal inheritance of freedom".

At a Catholic dinner on 7th July, Lord Fingall took the chair. After the loyal and other toasts had been drunk, Daniel O'Connell rose and said that whatever differences there might be amongst Catholics on some questions, they could unite in celebrating the public virtue and private worth of Lord Fingall. The *Dublin Journal* on 7th June had congratulated "the country and the Catholic body, on that rational tone of moderation and good sense which characterise the proceedings of the distinguished advocates of emancipation".

In 1821, the Catholic question was again raised, this time in the House of Commons by Plunket: "He who worships Osiris, the ape, the crocodile, the host of heaven, and the creeping things of the earth, is admitted to the privileges of the State, and our abhorrence is reserved for the Roman Catholic, who believes all that we believe, and differs from us only by believing something more".[62]

Peel, now Home Secretary, was as usual opposed, but on this occasion, he was unsuccessful, and the House went into Committee. Plunket's resolutions were agreed to *pro forma*, but when his resultant Bills came to be read, there were a number of petitions against the Catholic claims, including one from Catholics in Staffordshire and Warwickshire. O'Connell denounced them in a letter to the *Dublin Evening Post*[63]. Plunket blamed Dr Milner, one of the signatories, who he said had frustrated matters in 1813. Neither of his two Bills included the principle of the Veto in terms, but one of them did propose to regulate the manner in which the Catholic clergy should treat with the Pope. Wherefore the bishops of Ireland and some of the laity were said to be against the measure, calling it "the slavery Bill' and the "Bill of insults"; nevertheless it was consolidated with the other and duly passed the House of Commons, only to be rejected by the Lords.

On 12th August 1821 the new King landed at Howth. His arrival had been preceded on 10th July by a meeting of Catholics at which an emissary from the Corporation of Dublin was present, to arrange for an Address to be presented without any controversial proceedings. Fingall conferred with the Lord Mayor; there were promises (not in the event, realized) not to dress King William's statue on the Twelfth; and all was amicably arranged for a joint coronation dinner. The press was so great at the King's landing that Dennis Bowes Daly, as he shook hands, had his pocket picked. Protocol was carefully arranged: the Addresses of the Church of Ireland, Trinity College, and the Dublin Corporation only were received "on the Throne"; a somewhat lesser mark of distinction, reception "in the Closet" was accorded to the other three, the Roman Catholic bishops, the Presbyterians, and the Quakers. Others, some 270 in number, had to be content with the more public "levée". The anonymous writer of *The Royal Visit* (Dublin, 1821) stated that three out of the four Catholic archbishops were present at the Closet reception on 20 August, together with Dr Murray and six other bishops, including Doyle. They were dressed in full episcopal robes, and wore golden crosses on their breast. The compiler of the account asserted that there had been a difficulty, not only in persuading the authorities to agree to a Closet reception, but in allowing the Address to be submitted by the bishops at all. "A certain nobleman" (he can only have been alluding to

Fingall) "fought this point most strenuously and successfully". At the levée, "His Majesty was pleased to address the Earl of Fingall in a most courteous and affable manner"; on 28th August, he was among those admitted as a Knight of St Patrick; and on his departure, on 3rd September, the King, "Laying his hand upon Lord Fingall's shoulder . . . [said], 'Tomorrow you shall see my letter, I think it will please you'".

This was, perhaps, an allusion to the one contretemps of the visit when, at the Corporation dinner, a toast to the "Glorious, Pious and Immortal memory" was duly drunk, despite the King's disapproval; but Alderman Darley, who had called for it, said he had been inebriated at the time and was very sorry. The King, in his letter to the Lord Lieutenant, expressed the hope that "not only the spirit of loyal union, which now so generally exists, will remain unabated and unimpaired; but that every cause of irritation may be avoided and discountenanced". Besides the formal Address of the Catholic prelates, another was presented at the levée, signed by Fingall and O'Gorman, from the "Roman Catholics of Ireland". Drafted by Sheil, it stated that "In other parts of the great Empire over which you are appointed to rule, you will behold more gorgeous evidence of wealth and grandeur, and power, but in none will you ever find a more exalted or deeply-rooted attachment to your Royal Person".

At the King's departure, O'Connell presented him with a laurel crown, on bended knee; but a reaction set in and later in the year there were serious disturbances in Limerick, Mayo, Tipperary and Cavan. Wellesley replaced Talbot as Lord Lieutenant; and Plunket became Attorney-General. Both favoured Catholic claims.[64] But the Cabinet in London was not favourable to further emancipation. On 8th January 1822 Wellesley was presented with two Catholic Addresses of congratulation. The Dublin Corporation continued adamantly anti-Catholic, and a Mr Hugh O'Connor was refused admission at the quarterly guild of the merchants of Dublin.[65]

Outrages multiplied, especially in Munster; Cork County was particularly affected, and the Whiteboys were evilly prominent. Large rebellious bands retired into the mountains and descended upon the military. The Insurrection Act was re-enacted, and Habeas Corpus suspended. These measures had some effect; but the disturbances spread from Cork to Waterford, Wexford and Carlow; to Limerick and Tipperary, and to Donegal in the north. Later in the same year there was an Act for a more effective civil police. Constables were now to be appointed by the Crown and not by Grand Juries, and resident magistrates ("R.M."s) to supplement the Justices of the Peace.[66]

According to the *Annual Register*, the insurgents could be divided into three classes; the poor, the politically disaffected and the superstitious. Only a few of the second category remained, left-overs from 1798. The third category were the "Papists". The *Register* argued that tithes and taxes were not the "sole or principal inciting cause" of these problems. In the case of tithe, no agistment was paid, nor was any tithe paid on calves, lambs, pigs or livestock — "and even the tithable articles — corn, hay, and potatoes — were not rated at any thing like their full value". Moreover the Irish husbandman paid no direct tax to the State; he was not liable to duty for fewer than six windows. A small indirect tax was levied on leather, but the duties on alcohol and tobacco could be avoided. It was the local charges that were the chief grievance; grand jurors and J.P.s were often "jobbers" and laid them on thick. In the absence of any scientific survey, a farmer with 300 acres might be charged as much as a neighbour with 1,200 acres of similar land. It was widely believed that the troubles were stirred up by tobacco smugglers and operators of unlicensed stills in the south-west of Ireland, in order that the military could be diverted and arms smuggled in.[67]

By April 1822, the disturbances were at an end, but famine supervened. The potatoes rotted in the ground, and became very dear. Oatmeal soon ran out too, and many in Connaught and Munster starved. Even the seed potatoes were eaten, and the cattle went short of hay. The other provinces were not affected; but the mass of the people in Connaught and Munster had no money to buy food for man and beast. There was the will to bring in relief, but the Government shrank from furnishing the enormous sums necessary to feed the starving. A programme of public works was instituted, and funds were raised on both sides of the Irish Sea to ease the distress. By September, the worst was over, and considerable relief funds remained unspent. An attempt was made to deal with the tithe question by empowering the proprietors of tithes to lease them to the land's occupants. But the Act had little effect.

Wellesley's Catholic sympathies were shown when he forbade the customary silken adornment of William III's statue in College Green on 4th November. On 14th December, he was hissed at the theatre, and a bottle was thrown at the viceregal box. Juries refused to convict the culprits, and the sheriff was alleged to have said that "the traversers need not be under any apprehension of a conviction, for he had an Orange panel in his pocket, ready for the trial". It was subsequently resolved in the Commons that the sheriff's conduct should be inquired into at the Bar of the House; but the inquiry was inconclusive.

The Catholic question was raised only in Canning's motion for a Bill to enable Catholic peers to sit in the House of Lords. He argued that the Act of 1678 had been passed primarily in order to exclude James Duke of York, as he then was, though in practice he was excepted from it, and that it was not intended to be permanent. The Elizabethan Act excluding Catholics from the (English) Commons did not apply to the other House, for the Lords were expressly excluded from the requirement to take the Oath of Supremacy; and even in the Commons some Catholics had contrived to evade it. An Act of 1791 had enabled the Catholic peer to have access to and advise the Monarch provided he denied the civil and temporal power of the Pope within the realm; and at the coronation of George IV, Catholic peers were summoned to attend for the first time in 150 years. Canning's motion was carried by a small majority.

Peel opposed the Bill but expressed willingness to make other partial concessions such as allowing Catholic barristers to become King's counsel. The Bill passed all its stages in the Commons, but was defeated in the Lords.[68]

In the spring of 1823 Lord Killeen, Fingall's son and heir, accepted O'Connell's invitation to preside alternately with Sir Edward Bellew at the monthly meetings of the now reconstituted Catholic Association. Gormanston and Kenmare also lent their support.[69] Killeen soon found, however, that the lawyers were setting too fast a pace, and retired with his associates when he found that extraneous matter, quite apart from the petition to Parliament relating to emancipation, was being introduced into the discussions. It was nearly a year before this breach was healed. Although Goulburn, then Chief Secretary, took the view in October 1824 that both Fingall and Sir Edward disapproved privately of the Association but dared not come into the open about it, O'Connell claimed that only Lord Southwell ultimately refused to join the emancipation movement.[70]

The new Association first appeared upon the Parliamentary scene in June 1823, when Brougham introduced a petition from an association calling itself "The Irish Catholic Body", complaining of unequal administration of justice. Another member, Colonel Barry, identified it as emanating from the Catholic Association. Even the Parliamentary advocates of emancipation were becoming desperate. Plunket, formerly their staunchest helper, had in 1822, as Attorney-General for Ireland, declined to bring forward the question, and in 1823, despite assertions by Sir Francis Burdett in a debate on 17th April that the "once terrible triumvirate of the Pope, the Pretender, and the Devil was at an end", and that the Pope himself was "now considered as harmless as any other old woman in Christendom", the motion for emancipation was not only lost, but at least one other speaker treated the debate as a sham, a farce, and a foregone conclusion.[71]

We have seen that even Peel had shifted his ground and was prepared to admit some concessions. Indeed after emancipation he was an advocate of what would nowadays be called "positive discrimination" in favour of Catholics.[72] In May 1824 Goulburn, Chief Secretary from 1821 to 1827, denied that even then Catholics were excluded from appointments for which they were eligible. Of 1,800 persons on the police establishment, he said, 900 were Catholics, and official appointments to the value of £3,000 a year, out of a total of £8,700, had been given to them since the Marquess Wellesley had taken office three years previously.[73] Of other offices, however, it has been shown that Catholics in 1828 occupied only thirty-nine out of 1,314 in the judicial, and 134 out of 3,063 in the civil field, despite the fact that they comprised six-sevenths of the population.[74] All these were offices for which they were already eligible; emancipation would open to them only a further 250 posts in the judicial, and 650 in the civil fields, including Membership of Parliament. They had much more, therefore, to gain from improved education and greater fairness in selection procedures than from emancipation *per se*.

The new Catholic Association, from small beginnings in 1823, had burgeoned, and on 31 May 1824 Plunket presented a petition from about 1,800 members. On the same day a counter-petition from a body of freeholders and freemen in Dublin complained that the Association was sitting virtually as a Parliament; it held regular meetings, nominated committees, received petitions, ordered a census to be taken of the people, and had even levied a tax, "appointing collectors in every district for the receipt of imposts, to which they gave the name of the 'Catholic Rent'". The purpose of the fund was not clear; but amongst its avowed aims was to improve the supply of priests in America and England and to buy up those periodicals which seemed to be anti-Catholic. Why did the Government do nothing, asked Charles Brownlow (a member of the Orange Society)? The Attorney-General for Ireland had been very anxious to get hold of the bottle-throwers in the theatre; why was he so supine in regard to the Association? Plunket, mindful no doubt of the failure of the earlier prosecutions, agreed merely to keep the Association under watch.[75]

In 1825, the proceedings of the Catholic Association dominated Parliament. The Gracious Speech of 3rd February proposed to remedy the evil of "associations" which were irreconcilable with the spirit of the constitution and which exasperated animosities. Most speakers thought that the Catholic Association only was meant.

On 10th February Goulburn introduced a Bill to supplement the convention Act of 1793 and an Act against Orange Societies and processions which had been passed in 1823. Whether or not the Catholic Association aimed at repeal of the Union was a matter of some doubt; what was not in doubt was that the means it was using were incompatible with good government. True, the Association contained a large proportion of the Catholic gentry and aristocracy, but their connexion with it was not entirely voluntary; and many of them were extremely alarmed at its proceedings. The "Catholic Rent", though in form voluntary, was an exaction; parish priests were virtually instructed to keep registers of those who paid and those who did not, and landlords who advised tenants not to pay and opposed the "Rent" were being held up to reprobation and scorn. The Association was even conducting its own murder inquiries and coming to conclusions independently of the courts. In its "Address to the People of Ireland" (December 1824) it had referred to "the affectionate reverence you bear for the gracious Monarch", but added also "the hate you bear the Orangemen". At the same time, secret and illegal societies and Whiteboyism were condemned.

Tierney replied to this and other arguments by Peel and Plunket that the Association had raised only £10,000. The debate went on for four successive nights, and some of the more moderate Catholics began to feel they had gone too far. The Catholic Rent as such was abandoned and replaced by "British Catholic Free Gifts".

On 17th February Brougham introduced a petition against the mooted Bill. It declared that the Rent was subscribed to by many Protestants; the money was applied to lawful purposes; and the petitioners in no way claimed to "represent" any portion of their countrymen. Brougham failed to obtain leave for the petitioners to appear in person at the Bar of the House.

The Association consistently denied that it was "representative" (an attribute proscribed by the convention Act). So the new Act forbade the setting up of bodies which purported to redress grievances, assisted in legal processes, renewed their meetings for more than fourteen days, or collected or received money. An attempt was also made so to draft the Bill as to preclude the Association's being set up under another name.

The Catholic Association accordingly "expired without a struggle", as the *Annual Register* put it, vesting its funds in Lord Killeen.[76] But an aggregate meeting of Catholics did appoint a "Committee of Twenty-One" to see if another body could be set up within the new law, and on 13th July Killeen reported that this was admissible. The proposed "New Catholic Association" was to be open to Christians of all denominations and to have as its first object the promotion of "public peace and tranquility, as well as private harmony and concord, amongst all classes of His Majesty's subjects throughout Ireland". The other objects were to encourage education; build new Catholic churches; and carry out a religious census, to counteract anti-Catholic propaganda. The subscription was to be one pound.

The Committee decided that in order to comply with the fourteen day rule and other provisions of the new Act petitions should be drawn up in aggregate meetings county by county, and not by the new Association or by a large meeting in Dublin. The *Annual Register* regretted that Lords Gormanston and Killeen should submit to such treasonable language as was to be heard from O'Gorman and others upon the presentation of this Report.[77]

The Catholic Association having been, for the present, disposed of, Parliament turned its attention once more to the subject of Emancipation. A petition was presented on 1st March by the Tory radical Sir Francis Burdett; his motion was carried by a small majority, and a Bill was introduced on 23rd March which, first, dispensed with the Declaration against Transubstantiation as a qualification for most offices; secondly, substituted a modified Oath of Supremacy; and, thirdly, empowered a Catholic Board consisting of Bishops to advise the King on episcopal appointments. The Bill seemed likely to succeed; but on 25th April His Royal Highness the Duke of York, then heir presumptive, in an impassioned and moving speech, presented a petition against it from the Dean and Canons of Windsor. The result was that in the Lords the Bill was rejected by forty-eight votes. Two auxiliary measures were also considered. The first was to raise the voter's qualification from forty shillings to ten pounds and the second to make some public provision for the Catholic clergy.[78] Both these Bills were abandoned after the Lords division.

By 1826, the Act of Parliament directed against the Catholic Association had proved ineffectual; but there were few outrages, and the Catholic question was not raised in either House. Petitions were however submitted: one from Drogheda replied to the allegation made the previous year by the premier, Lord Liverpool, that the Catholics were divided in their allegiance, by asserting that they swore it to the King alone. Liverpool answered that although he did not doubt the sincerity of the Catholics in disclaiming *civil* allegiance to any foreign power, *spiritual* obedience to the Pope was inconsistent with *civil* obedience to the King, who, as the Duke of York had said, was bound by his Coronation Oath, taken independently of Parliament, to uphold Protestantism.

At the general election in the summer many Catholic priests as well as laymen took an active part in persuading electors to vote for pro-emancipation candidates.

At the beginning of 1827 the Duke of York died. The failure of the Administration to enforce the law against the Catholic Association made its members bolder; some, such as Sheil, openly hoped for a foreign invasion.[79] There was a reaction in England; the priests were seen as self-interested men who were concerned to secure the re-establishment of their own hierarchy; and crowds of anti-emancipation petitions flowed in. In Ireland itself, by contrast, the Protestants were more divided. On 5th March Sir Francis Burdett introduced a resolution in favour of the Catholic claims. Clerical interference in the previous year's elections was raised during the debate with particular reference to Lord George Beresford's candidature at Waterford. Villiers Stewart, his successful opponent, admitted that the clergy had interfered, but only in "self-defence". Other speakers, such as Richard Martin, also justified clerical intervention; but the latter was subsequently ousted by a petition then being heard.

The Master of the Rolls, Copley, was against the resolution. The issue of emancipation fed the flames of dissension. Multiplying present concessions would merely strengthen the precedent for future demands. Plunket, still Attorney-General for Ireland, replied in a notable speech. He agreed that there was a "set of restless demagogues and agitators", but drew the nice distinction that their intention was, not to "excite the people to acts of outrage or rebellion, but to rouse them to a state bordering on fury".[80] Plunket conceded that "there are the men, match in hand, who may in a moment set the whole in a blaze". Thus one had to look, despite the abuse which had been loaded upon them, to "the exemplary character and laborious exertions of the men who constituted the Roman Catholic hierarchy". Plunket went on to say that he could not condemn the priests for their interference, such as it was, in the recent elections. "Had they not a right to say to their parishioners, 'Here is a man, wishing to go into Parliament, who will there vituperate you — who will describe you as an idolater . . . If you like him, vote for him; but he is not a man that will do you justice'". Peel feared that Emancipation would bring Catholic and Protestant into greater conflict than ever before. If it were true, as Plunket had asserted, that the Catholic hierarchy were to be depended upon, why had they published no declaration against agitators? Eleven of the prelates were members of the Association.

Episcopal opinion had certainly hardened since 1824, when the Archbishop of Armagh, Patrick Curtis, had written to the Iron Duke deploring the open letters of "J. K. L.", the second of which warned the Government that they could not depend upon the Catholic hierarchy to prevent rebellion.[81] Curtis had promised the Duke that unless the author, James Doyle, Bishop of Kildare and Leighlin (hence the intials) atoned, the rest of the episcopal bench would disavow and silence him. Doyle was not however either disavowed or silenced. At least three Bishops supported the Catholic Rent, including ultimately even Curtis himself. In 1826 Peel had commented to J. L. Foster that Curtis "used to profess great alienation from the Roman Catholic agitators, lay and ecclesiastical. Now he seems, probably from his unmerited station only, a convenient tool in their hands".[82] Nonetheless, in a letter to Lord F. Leveson Gower (27 September 1828) in B. L. Ad. MSS 40335 fos 224–5 he promised to continue to "restrain and put down, by every proper means in my power" any "irritation and disturbance".

There were nonetheless solid grounds for Peel's opinion. His speech made a great impression, and the motion was lost by four votes. The Cabinet were divided; Canning favoured emancipation; Liverpool did not, but throughout his long premiership had declined to make the issue a "Cabinet question". In other words, Ministers were left free to differ. Liverpool was ill, and Peel feared defeat. A general meeting of Dublin Catholics, after expressing the "regret, and awful forebodings" with which they viewed the vote, went on to exhort the people to exercise "peace, perseverance, and Christian piety"; but a boycott of British goods was mooted. It was also proposed that petitions should be presented praying for a Repeal of the Union.[83]

Lord Liverpool having resigned, the Foreign Secretary, Canning, a supporter of emancipation, was appointed Premier after some delay. Peel and other opponents of emancipation, the Iron Duke included, declined office in the new Administration. Even supporters of emancipation like Melville would not serve. The new Cabinet consisted of those who resisted emancipation such as Copley (now Lord Lyndhurst), and also of those who favoured it; but the Prime Minister's Parliamentary support depended on the Whigs and to some extent, the Radicals. It was not long before Canning was dead. He was succeeded by Goderich, who lasted only until January 1828. The Duke of Wellington was then sent for. He formed a Ministry which consisted principally of those members of Liverpool's Cabinet who had refused to serve under Canning. These replaced the Whigs with whom Canning had coalesced. Wellington's Cabinet was as divided on the subject of emancipation as was Liverpool's.

On 8th May 1828 Sir Francis Burdett moved for a Committee on emancipation. The motion which in the previous year had failed by six votes was now carried by six votes, and the Lords considered it on 9 and 10 June. The Duke spoke on the subject for the first time as Prime Minister. His speech was absolutely consistent with what he had said in conversation with Lord Fingall twenty-one years earlier. He considered the question, he said, as merely one of expediency; but safeguards against the possible destruction of the Protestant constitution there must be, and the resolution did not even hint at them. The motion was lost.

Meanwhile in Ireland the Catholic Association continued to meet. Wellington's arrival in power produced inflammatory speeches: indeed the very word "agitation" in the political sense was now used for the first time by the Association.[84] Vesey Fitzgerald, the pro-emancipation Member for Clare, vacated his seat on being appointed President of the Board of Trade. Daniel O'Connell stood at the by-election, relying on the Catholic forty-shilling freeholders. Legal opinions were issued purporting to prove that, if elected, O'Connell could take his seat without swearing the oaths. Election day was 30th June. Bands of forty-shilling freeholders were marched into Ennis to vote for "God and O'Connell'. One priest refused to be dragooned by the Association and sent his flock to vote against O'Connell. But they were stopped and harangued by the mob, and the priest was denounced by the Association and removed from his parish. One of O'Connell's pledges was to vote for "reconsidering the abominable measure of the Union". He was duly elected, and it was reserved for Parliament itself to exclude him.[85]

In July the Act against illegal meetings expired, and the Association began to meet as before its enactment. Wellington's concern at the high proportion of Catholics in almost every Irish regiment was such that in the autumn, 25,000 men of the regular infantry strength of 30,000 were stationed either in Ireland or on the west coast of England in readiness for Ireland. In some instances parish priests, trying to prevent unauthorized meetings or processions, were repulsed by their congregations.[86]

Anthony Blake was a Catholic born about 1786 who had begun his adult life as an ensign in a Galway regiment of militia, and then practised at the English Bar. He rendered some service to Lord Wellesley, and was appointed in 1823 to the office of Remembrancer of the Exchequer, perhaps the first Catholic to hold it since the Reformation. "A remarkably agreeable, gossiping man, who knew everything and everybody", he received little courtesy either from O'Connell or from the newspapers of the day, but there can be little doubt of his honesty or that "in his multifarious exertions he had the interest of the country sincerely at heart". Thus wrote Doyle's biographer, W. J. Fitzpatrick. Now, in 1828, Blake published his *Thoughts Upon the Catholic Question*. Dedicated to the twelfth Duke of Norfolk, who by Act of Parliament in 1824 had been enabled to act as Earl Marshal of England despite being a Catholic, the work professed to discuss the subject not by reference to abstract ideas of right, but to the circumstances of Ireland. Since the Union, Catholics had prospered and resented all the more their remaining disabilities. Blake quoted Pitt's letter of 31st January 1801 and concluded by saying to Parliament, "Do what is right without delay; do it, and fear not."

"A Roman Catholic barrister"[87] took a similar line:

Would the State be more secure, were there men sufficiently abandoned to obtain political power, through the medium of perjury and fraud? A system of *tests* tends to do both. Let a man be profligate and they oppose no obstacle; let him be honest and conscientious, they exclude him from the service of his country.

Through the denial of full emancipation, he added, O'Connell had "acquired a power far *too great* to be wielded by an individual in such a country as Ireland".

1829 opened with the Catholic question still undecided. Wellington had declared as late as 11th December 1828 that the question could not be settled that year; it was the more surprising, therefore, that the Gracious Speech on 5th February referred to a measure for Emancipation, to be preceded by the suppression of the Catholic Association. On 10th February, Peel said that the 1825 Act, which had been passed for that purpose, had proved unsatisfactory; meetings said to be for excepted purposes — agriculture, commerce and so on — had been used to promote political objects and the law had been brought into contempt. It was now proposed that the Lord Lieutenant should have the power to ban any meeting or association which he thought dangerous to the public peace, or inconsistent with proper legal administration. Such associations or meetings were not to receive money.

The Bill received the Royal Assent on 5th March and almost immediately the House of Commons, at Peel's behest, went into Committee to consider Emancipation. Peel lost his seat as Member for Oxford University because of his change of opinion; but another was soon found for him. The Duke of Wellington, when the Bill came up for second reading in the Lords, put the alternatives starkly. (2 April 1829). Whereas in 1798 the vast majority of the country and its Parliament were prepared to support the sternest possible measures to put down rebellion, the boot was now on the other leg. Many Protestants of rank and standing favoured emancipation, and to refuse it now would be tantamount to inviting Civil War. Later (15th February 1833), he was at pains to deny that emancipation was conceded from fear; but his mind had never been closed against it. In conversation with the fifth Earl Stanhope, he made it clear that he had always, *as a private individual*, been in favour of the measure. In a public capacity he had felt, however, that he could not support it when the Monarch was opposed.

After extensive debates in both Houses, the Bill received the Royal Assent on 13th April. At the same time, the qualification for the franchise was raised from forty shillings to ten pounds. The Emancipation Bill itself contained no veto provisions; and it opened virtually every office in the realm to Catholics, except the Lord Lieutenancy of Ireland and the Lord Chancellorships of Great Britain and of Ireland. The idea of a state financial provision for the Catholic Church was turned down. There were restrictions on the wearing of civic regalia in Catholic chapels and of priestly robes outside the place of worship. Members of the Society of Jesus and monastic orders were to be registered and any who entered in the future were to be banished; bequests to religious orders were declared invalid; and Catholic ecclesiastics were denied the right to assume the titles of Archbishop, Bishop or Dean. Little notice was taken of the last of these; but some disabilities remained. Marriages before Catholic priests continued to be invalid at law until 1836; Catholic soldiers and sailors were still in theory obliged to attend Protestant worship; and Catholic charities continued to be treated as "superstitious uses". Monsignor Bernard Ward went so far as to argue that the Catholic clergy were better off under the Act of 1793 in Ireland than they were as a result of "emancipation". The main result of 1829 was psychological. As the Duke of Wellington said, "the great advantage of the measure was that it would unite all men of property and character against the agitators". In a letter to Maurice FitzGerald (6th November 1829) he wrote that

> It is very desirable that this country should be sensible and that the high and middling classes of the Roman Catholics in Ireland . . . are opposed to the system of conspiracy, intimidation and murder, of which we see too many instances every day. I don't doubt that they are so. But it is desirable that the world should be aware of the truth.[88]

Catholic opposition to the Repeal agitation which followed was to make his words good.

CHAPTER EIGHT

The Repeal Agitation

Before the year was out, O'Connell was advocating a repeal of the Union[1]. Meanwhile the Catholic Association was wound up "first by its own deliberate suicide, and secondly by an Act of Parliament".[2] In its place anti-Union societies had already begun to be formed in various parts of Ireland, and on 7th January 1830 O'Connell announced the formation of a national "Parliamentary Society, to form the basis of that great national society which I contemplate, in order to render the Repeal of the Union peaceable and tranquil, as it is, I think, inevitable".[3]

O'Connell's new society met on 29th March 1830. At first named as one for the "Improvement of Ireland', it was subsequently called the "Society of the Friends of Ireland", and opened to all denominations. After its suppression, the "Parliamentary Intelligence Office" remained the centre of O'Connell's activities. The chair at the first meeting was taken by Edward Berwick. Catholics of rank stood aloof.[4]

The general election of 1830 was foreshadowed by the death of George IV. Of the Irish Members returned to the new Parliament, nine were Catholics: Daniel Callaghan (Cork City), O'Gorman Mahon (Clare County, Sir John Burke (Galway), the Hon. William Browne (Kerry), Richard More O'Ferrall (Kildare), Lord Killeen (Meath), The O'Conor Don (Roscommon), Thomas Wyse (Tipperary) and O'Connell (Waterford). Not all of these favoured repeal; for example Lord Killeen, speaking in the House of Commons on 14th December 1830 said that

> he took leave to differ . . . as to the question of repeal, and he felt bound to express his opinion, though he knew it might expose him to some odium at a future election, where he knew this subject would be made the touchstone of popular excitement.[5]

Not only were there individual opponents of repeal amongst Catholic M.P.s, but a Catholic solicitor, Pierce Mahony, played a leading part in organizing a "Declaration of the Friends of the Union" which was opened for signature under the patronage of the Duke of

Leinster and which drew the support, amongst many others, of such leading Catholics as Lords Southwell, Gormanston, and Kenmare, and of Anthony Blake. The *Dublin Evening Post* (11 November 1830) stated in a leader that "Reformer, Whig, Tory, Catholic and Protestant" had unanimously decided against the question by signing this "Leinster declaration".[6] Some Catholic M.P.s, however, hesitated; thus although William Browne, one of the Kerry Members, signed, The O'Conor Don on 14th January 1831 deferred to the opinion of a County Roscommon meeting and decided to support O'Connell. He did not however long survive his re-election to parliament and died on 13th June 1831 at the age of sixty-nine.[7]

John O'Connell was much displeased with his brother Daniel's attitude. Repeal, he wrote to Maurice FitzGerald, "would result in a separation or a constant collision between the parliaments of both kingdoms. A ferment would be kept up which would preclude every chance of employment for our people or improvement in the country".[8]

On 8th February 1831 notice was taken of a declaration from the "Unionists of Cork" against repeal. The word *Unionist* had been used before, during the run-up to the Union, but now it was taking on new significance. There was a loyal Address, too, to the Lord Lieutenant (now Lord Anglesey), from the Catholics of Ballymena, Kirkinriola and Ballyclug. At Cloghenry in Tyrone 436 Protestants and 265 Catholics came together to assent to an anti-repeal declaration. Meanwhile, O'Connell had been arrested and prosecuted and the agitation, for the present, ceased. Further Addresses of loyalty from Catholics were presented. Lord Gormanston and his heir the Hon. Edward Preston signed the County Dublin Address, which expressed the conviction of its signatories that the dissolution of the Union would lead to complete separation.[9]

On 23rd April 1831, parliament was dissolved for the purpose of ascertaining the view of the country on parliamentary reform. The result was a considerable victory for the reformers. Lord Killeen, Daniel Callaghan, Thomas Wyse, O'Connell and The O'Conor Don were re-elected. Also elected was Henry Lambert, member of an old Catholic family whose ancestor had come over with Strongbow. He had already made his mark by opposing Malthusian doctrine at the general election of 1830 and by making it clear that he was in favour of repair and amendment, not destruction. He was also, he had said, against landlords "driving their tenants like pigs to the poll".[10] Now, in 1831, he was a fervent supporter of reform.

The Irish members in the new parliament continued to meet as a body when specifically Irish topics were under discussion, but they did not form an "Irish Party". In the *New Monthly Magazine* it was stated that although O'Connell had "long been yearning" after the leadership of such a party, "among the Irish Catholic Members he has not a friend. They knew too well his intolerant, voracious vanity".[11] But there was overwhelming support among Irish Catholic M.P.s for parliamentary reform. In the Lords too Lord Fingall, now a peer of the United Kingdom, voted in favour; but nineteen of the Irish representative peers were against, and voted in the majority which rejected the Bill in the Upper House. Sheil, speaking in the Commons on the Irish Reform Bill (25th May) stated that "the surest way of preventing the agitation of the Repeal of the Union would be, to do complete justice to Ireland, in granting her a reform as extensive as that which had been yielded to the wishes of England". Writing much later, "A Roman Catholic" claimed in 1852 that if it were not for the Irish M.P.s, the Reform Bills would not have passed, as there were majorities against them among Great Britain members.[12]

The Reform Bills became law in June 1832 after the peers' veto had been overriden by a threat to create sufficient new Lords of Parliament to swamp the opposition; and yet another general election followed. Repeal was now a major issue, and Catholic Unionist candidates like Lord Killeen and Thomas Wyse lost their seats.

There was an interesting situation in Wexford, where Henry Lambert refused to pledge his support for repeal, though it was announced at Tintern on 6th December that he had written a letter saying that "if a majority of the freeholders required him to vote for the repeal, he would not put his private opinions in competition with the entire county".[13] There was a great deal of popular excitement about the issue, and, as the *Wexford Freeman* asserted, there were people "who would shout for a repeal of the moon if the word was only put in their mouths".[14]

Lambert was against the tithe system whereby the Catholic peasantry was taxed to support a Protestant Church. But, equally, "if the Catholic Church had the enormous wealth of the Establishment, he would use even greater exertion, to strip her from those abominations".[15] He was impartial between Whig and Tory, and "he looked with confidence to a reformed parliament to do justice to Ireland". It was, after all, a Protestant parliament which had rescued his ancestors from "degradation and bondage". As to repeal, however, they should "first call for redress of public grievances", and go to repeal only if that were to be denied.

He wished to reform, not destroy, and was against the idea of a pledge "upon constitutional principles"; a man's best pledge "should be his honesty".

After his election, Lambert again repeated that he went to parliament "unpledged and unfettered". Anonymous correspondents vituperated. "Henry Lambert" was "a pompous name, replete with vowels and liquids", complained "Mentor" of Castlebridge, whilst "Junius" attributed his election to the county's "hatred for Conservative nuptials", not to its "love for your 'wait-a-while devotion' ".[16]

O'Connell wanted to postpone consideration of repeal by parliament because he was not really in a strong enough position. Of the 105 Irish members, twenty-seven were Conservatives, and although over thirty-eight of the remainder were pledged repealers, the others had not been fully won over. The government astutely forced O'Connell's hand by referring to the subject of the repeal agitation in the Gracious Speech at the beginning of 1834. Only the thirty-eight repealers voted against Spring-Rice's amendment to the Address in support of the Union, and the cause of Repeal received, according to O'Connell's biographer Fagan, a "stunning blow".[17] In a revealing passage he stated that in a question like repeal, "agitation is its vitality . . . if the Agitation of it be abandoned, it becomes weak and sickly". This is as good as an admission that there was no real "steam" behind the repeal movement, with which O'Connell had identified himself so single-mindedly.

To argue, as Sir Charles Gavan Duffy later did, that Lambert had been elected as a repealer, is absurd; he had made his position fairly clear during the election campaign, and, in parliament, made it even clearer. On 12th March he spoke out against O'Connell.[18] There was no doubt, he said, that distress, "to a melancholy extent", existed in Ireland, but he failed to see how it would be relieved by repeal of the Union. Distress had existed before the Union and measures of great injustice to the poor had been passed by the Irish parliament. "Employment was all that was wanted to relieve the distress of the people" and measures should be taken with this effect.

On 25th April[19] he spoke at greater length. O'Connell had asked for two million signatures in favour of repeal, but only 100,000 had been obtained. He had looked back to Grattan's Parliament of 1782–1800 as a "green spot" in the history of Ireland but Wexford's position at least had improved since the Union; she now had a hundred coasting vessels compared with only ten or twelve before. A powerful mimic, Lambert imitated at this point one of O'Connell's declamations with considerable effect. With the House on his side, he continued by pointing out that any repeal parliament was likely to put prohibitory duties on imports. England would follow suit, and Irish agriculture would be ruined. Quite apart from this, he continued, as repeal had been consistently refused by the House, what was the point of continuing the agitation? Ireland was being "torn, without the slightest prospect of any good". The agitation for repeal was of a profoundly different character from that in favour of emancipation or the Reform Bills. These were supported by people of standing and "produced no outrage". In this case however an election in Kilkenny had made it necessary for a Coercion Bill to be passed for the first time. The Roman Catholic Bishop of Waterford had been assailed and pelted with stones, and another bishop had been protected solely by the intervention of the sheriff and lower clergy had also been roughly treated.

What was O'Connell's object, his "real object" in exciting such agitation? It was not repeal, but "to stir up a hatred of the English, to excite in the lowest of the populace a thorough contempt and hatred of the English parliament, and to hold it up as totally incompetent to do justice to the people of Ireland". As for the "national tribute", it was in truth "an intolerable national nuisance". Lambert yielded to no one in his admiration of O'Connell's efforts to secure emancipation, and had freely supported the tribute raised for that purpose. But this was not a "voluntary effusion"; it was an "exaction of contrivance and a management of tact and business". Dr Murray, the Catholic Archbishop of Dublin, had written to him that he could no longer pay what was called the O'Connell tribute, and that his family were obliged to abstain from attending a place of worship "merely to avoid Mr O'Connell's jackalls, who, during the whole Sunday, were enforcing the tribute".[20] Both Catholics and Protestants were "embarked in the same cause. The property of both was alike in jeopardy, and they were now called upon to forget all past animosities . . . for, if the object of the agitators prevailed, neither Catholic nor Protestant would be spared." Lambert compared the agitation for repeal with the disturbances of 1798, when attempts were made to seduce soldiers from their duty. "Look at the treatment that had been experienced", he said, "by those upright and honourable men, the late Members for Meath, Dublin and Kilkenny, who after struggling to accomplish the great measure of Reform . . . were expelled from that House by the influence of unprincipled agitators as the reward for their services". The member for Meath had indeed been another Catholic, Lord Killeen, the Earl of Fingall's heir, who as we have seen had refused to support repeal.[21] Lambert concluded by saying that he was likely to suffer a similar fate for speaking out: he well knew the implacable vengeance he was bringing down upon his head"; yet speak out he must, for the honour of his country. The speech was received with "loud and enthusiastic acclamations".[22]

The Reverend David O'Croly was another Catholic who was disgusted by O'Connell's activities. Born in Cork, ordained in Cork, and ministering to his flock there, he was, in October 1834, suspended by his bishop on the grounds, first that he had "tried to bring about a reunion between Catholics and Protestants" and secondly that he wanted a state provision for the clergy. He had undermined Catholic doctrine, according to the bishop, by suggesting that the difference between the faith of "enlightened" Catholics and that of Protestants was small.

O'Croly was certainly what today would be termed an ecumenist. His reply to the bishop, however, besides dwelling on points of doctrine, expressed his disgust at the fact that some priests were "more prompt to pay obedience to an instruction from Daniel O'Connell than to a rescript from his holiness the pope". In times past, priests had always been opposed to disorder and violence. Yet now even Daniel Murray, Archbishop of Dublin, was not "safe". Kinsella, Lanigan's successor as Bishop of Ossory, was opposed to his views, and Murphy, Bishop of Cork, to the "venerated Moylan".

O'Croly was, perhaps, a crank, though today's ecumenists might well pay him some attention as one of their pioneers; and he became a member of the church of Ireland. Moreover, he was probably unfair to prelates like Murray, who from a twentieth century standpoint seems much sounder on law and order than he no doubt appeared at the time. Nonetheless, he had a point about O'Connell having turned the Catholic Church in Ireland, as O'Croly put it, into a "politico-religious society". It has certainly been the view of many subsequent commentators that O'Connell "brought the priests into politics", and whilst we regard that statement only as a half true generalization, no truer than similar adages about Parnell, there is no doubt that he had drawn in many who would otherwise have remained aloof.

By contrast to repeal of the Union, tithes presented a real grievance, and a Tithe Bill was introduced to convert them, in effect, into a land tax payable through the crown. Grey was succeeded by Melbourne as Prime Minister; the Coercion Act was modified, and the Tithe Bill thrown out by the Lords. Once again, a government in London had been broken up by an "Irish difficulty". O'Connell announced himself to be a "Ministerialist", i.e. a supporter of the new Whig government. The Tithe Bill had been thrown out "because it was approved of by Daniel O'Connell".

In November 1834 the Melbourne Ministry was dissolved by the Monarch after the death of Lord Spencer had deprived it of its principal mainstay in the Commons, his heir Lord Althorp. *The Times* announced (the statement was later retracted), "The Queen has done it all".[23]

The Duke of Wellington was sent for; but nothing could be done without Peel, who was then relaxing in Rome, particularly as, in the Duke's view, it was necessary now for the Prime Minister to be in the Commons. O'Connell's response was to form an "anti-Tory" association in Dublin. Repeal was, for the nonce, abandoned.

Peel's celebrated Tamworth manifesto followed. It was in December of that year that Orange Societies first began to chant John M'Cree's hymn, the refrain of which runs, "So put your trust in God, my boys, and keep your powder dry."

The second Earl of Kenmare was no friend to what he called "Ultra-fanatical Orangeism"; but he did not much care for O'Connell either. In a letter to Christopher Gallway (3 January 1835) he made his views plain:

It is now a matter of politics. The question at issue is, whether we are to bow our heads to a system of insolent dictation and intimidation, whether those freeholders who will not submit to be used as mere puppets by Mr O'Connell are to be pointed out with inpunity as objects of insult and assassination.[24]

Early in the election campaign, O'Connell had proclaimed there was not a Catholic voter in County Kerry who supported the Knight of Kerry "who shall not have upon his door a death's head and cross bones painted, to show what a miscreant that Catholic must be".[25] Kenmare decided to swing his supporters behind the knight, and he thus described a visit by O'Connell to Youghal in the course of which the latter passed through Killarney:

He is outrageous, and goes about like a roaring lion. He loses his temper woefully . . . He sent for David Murphy, a shopkeeper here, and abused and threatened him in a shocking manner . . . Murphy is a shrewd and firm man, and by his replies to O'Horrid, as Fairfield calls him, put him into such a rage that he . . . stamped about the room".

Augusta Lady Kenmare wrote to Maurice FitzGerald on 11th January 1835 that she feared the "priests" influence would be greater than the landlords". There was a strong feeling in the country against the new administration. "Would to God that Sir R. Peel and the Duke would take into their serious consideration the adjustment of that dreadful grievance [tithes]. As long as it remains in its present state, they put fearful weapons into the hands of the priests and demagogues."

On 13th January her Ladyship wrote again to FitzGerald informing him that his prospects were worsening. The priest, "Mr Tuomy" had harangued his flock "in the most violent manner".[26] Not all parish priests however were so disposed. Peter Foley wrote from Tralee on 15th January that although some of the Catholic clergy were "shamefully" using their influence against him, his own, Dr McEnery, had manifested no such hostility. On 29th January he mentioned another priest, Dr Foley of Dingle, who had refused to vote or interfere against the knight.[27]

The Revd A. B. Rowan wrote to FitzGerald on 23rd January that his opponent's majority would probably be about 150. Every kind of intimidation had been exercised. "Dan" appeared to be

> absolutely losing reason . . . Conceive his coming near me today in the assessors' room for the purpose of coughing in such a manner as to spit upon my hands and clothes and then turning to one of his train and saying, 'That's a cough that does me good.'.

In the event, the majority against FitzGerald was 200. Catherine FitzGerald, one of Maurice's daughters, described in a letter of 26th January how one of O'Connell's nephews had voted for her father; out of spite, his opponents "put the bribery oath to him; which so enraged him that he swore, as long as he lived he would never vote for an O'Connell".[28]

The Whigs had a majority of about ten. Of the Irish seats, both Conservatives and liberal Unionists improved their position with thirty-seven and forty seats respectively; committed repealers numbered only twenty-eight. Thomas Wyse, who had lost his seat in 1832, was re-elected.[29] Nevertheless, the repealers were in a commanding position;

they met the Whigs at Lord Lichfield's house, and agreed to support them on certain conditions. This "Lichfield House Compact" was honoured as much in the breach as in the observance.

In the House of Commons there was stalemate, despite what seemed the impending accession to the Conservatives of the "Darby Dilly carrying six insides" as O'Connell, echoing Canning, dubbed Lord Stanley and his little band of supporters. But, as George Saintsbury wrote in his biography of Derby (as Stanley afterwards became), "a feebler joke never was"; for Stanley could have filled the vehicle many times over.[30]

Haddington replaced Wellesley as Lord Lieutenant, and in March 1835 Peel re-introduced the tithe measure, almost in the same form as that in which it had been introduced by the Whigs. The Lichfield House Group however met, and decided to divide the House on the question of the manner in which any surplus accruing to the established Church of Ireland should be disposed of. Sir Robert Peel said that he would never agree to any such surpluses being applied for the benefit of persons other than those of the established religion, and the government was defeated by a majority of about thirty. Melbourne then formed an administration, with Mulgrave as Lord Lieutenant of Ireland, and Lord Morpeth as Irish Secretary. Melbourne was almost immediately asked whether he agreed with O'Connell's views on repeal, and replied that he did not. But O'Connell was soon to be unseated; not before Disraeli had described him in a letter as a "very amusing, a very interesting, but a somewhat overrated man".[31]

The Government's Irish Bills were rejected by the Lords. O'Connell, despite the "Lichfield House Compact", repeatedly voted against the government, and at the end of the session returned to Dublin to contest an election petition.

In 1836 his theme was "justice for Ireland". The Gracious Speech included promises to legislate on the tithe question and to extend municipal reform to Ireland. The Conservatives opposed the latter, attempting instead to abolish the corporations, fearing that if they were opened to Catholics they might become hotbeds of agitation. The Bill passed the Commons, but was "wreckingly amended" by the Lords. O'Connell was unseated as member for Dublin, but almost immediately returned for Kilkenny.

In 1837 municipal reform and church reform in Ireland were again brought forward as government measures, together with a Poor Law Bill for Ireland. They were withdrawn with the death of William IV.

O'Connell, curiously enough, opposed the latter bill, though the Catholic hierarchy, including Dr Murray, Archbishop of Dublin, were in favour. In a speech in Dublin at the beginning of the new reign, O'Connell promised to abandon repeal if he could obtain from the English Parliament such measures as an independent Ireland would have called for. Ever royalist, he rallied to the support of the new Queen against the onslaughts of *The Times* newspaper. "We have lived to see upon the Throne, a Monarch who will do us justice".[32]

At the general election the Whigs had a majority of about twenty-five. Repeal was forgotten at the hustings, and the cry was: "The Queen and her Ministers". Some Orangemen favoured the Duke of Cumberland, who under Salic law would have inherited the United Kingdom, as he had inherited Hanover. O'Connell, at Rathcormac in Cork, asked the crowd if they would fight for the queen against the King of Hanover, and obtained a rapturous response. He even went so far as to dissolve the latest of his many associations,[33] quite voluntarily. At the end of the year, once again elected for Dublin City, he stated at Westminster, "I wish not to agitate the question of the Repeal of the Union again. I wish the people of Ireland to be part and parcel of the British Empire".[34]

The Dublin Trades' Union was one of the first to be founded. The Webbs, in their *History of Trade Unionism*, virtually ignore it, though they did point out[35] that the difference between a *Trade* Union and a *Trades* Union is, strictly speaking that the first is a combination of the members of one trade and the second is a combination of different trades. In 1832 O'Connell came into collision, not for the first time, with the "Trades Political Union", although he was in many places supported by individual trades. Again in 1837 in a speech to the "Trades Political Union" he came out against illegal combinations, especially where they led to bloodshed.[36] The Trades countered by accusing him of buying a carriage in London. In 1838 there were further meetings and O'Connell was heckled. Archbishop Murray too came out against the Unions, but the spirit of "combination" was too deeply rooted.

The accession of Queen Victoria was followed by a "honeymoon period". D. O. Madden wrote:

> with the Liberals and Catholics everything was in those times quite *couleur de rose. The whole people went to Court.* The Aristocracy *cut* Lord Normanby, but the people enthusiastically paid him homage, and if Dublin Castle was deserted, his Excellency held monster Levées throught the country.[37]

It was in 1838 that the expression "Property has its duties as well as its rights" was first used; not, as is sometimes supposed, by Stephen Woulfe, Attorney-General and afterwards, Chief Baron of the Exchequer in Ireland, but by Thomas Drummond, the Under-Secretary.[38]

Woulfe, a Catholic from Ennis, County Clare, was educated at Stonyhurst, as was his contemporary, Thomas Wyse. One of the earliest Catholics to pass through Trinity College Dublin, he had been called to the Bar in 1814. Although he was an active supporter of emancipation and in 1819 published a pamphlet on the subject, he had broken with O'Connell on the veto question; indeed, Madden goes so far as to describe him as the "organ of the Vetoists".[39] "He never fawned upon the great, he never flattered the people. Unlike those who are 'always valiant on the stronger side', Woulfe never spoke better or more fearlessly than when struggling in a minority". In 1835 he was elected member for Cashel and in November 1836 appointed Solicitor-General for Ireland; in February 1837 he was promoted to Attorney-General and on 11 July 1838 Chief Baron of the Irish Exchequer. He was the first Catholic to hold that office, although he had been preceded as first Catholic law officer since the time of James II by Sir Michael O'Loghlen (1789–1842), who for a few months in 1834 was Solicitor-General for Ireland and in 1836 became a Baron of the Exchequer. In 1858 W. J. O'Neill Daunt was told that when O'Loghlen went circuit for the first time at Ennis, the Catholic criminals expected some favour from a Catholic judge, but soon found that "he hangs them like any Protestant".[40] The post of law officer in Ireland had an administrative, even a political content not present in England, since except for a brief period in the late 1880s the Chief Secretary for Ireland had no deputy other than one of the law officers to answer for him in the House of Commons.

"It has been well said", wrote D. O. Madden, that "Woulfe was the first mind amongst the modern Irish Catholics". He had received a theological training at Maynooth, and was singularly "'unhating' for one bred in times of agitation". He was never a repealer, and between 1829 and 1835 virtually seceded from politics. Woulfe was succeeded as Attorney-General for Ireland in 1838 by Nicholas Ball, another Catholic of similar background, and an earlier associate of Wyse. Madden was contemptuous of Ball, who in his opinion was unjustifiably promoted over the head of Richard Wilson Greene, just because of his Catholicism. J. R. O'Flanagan, writing in the 1870s, however, paid tribute to his "agreeable manners and convivial disposition":[41] in 1839 he became a Judge of the Common Pleas Bench, where he was noted for the clarity of his addresses to juries at *nisi prius*. Bruce Austin in the *Dictionary of National Biography* described him as a "sincere Roman Catholic, but no ultra-montanist, a zealous Irish liberal, but strongly opposed to the disintegration of the empire".

Ball's successor as M. P. for Clonmel was David Pigot (1797–1873), another Catholic. Pigot was the son of a County Cork physician, and was educated at Trinity College Dublin and Edinburgh University. He had been sworn a King's Counsel in 1835. His adoption meeting was presided over by a Catholic priest, and another proposed his adoption. His election Address advocated the extension to Ireland of "the system of self-government, now enjoyed by the free municipalities of Great Britain", but made no mention of repeal. This did not prevent the *Tipperary Constitution* (19th February 1839) describing him as "the nominee of O'Connell, the Priests, and the wretched *clique*, who are allowed to *lord it* over the miscalled liberal constituency of Clonmel".

Pigot was already Solicitor-General for Ireland, and in the following year became Attorney-General, so necessitating a by-election. But he was unopposed. Again his election Address referred to his support for municipal franchise and again the *Tipperary Constitution* was scathing. There had been a rumour that a repealer would stand for the borough, but in the event none appeared. At the general election of 1841 the paper was more gracious, and quoted a report congratulating "the Protestant and Roman Catholic Conservatives of Ireland, and of the United Kingdom in general" on their victory.

In 1846, Pigot was made Chief Baron of the Exchequer in Ireland. At his swearing-in as Attorney, Christopher Fitzsimon was present as Clerk of the Hanaper, and O'Loghlen was acting as Lord Chancellor. All three were Catholics. There were doubts when O'Loghlen was raised to the Exchequer Bench in 1836 because of the tithe writs which had to be issued by that Court; but even the *Dublin Evening Mail* was ultimately constrained to agree that the appointment, which O'Connell had refused, was a good one.[42] Catholics numbered thirteen out of the thirty-four appointments to the stipendiary magistracy between 1835 and 1839.[43]

The effect of the Reform Bill had been to consolidate the party system, and to lessen Royal influence. The *Annual Register* for 1839 commented that the popularity of the Whigs had become materially lessened by their connexion with O'Connell, for suspicion of Catholics was still strong, and "Ireland is still . . . the cardinal point of English domestic politics".

1839 opened with the assassination of Lord Norbury within a mile of his house, in broad daylight. At a meeting of magistrates it was asserted that the cause was the Lichfield House compact; the dependence of the Whig administration on "agitators" had encouraged violent men in Ireland. The very maxim "property has its duties as well as its rights" was criticized by Lord Charleville as a contributory cause. O'Connell, for his part, insinuated that the earl had been murdered by his heir. The assassination was regarded as particularly shocking, since the earl had been a model landlord; the Catholic priest had eulogized him at a public meeting. One motive could have been that it was Norbury's father who had tried Emmet in 1803. The ministry were accused by Shaw of having slighted the judges and insulted the magistracy, "and when the resident gentry, struggling to preserve their properties and their lives amidst difficulties the most trying, and dangers the most imminent, had not the Government taken that most infelicitous opportunity to insinuate, that their duties as landlords had been neglected?" Lord Morpeth asserted in his reply that the Government "would not withdraw their deliberate opinion, that property had its duties as well as its rights".[44]

One of the charges made was that Roman Catholics were being excessively favoured by the administration. To this Normanby replied that there was still a slight preponderance of Protestant appointments in various legal and constabulary departments. O'Connell's most recent creation, the Precursor Society, also came in for criticism. Lord Fingall said that in spite of the prevalence of crime and conspiracies, the condition of the people was gradually improving.

In 1840, the Precursor Society, with its local counterparts had given way to the Repeal Association, renamed the Loyal National Repeal Association early in 1841. This had the support of Archbishop MacHale of Tuam and other bishops. Many, however, held aloof, including Frederick Lucas, founder of the *Tablet*, who at this time opposed O'Connell. Repeal, he wrote, might or might not be beneficial to Ireland, but for English Catholics it would be disastrous.

> Those who know and have seen the increased activity which had been communicated to every Catholic enterprise in Great Britain and the colonies during the last twelve years, can best appreciate the grievous loss which Catholicism would have sustained if the Act of Union had never passed. In the Supreme

Legislature of the empire the Catholic church would be shorn of nine-tenths of its strength . . . We cry loudly for union; union not to the injury of Ireland, but to the common benefit of us all; a union . . . among the votaries of a common faith, that our enemies may not triumph over us; a union for the benefit of Ireland, unless Irishmen care nothing for the thousands, or rather millions, of their countrymen who are peopling England and Scotland and every distant corner of the empire . . . United the Catholics are one-third of the empire . . . Separated, what are we?[45]

Similar thinking lay behind Archbishop Murray's support for the system of national schools established in 1833. Dr MacHale carried out active propaganda against the schools, and in 1839 the Sacred Congregation of Propaganda at Rome was considering coming out against them. Dr Murray, with Pope Gregory's permission, sent two priests to remonstrate with His Holiness, and it was finally laid down that each bishop should accept or reject the national system as each should consider wise.[46] At a general meeting of Catholic prelates held in Dublin in February 1840, eighteen were favourable to the national schools, which provided for Catholics and Protestants to be taught together, and only ten were against, though much later, in 1869, the system was condemned.[47]

In 1841, the subject of the repeal agitation was brought up by Sir Robert Inglis. Large meetings had been held by O'Connell, and troops had had to be moved in to support the civil power. Lord John Russell was facetiously asked whether he was a Conservative or a repealer, as the "Agitator" had asserted that everyone must take his stand on one side or the other. The Government were defeated in the Budget debate, and Parliament was dissolved. O'Connell himself lost his Dublin seat at the ensuing election, though another was speedily found for him; and his fellow-repealers too were unsuccessful. Only eighteen, according to one account, and "less than a dozen" according to another, were elected; and Peel replaced Melbourne as Prime Minister. In a letter to Archbishop Murray in August 1841, the Catholic Primate of All Ireland, William Crolly, referred to Repeal as "a desperate and dangerous infatuation".[48]

1843 was "Repeal Year" in Ireland. The Loyal National Repeal Association consisted of associates, members and volunteers. Repeal wardens, general inspectors and collectors completed an array very reminiscent of the "Catholic Rent" of the 1820s. An innovation was the holding of "monster meetings", as they came to be called, the first at Trim on 16th March, and another at Mullingar on 14th May with two Catholic bishops present. At Ballina on 19 February the local priest even went so far as to say he would not marry people who were not enrolled repealers, but Catholic support was by no means solid. Bishop Higgins of Ardagh was severely criticized in the House of Lords by Lord Beaumont, himself a Catholic, for his speech at the banquet at Mullingar, where it had been freely asserted that every Catholic bishop in Ireland was a repealer. It was stated in debate that the Catholic clergy were not, as a body, opposed to the Union, and the Earl of Wicklow denied that Archbishop Murray favoured repeal. The latter, in a statement to the press, asserted that he had taken no part whatever in the movement; and that in January 1834 he had agreed with a resolution unanimously passed by the Irish Catholic bishops, exhorting their clergy to abstain in future from taking any prominent part in politics. This was a declaration of aloofness and not of opposition, yet although O'Connell managed to enrol fourteen bishops into the association, nine refrained from membership, as did the Archbishops of Armagh and of Dublin.

Murray was concerned enough to write to Paul Cullen, then Rector of the Irish College at Rome, asking for the Vatican to issue another warning. "Many of the clergy and even several of the Bishops", he wrote, "are keeping alive this dangerous excitement . . . If they were more deeply imbued with horror for the calamities which entered from the French Revolution and the Irish Insurrection they would be slow to adopt it".[49] At the same time (August 1843) Wyse presided over a committee which drew up what has been described as a "remarkable Liberal-Unionist document"[50] warning that "every day's delay" in meeting the various grievances rehearsed, "increases the difficulties of the task and gives additional strength to those who maintain that there is no hope of good government for Ireland, except in the restoration of her National Parliament".[51]

The subject was aired in Parliament, and the Government enacted an Irish Arms Bill in order to secure registration and licensing, and further to restrict the sale of gunpowder. Magistrates found to be attending or participating in Repeal meetings were to be removed from the Commission of the Peace. Lord Ffrench was among those who incurred this penalty. Thirty-five thousand troops were quartered in Ireland as a preventive measure.[52]

The agitation continued, and O'Connell grew bolder. On 15th August he addressed at Tara a mammoth gathering estimated at over a quarter of a million and predicted a Parliament in Dublin within twelve months. His hearers were instructed to boycott the petty-sessional Courts. After a series of other meetings, arbitration courts were set up by the Repeal Association. The Government decided to act; but a meeting planned for Clontarf on 8 October was not "proclaimed" (i.e. banned) until the afternoon before it was due to take place.[53] O'Connell immediately summoned his Repeal Association, and tried to call the meeting off. Despite a large attendance, both of his followers and of the military, the day passed off peacefully; O'Connell was nevertheless arrested on the fifteenth with nine others on charges of sedition, conspiracy and unlawful assembly. His trial was put off until 1844.[54]

Why did the repeal agitation make such advances in 1843 when electorally its fortunes were sinking? Sir Charles Gavan Duffy attributed its success to the activities of a small number of Protestant lawyers and law students who joined the association in 1841. Of these the most notable were John Blake Dillon and Thomas Davis. With Duffy's assistance, a weekly paper, *The Nation*, was founded in 1842. It took for its motto a saying of Stephen Woulfe with regard to municipal corporations, which were just then being opened to Catholics: "To create and foster public opinion in Ireland, and make it racy of the soil". The founders of the *Nation* felt that O'Connell was over-emphasising Ireland's economic difficulties; they sought to redress the balance by emphasising nationality. They differed from him in favouring the retention of the Poor Law, which he opposed; and on the national schools. The Young Irelanders, as they came to be called, also favoured a combined University education for Catholics and Protestants. These inheritors of the tradition of the United Irishmen also genuflected to Grattan and harked back to the Gaelic and Norman past. They cherished the cult of "the dark Rosaleen".[55] Romantic liberals of their number quaffed the heady wine of Kosciusko and of Garibaldi, no friend of Papalism. They were anti-clerical, like Tone and Emmet. The Unitarian, John Mitchel of Derry, declared society dissolved because of the intolerable suffering of the people. Young Ireland abhorred the British connexion which O'Connell upheld. They resented his autocratic leadership.

O'Connell visited Belfast in January 1841, but so strong was opposition to him there that he was soon forced to withdraw. Huge conservative demonstrations were organized against him on 21st and 23rd January; and although there were no Catholic speakers, a number of references were made to Catholic support for the Unionist cause. In a letter to Stanley agreed at the meeting on 21st January, it was stated that the anti-repeal petition was signed by Roman Catholics as well as by Episcopalians, Presbyterians and Methodists.[56] This had also been true in 1830, when an anti-repeal meeting was held in Belfast.[57]

In 1844 controversy centred upon the Charitable Bequests Act.[58] O'Connell made muddled accusations which were answered by "A Lay Roman Catholic" in *A Letter to the Most Reverend Doctor Murray*. The Act had "done good by giving to the faithful and pious Roman Catholic people, a simple and easy method of conveying their property for religious or charitable uses". The Archbishop and other Catholics, "clerical and lay, of the highest respectability", had refused to declare against the Act. They were urged to persevere, for "if you give way to *Mr O'Connell*, the enemies of our creed will tauntingly exclaim,

There, ye wise saints, behold your Light, your Star,
Ye would be dupes, and victims, and ye *are*.

Despite O'Connell's opposition, a number of prominent Catholics, including the Archbishops of Armagh and Dublin, with Dr Kennedy, Bishop of Killaloe, accepted seats on the Board of Commissioners set up by the Act. Blake and Bellew were also members. It is indeed difficult to understand O'Connell's opposition, for the Act introduced a distinct improvement on its predecessor, the Bequests Board, which had no Catholic members at all.[59] Archbishop Walsh made this clear in a book published in 1916; and pointed out further that at least one of O'Connell's professional "opinions" against the Act was based on features of the Bill which were amended as it passed through parliament, and did not relate to the Act at all. The Act, amended in 1867 and 1871, had then been operating quite successfully for over seventy years, "in an atmosphere of practically unruffled calm".[60]

The essence of the problem lay in the occasional "concealment or misapplication" of charitable donations or bequests.[61] It was clearly wrong for a purely Protestant body to supervise the application of funds which might be intended for purely Catholic purposes, and such was the discretion conferred upon the board of 1800 that they could not escape the charge that they were acting with partiality in certain cases. Apart from introducing Catholic members, the main improvement made by the Act was to enable property assigned for Catholic religious purposes to be held in trust by the new commission in perpetuity, thus removing the necessity to set up a private trust. In the event, the Catholic bishops of Ireland took the same view of this Act as they had of the question of national education; each was allowed to decide for himself.[62]

1845 brought to the fore the question of an increase in the grant to Maynooth. As we have seen, the Royal College of St Patrick at Maynooth, in County Kildare, had been established in 1795 in order to replace the seminaries abroad which had existed for candidates for the Catholic priesthood before the French Revolution. It was supported by an annual grant of public money, which in 1808 had become fixed at £9,250. In 1844, Peel planned to increase the grant and make it permanent, partly in order to "detach a considerable portion of the moderate Roman Catholics from O'Connell, by timely concessions".[63] Some Catholic laymen, such as Blake, were consulted, but Peel pressed ahead and Gladstone, for one, resigned from the government, an important step in the course that was to lead him to the leadership of the Liberal Party. Much other Protestant opinion was outraged, and a central anti-Maynooth committee was formed. The anonymous publication of a book on Ireland by Charles Greville led to fears that this was but the prelude to a policy of concurrent endowment both of the Catholic Church and of the Protestant Church of Ireland. Even such men as Christopher Wordsworth feared this, and Disraeli was scathing.[64] The fear had some basis in Empire practice; not only in Quebec but in Mauritius, Newfoundland, India, the West Indies, Gibraltar, Malta, Australasia and the East Indies there were state hand-outs to Catholic priests, as there were to Protestant Dissenters, although some of these were "voluntaryists", that is to say, they disapproved of all state grants on principle.

As we have seen, Thomas Wyse had broken with O'Connell on the subject of repeal, and may well claim to be regarded as the type of a Catholic Unionist. Born in 1791, of Anglo-Norman stock, he was educated at Stonyhurst, the great Jesuit college which had been transferred to Lancashire in 1794, and at Trinity College Dublin, which had been opened to Catholics (subject to certain limitations) in 1793. Besides Woulfe, Sheil, and Ball, his early associates included John Talbot, Earl of Shrewsbury, a large landowner in Wyse's native county, Waterford. At Trinity Wyse won the Chancellor's prizes in Greek and Latin, and was active in the Historical Society founded by Burke, whose gold medal he won. He read for the Bar at Lincoln's Inn, and in 1815 proceeded on the Grand Tour with Woulfe and Ball. At Rome he met Lucien Bonaparte, and subsequently visited the Near East and the Sudan. He returned to Italy in 1820 and in the following year married one of

Lucien's daughters. At first the marriage was idyllically happy, but difficulties of temperament soon became apparent. Wyse was studious, serious, and puritanical; his wife was beautiful, fond of society, and very conscious of her status as the niece of a former emperor and the daughter of one who had been offered kingdoms. For a time she was shut up in a convent, but in 1825, the couple, with a child and Wyse's sister, returned to County Waterford where Wyse immediately became active in politics. In 1826 he was instrumental in securing the election of Henry Villiers Stuart as member for the constituency. He then wrote a history of the Catholic Association which appeared, appropriately enough, in the year of Emancipation; but the writing of it took him to Dublin a great deal, and the rift with his wife widened until eventually she left him. One day in London she threw herself into the Serpentine, but was fortunately unharmed. For the rest of his life Wyse avoided meeting her, and his two sons caused him great embarrassment when they sometimes, despite all his efforts, fell under her spell.

Wyse's finances were as parlous as his private life. In 1830 he was elected to parliament for Tipperary in the Liberal interest, and duly voted in favour of the Reform Bills. On repeal, however, as has been said, he refused to give the unconditional pledge which O'Connell required, unlike weaker men who deferred, if not to him, then to pressure-groups within their constituencies[65]; and at the general election of 1832 he was defeated at Waterford after failing to give a "satisfactory" answer to the Political Union there on the subject of repeal. Nevertheless he believed in subordinate legislature for England, Wales and Scotland as well as Ireland — "Home Rule all round", as it was afterwards to be called — and in alterations to the ecclesiastical and educational systems. For the next three years he studied educational reform, and in 1835 he was elected for Waterford City at the head of the Poll.

In 1836 Wyse published his *Education Reform*. This retailed the views of the Catholic prelates, who in 1826 had adopted resolutions permitting the education of Catholic and Protestant children in the same schools, provided that there were proper safeguards for their religious instruction. On 9th December 1830 Wyse submitted to the Chief Secretary, on the basis of these resolutions, a detailed plan for Irish primary education, a plan which afterwards bore fruit in *Mr Stanley's Instructions to the Lord Lieutenant*. These envisaged an annual grant of £30,000, to be administered by a Board of Education of which the Protestant and Roman Catholic Archbishops of Dublin and the Ulster Synod's Moderator should be *ex-officio* members. This National Board of Education, to which there was no counterpart in England until the 1870s, was to refuse applications for assistance unless they came from the Catholics and Protestants of a district combined. Unfortunately the scheme was non-statutory and, as we shall see, ultimately came to grief.

In 1835 Wyse was appointed to a select committee on Irish education, which recommended, amongst other things, the foundation of provincial colleges to improve higher education. There was considerable enthusiasm for this proposal, especially in Cork, and in 1845, in a speech in which he went out of his way to praise Wyse's efforts, the Home Secretary, Sir James Graham, introduced a Bill to set up such non-denominational colleges. The Bill was furiously attacked; Archbishop MacHale, adopting a phrase of Sir Robert Inglis, christened the colleges "Godless"; but the Primate, Crolly of Armagh, approved, as did Murray of Dublin and Bishop Murphy of Cork.[66]

Division within the Catholic hierarchy followed similar lines to that on the Charitable Bequests Act. But the Young Irelanders supported Wyse's view, and O'Connell's opposition was somewhat less strident. He conceded that there were circumstances in which mixed education was advisable. In 1849 the new colleges were opened, at Belfast, Cork and Galway; and in 1850 the Queen's University of Ireland was formed to unite them and to act as a degree-awarding body.[67]

Wyse's political activities in the strict sense ended with his appointment as British Minister Plenipotentiary in Athens in 1849, but before that he had become a prominent speaker on educational subjects throughout England. He was appointed to the Royal Commission set up to advise on the decoration of the new Houses of Parliament after the fire of 1834, and served on a committee on legal education. In the House of Commons he was in the words of his biographer:

> the consistent supporter of the ideal of the United Kingdom, and though he was willing to support some measures of devolution, particularly as he was a strong supporter of decentralised government by county boards and district commissions, he was at all times an avowed opponent of any extreme tampering at the fundamentals of union. This does not mean that he did not frequently lose patience with the attitude of successive British governments towards Ireland. Far from it! At times his rage and despair were overwhelming, but he looked forward to a glorious future in which the partnership

should really be a partnership undisguised by any measure of coercion.[68]

In February 1844, following the banning of the repeal meeting at Clontarf, and the arrest of O'Connell and his associates, the repeal defendants were fined £2,000 and sentenced to a year's imprisonment. But in September the Law Lords reversed this decision and O'Connell, released from comfortable internment at Richmond gaol, was received as a conquering hero.

Heytesbury, who had become Lord Lieutenant in July, had meanwhile learnt that a number of prominent Catholics who were out of sympathy with the repeal movement were willing to declare their Unionism on certain terms: the validity of diocesan titles for bishops, some financial provision for the clergy, and diplomatic relations with the Vatican. Peel thereupon ordered a collection of the more pro-repeal speeches, such as those of Archbishop MacHale and Bishop Higgins, to be made up for presentation to the Pope and to Metternich in an attempt to persuade the former, perhaps through the latter, to come out against the repeal agitation. The result was a letter from the Prefect of Propaganda, Cardinal Fransoni, dated 15 October 1844, which began by reminding the Primate of All Ireland, Archbishop Crolly, of an earlier warning sent by the Vatican to the effect that bishops should concern themselves with the spiritual life of the faithful and not with secular concerns. Sermons should be concerned only with Christ crucified.

Although the letter carefully avoided mentioning the repeal agitation in terms, it was stronger and more insistent than earlier letters. The hierarchy received it respectfully and pledged themselves to carry its spirits into effect. O'Connell asserted in *The Nation* that the letter was "uncanonical" and challenged Crolly to publish it. He later withdrew his objection, but differences of interpretation persisted, and some Bishops continued with their active support of Repeal. In a letter to Archbishop Murray from fifty-four of his priests, published in the *Dublin Evening Post* of 14th January 1845, a pledge was made of support to him and to the Holy See. Regret was expressed at the attempts that were being made to alienate the people from their clergy and to force the clergy to adopt opinions under pressure of popular clamour.

In 1846 the Repeal movement split on the question of physical force, the Young Irelanders claiming that armed insurrection was legitimate. The clergy took the side of O'Connell; even Bishops Higgins and Cantwell denounced the "physical-force" men in *The Pilot* of 5

August. In 1848 a band of Young Irelanders attempted such an uprising. But the conspiracy was broken up. Convicted ringleaders were transported. They ended up, and some of them became politically prominent, in America, Canada and Australia. From such as these, and their descendants, separatist Ireland would draw money and arms and encouragement to resist and persevere. The rapid collapse of the uprising was attributed by contemporaries largely to priestly intervention. By then, O'Connell was dead, and famine was decimating the population.[69]

CHAPTER NINE

Famine and Fenianism

The Melbourne Government had taken the view that the most effective method of alleviating poverty in Ireland was to extend to it the "Workhouse" system, which had been introduced in England in 1834. In 1838 such an Act was passed, despite considerable opposition, not on the ground that workhouses were inhuman, but because it was felt that too great a sum would have to be expended in setting up and maintaining such a system. It did indeed take seven years to bring the Act fully into force, and under the impact of famine, the system broke down.

Those principally affected by the famine were in the south and west of Ireland and could be divided into three classes; the absolutely landless, who had to hire out potato-ground from some farmer from year to year; people living on the land of the farmers for whom they worked, with small plots of their own ranging up to one acre; and small farmers with land up to five acres. The Devon Commission, named after the Earl of Devon, its chairman, was appointed in 1843 to investigate land holdings in Ireland, and reported in 1845. "In many districts", it stated, "their only food is the potato, their only beverage water . . . their cabins are seldom a protection against the weather . . . a bed or a blanket is a rare luxury . . . nearly in all cases their pig and manure heap constitute their only property".[2]

In 1845 an extensive disease of the potato crop appeared in various parts of the United Kingdom. It caused the resignation of the Peel Government, because Sir Robert felt that farmers ought not to be protected against cheap imports of wheat; and the Corn Laws ought to be repealed. There was considerable opposition to the proposal within his own party; he resigned; Lord John Russell was sent for, but fared no better, and the "poisoned chalice" was returned to Sir Robert.[3] The Queen's Speech of January 1846 referred in some detail, both to the potato failure — "the disease by which the plant has been affected has prevailed to the utmost extent in Ireland", and to the "very frequent instances in which the crime of deliberate assassination has been of late committed in Ireland". The repeal of the Corn Laws was carried; but immediately afterwards the protectionists led by Lord George Bentinck and Disraeli coalesced with the Whigs and threw him out on the Irish Coercion Bill. Escorted by a great crowd, who took their hats off as he passed, Peel retired from his defeat: he had "lost a party but won a nation".[4]

In August his successor, Lord John Russell, began a speech by pointing out that the previous Government had already spent over £850,000 on relief works and on the purchase of maize and other necessaries. The potato crop was even worse in 1846 than it had been the previous year. In announcing further measures, he added that he "considered the present as a special case requiring the intervention of Parliament, and rendering it imperative on the Government to take extraordinary measures for the relief of the people".[5] There was no opposition in either House, and Labouchere paid tribute to the "clergy of all denominations, Roman Catholic and Protestant", who had used "their best efforts to check that spirit of exaggeration and panic which, if spread abroad, might lead to the most evil consequences'.[6]

It has been the fashion over recent decades to decry the efforts which governments in London took to meet the emergency, and they were not wanting critics at the time who saw them as "too little, too late"; but by the beginning of 1847 it was impossible for anyone to ignore the seriousness of the situation. The Queen's Speech on 19th January was almost all devoted to the famine and its relief. Especial tribute was paid to the "patience and resignation" of the people in many of the most distressed districts. "It was observed", stated the *Annual Register*, "that the passages relating to Irish distress were delivered by Her Majesty in a rather subdued tone, and with an accent of sympathy for the sufferings described".[7] According to Lord John Russell, speaking on 25th January, at least £700,000 a month was being spent by the government on public works. In order to avoid abuses, it was planned to set up relief committees in affected districts. These would open soup-kitchens and employ labourers. Workhouses were to be kept as tests of destitution; but they were often beseiged by those seeking admission; and in certain cases out-door relief was to be given even to the able-bodied, in the form of food. There were to be increased facilities for Irish emigrants landing in America; but otherwise nothing was done to encourage emigration, as in the Government's view Ireland was not over-peopled.[8] Crime gave rise to concern. Fewer offences were committed than in the previous year, but homicides had increased by nearly half and attempted murders by shooting had more than doubled, as had armed robberies and arson. More than seventy per cent of these crimes were perpetrated in Clare, Limerick and Tipperary, which counties contained only thirteen per cent of the population. Assassination in broad daylight was the most frequent crime, and, it was asserted as so often in Ireland through the centuries, the public would not help the police as they did in England.

One pillar of law and order was the Catholic priest, Theobald Mathew. Born in 1790 at Thomastown, Tipperary, he was educated at Kilkenny, Maynooth and Dublin. In 1841 he was ordained by Archbishop Murray and proceeded to Cork, where one of his predecessors had been Arthur O'Leary. Mathew opened Free Schools and held aloof from political, and even from theological, controversy. Thackeray described him as almost the only man in Ireland whom he had encountered who, in speaking of public matters, was not a partisan.[9] One of his achievements was an interdenominational cemetery, intended to avoid quarrels at the graveside between clergy of rival denominations.

In 1838 Mathew was persuaded by some Nonconformist friends to sign a pledge of total abstinence. His influence on his fellow Catholics was enormous, and the duties paid on alcohol in Ireland are said to have fallen by over forty per cent in five years as a result of his teachings.[10] In 1843 he came to London, and was kindly treated by Peel. At the height of the famine (30th September 1846) Mathew wrote to Charles Trevelyan that

> the late provision riots have occurred in the districts in which the temperance movement has not been encouraged. Our people are as harmless in their meetings as flocks of sheep, unless when inflamed and maddened by intoxicating drink . . . Were it not for the temperate habits of the greater portion of the people of Ireland, our unhappy country would be before now one wide scene of tumult and bloodshed.[11]

We have already described how the Young Irelanders broke with O'Connell on the subject of mixed education and, ultimately, on the question of physical force. Yet until February 1848 neither "Conciliation Hall" as O'Connell's section was known, nor the Irish Confederation (the Young Irelanders' Association) were in favour of disturbing the peace. John Mitchel's views were denounced at a meeting of the latter, and Mitchel was forced off the *Nation* newspaper. Instead he launched a rival to it called *The United Irishman* on 12th February.[12] This preached treason openly in the city of Dublin. Clarendon, the Lord Lieutenant, was urged in parliament to act, if only to encourage loyalism. On 21st March, three weeks after the revolution in France, warrants were issued against Smith O'Brien, Meagher and Mitchel for seditious speeches. But the *United Irishman* continued to describe Clarendon as "Butcher General of Ireland" with impunity; the ladies of Dublin were invited to throw acid at the troops, and methods of upsetting horses were described. Lectures upon street-firing and the manufacture of pikes were also included. As a result Dublin was put in a state of siege; important buildings were taken over by troops and bullet-proof shutters were fitted everywhere. But the insurrection came to nothing.

In 1849 the Habeas Corpus Suspension Act was renewed. There were fears about the (for then) massive sums being spent on poor relief. Prosperous estates were being forced, said Peel, to subsidize the unprosperous. The effect "would be to merge the solvent estates in one common ruin with those already insolvent".[13] A cereal crop should replace the potato. Disraeli's remedy was the substitution of an income tax for the poor rate, and a stringent "poor-law test", by which he seems to have meant a means test.

The Queen's visit to Ireland began with a landing at Cove (re-named Queen's Town in her honour) where she proceeded to neighbouring Cork and to Dublin. As she left Dublin "the royal standard was lowered in courtesy to the cheering thousands on shore; and this stately obeisance was repeated five times".[14] Thence to Belfast and, stated the *Annual Register*, "if Her Majesty's reception at Catholic and repealing Cork was as enthusiastic as imagination can conceive, what can be said for that of the Protestant capital of Ireland?"

Specifically Catholic Addresses were presented by the Roman Catholic Bishop and clergy of Cork, and by the "Undersigned Archbishops and Bishops professing the Roman Catholic religion in Ireland". The second made no reference to the famine except in passing; the first was more specific, and bore witness, not only to the "heroic patience" with which the "poor and suffering portion of the community" had borne "those chastening visitations of providence, which so overshadowed the land", but to "their loyal, peaceful, and orderly conduct under privations and afflictions the most severe that have ever fallen to the lot of humanity".[15]

The *Belfast News-Letter* complained on 17 August that whilst "the Romish address is received with more than usual cordiality, that of the Presbyterian clergy is responded to with a sort of *insouciance* and unmeaning vagueness". The former, it added, was subscribed to by fourteen only out of the twenty-seven prelates; four from Armagh, two from Cashel and all from Tuam (MacHale's province) had disassociated themselves from it. "The Romish Church in Ireland, in short, came to the foot of the throne like a paralytic cripple — one half of the body showing a sickly vitality, and the other half morally and physically dead". This was somewhat unfair. Controversy behind the scenes had centred merely upon the form which the Address should take, not upon the principle. As to the complaint that the Presbyterian Address was treated with *insouciance*, it is true that it was received merely with "great" satisfaction, a opposed to the "heartfelt" satisfaction with which that from the all-Ireland Catholic prelates was met. The Catholic text was slightly longer because of a reference to the famine, which also appears in the reply to the Address from the United Church of England and Ireland of approximately the same length. The Presbyterian Address made no reference to the famine. The Catholic archbishops and bishops also presented a loyal Address to Prince Albert, as did the church of Ireland.[16] In Belfast, another received by Her Majesty from Cornelius Denvir, Catholic Bishop of Down, who signed for "self and clergy",[17] asserted that "among the numerous subjects of this extensive realm, we yield to no class or portion in warm attachment to your Majesty's person, or devoted loyalty to your Majesty's Throne". A similar, but shorter, Address was presented to Prince Albert.[18]

That there *was* controversy about the all-Ireland Catholic Address appears from correspondence between MacHale and Murray published in 1885.[19] Murray's Address, as originally drafted, left out the famine; he was prepared to compromise, and did, but MacHale's alternative went too far in its criticism of ministers. Nevertheless, it contained some fine passages; for example, it made reference to the "fealty challenged by the Sovereign" being "transformed into filial attachment towards the parental heart of Queen Victoria who has condescended to come in the hour of their affliction, to cheer and to console the desponding hearts of her loving children".

Differences of opinion among the Catholic bishops were nothing new. They had developed gradually in the course of the 1840s over such questions as national education, repeal, and charitable bequests. In January 1850 a group of "moderates" (the Bishop of Raphoe and others) wrote to Rome that although they believed that benefits conferred by a Protestant government might contain risks from a Catholic point of view, those risks had to be run and in general were due to ignorance, not bad faith on the part of the Protestant ministers. T. H. Whyte[20] has likened the difference between the two parties in the Irish Catholic Church to those between Gallicans and ultramontanes in France, the moderates (Murray and others) acting as the counterpart of the Gallicans; but, as we have tried to show, the comparison does not hold for the Repeal period when it was Murray, not MacHale, who secured Vatican support for his views. Thus the priests who rallied to his support in January 1845 were at pains to point out that

> when we see the people publicly, and, as we know, still more privately, taught to distrust the integrity of the Holy See, and to imbibe doctrines regarding the authority of the Pope, which are plainly at variance with the Catholic faith; when we see all this, and behold your Grace exhibiting the same apostolic courage in opposition to the tyranny which enslaves us now [i.e. the Repeal Agitation], which you exhibited against the tyranny that threatened to enslave us in former times, we return our fervent thanks.[21]

"You will cling to the 'successor of Peter and Damasus'", they added, "and we will cling to you". A truer picture of Archbishop Murray's position is given in *Ultramontane Designs in 1865*, where three parties are distinguished.[22]

Archbishop Machale's problem seems to have been in part at least that he liked to be contrary and "agin" everyone. Master in his own domain, he was not for nothing known as the "Lion of the fold of Judah" and "The Patriarch of the West". Archbishop Cullen complained to Propaganda in May 1854 that

> the sole obstacle to perfect harmony in the episcopal body is Mgr the archbishop of Tuam, who cannot resign himself to thinking like his colleagues, and who even changes his own opinions when they come to be adopted by others, so as to remain always in opposition.[23]

On 24th February 1850 Cullen became Archbishop of Armagh, and thus Primate of All Ireland. His co-primate, the elderly Archbishop Murray of Dublin, though technically of lesser rank, since his primacy was of "Ireland" rather than of "all Ireland", retained the primacy of honour as is shown by Cullen's translation to Dublin after Murray's death two years later.

Yet Cullen, throughout the period of his primacy, exerted immense authority, partly because of his personal qualities, and partly because of his eighteen years as Rector of the Irish College at Rome. At the Synod of Thurles in August, battle was joined on the subject of the Queen's Colleges. Murray declared that, despite the rescripts of the Holy See, he would not exhort the faithful to stay away from these colleges, or to keep their sons away from them. The government had made concessions; the colleges were not wholly "Godless", for Catholic prelates could be named among the college visitors, and Catholic halls of residence were to be established under deans appointed by the local Catholic bishops. But, for once, the archbishop found himself in a minority, and he and others were forced to appeal to Rome.

Events were also moving swiftly in England. In September 1850 the Pope purported to re-instate a Catholic hierarchy of bishops and archbishops such as had not existed since the reformation. Much Protestant opinion was outraged, especially when the new Archbishop of Westminster, Cardinal Wiseman, in his first pastoral declared that "we govern . . . the counties of Middlesex, Hertford and Essex as ordinary thereof". Some Catholics in England disapproved of the change, notably Lord Beaumont and the thirteenth Duke of Norfolk, who thought it "totally incompatible with allegiance to our Sovereign and with our constitution". He left the Roman Catholic Church in September 1851 and was reconciled to it only on his deathbed.[24]

Lord John Russell himself led the protests in his celebrated *Letter to the Bishop of Durham*, and in 1851 the government carried an Ecclesiastical Titles Bill making it a penal offence for Catholic bishops to adopt territorial titles. This had the effect of uniting the Catholic prelates of Ireland, and Archbishop Murray was foremost in issuing a pastoral condemning the Government's action. The Catholic members of the Bar also opposed the ·measure, and their protest in Ireland was signed by two out of the three serjeants, twelve Queen's Counsel, and about eighty other barristers.[25] Lord Gormanston, always a significant barometer of Catholic Unionist opinion, joined the protest. The Chief Secretary for Ireland, now Sir William Somerville, reported that county meetings were being organized, and that "there are names attached to that document which nothing short of what the parties think a religious obligation would have detached from my interests".[26]

The Ecclesiastical Titles Bill was never enforced, and it was repealed in 1871, but it had weakened the Catholic Unionist position. The Holy See rejected Murray's appeal against the Synod of Thurles, and Murray himself died in February 1852. He was a man whom even *The Tablet* (which had by now become hostile to the Union) respected for his piety, gentle manners, disinterestedness and skill in administration.

Cullen was translated to Dublin and after the next synodical meeting of bishops was able to report that "even the Bishops of Cork, Limerick, and Down and Connor, who were the most recalcitrant — declared themselves in this assembly ready to contribute to the setting up of the Catholic University".[27]

A committee for this purpose had, indeed, already been formed by the Synod of Thurles, and in November 1851 Newman had accepted the office of Rector.[28] The next year he occupied in writing the first part of one of the best-known of his treatises: *The Idea of a University*. By 1854 he was in Ireland, finding that not all Catholics favoured the scheme. Thomas O'Hagan, for example, wrote to him on 27 June that many of the Catholics he knew felt that to support the new University would mean the abandonment of the principle of mixed education. Other members of the Bar, too, had scruples, as Monsell informed him; and Lords Kenmare, Castlerosse, and Fingall also objected. Newman thought that there was an element of anti-clericalism about these lay Catholic objections.[29] He found the Catholic bishops in general somewhat stand-offish; and the Unionist Bishop Moriarty was the only one who gave him any real help. In several of his letters he expressed the view that Moriarty, with whom he had made friends in 1849, should replace him as Rector.[30]

Nevertheless the Catholic University had been, after a fashion, formed; but now a fresh point of controversy arose. In August 1850 a Tenant League had been started to combat high rents and evictions. Several of the Catholic hierarchy, including Archbishops Cullen and MacHale, gave it their support. In England, the Ecclesiastical Titles Bill caused Lord John Russell to resign within a year because of the loss of Irish Catholic support. For a few months of 1852 Derby became Prime Minister in the "Who? Who?" Ministry, so called because the now aged Duke of Wellington had to have the names of its members shouted into his ear. He was succeeded by Lord Aberdeen, a Peelite governing with mainly Whig support. Catholic feeling was further alienated by British support for Garibaldi and Victor Emanuel in Italy in their attacks upon the Papal States. Even so late as 1860, when Palmerston tried to advance to the Solicitor-Generalship a Mr O'Hagan, "one of the most accomplished and deservedly popular Catholic barristers"[31], his nominee was virtually sent to Coventry by the extreme party. In 1862 an anonymous Catholic writer was led seriously to consider an alliance between the Conservatives and the Roman Catholics. "Abstractedly", he was prepared to concede, "the genius of Catholicity is doubtless Conservative".[32]

In the 1850s, however, attention was concentrated on the development of an independent Irish party. Although this had it roots in the Tenant League as well as in the Catholic Defence Association (a United Kingdom body founded in August 1851 in order to secure the repeal of the Ecclesiastical Titles Act)[33], its main strength lay in the fact that many Catholics felt themselves to have been betrayed by the Liberals. Nonetheless, there were Catholics who refused to abandon their political allegiance and declined to pledge themselves not to support any party in parliament which refused to legislate in favour of tenant-right. Among these was William Monsell, afterwards Lord Emly, who had been elected for Limerick in 1847. In 1850 he became a Roman Catholic under the influence of the Tractarian movement (Newman's *Essays and Lectures on University Subjects* of 1859 is dedicated to him); but although he supported tenant-right, he was not prepared to give the pledge required by members of what came to be known as the "Irish Brigade" or, more euphoniously, the "Pope's Brass Band".

The Parliamentary position in the early 1850s was complex. Over sixty of the 105 Irish M.P.s were Liberals, four were Peelites, and over thirty were Conservative. The Liberals were divided equally between Catholics and Protestants and the others were all Protestants. The over-all balance of parties in the House was similar.[34]

The Tenant League's Bill, in essence, provided that tenants who had made improvements to the property which they had rented from landlords should be entitled, when their holding next changed hands, to charge incoming tenants the value of the improvements which they had made. This was already the custom in Ulster, and the object of the League was to place it on a statutory footing in all parts of the country. Sharman Crawford's Bill had, in 1847, attempted to do this, but had been defeated by a large majority.[35]

The general election of July 1852 was preceded, on 15th June, by a proclamation reminding Catholics that it was illegal for them to exercise their religion in public, or for their ecclesiastics to wear in public the habits of their order.[36] Whatever its ulterior purpose, many took this reminder of a law which was virtually a dead letter as an insult. On 27th June twenty-four Catholic houses were looted at Stockport, and two chapels wrecked after a procession of Catholic schoolchildren. The government were accused of causing these events by their proclamation, and a number of prominent Catholics in Ireland who had hitherto been opposed to the Liberals decided to change their allegiance.[37]

At the election itself, both landlords and clergy were accused of intimidation. J. P. Somers, Catholic Whig M.P. for Sligo, who refused to pledge his support for the Tenant League, was accused by his priest *coram publico* of being "a traitor to my religion and my country, and that any man who voted for me voted for hell and the devil; and that every man who voted for my opponent, voted for God and for Heaven".[38] A Catholic Conservative wrote to a London newspaper that William Kenny, unable to vote because of a fall from his horse, was held up to the congregation as an example of God's wrath because he had presumed to vote against the candidate supported by the priest.[39]

These were isolated incidents, and too much should not be made of them. They do however indicate the strength of feeling that had been aroused. The Catholic laity were sometimes divided between rival candidates. At New Ross, the parish priest and his supporters backed Sir Thomas Redington, who had been M.P. for Dundalk since 1837 and, from July 1846, Under-Secretary for Ireland in the Liberal Government. Although a Catholic, he had remained in office when the Ecclesiastical Titles Bill was passed. The senior curate and other members of the laity however backed the Young Irelander, Charles Gavan Duffy, who was elected. The priestly quarrel waxed bitter, and mutual denunciations were exchanged. In the event, Redington decided to withdraw from the contest, and Duffy was opposed only by Henry Lambert, whom we have already encountered as a vigorous Catholic opponent of O'Connell's movement for repeal.

Lambert had by now moved on from Liberal Unionism and become a Conservative. In a notable book published the previous year under the title *Memoir of Ireland in 1850* ("By an ex-M.P.") he had reviewed the history of Ireland in his time. For a series of years, he had asserted, Ireland had had no government for any useful or salutary purpose. "Paltry backstairs intrigue" and the "judicious management of patronage" had been the order of the day. "Democracy tinged . . . with the principles of what is termed communism" (then a new word, only recently invented), "appears to have taken a strong hold of the popular affections." "From a horde of crouching slaves, we have become a nation of rampant grievance-mongers . . . overlooking the evils that weigh heavily on the State, we clamour for impossibilities." Wellesley had been a good Governor, but Lambert had little good to say of others such as the "bland and polished Normanby", who had "opened the gaols for felons and the Castle to the canaille".

Repeal of the Union had never rested on its merits, but on the demerits of government. If granted, it would ultimately have led to a collision, for an Irish parliament would have made short work of commercial arrangements and of the aristocracy nor could England have tolerated an enemy so near her. The criminal courts were "tiltyards of chicanery" and "crowds looked on with indifference at the noon-day slaughter of their fellow-creatures". Whereas in England lawful authority was generally revered, in Ireland it was "despised and detested, evaded, or violated with perfect impunity".

Father Mathew's temperance pledge had been effective for a time; but in many cases there had been a reaction. Nonetheless, it had done some good. The national scheme of education had been on the whole a success. But these were the only two bright spots in a picture of almost universal gloom.

In the second chapter of his book, Lambert discussed the famine. It was an "inscrutable dispensation of divine Providence"; but the Whig measures to meet it had been thoroughly bad. Her Majesty's Ministers had undoubtedly meant well, but they should have tried to keep down the price of food. Instead, in "their zeal for the rights of money, they entirely forgot the rights of humanity". Obsessed by the doctrine of *laissez-faire*, they had abandoned the provision of food to private speculators: "never before did it occur to rulers in any country to consider a period of such affliction as a suitable season to indulge in working out abstract theories and constitutional experiments". During a previous famine early in the reign of George III, Chatham had embargoed provisions at the ports; but the Whigs would not take so obvious a step. Nonetheless, "with all their professions of philosophical non-interference", the Whigs *had* interfered "largely, fatally", with the labour-market. They had "squandered on wilful, sturdy idleness, the funds that should have been sacredly reserved for the destitute and deserving poor".[40] The evil became so glaring that a sudden stop was put to the waste labour scheme. Funds were advanced for the purchase of food to be distributed by local committees. This was an improvement. Lambert's own committee found that two hundred pounds between March and August sufficed to relieve real destitution where several thousand spent on unprofitable public works had failed.

The Poor Law was then extended to "indiscriminate out-door relief". This ruined some of the more distressed Poor Law Unions because of the resultant increase in the poor rate. But the system was "rigidly enforced while a shilling remained to the industrious and well-disposed portion of the community; as if the object to be attained were the reduction of all to a common level of beggary and demoralization".[41] The workhouse system was, in Lambert's view, no use; it bred demoralization though in a few cases it imposed discipline.

Next the government tried a "rate-in-aid" to be levied all over Ireland including the wasted and insolvent Unions. Lord George Bentinck's "wise and beneficient project" to employ the starving Irish in railway construction was rejected. The only effect of grinding down relatively prosperous people, whether landlords or tenants, was to drive them to emigrate, as was already happening. Landlords were constantly being exhorted to employ the poor but where were they to find the money to pay them?

In his third chapter, Lambert discusses the financial aspects in detail, and the arguments have a curiously modern ring. The "bullionists", who were the monetarists of the period, favoured what was called a "sound and wholesome currency". But Lambert was what we may, over-simplifying, call a Keynesian. He favoured a policy of expanding credit such as had been pursued by Mr Pitt up to 1819. The Bank of England had, up to then, been released from its obligation of paying notes on demand and was thus, in a way, "off the gold standard". The Directors of the Bank had remonstrated against any change and the Act of 1819 had, according to Lambert, produced great agricultural distress. Silver had been abolished as legal tender in England and replaced by a "gold standard". Lambert argued that this was absurd and would produce great fluctuations in monetary values; but he was not proved right over the long term. For nearly a century there was in fact considerable stability in the value of money, though some economists have argued that this was due to other factors.[42] In any event, Lambert asserted, the adoption of a gold standard led to considerable hardship in Ireland; from eight or nine million, the paper circulation of Ireland had been reduced to four million, and the poor rates alone were two million pounds annually. It was true that paper money could be abused, but it could be contracted as soon as it had ceased to have any salutary effect upon the action of industry. There was, however, now no "discretionary power to afford relief" because of the Bank Charter Act of 1844, which restricted the powers of local banks to produce their own notes.[43]

What was needed was an import levy; "the unlimited influx of foreign grain, rushing at once into the home market, gave the finishing blow to the struggles and to the hopes of the afflicted Irish people".

On the subject of landlord and tenant, Lambert concluded that the advantages were not all on one side; a "dishonest and litigious tenant with an unscrupulous and smart attorney" could often plunder and defy his landlord. On the other hand, it was also true that merciless and unprincipled landlords could oppress well disposed and industrious tenants. Lambert favoured tenant-right, by which he understood the payment to the tenant, on the expiration of his lease, of the value of his permanent improvements to the property. The Tenant League, however, as he understood it, went further, advocating a compulsory valuation of land according to its own rules, and a perpetuity of tenure. To the former he was opposed, though he might have been able to accept a more impartial assessment.

But even in 1850, landlords could not always do what they liked with their own. They were for example, legally bound by any covenants, and were already "a fixed mark for condign punishment, should they exceed by the smallest tittle the exact limit of their legal rights; whereas the tenant may violate every contract, and set at nought every principle of law, leaving to the landlord enormous costs to pay, and a 'dissolving view' of his prosecutor in full march for the United States". These were events, added Lambert, of everyday occurrence in Ireland. Moreover, English M.P.s were not easily persuaded by tenant-righters. They had a formal, John Bullish notion that a bargain is a bargain.

The government's monetary policy and pursuit of free trade had reduced the value of land by two-thirds. Landlords were also made victims of character assassination — "destruction of character" was Lambert's phrase. They were accused of atrocities, and they often felt that they were being hunted "to extermination". Certain evictions had been justly reprobated, but what had caused them? some landlords too had been obliged to leave, but they had no "Debtor Right League" to protect *them* from the Confiscation Court.

As to emigration generally, it had long since "passed the salutary point". It was now "the fatal depletion of an already sinking patient. The able-bodied, intelligent farmers, with some capital, a class of men whom it would take a century to replace, are quitting us every day by hundreds for the United States, there to cherish, extend and bequeath a deadly, implacable hatred to England".

Irish estates had already become "almost unsaleable". Landlords had no security for life or property. They were "perpetually on trial for character or life, in a court where no evidence is admitted for the accused, and where execution frequently precedes conviction". Few would choose to reside on such terms. The "generous sympathies of the modern public" were exclusively reserved for "overholding tenants, squatters, and crop-lifters".

Here then was the landlords' view, forcibly and convincingly expressed, and nearly thirty years before the foundation of the Land League, Lambert indeed portrays a situation remarkably similar in kind if not in degree to that of landlords in the 1880s, when their plight became better-publicized.

Why should Roman Catholics support the Whigs? This was the title of Lambert's fifth chapter. He began it by pointing out that the devotion of Catholic M.P.s was understandable enough when they could obtain preferment. Although there had once been an independent and high-minded Irish party capable of resisting Treasury blandishments, O'Connell had broken it up. But why should they support the Whigs, when "every concession made to Roman Catholics, from the first dawn of toleration to the repeal of the penal laws in 1829 was the work of the Tories exclusively"? It was the Conservatives who had conceded promotion in the armed services to Roman Catholics, and the attitude of English Catholic peers in supporting the Whigs was particularly difficult to understand. Lord John Russell, in his *Essay on the English Government and Constitution* (1821) had expressed the view that the penal laws were just, if not wise. Dr Johnson had thought otherwise.[44] Lord Russell, one of the founders of the Whig Party, had been beheaded for treasonable conspiracy in the reign of Charles II. He had pursued to death Lord Stafford and Archbishop Oliver Plunket, yet Lord John praised his ancestor whose "religious creed was that of a mild and tolerant Christian". The whole object of the Whig exclusion plot had been to prevent a Catholic from ascending the throne. The iniquitous and cruel laws against Catholics had been unquestionably "the invention of the Whigs, who enforced them with remorseless perseverance, until it suited their political purpose to take up emancipation and confer on it a "factitious and barren support". Nevertheless, a glance at House of Lords division lists might incline one to believe that "passive obedience to a Whig Ministry was an article in the creed of Pope Pius, or had been enjoined by a decree of a National Synod". Yet the Tory party took its very origin from its refusal to concur in excluding a Roman Catholic prince from the throne. Hatred of Catholicity still rankled in Whig hearts, "and it is tolerably certain, that they would raise the old No Popery cry to-morrow, if they thought it would, by any means, tend to prolong their possession of office". Lambert added in a note that this passage was written in October 1850, before the crisis caused by the re-establishment of the Catholic hierarchy, and before Lord John Russell's Durham letter. But not only that and the Ecclesiastical Titles Bill, but Gladstone's attack on the Vatican decrees in the 1870s, may be seen as part of the same Whig tradition. Would the noble Lord, asked Lambert, now require His Holiness to "unfrock" his bishops, and, failing this, is a fleet to be sent to Civita Vecchia, as it was to the Piraeus? The former but not the latter course was in the event adopted. Lambert went on to point out that colonial bishops with territorial designations had been appointed by the Pope and officially recognized by the British government; a new Roman Catholic see at Galway had been created without remonstrance; while "the Viceregal supplication to the Pontifical throne, in the affair of the Irish colleges, seemed almost to invite the aggression that certain diplomatic doings in Rome were directly calculated to provoke".[45]

The Whigs had compelled William III, who was naturally of a humane and liberal disposition, to violate the Treaty of Limerick; and modern Ireland had suffered from the Whig poor laws and other demoralizing pieces of legislation.

Yet there was a worse charge against Whiggery. Deists and Latitudinarians of every kind had been granted preferment in the Church of England. Catholics might be disposed to welcome this as tending to that Church's destruction; but they should recall the many points of resemblance and above all that it was "one of the great bulwarks of Christianity itself against atheism, infidelity, and the abominable doctrines of materialist and utilitarian philosophy".

Now, in 1852, Lambert's candidature at New Ross attracted the support of the *Dublin University Magazine*, whose anonymous writer was scathing about Catholics like William Keogh, Lord Arundel, and More O'Ferrall, the first for his inconsistency (he had begun his political life as an opponent of O'Connell and a supporter of Peel and was now a member of the "Brigade") and the last two for having "truckled to the Papal authority".[46]

Lambert, by contrast, was "a man of high talent, and high family — a Roman Catholic in religion, a consistent Conservative in politics". In Parliament, the repealers had "winced under his rebukes". Redington, by contrast, was "the most degraded" of the three candidates. Why? Because when High Tories such as Lord Derby and Croker writing in the *Quarterly Review* had rebuked Lord John for the views expressed in his Durham letter, "Sir Thomas Redington pocketed the affront and the salary together". According to the *Magazine*, Redington had also taken part in jury-packing.

Thus did Lambert receive praise even from a source hostile to Catholics, and especially to "Castle Cawtholics", as they were dubbed in Duffy's *Nation*. Duffy, having won by eighty-two votes to thirty-one after Redington's withdrawal, commented unfairly and in retrospect upon Lambert, who had, he alleged, "been elected as a Repealer in O'Connell's first repeal movement in 1832 but had deserted the party in the House of Commons". This despite Lambert's assurances made during that election campaign and after that he was not pledged to repeal. Duffy went on to say that Lambert was "known to the people" (by which, presumably, he meant his own followers and the mob) as "Luttrell Lambert", after the Jacobite commander at Aughrim who sold a pass to the Williamite forces. This gibe originated in a speech made by Joseph Kennedy at Newtownbarry, 26th January 1834, after Lambert had voted against repeal in the House of Commons. Lambert had brought a libel action against Kennedy for this speech, heard before the King's Bench in Dublin on 29 November 1834, an action which he won before a jury despite an eloquent and witty speech by O'Connell in Kennedy's defence.[47]

The elections of 1852 were a success for the "Brigade" and by December they could number nearly fifty adherents in the new House of Commons. Nevertheless, at least ten of the fifty Catholic M.P.s elected to, or during, this parliament are known not to have given a pledge. Besides Monsell, they were Valentine Browne (Kerry) (who became Lord Castlerosse in 1853), Maurice O'Connell (Tralee), Vincent Scully (Cork County), and others returned at by-elections, such as Daniel O'Connell (Junior), elected in July 1853 on the death of his brother; John O'Connell, third son of Daniel Senior, returned for Clonmell, 21st December 1853 and afterwards appointed Clerk of the Crown and Hanaper in Ireland; Sergeant James O'Brien, elected for Limerick City in October 1854; Stephen de Vere (Limerick County, December 1854); R. Deasy (Cork County, April 1855); and H. G. Hughes (Longford, May 1856). After the election of 1857, the proportion was much higher; at least twenty-one out of the thirty-six Catholic M.P.s at that period were uncommitted.[48]

In 1852, in the United Kingdom as a whole, the Conservatives had slightly increased their majority; but although they made sincere attempts to conciliate the "Brigade" by introducing a Tenants' Improvement

Compensation Bill which went further than any previous such measure, it annoyed its own supporters. The government retreated, offended the Brigade, and was defeated on 17th December 1852 on the budget. A coalition of Liberals and Peelites then took office, with Aberdeen as Prime Minister. Two of the "Brigadiers", William Keogh who became Solicitor-General for Ireland, and John Sadleir, accepted office, thereby incurring the wrath of many who saw them as "pledge-breakers". There were some, however, who supported them. For example, at a meeting of the electors of Athlone when Keogh stood for re-election, the Vicar-General of the Diocese of Elphin and seven other Catholic clergymen concurred in satisfaction at his "prudence and consistency".[49] A third office-taker, Monsell, came in for no criticism because he had taken no pledge.

That the three were no place-seeking ciphers is shown by the fact that within a year they were offering their resignations because of unguarded remarks by Lord John Russell. On 31st May 1853 he hinted that the political activities of the Vatican were placing the loyalty of Catholics in some doubt. In his reply to Monsell, Aberdeen was at pains to point out that Lord John's views were not shared by himself nor by many of his colleagues. Furthermore, "Ld John Russell desires me to say that he did not impute want of loyalty to the Roman Catholics, and that he expressly said that political and social equality ought to be maintained".[50] Monsell then withdrew his resignation. Whatever might be his feelings about other members of the government, "I have trusted, & do trust your Lordship as a highminded statesman, resolved to deal justly & liberally with a religious Communion which has long suffered from opposite treatment".[51] Keogh and Sadleir also agreed to remain in office. They were denounced as pledge-breakers, and the vendetta especially against Keogh, who became a judge in 1856 and tried Fenians in the 1860s, continued relentlessly; but they had shown, as had Monsell, that Catholics in office were influential, and they thereby weakened the case of the Brigade for refusing office except on rigidly-defined terms. "An Irish Catholic" wrote in 1853 of these appointments that Aberdeen had "distributed the posts of office, within his gift, fairly, and without regard to religious opinions". Sir Thomas Redington was Secretary to the Board of Control; and another Catholic, John Corballis, was law adviser at the Castle.[52]

The Brigade was also weakened by a quarrel with the bishops. We have seen that Archbishop Cullen, who had been translated to Dublin on Murray's death, was less sympathetic to Unionism than his predecessor. Nevertheless he was also against revolutionaries, having had recent experience of them during the 1840s as Rector of the Irish College at Rome; and in the autumn of 1853 Newman, then Rector-designate of the new Catholic University in Dublin, received a letter from Ambrose St John stating that the Archibshop was beginning to surround himself with "Dr Murray's people". Father Doyle, Duffy's supporter at New Ross, had already been transferred to an inferior parish; and in Ossory the curate of Callan who had been campaigning for a "Brigadier" or "Independent" as the party was now beginning to be called, was reprimanded by his bishop. In 1854 resolutions of a national council of the Catholic prelacy contained clauses limiting the clergy's political activities,[53] and in 1855 Cullen wrote to David Moriarty, Bishop of Kerry, that Duffy "acts as the life & soul of a most dangerous party, the Young Ireland faction . . . It is most dangerous to do anything tending to give him or his faction an influence in the country which his party would not fail to exercise against church or state".[54] The Independent party appealed to Rome, but were unsuccessful; and in 1855 one of their leading proponents, Frederick Lucas, founder of the *Tablet* and M.P., died. Duffy had always said that if Rome found against him he would resign his seat in Parliament, and in November he accordingly sailed for Australia.[55]

The Resolutions of the prelates had some influence on the methods by which clerical influence was exercised at elections, but little on the actual fact of intervention. In the election of 1857 it was only at Waterford that a prelate actually used his episcopal authority to ban a priest from taking part; and an Independent was, nonetheless, elected. The true causes of the decline of the Independent party, a leading authority has concluded, did not include the disapproval of the hierarchy, but a decline in the quality of leadership, the increasing prosperity of the country due to a succession of good harvests, and the decline in anti-Catholic activity. Local issues became more important. The Catholic proprietors were concerned at the influence of Archbishop MacHale and made determined efforts, for example in Galway, where Sir William Gregory, a Protestant, was elected with the support of two out of the four Catholic bishops.[56] Bellew, his opponent, was supported by the other two and the archbishop. Dr Fallon, bishop of Kilmacduagh, even wrote Gregory's letters for him when he was in bed with a cold, and McEvilly of Galway was equally strong in his support. On one occasion, when a member of the crowd abused him as a Protestant, a priest who was by his side "sprang into the thick of the throng, and then and there, amid general acclamation, administered to him a sound castigation with a stick".[57]

The Aberdeen Ministry had fallen early in 1855 over its handling of the war in the Crimea. Palmerston then became Prime Minister with a virtually identical cabinet, but after a few days the Peelites, including Gladstone, resigned. Nevertheless the ministry successfully remained in office for over two years. In 1857 Palmerston decided to ask for a dissolution because of a defeat in the Commons over a case involving British subjects in Canton; in the course of his election campaign he stressed that national honour was at stake, and Peelites and Radicals alike suffered severely.[58] In 1858 national prestige was again affected. An explosive attempt on the life of the Emperor Napoleon III was traced back to a conspiracy by foreigners in London, and Palmerston introduced a Bill at the French Government's behest making conspiracy to murder a felony punishable by penal servitude for life. A vote of censure was carried against the Bill, and Derby was sent for. Disraeli became Chancellor of the Exchequer, and Lord Eglinton Lord Lieutenant. A year later however the Government was defeated on a Reform Bill, opposition to which was skilfully led by Lord John Russell, and an appeal to the country followed. The Conservatives gained about twenty-five seats over-all, and one of the new Members was John Pope Hennessy, who was returned for King's County "in the unique role of an Irish Catholic and Nationalist who was also a Conservative".[59]

Pope Hennessy was born at Cork in 1834 and educated at the Queen's College there, afterwards at the Inner Temple. He was still a law student when elected to parliament. In a statement after the election, published in the *Cork Examiner*, he began by asserting that "of the two great parties, the Liberals and the Conservatives, I am naturally inclined, as a Catholic and an Irishman . . . to join the latter". Although it had been assumed that the Liberals favoured tenant-right and the Conservatives did not, in fact "the very reverse is the case". One section of the Liberals viewed any interference between landlord and tenant as an infringement of the principle of Free Trade, whilst the other had no very clear reason except that their leader, Palmerston, was against it.

> On the other hand, the alliance which has at all times existed between the Conservatives and the agricultural classes, as well as those principles of Conservatism which tend to encourage legislative enactments of a protective kind, render the Conservatives more friendly to our cause than the Liberals, and accounts

for the fact that under both the administrations of Lord Derby a Tenant Right Bill was made a Cabinet measure.[60]

In the educational field, Pope Hennessy was an advocate of separatism and could, again, find greater support for this as a principle among Conservatives than among Liberals. Similarly, Conservatives had, he asserted, been more active in protecting the exercise of the Catholic religion in public establishments; whereas commissioned chaplains for Catholic soldiers were urged "year after year" upon a Liberal Government, it was only under the Conservatives that Catholic priests were appointed.

The *Saturday Review*, for its part, sneered at what it saw as this new alliance between Catholicism and Conservatism in Ireland; it was reminded of the Lichfield House compact of 1835, under which O'Connell's Repealers had agreed to support the Whigs on certain conditions, and which had been honoured as much in the breach as in the observance. "The allegiance of Mr Bowyer", it wrote, "to the Ministerial ranks had been welcomed by the sacerdotal tribunes who 'hold the keys' of the borough of Dundalk".[61] MacEvoy, Corbally, Blake and Maguire also owed their seats entirely to the Catholic Church's influence. "The vinegar of Derbyism and the oil of Romanism have, in Ireland, coalesced into a mixture which . . . is very unpleasant to well-regulated consciences." Using a favourite analogy of the day, it went on to describe Derby as the "leader of a thimblerig Cabinet, which shifts the pea from 'Protestantism' to 'Popery' at its convenience". The reason for the present alliance, in its view, was that ever since 1846 Derbyism had been associated with the "communists of the Irish tenant-right league, who after 1848, transferred their allegiance to the Irish priesthood from Smith O'Brien". On the other side, the Durham letter had alienated the mass of Irish Catholics from Lord John Russell, and the Irish Government from 1846 to 1851 was "occasionally marked by discourtesy and harshness". Derbyism, in 1859, "has somehow contrived to identify itself with the name of Sir Robert Peel, which in Ireland is beloved by the Roman Catholics like a household word".

Despite Conservative electoral gains, the Government was defeated in the House, and Palmerston again became Prime Minister, and so remained until his death in 1865. Gladstone became Chancellor of the Exchequer.

In 1858 an American Society, known as the Fenian brotherhood, had been founded. the name is said to have been taken from the Fianna, or armed force supposed to have defended Ireland in legendary times, though it is more likely to be derived from *fene*, a name given in Old Irish to one of the ancient populations of Ireland.[62] Dr Edward Norman has pointed out that it owed its origin in the United States to the activities of certain American political groups such as the Know-Nothing party against Catholic Irish immigrants.[63] In the same year, in Ireland itself, the attention of the authorities was drawn to the existence of a secret body known as the Phoenix society of Skibbereen, which had an oath running somewhat as follows:

> I . . . swear in the presence of God, to renounce all allegiance to the Queen of England, and to take arms and fight at a moment's warning, and to make Ireland an Independent Democratic Republic, and to yield implicit obedience to the commanders and superiors of this secret society.[64]

Many of the Phoenix men were arrested and tried, but James Stephens escaped the net. Stephens had been an active Young Irelander in 1848, and on 17th March 1858 had founded in his Dublin lodgings another secret society later to be known as the Irish Republican Brotherhood.[65]

These various groups differed from Whiteboys and Ribbonmen in that their political aspirations were precise; they differed from the United Irishmen of the previous century in their superior methods of security, so that no member was known to any other member except in a limited circle. Their activities in Ireland itself were limited until the end of the American civil war in 1865 released from the Federal Army large numbers of restless and battle-trained Irish Americans. A plan for an outbreak to set up an Irish republic was ill-concealed. The leaders were arrested in September; but James Stephens escaped from prison, made his way to America, and announced a general rising. In 1866 it became known that Fenian agents were swearing in recruits and smuggling arms into Ireland; Habeas Corpus was suspended on 17th February. After an abortive raid by some American Fenians across the Canadian border in May, Stephens was deposed from the leadership. In February 1867 a body of men believed to be Fenians assembled at Chester, and the military had to be called in to protect installations. In September two Fenians who had been arrested in Manchester were abducted from a prison van. A police officer was killed, three out of his five attackers were hanged, and the five became known as "the Manchester martyrs".

In an attempt to release two prisoners at Clerkenwell gaol in December, a barrel of gunpowder was blown up against the outer wall, killing twelve people and wounding about 120 others.

Killarney was the scene of the first of the Fenian outrages in Ireland itself. Ironically enough, it was also a centre of Catholic Unionism, and in 1861, during the course of the third of her visits to Ireland, the queen had explored the lakes of Killarney with her beloved Prince Albert, and had been received by Lord Castlerosse at Killarney House, home of the Earls of Kenmare. The first Earl, Valentine Browne, who had played such a prominent part in Catholic affairs in the latter part of the eighteenth century, died in 1812 and was succeeded by his son who died childless in 1853. The Irish earldom thereupon devolved to the latter's brother, but the United Kingdom peerage became extinct and was not revived in his favour until 1856. The third Earl's son, Valentine Augustus, was born in 1825. In 1851 he became High Sheriff of County Kerry and was a member of Parliament by 1852. When his father succeeded to the earldom in 1853 he became Viscount Castlerosse.

The queen, therefore, had been very much in "Kenmare country" and the earls were greatly respected as landlords. Her reception there had been 'the most hearty and genuine that the Queen has had in Ireland'', wrote *The Times* correspondent. Although the visit was supposed to be informal, wherever the royal party went, they had been cheered at every turn; and the outstanding beauty of the surroundings must have greatly impressed Her Majesty. The queen had met Catholic prelates before; Archibishop Murray, whom she had described in 1849 as a "fine venerable-looking old man of eighty"[66]; and Bishop Denvir in Belfast ("an excellent and modest man"); but here in Kerry was a still more redoubtable champion of the Unionist cause in the person of David Moriarty, Bishop since 1856. Early on in his episcopate, he had denounced the Phoenix conspirators at Tralee, after successfully persuading some of them to give up their activities. "I protest", he had said, "against the members of this so-called conspiracy being canonised as patriots. I protest against the nationality of Ireland being represented by a company the only avowed and self-confessed members of which are certainly no credit to the old Milesian stock".[67] *The Times* had even mentioned the possibility of a regular royal visit to Ireland every autumn, but all was changed by the death of the Prince Consort in December 1861. Not for nearly forty years did the queen visit Ireland again; and when all the possible political reasons for this are examined, the thought remains that Her Majesty could not bear to revisit the scene of her last holiday here on earth with her beloved husband. As during the visit of 1853, which took place under the shadow of the Ecclesiastical Titles Act, the protocol was so arranged that no Catholic Addresses were allowed to be presented; but on neither occasion could anyone seriously deny the loyalty and enthusiasm of the Catholic population. Why was it, *The Times* asked,[68] that "the mere presence of a queen should awake in every heart the liveliest sympathies, and call forth expressions of unbounded attachment from the people, who but a few days before were sedulously engaged in traducing every act of her Ministers, and endeavouring at least to bring her Government into disrepute and contempt?"

The popularity of the sovereign was such that it has often been argued that the lack of a regular visit between 1861 and 1900 reinforced the Home Rule movement. This may be an exaggeration, yet it is certain that the queen was sorely missed by Irish Unionists, and that the Fenians filled the vacuum. In February 1867 some hundreds of them warred at Cahirciveen, sacked a coastguard station at Kells, and shot a mounted policeman bearing dispatches, robbing him of his horse and arms. They then cut the telegraph wires, severing the Atlantic cable for about five hours. Troops were sent from Cork to Killarney, and on the 14th the terrorists withdrew into the Toomes mountains.[69]

Moriarty was quick to denounce the rebels, reminding his auditors that because their avowed object was to make war upon the queen, "they purchased for themselves damnation".[70] They had demanded papers of the policeman, who happened to be a Catholic, and when he had refused and ridden on at them, "they let him pass — the man they dare not face in front — and, standing at his back, they shot him". "The blood-guiltiness of the act", he went on, "is surpassed only by its baseness and cowardice. When that Christian man lay weltering in his blood at the roadside he turned to his murderers and asked for a priest." A local priest then attended the wounded man, and with great courage went off to the police barracks at Ross Bay to warn them of a possible attack. Returning, he fell in with some of the miscreants again, and undeterred, assured them that if they attacked the barracks they would be staunchly defended. The Fenians thereupon accused him of having informed on them. He did not deny this, but was nevertheless allowed to pass after further abuse.[71]

Bishop Moriarty continued his sermon by excoriating the supineness of his own people. Although none of the peasantry, he said, had joined the Fenians, and many had fled at their approach, "there is an absence of manly, out-spoken, public spirit amongst you. You hate outrage and disorder, but you do not show yourselves like men on the side of law and order. You do not make Fenians afraid of you. You seem to halt between two sides as if you were afraid of them." He praised the family of Lord Kenmare especially for their kindness and bounty to the poor. Despite private assurances from him, the children of Lord and Lady Castlerosse had been removed to safety in England. "Yet there is not a man or woman in Killarney who would not part with life to defend these loved ones, yet you are afraid to show what you are. You are afraid of the Fenians".

All this must change, he asserted, and the tables must be turned on the evildoers. "If we must condemn the foolish youth who have joined in this conspiracy, how much must we not execrate the conduct of those designing villains who have been entrapping innocent youth, and organizing this work of crime". He was thankful that the Fenians were not truly Irish, or if they once had been had lost their Irish character in the cities of the United States; but beyond them were

> criminals of a far deeper guilt . . . fattening on the spoil in Paris and New York whilst sending their dupes into danger . . . The execrable swindlers who care not to endanger the necks of the men who trust them, who care not how many are murdered by the rebel or hanged by the strong arm of the law, provided they can get a supply of dollars either for their pleasures or for their wants. O God's heaviest curse, his withering, blasting, blighting curse is on them. I preached to you last Sunday on the eternity of Hell's torments . . . when we look down into the fathomless depth of this infamy of the heads of the Fenian conspiracy, we must acknowledge that eternity is not long enough, nor hell hot enough to punish such miscreants.

This was strong language, which with its reference to Irish America, has echoed down to the present day.[72] Archbishop Cullen thought it was too strong; and J. F. Maguire stated his belief in parliament that the Catholic clergy "had stood between the people in Ireland and the counsels of violent men, thus compromising to a certain extent, their influence with their flocks".[73] Yet Bishop Moriarty was no Castle hack. At the Tralee meeting in the late 1850s, in the aftermath of the discovery of the Phoenix conspiracy, he had denounced the setting aside of jurors merely because they were Catholics, stating that the then Government of Lord Derby had inflicted a grievous insult upon the whole Catholic community.[74] There were further risings, and masses were said for the "Manchester Martyrs", but by 1870, when the bishops and the government succeeded in securing from the Vatican a definite pronouncement against Fenianism as the "enemy of Church and State", it had become a spent force.[75] The Lord Lieutenant stated in February 1872 that whereas in 1870 agrarian outrages had numbered 1,329, in 1871 they were reduced to 373.[76]

The Catholic Unionism of the day was not confined to County Kerry. Thomas O'Hagan was born in Belfast in 1812, the son of a Catholic trader. He was educated at the Belfast Academical Institution, where he was awarded a gold medal for an essay on the history of eloquence. A protégé of O'Connell, he was called to the Irish Bar in 1836 and resided at Newry for four years, where he edited an O'Connellite paper as well as practising on circuit. In 1842, having moved to Dublin, he defended Gavan Duffy as O'Connell's junior; but he had largely given up politics, and, as J. D. Fitzgerald pointed out in the *Dictionary of National Biography*, he was opposed to repeal of the Union, preferring instead a local legislature for local purposes, with continuing Irish representation in the Imperial Parliament.[77] Having broken with O'Connell and his fellow-repealers on this issue, he became assistant barrister of County Longford and in 1849 a Queen's Counsel. In 1857 he came back to Dublin as Assistant-barrister and was appointed third serjeant in 1859. Solicitor-General for Ireland in Lord Palmerston's Administration of 1861, he became Attorney-General and an Irish Privy Counsellor the following year. He also sat on the Board of National Education. At a by-election for Tralee in 1863 he was returned despite the combined opposition of three candidates, one of them the Lord Mayor of Dublin, J. P. Vereker. The others were A. M. Sullivan, editor of *The Nation*, and Captain Knox, proprietor of the *Irish Times*. In a vigorous speech, O'Hagan acknowledged the help he had received from James O'Connell, Daniel's brother, and made it plain that he had not much desire for a political career.[78] He had, he said, "been content to do my duty in the quiet walks of my profession; and I have not sought promotion through the avenue of Parliament". Having attained the office of Attorney-General for Ireland, he had not come to apologize for the fact. "I hold no terms with the preposterous doctrine, that a Catholic Irishman, faithful to his Church and true to his country, is to ostracise himself, and decline a position of dignity and power which he may have won by honest effort and fair capacity". On the subject of the National

Board for Education, he pointed out that when he was first given a seat on it, it had a small minority of Catholic commissioners; it now had an equality as a result of the efforts of Cardwell, Chief Secretary from 1859 to 1861, assisted by himself; and yet, "because I aided him to the utmost of my poor capacity, you have been told that I am unworthy to be your representative". He roundly defended the national education system as "the greatest boon and blessing which since emancipation was ever conferred on Ireland by the Imperial Government".[79]

In January 1865 O'Hagan was appointed to a vacant judgeship in the Irish Court of Common Pleas. In October of that year Lord Palmerston died, and was succeeded as Prime Minister by Lord John, now Earl, Russell, whose Ministry lasted only until the following year, when it was brought down by a combination of Conservatives and Adullamites voting against a new Reform Bill. Lord Derby came into office to form his third minority government, and another Catholic Unionist, Michael Morris, who had been elected for Galway in 1865, became solicitor-General for Ireland.

Derby's Government faced a serious situation. There was considerable agricultural distress, and a meeting called by the Reform League in Hyde Park on 23rd July became violent and tore down the railings, the gates having been closed against them. The next year a Reform Bill was introduced; but three members of the Government, including Lord Cranborne, afterwards third Marquess of Salisbury, would have none of it and resigned. The Fenian troubles added to the Government's difficulties; and after Disraeli had succeeded Derby as Prime Minister because of the latter's ill-health, early in 1868, Gladstone moved resolutions which were successfully carried against Government opposition, pledging the House of Commons to introduce a Bill to disestablish the Protestant Episcopal Church of Ireland. Thereupon there was a general election which the Liberals overwhelmingly won.

One of the Acts passed during Lord Derby's period of office had opened the Irish Lord Chancellorship to persons of all religious belief, and Gladstone took an early opportunity of offering O'Hagan the post. In his letter of acceptance the latter wrote that he rejoiced "to be permitted to assist, however humbly, to the accomplishment of the glorious work . . . for the redemption of Ireland & the consolidation of the Empire".[80]

The redemption process began with the disestablishment of the Church of Ireland in 1869, followed by a Land Act in 1870 which gave the small tenant an interest in any improvements which he might make to his property, and provided him with compensation if he were evicted.

O'Hagan was raised to the peerage in 1870, and he resigned his office in 1874 when Disraeli succeeded Gladstone as premier. First Vice-Chancellor of the Royal University of Ireland in 1880, he again became Lord Chancellor of Ireland on Gladstone's return to office and supported the Irish Land Bill of that date in the House of Lords. In 1881 his health gave way and he was obliged to resign.[81] He was made a Knight of St Patrick, and died in 1885. He had shown that Catholic loyalism and Unionism was a powerful force working for the good of Ireland.

PART II

The Assault on the Union

CHAPTER TEN

The First Home Rule Bill

Fenianism had thus failed to produce an Irish revolution, but it had forced men and women "furiously to think" about the Irish future. Some Conservative Protestants feared lest the disestablishment of the Church of Ireland and the revolutionary tendency revealed by the rise of Fenianism might lead on to anarchy if conciliatory steps were not taken. One such was a lawyer called Isaac Butt who, born in 1815 in County Donegal, became a Professor of Political Economy in 1837 and a Queen's Counsel before he was thirty. In his early days Butt had opposed O'Connell, believing that the Union experiment had not been fully tried, but 1870 found him the leading speaker at a conference which brought together at the Bilton Hotel on 19th May over sixty prominent men from all parties. He concluded by proposing "That it is the opinion of this meeting that the true remedy for the evils of Ireland is the establishment of an Irish parliament with full control over our domestic affairs."[1]

The resolution was passed unanimously, and resulted in the formation of an organisation to be called The Home Government Association of Ireland. It differed from O'Connell's repeal movement mainly in being considerably more precise in its aims and to some extent more limited: thus to the imperial parliament were to be reserved all questions affecting the crown and government, legislation regarding colonies, foreign affairs and defence; and the control of the proposed Home Rule parliament over Irish resources was to be subject to "the obligation of contributing our just proportion of the imperial expenditure".[2]

The representatives of all parties at the Bilton Hotel included some who described themselves as "Protestant Conservatives", "Liberal Catholics" and so on. What speedily became clear, however, was that the Home Rule movement, as, from 1871, it began to be called, did not command the loyalty of all Catholics. For example, Lord Fingall's brother refused to declare for Home Rule at a bye-election at Meath in 1871. In County Kerry, when Viscount Castlerosse succeeded to the earldom of Kenmare, the new earl's cousin, James Arthur Dease, put up a valiant fight against Blennerhassett, then a Home Ruler, with the support of Bishop Moriarty and the family of Daniel O'Connell, who were active supporters of the Unionist cause.[3] At the Meath nomination in 1871, Plunkett's friends included about thirty Catholic priests[4], and the Dublin correspondent of *The Times* went so far as to describe the contest as one between priests and people. The mob would not allow Plunkett to make a public speech; but he recalled to the Press the family services to the Catholic cause in penal days. Referring to the Land Bill then before Parliament, he said it was not perfect, but should nevertheless be tried. Plunkett's opponent was elected by 1,128 votes to 642.[5] A line similar to his was taken by Dease in the Kerry election of 1872. Bishop Moriarty looked forward to the day when, under the Union,

> the old feud between Catholic and Protestant shall have been forgotten in religious equality, when a common interest, well understood, shall have obliterated the antagonism between landlord and tenant, when Ireland shall have a united people, north and south; but in her present state of disunion, self-government could only be a war of faction and of class.[6]

Not all the bishop's clergy supported him, but they were commanded not to interfere "by canvassing, speeching, attending meetings, or other public action, in another parish", unless by leave of the parish priest.[7] The chairman of Dease's committee was Sir James O'Connell, Daniel O'Connell's brother. When the result was declared, with a majority for the Home Ruler of 820, the *Dublin Evening Post* commented that the roads had been scoured by armed mobs, people had been dragged from their carriages and beaten, the voters of whole estates had been intimidated into non-attendance and houses smashed in order to secure the return of the Home Rule candidate. Sir James O'Connell, as *The Times* put it, "notwithstanding his advanced years, entered personally into the struggle with great ardour, and incurred some risk of violence from the populace". A few years later Dease died as the result of a blow on the head from a stone thrown at him on the hustings.[8]

Another Catholic Unionist of the period was Aubrey de Vere, the poet (1814–1902), who was converted to Catholicism in 1851. Before that he had published *English Misrule and Irish Misdeeds* (1848), which combined support of the Union and loyalty to the Crown with intensely Irish sympathies. In 1882, after the Phoenix Park murders, de Vere published his *Constitutional and Unconstitutional Political Action*. Fenianism he early on denounced as being "equally out of sympathy with the old Catholic instincts of Gaelic Ireland, and with those purely *Constitutional* exertions by which alone Ireland can get what is lacking to her". In 1866 he wrote to congratulate Bishop Moriarty for speaking out so strongly to his clergy against the Fenians.[9] Favouring disestablishment of the Church of Ireland, de Vere opposed the secularization of Church property which Gladstone ultimately came to regard as essential in the face of the refusal of the Catholic clergy to accept concurrent endowment, i.e. state provision for both Churches. Later he wrote to a friend, "If Statesmen continued to resist just demands, like that for a Catholic University Education, and wise concessions, . . . they would end in making nearly unlimited concessions which, far from averting 'Repeal', will tend to bring it about".[10]

Home Rule, he wrote in January 1887, meant "misrule and ruin both to Ireland and England".[11] Disaffection could only be cured "by winning a people's affections"; not however through a policy which professed to "'govern through love' alone" and disparaged as "coercion" a Government's first duty, to enforce obedience to law.

As a means of resolving grievances, de Vere advocated a measure of land purchase, but of a moderate nature; if half the land of Ireland passed into the hands of peasant proprietors, more than three quarters of existing occupiers would become owners; "while that anti-revolutionary spirit which is the only guarantee for the safe use of the political privileges created, would be effectually called into existence, both by the possession of property and by the prospect of possessing it later".[12] His other remedies for Irish troubles included denominational education, state-provided residences for the Catholic clergy; an Irish Board for matters such as railways; state aid for industrial enterprises; and loans for emigrants from the west of Ireland. In a pamphlet (*Ireland and Proportionate Representation*, 1885) he argued that the third and last of the great pieces of reform legislation of the nineteenth century, that of 1884, had enlarged the franchise to a much greater degree in Ireland than in Great Britain. It was therefore essential to introduce some kind of proportional representation in order to give a truer balance to the will of the nation as expressed in Parliament. Disraeli in the 1860s thought some such system to be essential in England if universal suffrage was ever reached.[13]

In his *Recollections* (1897), Aubrey de Vere paid tribute to the work of his brother, Sir Stephen E. de Vere. Both were sons of Sir Aubrey de Vere (sometimes confused with his younger son), who was also a poet and had been a friend of Wordsworth. Born at Curragh Chase in 1812,

Stephen was educated at Trinity College Dublin and became a Catholic in 1848. From 1854 to 1859 he was M. P. for Limerick and, as has been noted, was amongst those who refused the pledge not to take office or support a Government which failed to undertake to introduce tenant-right. In 1847 he had taken ship to investigate for himself what life was really like for emigrants, many of whom perished from disease, both on board ship and on landing. A letter he wrote describing their sufferings was read in the House of Lords by Earl Grey and the Passengers Act of the time was amended so as to take account of his criticisms. It has been said[14] that whereas Aubrey de Vere the younger took his Catholicism from Newman and his philosophy from Coleridge, Stephen joined "from simple admiration of the religion of the Irish peasantry, and from a desire to be in harmony with them". With all classes in County Limerick, stated *The Times*, he possessed, until the Land League troubles, a "remarkable and unique" influence. Translator of the *Odes* of Horace and a minor poet, he was "an excellent man and citizen, tender-hearted, but no sentimentalist; passionately anxious for the welfare of the Irish people, but resolutely opposed to Parnellite and Gladstonian Home Rule".

Aubrey de Vere made the criticism of the land laws as they developed in the 1870s and 1880s that although something had rightly been done for the tenant, there had been too much interference with "free trade" in land. The effect of Mr Gladstone's Land Act of 1881, in particular, and of the Reform Act of 1884, Derby's "leap in the dark", against which de Vere wrote his pamphlet on proportional representation, had been hard on the "gentlemen of Ireland". The 1884 Act had doubled the English Parliamentary constituency, but tripled that of Ireland.

Cardinal Cullen had, he said, opposed Home Rule, writing that:

France was once as Catholic as Ireland, but the Revolution undermined her faith. Should an Irish Parliament, whose strength, I believe, will come from revolutionary sources, pass laws that are subversive of justice, morality, or religion, it will be the duty of the bishops to speak out to warn their flocks, and to condemn such acts. Such a Parliament will at once pass laws to weaken and destroy the Church's action, and to restrain the bishops in the performance of their undoubted duty. With this conviction in my mind, I, for one, can never advocate this revolutionary movement, as I believe it to be, for Home Rule.[15]

Cullen's successor Cardinal M'Cabe died, according to de Vere, of a broken heart caused by revulsion from such vile crimes as the murder of Lord Frederick Cavendish and his Catholic Under-Secretary in the Phoenix Park. "The great Dominican preacher", he added, Father Tom Burke, "perhaps the man most venerated in Ireland, then dying of an excruciating malady, continued as long as he could stand to denounce those crimes, though warned that if he persisted in doing so he would be shot in his pulpit". Bishop Moriarty was not alone in speaking out fearlessly. Edward O'Dwyer, Bishop of Limerick, "rebuked the false casuistry, wholly opposed to the teachings of Catholic theology, and that of the present Pope, by which a plea was set up in defiance of the plainest engagements respecting property".

De Vere himself wrote extensively, especially in the *National* and *Edinburgh* reviews. He "recalled to the recollections of those led astray the solemn admonitions issued at as early a period as 24th June 1880 by the Catholic archbishops of Ireland:

> We declare it our duty . . . to warn our devoted flocks against allowing themselves to be driven by their sufferings or persecutions to the employment of unjust or illegal remedies; and to exhort them to be on their guard against such principles and projects as are contrary to the teachings of Religion and Justice.[16]

De Vere himself added:

> There is an Ireland larger and better than that of the Tenant-League . . . The Ireland of Catholic principles, not of casuistry misapplied; the Ireland that suffered during centuries for the faith; the Ireland that did not confound licence with liberty, that reverenced law, and therefore made no man judge in his own cause. That Ireland survives.

In the new situation, the highest duty of landlords would be:

> to remain among their poor, no matter how wronged or defamed, there or elsewhere . . . and to resist the progress of that Jacobinism from which Ireland has suffered so much. Their duty to both England and Ireland will be to cement their union

and make it become at last, if possible, a union alike of hearts
and of interests.

In 1893 he published a poem "To the Liberal Unionists of 1887"[17]:

Ye, who, to Virtue and your Country vowed,
Reject, denounce dishonoured party ties
And side by side with ancient enemies
Confront the Jacobin onset blind and loud
Nor snared by sophist tongue nor clamour-cowed . . .
Against you march Revolt and Rapine's brood: —
That sect its scope remoter knows not yet:
In France its axe is red with brother's blood:
Firm as a flint your face 'gainst such is set:
Old friends change faith: to old convictions true
Ye change but place. Changelings are they not you.

In the 1870s the former Conservative, Isaac Butt, led a comparatively
moderate Home Rule movement. Even then, however, it embraced
"obstructionist" members of parliament who were prepared to abuse the
then very tolerant parliamentary forms so as to hold up government
business, and particularly Irish business. It was not long before
Conservative Home Rulers began to resign from the association, for
example after the Galway judgement of 1872 when Keogh, now a judge,
unseated Captain Nolan, the Home Rule candidate, on grounds of gross
intimidation on the part of his supporters, who included three Catholic
bishops. Perhaps unwisely, Keogh reported all three together with
thirty-one priests, to parliament as guilty of undue influence.[18] When
Gladstone announced that they would be proceeded against, Father
Healy of Little Bray was the only parish priest who failed to attend a
protest meeting of the clergy of the Dublin archdiocese summoned by
Cardinal Cullen. The manifesto issued after the meeting used strong
language against the judge, and an effigy of him was burnt before Father
Healy's door. In February 1873 Dr Duggan, Bishop of Clonfert, and
two priests were acquitted, and the remaining prosecutions abandoned.
Butt brought forward in Parliament an abortive motion for Keogh's
dismissal. The judge's life was thereafter in danger, and the train by
which he travelled to open the Assizes at Longford contained a
detachment of military and was preceded by a pilot engine. At nearly

every station the constabulary were drawn up, and on his arrival at Longford he was guarded by cavalry.[19]

In 1872 the programme of the six Home Rule members was fixity of tenure, denominational education, and amnesty for Fenian prisoners. Only a few Conservatives remained in the movement.[20]

In February 1873 Gladstone produced his University Bill. This proposed to establish a Catholic college, but it was to be unendowed. Catholic Unionists like Monsell and the de Veres tried to persuade the hierarchy to accept the measure as an instalment of justice; but after consultation they rejected it, as did the Conservatives in parliament, who complained that it went too far in the direction of denominationalism. The handful of Home Rule members joined with others to defeat the ministry, which resigned after the second reading. J. A. Dease wrote to Monsell, "I forsee uneasy times before us and a melancholy strengthening of the hands of Home Rulers".[21]

At the next election William Delany thought that the Catholic Unionist position would be a hopeless one. They would be caught between the clergy and the Home Rulers. Monsell accepted a peerage. He had been Postmaster-General since January 1871, the first Catholic cabinet minister since the seventeenth century.

Later in the year a Home Rule conference was held at the Rotunda, Dublin. Of twenty-five M. P.s present, fourteen were Liberals supporting the cause for the first time. The Home Government Association was dissolved, and the Home Rule League formed in its place. In the 1874 elections, of fifty-nine Home Rulers returned, all had pledged themselves to support denominational education and tenant-right. Forty-six of the Home Rulers were Catholics; only three Catholics remained unpledged to Home Rule.[22] The hardest blow received by Gladstone was at Louth, where the anti-Home Ruler Chichester Fortescue, formerly Chief Secretary for Ireland, was supported by the Catholic Archbishop Daniel McGettigan of Armagh, who praised his efforts on behalf of Catholic education and asked the lower clergy to persuade Home Rulers to withdraw from the contest. But at a meeting at Dundalk his lower clergy refused to support him, and both Fortescue and Mathew O'Reilly Dease, a mild Home Ruler, lost by substantial margins.

Ireland was excited by the movement and many of the Irish were attracted by firebrands. At the by-election at Limerick following the elevation to the peerage of Monsell as Lord Emly, all three candidates, James Kelly, W. H. O'Sullivan and E. J. Synan, the former member, were Home Rulers. The bishop, George Butler, and his clergy favoured

Kelly; the Archbishop of Cashel refused formally to meddle, but his clergy, a few of whom were in Limerick County, favoured O'Sullivan, a Fenian. Again, priestly feelings ran high; O'Sullivan and Synan were elected.

Gladstone wrote a pamphlet against the claims of the Vatican, to which he ascribed responsibility for episcopal opposition to the University Bill of 1873. John Henry Newman replied in a letter addressed to the young Duke of Norfolk, afterwards to become a noted Catholic Unionist.[23] Monsell was closely concerned with Newman in these moves and himself wrote a letter of protest to Gladstone against his charge, initially made in a *Contemporary Review* article entitled "Ritualism and Ritual", that Catholics were unworthy of trust and that their civil loyalty could not be depended upon.[24]

Another who wrote against Gladstone's pamphlet was Father Robert O'Keeffe. O'Keeffe was born at Callan in 1814 and was educated at the Bishop's College, Kilkenny, and at Maynooth. He afterwards taught science and classics at Kilkenny, and in 1860 was appointed parish priest at Rathdowney, being transferred to Callan in 1863. In 1867 he laid the foundation of the Christian Brothers' (Ignorantine) school at Callan; the Brothers opened it the following year. But besides supporting this avowedly Catholic school for the education of poor children, he was also a patron of the National School, which he managed to associate with the Science and Art Department, South Kensington, and it was his success in this field which proved his undoing. The Christian Brothers and the bishop were offended by such exhibitions of learning as the proving of Euclid's propositions in French by his pupils, and the school was denounced as "godless" by his curates to the congregation. He was accused of making statements, and even of misappropriating funds.[25]

Father O'Keeffe's subsequent actions for libel, in which even the name of Cardinal Cullen was joined, may have been misconceived, but they did arouse widespread public sympathy, and presented the hierarchy in a bad light. The Vicar-General of his diocese purportedly suspended him from office, and also deprived him of his Workhouse chaplaincy. The Board of Guardians of the Callan Union could not be prevented from issuing a declaration in his favour; but a mob of roughs were instigated to break into his chapel, which they seized; and he was besieged in his house, where he had to be guarded by twenty policemen, day and night.

A substantial body of lay Catholic opinion was alienated by the tortuous manoeuvrings of Mr Gladstone's mind. O'Keeffe's view, as expressed in his book and in the case which he brought, was that there was nothing in the laws of their Church to prevent Catholics from being loyal, and that he for one was. The lay courts were entitled to take cognisance of disputes between individual members of the Catholic Church and the National Education Commissioners in Dublin had no right to depose him from his post as commissioner of the national schools merely on the say-so of his ecclesiastical superiors and without giving him the chance to be heard. Gladstone took the view that the commissioners had not acted improperly; but the courts were of the opinion that O'Keeffe was entitled to bring his action, and that the Papal Bull purportedly prohibiting the bringing of such actions before the civil courts could not be enforced. By implication, Chief Justice Whiteside too had answered Gladstone's sneer that the laws of the Catholic Church prevented Catholics from being loyal to the civil power. Led by the young Duke of Norfolk, who cast his first vote in the House of Lords in 1879, there was a movement among Catholics towards the Conservatives; and in 1880 his Grace's brother, Lord Edmund Talbot, stood at the general election as a Conservative candidate.

This movement was not entirely the result of disgust with Mr Gladstone. Sir Michael Hicks Beach's education policy, carried into effect by his successor as Chief Secretary, James Lowther, had pleased many Catholics because it did not insist, as had the policy of National Schools for primary level children earlier in the century, on an undenominational framework as a condition for the provision of public funds.[26]

The Liberals triumphed in the general election, winning a majority of fifty over Conservatives and Home Rulers combined. Fifty-one Catholic Home Rulers were returned, five more than in the previous election. Nevertheless, four Irish Catholic Liberal M. P.s remained uncommitted to Home Rule, namely Sir John Ennis (Athlone), Robert Lyons (Dublin), Charles Russell (Dundalk) and The O'Donoghue (Tralee).[27] Gladstone hoped to govern Ireland by the ordinary law, and let "coercion" lapse. The Land Act of 1870 had protected tenants' improvements and provided compensation for disturbance within limits, but not when the ejectment was for non-payment of rent. There were grumbles, but the scheme worked satisfactorily until foreign competition and a succession of bad harvests renewed in 1879 the threat of famine and distress in the west of Ireland. The Land League was then formed under the inspiration of Michael Davitt. The President of the League was the Protestant Home Ruler, Charles Stewart Parnell, the Member for Meath. Parnell collected 200,000 dollars in a three-month tour of the United States. At Cincinnati he declared that "none of us, whether we be in America or Ireland, or wherever we may be, will be satisfied until we have destroyed the last link which keeps Ireland bound to England".[28]

Parnell would not have "taken off his coat", he told them at Galway on his return, to help the tenant farmers had he not known that that was the way to legislative independence. Disraeli, now Earl of Beaconsfield, gave warning in his election Address, which took the form of a letter to the Duke of Marlborough, of a party in Ireland "attempting to sever the constitutional tie which unites it to Great Britain in that bond which has favoured the power and prosperity of both", and that such an agitation might in the end be "scarcely less disastrous than pestilence and famine". The incoming Liberal Government tried to introduce further reforms, even to the introduction of a Compensation for Disturbance Bill. This measure attempted to justify the principle that a landlord who had already lost his rent should have to pay the defaulting tenant before replacing him or making the farm profitable by taking it into his own hand. Not surprisingly, the Lords threw out the Bill.

Speaking at Ennis on 19th September 1890, Parnell called for a people's punishment of anyone who took a farm from which another had been evicted. Let him be isolated "from his kind as if he were a leper of old". Captain Boycott gave a new word to the language by becoming the first victim. Parnell and some associates were indicted for conspiracy, but the jury disagreed, and thenceforward no landlord's life was safe.

In 1881 Parliament was dominated by Ireland. In January a Bill was introduced empowering the government to arrest suspected persons and detain them without trial, the Act (known as the Coercion Act by its opponents) to expire in September of the following year. There had been parliamentary obstruction before. In this session there were unparalleled scenes, and Mr Speaker Brand had to close the debate on his own responsibility after twenty-two and forty-one hour sittings merely to obtain a First Reading. The parliamentary rules were permanently altered, and at one stage Parnell and thirty-five of his colleagues were suspended.

Gladstone was not content merely to hold down the lid of the simmering pot. A Land Law (Ireland) Act was passed embodying the "three Fs": free sale, fixity of tenure and fair rents. Under the first principle tenants were empowered to sell their tenancies, subject to a right of pre-emption by the landlord; under the second, tenants were secured from eviction except for non-payment of rent; and under the third, the tenant was given the right to have a "fair rent" fixed by a newly formed Land Commission Court. Despite these sweeping reforms, Parnell and his followers continued to breathe defiance, and in September 1881 a Convention of the Land League announced that it would refuse to co-operate in working parts of the new Act. Many individual farmers did so, however, and on 7th October Gladstone announced in a famous speech at Leeds that "the resources of civilisation are not yet exhausted", and that Parnell "stood between the living and the dead, not like Aaron to stay the plague, but to spread the plague". Four days later he was arrested under the "Coercion Act" and lodged in Kilmainham gaol. The Land League retorted by ordering tenants to pay no rent at all; speaking at Liverpool on 27th October, Gladstone said that they were "marching through rapine to the disintegration and dismemberment of the Empire".

Whereas the Land Act, despite opposition, was a partial success, the "Coercion Act" was an almost complete failure. The ten months that followed its enactment saw a sixty per cent increase of agrarian outrages over the period preceding it, and cruel mutilations of cattle. The Land League having been banned, a Ladies' Land League was formed to carry on, and there was even an attempt at a Children's League — a sad foretaste of I. R. A. methods in the 1970s.

In December 1881, Gladstone wrote to Cardinal Newman in prophetic vein that although the state of Ireland was not without "favourable features", it was, "in all its darker parts", "the main impediment to my fulfilling the only dear earthly wish I entertain for myself that of bidding adieu, after half a century, to the arena of political contention". Perhaps with the rejection of his Irish University Bill in mind he added that "I have a feeling that mankind is not now principally governed from within the walls of Cabinets and Parliaments . . . We have lived through a quiet period, the next half century may perhaps be quieter still: I think it looks more alarming".[29]

Newman replied that he would "gladly find myself able to be of service, however, slight it might be, in a political crisis, which must be felt as of grave anxiety by all who understood the blessing of national unity and peace".[30] He thought that Gladstone overrated the Pope's power in political and social matters. So did Lord Emly in 1874 when Gladstone had denounced Ripon's conversion to Rome. "Does he really mean", Emly had written,

that Dr Newman & Hope Scott & Robert Wilberforce & you &
I have placed our civil loyalty & duty at the mercy of any
one — that we are less loyal subjects & lovers of our country
than he is himself — What circumstances occurred . . . in the
last 27 years, in which I have to sacrifice one jot or tittle of my
. . . freedom, & in which I have to seek any other guide than
my own conscience. Take a . . . test. The Irish University
question — did any one presume to hint that I had done
anything inconsistent with my duty in voting for it, & is it not
notorious that the mass of Catholics who voted against it so
voted partly from indignation at Cardwell's speech & a partly
from the same motive that used to make many men, Liberal in
their hearts, vote against Maynooth, viz fear of losing their
seats"? Did Mr Gladstone believe that if the Pope preached a
crusade against England Catholics would join him or would do
otherwise than resist him to the death?[31]

Gladstone was thus incorrect in assuming that Catholics could not be
loyal. There were however some grounds for his concern that following
the defeat of his Universities Bill the balance of hierarchical opinion in
Ireland was tilting away from the maintenance of law and order. In an
attempt to redress this balance, the government of 1880 attempted to
renew relations with the Vatican, which had been in suspense since the
failure of the Conservative government in 1874 to replace Sir Henry
Jervoise, who from 1870 had been Her Majesty's government's
unaccredited resident agent at Rome, having succeeded Odo Russell,
later Lord Ampthill.[32]

For obvious reasons, the English Minister to the Kingdom of Italy
could not be used directly, but by the end of 1880 Sir Augustus Paget
was using an English Cardinal resident at Rome, Edward Henry Howard
as an intermediary. By then Parnell was effectively leader of the Home
Rulers and the Association as a law-abiding body had become suspect,
particularly since the formation of the Land League in Ireland. Parnell
was believed to countenance, if not actually inspire, atrocities. On 5th
January 1881 Pope Leo XIII issued a public letter addressed to Edward
M'Cabe, Catholic Archbishop of Dublin, who had succeeded Cullen in
1878. The letter expressed His Holiness's confidence

in the justice of the men who are placed at the head of the
State, and who, certainly, for the most part, have great practical

experience, combined with prudence in civil affairs. Ireland may obtain what she wants much more safely and readily if only she adopts a course which the laws allow and avoids giving cause of offence.[33]

In commending the Pope's letter to his clergy, M'Cabe said that whilst the Holy Father knew of the injuries caused by the land code, he did not approve of certain aspects of the agitation against it. But neither Papal denunciations nor the Coercion Act were of avail in reducing violence, and early in 1882 the Government decided on a change of policy. On 10th April 1882 Parnell was given leave from prison to visit a married sister whose son was dying in Paris. On his way back he saw Captain O'Shea, through whom negotiations were opened with Gladstone and Chamberlain. Parnell agreed to use his influence to end crime and disorder, whilst the Government would introduce a Bill to wipe out arrears of rent with a contribution of money from some public source. The Lord Lieutenant, Cowper, and Forster, the Chief Secretary, who had been the recipient of at least one letter-bomb during his term of office[34] resigned upon the release of Parnell and certain of his associates in May 1882, and were succeeded by Lord Spencer and Lord Frederick Cavendish respectively. All seemed set fair for an improvement.[35]

Tragedy, however, was to strike again. On 6th May 1882, the very evening of his arrival, Lord Frederick and the Permanent Under-Secretary, Thomas Burke, a Catholic, were stabbed to death in the Phoenix Park in broad daylight. An article in the *Freeman's Journal* had declared that a "clean sweep" should be made of Castle officials.[36] Archbishop M'Cabe was at the time returning to Dublin after receiving his Cardinal's hat and the murders came as a great shock to him as they did to many others. A retiring man compared to Cullen, he nevertheless followed his predecessor's policy, and was if anything, a firmer Unionist. One of his last public acts was to officiate at a requiem mass for Lord O'Hagan, a kindred spirit "whom he regarded with honour and affection".[37] "His spiritual regime", wrote his *Times* obituarist, "was characterized by a quiet power which was unseen but felt, and the more willingly obeyed because it appealed not so much to the fears as to the consciences of his spiritual subjects".

But, of course, his prayers were unavailing in certain quarters. "His house at one time", wrote P. J. Walsh, the biographer of his successor, who was by no means in such sympathy with the Unionist cause, was the object of attack, the escutcheon at the door being battered and defaced, and his life, it is said, was once threatened. But none of these things moved him, nor did he count his life dear to himself. Almost throughout his episcopate he was most unpopular politically with a large section of his people, whom he loved . . . He entertained no bitterness or resentment towards them; he regarded them as misguided members of the household of the Faith, the dupes of cunning and wicked men.

Although a modest man who had tried to refuse his Cardinalate, he was, nonetheless, a man of undaunted courage and dogged perseverance. After the 1880 election he had warned of patriotism being "invoked as a spirit of disunion between priests and people, and the evil genius of Communism, which has brought such fearful wars in other lands, is only watching the opportunity the disunion may give it to try and establish its hideous throne among us".[38]

George Errington, Catholic M. P. for Longford, was now also a Unionist. Born in 1839 in Ireland of mixed Anglo-Irish parentage, he was educated at Ushaw College, Durham, and at the Irish Catholic University set up by Newman. In 1874 he was returned for Longford on a "Catholic and Home Rule" platform, but he was against Parnell and in January 1881 resigned from the Home Rule party. Errington used to winter in Rome, and in 1881 he proposed to Lord Granville, the Foreign Secretary, that formal diplomatic relations should be established with the Vatican. Lord Spencer, who had been appointed Lord Lieutenant of Ireland from 1868 to 1874 and was to be re-appointed in 1882, acted as intermediary, and in October 1881 Errington proceeded to Rome almost as a formal envoy. He remained until the following May, and undertook three further missions in subsequent winters.

There were occasions when his interventions were effective. Thus when in November 1882 Thomas Nulty, Catholic Bishop of Meath, sent a carriage to the local railway station to collect Michael Davitt, a prominent Land Leaguer, the Papal Propaganda at Rome wrote in reproof. Nulty replied that the carriage was an old one and had but taken Davitt to Mass, whereupon Propaganda authorized Errington, who happened to be on the spot when the reply to this rejoinder was being drawn up, to "answer Dr Nulty's reply . . . and adopted even my language in their rejoinder".[39]

In August 1882, and again in January 1883, public letters were addressed by the Holy See to the Irish hierarchy on the subject of

Granville asked him directly His Grace wrote to Cardinal Howard, who presented the appeal to His Holiness.[46]

Other Catholic moves were made against Walsh, who was known to approve of the Land League. Errington regarded him as "a most dangerous man". Sir Rowland Blennerhassett, a Catholic member for Kerry, wrote to Spencer on 1st March 1885, and as a result Granville seriously contemplated asking William White, a Catholic diplomatist serving as Minister in Bucharest, to go secretly to Rome and plead against Walsh's appointment.

Meanwhile Errington had been seriously undermined in Ireland, and despite the efforts of Bishop Woodlock of Ardagh, in April 1884 the re-adoption meeting rejected him as candidate for Longford. One of his letters to Granville was "leaked" and the Government repudiated all responsibility.[47] Dilke and Chamberlain were strongly opposed to Government pressure at the Vatican, and the matter received a widespread airing in the public press. Dilke expressed the view to Gladstone that Errington's policy had back-fired. He was opposed "not to diplomatic relations with the Pope, but to the extraordinary anomalies involved in the Mission that was no Mission".[48]

Walsh was consecrated Archbishop of Dublin on 2nd August 1885. In his reply to a welcoming Address from the Mayor and Corporation of Dublin he made it clear first that he was in favour of a separate Irish legislative (without mentioning Home Rule by name) and, secondly, that he would not differentiate in his ministry between those who supported that policy and those who did not. The Lord Mayor and Corporation of Dublin were less gracious when in April their Royal Highnesses the Prince and Princess of Wales visited Dublin.

For a generation the project of a Royal residence in Ireland had been under discussion. Disraeli had recommended it in March 1868 and in 1871 Gladstone put forward the idea again, combining it with a proposal that the Lord Lieutenancy should be made non-political and granted to the Prince of Wales.[49] The queen disapproved, adding her fears that the prince's equerry and friend, Lord Hamilton, was infecting him with Orangeism. In vain did the prince plead with his mother that "a permanent royal residence in Ireland would do more good than any political measure". Again in 1885, during Spencer's second term of office as Lord Lieutenant, the matter was raised at Windsor; but although Her Majesty showed "illusive signs of yielding", she rapidly resumed her former opposition to the proposal. Lord Spencer felt inclined "to throw up the sponge and retire to my plough in Northamptonshire", as he wrote to the queen's secretary. The project was raised later in the queen's reign, but never pursued.

The prince first visited Ireland in May 1865 to open an international exhibition. This visit was a success, and early in 1868 Disraeli urged another, pleading that "during two centuries the sovereign has only passed twenty-one days in Ireland".[50] The suggestion was accepted, and the prince and princess were well received. The Lord Lieutenant wrote: "I was hardly prepared for the progressive increase of welcome, amounting to real enthusiasm".[51]

In December 1868 the Prince's friend, Lord Spencer, was appointed to the Lord Lieutenancy. His Royal Highness was soon being pressed to visit Ireland again, which he willingly did in August 1871, spending a few days in Dublin. This was, perhaps, his first real contact with Irish unrest for, as he wrote to the queen on his arrival, "the cheering in the streets mingled with some hissing, chiefly in those quarters where Fenianism is said to exist".[52] But his popularity steadily grew, no doubt in part because of his exquisite tact; and at the review in Phoenix Park, all records of Dublin crowds were, in Lord Spencer's estimate, broken. Nevertheless, it proved impossible to prevent a "monster meeting" of Fenians in the Phoenix Park, which had to be broken up by police within sight of the prince. Despite this, he was keen in urging his mother to visit Ireland in the following year to unveil a statue of the Prince Consort. The queen declined to do so; and in May 1872 an attempt was made to blow it up.

In the autumn of 1884, Lord Spencer, once again viceroy, urged the queen to allow a tour by the prince of the south as well as the north of Ireland. Her Majesty ultimately agreed. Campbell-Bannerman, who succeeded Trevelyan as Chief Secretary in October, was unenthusiastic; and the United Irishmen of America offered ten thousand dollars for the prince's body "alive or dead".[53] By forty-one votes to seventeen the City Council of Dublin resolved on 16th March 1885 that the prince should be given no official reception, and in the event it was a "City Reception Committee", headed by a prominent Catholic Unionist, Richard Martin, which welcomed their Royal Highnesses to Dublin.

Martin, born in 1831, was president of the Dublin Chamber of commerce, a shipowner and merchant, member, in fact, of one of the oldest timber and shipowning firms in Ireland.[54] The Address which he presented, with Edward Guiness and others, asked the prince and princess to "honour Ireland hereafter by visits of more frequent occurrence and of longer duration". Following the precedent of the official welcome in 1868, a permanent royal residence in Ireland was also suggested; and an Address later received at Killarney specifically suggested that place as its site.[55]

Despite a few ugly incidents, on the whole the royal couple were received with enthusiasm. On their departure from Dublin the Lord Mayor was heard to remark that the visit was an insult to the people. When he was hissed by loyalists he declared that "he would telegraph to Mallow that he had been hissed by Orangemen and Freemasons' landlords and bailiffs". "He then called for a cheer for Mr Parnell, to which there was a very faint response".[56]

At Mallow the nationalists were out in force, but a confrontation was averted, and the main welcome was cordial. Black flags flew in a few places, and a few faint counter-cheers were raised for Parnell. In Cork, "a body of men in military array . . . passed through the streets singing 'God Save Ireland' and hissing"[57]. But there were cheers at Cork too, and the prince and princess were received at a house of refuge and industrial school by the Catholic bishop, Dr Delany, and by eighteen clergy.

At Killarney the prince and princess were received by Lord Kenmare, Sir Rowland Blennerhassett, M. P., Mr R. P. Blennerhassett, M. P., and other Catholics, including Sir M. J. O'Connell and "Mr Daniel O'Connell, D. L., Derrynane Abbey, grandson of the Liberator". Loud cheers were given at several points along the route. At Belfast the welcome was particularly warm-hearted.

The Coercion Act of 1881 had not been a success, and in 1882, after Parnell's release, a much more comprehensive piece of legislation, the Crimes Prevention Act, came into force for a period of three years. This measure was, to some extent, effective, but on its expiry there was a renewed upsurge of agrarian crime. The Liberal Government fell on a financial matter in which Parnell voted with the Conservatives. Lord Salisbury came into office at the head of a minority government. It only lasted seven months, but it carried a state-assisted scheme of Irish land purchase known as Lord Ashbourne's Act after the Irish Lord Chancellor of the day. It was an advance on its predecessor, the Land Act of 1881, in providing that tenants who were able to agree with their landlords on the purchase of their holdings could borrow, through the Land Commission, the whole of the purchase money, to be repaid in forty-nine annual instalments of four per cent. Five million pounds was granted to the Land Commission for this purpose.

The new viceroy, Carnarvon, had introduced the British North America Act of 1867 1982 and favoured giving Ireland Home Rule status similar to that of a Canadian province inside the Dominion; in July and August 1885 he held secret conversations with Justin McCarthy and with Parnell. The Conservative party subsequently denied that these conversations were other than tentative; but Gladstone had come to the conclusion early in August that Home Rule had better go ahead, and who better to proceed with it than Lord Salisbury, with his command of the House of Lords?[58] Overt Liberal support would antagonize Salisbury's supporters, so Gladstone bided his time, maintaining what R. C. K. Ensor, whose account has been followed here failing convincing refutation by his recent critics, called a "Delphic ambiguity". In November 1885 Parnell was sufficiently encouraged to urge his followers in Great Britain to vote Conservative.

Yet it was the Liberals who were successful, (though in Ireland they were wiped out) partly because of the wider franchise introduced in 1884 and partly because of Joseph Chamberlain's "Unauthorised Programme"; and in the new Parliament, Parnell and his party held the balance with 86 Members, as against 331 Liberals and 249 Conservatives. The Conservatives continued to hold office until January 1886, relying on their alliance with Parnell, but were defeated on an issue not directly connected with Ireland, and Gladstone became Prime Minister, with Aberdeen as Lord Lieutenant and John Morley as Chief Secretary. The split between Parnell and the Conservatives had been precipitated by Gladstone's son Herbert, who had disclosed to certain editors in the preceding December the secret of his father's conversion to Home Rule.[59] On 17th February Walsh and a number of other Catholic bishops also came out in its favour. They also supported land nationalization and the suspension of all evictions.[60] The Primrose League and the Primrose Dames as well as the Irish Loyal and Patriotic Union led the opposition to Home Rule. At the end of February the Duke of Norfolk, addressing the second of these bodies, said that the action of the bishops had caused him "special grief and shame". Walsh differed from Parnell only in thinking that some Irish M. P.s should continue to sit at Westminster.

The Government of Ireland Bill brought in in April proposed to exclude them. The new Irish legislature was to consist of two sections sitting and voting together, but able to elect to sit separately if required. The first section, or "order", was to consist of the Irish representative peers and seventy-five other members with a minimum property or income qualification, to be elected by £25 occupiers for ten years. The second order was to consist of 204 members elected for five years by the normal electorate. The new Irish parliament would eventually control the police; customs and excise, trade and navigation, postal matters, coinage and legal tender were to remain with the imperial parliament as well as defence and foreign affairs. The Bill never reached the Lords. On 7th June 1886 ninety-three "dissentient Liberals", as Gladstone called them, voted against its second reading. In July the ensuing general election returned seventy-four Liberal Unionists who formed with the Conservatives a Unionist party that outnumbered Gladstonians and Parnellites combined by over a hundred.

A leading Catholic and Unionist of this time was Thomas Maguire, the first of his faith in modern times to become a Fellow of Trinity College, Dublin. Under its seventeenth century statutes Catholics had effectively been precluded from holding Fellowships and from taking degrees, although care was taken to avoid making any inquiry into the religious beliefs of undergraduates and until 1794 no student was required to declare his creed on entrance. As D. G. Heron, a Catholic, wrote in 1847, "Catholics were permitted to enter College, because the fees which they paid were profitable to the Fellows, and because there was hope that they might see the error of their ways, and become good Protestants."[61]

They were not compelled to attend chapel, especially if resident outside, unless they became scholars; but Fellowships remained closed to them. Even scholars were sometimes Catholics, as the case of Mr Martin Toumy and others in 1791 shows. Three such scholars had voted for the College's member of Parliament, claiming that they had turned Protestant beforehand; it was established that before their conversion they had remained Catholics whilst holding scholarships.[62]

Following the Act of 1793, Catholics could take degrees at Trinity; but the bar to their obtaining scholarships remained, and was perhaps more rigorously enforced. Even so, some Catholics protested against the idea of a separate Catholic college, first because they valued what they called "the permission of having their youth educated along with the Protestant youth of the Kingdom", and secondly because they saw "with deep concern the principle of separation and exclusion, they hoped removed for ever, now likely to be revived and re-enacted".[63] In 1847 D. C. Heron, who in 1843 had been passed over for a scholarship, inveighed against the continued exclusion of Catholics from positions involving payment. "There have been many", he asserted,

amongst the Fellows of Trinity College, who dated their
Protestantism from the time when they 'turned for Scholarship'
. . . Of those who thus conform, some remain in their new
creed . . . others . . . return to . . . the Catholic faith . . . How
long, Irish Catholics, will you endure, without remonstrance,
that you should be thus, in your national University, excluded
from the rewards of learning, and tempted to hypocritical
conversion?[64]

In 1854 non-Foundation scholarships open to all were established and
under what was called the "Fawcett Act" of 1873, all religious tests were
abolished and all offices and emoluments opened to Catholics and others.
"In 1880 and again in 1890", wrote one of her historians, "she elected a
Roman Catholic Fellow".[65]

The first, as has been said, was Thomas Maguire. Born in Dublin,
the son of a Catholic merchant, he accompanied his father to Mauritius,
where the latter had been appointed a stipendary magistrate, at the age
of fifteen, and returned to enter Trinity in 1851. After gaining high
honours in classics and metaphysics he graduated in 1855 and was the
first holder of the new scholarships. In 1861 he obtained the law
studentship at Lincoln's Inn and in the following year was called to the
Bar. Maguire did not, however, practise law. Instead he became a
private teacher at the University, where he took his doctorate of laws in
1868. In 1869 he was appointed to the Chair of Latin at Queen's
College, Galway; and after the passing of the 1873 Act he became a
Fellow of Trinity in May 1880.

A zealous Unionist, in 1886 he published three pamphlets: *England's
Duty to Ireland*; *The Effects of Home Rule on Higher Education*; and *Reasons
Why Britons Should Oppose Home Rule*. The last of these, dated as 6th
May 1886, began by pointing out that every scheme of Home Rule
involved the expenditure of large sums of English, Scots and Welsh
money. "It may be taken for granted that Home-ruled Ireland will have
to contribute *something* to the Imperial Treasury . . . But the Briton may
rest assured that once Home Rule is granted not a penny will ever be
paid".[66]

What the loyalists claimed was

merely their birthright . . . Magna Charta and its complement
the Petition of Right, the Bill of Rights and the Act of
Settlement . . . These Acts are the Bible of British Freedom: all

others are mere comment. The Irish . . . have had Magna Charta from the very beginning — in fact one of its signatories is the Bishop of Dublin. And, accordingly, the Loyalists of Ireland now call for the aid of all our brother Loyalists — from the Prince of Wales down to the lowliest of his fellow-subjects.

Morley's arguments for Home Rule were in reality

the most severe reflections on the Parnellites. Home Rule is to be granted, because the Parnellites are estranged from England, and in default of getting what they howl for, threaten, like Archbishop Walsh, the *Irish World*, J. B. O'Reilly, and the *Freeman's Journal*, daggers and dynamite. As to estrangement, if the Parnellites cannot appreciate British Freedom — the largest the world ever saw — it shows they are not fit for Home Rule; and if they were fit for Home Rule, as the Scotch are and they are not, they would not howl for Home Rule. A man in good health does not get a doctor to examine him every morning.

The Irish loyalists, under the Bill, were to "change the old flag, which has wavered over the united valour of the men of the two islands in many a fight, from Namur to Tel-el-Kebir, for the green abomination — the symbol of murder".

"Mr Gladstone's manifesto", he concluded, "is the most gigantic fallacy that has yet appeared. In plainer language, it is the biggest swindle. It says, give up details and affirm the principle". But "there can be no Home Rule without determining what is English, what is Irish, what is Imperial. And granting that we could settle the present details, no man can warrant the future . . . Who can foresee the complications arising out of the relations of England, rebel Ireland, and Fenian America?"

Shortly after writing this pamphlet, Maguire became involved in the unfortunate incident of the Pigott letters. Edward Caulfield Houston, Secretary of the Irish Loyal and Patriotic Union, had become convinced that Parnell and his associates were in some way involved with the Phoenix Park murders, and after prolonged investigation thought he was on the track of letters written by Parnell which proved his complicity. But they had been forged by one Richard Pigott; forged so cleverly, however, that both Houston and Maguire were taken in, not the last time that this has happened to eminent academics acting in association with *The Times* newspaper. *The Times* duly published one of the crucial letters under the heading "Parnellism and Crime". Parnell asked for a Parliamentary Select Committee to investigate the allegations against him; the Government responded with a Special Commission of three judges. Parnell was represented by a great Ulster Catholic, Sir Charles Russell (afterwards Lord Russell of Killowen and Lord Chief Justice of England), who mercilessly exposed the Pigott forgeries and added greatness to an already distinguished reputation; but Maguire was a broken man. Though innocent of any deception, his judgement in the affair was suspect, and some saw his death, three days before Pigott shot himself in Madrid, as more than a coincidence. *The Times*, however, concentrated on the bright side, paying tribute after Maguire's death to his "guileless and generous nature, genial manner, and unobtrusive but impressive talents" which had made him "a generous favourite in social as well as academic life".[67]

Another prominent Catholic Unionist of the day was Sir Rowland Blennerhassett, who was one of those who received the Prince of Wales at Killarney in 1885. Born at Blennerville, County Kerry, he succeeded to his father's baronetcy at the age of ten, and was educated at Downside, Stonyhurst, Oxford, and the University of Louvain, where he took a doctorate. In the 1860s he became friends both with the German theologian Döllinger, and with his former student, afterwards Lord Acton, both strong opponents of the doctrine of Papal infallibility as promulgated by the First Vatican Council. Blennerhassett very largely financed a magazine called the *Chronicle*, which in 1867 succeeded Acton's *Home and Foreign Review* as a journal of moderate Liberal Catholic opinion. The *Chronicle* however died in February 1868 after being an early advocate of Home Rule.

In 1865 Blennerhassett was elected M. P. for Galway along with Michael Morris, another Catholic Unionist and later a Lord Chief Justice of Ireland. Blennerhassett's friendship for Döllinger and Acton, having lost him the support of the priesthood at the time of Vatican I, he transferred in 1874 to Kerry, which he represented until 1885, in association with his cousin, Rowland Ponsonby Blennerhassett. During this period his attitude towards Home Rule began to change, especially when the leadership of the movement was taken over by Parnell; and he became an active opponent. He was defeated at the general election of 1885. He had strong views on University and land questions; he admired German University methods and supported Gladstone's Bill of 1873. On agrarian problems, he advocated as early as 1884 the purchase of land from landlords in order to transfer it to peasant proprietorship. In later life he was actively associated with educational administration in Ireland as President of Queen's College, Cork, and senator of the Royal University.[68]

The Catholic University of Ireland, of which Newman had been first Rector, had declined after his resignation, and in the 1870s only about twenty students were in residence at the University College in Dublin. Yet the bishops shrank from closing it down.[69]

In May 1879 The O'Conor Don introduced a Bill to create a new University for Irish Catholics, as a rival to the Queen's University with its colleges. The government then introduced a Bill of its own to provide for an examining University so constituted as to be unexceptionable to Catholics, instead of the Queen's University. Unlike The O'Conor Don's Bill, the government measure at first proposed no assistance to Catholic colleges, students or professors. The Bill was however subsequently modified so as to provide for such grants and became law the same year. Some Catholics, such as Father Delany, thought the Act should be accepted and worked for what it was worth; others, such as Archbishop Walsh, disliked it but did not publicly oppose it. Rather more than half the senators of the new University were Catholics: they included such prominent Catholic Unionists as Lord O'Hagan and Chief Justice Morris.

Michael Morris was born in 1826, the son of Martin, a Galway Justice of the Peace, and was, in 1846, gold medallist in ethics and logic at Trinity College, Dublin. In June 1849 he was called to the Irish Bar. A born humorist, he was also a fine athlete and rackets player. From 1857 to 1865 he was Recorder of Galway. "No man more familiar", said the *Irish Times* after his death, "with the life of the city of the tribes[70], no man in whom its people took greater pride. No fisherman of the Claddagh" (a suburb traditionally inhabited by men of this fraternity) "ever thought of speaking of him except by his Christian name, and, as he would have said himself, he returned the compliment."[71] In July 1865 Morris stood for Parliament, declining to issue the usual type of election Address. "You do not require from me", he asserted grandly, "any profession of politics". This was one of the last of the elections caricatured as "Eatanswill" before the ballot Act, and he was not unopposed. Indeed at one stage there were no fewer than six other candidates in the field. "Stump orators", wrote a correspondent of the *Galway Vindicator*, "kept the claims of their favourite candidates before the public at each corner of the Square. Mr Stubber, Mr Dolphin, Mr

Power and others thundered from the steps of the Railway Hotel".
Trouble was expected. "The police are bivouacing by the corner of the
Square and along the streets — 'tis midnight before polling day." Mr
Stubber and the others were however unsuccessful, and Morris, without
a declared policy, was elected with a margin of over 100 over his nearest
opponent.[72] The following year Morris was appointed Solicitor-General
for Ireland in Lord Derby's administration, and under the law as it then
stood had to seek re-election. Again Mr Stubber was defeated, this time
by a much more considerable margin. Yet a third election took place in
February 1867 when Morris was appointed Attorney-General for Ireland.
His speech on this occasion shows the emphasis which he placed upon
local issues, and the reason for his success. He began by pointing out
that

> on the last day, the 3rd August, when you elected me, I stated
> in my address on the hustings that my politics always were in
> favour of the persons, whoever they might be, who were ready
> to introduce measures useful to the country and advantageous
> to its material prosperity and not to pin myself to persons who
> merely intend to relieve sentimental and theoretical grievances
> . . . while there were other matters which admitted of no delay.

He then went on to discuss depopulation. Three million of the eight and
half million population of Ireland had left in twenty years. In 1846 her
people grew four and a quarter million acres of corn; in 1866 they
produced only two and a quarter million. "The repeal of the corn laws
was a necessary measure, but when it was passed, it was passed with an
utter absence to the interest of Ireland." In 1846 there had been three
million acres of potato, flax and green crops; in 1866 only a million and
three-quarters. In 1845 three and a quarter million quarters of corn had
been exported from Ireland; in 1866 only a million and a quarter.
Economic revival was therefore a necessity. "It is much more important
for the people of Cork, that there should be a great naval station, than
whether the mayor is to be allowed to wear his chain going to Mass."[73]

Only a few months later, Morris was appointed a puisne Judge, and
his brother George fought and won the seat, arguing, during the
campaign, that the tenant was entitled to full compensation for his
improvements.[74] One of George Morris's achievements in Parliament
was to carry through an Act making leaseholders owners in fee of their
properties.[75]

George Morris was less stalwart a Unionist than his brother Michael, and in 1868 ran into some pretty rough opposition. He had rendered the local community considerable service. For thirty years the Board of Works had held a mortgage on the Harbour dues and no improvements were made. A Bill, for which the foundations had been laid by Michael Morris, abolished £12,000 worth of debt and restored local control over the harbour. Authority was given for the Harbour Board to borrow for the construction of a graving dock. But such achievements availed nothing in the eyes of the priests against his declaration on 7th September 1868 that he was "entirely independent of any political party".[76] At a meeting of the clergy of Galway on 18th September, with Bishop MacEvilly in the chair, it was resolved to ask candidates to pledge themselves to support Gladstone's Irish disestablishment resolutions and security of tenure for tenants who paid rent. This was interpreted as a move against Morris.[77] In a letter of 3rd October, George Morris began by pointing out that he had voted in parliament on every occasion in support of Gladstone's resolutions. As to the clergy's requirements, he replied that he had been elected to parliament by the people of Galway, not by the "College House" (a reference to the place where the meeting of the clergy had been held). "In no county or town in the Kingdom", he went on, "has the existence of the Catholic laity been ignored except in yours, and if the Catholic 'City of the Tribes' is satisfied to register the edicts of the College House, I shall be no party to the process".

MacEvilly replied in an ill-natured letter published in the *Galway Vindicator* of 7th October. He described Morris's Address as "better suited for an Orange than a Catholic constituency", the leading questions of the day being "utterly ignored". The final paragraph was remarkable for its spite:

> Whether the "City of the Tribes" would "Register" what Mr Morris politely terms "the edicts of the College House" will remain to be seen . . . One thing however is certain, that every well-minded man in Galway will know how to "Register" in his memory Mr George Morris's Third Address, which would better answer "a no Popery cry" than the calm pronouncements of either a former or present legislator of our country . . . From the whole tone and supercilious bearing of some men, who utterly forget themselves, a stranger to this neighbourhood could arrive at no other conclusion; but that Galway was a family borough; that the whole gentry of the locality were men

of some inferior caste, only destined and fitted to be so many
attendant satellites of the illustrious and historic house of Morris

George Morris thereupon decided to stand down.[78] But his parliamentary
career was not over. In 1874 he was again elected, on a platform which
included support for Home Rule, although he gave it less prominence in
his Address than he accorded denominational education and a charter of
endowment for the Catholic University.[79] In 1880 he decided to retire
from Parliament because of "pressure of private business". An attempt
was made to dissuade him by a requisition from over four hundred
electors. In his reply he thanked, amongst others, the Bishop and clergy
for their support and confidence. The *Galway Express* (13th March
1880), whilst congratulating him on his past record and expressing
regret at his retirement, was also sorry that he had taken up Home Rule.
No candidate should be supported, it said, who "will not prove of
practical benefit to the town and neighbourhood".[80] After his retirement
from parliament, George Morris became a commissioner of the Local
Government Board for Ireland, and was its vice-president from 1890 to
1898, when he was made a Knight Commander of the Bath. At his
death in 1912 the *Galway Express* declared that George Morris had done
more for his native city than all his successors. The obituary also recalled
the father of the two brothers as a man who was never known to evict a
tenant. People then still living could testify that in the famine years
Martin Morris was the means of saving many from starvation, even
outside his own tenantry.[81] Martin had been the first Catholic High
Sheriff of County Galway since the Battle of the Boyne.[82]

Meanwhile Michael Morris, the elder of the two brothers, had in
1876 been made Chief Justice of Common Pleas, and in 1887 Lord Chief
Justice of Ireland. He was a strong and uncompromising Unionist, and
according to his daughter, regarded Gladstone as "the author of much
mischief in Ireland".[83] Though an Irishman to the backbone and
belonging to an old Catholic family (a Richard Morris had been bailiff
of Galway in 1486), Michael Morris began life as a Conservative and
remained one to the end. He was a strong anti-Home Ruler.[84]

His daughter wrote that because of his background "Himself" (as
she calls him throughout her book) "was more Irish than any of their
so-called patriots in Dublin and elsewhere, so it was not possible for
them to vent their animosity by calling him a 'sassenach' or a 'West
Briton' ". "My father", she wrote,

clear headed and devoid of romantic or sentimental delusions or
cliches . . . saw only too well how Home Rule would work out
for Ireland. Separation from her rich and steady partner would
only drive Ireland back into the seething pot of factions . . . all
pauperised. He also foretold it would mean the cutting up of
Ireland into two parts.[85]

Michael Morris was no sycophant. He said of the Irish question: "the
difficulty lies in a slow-witted race trying to govern a quick-witted
one", and of the complacency of some Chief Secretaries for Ireland, that
he had known twenty-six of them, "and I declare to God there is not
one of them who, after he has been in Ireland three days, would not
undertake to show me up my own backstairs". On one occasion he is
reported to have said to a Scottish M. P.: "Did you ever know a
Scottish Secretary who was not Scottish, or an Irish Secretary who was
Irish?" "No", said the Scotsman. "Well, go home and moralise over
that as a possible solution of some Irish difficulties, for may be, if an
Irishman was sent over, by accident, to be Chief Secretary, the official
would not fall into the mistake of trying to reconcile the irreconcilable."[86]
The playwright Lady Gregory described him as Chuchullain, the great
Irish chieftain,[87] come to life again; and his neighbours often regarded
him as omniscient as well as omnipotent.

Morris was one of Lord Randolph Churchill's Irish friends, and he
visited him as he lay ill in Grosvenor Square. There he met the young
Winston. "A chip of the old block with a dash of the Yank", was his
comment: "but I think he will get there all right".[88] He was consulted
by Lord Randolph on Conservative tactics during the proceedings on the
first Home Rule Bill and afterwards, in 1889, accepted a life peerage as a
Law Lord and went to live in London. In 1900, on his retirement from
the law, Lord Morris was created a United Kingdom hereditary peer,
and took the title Killanin, which his son Martin, named after his
grandfather, succeeded to when Michael died in 1901.

Michael lived long enough to re-enter the fray when Martin stood
for Parliament in 1900. At a meeting at the Claddagh, where his old
friends the fishermen lived, he asked rhetorically:

Who was there that could say a word against the name of
Morris? There was one man who had done so at a recent
meeting — Father Dooley. Were the Morrises . . . to be
attacked by a clergyman? There was no family in Galway

whose money had been expended more freely in the support of Catholic institutions . . . Why should they bring a man from Antrim or Waterford to oppose Martin Morris? . . . Would he (Lord Morris) be listened to if he went to Waterford and indulged in 'platform spouting' as one of their opponents termed it?[89]

In the championing of local causes lay the great strength of the Morrises. Yet Martin had been defeated in 1895; and it is difficult to avoid feeling that in 1900 it was the release of "Himself" from the political restraints imposed upon him by his Law-Lordship which was responsible, in part at least, for his son's success. The voters of Galway were above all "Morrisites"; left to themselves, they voted with the trend, that is to say for the nationalists, as Sir Horace Plunkett found when he fought the seat after Martin's elevation to the Lords on his father's death. Michael Morris stood for something in Ireland which had not yet been wholly extinguished.

Another Catholic Unionist of the day (though some said he had no politics) was Father James Healy of Little Bray (1824–1894). "One of the pleasantest faces in life has Father Healy", wrote "Amazon" in *The Ladies Pictorial* (22nd October 1881)

and the most intellectual, with firm mouth and keen and searching eye, and as we walked to the station together I thought what a nice portrait he would make. His intellect is as bright as his glance, his converse lively and full of wit, his hospitality proverbial, his charity unbounded. No wonder that he is a favourite with all ranks and creeds, and there is no greater proof that he is so than the fact that, when he got heavily dipped some time ago through an unwise speculation, the money subscribed to release him from his difficulties flowed quite as freely from Protestant pockets as from those of his own faith. He is famous for his kindly hospitality, but his entertaining is ever the simplest. The best people dine at his table, but it is off a simple joint, preceded by soup or fish — never both — and followed by such fruit as is not to be bought for money: rich, luscious, ripe — the produce of hot-houses and gardens of surrounding friends and neighbours. His cellar is of the best, no inferior liquid disgraces his board, and his cigars are such as to remind one of those to be had only in an exclusive little club

not a hundred miles from Waterloo Place . . . At humorous
story-telling Father Healy has few compeers, whilst his ready
wit, which never degenerates to vulgarity, is ever keen and
bright.

Healy was, in the words of Field Marshal Lord Wolseley, "a link
between the many sections into which we Irish are unhappily divided,
and he had the moral courage — a rare virtue in Ireland — to express his
opinions very plainly, even when he knew that his views were
unpalatable to the majority of his own cloth in this country". [90]
Labouchère wrote that Healy was as popular with Nationalists as with
Unionists, but of all the Catholic priesthood of Ireland he alone, towards
the end of his life, continued to attend the Lord Lieutenant's levée.
Cullen, on succeeding Murray as Archbishop of Dublin, avoided going,
as did his brother Bishops; and the three priests who, with James Healy,
continued to attend (Canon Pope, John Murtagh and Christopher Burke)
died before him. [91]

Healy was a great friend of Henry Neville, sometime Catholic Dean
of Cork, Pastor of St Finbars, and Rector of the Catholic University in
Dublin. Neville sometimes acted as *locum tenens* for Healy at Little Bray
(a place quite unconnected with the Bray whose Vicar became infamous
for turning his coat), and nowhere was he more at home. Other
associates included Tom Burke, Dan Griott, and John Egan, who
succeeded Neville at the Catholic University, and in 1889 became Bishop
of Waterford. All these priests were Conservative in politics. Neville,
indeed, published a reply, by some considered superior to Newman's, to
Gladstone's attack on the Vatican I decrees, and was considered both for
the archbishopric of Cashel and, on Cullen's death in 1878, for that of
Dublin. He was passed over. At his death in 1889 the *Cork Examiner*
paid him eloquent tribute, and in his own *Letter to the Duke of Norfolk*,
Newman wrote that Neville's pamphlet was "the best and most thorough
answer to Mr Gladstone on the points with which it deals". [92]

CHAPTER ELEVEN

The Pope and the Plan of Campaign

The Plan of Campaign began in 1886 in response to the defeat of Parnell's Tenants' Relief Bill and in resistance to evictions. Although it was not a "no rent" manifesto,[1] its contrivers were well aware "that their enterprise would turn many a farm into a wilderness, many a comfortable home into a roofless ruin, above all else many an honest Irishman into a trickster and a rogue".[2]

The tenantry on every estate were invited to resolve on an abatement of rent. The reduced rate so decided upon was to be offered to the landlord's agent at the appropriate time through the chairman of the tenants' committee. If it were refused, it was to be deposited with someone known only to the committee whose estate was reasonably secure from attachment. This "estate fund" was then to be distributed to dispossessed tenants.

The plan was, eventually put into effect on over a hundred estates. In sixty of these the landlords gave way; on twenty-four others there was an eventual compromise, but seventeen stood out. At Killarney a landlords' syndicate enabled Lord Kenmare to settle on his own terms.[3]

The Kenmares were good landlords. In the time of the second earl, who died in 1853, a guide-book writer had this to say:

> Every visitor to Killarney owes a debt of gratitude to his Lordship for the facilities which, at a great expense, he has afforded for the comfort and convenience of strangers — for the generosity and cheerfulness with which every portion of his estate . . . is thrown open . . . The Earl of Kenmare is universally spoken of as a humane resident, and to the extent of his power (which is crippled by leases for ever, and the class of middle men) an improving landlord; a very amiable and charitable private character, and, as head of the Catholic Aristocracy, when occasion requires, an independent and public-spirited individual.[4]

The third earl was his brother, who lived until 1871, and the fourth was his nephew, known as Viscount Castlerosse between 1853 and the time of his father's death. Castlerosse was M. P. for County Kerry in five Parliaments between 1852 and 1871, and became a Liberal Unionist in 1886.[5] At the time of his death in 1905, local public bodies passed resolutions of condolence and Killarney was in mourning. The Catholic Bishop of Kerry said at his funeral that during the years of tension and friction, of strain and stress, the Earl had hurt nobody's feelings. "He was possessed in a rare degree of that Christian self-control which made his life an example" and of "a rare combination of Christian humility . . . which always made all, even the poor and lowly, very well at their ease with him, while at the same time, unconsciously, they never forgot and never could forget the respect that was due to his high position".[6] It was indeed widely accepted that by his death the poor of Killarney had lost a friend; his demesne was freely open to them and they were allowed to take timber from his woods.[7]

Perhaps for this very reason, and because he was Lord Chamberlain, "the political agitators made a special set at him & he was accused of every kind of enormity & cruelty in speech & in the popular press". "Yet even with all this", wrote Edmund Dease to Gladstone in 1890,

> I was greatly impressed by seeing the demeanour of the people around Killarney towards him. What particularly struck me was seeing — early one morning — when I was passing through the town with him, hundreds of school children going to their schools, & when they saw Lord Kenmare driving by they all ran after him cheering him most enthusiastically . . . These children cannot have heard him abused in their own homes.[8]

In February 1887 the Cowper Commission reported that the fall in prices had made it difficult for tenants to pay full rent. The Land Commission had accordingly reduced the "judicial" rent which they fixed. The year 1886 had been "the worst year of the century" for farmers.

In an interview he gave the *Pall Mall Gazette* in December 1886[9], Archbishop Walsh refused to condemn the Plan; but *The Tablet* saw the issue clearly. After pointing out (11th December 1886) that Parliament had already ruled in favour of the existing settlement, it added:

> Let the leaders of the League be ever so convinced of the truth of their statements and the equity of their claims, and the

question will remain — are they justified in counselling the tenants of Ireland to take the law into their own hands?

The Tablet went on to condemn the doctrines of the League: they were "doctrines of anarchy and revolution". Tenants on estates which were the object of its action were prohibited from paying unreduced rents even should they wish to do so. Edmund O'Dwyer, Bishop of Limerick (1842–1918), then coadjutor to the Bishop of Clonfert, also expressed dissent from Walsh's views. But Croke, Archbishop of Cashel, supported him: indeed a cynic said that the difference in the attitude of the two Archbishops towards the plan was that whilst each was in sympathy with the general aims, Dublin drew the line at the maiming of cattle, and especially the "curtailment" of cows. Aubrey de Vere wrote to the Duke of Norfolk on 16th January 1887 that "the half-hearted & vacillating administration of Ireland in connection with the Land Question is every day aggravating that *Demoralization* which is Ireland's worst danger & if connived at much longer will be a blood-poisoning that nothing can cure".[10]

In March 1887 Arthur Balfour, who had replaced Hicks-Beach as Irish Secretary, introduced legislation on lines similar to those proposed by Parnell in the previous September. Judicial rents fixed between 1881 and 1886 were to be revisable by the Land Commission to take account of the fall in prices, and leaseholders were enabled to benefit from the Land Acts passed in 1870 and 1881. A "Coercion Bill" was enacted, and in September three men were killed when the constabulary fired on a crowd of between five and ten thousand persons who had assembled in protest against it: this became known as the "Mitchelstown Massacre". Carson, who had, earlier in the day showed considerable bravery by walking openly from the courthouse through the middle of a hostile crowd, thought the affair had been mishandled.[11]

The fifteenth Duke of Norfolk had come to occupy an important role in the minds of Catholic Unionists. Disraeli wrote to him on 18th October 1879:

> Always write to me on all matters when you like . . . From our first acquaintance I have entertained for you a sincere regard & have complete confidence in your straightforwardness, truthfulness, & Honor.

Disraeli's death had not diminished the esteem in which he was held in

Conservative circles, but he was not always successful in his interventions. Thus in August 1887 he was unable to secure the appointment of Sir John Ross-of-Bladensburg as Under-Secretary for Ireland, though Hicks-Beach had written to him in February that he would be glad to find a Catholic if possible. It was well known that the duke regarded the Irish priests' and Bishops' support for Home Rule and the League as shameful. In a speech to the Ladies' Grand Council of the Primrose League on 20th February 1886 he said that while he was convinced that there were very many thoroughly loyal Catholics in Ireland who would gladly range themselves on the side of law and order, it was a "special grief and shame" to find that "some of those whom one would naturally look to to guide the people in a dark and dangerous hour had given their countenance to so much which all must deplore and detest".[12] The Earl of Ashburnham, a Liberal Catholic, protested against the Duke's words: but Viscount Bury, another Catholic peer, sprang to His Grace's defence.[13] The action of the Catholic bishops, he wrote, "is not religious", for they "teach rebellion . . . The political *dicta* of the Irish Bishops are *ultra vires* as regards their ecclesiastical functions". After denouncing the "brutal terrorism of the Land League", he condemned Gladstone's negotiations with Parnell, Davitt and O'Donovan Rossa. These "bloodstained mandatories" of the League were supported by "paid agitators, by the gold of the American dynamiters, and by the whole riff-raff of the socialistic enemies of England". "The so-called demand for Home Rule" was kept up by "hireling agitators alone; and the concession even of the outrageous demands now formulated will not satiate their rapacity. Be not misled by the idea that this is a religious dispute", he added. "They know better in Ireland".

Walsh wrote privately to Herbert Vaughan, *The Tablet*'s proprietor, complaining of Lord Bury's article. Vaughan, afterwards Cardinal and Archbishop of Westminster, had taken over *The Tablet* in 1868 after a period during which J. E. Wallis, who had succeeded Lucas, the journal's founder, in 1856, had turned it virtually into a Conservative journal. Wallis, an English Catholic barrister, had begun by proclaiming the paper's politics to be "Liberal, by which I understand a thorough repudiation both of Whiggery and of its near relative, the false Liberalism of Continental infidelity".[14] He had advocated the formation of an independent Catholic party, and was opposed both to Orangeism and to Toryism. However, by 1868 he had managed to offend both Liberal Catholics and the Hierarchy. The part which he had felt obliged to make *The Tablet* take "ran counter to the feelings of many of its old supporters, and procured for me sundry comforting assurances that the *Tablet* was uniting the extremes of religious Liberalism and of political Conservatism, and presenting the public with a maximum of Toryism and a minimum of religion".[15] His own opinions had not changed, but he felt that many Catholics had moved, and that "the movement has been towards absolutism in religion and towards democracy in politics". Wallis was loyal to the old English Catholic tradition, which, as he understood it, consisted of "active loyalty to the Crown, sincere attachment to English institutions, and complete identification with the national and imperial fortunes".

Herbert Vaughan continued this tradition, with greater support from the hierarchy. To Walsh, in 1886, he replied tactfully but to the point:

> Why do not the bishops speak out more plainly and also frequently against crime? . . . I know that if the Bishops were loud on the side of virtue and order — I mean if they denounced evil — they would stand better on this side of the water.[16]

Walsh then denounced *The Tablet* in an interview with the *Pall Mall Gazette* (4th April 1887). Meanwhile an attempt was made by a group of Irish Catholic laymen, including Lord Emly and the de Veres, to memorialize the Pope on the subject of the Irish episcopate.

In February 1887 Archbishop Croke of Cashel wrote publicly recommending or at least suggesting the non-payment of taxes.[17] Cardinal Howard, in particular[18], was incensed and asked for an equally public rebuke. Archbishop Kirby, Rector of the Irish College at Rome, since Cullen's promotion to the Archbishopric of Armagh in 1850, was an old friend of Pope Leo and wrote to Croke in terms of mild remonstrance. It was to no avail. He had written, Croke wrote to Walsh, "as if I were still a student in the Irish College". Croke justified his opinion in another letter to the *Freeman's Journal* (7th March 1887) denying that he had recommended "a general uprising against the payment of taxes".

On the occasion of the Queen's Golden Jubilee, a Papal delegation paid a congratulatory visit. There was renewed talk of the establishment of British diplomatic representation at the Vatican, and Archbishop Persico and Dr Enrico Gualdi (a former missionary in London) received a Papal Commission to visit Ireland and report. Persico, a Neapolitan by birth, had been a bishop in British India and in the United States. Views about him differed. John Ross-of-Bladensburg, a Catholic Unionist, had written to the Duke of Norfolk in 1885 that he would be the ideal candidate for the post of Apostolic Delegate in Ireland. Such a delegate required full powers "to correct, enforce, and preserve religion." Without it there would be "chaos, hopeless and irreligious chaos." "The fact was", he added "that there is a party of action who oppose the Pope tooth & nail, and the remainder are in a state of flabby collapse, afraid of moving, afraid of action, afraid of their own shadows". A delegate "would rally this party who are like a flock of sheep without a shepherd, & the remainder who are now leading the rebellion would have to give up their revolt".[19] Similarly, Manning wrote to Walsh on 25th June 1887 expressing confidence in his impartiality and that of Dr Gualdi. Croke had, however, written to Walsh, *Persicos odi*[20], a comment repeated in jest by Father James Healy of Little Bray. Not that even Croke favoured complete separation from England.

After about a fortnight in Walsh's company, Persico visited Limerick, where he stayed with Emly at Tervoe. Thence to Armagh, Dundalk, Tuam and Cashel, where Croke found him "friendly". Edmund Dease, who had been Liberal M. P. for Queen's County from 1870 to 1880 and was to sign a Catholic Unionist petition against the Second Home Rule Bill, wrote to the Duke of Norfolk in October that Persico seemed to him "to have taken in the situation with wonderful exactness — I much doubt, if England had ever seen a prime minister who seemed so complete a master of our past history with its present lamentable outcome". "I also think", he added, "that he sees fully that the present *unrest* & revolutionary principles are coexistent with the greatest freedom we have ever enjoyed & with the unquestioned fact that England is doing all she can to blot out our past history by the removal of every just cause of complaint".[21]

On 24th October 1887 Persico returned to Dublin and took up residence with the Capuchin Fathers, Gualdi having returned to Rome. On 20th November Persico left for Cork. There were rumours in the press that he had been given the hint that the Government intended locking up the priests who took part in the National League, and that he was being enlisted to put "the screw on the priesthood in the interests of Dublin Castle".[22] The Bishop of Limerick (Edward O'Dwyer) and John Healy, then Coadjutor Bishop of Clonfert, were labelled "Landlord Bishops". O'Dwyer indignantly denied that he was a Unionist, and indeed he later became a supporter of the Sinn Fein[23]; but he considered "boycotting" to be irreligious and the Plan of Campaign to be unjust.

Dillon and O'Brien "organised a meeting under his windows to insult and to intimidate him".[24]

In December 1887 Walsh left for Rome to take part in the Pope's sacerdotal jubilee. His departure coincided with the death of the Archbishop of Armagh, Dr McGettigan, who was succeeded by Logue as Primate of All Ireland. Also for Rome were the fifteenth Duke of Norfolk and Captain Ross-of-Bladensburg, grandson of the Major-General Robert Ross who defeated the Americans at the Battle of Bladensburg in 1814 and afterwards captured Washington, where the White House was burnt. The author of a book about the Coldstream, John Ross served as Additional Military Secretary for Ireland, and was responsible for conveying the special despatch on the Phoenix Park murders to the Queen at Windsor Castle. In 1885 he had taken part in the Sudan expedition.[25] Some time after 1876 he had become a Catholic, following the example of his wife.[26]

The missions neither of Walsh nor of the duke were wholly concerned with formalities. The latter's papers contain notes of two interviews with Cardinal Rampolla, the Secretary of State. At the second of these, it seemed pretty clear "that Mgr Persico had reported *against* the clergy and their acts in Ireland. Mgr Persico's opinion appeared to be shortly this: 'The Holy See would have a most difficult task to prevail upon the clergy to adopt a moderate and loyal course of action. They were very excited & very fanatical. To curb them too suddenly might only succeed in inflaming them & perhaps produce a schism — without any benefit accruing to the civil power.' Persico "probably talked of some concession being given" and this Cardinal Rampolla too seemed to favour; "but it was pointed out that reform had followed upon reform without any ostensible result — except to enable the agitators to have more power in the country and to ask for something more, which would strengthen the hands of the revolutionary party". Rampolla was finally persuaded to limit himself "to the hope that the Govt of the Country should not be too exclusively in Protestant hands. It was however pointed out that this was scarcely a remedy that would do much to tranquillise the Country, that Catholics were as unpopular as Protestants when they thwarted National aspirations. It was further suggested that suitable Catholics were not easy to find".[27]

On 1st February 1888 the Pope, speaking in Latin, re-iterated his adherence to the letter of instruction which he had sent to Cardinal M'Cabe at the time of earlier troubles; and his speech was interpreted as advice to Irishmen to try to reach a settlement with England. At a meeting with the Pope on 13th February, Walsh made it clear that he was a "staunch Home Ruler, but not a separatist", and was invited to compose a memorandum on the Irish land question. This he did in a volume of over 320 pages completed in the middle of April 1888; but in the mean time a Reply or Decree (as the document was variously called) was issued by the Congregation of the Holy Office stating in terms that "it is not lawful in the disputes between landlords and tenants of farms and estates in Ireland to make use of the means commonly called the Plan of Campaign and Boycotting".[28] "A rent fixed by mutual consent", it stated, "cannot, without violation of contract, be reduced at the arbitrary will of the tenant alone". Boycotting was "foreign to natural justice and to Christian charity". In a letter to Salisbury, the Duke of Norfolk gave Ross the credit for the timing of the Papal Decree.[29]

His Grace also tried to persuade Rampolla that Persico should remain in, or rather return to, Ireland (he had retired to England for reasons of health), in order to see the decree enforced. But Persico was in distress. "The Papal decree", he wrote,

> has been received very badly in Ireland. Its subject matter is attributed to my report, and I am now under constant attack. My post is full of threatening letters . . . the Irish newspapers . . . write most offensively about the Holy Father himself.[30]

After a visit to Scotland, he was allowed to return to Rome, where he afterwards became a Cardinal. Catholic Nationalist M. P.s protested on 14th May 1888 that they could recognize no right in the Holy See to interfere in their political affairs. Walsh, from Rome, sent an emollient telegram, and the Irish hierarchy affirmed, on 30th May, that the decree was intended to affect "the domain of morals only". *The Tablet* (12th May 1888) was firmly of the opinion that the decree, while not "Dogmatical", i.e. relating to dogma and thus falling within the doctrine of Papal infallibility, was a judicial act resting "upon the supreme authority of the Holy See and its right to adjudicate without appeal on all cases relating to the moral law and the moral conduct of its subjects", and was thus not merely an exposition of the law as the *Freeman's Journal* had claimed. Walsh took a different line, denying that freedom of contract existed between landlord and tenant in Ireland, and pleading for a stay of evictions. The Pope sent an encyclical letter which was read in all the Catholic churches of Dublin on 15th July 1888, reaffirming the decree.

The O'Conor Don wrote to Ross from Sligo on 14th August that in the diocese of Elphin neither the decree nor its accompanying letter had been published in the diocese and that boycotting was as rife as ever. Of the Plan of Campaign, The O'Conor Don's shrewd opinion was that it "is nearly extinct, but not on account of the papal condemnation, but because the people would not join in it a second time on any estate where it had been tried". "What is really required in this country", he added, "is some ecclesiastical head, who would enforce the popes decrees & make the bishops obey".[31] The O'Conor Don was among many Catholic laymen of moderate opinions who supported the principle of a strong apostolic delegate able to take the lead, as Archbishop Walsh was conspicuously failing to do, in combating lawlessness.

In the following year Sir Lintorn Simmons headed a further mission to the Vatican. Simmons, who had had a distinguished military career and was a field marshal, had been Governor of Malta from 1884 to 1888, and the mission was principally concerned with the position of the Roman Catholic Church there. But he was accompanied by Ross, and Ross remained in Rome after Sir Lintorn's departure.[32] His letters to Balfour during this second mission are preserved in the British Library. In one dated 10th December 1889 he wrote that "since we left Rome last year, we have so to speak lost headway". The impression in Rome seemed to be "that things are improving in Ireland, that the Bishops have generally done their best to enforce the Decree; in fact that moral teaching has had its effect, & that political excitement more or less is all that remains".[33] Ross tried to correct this view, pointing out that Bishop O'Dwyer in particular was isolated and ought to be supported.

On 17th January 1890, Ross was accorded a private audience of the Pope, who "seemed disinclined to talk to me on Ireland". When he did speak, the talk was all of "concessions"; of a "Diet", of "Agrarian Reform" and of Higher Education. However, Cardinal Rampolla, at a later interview on 6th February, "sees that Walsh and Croke are both incorrigible, & spoke to me quite openly about them, as the two pillars of much of the evil that prevails in Ireland".[34]

Nevertheless, although the "land war" was continuing, "Bloody Balfour" was beginning to bring it under control. Whereas in 1886 the total number of outrages had been over a thousand, by 1889 it had almost halved, and boycottings fell from 4,900 in June 1887 to none in January 1891.[35]

Bishop Healy had not only denounced the Plan of Campaign from the outset but in December 1886 wrote to the Prefect of Propaganda at Rome complaining about Dr Walsh's interview with the *Pall Mall Gazette*.

He was a courageous prelate. Born at Ballinafad, Sligo, in 1841, the son of schoolteachers, he was educated at Sligo and at Summerhill, Athlone, where one of his classmates was the future Under-Secretary, Sir Anthony McDonnell. Two years later, in 1861, he entered Maynooth, where Edward O'Dwyer and James Murphy of Dublin were fellow-students. After his ordination he became a member of the staff of his old college, Summerhill, and then a curate at Ballygar. Healy delivered a notable speech at Sligo expressing sympathy for Pius IX, then a prisoner in the Vatican. In 1871 he was transferred from Ballygar to Grange, between Sligo and Bundoran; in 1878 he became Rector of a classical school at Elphin known as St Asaph's. The following year saw his return to Maynooth as a Professor of Theology. His biographer, P. J. Joyce, wrote that he first saw him at a gathering there twenty years before his death.

> His massive frame, his flashing eyes, his ruddy complexion . . . attracted the amused attention of the students in the hall, notwithstanding their belief that his political views were agreeable to the British Government.[36]

John Healy was a profound, though not outstandingly original, theologian who held, not only that all power was from God, but that this power was vested by God not directly in the people but in the Government. The character of the civil ruler, he wrote:

> is sacred; their persons are inviolable; they are the annointed of the Lord, if not with sacred oil, at least by virtue of their office. Their power is broad — based upon the Will of God, and not on the shifting sands of the people's will . . . They will be spoken of with becoming reverence, instead of being in public estimation fitting butts for all foul tongues. It becomes a sacrilege to violate their persons, and every indignity offered to them in word or act, becomes an indignity offered to God Himself. It is this view of Kingly rule that alone can keep alive in a scoffing and licentious age the spirit of ancient loyalty, that spirit begotten of faith, combining in itself obedience, reverence and love for the majesty of kings, which was at once a bond of

social union, an incentive to noble daring, and a salt to purify the heart from its grosser tendencies, preserving it from all that is mean, selfish and contemptible.[37]

After a controversy with Cardinal Newman on the subject of the Inspiration of Holy Scripture, in which Healy upheld the traditional view, he was, in June 1884, appointed titular Bishop of Macra and coadjutor to the Bishop of Clonfert. Newman sent him a specially-bound copy ofthe *Ceremoniale Episcoporum* to close the correspondence; and after Newman's death in 1890 Pope Leo issued, in 1893, his encyclical *Providentissimus Deus*, in which Healy's view was upheld.

Dr O'Brien, an ex-professor, at the banquet following Healy's consecration, described him as a "rough diamond when he came to Maynooth, and many thought he was destined to remain one". But "he is now, as you see him, a gem fit for any crown".

As his biographer wrote, Healy's arrival at Clonfert was comparable to St John falling into a cauldron of boiling oil. The bishop to whom he became coadjutor, Patrick Duggan, was a favourite with the Land-Leaguers; and when some laymen greeted Healy with an Address a letter in *United Ireland*[38] described them as "a few of the nobs and snobs of South Galway". Nevertheless Healy managed to maintain correct and even friendly relations with his diocesan, who by 1890 had delegated to him virtually all his administrative powers. In 1885 they wrote sadly of the bad relations existing in the diocese between certain Catholic landlords (among whom were the Earl of Westmeath and Sir Henry Burke) and their tenants, and of "some political clerics who deliver wrathful harangues, and who are negligent in preaching to the people, especially on days of political meetings". Ten years later the note was more cheerful. The political harangues of the priests had largely ceased, and they kept "far away from political faction and public meetings". "Formerly the coadjutor-bishop for giving such advice lived not without a certain risk of his life. Now, however, he is esteemed by all".[39]

Within the diocese, on the shores of Lough Derg, lay the Clanricarde estate. The Marquess, whose ancestors had been Catholics, was an absentee residing in London, and was unpopular with his tenants. Healy never saw him, and did not approve of him. He got on well, however, with such as Lord Emly and Aubrey de Vere. At one party at Tervoe, he and de Vere, "told us wild and romantic stories from Irish history and folk-lore till past midnight".[40] He was neither a valetudinarian nor a dyspeptic, wrote his biographer. "It was readily believed that he sat down to his meals with enjoyment". When described obliquely as a "good trencherman" he took it as a compliment; "for I never knew a man who could not do well at dinner to be much good anywhere else". A considerable scholar, he read widely and deeply, especially in Irish history and theology; "He sallied forth from his library, in which many have lost the priceless pearl of faith and many have been petrified into pedants, more Christian, more human and more manly than before". He disliked radicalism in any form, and in 1897 lectured at Maynooth on "The Priest in Politics", pointing to the similarities between the situation in the Holy Land in our Lord's day and that of Ireland in his own, and adding that "if the life of our Saviour is to be the model of a good priest, no one can blame the priest for declining to take a prominent part in the political struggles of the hour, no matter how the 'patriots' may declaim against him".[41]

In 1886, Healy challenged the Land League with its episcopal backing. His diocese of Clonfert was prominent in their agitation. Clanricarde's agent, Mr Blake, was shot dead, posthumously disentombed and his remains mutilated. Healy himself was shot at through his bedroom window when on episcopal visitation. He did not approve of Clanricarde, but disapproved of the Plan. For this he was castigated as a "Castle Bishop" and so forth, most notoriously in *Letters of an Irish Catholic Layman*, first published in *The Nation* and afterwards as a book. "Here, I say", wrote the author, "is an Irish ecclesiastical deliberately entering Dublin Castle, which he knows or ought to know is an ante-chamber of hell, and in the sight of his outraged flock, making peace and alliance with anti-Christ seated therein".

Healy did not reply to such diatribes. In the eyes of the Nationalists he "loomed on the horizon as a landlords' man".[42] Yet he was in favour of peasant proprietorship and at a dinner party in Galway drove a number of landlords from the table with a blunt declaration that they would, as a class, eventually have to disappear from Irish life.

In 1872 the Home Rulers made electoral gains. The tenants refused to vote for the old Marquess of Clanricarde's nominee. Clanricarde died in 1873, but not before imposing a twenty per cent rent increase at Woodford which was continued by his son and heir, who was "*par excellence*, an absentee landlord". Chief Baron Pallas thought him mad.

In 1885 Healy twice appealed to him for an abatement of rent to his tenants; and in 1887 and 1888 again attempted to intervene. After Balfour's arrival as Chief Secretary, he met Healy twice at Michael Morris's house. Evictions were postponed for a considerable time in response to a letter Healy wrote in 1888. His efforts were, however, only partially effective and he complained in the columns of *The Times* that Mr Tener, Clanricarde's agent, had not behaved justly towards them.[43] From 1879 to 1892, 206 tenants were evicted from the estate, the majority in the years following 1888. As in other places, the Plan of Campaign had failed at the cost of untold hardship.

1889 was on the whole a good year for Ireland. "The law", in the words of the *Annual Register*, "was firmly though dispassionately administered. Agrarian outrage rapidly diminished, the Plan of Campaign languished, and even boycotting showed signs of a wasting energy".[44] The harvest was good and agricultural prices rose. In 1890, the Bishop of Limerick, Edward O'Dwyer, at a conference with his clergy, announced that he had decided to make boycotting and participation in the Plan of Campaign reserved cases, withdrawing the power from all priests of his diocese to give absolution to those taking part. The nationalists attacked him on the subject of events at the Glensharrold estate, claiming that he had distorted and suppressed evidence; Tim Harrington claimed that O'Dwyer's own surveyor had reported back to him that the reduction demanded by the tenants was just.[45] This O'Dwyer indignantly denied as "shockingly and disgustingly untrue, and made recklessly to deceive the public".[46] His surveyor had agreed that thirty per cent, not forty per cent, would be a fair reduction. Dillon subsequently accused Salisbury and Balfour in parliament of "offering bribes to His Holiness to aid them in evicting the people of Ireland" and of "succeeding in getting His Holiness to send an agent to trade on the revenue of Irish people". O'Dwyer replied by pointing out the immorality of boycotting and the Plan of Campaign, and the "anomalous position of those priests and laymen who encouraged methods condemned by the Head of the Church". Nationalist bodies in all parts of the country passed votes of censure on O'Dwyer; and when the Corporation of Limerick refused to do so, the Mayor and several other of its members were expelled from the National League. Archbishops Walsh and Croke washed their hands of the matter, and although the Bishops of Cork and of Clonfert (Drs O'Callaghan and Healy) used their best endeavours, the Papal rescript had little effect in 1890, especially as the potato crop was not good. Dillon and O'Brien were arrested for preaching the non-payment of rent. They were tried at Tipperary, but after some days it was found that they had jumped bail and gone to the United States. They were condemned in their absence to six months' imprisonment. Balfour and Jackson, the Secretary to the Treasury, carried out a series of tours to affected districts, and were on the whole well received.

Edmund Dease (1829–1904) was a Catholic who in January 1870 had been elected Liberal M. P. for Queen's County. In 1880 he resigned his seat and was later to emerge as an active opponent of Gladstone's Second Home Rule Bill. In June 1880 he wrote to his old chief that he had hoped that the Act of 1870 "would have settled our agrarian troubles on a sound and lasting basis". The problem was, however, that *some* landlords, "with little sense of justice or of wisdom", "constructed leases so as to render nugatory all that the great Act was intended to achieve". This had caused the political pendulum to swing against the landlord, and "now under a conservative government, we see a Bill introduced into Parliament, for the purpose of *banishing* under the name of purchase — the present landowners from their own country". It was not true that all landlords were bad: they had been "given a far worse name than they deserve — as a class". Yet "too many of them — but still a very small minority" had by their misdeeds "brought all this obloquy on an entire class . . . To read the public papers, one would suppose that the feeling of the public & the tenant farmers against the landlords was general & extreme."In many districts however, there was "the best feeling between the classes", even in places "where every effort is used, to create hatred, and ill will".

Dease gave a number of examples, including his fellow Catholic Unionist Lord Kenmare, with whom he had recently stayed at Killarney. "This is a country", he went on,

> full of anomalies & even for those living all their lives here & knowing the people well it is not easy to thoroughly understand all that goes on. In this respect, we are so different from the English and Scotch in character & national peculiarities, *some* of which, are the outcome of centuries of *misrule* . . . I always, deeply regret, that your personal knowledge of my country is not greater, & that you have been able, to *see so little* of a country with which your name must ever be associated.[47]

Authors such as B. L. Solow have questioned the notion that the system of land tenure lay at the root of the Irish troubles. She argues in her book *The Land Question and the Irish Economy 1870–1903* (1971) that in post-famine Ireland, "eviction was rare, rents were moderate, and tenant investment incentives were established". Tenure customs were at fault principally because they acted as a disincentive for landlords to invest, but "impressive progress" was nonetheless made.[48] More important to the development of Ireland and to the maintenance of the Union through the happiness of her people were such measures as drainage, flood control, improved communications, harbour improvement, and the extension of industries to the South, all of which, it may be noted, were strenuously advocated by such as the Morrises of Galway. Land legislation not only "did not ameliorate economic conditions", but at a critical time it "pre-empted the field of economic policy; and in the course of this, its working exacerbated landlord-tenant relations by focusing on a point of conflict of interests; finally . . . it eventually resulted in the end of landlordism in Ireland". Once the landlords were gone, she argues that the island "became much less important to the English".[49]

Not all the landlords, of course, did go; many stayed behind and suffered. When in 1881 The O'Donoghue forced an adjournment debate on the subject of Lord Kenmare's estates, about which there was much nationalist propaganda at the time, his land-agent, Hussey, wrote to *The Times* in reply, pointing out that during the years of distress Kenmare had spent more in the decade 1870–1880 than he had received out of his Kerry estates, and that rents were a quarter lower in 1880 than they had been in 1840. When, eventually, the earl was forced temporarily to leave Ireland because of intimidation, the effect was that employment was lost because his labourers were all discharged. Despite a substantial round-the-clock police guard, Hussey was awakened one night by a bomb exploding at the back of his house. With grim humour he is said to have gone back to sleep asking his wife to wake him up at the next explosion, or, as he himself put it, "I do not think the ruffians will trouble us again tonight".[50] S. M. Solow thinks that all this economic hardship, murder and marauding was worth it from the Irish point of view; but there were Irishmen who took leave to doubt it, and not all of them were Protestants. A. M. Sullivan, father of the "last Serjeant", and in his day a strong nationalist and Home Ruler, was one such Catholic who was not deceived. His son wrote; No matter what folly or crime a man was advocating, if the British Government prosecuted him, the Irish people were bound to allow him to ruin their country. Such was the unwritten law.

"The substitution of the capacity to read for the capacity to think", he added, "left these people at the mercy of agitators and the Press. Their 'illiterate' parents would not have been led to ruin by false and empty phrases".[51]

Another was William Cogan (1823–1894), who was Liberal M. P. for Kildare for nearly thirty years between 1852 and 1880. Born in Dublin and educated at Trinity, he was called to the Irish Bar in 1845. In 1874, he had been one of the twelve out of thirty-eight Liberal M. P.s seeking re-election who refused to endorse Home Rule at a time when the cause was popular and even fashionable among those who became Unionists in 1886; and he voted against Butt's subsequent Home Rule motion.[52] At some time in his Parliamentary career he was offered, but refused, government office, and in 1886 was sworn a member of the Irish privy council. A member of the Loan Fund Board (1860) and Sheriff of Wicklow (1863), he was, from 1880, a Commissioner of National Education. His quiet but distinguished career in parliament was ended in 1880 when *The Times* attributed his retirement to the Land League agitation.[53]

In July 1886 he wrote to the Duke of Norfolk approving of the Duke's letters to *The Times* on the duties of English Catholics. He enclosed a letter he had written at the time of the previous election for which he had been "most vehemently attacked" by Archbishop Walsh. However, "I have reason to know that I only expressed the opinions of the Catholics of the educated classes all over Ireland. It is most lamentable. I think of the hurt to our religion the conduct of the clergy here had done and is doing. The result must be most devastating."

The letter he enclosed was dated 27th November 1885 and was published in the *Freeman's Journal*, which had described him as an "Orange Tory Catholic". On the contrary, he replied, he was "a member of the party of moderate Liberals, and on principle opposed to the Orange, Tory, or Parnellite parties". However, it was "the duty of every man to come forward and take his side; it is the part of a coward to shirk it." One must be in favour of law and order and loyalty, and "the continuance of the sovereignty of the Queen or in favour of an illegal conspiracy which has already worked its end by acts of the most terrible cruelty". If not grappled with in time, "a flood of socialism and infidelity will deluge our unhappy country, and possibly sweep away, as it did in France, both the altar and the throne". The danger was "formidable and pressing" and Cogan ended by urging people to vote against Parnellite candidates for parliament.[54]

Cogan's claim that he "only expressed the opinions of the Catholics of the educated classes all over Ireland" was no empty boast, as readers of Trollope's *Land Leaguers* will readily appreciate. Their dilemma was eloquently expressed by William Bonaparte-Wyse in his *Vox Clamantis*, published in 1880. The Irish Catholic estated gentleman and landlord was in a difficult position. If he combined with his mainly Protestant fellow-landlords, he would be against the majority of his co-religionists. "In one case he is liable to be disliked and labelled as a 'toady' or sort of 'Orange Catholic'; on the other, he becomes a voluntary sapper away of the rights and influence of his class". Nonetheless, "the Catholic landlord should sally forth with his Protestant brother to face, attack and annihilate the common enemy, whose eye is fixed upon the twain, and to vindicate, as he may, eternal laws long anterior to either sect or dogma." When Parnell was invited to Waterford, he, as a Catholic layman, asked the clergy at least to "have the courage and the 'nous' to keep away" from his meeting. He asked them with something of an hereditary right,

> for it was a lineal ancestor of mine who left me a goodly share
> of his heritage; it was a lineal ancestor of mine who, at the peril
> of his life, in the woeful penal days, forced open the gates of
> their chapel, now their Cathedral Church, in Barronstrand
> Street; and it was also he with O'Connor and Curry . . . who
> forestalled O'Connell in the plans and projects of his victorious
> Association.

Wyse was indeed, one of the few landlords, who, "scorning to 'pop' at his opponents from behind the hedge of an 'anonyme'" had dared to sign his name in letters to the press. He received no end of threatening letters for his pains.

The silence of Catholic Unionists has often given the false impression that they are few in number, mere exceptions to the general rule, "converts" and the like. Yet the evidence shows that Catholic Unionism was widespread and not confined to office-holders and toadies. For a view of such "casual" Catholic Unionism, we cannot do better than to turn to the case of Frank Power, whose father was no estated gentleman, but the mere manager of the National Bank of Ireland in Dublin. Young Frank, born in 1859, showed early talent both as an illustrator and as a journalist; he was "broad-shouldered, strong-limbed, round-headed" and dark-eyed. "His carriage, erect & firm & decisive, all suggested the *beau sabreur*."[55]

In 1883 Power was appointed *Times* correspondent in the Sudan, and was in Khartoum from 1st August 1883 to 10th September 1884, when he was ordered back by Gordon and murdered on the way. The story is well told in Arnold Power's preface to his brother's posthumously published book of letters home.[56] The British Library manuscripts contain the following epitaph:

Thy chief was sent by Government and Queen
Watched by the world, on splendid enterprise
Thou, only of true heart, thy worth unseen
didst share the task before his lonely eyes.
Others are laid beneath frequented aisle
Soothed by soft hands, to calm and honoured rest
Above thee rolls the dark, forgetful Nile,
Its cold sand gathering in thy murdered breast.[57]

Gordon was his chief because by the end of 1883 Cromer (then Sir Evelyn Baring, and as Consul-General, effective ruler of Egypt) had appointed Power British Consul at Khartoum. Indeed the great proconsul seems to have been very kind to him, sending him pipes and tobacco at Christmas. Power was allowed to retain his *Times* correspondentship, and although Khartoum gradually became invested by the Mahdi and his men as 1884 wore on, many of his telegrams to the paper got through. Even before Gordon's arrival Power had become convinced that Khartoum could not be held, and it was said after his death that although the government made soothing noises the queen had said to Gladstone: "I believe they are in great distress & I believe all Mr Power's dispatches."[58]

Power remained robust and cheerful despite severe attacks of dysentery. He learnt to speak the language of the servants, and even when they stole from him and had to be dismissed, interceded with the Egyptian authorities to prevent them from being flogged. The Europeans gradually left; Hicks Pasha's expedition was massacred, and when Gordon arrived there were only two of them left in the palace at Khartoum. The Egyptian army was unreliable; there were only 2,000 men to guard four miles of perimeter, and as the Hicks expedition had shown, even when they were numerically superior to the Mahdi's men, they would run at the sight of them. Only the few Negro troops were reliable.

The formal siege began on 18th March, a month after Gordon's arrival. Power's dispatches ceased, the wires having been cut; but on 29th September 1884, after six months' silence, a telegram was published in *The Times* carrying the story down to 31st July. Berber had by then been captured and Khartoum completely isolated. Colonel Stewart, Frank Power and the French Consul were sent down river to bring news to the relief force. Berber was safely passed, despite being in enemy occupation, but further down river towards Cairo their ship struck a rock, and they were decoyed ashore and murdered on 18th September. Their bodies were thrown into the river. Lord Randolph Churchill asked the War Office for a report on their fate; Evelyn Baring wrote letters of sympathy; and Colonel Swaine, Military Secretary to Lord Wolseley, was instructed to write that "after the gallant defence made in Khartoum, in which Mr Power, your son, played so distinguished a part . . . his death has become a national loss".

Gordon and he hit it off. Gordon gave him a copy of Newman's *Dream of Gerontius*, and they discussed à Kempis. Power was a caricaturist of ability, and some of his sketches sent to an illustrated paper got through. Gordon described him in his Journals as a "chivalrous, brave, honest gentleman", though he thought that both he and Stewart should have resisted the lure to go on shore when their vessel was stranded.[59]

Power's letters to his family contain a number of references to Ireland. Thus on 11th October 1883 after describing the wretched life of the Sudanese people, to whom "envy and ambition" were "unknown", he expressed his wish that "some of the Irish agitators had a year of it". Again on 14th December 1883; "I am glad to see that Orangemen are meeting the Land League on its own ground; but they are foolish to resuscitate their obsolete old war-cries too much, as they will repel the respectable Catholics, who, being honest, do not believe that 'Parnell is Allah, and Healy is his prophet'". And on 18th January 1884, in ironical vein: "So Parnell has 'stowed the swag'; it is well to give up everything you have for your country, and become a patriot-martyr for a little time in Kilmainham". On 1st October 1883: "remember me to Mr and Mrs M.; I was so sorry he was beaten in his election by a Land Leaguer".[60] Frank Power's Unionism was not due to his appointments oversea; rather, it was a sincerely held opinion which he shared with numerous middle and upper class Catholics all over Ireland. If literacy had been more widespread, the view that Catholic Unionism was "exceptional" might be even more difficult to sustain.

CHAPTER TWELVE

The Second Home Rule Bill

Parnell had survived the Special Commission set up in the summer of 1888 in order to establish whether or not he was actively engaged in fomenting crime in Ireland, as alleged in certain "revelations" in *The Times*. In the event the letters on which *The Times*'s case was based turned out to be forgeries; and their forger, Pigott, as related, committed suicide. Lord Randolph Churchill denounced the government in a bitter speech: the result of their "mountainous parturition" had been "a ghastly, bloody, rotten, foetus — Pigott! Pigott!! Pigott!!!"[1]

But on 6th December 1890 in Committee Room Fifteen at the House of Commons the Nationalists split over the O'Shea divorce case, in which Parnell was cited as co-respondent. Justin McCarthy, with forty-four other dissidents, withdrew, leaving Parnell with twenty-seven followers. Archbishop Walsh wrote that in selecting a leader a party had no duty to consider moral questions. Only later did the Irish hierarchy come out with a firm denunciation of Parnell's conduct. On 6th October 1891, Parnell died; and John Redmond succeeded. The split widened.[2]

There was in the first place a division between Parnellites who argued that Ireland would be better served if its M. P.s were completely independent of mainland politicians and those who thought that Gladstone, if supported, and only if supported, would bring in Home Rule. In the second place, those who thought that Parnell's involvement with Mrs O'Shea disqualified him from the leadership broke with those who did not. It was Gladstone's clearly expressed moral disapproval of Parnell which tipped the scale on both counts.

Lord Salisbury took a philosophical view. In a speech at Cambridge on 21st January 1891 he said that though the discontent or disaffection in Ireland might take a political form, at bottom it was the poverty and suffering of the Irish people which for many generations had caused the connexion between England and Ireland to be so disturbed. Natural resources, he pointed out, were lacking in Ireland. There were scarcely any islands on the wrong side of fifty degrees of latitude in either hemisphere. "I put aside the Falkland Islands and Iceland, you will scarcely call them habitable; but Ireland stands by herself in this that she is in a geographical position singularly unfitted for production, and she has a population tending to increase with great rapidity, and that she has no mineral resources to sustain her".[3]

At the general election of 1892, the Parnellite following was reduced to nine. About half of all adult males, or one sixth of the population, had the vote; sons or servants living in a household were excluded. Four Irish seats were won by Liberal Unionists, nineteen by Conservatives and seventy-two by anti-Parnellite Home Rulers. One of the Liberal Unionists was William Kenny.

Kenny was born in Dublin in 1846, the son of a solicitor. After an initially private education, he went to Trinity College, now more widely open to Catholics, and was called to the Irish Bar in 1868, at the age of 22. Five years later he married Mary, elder daughter of David Coffey, a Master in Chancery. In 1885 he became a Queen's Counsel.

The atmosphere of the Irish Bar of the day is well described in Edward Marjoribank's *Life of Carson* (1932). Barristers tended to congregate in the Library of the Four Courts. They were overcrowded compared to their brethren in London, but this very overcrowding led to a much closer association: "jealousy and backbiting were so uncomfortable as to become really impossible, and . . . friendship and good-fellowship were not only general but necessary in such conditions".[4] At the entrance to the main room in the 1870s stood an ex-trooper named Bramley, with a clear, powerful voice. Solicitors or their clerks needing to see a barrister, or to summon him to Court, came to the library door and mentioned the name of their counsel. Bramley then shouted the name — his voice would have reached far beyond the uttermost corner of the library — and the barrister immediately stopped his drafting or reading and went to the door. "Bramley's voice retained its power from early morning till the shadows fell", added Marjoribanks, "and, in justice be it recorded, the ex-trooper's throat needed very little lubrication".

Such was the atmosphere, predominantly Protestant and Conservative, of Carson's, and indeed Kenny's day. But Kenny, like Carson, was a Liberal; and it was not until the shock of Mr Gladstone's Home Rule Bill of 1886 fell upon the country that he began to take a prominent part in politics. In 1887 the Bill was defeated and a number of prominent Unionists in Great Britain quit the Liberal party. A meeting was held at the Shelburne Hotel to form an Irish branch of the Liberal Union, and Kenny and Patton were elected Honorary Secretaries. The *Irish Times* wrote in a leader that "such names as Jellett, Cogan, Piers White,

Kenny, Dowden, Holmes, Hogg, Wilson, Wigham, Blennerhassett and Bewley, are a guarantee that this is really what it professes to be — a society formed for the purpose of safeguarding the integrity of the Empire, in our part of Her Majesty's dominions, and of protecting the interests of all ranks and classes against socialistic revolution".[5]

On 11th November, a Unionist meeting was held at the Leinster Hall. Thomas Maguire, Catholic Fellow of Trinity College, was there, as was Kenny; the latter, as joint honorary secretary, was mainly instrumental in organizing a visit later in the month by Lord Hartington and Goschen, in the course of which another meeting was held on 29th November, attended by an estimated 10,000 people.[6] Among those on the platform were the Earl of Fingall, Maguire, and at least two other prominent Catholics.[7] At the overflow meeting a Mr Hussey Walsh said that

> He stood on this platform an Irish Catholic . . . to bear witness to the strength and sacredness of their Unionist feeling. They believed that, instead of the ascendancy of one creed there had now come to Ireland an ascendancy of honest men. That was the ascendancy for which they struggled, that was the ascendancy which they would defend.

After reviewing the strength of the forces ranged behind Mr Gladstone, he stated that in opposition to this policy,

> the Unionists had a consistent policy . . . they believed in the policy of the Union. By Union they meant union between all classes and sections of the community; union between Catholics and Protestants; union between the rich and the poor; union between landlords and tenants; and union between Great Britain and Ireland.[8]

At the subsequent banquet in the Leinster Hall, both Kenny and Lord Emly, by now Vice-Chancellor of the Royal University, are mentioned as among the more prominent guests. Hartington presided and proposed the loyal toast, and the next, "the Unionist cause" was proposed by Kenny:

> To England the independence of Ireland means Imperial danger, and nothing more. To Ireland it conveys but the one idea of

utter and complete ruin — ruin not by slow degrees but by a quick and sharp process touching every individual interest. To none has that idea presented itself with more convincing reality — with more solemn seriousness — than to the mercantile, professional and industrial classes of Dublin . . . We are now determined to show that Unionist Ireland is not represented by Ulster alone, and that in the metropolis of the country the cause of the Union is as dear to us as it is to our friends in the North.[9]

Kenny had thus become a formative influence on Unionist thinking in southern Ireland. He was an active and consistent champion of the cause. Whether he was the author of an article in the *Dublin Review* for April 1886, when the Home Rule controversy was at its height, cannot now be determined. Certain it is, however, that the "Irish Catholic Barrister" who wrote that article was seized of similar sentiments:

There was no reason whatever to suppose that Mr Parnell and his Socialistic followers will be converted to the moral law by finding their iniquities unrestrained and unopposed. We might as well expect to find the butler taking the pledge after he had just broken open the cellar . . . Well-meaning but short-sighted persons, carried away by the poverty and sufferings of a particular class, have unfortunately sowed the seeds of Communism in a fertile soil. A doctrine at once so dangerous and attractive cannot fail to delude and to destroy a people once generous and virtuous, and to blight the fair prospects of Ireland with the double curse of cupidity and poverty.[10]

The *Northern Whig* wrote on 29th November 1887 that attachment to the Union was

not confined to Protestants; it is shared in by the most respectable Catholics, who, though seats in Parliament are considered social distinctions, have turned disdainfully away from purchasing them from Mr Parnell and other Irish Nationalist leaders at the price of their surrender of all independence of mind, of all that gives dignity to a popular representative in the House of Commons. Lord Hartington's host in Dublin is a Catholic, and not one of Mr Healy's dukes or lords, not one of Sir William Harcourt's landlords anxious to collect his rents. Mr Goschen's host is also a Catholic, who is not afraid of showing his sympathy with the cause of the Union.[11]

After his death, the *Irish Times* wrote of Kenny that, "with characteristic independence of mind, he wholly disregarded bitter and persistent personal attacks, defending the Liberal-Unionist policy, in speeches of remarkable vigour, and the solidity of his arguments, together with the signal skill with which they were constructed, had the effect of powerfully influencing a great body, not only of local, but of general electoral opinion".[12]

The Liberal Union of Ireland was not the only Richmond in the field. The Irish Loyal and Patriotic Union (ILPU), in some ways a more important body, was founded in May 1885. It proclaimed itself to be unsectarian, and willing to support any Unionist candidate prepared to fight Parnell.[13] The Duke of Norfolk was one of its first presidents, and Colonel Gerald Dease, a Catholic from Celbridge, County Kildare, and a Director, subsequently Governor, of the Bank of Ireland, was a Vice-President. The Union fielded nearly fifty candidates in the general election of 1885, and although none of these won, its impact was not entirely lost.[14]

The activities of the ILPU were at first confined to the three southern provinces; Ulster had its own body, the Loyal Irish Union (LIU) founded in August 1885 at Belvoir Park.[15] But in January 1886 the ILPU began to extend its activities to Belfast, and the LIU was soon disbanded. Nevertheless Unionism in Ulster continued to develop on different lines; a rival organization, the Ulster Loyalist Anti-Repeal Committee, virtually confined to Protestants, was soon set up, whilst the ILPU supported an organization in Tyrone called the Northwest Loyal Registration and Electoral Association.[16] The Orange Order was particularly associated with the Anti-Repeal Committee. There was serious rioting in Belfast after the rejection of the first Home Rule Bill; thirty-two died, and thirty-one public houses were wrecked.[17]

This did not prevent some Ulster Catholics from supporting the Union. On 17th June 1892 an enormous convention was held in Belfast, for which a special pavilion had to be constructed. Presided over by the Duke of Abercorn, and consisting of thousands of delegates from every part of the province, the meeting was partially organized by Catholics, and there were even Catholic priests on the platform.[18] Dr Kane, Grand Master of the Orangemen of Belfast, is reported as asserting that

> we hail their presence here with sincere pleasure, not because we wish to make use of them for the purpose of fastening a yoke of slavery upon them and their co-religionists; but because we acknowledge to the full their right to all the privileges of British citizenship, and because their presence here as fellow-soldiers with us in the cause of the unity of the kingdom and the supremacy of the Imperial Parliament gives a bright promise of the speedy advent of the day when Irishmen, as well as Englishmen and Scotchmen and Welshmen, will be content to live and to work and to prosper under the aegis of an Imperial Constitution and Parliament which secures the utmost civil and religious liberty for all and, with a strong hand, puts down arbitrary dictation, whether of the hired agitator or of a domineering clericalism.[19]

This was conciliatory and even handsome; other speakers were sometimes a little disparaging of Catholics, although Lord Arthur Hill, M. P. is reported to have written that: "After the Convention . . . I had a chat with some representative Roman Catholics who had been present, and they assured me that they were both pleased and satisfied with the tone adopted towards Roman Catholic Irishmen".[20]

A similar convention for the three southern provinces followed on 23rd June in the Leinster Hall, Dublin. Not only were Catholics present, but the Chairman was the eleventh Earl of Fingall (1859–1929). In introducing him, David Plunket, First Commissioner of Works, said that:

> The name of the ancient house of Fingall has been for centuries an ornament to the Catholic community of Ireland, and I am proud to remember that your and my ancestors were foremost, side by side, amongst the men who, in the earlier years of this century, struggled for and achieved the great measure for the enfranchisement of the Catholics of Ireland. Yes, and many others of your faith are here, and some of them will no doubt address this meeting, Catholics who do not recognise in the violent appeals of clerical agitators the true teachings of their religion, and who believe that the best interests and the freedom

of their Church are more secure in the keeping of the Imperial Assembly than they would be under any separate legislature which might be set up in this country.[21]

Fingall himself said:

I must be careful to recognise that the selection as chairman of a Catholic and Liberal Unionist has a significance which throws all personal considerations into the background. I hasten on behalf of loyal Catholics and Liberal Unionists to assure our Protestant and Conservative companions in arms that we will stand by them as long as they stand by us . . . No doubt we shall be told that our coming here is a mere political move, an election device . . . I state emphatically that our action is spontaneous . . . So far as Catholics are concerned I cannot help thinking that if our faith can be said to have any political tendency at all it is rather towards the maintenance of the Union than towards Home Rule. This was illustrated a few years ago when Home Rulers called to their aid the most inhuman political agencies, which the head of my Church was constrained to condemn.[22]

He alluded to Gladstone's assertion made at Clapham on 17th June 1892 that the whole mass of Irish Roman Catholics except a portion of the upper class opposed the Pope's "rescript". They included the clergy and almost every Bishop. Fingall, correcting Gladstone, pointed out that it was not a rescript but a decree. It was promulgated in the diocese of Dublin by the archbishop, who ordered it to be read out in all churches. Fingall interpreted Gladstone as suggesting that Irish M. P.s should lead the priests against the Pope. For his part, he preferred "to follow the simple instincts of an inherited faith rather than the guidance of even such an intellectual giant as Mr Gladstone, and thus I come by the belief that the Catholic religion is better safeguarded under the protection of the Imperial Parliament than it would be under any form of Home Rule Government which Mr Gladstone can devise". "Whatever claim individuals may assert", he added, "neither my creed nor any other creed represented here . . . contains any tenets or provisions which either directly or by implication can be held to justify 'clerical domination' or 'religious ascendancy'". In conclusion, "so long as our birthright is being offered for sale to an English party, and the empire which has risen by union is being hurried along a downward course, we give notice to all who would tamper with our freedom, our fortune, and our lives that Ireland will block the way".

A general election was imminent. William Kenny, parliamentary candidate for the St Stephen's Green Division of Dublin was at the Leinster Hall gathering and proposed a vote of thanks to the president of the overflow meeting, T. Plunkett Cairnes. "Warnings may have been given of what we believe to be the unquestionable results of any attempt by any future administration to force a measure of Home Rule upon this country, but the language of tonight has been temperate, weighty, and dignified". On the next night, in the course of a speech in his division, he mentioned seeing a large number of Catholics in the Minor Hall, when the meeting took place. The Earl of Fingall had taken the chair in one hall; in the second the "second chair was taken by a well-known Dublin gentleman, who had filled the chair of the Chamber of Commerce, and who was also a Roman Catholic".[23] As to his two opponents in the division, "he would not say a word against the Lord Mayor" (Dr Joseph Meade), "but the Lord Mayor was a Parnellite . . . Every Unionist voter who voted for the Lord Mayor, as some might be disposed to do from a feeling of friendship, should remember that in doing so he was voting against his principles". As for Pearson, the second Nationalist candidate at St Stephen's Green, people "were asking who he was". Kenny "dared to say that wherever Mr Pearson was known he was respected, but he was a member of that heterogeneous and highly select body known as Protestant Home Rulers".[24] Kenny was always scrupulously fair to his opponents, and it may well be that his refusal to sling mud stood him in good stead with the electors, with whom the Lord Mayor, his principal opponent, was justifiably popular.

On 25th June, Horace Plunkett spoke in his support.[25] "Protestants had often felt", he is reported as saying, "that Home Rule would endanger their religious views, and the Leinster Hall meeting was the first occasion on which they had found a prominent Roman Catholic agreeing by word and announcement that it was likely to endanger his religious views as well. Therefore, although he was a Protestant himself he said without hesitation, and without fear, that it was gratifying to see them at St Stephen's Green selecting as their representative an able, eloquent, and well-known Catholic . . . in order that the Protestants and Nonconformists could show to Roman Catholics that they were prepared to be just as liberal as Lord Fingall".[26]

Kenny himself spoke of the effects of the 1886 Home Rule Bill and of Gladstone's preceding "pilot balloon" (more often referred to as the "Hawarden Kite") of 1885 on bank and other stock in Ireland. He returned to this theme after his election to parliament. Business confidence had begun to revive under Balfour's administration, but had slumped again more recently under the impending threat of a dissolution and the return of a Gladstonian majority. Kenny repeated that he had no personal animus against the Lord Mayor or the other candidate; but the former (Meade) "was one of the directors of the *Freeman's Journal*, when that journal sent a special reporter to stand at the door of the Balfour banquet to take down the names of every Unionist who attended it for the purpose of having them boycotted".[27] On 30th June, he added that not only was Mr Meade an extreme Parnellite, but he was "anxious for the release of men whom he called political prisoners, but who were persons who had been justly convicted of an attempt to destroy English buildings by dynamite, and who were convicted by fair-minded English juries".[28] Referring to the Leinster Hall Convention of 23rd June, he stated that "he had been speaking to a gentleman who had come up from the west with fifteen delegates, and out of that number thirteen were Roman Catholics. Such a thing would not have been possible some years ago, not because those men would be unwilling to come, but because there was a reign of terror through the country, and the people could not profess their politics, or other opinions".

In conclusion, "Mr Kenny asked those present not to think anything of him personally, except that on Thursday next he would bear the flag of Unionism in this contest. They should think of him as one of themselves, whom they could trust to bear the standard of the Union".

On 4th July, an *Irish Times* editorial came out in strong support, and when Kenny was elected, by a majority of only fifteen votes over his principal opponent, commented that he had been opposed "by the strongest candidate who could be found in Ireland, our universally admired and respected Lord Mayor . . . Mr Kenny will be an excellent member. He has acted throughout with a high and chivalrous aim . . . In the House of Commons he will be no dumb representative, but will prove that Irish Catholics can be, as a larger number every day are, thorough Unionists". Lord Salisbury wrote congratulating him on his "great victory", whose "moral effect . . . will be enormous".[29]

At the declaration of poll, Pearson, the anti-Parnellite Home Ruler, was blamed for the Lord Mayor's defeat[30], "some person" calling for a cheer for "the man who had sold St Stephen's Green". The declaration was held for all the divisions simultaneously, and Kenny's namesake, J. E. Kenny, elected in the Parnellite interest for the College Green constituency, referred to the "treachery by which the St Stephen's Green Division was handed over to the enemy". One feels sorry for Pearson, whom the *Irish Daily Independent*, a bitterly pro-Parnell journal, described as "the Whig candidate". His opponents (though not, be it noted, Kenny himself) made great play with the fact that he had been present on 25th June at what the *Independent* described as "a Unionist Prayer meeting" presided over by the Protestant Archbishop of Dublin. At a meeting held on 4th July Timothy Harrington[31] asserted that "he had no other feeling for Mr Pearson than a feeling of regret that such a glorified idiot should have been brought into Irish politics". Harrington did not assert in terms (no doubt fearing legal action) that he "had the wickedness or the trickery to make a bargain with the Tories", but he did hint that a "gentleman from the North" had come down to make a corrupt bargain with him.[32] The *Independent*'s account of the declaration was headed; "The Answer to Pearson's Prayer — Selling a Seat to the Enemy".[33] The Parnellite journal defamed Kenny as "the coercionist place-hunting lawyer", and printed an anonymous letter which asserted that he had "no property or any stake here except his profession, and if he had not, and did not, sell his party would never have been taken up by wirepullers".[34]

While it is not certain that Kenny's election in 1892 was the result of a split among the Nationalists, there is no doubt that his cause was advanced thereby. He was also assisted by his popularity, and his conduct of the election, which the defeated Lord Mayor described at the declaration as "strictly honourable and straightforward, and in the highest degree creditable".[35]

Two other Liberal Unionists, Hugh Arnold-Foster (West Belfast) and Thomas Lea (Londonderry South) won seats from the nationalists at this election, and a fourth, Thomas Russell, who had won South Tyrone in 1886, was also returned. But in the United Kingdom as a whole the Liberal Unionists lost thirty-one seats, and the Conservatives forty-eight. Home Rule Liberals and nationalists had a majority of forty.[36]

Salisbury, in the short period left to him before his administration's inevitable defeat during the debate on the Address, made the newly-elected Carson Solicitor-General for Ireland, a post Kenny himself was to occupy three years later. After the defeat of the government in August 1892, Carson and Kenny took up the cudgels in Dublin on behalf of the unpopular and elusive Marquess of Clanricarde, whose conduct was being inquired into by the Evicted Tenants' Commission in Dublin. This body was set up by John Morley, the new Liberal Chief Secretary. At its head was Mr Justice Mathew, who was a collateral descendant of Father Theobald Mathew, who had such an influence for good in Ireland during the famine years. The judge had a reputation for impartiality, and his sympathies are revealed in the best-known saying attributed to him that "in England, justice is open to all, like the Ritz Hotel"; but according to Marjoribanks, he became a prejudiced person the moment he set foot in Ireland. Clanricarde, too, had distinguished ancestry; the first Marquess, a Catholic, was the last King's Lieutenant in Ireland before the Cromwellian take-over. But the family had now turned Protestant.[37]

Failing to observe Clanricarde in Court, Mathew now demanded the reason for his non-attendance, and was dissatisfied with Carson's explanation. He then refused to allow Carson to cross-examine John Roche, a nationalist M. P., and when Carson pressed the matter declared to him: "When you have taken off your wig and gown, you will see that it is most convenient and best. You are here at present as an *amicus curiae*" (friend of the Court) "and in no other capacity". Before luncheon Mathew had told Carson that he would allow him to cross-examine later; now, refused permission to do so, Carson, still on his feet, his brogue slower than usual, said:

> My Lord, if I am not at liberty to cross-examine, I say the
> whole thing is a farce and a sham, I willingly withdraw from it.
> I will not prostitute my position by remaining any longer as an
> advocate before an English Judge.

"I am not sitting as a Judge", retorted Mathew. Carson then rejoined in a low voice, but loud enough for the court to hear: "Any fool could see that". He was told that his observations were "disgraceful". Kenny, also briefed for Clanricarde, entirely concurred with Carson's protest, to be told that his remarks were "equally impertinent and disgraceful". Carson then threw down his papers on the desk and walked slowly out of court, followed by every member of the Irish Bar present.

The London *Times* devoted its first leader on the following day to the subject, declaring that Mathew had refused "to be bound by any of the rules of judicial procedure". The evidence of a witness, not himself a tenant, was purely hearsay, and not to allow this person, a plan of campaign organiser, to be subject even to cross-examination, after a promise had been given that this would be permitted, was a method of inquiry for which no precedent's existed since James II. "We do not believe that Sir James Mathew's harsh and irritable observations on the conduct of the distinguished counsel who appeared in the case of the landlords in urging their right to cross-examine will command the sympathy of the English Bar".[38] In subsequent correspondence, Carson wrote that "if I erred it was because I am accustomed to practise in Courts where parties are heard before they are condemned, and where Judges never complain if they are in a respectful manner corrected as to a misapprehension of a matter of fact".[39]

The commission became discredited, but sat on to produce a report which was debated in the House of Commons on 13th March 1893. An Act of 1891 provided for the voluntary re-instatement of evicted tenants, who could then apply to the Land Commission for a loan to purchase their holdings. This was not unreasonable; but the issue raised by the *Report of the Evicted Tenants' Commission* of 1893 was much more controversial. It called for the *compulsory* reinstatement of such evicted tenants, whether their former landlord liked it or not. The report of the commission "really placed", said Kenny,

> a premium upon dishonesty. The tenant had been evicted — he had been out of his holding for several years — he had been living in an evicted hut upon the scanty means offered him by the hon. Gentleman opposite — what capital he had had been lost — but now under the finding of the Evicted tenants Commission that tenant, without one farthing in his pocket, was to be compulsorily reinstated in his holding.

After recalling Sir James Mathew's refusal to allow Carson to cross-examine witnesses before him, he added that Sir James was himself an avowed Nationalist, and that the other members of the Commission included no one representing Unionism.[40]

It remained for Wyndham to settle the Irish land question in the early part of the next century; but we may pause here to note that despite the evident unfairnesses of the Mathew Commission, the government introduced a Bill to restore evicted tenants on the lines which it had suggested. Kenny spoke to the Evicted Tenants (Ireland) Arbitration Bill on 19th July 1894 and later moved amendments; it was rejected by the Lords.[41] The following year Morley introduced a Land Bill which was to deal with the continuing allegation that "the Irish tenant was rented on his improvements".[42] Kenny however, asserted that the consensus of evidence was that before the landlord got any increased letting value the tenant received between five and ten per cent on his improvements. The sub-commissioners had claimed that an extra five per cent was given to the landlord; whereas three lay commissioners had observed that the tenant got every farthing. On balance, however, Kenny came down in favour of leave being given to introduce the Bill, which appears to have been caught by the dissolution.[43] At the beginning of the 1892 to 1895 parliament, however, all Irish matters were overshadowed by the second Home Rule Bill.

In 1891 the Irish Loyal and Patriotic Union became the Irish Unionist Alliance.[44] The latter had a central organization on which the Primrose League, the Orange Body, the Liberal Union of Ireland, and the Unionist Clubs Council were represented and sometimes affiliated. Ulster Unionism for its part tended to go its separate way. This weakness in the movement was to have serious consequences.

The second Home Rule Bill differed from that of 1886 in providing that Ireland should continue to be represented in the imperial parliament. Her Members would, however, only vote at Westminster on subjects concerning Ireland or the empire; army, navy, customs and excise, trade and foreign affairs were excluded from discussion by the new Irish legislature. Although the Bill was rejected by the Lords on 8th September 1893, and Gladstone was restrained by his colleagues from going to the country, his efforts, "whether for good or evil", were not useless.

> The Home Rule Bill of 1886 had only been a flash in the pan. The commons had rejected its bare principles; its details were not reached. Had it lacked a sequel for nineteen years, there might never have been one. But the bill of 1893 went through all its stages in the elected house. It emerged a complete measure which, but for the veto of the house of lords, would have come into force. It was almost bound to be revived if and when a majority of the nation took the view that the lords had used their vote unfairly.[45]

Irish Unionists had reason to be alarmed. A petition was sponsored by six Catholic peers, including Fingall, Kenmare, and Emly, and thirty-six others of rank and station. They included Ross-of-Bladensburg, Stephen de Vere, William Kenny, Richard Martin, Maurice and Daniel O'Connell, and Gerald Dease. "As a false impression has been created", they proclaimed,

> that the contest upon the Home Rule Bill is, in reality, only a contest between a Roman Catholic majority and a Protestant minority, we have thought it right, in order to make the position clear, that Irish Roman Catholic Unionists should have an opportunity of joining in a separate and distinct petition to Parliament against the Bill. While deprecating certain anti-Catholic utterances to which the excitement of the moment may have given rise, we are, so far as our objections to Home Rule rest upon purely secular considerations, heartily in accord with our fellow Unionists. More than this, we believe that Home Rule, if imposed upon Ireland, would, under the peculiar conditions of the country, foster a revolutionary spirit disastrous to the true interests of our religion. We therefore invite our fellow Roman Catholics in Ireland to join us in signing the petition, a copy of which is appended to this letter.[46]

The petition itself read as follows:

> To the Honourable the Commons of the United Kingdom of Great Britain and Ireland in Parliament assembled The Humble Petition of Roman Catholics in Ireland Sheweth —
> That we entertain unshaken allegiance and devotion to the Crown and Constitution under which we live and enjoy full civil and religious liberty. That we regard the maintenance of the Union between England and Ireland as a necessary safeguard of that liberty. That we believe the establishment in Ireland of a separate Legislature and Executive in the manner proposed in the Government of Ireland Bill recently introduced into your Honourable House would be most prejudicial to our religion, and disastrous to the best interests of Ireland.
> We beseech your Honourable House to reject the said Bill . . .

Professor Edward Dowden, a Liberal Unionist, discussed this petition in the *Fortnightly* of May 1893:

> The free expression of opinion by Roman Catholics is checked by a system of intimidation and terrorism, of which abundant

evidence has been in my own hands. Thousands of signatures have been attached to the Roman Catholic petition against the Bill; but some of these have been volunteered secretly and at night; others have been cancelled in consequence of the terrified entreaties of those who signed; others have been refused by persons who desired to sign, but who declared that they would be burnt out of house and home if they ventured to do so. Servants who voluntarily signed have, on returning from chapel, announced that they must withdraw their signatures or leave their situations. There is an impression abroad among the peasantry that the names will be got at by Nationalist Members of Parliament and that those whose names are attached to the petition will be made the victims of social persecution. Notwithstanding this system of terrorism, thousands of names already stand at the foot of the petition.[47]

Professor Dowden also quoted from a Mr E. O'Ryan, of Larne Harbour, who had said that "We, loyal Catholics, could never submit to Mr Gladstone's ticket-of-leave men placed in power over us in this country, and rather than submit to them, we are prepared for the worst, and ready, if need be to die with the words 'No Surrender' on our lips".

Meetings were organized to protest against the Bill. Lord Dunraven spoke thus at Limerick on 22nd March:

It is usually supposed by the constituencies of Great Britain that Unionism in the south is the political creed of a few fanatical county gentlemen . . . It is not true. Consider that petition against Repeal signed by many Roman Catholics of position in the country, and by numbers of their co-religionists. Look at this great meeting. Of what is it composed? Both religious creeds represented on this platform, and representative of all classes and creeds in the body of the hall. It is absurdly false to pretend that devotion to the Union burns in the breasts of country gentlemen and Protestants alone.[48]

According to the *Daily Express* of Dublin there were present "a conspicuous group of Roman Catholic noblemen and gentlemen . . . There is no desire for ascendancy on the part of any Irish Unionists, and the Unionism of Lord Emly, the Earl of Fingall, Lord Gormanston, Mr Cogan, Mr More O'Ferrall, Colonel Dease, and so many others of the leading Roman Catholic laymen proves that they, at all events, acquit their Protestant countrymen of any such desire".[49] The adhesion of Catholics to the Unionist cause was explained away by calling them Castle officials and insinuating that their allegiance had been bought. But surely that argument cut both ways, for an official was in an unrivalled position to observe for himself whether any discrimination was being exercised against Catholics, and the adhesion of noble-minded and disinterested officials could be seen as proof that it was not and that the days of the ascendancy were dead.

Dunraven had summed up what was likely to happen when he wrote on 6th March:

> By the Home Rule Bill, Ireland will be degraded from a sound and honourable position of co-partnership with a great and prosperous nation to the ignominious attitude of a tattered poor relation, alternately whining for charity and threatening blackmail.[50]

Evidence of the intimidation of voters was forthcoming from the Cliffoney division of Sligo, where at an election of Poor Law Guardians in March, Roman Catholic tenants wishing to vote for their landlord were prevented from doing so by the mob. Several voters testified that their houses had been attacked, and voting papers extorted by threat. In one case, there had been serious personal injury following refusal. The facts were not in dispute, and the Lord Chief Baron, himself a Catholic, referred in his charge to the occurrences as conclusively proved. Two of the prisoners were found guilty.[51] As Mr Barrett, another Catholic, said:

> The reason that the great bulk of the middle class of Roman Catholics were standing aloof at the present time was because they had a distinct recollection of the terrible time they passed through from 1880 to 1886 . . . They then passed through an ordeal that was, perhaps, unequalled in any part of the world. Roman Catholic men were dragged out of their beds at night and murdered in the presence of their wives and families . . . Roman Catholic farmers' houses were burned . . . and they themselves were maimed and injured . . . and their cattle destroyed, and simply because these men would not become members of the Land League or subscribe to its funds. That

was the reason Roman Catholics were not coming forward in great numbers now.[52]

On 8th April Lord Emly spoke at Dublin in support of Mr Balfour[53]; but perhaps the most impressive Unionist demonstration of the year was one held at the Albert Hall, London, on 22nd April. The Church of Ireland Bishop of Derry's references to Catholic support for the Union were magnanimous:

> Our Roman Catholic friends are, as a general rule, entirely on our side . . . We have instances of it, I am thankful to say, upon this very platform. The farmers who have large farms are in many cases coming forward. They have written letters in the Irish papers, and have placed their names at the bottom of them . . . All the religions in Ireland are represented on this platform . . . Loyalty has, thank God, ceased to be a sectarian word . . . Noble-minded Roman Catholics are as loyal to the Queen and Constitution as we are.[54]

Lord Fingall is recorded as saying:

> Irish liberties are safer under the British Empire than they would be under any Government in the world. I am sure that Protestant England will increase her efforts in resistance to the Bill when she realises that almost all the English Roman Catholics and a large number of Irish Roman Catholics are bitterly opposed to it.[55]

The leading English Roman Catholic layman of the day was Henry Fitz-alan Howard, fifteenth Duke of Norfolk. His shining integrity was likened by *The Times* newspaper of 12th February 1917 to that of Sir Thomas More.

> Both had a passionate love of their country and a profound loyalty to their sovereign. None could be found more typically English, none ever loved their country better, none were ever more devoted to the See of Rome than were Thomas More and Henry Fitzalan Howard.

His simple and traditional Catholic piety remarked on by Father Bernard Vaughan and his special devotion to Our Lady of Lourdes may have seemed to some Protestants as "un-English". But, unlike Sir Thomas More, he was spared the grave conflict of loyalty to Caesar and loyalty to God. In the *Daily Telegraph* of 17th February, 1917 he was described as "Elizabethan in his patriotic fervour and zeal, in the adventurous temper of his mind, and also in his intuitive belief in the true functions of a ruling class in the State". In his day Norfolk could be, like More, "the King's good servant but God's first", without braving the fearful Tudor penalties; but the ancestral prejudices against Papists lingered and in Norfolk's time much that was said and done in Catholic Ireland did little to dispel them. *The New Witness* testified thus: "No man loved England better or served her more faithfully." Referring to his resignation of the Postmaster-Generalship in Salisbury's administration in order to volunteer, though "already past the prime of life", for active service in South Africa, the eulogy continued:

> As Earl Marshal of England he was responsible for two Coronations. And he was a Roman Catholic. Curiously enough, his fellow-countrymen saw no incongruity in this circumstance. This was perhaps the Duke's greatest triumph. Here was a man professing a religion which little more than a generation ago was generally both detested and distrusted in this country. And the man was a patriot! That was the wonder of it! As time went on the thing became less wonderful. That the Catholic Church is no longer regarded in England as "the enemy" is due in no small measure to the late Duke.

The Month attributed the Cardinal's hat bestowed on John Henry Newman to the influence of Norfolk. He dealt on Queen Victoria's behalf with the Holy See and entertained Papal Nuncios in England; but, according to *The Times*,

> There was a John Bull element in his nature that made the details of entertaining foreigners somewhat of an effort to him. He did not care to give bow for bow or compliment for compliment in the grand Italian manner!

More important for our purpose was the duke's staunch opposition to Home Rule for Ireland. His criticism of the plan of campaign brought him into conflict with some Irish bishops. But he fought persistently for Catholic schools and, although his motives were not always understood throughout Ireland, he believed that Home Rule would spell disaster to her people. "For the Protestants of Ireland", he said on the second reading of the Home Rule Bill of 1893,

> the Government would be wielded by those whom they feel they cannot trust; and for the Catholics the Bill dangles before them dangerous temptations to a power and opportunities which can only be grasped by an unholy alliance with a movement whose strength is founded on means condemned by the Church, and whose leaders have openly defied the strength of the Holy See.[56]

Like Lord Fingall, the duke was always ready to speak out against those who used the cloak of Unionism to make attacks upon his religion. Thus in a letter to Colonel Saunderson, M. P. for Portadown, he complained of the Colonel using "Rome" and "Popish" as terms of reproach. "Have you forgotten", he wrote,

> that when British statesmen were condoning Boycotting and palliating the Plan of Campaign, it was the Pope who uncompromisingly condemned both? . . . The great body of Catholics who are at this moment standing by the Loyalists of Ireland may claim to have their religion respected . . . We have a hard, and, it may well be, a long fight before us for justice, law and freedom. Do not let us sap our vigour by words and arguments which only undermine the mutual trust on which our strength should rest.[57]

Saunderson's reply is in the archives at Arundel. He regretted that his remarks at Liverpool had been understood as implying disrespect, and offered to avoid the terms "Romish" and "Popish" in the future. "My criticism of the action of the Roman Catholic priests in Ireland at the Late elections was not aimed at them as Roman Catholics but as Politicians . . . the last desire I entertain would be to give offence to those who have so loyally stood by the cause of Imperial unity."[58] In similar vein, the Duke's brother, Lord Edmund Talbot, afterwards first Viscount FitzAlan of Derwent and the last Lord-Lieutenant of Ireland, wrote to Craig in 1912 with a donation for his fighting fund, explaining that "if I find it is being used in an attack on orthodox, and not

Hibernian, Popery, I shall have to come over and study the best means of incendiarism on Craigavon".[59]

Indefatigable in presiding at anti-Home Rule meetings, the Duke was even prepared to appear on Orange platforms. Some called him "the Orange Duke". There were many who felt, with Sir John Ross-of-Bladensburg, that his immense courage, profound piety, and great position, should have been recognized by the Salisbury Administration which succeeded the Liberals in 1895. A short Act could have been passed opening the viceroyalty to Catholics, as was done later for the duke's brother, and His Grace could then have been appointed Lord Lieutenant. Instead he was made Postmaster-General according to the precedent Gladstone had created in the case of Lord Emly. "I have always felt", wrote Ross,

> that he was especially endowed with qualities to enable him to cope successfully with the Irish difficulty. However much he may have differed with the aspirations of the Irish, he was ever respected (and really respected) by even the most "advanced" among them . . . and they were ready to trust him. They would have done so all the more had they known him better than they did. My firm belief is that he was the one man who could have reconciled the Irish, and that he would have been highly successful; but bigotry intervened, and that opportunity has been lost.[60]

No fewer than 459 speeches were delivered for and 938 against the second Home Rule Bill; the Commons gave it over 210 hours of parliamentary time.[61] Carson was pre-eminent in opposition; but he was ably assisted by Kenny, who in a speech on 16th February 1893 asserted that his constituency "protested as strongly against the initial principle of Home Rule . . . as did Belfast, Londonderry, or any other part of Ulster".[62] He went on to say: "The loyal minority said, 'we represent the intelligence and the wealth of Ireland'". Gladstone had accused the Conservatives of trying no other policy but coercion; but Ireland had prospered since 1886, and the number of paupers in receipt of indoor and outdoor relief had decreased considerably. The measure attempted to conciliate two parties, one of which was known as the Gas and Water Party, and the other the Parnellite Party. Gladstone had "thrown a sop to the Nationalists of Ireland by giving the Lord Lieutenant a veto on the advice of the Irish Ministers, while to the Gas and Water Party he had urged that whilst there was undoubtedly this veto in Ireland, there was another veto in England". He omitted to say that he had retained the Irish members in the imperial parliament to prevent an English veto. Moreover, Mr Gladstone seemed to lack confidence in the legislative authority to be set up. He reserved the land question for the imperial parliament for three years and for six years the constabulary; and the judges were to remain within the imperial domain. As for safeguards for the minority, the proposed Legislative Council of forty-eight would not, he believed, contain more than four or five Unionists. The supremacy of the English parliament was, moreover, rendered a nullity by the presence of the Irish members. "If the veto was refused by the Lord Lieutenant on the advice of his Irish ministers in Dublin, the Irish members to the number of 80 or 81 would be in attendance at Westminster and put any ministry out of office that dared to apply the imperial veto when the Lord Lieutenant had refused to apply it in Ireland. The Bill was "really but a lever for further agitation in the Imperial Parliament".

In his next major speech on the Bill on 21st June, Kenny spoke to an amendment moved by David Plunket, afterwards Lord Rathmore, seeking to exclude Trinity College Dublin from the purview of the proposed Irish legislature. Redmond, speaking immediately before him as a "Catholic Nationalist" denied that Irish Catholics wished to destroy the college or that the Home Rule Bill would enable them to do so, to which Kenny replied that whereas Redmond had asked to be heard as a Catholic nationalist, he "asked the Committee to hear him as a Catholic Unionist who had graduated in the University of Dublin". He supported the amendment, "because he had been through Trinity College, and he knew how free that College was to every denomination at the present time, and on what a basis of perfect equality all the alumni stood, and had stood for years". Whilst he agreed with Redmond to the extent that it was unlikely that a future Irish parliament or people were likely to destroy or despoil Trinity College, Redmond "had not for one moment said that the Irish Parliament would not deal with it in some way or other". Gladstone had complained that the amendment proposed to remove the University of Dublin altogether from the control of the Irish parliament. But this was exactly what the premier had himself proposed in 1886 in respect of corporations incorporated by charter or Act of Parliament. "They were told that this Bill bristled with safeguards", he concluded, "and was saturated with supremacy. He ventured to say it was pervaded with distrust of the Irish Parliament from beginning to end . . . As a graduate of Trinity College, who did not want that ancient University touched or meddled with in any degree, he heartily supported the Amendment", which was, however, lost.[63]

On 12th July Kenny again spoke on a University subject, the proposal to abolish the University Members for Dublin, of whom Carson was one.

> The Chief Secretary had told them that this disfranchising proposal was inserted in the ninth clause because there was a monotony in the representation of Dublin University, the University always returning not only lawyers, but Tory lawyers. He would ask the right hon. Gentleman if, supposing there existed a University in Ireland called, say, the St Patrick's University, and returning Members of the Party to which the Chief Secretary belonged, he would have been as eager to disfranchise it as he was to disfranchise Dublin University. He ventured to think that what had induced the Government to insert this provision in their Bill was that it would deprive the Irish representation in Parliament of two Unionist Members. They had had to listen to a long string of sneers and reflections upon the distinguished men who had from time to time represented Dublin University in Parliament from the hon. Member for S. Donegal [J. G. S. MacNeill] who had shown not a little bias. But he would point out that the Dublin University constituency was unique in Ireland, inasmuch as it did not contain a single illiterate; and in that respect it contrasted favourably with the constituency of the hon. and learned Member for South Donegal which contained, he believed, a larger percentage of illiterates than any other Irish constituency.[64]

Literacy of a sort has spread since Kenny's day. Yet these arguments might well be advanced in defence of the University seats abolished in 1948. One may wonder whether Gladstone, in approving of this provision, had in mind his own ousting from the representation of Oxford University in 1865.[65]

In his final speech on the Home Rule Bill made on third reading on 31st August, Kenny pointed out that the measure was regarded, both by the nationalists and by certain members of the government itself, as lacking in finality. He complained that important changes, largely undiscussed, had been made to the Bill by the government since its introduction. One such was the so-called "in-and-out" clause governing the circumstances in which the Irish members of the imperial parliament would be able to speak and vote. This clause had been altered by the prime minister on his own motion, the night before the closure was to be applied. Nevertheless the Bill passed, as we have seen, only to be defeated by the Lords.

Apart from numerous interventions at question time, Kenny's other speeches during the 1892 to 1895 parliament concerned the County Councils (Ireland) Bill and the Municipal Franchise (Ireland) Bill.[66] The general election of 1895 found him strongly placed again to contest the St Stephen's Green constituency, and despite formidable opposition, this time from a single nationalist candidate, Count Plunkett, Kenny was once again placed at the head of the poll, with an increased majority. The Unionist vote improved from 2,893 to 3,661.[67] This result was all the more remarkable in that of the four Dublin city constituencies, only St Stephen's Green was contested. In the other the nationalists (all Parnellites) were elected unopposed.[68] The entire weight of local nationalist effort could therefore be concentrated on Kenny; but one factor in his favour was the success of his agent in persuading absent voters to return from holiday. Above all Kenny's personality shines out as in 1892 from the old newspaper reports of this election. Speaking in his support on 11th July David Plunket said that "it had been stated that some Protestants would not vote for Mr Kenny in St Stephen's Green Division. He was as strong a Protestant as they could wish and he was going to vote for Mr Kenny, and would ask these superfine Protestants what would have become of them if they had not had men like Mr Kenny to stand up for them?"[69]

The election was marked by trying personal attacks. At the declaration of the poll the *Irish Daily Independent* reported that there were "loud groans and cries of 'Orange Kenny' and 'Judge Kenny'", and the *Freeman's Journal* added that his speech was interrupted and the Count Plunkett and his namesake Dr Kenny, who had been elected unopposed, had to call for a fair hearing for him. Speaking immediately afterwards at Kingstown, Kenny attributed his success to the work of the Unionist Registration Association. However,

> it may be said that we are indebted to our opponents for some votes given for me . . . We may be indebted for a few, because I have seen it stated during the week that oil and water would sooner combine than Parnellite and M'Carthyite . . . I have been speaking in the open air, a thing which is very unpleasant,

particularly when it is raining upon you. I confronted today as ugly a meeting as ever I confronted in Green Street Courthouse [The Dublin Criminal Court] and I would not wish my worst enemy to have had the bad quarter of an hour that I had today. But despite all that we have won.[70]

The *Freeman's Journal* expressed its puzzlement at the result of the election, concluding tentatively that it was due to continued factionalism amongst the nationalists. "A well-founded rumour exists that a large body of Mr Redmond's own stalwarts voted for the coercionist for selfish reasons."[71] The *Independent* was, as might be expected, much more sure of itself. It roundly declared that "by an enormous expenditure of money in Registration, and by the manufacture of fictitious qualifications in this Division", the Unionist Party had increased their strength. "A vast proportion", it asserted, of Unionist electors, "had travelled from England", and "not a few" from the continent. Some anti-Parnellite nationalists had stayed away because of the candidature of Count Plunkett.[72] The charge of manufacturing votes was of course absurd, and no doubt the *Independent* knew it to be absurd. That some voters had travelled back from England and the continent was a tribute to the efficiency of Kenny's organization. There was nothing fraudulent or illegal about it. Indeed the paper was reduced to repeating its 1892 cry that Kenny "had nothing to recommend him except his greed for place".

The only way that Kenny could have avoided that particular charge was by refusing the offer shortly to be made to him to serve in Lord Salisbury's administration as Solicitor-General for Ireland, which was the post which Carson had held in the short-lived Conservative government of 1892. To refuse would have made him no friends among the nationalists, and would have rebuffed the party he was proud to serve. Kenny did not refuse, though under an Act of 1707 whose provisions were not repealed until 1919[73] it meant another contest. The appointment was duly announced on 22nd August.[74] This provoked a further howl from the *Independent*, which declared on 28th August that "when Mr Kenny stood last July he expressed great annoyance at being described as a placehunter. He is now a placeman, and in a few months more . . . he will be on the Bench . . . He is a mere bird of passage on the lookout for a comfortable nest for himself . . . and even Dublin Conservatives may well ask themselves why they should put themselves about to secure the success of a man whose candidature is thus more or less a piece of audacious cynicism". Nevertheless, "put themselves about" they did, and even the *Freeman's Journal* contented itself with observing on 24th August that "the Liberal Unionists have grabbed another prize". The newspaper was rewarded for its lukewarmness about Mahony, the Parnellite candidate, by the *Independent's* accusation of going "as far as it dared in support of the Unionist".[75] The latter paper descended to the depths of vituperation during the course of this by-election, and in a second leader on 30th August referred to Kenny as one of those "renegade Irishmen who are ready to bow the knee to our foreign rulers and to use the necks of their own countrymen as stepping stones to their own advancement". The following day he was described as "one of the bores of the House of Commons", and the editorial concluded with an attack on the Jews, an easy target for bigoted persons of all ages and countries, who "were reported to have helped to ensure the defeat of the Nationalist candidate at the previous two elections".

The invective over-reached itself and may have done as much to ensure Kenny's success with the fair-minded electorate of St Stephen's Green as did the superior organization of his campaign; but there was more substantial opposition. Redmond spoke in Mahony's favour on 30th August, describing Kenny, somewhat unconvincingly, as "an almost absolute and dismal failure" as a parliamentarian, and as "absolutely useless to his constituents and his party".[76] Kenny replied to the accusation of being a placeman at a meeting held on 30th August and reported in the *Irish Times*. He reminded the audience that Mahony had himself been a Land Commissioner, but had been dismissed, so that it ill became him to bring the charge. In the event, Kenny was returned with an increased majority in relation to the total poll.[77] Thus, as the *Irish Times* wrote after his death,

> on three successive occasions he attacked, and captured, what had aforetime been regarded as an impregnable nationalist stronghold. All of these electoral battles were fought with the utmost pluck and determination. Fearless of criticism, the Liberal-Unionist candidate carried all before him by sheer force of personality, and his triumph afforded extraordinary gratification to his friends and supporters on both sides of the channel. The atmosphere of the House of Commons was congenial to the new Solicitor-General. His marked abilities, strength of character and modesty of bearing were justly appreciated upon all sides.

On 29th December 1897 Kenny was appointed a Judge in the King's Bench Division of the High Court. He is described as "painstaking almost to a fault" and his charges to juries were always strictly impartial, as was attested by his political opponent T. M. Healy,[78] who described him as "an ornament to the Bench", The *Irish Times* referred to his "eminently dignified, while wholly unaffected manner, and his urbanity and courteous consideration for others". Made a Privy Councillor in 1902, Kenny became Chairman of the Irish Railway and Canal Commission in 1919.[79]

In sum, it may be said that he reflected Dublin society at its best. Had there been more Catholics like Kenny, is it possible that despite the shortcomings and blunders of successive British governments, the whole of Ireland might have been saved for the Union?

CHAPTER THIRTEEN

Land and Education

The commission appointed when Rosebery was premier to consider the financial relationships of England and Ireland issued its report in 1896. It was signed by eleven out of its thirteen members. The conclusion was that Ireland had borne too heavy a burden of taxation since the Union and that the tax-revenue, instead of being one eleventh that of Great Britain as it was, ought not to be more than a twentieth.[1] On 12th December a meeting at Cork called by the Lord Lieutenant and addressed by landlords, Unionists and nationalists in the presence both of Church of Ireland and of Catholic bishops endorsed the Report.[2] So did the Dublin City Council on 14th December. The *Annual Register* commented tartly:

> Both meetings assumed as certain that the true financial rule was not that an Irish peasant making £100 a year should pay the same as an English peasant making £100 a year, but that an Irish peasant should either pay considerably less . . . or receive back the difference.[3]

Other such meetings were held, for example at the Mansion House, Dublin, on 28th December, when both the Church of Ireland and the Catholic archbishops were present, together with at least one Catholic Unionist, Sir Percy Grace.[4] Next day Dunraven took the chair at a gathering at Limerick. Bishop O'Dwyer also spoke. The latter had been a vigorous opponent of the Plan of Campaign, but was now "quite on the Irish side, and expressed his impression that if the Unionist Government were not willing to pay back the over-taxation of the Irish people, Irish Unionists might find it necessary to withdraw their support from the Unionist Government. Indeed, it was a question whether union with England was not 'dear at any price' ".[5]

The signatories of the minority report were Sir Thomas Sutherland, Unionist M. P. for Greenock, and Sir David Barbour.[6] In their reading of history, although the Act of Union had made special provision for the separate financial treatment of Ireland, the fact remained that in 1817 the English and Irish national debts were amalgamated, in 1819 the tobacco duties equalized, and in 1824 the stamp duties were placed on an equal footing. In 1853 income tax was imposed on Ireland and in 1858 the spirit duties were equalized. Further, both national education and the police were in Ireland maintained out of exchequer money. But there were few people in Ireland, whether Unionist or not, who supported the minority view.[7]

The next year, 1897, was the queen's diamond jubilee. The *Annual Register* noted that except in Ulster there were few demonstrations of enthusiasm. This was in marked contrast to 1887.[8] On the other hand, the Duke and Duchess of York, afterwards King George V and Queen Mary, were warmly received in Ireland; and the idea of a permanent royal residence was revived. The cabinet approved, but the queen again refused to consent. Salisbury wrote from Hatfield to the Duke:

> The devotion to your person which you have inspired is not only a result gratifying to yourself . . . but it will have a most valuable effect upon public feeling in Ireland, and may do much to restore the loyalty which during the last half a century has been so much shaken in many districts.[9]

According to *The Times'* special correspondent "not during the Jubilee of 1887, nor during the Diamond Jubilee, nor in Wales when the Queen made her progress through the Principality . . . have I ever seen the entry of Royalty into a great city accompanied by greater demonstrations of loyalty or of a more cordial regard for the Royal Family". Sir Percy Grace, a prominent Catholic Unionist, was among those present to greet their Royal Highnesses, and Sir Gerald Dease, Chamberlain to the Lord Lieutenant and a Catholic, was among those who saw them off from Dublin.[10] At Killarney they were met by Lord Kenmare and his son Lord Castlerosse and even the ultra-nationalist Board of Guardians condescended to present an Address. The visit to Killarney was seen as particularly appropriate because one of the Duke's titles was Baron Killarney.[11] At Newton Stewart the brass bands, Orange and Catholic, united together to play "The Queen", and both the Catholic and the Church of Ireland bishops of Derry were present at Baronscourt together with many clergy, both Catholic and Protestant, including Cardinal Logue of Armagh and the Very Reverend Monsignor O'Hagan.[12] The *Cork Constitution* noted (7th September 1897) that only at Tralee did the governing body not present an Address of welcome, and even there the local people organized a remarkable demonstration of loyalty.

1898 saw the passage of an Irish Local Government Act and the appearance of the *Report of the Royal Commission on the Irish Land Acts* backed by Sir Edward Fry.[13] This was the centenary year of the 1798 rebellion, and in County Mayo William O'Brien launched the United Irish League on 23rd January.[14] This was intended to further by constitutional means the re-distribution of land to peasants for tillage as opposed to grazing, work which had been started by the officially sponsored Congested Districts Board, founded in 1891, but in practice its methods were not always constitutional.[15] Nevertheless it led the way towards a reunion of nationalist politicians, who had become split three ways since Parnell's fall. T. M. Healy and his followers, who numbered some twenty-five M. P.s in 1895, stood out against the new movement, and were supported by many of the Catholic clergy. Nevertheless they were strong only in a limited number of areas, and after the 1900 general election all except himself submitted to Redmond.[16]

More sensational news was the conversion of the second Lord Emly to nationalism of "an aggressive and exclusive type".[17] Standing for Limerick County Council, he undertook to represent labour. In the local government elections held in 1899 the nationalists swept the board except in the Six Counties. The Limerick Corporation, followed by a number of others, adopted a pro-Boer resolution; the Cork District Council went further, accusing England of "rapine, murder, pillage and other crimes".[18] The authorities took little notice, although several chairmen of district councils were removed from the Commission of the Peace and Lord Emly was deprived of the deputy lieutenancy of County Limerick.

In 1900 Queen Victoria made her first visit to Ireland for nearly forty years. It was quiet, and confined to drives around Dublin. The corporation refused to follow the discourteous precedent of the Prince of Wales's visit of 1885, and adopted an Address by thirty votes to twenty-two.[19] The ceremonial observed is described in the *Dublin Gazette* of 13th April 1900. Athlone Pursuivant appeared at an especially erected city gate at Leeson Street Bridge and formally demanded admission to the presence of the Lord Mayor. The Lord Mayor having directed the gate to be opened, Athlone, uncovering and bowing, said: "My Lord Mayor of Dublin, I seek admission to the City of Dublin for Her Most Gracious Majesty the Queen". The Lord Mayor replied:

> On behalf of the City of Dublin I desire to tender to the Queen
> a most hearty welcome to this Her Majesty's Ancient City, and

on the arrival of Her Majesty the City Gates shall be thrown open on the instant.[20]

The queen wrote in her journal that "the whole route from Kingstown to Dublin was much crowded, all the people cheering loudly. At the archway the old city keys, 12 in number and 600 years old, were presented, as was the city sword . . . Even the Nationalists in front of the City Hall seemed to forget their politics and cheered and waved their hats."[21] "Wherever I go", Her Majesty added on 16th April, "the people come out and cheer, and call out, 'God bless you'".

Lord Denbigh was in waiting, though it was not his turn for duty; and he stated later in the *Universe*[22] that he had been particularly commanded because, "being a Catholic, she wished me to go to Ireland in attendance". The queen, he added, as had been shown during her previous visits, was "most anxious to do all that she could to draw classes in Ireland together, and soften the religious bitterness between Catholics and Protestants". This gives the lie to those who, like the late Sir Shane Leslie, sought to propound the notion that the queen failed to visit Ireland for forty years because she disliked Ireland and feared her Irish subjects.[23] King Edward VII may have been more popular in certain quarters in Ireland; but the queen disapproved of his Ulster connexions; and if she had a bias, it was towards her loyal Roman Catholic subjects. This had been amply demonstrated during her previous visit a few months before the Prince Consort's death in 1861; and now again Her Majesty made strenuous efforts, despite failing health, to invite prominent Catholics to Viceregal Lodge and make them welcome. There was no visit to Belfast, and a scrupulous avoidance of any appeal to Orange sentiment. Sir Gerald and Lady Dease, Sir Richard Martin and Lord Morris, were among those invited to Viceregal Lodge; and before leaving, Her Majesty was presented with a model of the Cross of Cong by the wife of The O'Conor Don.[24] Cardinal Logue, too was invited. The Queen found him "very unassuming and pleasing in manner, though hardly in looks . . . He seemed to be on very good terms with our Archbishop of Armagh". And, at the conclusion of the visit:

I felt quite sorry that all was over, and that this eventful visit . . . had . . . come to an end . . . I can never forget the really wild enthusiasm and affectionate loyalty displayed by all in

Ireland, and shall ever retain a most grateful remembrance of this warm-hearted sympathetic people.[25]

Nevertheless the Catholic Church as such conspicuously abstained from presenting a loyal Address, though others were duly received from the Church of Ireland and from the Methodist and Presbyterian Churches, and Catholic Unionists such as Lord Morris and Sir Rowland Blennerhassett were prominent in presenting Addresses from such bodies as the Royal University and Queen's College, Cork. There were citizens' Addresses too from Cork, Limerick and Waterford.[26]

The queen's departure for Holyhead on 26th April marked the end of an era. There were few who could foresee that in a little over twenty years it would no longer be possible for the monarch to visit Dublin.

The general election returned eighty-one nationalists, nearly all of whom were willing to back the United Irish League, which stood for compulsory sale to tenants of their land-holdings. John Redmond, now titular leader of the re-united nationalists, supported O'Brien. Tim Healy alone stood out and was re-elected at Louth. His supporters however fared badly, and at a nationalist convention held in Dublin on 10th December both Healy and Carew were excluded from the party, despite protests from Tim Harrington and even from Redmond himself.

The Unionist Party too had its dissensions. Some members had little confidence in Gerald Balfour, now Irish Secretary, and felt that "the injustice and hardship previously inflicted by Gladstonian measures on the proprietary had been not only continued but enhanced".[27] Balfour had appointed T. P. Gill as Secretary to the new Agriculture and Industries Department. The latter had been connected with the plan of campaign and had made no public recantation and as Balfour himself, who sat for Central Leeds, could not easily be fought on his home ground, an Independent Unionist, Mr Elrington Ball, stood instead for South Dublin County against Horace Plunkett, Vice-President of the Agriculture and Industries Department. A nationalist was elected on the split vote. Unionist disunity also lost the party the St Stephen's Green division of Dublin City; one bright spot was Galway City where Martin Morris was returned.

Morris was the son of Lord Morris and Killanin, perhaps the most prominent Catholic Unionist of his day. His success was all the more remarkable in that in 1895 he had come third.[28] The Marquess of Hamilton, the Duke of Abercorn's son, recovered Derry City for Unionism. The Duke disapproved of the attack on Plunkett; and although no Unionist seats were lost in Ulster, two or more might have been gained had it not been for the split. Presbyterian Unionists in the north had a tendency to support the principle of universal compulsory purchase of land by or for the benefit of tenants, and T. W. Russell, re-elected for North Tyrone, was removed from the Local Government Board for advocating this policy. His followers are sometimes known as "Russellites".[29] A Captain Craig was to defeat a Russellite in the Down East division in 1906.

1901 showed signs of great growth in Irish industry, especially in the north. Record quantities of Irish butter and eggs were exported to Great Britain. Shipbuilding boomed, and Harland and Wolff's of Belfast stood first in the world for individual output.[30]

Prosperity notwithstanding, the United Irish League continued to extend its tentacles, and although there was little overt criminality, the government were criticized by some Unionists for allowing a system of intimidation to prevail. The new Chief Secretary, Wyndham, advised Unionists on 10th December to avoid giving advertisement to the League by using the language of exasperation and fulmination. The economic and social regeneration of the country should be their aim.

Wyndham's estimate that there were only forty branches of the League in the whole country was received with derision. Swift action was taken by the Government in the latter part of December against certain Irish M.P.s for participating in unlawful assemblies intended either to force farmers whose tenants had been evicted to give up their farms or to intimidate tenants on other estates into refusing to pay their rent. When some of these cases came up for appeal in February 1902, Chief Baron Palles, a Catholic, gave as his opinion that the action of the assemblies was illegal and void.[31] At the spring Assizes a number of judges, including Kenny at Carrick-on-Shannon, drew attention to the prevalence of boycotting and combinations interfering with personal liberty.

When the Irish Unionist Alliance held its Annual General Meeting on 10th April a number of speakers urged the Government to bring the Crimes Act of 1887 into operation, and this was done in nine counties and in the cities of Cork and Waterford. It had just been announced that King Edward would not be making his intended visit to Ireland. This decision was widely thought to have been influenced by an incident in the House of Commons in March after the Boers had routed a force under Lord Methuen near Tweebosch, wounding him in the thigh and taking him prisoner. When the relevant telegrams were read, there were cheers and laughter from some Nationalist Members.[32]

In the summer of 1902 there were evictions from the Frenchpark estate of Lord De Freyne in County Sligo. The question at issue was not that the tenants concerned were unable to pay, but that they felt aggrieved that their rents were higher compared with their neighbours' purchase instalments on the former estate of Lord Dillon, which were subsidized under a Government scheme administered by the Congested Districts Board. This Board had been set up in 1891, and its powers were exercised mainly in certain counties in the West (Donegal, Sligo, Leitrim, Roscommon, Mayo, Galway, Clare, Kerry and Cork), where more than twenty per cent of the population of a county lived in electoral divisions (the Irish equivalent of parishes in England) of which the total rateable value, divided by the number of inhabitants, gave a figure for each individual of less than thirty shillings.[33] These divisions could then be formed into congested district counties, in which the powers of the Board became exercisable. In 1896 these powers, which included the assistance of emigration and the development of agriculture and forestry, were extended so as to enable the Board to purchase land with government assistance and sell it to the tenants. These purchase instalments were thus not only lower than the rent which might be payable in adjoining areas, but they would also end altogether in a measurable period when the purchase was complete. A Landlord's Trust was formed to fight the intimidation of tenants and on 1st September 1902 the operation of the Crimes Act was extended to more than half of Ireland, including the city of Dublin. Wyndham lost popularity but check was given to the League excesses.[34]

Some small proprietors now moved for a conference with tenants in order to end the land war; but at the landowners' convention on 10th October 1902 an amendment against this proposal was carried by a substantial majority.

In November in the Tallow conspiracy case a tradesman in County Waterford obtained from a special jury in Dublin County a verdict of conspiracy against ten boycotters. Chief Baron Palles spoke out strongly against the conspirators; and when he was attacked in the *Freeman's Journal* Archbishop Walsh spoke up in defence of his co-religionist.[35]

Despite the disapproval of the landlords' convention, the proposed conference between landlords' and tenants' representatives was held on 20th December with Dunraven in the chair. The conference was a success and the next year an Irish Land Bill was introduced.[36]

Martin Morris is not known to have addressed the House on the subject of this Bill. He made his maiden speech on education.[37] He had, he explained, been educated in England at the school presided over by Newman, and was subsequently at Trinity College. He might have added that he had been called to the Bar both by the King's Inns, Dublin, and by Lincoln's Inn, London, and had at Trinity won the University Philosophical Society's Gold Medal. Before becoming Member for Galway he had acted as private secretary for his father. "I am", he declared, "the sole Unionist in the House of Commons out of three provinces of Ireland and I am the only Catholic Unionist in the House for Ireland. Practically speaking, Irish Catholic Unionists are unrepresented in the House of Commons, because, though a large, they are a scattered body, and at no place do they exist in sufficient numbers to return a representative to Parliament". "I think", he added,

> they have some claim upon the Government, and upon Members on this side of the House, because as in the past they have remained loyal, in spite of terrible laws and the loss of their position and property, to the faith of their country, so in recent years they have, in the face of an immense amount of undeserved unpopularity and loss of local influence remained loyal to the Throne and the Constitution.

On the University question, Morris took no issue with the nationalists. Trinity was, he said, despite its being opened to Catholics still "a Protestant institution". It was, moreover, "exotic and unnational".[38] The Royal University was "not a University at all"; merely an examining body. The Queen's Colleges were secular and there was no University for Catholics. "I consider, for my part, that the penal laws of Ireland may be said still to exist to a certain extent so long as you prevent Irish Catholics from having University education". Later in 1901 Morris took the lead in questioning Balfour on the composition of the Royal Commission on Irish University education, but by the beginning of the following session he was called up to the House of Lords on the death of his father.[39]

In 1908, as Lord Killanin, he spoke on the Second Reading of the Irish Universities Bill. Introducing it, Lord Crewe recapitulated the complex history of University education in Ireland.[40] The Queen's Colleges of Cork, Belfast and Galway, founded in 1845 to provide non-denominational education, were condemned by the Catholic hierarchy as "Godless" and there were only about 250 Catholics in the three of them.

The Catholic University started by Newman in the 1850s was a "private enterprise" institution, "never succeeded as a University, and it now only exists, so far as it can be said to exist at all, as an association of Roman Catholic colleges", including Maynooth. Nevertheless, under the Royal University scheme of 1879 which superseded the Queen's University of 1845, some fourteen Catholic University Fellows in Dublin were paid out of public funds whilst a similar number in the three "Godless colleges" received only a small addition to their existing stipend. This arrangement for a "secret subsidy" is widely believed to have been due to Disraeli.[41]

The Royal Commission of 1901 reported against the examining University system and its methods of indirect subsidy, and advocated instead the foundation of a wholly new College in Dublin.

In 1906 a fresh Commission was appointed which included Trinity within its purview and numbered Chief Baron Palles among its members. It recommended the establishment of a new college in Dublin, but its members were divided on whether or not Trinity should form part of it. In view of the known opposition of Trinity, the Government had decided to proceed without her. "We propose to form two Universities", said Lord Crewe, "one with its seat in Belfast, and the other with its seat in Dublin, consisting of a new College in Dublin and the old Queen's Colleges at Cork and . . . Galway".

Killanin began by saying that the question of Irish University education for Catholics had always interested him and for many years had seemed to him "far and away the most important question in connection with Irish matters". As a senator of the Royal University and a Commissioner of National Education in Ireland he welcomed the Bill. A small section of his own party had defeated Balfour's efforts to settle the question. "Many of us in Ireland felt that very much", not only because the grievance was a just one, but also because it was felt that "the duty of settling that question devolved especially on that Party in the State whose principal maxim and pledge was, in reference to Irish affairs, that the Imperial Parliament was willing and capable of dealing with any real Irish grievance, which is to my mind the only possible position for any feasible Unionist policy in Ireland".[42] "Many of us in Ireland", he added, "winced under what we felt was a true indictment, namely, that the treatment of this question by the official Unionist Party had furnished an unanswerable argument in favour of Home Rule, and had struck a heavier blow at the Union than it had ever received before". Now that the question was finally being settled it is almost too late. I say it is almost too late because, although it is impossible to exaggerate the injury that has already been done in Ireland by the neglect of this question, the whole of the higher and nobler life of three-quarters of the population of Ireland has been thwarted and stunted during that period. A bitterness has been created in the Catholic class in Ireland that did not exist and need not have existed.

At the same time Killanin regretted the absence of provision for residential quarters. Another Catholic speaker, Lord MacDonnell of Swinford, believed that a better way forward would have been to combine the Royal University with Trinity, or at least to associate a new Dublin College with it. Quoting from Newman, he too endorsed the principle of residence as being all-important.

Dr John Healy also championed a Catholic University, and had praised A. J. Balfour's intentions in this regard as long ago as 1890.[43] The privately-endowed Catholic University in Dublin had not been altogether a failure. In 1883, it was handed over to the Jesuits and under their auspices by 1894 had a better academic record even than Queen's College, Belfast. Dr Healy was not behindhand in commanding his flock to matriculate in the Royal University. At the silver jubilee celebration of the Catholic college he reminded his audience that the Royal was not merely an examining University, for its twenty-nine Fellows set a high standard. The total number of its candidates had increased from 1,500 to about 4,000; and it had pioneered female education by being the first to award degrees to women.

Healy had been a member of the first of the two Royal Commissions on Higher Education in Ireland. On St Patrick's Day 1903 he became Archbishop of Tuam, succeeding MacEvilly, who had himself succeeded McHale. MacEvilly, like Cardinal M'Cabe, had been opposed to the Land League from its inception, and was among those assailed in *The Nation* as a "Castle Bishop". Addressing the Mayo County Council Healy said, apropos of the Land Bill then before Parliament, "When I got an opportunity I told the landlords at their own tables, and I told statesmen themselves, that land reform on lines now about to take place was an essential, necessary and proper movement."[44] And at a banquet in the evening:

I hope, especially when the urgent question is settled, that we shall all learn to live together in Ireland as fellow-countrymen in a thorough spirit of Christian union, working for the common good. We have in the past suffered much from the spirit of exclusiveness and the spirit of ascendancy . . . We are seeking to destroy all these things . . . But let us take care that . . . we do not ourselves fall back into those courses that we so sharply reprehend in others." Home Rule "can never come until the land question is settled; and I believe it will never come, and I doubt whether it ought to come, except we strive to act on those principles of large and liberal toleration for all which I have just enunciated.

Healy's diagnosis of the essential problem was profound, simple and accurate. Emigration must be stopped, he said in another speech,[45] and "the most efficacious means of stopping the depletion of the life-blood of the population, and the most expeditious means, is to sub-divide those grass prairies [i.e. extensive areas of pasture land] and to place upon them men who are able and willing and anxious to till them. This was a question of life and death for the people of Ireland, especially in the West".

And, at Castlebar:

I should despair of my country in the future if I thought the new Ireland . . . was to be an Ireland for one Church or one class or one section of the people. There is room in our ancient land . . . for the Catholic and the Protestant; there is room for the rich as there is for the poor; there is room for the learned as there is for the simple-minded.

Healy then, despite "fairly advanced views on the land question, had never made any pretence of being a Home Ruler". Thus David Miller in his *Church, State and Nation in Ireland* (1973),[46] After some nationalists had refused to toast the king on an occasion in Sligo, Healy lectured an audience of school teachers on loyalty:

We, in the West of Ireland here, have always been genuine loyalists, in spite of much foolish talk; but the Orangemen of Belfast are not genuine loyalists at all: they only prate about loyalty to the King . . . Our forefathers were loyal to Charles I . . . because he was the King. They were loyal in their day to James II — unworthy as he was — because he was the King,

whilst the ancestors of those blatant loyalists sold their King —
a King of their own blood — and drove his children into exile.
We are loyal to King Edward, their descendant, because he is
King. We owe him an absolute and unconditional loyalty as
King *de jure* and *de facto* . . . I hope no Irish teacher or true
Irishman will ever fail to pay due honour to the toast of
Edward VII, who not only royally but personally deserves that
honour at the hands of every Irishman.[47]

Healy lived to witness and acclaim Redmond's plea to his countrymen in
1914 to rally to England's side. He was the last of a long line of Irish
Catholic prelates who valued the British connexion and who saw how
Irish aspirations, if strenuously furthered, could be met by a combination
of boldness and patience, within the four walls of the Union, to the
furtherance of Ireland's greatness as well as to Britain's.

CHAPTER FOURTEEN

The Third Home Rule Bill

King Edward VII paid three visits to Ireland as King, in 1903, 1904 and 1907. At the beginning of the reign, there was renewed talk of the Lord Lieutenancy being made non-political and granted either to the new Prince of Wales or to the Duke of Connaught. It was Lecky who convinced the cabinet that, since Lords Lieutenant were invariably unpopular, the proposal was unwise. In 1905 the king favoured the abolition of the office.

This proposal was not new. It had been mooted occasionally in the nineteeth century, when it was discovered in the years following the Union that the duties of the post had decreased and that it had lost most of its patronage. In 1823 Peel responded to a motion for abolition that a local executive in Ireland "was an essential and necessary check". The Home Office, to which it was proposed to transfer the viceroy's functions, was already overburdened, and if a separate Secretary of State for Ireland were appointed, "his absence from that country would be highly injurious, and yet it could not be avoided, for he must sit in parliament". The motion was negatived without a division.

Then in 1847 it was rumoured that Lord John Russell had decided on abolishing the post on the departure of Lord Bessborough. In 1850 Greville wrote categorically that the viceroyalty was to be abolished on 1st January 1851. Clarendon (by then viceroy) was to become "Secretary of State for Ireland". Russell's idea was that the queeen should come "about every other year" to stay in Dublin. But, as Lady Clarendon pointed out, the government's Bill as drafted made no provision for the proposed Secretary of State to reside in Ireland and contained no plan for a resident secretary at all.

Nonetheless, a motion for leave to introduce a Bill was moved by Lord John on 17th May 1850. Disraeli ridiculed it. Clarendon, he said, according to Russell, had been "the most successful governor that ever flourished"; but he was proposing to "take him away". The Duke of Wellington, in the Upper House (27th June 1850) was similarly opposed. Withdrawing the Lord Lieutenant would mean that the chief civil authorities would become the Lord Mayor of Dublin and other civic dignitaries who might be "very nice" people, but could not necessarily be depended upon in case of serious trouble. The Bill was quietly dropped.

Although in 1905 King Edward VII was in favour of abolishing the office, in March 1902, after a nationalist demonstration in the House of Commons, he commented to Lord Cadogan that:

> There is no disguising the fact that the state of affairs is far from satisfactory and can only be met by firmness on the part of the Executive, and that loyal and well-disposed Irishmen should be protected.[1]

It is not at all clear that the replacement of the viceroy by a member of the royal family who would reside in Ireland for a few weeks in the summer and entertain would have averted, for example, the events of 1916, which can be viewed as having been caused by the weakening of the viceroy's position rather than the fact of his existence; nonetheless a full-time viceroy who was also a member of the royal family might have been able to avert that particular rebellion.

The king's 1903 visit to Ireland took place in July and August. At Kingstown their Majesties were duly received by a deputation from what was now the Urban Council. The welcoming Address contained yet another plea for a permanent Royal residence. The king in his reply referred to the sadness caused by the recent death of Pope Leo, remembering as he did "the kindness with which His Holiness recently received me at Rome and the interest which he took in the welfare of my people", and entrusted Cardinal Logue with a message of condolence. The action was not lost upon his Irish Catholic subjects. A little girl said in George Wyndham's hearing: "I am so glad that we may love the King now because he spoke so nicely about the Pope".[2] Ross-of-Bladensburg, who had been passed over for the post of Under-Secretary in 1887, and was now the Chief Commissioner, Dublin Metropolitan Police, was on duty with Wyndham when the Urban Councils of Pembroke, Rathmines and Blackrock presented Addresses. The Dublin City Corporation refused to present an Address and there was no ceremony of the keys or presentation of the civic sword.

Eighty-two Addresses were presented in all. Charles Martin, D. L. and James Talbot Power, D. L., both Catholic Unionists, were among those who presented the Address from the Citizens' Committee formed on 16th June. Unlike, however, the Church of Ireland, the Methodists, the Baptists, the Jews and the Society of Friends the Catholics of Ireland as such presented no Address.[3] Nevertheless the Catholic Archbishop of Dublin, Dr Walsh, condescended to grace His Majesty's levée. This was his first appearance at the Castle. George Wyndham described how, in a drive to Trinity College, "every woman with a baby in Dublin was there to jump him up and down at the King . . . They do not say 'God Save the King' as we do . . . They lift their hands to heaven to imprecate 'God BLESS the King', as if adjuring the Deity to fulfil their most ardent desire and His most obvious duty".[4]

On 25th July, the royal couple left for Belfast, where a statue of Queen Victoria was unveiled. After Londonderry, a visit was paid to Connemara, the most westerly district of Galway. At Tully Cross Father Glynn called on "every man woman and child" to do what they could in the way of loyalty. Across the gate of the chapel was a blue banner with the inscription "Friend of our late Pope", opposite which Fr Glynn had drawn up the children of the neighbourhood. The royal car stopped, and the queen accepted a bouquet. As they drove out of sight the remark "What a nice homely gentleman" was heard.[5] At Galway itself, many Catholic priests were in the welcoming party and at Dereen House, Kerry, the parish priest of Lauraugh, James Beazley, read a welcoming Address, as did another, the Very Revd Canon M'Donnel at Castletown-Berehaven.[6] At Cork, the Lord Mayor attended in state when their Majesties arrived, and the reception was ecstatic. Both the Protestant and Catholic bishops were present at the opening of the Cork International exhibition.

The King's landing at Kingstown had coincided with the third reading in the House of Commons of George Wyndham's Land Purchase Bill. This Bill provided that landlords who chose to sell would be compensated by a sum which, invested in three or three and a half per cent gilt-edged stock, would yield them an income equal to their rents after deducting ten per cent, representing the former cost of collecting. As the annuities payable by the tenants were so calculated as to allow a reduction of some fifteen to twenty per cent on their former rents, there remained a gap which was filled by a subvention of twelve million pounds from the exchequer.[7] A weakness in the scheme was that the guarantee fund which was intended to meet any liability to former landlords arising out of a possible depreciation of government stock, was charged on the Irish ratepayers; an Act passed in 1909 transferred this liability to the general taxpayer of the United Kingdom as a whole, but, even so, the possible depreciation of stock was not fully provided for, and owners, in time, became reluctant to sell. Nevertheless, by 1920, 420,000 out of 470,000 holdings had been disposed of.[8]

In the spring of 1904 the king visited Ireland for a second time. For a second time, the corporation of Dublin refused to present an Address of welcome, unlike Waterford, Kilkenny and Kingstown. Sir Antony MacDonnell, Wyndham's Under-Secretary and a Catholic who was shortly to incur Unionist odium because of his flirtation with the "devolution" proposals of Lord Dunraven, wrote to Lord Knollys on 11th May that the visit "has produced a very good effect and that the manifestations of goodwill towards his Majesty were quite natural and spontaneous.".[9]

Dunraven's Irish Reform Association was, superficially at least, non-party. Its preliminary manifesto, issued in August, advocated "such effective control for Ireland of purely Irish affairs as might be compatible with maintenance of the legislative Union between Great Britain and Ireland and with the supremacy of the Imperial Parliament".[10] A devolution scheme was then published on 26th September, and as it had been drafted on Dublin Castle writing paper the impression was created that it had Wyndham's approval. It proposed the formation of an Irish Financial Council, part nominated, part elected, which would control some purely Irish expenditure, subject to supervision by the United Kingdom House of Commons. Irish business was to be delegated to a new statutory body to be created by parliament. Unionists came out strongly against the scheme, and Wyndham himself criticized it in *The Times*.[11] He made it clear, in an interview with MacDonnell on 1st October, that he disapproved of his behaviour. But this was not enough. Edward Carson, then Solicitor-General, threatened resignation, and the cabinet issued an *aide-mémoire* expressing its disapproval of Sir Antony's having aided Dunraven in drawing up his scheme. But a parliamentary storm was brewing, and in March 1905 Wyndham resigned.

The Liberal Party, which in 1906 had a landslide victory at the polls, obtained the appointment of Lord Aberdeen as Lord Lieutenant. The King thought him too pro-nationalist and not firm enough against lawlessness. There were rumours that the new viceroy's household was ultra-democratic; nothing more harmful emerged than meetings of the Haddo House club, where his Lordship would lecture on "Railways and Railway work", his valet would sing "Will o' the Wisp", whilst an odd-job man would recite "Caught in his own Trap". A more serious defect was that his relations with Augustine Birrell, the new Chief Secretary, were poor. And a story ran the rounds that when Lady Aberdeen asked

Lord Morris, at one of the viceregal receptions, if he would have the hardihood to tell her that there were no Home Rulers at all in that assemblage, he replied, "Oh, no; there's His Excellency and the waiters".[12] The earl was to become, on his retirement, "Marquess of Aberdeen and Tara". There was a chorus of protest, led by Georgiana, Viscountess Gormanston, who in *The Times* of 19th January recalled that the title of Tara had been held by at least two members of the Preston family. The *Irish Times* (18 January) was blunt in its reference to "a Scottish nobleman who does not own as much of the soil of Tara as in the saying of the County Meath peasantry, would sod a lark" and after further criticism in the Press, it was announced that the title would be "Aberdeen and Temair". All were satisfied except a lady who received from Lady Aberdeen a photograph of herself with a dog, signed "Ishbel Aberdeen and Temair". "I suppose Temair is the name of the dog", replied the lady gratefully.[12]

On 31st May 1907 Aberdeen wrote urging the king to visit Ireland again, and His Majesty accordingly arrived at Kingstown in the royal yacht on 10th July. He toured the Dublin International exhibition, but the warm welcome accorded him was marred by the discovery four days earlier that the State jewels of the Order of St Patrick had been missing from Dublin Castle since 11th June. An incensed monarch called for the suspension from office of Ulster King of Arms, Sir Arthur Vicars who, with his assistants was asked to resign. Vicars appealed, but a commission, which held its sittings in public on the king's insistence, found that he had not exercised due care and vigilance in his custody of the keys of the safe, and he was duly removed in January 1908.[13] The Dublin correspondent of *The Times* thought that the warmth of the King's welcome in 1907 was greater than that of the two previous visits.[14]

One of the consequences of the devolution crisis of 1904–5 was the formation of the Ulster Unionist Council.[15] Not that the now Liberal Government was in a hurry to bring about the Home Rule that featured prominently in the King's Speech of 1906. Its majority was substantial, and there was no need for hurry. But the "People's Budget" of 1909 was rejected by the Lords. Two general elections followed in quick succession in 1910. The first returned 275 Liberals and 273 Conservatives, and the result of the second was similarly close. More ominously, the 1911 Parliament Act made it impossible for Unionists to look to the House of Lords to throw out a Home Rule Bill passed by the Commons. It was time for drums to beat. The northerners lived up to Lord Randolph Churchill's prophecy of 1886: "Ulster will fight — Ulster will be right"; Edward Carson and James Craig headed a great meeting at Craigavon attended by an estimated hundred thousand people. On the following Monday, 25th September 1911, the Ulster Unionist Council, meeting in Belfast, resolved to set up a Provisional Government for Ulster in the event of any Home Rule Bill going through Parliament.[16]

On 10th October there was an anti-Home Rule meeting in Dublin, and on 9th April 1912 Southern Unionists took part in a demonstration at Belfast. Among them was Mr J. C. Coffey, a Catholic who

> knew he differed from the great majority of those present on religious matters, but he was pleased to be there that day with his Protestant friends in Belfast. He might tell them that in Dublin they had loyal supporters . . . He was certain that there were thousands of Catholics in Ireland who wished them well in their campaign against Home Rule.[17]

Their numbers even exceeded those who took part in the September meeting. The four-mile long procession to Craigavon numbered a hundred thousand men in addition to the estimated quarter of a million at the demonstration itself.

Two days later, the third Home Rule Bill was introduced into the imperial parliament. It proposed a subordinate Irish parliament in Dublin, to consist of two chambers, and to control all subjects not specifically reserved to Westminster; the number of such reserved matters was however so large as "virtually to reduce the Irish National Parliament to the status of a glorified County Council".[18] The official nationalists, both those, the majority, who followed Redmond and those who followed William O'Brien, accepted the Bill with varying degrees of enthusiasm; but Patrick Pearse, leader of Sinn Fein, declared that Redmond had "sold Ireland's birthright for a mess of pottage, and a dubious mess of pottage at that".[19] At the committee stage in June, a proposal was made to exclude four of the counties of Ulster from its scope; but both Asquith and Redmond successfully resisted it. Augustine Birrell, better known as a littérateur, but then Chief Secretary for Ireland, made light of forecasts of civil war if the Act were brought into operation; but the leader of the opposition, Bonar Law, declared at a great meeting at Blenheim on 27th July attended by some 120 Unionist M.P.s and forty peers, including the Duke of Norfolk, that the government were "a Revolutionary Committee which has seized upon despotic power by fraud". If an attempt were made to force Ulster loyalists to submit to Home Rule, he could "imagine no length of resistance to which Ulster can go in which I should not be prepared to support them, and in which, in my belief, they would not be supported by an overwhelming majority of the British people".

Unionist meetings were held throughout Southern Ireland. As Lord Midleton wrote in *The Times* of 21st October,

> Ulster holds the field, but the Unionists outside Ulster have rallied as they have never done before, and at all their meetings Catholics of substance and repute have risked obloquy and ignored threats to show their alarm at the prospect of being governed by Nationalists, even though they be co-religionists.

Midleton described large meetings held during the previous six months at Cork, Waterford, Tralee, Sligo, Limerick, Kilkenny and other places. Resolutions of vehement protest had been adopted; at Limerick speakers were mobbed, "while the Catholics who intended to speak at Kilkenny were marked down and threatened".

A public meeting of the Unionists of Munster in the Cork Assembly Rooms on 20th April 1912 was described by the local Unionist paper, the *Constitution*, as "undoubtedly the largest and most representative expression of Unionist opinions ever voiced in the city of Cork".[21] An overflow meeting had to be arranged at the last moment in order to accommodate an unexpected number of guests. Lord Bandon was in the chair and the speakers included the Duke of Devonshire and the fifth Earl of Kenmare. Kenmare said that there were Catholics in the south, and all through Ireland, "who are as bitterly opposed to the granting of Home Rule, as are the people of the North, and who feel as strongly as I do, the injustice of subjecting a large and prosperous portion of his Majesty's subjects . . . to a form of Government abhorrent to them, and in which they would have an inadequate representation". "When I look around", he added,

> and see the benefits that have come to Ireland of late years from her connection with England; how her credit is strengthened and wrapped up in the credit of England, and how her trade and commerce have steadily increased, it seems to me . . . a tragedy that this forward movement should be checked, if not permanently stopped, and that the solid benefits which have come to Ireland of late years should be given up to embark on

an untried and dangerous experiment. The tendency all the world over of the prosperous go-ahead nations is for closer union, and I feel sure that the only chance of peace and well-being for Ireland is in the maintenance of the union with Great Britain.

Galway too saw representatives of all creeds and classes at Unionist meetings[22], and at Dublin on 29th November the Catholic Denis Henry, afterwards to become the first Chief Justice of Northern Ireland, moved the resolution against Home Rule.

Henry was born in 1864, the sixth son of James Henry of Cahore, Draperstown, County Derry. Educated at Chesterfield and at Queen's College, Belfast, he was called to the Irish Bar in 1885, took silk in 1896, and was Senior Crown Counsel for County Westmeath.[23] In 1898 he became a Bencher of King's Inn, Dublin, and was also a deputy lieutenant for Derry. In 1906 he contested North Tyrone, making it clear in his election Address that he was not in favour of any legislation intended to weaken the Union, whether it took the form of Home Rule or of Devolution. He advocated purchase by tenants of their holdings, and even compulsory purchase should the Wyndham Act prove inadequate. Tariff Reform, Sunday closing of public houses and the payment of jurors were other planks in his platform.

Henry's Presbyterian opponent, W. H. Dodd, who held the ancient office of serjeant-at-law, also favoured the last point. He was at pains not to use the words "Home Rule", but to refer merely to "a just measure of Self-Government for Ireland to the fullest extent consistent with the supremacy of Parliament and the integrity of the United Kingdom".[24] Dodd, said Henry at Glentimon on 13th January 1906, was "going about the constituency with two thimbles and one pea . . . and whenever a nationalist came along he lifted the thimble and there was his Home Rule pea; but if a Unionist came along he did a shuffle and lifted the thimble and there was no Home Rule pea at all".[25] Devolution, he said at Ardstraw, was "only Home Rule on the three-years [i.e. instalment] system". As to education, he did not believe in a sectarian University. "Mixing was good for everyone, as it broadened their views and let them see that other people held as honest opinions as themselves". David Craig, introducing him at Ardstraw, declared that the candidate had always been a Unionist and his father before him. Another speaker said that by returning Henry they would show that they were not Orange bigots, as some supposed. The Liberals in 1891 had offered him a good appointment if he would join them, but he had refused the offer. Another speaker pointed out that Henry had attracted the support of Protestant clergymen and also of "Mr Dan Holland, whose name was one to conjure with in the Orangeism of Derry city".

At a meeting held at Newtownstewart on 8th January 1906 a Reverend Professor Henry of Magee College, and an old college friend of Serjeant Dodd, spoke with effect. The Professor conceded that Dodd was an amiable, able and accomplished lawyer and as a Nationalist M.P. would be bound to exercise a moderating influence. Nevertheless he felt bound to oppose him. In University education, "the Roman Catholic Church has equality, but demanded privileges. Mr Henry, Roman Catholic though he was . . . wanted 'strict justice all round and no pampering of pet sects'." Denis Henry was also officially supported by the Ardstraw Orange Lodge, in full conclave.[26]

At Baronscourt on 11th January, a number of Roman Catholics were present. Lord Frederick Hamilton paid Henry eloquent tribute. "There was no sailing under false colours with him. As a true Irishman, he had the good of Ireland at heart." It was a bitter disappointment when the declaration showed 2,966 votes for Serjeant Dodd and 2,957 for Denis Henry. Yet the latter had reduced the two previous majorities against the Unionist candidate from eighty-eight and fifty-five to only nine. "You have today shown conclusively that the North of Ireland is as tolerant as any other part of the United Kingdom".[27]

In 1907 Serjeant Dodd's elevation to the Bench brought on a by-election. Henry stood again against Redmond Barry, Liberal Solicitor-General for Ireland, and a co-religionist. Like Dodd before him, Barry was careful not to mention Home Rule in terms, referring merely to the "concession to Ireland of the full power to manage Irish affairs, consistently with the supremacy of the Imperial Parliament".[28] He was in favour of compulsory purchase if necessary and of the restoration of evicted tenants. On the 6th March Henry was met in the Grain Market at Strabane by mingled cheers and hisses. A strident female voice cried: "Away and get a good Presbyterian wife" (he was a bachelor). "What are you going to do for Ireland?" ejaculated another interrupter. "I am going to try and keep the disorderly elements in subjection", rejoined Henry, whereupon the crowd, "scenting a personal allusion", became more disorderly than ever. However, the Orange Lodges gave Henry unanimous support, and on 8th March 1907 the Ulster Unionist Council in Belfast expressed its confidence in him as "a most faithful and exceptionally able defender of Unionist policy".[29]

Barry's majority was only seven (3,013 to 3,006) in the heaviest poll ever recorded in North Tyrone. It was a moral victory for the disappointed Unionist candidate. The nationalist *Ulster Herald*, throughout the campaign his bitter opponent, gave the headline "Tyrone Unionists routed", whereas the previous year it had been nearer the mark with "Neck-to-neck contest decided".[30] In fact, on a higher poll, the result was more "neck-to-neck" than that of 1906. The Unionists of Tyrone showed Henry their gratitude at a dinner given at the Guildhall, Derry on 28th March 1907. The Marquess of Hamilton said that "the Roman Catholic gentry, like their friend Mr Henry, were prepared to see fair play done their Protestant fellow-countrymen" and that "the Protestants of the North were not the narrow-minded bigots their opponents would make them out to be but they were proud and glad that they had a Roman Catholic like Mr Henry to stand by them and fight their battles".[31]

On 13th April 1907 at an endearing ceremony presided over by the Duchess of Abercorn, the Unionist ladies of North Tyrone presented Henry with pieces of plate, for which there had been 2,635 subscribers. Acknowledging the presentation, Henry admitted that defeat had been bitter, but "when the first lady in Ulster came . . . at great personal inconvenience" he regarded it as a compliment, not only to himself, but to the loyal women of North Tyrone.[32]

In 1912 he spoke in Dublin in graver vein, of the greatest crisis which had been confronted by any of them, "aye, the oldest of them". In the thirty years since he came to Dublin, no Unionist had held public office under the corporation. This was a bad augury for a future Home Rule parliament. The loyal minority would be subject to a combination of "metropolitan misfits and provincial pirates". The loyalists' fellow-citizens, he hoped, "would decline to hand them over to a party of disorder and a party of disloyalists". They protested against a system by which the English government proposed to become tax gatherers for the United Irish League, without giving to Unionists that protection for lives and property which they had a right to expect.[33]

Meanwhile in Belfast and throughout Ulster, the Solemn Covenant, reminiscent of the Solemn League and Covenant of 1643, whereby Scottish Presbyterians bound themselves to aid Cromwell, and of the earlier Covenants of 1557 and 1581, was signed. This new covenant, which bound its signatories to use "all means which may be found necessary to defeat the present conspiracy to set up a Home Rule Parliament in Ireland" secured the adhesion of nearly half a million people in the weeks following 28th September 1912.[34] Augustine Birrell might scoff, but in January 1913 the Ulster Unionist Council decided that all the loyalists who had already been drilling secretly would be formed into a single Ulster Volunteer Force, to be composed of 100,000 men who had already signed the Covenant.[35] Loyalists drilled too on the mainland. On 27th March 1913 the formation of a British League for the Support of Ulster and the Union was announced. By November it had enrolled over 10,000 men, some of them Catholics. The latter were on parade in Chelsea in March 1914.[36]

The House of Lords twice rejected the Home Rule Bill. Martin Morris, second Lord Killanin, spoke against it on 29th January 1913. Those who argued, he said, that Home Rule was objectionable because it would lead to the setting up of a Roman Catholic parliament on College Green were playing into the hands of their opponents or, as we might say today, "kicking own goals". They seemed to be opposing the Bill, not because they did not want Home Rule, but because they did not want Ireland to be ruled by Catholics. "I resent, as strongly as I can, and I deplore that way of arguing on this question . . . I think it does great harm . . . because Catholic Unionists in Ireland have openly ceased to be Unionists on account of such attacks made on Roman Catholicism".[37] After citing the names of Parnell, Grattan, John Mitchel, Thomas Davis, Wolfe Tone, Robert Emmet and Smith O'Brien, prominent nationalist Protestants, he added that "if the noble Lord wants a great Nationalist leader of the Irish people who, besides being a leader of Nationalism was loyal to the English connection and to the English Throne, and avowedly so, he must go to the few Catholic leaders of the Irish people — he must go for instance to O'Connell". As for Ulster: "Even if every Orangeman were a Nationalist, I would still have grave doubts about the necessity or the wisdom of the policy of Home Rule". He was not against Home Rule because Irishmen were *au fond* disloyal — they were not. Nor was he against it because Irishmen were unable to govern — for experience of the operation of local government institutions had shown that the contrary was the case. He was against Home Rule partly at least because he had never seen any scheme of it proposed except on terms disadvantageous to Ireland, and the present scheme was no exception. Over the past twenty-five to thirty years, "the Imperial Parliament had been capable and willing to do everything for Ireland that Ireland could do for herself, and in many very important respects able to do so better than an Irish Parliament could". Taking the example of education, agriculture and the institution of old age pensions, Killanin averred that "in the whole of Europe and America there is not a University founded on such a democratic basis as the National University of Ireland. Nor is there a Department of Agriculture founded on such a democratic basis". During the previous generation, the imperial parliament had "steadily removed all grounds for discontent, and all causes of injustice in Ireland".

Criticizing the Bill itself, Killanin complained that it reduced Irish representation in the imperial parliament from over a hundred to forty-three members, whilst still retaining important land, trade and taxation questions in imperial hands. "One of the 'asides' which I hear or overhear being whispered in this country" was that the Bill was a device to get rid of the Irish members. Secondly, it was being pilloried as a device for England to escape her just debts to Ireland by claiming that the Irish exchequer owed the English money, when on a long-term view the opposite was the case.

Under the Parliament Act a Bill passed in three successive sessions by the House of Commons would become law despite the opposition of the Upper House. The Lords could not therefore veto the Bill after 1914. Home Rule could thus only be defeated by some disobedience to the will of parliament. Here was a grave constitutional dilemma for loyal servants of the king. By the end of 1913 the Ulster Volunteer Force had over 90,000 part-time volunteers, with mobilization plans which included the use of motor cars, motor cycles, and even a nursing corps. Arms had at first been lacking, to some extent as a matter of deliberate choice; but in the course of the year Major Frederick Crawford and his confederates arranged for the importation from England into Ulster of several thousand rifles, six machine guns and a quantity of ammunition.[38] Thus far the importation was not, strictly speaking illegal, for in the heady days of 1907, when the egregious Birrell had said that "Ireland is at this moment in a more peaceful condition than she has been in for the last six hundred years", the Peace Preservation (Ireland) Act of 1881 had been allowed to lapse.[39]

In this menacing situation the Protestant Dean of Chester wrote to the Dublin *Daily Express* (17th October 1913):

> Neither Lord Ribblesdale nor the average elector takes into consideration that the people of Ireland are sharply divided, not merely between Protestants and Romanists, between those who are loyal to the Crown and those who hate everything English, but also between Churchpeople and Presbyterians, and between

educated Romanists and the rabble who to a man support Home Rule avowedly because they are told and believe that they will get a house and a bit of land for nothing, while the educated who have some stake in the land or in commerce dread the thought of Home Rule. It is appalling to think of the loyalists who are scattered through the South and West . . . To adopt a phrase from one letter — "Ulster may be able to defend themselves, but we, isolated as we are, wait in mute despair either to be driven from our homes or to be shot if we stay".

The Duke of Norfolk spoke at Norwich on 12th November on the same theme:

We know that an effort is being made to hand over the destinies of Ireland to those who have never made it any secret that they abhor the connection with Great Britain. We know, moreover, that owing to the action of the Government, those who have always been supporters of the connection . . . now find themselves very much at the mercy of those who have always been opposed . . . I think you will feel that this is an act of gross betrayal and one against which we ought to protest most strongly.

Religious feelings, the Duke said, were being aroused on both sides; and in Ulster at least the Catholics had quite as much cause for complaint as the Protestants. A great deal of the religious bigotry in Ulster rested on panic and sprang from a deep and widespread ignorance; nonetheless, the loyal population of the province were entitled "to look with dread to what may take place".[40]

Catholic Unionists, among them Lord Kenmare, John Blake Powell, Frank Martin, Sir George Roche and Denis Henry were active in the south, wrote the Irish Alliance's Secretary, R. J. Herbert Shaw, to the duke on 13th November.[41] There was a demonstration in Dublin on 28th November at which a letter from the duke was read out. Frank Martin seconded a resolution of thanks to Bonar Law and Carson, and Sir George Roche moved another for Sir Maurice Dockerell to take the chair at the Winter Gardens. Many Roman Catholics signed the protest of southern Irish businessmen against Home Rule.

On 25th November 1913 the Irish National Volunteers were formed as a Nationalist riposte to the Ulster Volunteer Force. The inaugural meeting was attended by delegates from Sinn Fein, the Gaelic Athletic Association, the Gaelic League, the Irish Republican Brotherhood, the Ancient Order of Hibernians (the nationalist counterpart to the Orange Order), and the United Irish League. More sinister forces were also at work. In August a damaging transport strike had begun in Dublin under the leadership of James Larkin. Larkin was arrested on 28th August, but released on bail. The next evening he declared to some 10,000 people in Beresford Place that he was going to burn the king's proclamation: "people make Kings", he added, and "people can unmake them". Rioting began the next day and on the Sunday, after Larkin had been re-arrested at the Imperial Hotel, some 200 policemen were injured by the mob; an event which, like a number of others in Irish, Russian and English history has become known as "Bloody Sunday".[42] William Kenny, now a judge, wrote to the Duke of Norfolk on 16th November that "Between the apprehension of Home Rule and Larkinism this country will soon be a good one 'to live out of' ".[43]

In England there were sympathetic strikes, leading to a "sympathetic lock-out".[44] The strike collapsed early in 1914, but during the previous autumn Larkin had begun drilling and organizing a "citizen army" which was to play a leading role at Easter 1916.

To counter this disorder the government issued two proclamations on 5th December 1913, the first under section 43 of the Customs Consolidation Act of 1876, the second under section 8 of the Customs and Inland Revenue Act of 1879. The former purported to prohibit importation of arms into Ireland, the second dealt similarly with coastwise traffic. But there was a snag. Three days later, on 8th December, "A Barrister-at-law" in the columns of the Dublin *Daily Express*, a Protestant, hard-line paper, corresponding roughly to the London *Morning Post*, questioned the legal validity of the proclamations, principally on the ground that the Customs Consolidation Act was intended to refer, and did explicitly refer, to the whole of the United Kingdom, and that consequently the banning of the importation of arms into only part of it could not be valid. Even if valid, it could be, according to the writer, lawfully evaded, since there was nothing to stop, on the face of it, a preliminary importation into England or Scotland. A case was then brought at Belfast Assizes by a firm of gunsmiths and, at first instance, the court found in favour of the litigants. An appeal by the government to the Dublin Court of King's Bench was sustained by a majority of two to one (William Kenny dissenting). Judgement was not however delivered until June 1914[45], so a considerable interval elapsed during which it might reasonably be argued that the importation of arms into Ireland remained legal pending the decision of a higher court.

In January 1914 Carson gave his consent to Crawford's plan to import a large quantity of arms and ammunition from Hamburg to Larne and other places in an operation which subsequently became known as the "Larne gun-running". But he was well aware that he might be arrested, and said to Crawford: "I'll see you through this business if I should have to go to prison for it".[46] Such feelings were widespread in England. The signature of the composer Sir Edward Elgar, a Catholic, was obtained for a letter of support for Ulster. *The Times* of 3rd March 1914 publicized a declaration drafted in remarkably similar terms to the Ulster covenant of 1912. The signatories declared that they would feel themselves justified in taking or supporting "any action" to prevent the Home Rule Bill being put into operation, and "more particularly to prevent the armed forces of the Crown being used to deprive the people of Ulster of their rights as citizens of the United Kingdom".[47] Elgar was also prepared to back his convictions with cash.[48] Lord Lovat was another Catholic who gave his support, and within a few days the declaration had attracted more than a million supporters.[49]

The government were now seriously alarmed. On 14th March Winston Churchill who had in January 1912 been prevented by Ulster Unionists from speaking at the Ulster Hall, Belfast, declared that these "grave matters" must be put to the proof and Seely, Secretary of State for War, drafted a letter to the Irish General Officer Commanding-in-Chief, Sir Arthur Paget, informing him of reports that certain "evil-disposed persons" might attempt to steal arms and ammunition from military stores. Paget replied that all was well, but that he was taking certain further precautions. He was then recalled for further consultation, and orders were given to reinforce the garrisons at Enniskillen, Carrickfergus, Armagh and Omagh. On 19th March the Third Battle Squadron sailed from somewhere off the coast of Spain to the Isle of Arran, only a few miles from Belfast. Paget did not like what appeared to be a panic attempt to overawe Ulster. He asked for his orders to be put in writing; and he went further. He asked for, and obtained, permission from Seely and from Sir John French, then Chief of the Imperial General Staff, to exempt officers domiciled in northern Ireland from playing any part in any operation which might be conducted there.

On 20th March 1914 Paget conferred with his officers in Dublin. A show of force was planned for the next day to overawe the Ulster Volunteers.[50] But Paget explained his orders so confusedly to his senior staff that fifty-seven cavalry officers, led by Brigadier Hubert Gough, decided that they would prefer to resign their commissions if ordered north. Gough explained afterwards that he had "never refused to obey orders. On the contrary, I obeyed them. I was ordered to make a decision, namely to leave the Army or to undertake active operations against Ulster . . . As I was given a choice, I accepted and chose the first alternative".[51] Which did not prevent the choice of the Curragh officers being widely described as a "mutiny". The operation was abandoned, and during the night of 24th–25th April some 35,000 rifles and over three million rounds of ammunition were landed for the Ulster Volunteers at Larne, Bangor and Donaghadee.[52] Carson and Craig expected arrest, which was seriously considered by the government. John Redmond was generally believed to have prevented this, and on 27th July he informed the Commons that "we thought it would have been a futile and an exasperating and a useless proceeding to enter upon a series of prosecutions in connection with that transaction".[53]

Catholic Unionists continued active. We have already mentioned the meeting in Dublin on 28th November 1913, which was described in *The Times* as "perhaps the most impressive and significant demonstration of Irish Unionists which has ever been held South of the Boyne".[54] At this meeting Frank Martin, one of the largest Roman Catholic employers in Dublin, seconded the resolution moved by Lord Iveagh to thank Bonar Law and Carson. In May 1914 a draft "Statement of British Catholic Unionists on Home Rule" was sent to the Duke of Norfolk. This pointed out that the Irish agitation since 1879 had been based largely on revolutionary principles condemned by the Holy See, and that the Irish ecclesiastical authorities had "failed to cope" with these revolutionary tendencies.[55] In a speech delivered at Leeds on 13th June the duke said that "we especially wish to protest against the whole possibility of the armed forces of the Crown being used to force the loyalists of Ireland out of the British Empire to which they are proud and happy to belong . . . We are determined to support the men of Ulster".[56] In the same month, Michael M'Cann, of Newtownforbes, County Longford, was selected for commendation by the secretary of the Irish Unionist Alliance. This Catholic farmer and Longford branch representative on the alliance's general council had often entertained at his house visitors from the mainland who were invited to see for themselves nationalist incompetence and intimidation. M'Cann was "severely boycotted" for his pains.[57]

It was now the turn of the Irish National Volunteers to engage in gun-running. On the morning of Sunday 26th July its Dublin contingent of about a thousand marched to Howth, some nine miles from the capital, where a yacht berthed, loaded with arms. Every one of them received a rifle, and the few police present were forcibly prevented from interfering. The volunteers then began to march back to Dublin. Meanwhile, in the absence of the Chief Commissioner, the noted Catholic Unionist Sir John Ross-of-Bladensburg, the Commissioner, Mr W. V. Harrel, was alerted. The proclamations were unequivocally in force, and there could therefore be no legal justification for the volunteers' exploit. Both as a magistrate and as a policeman, Harrel felt he had to act. But what was to be done?

Harrel's action was subsequently criticized, but in the after-light it can be seen that he had no alternative. He consulted the Under-Secretary, Sir James Dougherty, at the Castle, who asked him whether his police were armed. He understood the conversation to imply that he should take some action, and so he attempted to secure armed police to supplement the three tramloads of unarmed Dublin Metropolitan Police which he decided to send. This proved to be impossible in the time available, and there was accordingly no recourse but to the military.[58] Having called in the King's Own Scottish Borderers, and added a small force of the D.M.P., Harrel proceeded along the road to Howth.

At Clontarf they found the volunteers blocking both the main roads to Dublin. Harrel parleyed with the leaders; and upon their refusing to order their followers to give up their arms, he ordered his policemen to disarm them. There was a scuffle, and only nineteen rifles were captured. The remaining volunteers dispersed.

Marching back to Dublin, the troops were pelted with stones and other missiles. They did not retaliate until they had reached the corner of Liffey Street and Bachelor's Walk, by which time about a quarter of their number had been badly injured. Major Haig, who had taken command, ordered thirty of the K.O.S.B. to line the road with loaded rifles. Owing to a misunderstanding, twenty-one of them opened fire without being given the order to do so, killing three people and seriously wounding thirty-eight others. Such was the "Bachelor's Walk massacre" of nationalist legend. A commission of inquiry decided that the soldiers were not justified in firing, but failed to reach any conclusion on the question of whether or not the order to fire had been given.[59]

By dinner-time on the Sunday Augustine Birrell, the Irish Secretary, had become aware in London of what was happening. He telegraphed Dougherty, the Under-Secretary, asking first, whether the police had requisitioned the military entirely on their own initiative and if so, why; and secondly, why the military had fired on the crowd and moreover why were there no police with the military on the return journey. According to Birrell, Harrel's telegraphic reply was received on Monday morning. He had requisitioned the military entirely on his own responsibility. Birrell, after obtaining the Prime Minister's concurrence, suspended Harrel.

Meanwhile the latter had prepared a detailed report on Sunday's proceedings. This with a covering minute by Ross (who had now returned to duty) was sent to Dougherty on the Monday morning for onward transmission to London. According to Birrell, Ross's minute was not telegraphed to him until 6 p.m., some three hours after Harrel had been informed that he was suspended. So the suspension was somewhat premature, to say the least. In a letter to Birrell some three weeks later Ross pointed out that

> a suspension is a step taken against an officer when an offence of gravity is alleged against him, which is distinctly stated, and when there is prima-facie evidence that he is guilty of it. No last-joined Constable could be suspended unless he be charged with a clear offence ; . . and yet a contrary course was adopted in respect to Mr Harrel, who occupied the responsible post of Assistant Commissioner.[60]

Why had he been suspended? The charges against him were not at that date known.

> I might perhaps gather from your letter of the 17th instant that he was suspended because he felt it necessary to exercise his legal powers as a Magistrate to call out the military; but that could not be the reason, for the Commissioners, as Justices appointed for the preservation of public peace, have frequently exercised this power without question. Nor could it be because the Police had not been sent to escort the military back to their Barracks, for this has never been done in Dublin, and the unhappy riot that unfortunately provoked the soldiers to fire was wholly unexpected and was an entirely new feature in the relations between the military and the people of Dublin.

Ross decided to resign because he felt that the order to suspend Harrel was an act of injustice. Even if he were vindicated, he could never again resume his place in the department to which he belonged. His career was broken without even a preliminary investigation. "A great and undeserved wrong has been done to a highly meritorious and most efficient servant of the Crown, whose only desire was to carry out the wishes of the Government in an emergency when immediate action was necessary".

Ross's correspondence with Birrell was occasioned by the fact that in his statement to the House of Commons on the Monday evening Birrell had taken it for granted that Ross disapproved of his subordinate's action. Ross's minute of Monday morning, received at 6 p.m., should have made it clear that this was incorrect, but Birrell repeatedly stated in correspondence that this was not the impression that had been conveyed. It was in fact only at 8.29 p.m., half an hour before Birrell took part in the debate, that the Chief Secretary wired Ross asking him whether Harrel had consulted him and whether he approved of his action. Birrell could hardly have expected a reply before rising to speak. He learned afterwards that Ross's resignation had been tendered. The whole episode, the latter wrote subsequently to Balfour, "does not I think exhibit much sagacity, capacity for rule, nor even good feeling on the part of those who at this critical moment, have Ireland in their charge".

In a letter of 21st August 1914 Birrell asked Ross to wait until the report of the Royal Commission into the affair was published. In Ross's view, however, justice could not be expected from the commission. Two of its members were closely associated with the government and Lord Shaw was a friend of Sir James Dougherty. Shaw indeed seemed to be leading witnesses and suppressing evidence favourable to Harrel. The *Irish Times* (2nd October 1914) commented that Sir John Ross's evidence was not taken at all, because Harrel's friends feared that it might put the authorities in such a bad light that they might be tempted to inflict further injustice upon him. Dougherty was not cross-examined, and his failure to respond to a second telephone call by Harrel for three crucial hours was thus not inquired into. He knew at 2.35 p.m. on the Sunday that the volunteers had already left Howth for Dublin. But, instead of getting in touch with Harrel, he sent for the Lord Chancellor of Ireland and drew up a minute dissociating the executive from Harrel's action. This minute, with its almost ludicrously impossible direction that forcible disarmament should not be attempted but that the names of the men should be taken and the destination of the arms investigated, did not reach Harrel until 5.45 p.m. Yet a written message received before 3 p.m. would have averted the conflict. The report of the commission, upholding as it did Harrel's suspension and criticising the conduct both of police and military as being "tainted by fundemental illegality", strengthened the hands of those who were already planning rebellion.

Meanwhile the Home Rule Bill passed the Commons for a third time on 25th May. On 1st July a Government of Ireland (Amendment) Bill was introduced into the House of Lords. Next day Lord Denbigh spoke as "one of a small band of British Catholic Unionists".[61] Much irritation had, he believed, been caused by the "extreme people in the Orange Party"; but although he detested "the practices of these extremists in the North of Ireland", he sympathized "with their desire to remain under the British flag". The press, he said, was taunting Catholic Unionists for their allegiance and asking how they could associate themselves with such extreme utterances. His reply was that there were Protestant Unionists who detested such utterances as much as he did. He was a Unionist, "not because I do not sympathize with the Catholics of Ireland", but because he believed that a Home Rule parliament "could only have a weakening effect upon the position of Great Britain and the British Empire in the face of the world, and because I cannot . . . see how Ireland or England is going to benefit from a Home Rule Parliament".

The Amending Bill provided for exclusion by county option and for a six-year time limit. Lord Killanin, on 6th July, refused to support it. Partition was, he said, one of the worst solutions and would "accentuate every cleavage in Irish society".[62] The government should either drop the Bill or go to the country. In view of their appeals to him he would not however vote against it. The Bill was duly given a second reading and on 8th July went into Committee. There Killanin again spoke, this time against a time-limit for the exclusion of Ulster. He believed that to enact a temporary exclusion would be to harden opposition in Ulster against an all-Ireland solution.[63] The six-year clause was voted down, with Lords Fingall, Gormanston, Killanin and Kenmare (all Catholics) in the majority.

Lord MacDonnell of Swinford thereupon proposed to set up an autonomous Ulster with an Ulster Council subordinate to the Irish parliament in Dublin. This was voted down by 196 votes to 20. Catholic Unionists like the Duke of Norfolk, Lord Denbigh and Lord Kenmare were in the majority, but Lord Fingall voted in favour of the clause. An amendment was then voted on which excluded the whole of Ulster indefinitely, and this was agreed to by 138 votes to 39. Lord Fingall again found himself in the minority; unlike other Catholic Unionists such as Lords Bellew and Kenmare. MacDonnell's warning that Counties Donegal, Cavan and Monaghan were predominantly Nationalist was ignored, though Lord Lovat, another Catholic peer, later referred to it.[64]

On 9th July 1914 Lord Halsbury moved an amendment re-instating appeal to the House of Lords from all the Irish courts. This was supported by virtually all Catholic Unionist peers; and on 14th July Lord Dunraven proposed that a constitutional commission be set up if the Act were suspended for any reason. Killanin concurred.[65] He complained that there was still insufficient information; and that the Amendment Bill had made the entire Home Rule scheme "hateful to Ireland". Unlike that of the then government, Unionist policy was one of "national reparation" and by the bringing together of all parties there was a chance of reaching settlement.

The idea of a constitutional commission or conference was already in the air and on 1st May King George V had approached the Speaker and asked if he would be willing to preside over such a body. Three days after the House of Lords debate, Asquith wrote to His Majesty that, now that the amending Bill was to be brought before the Commons, he could see no way of avoiding a debate which would "accentuate and . . . emphasize differences . . . and . . . open the way to violent and regrettable action". He had no real confidence that the proposed conference would reach a solution, "but it will certainly postpone and may avert dangerous and possibly irreparable action".[66]

The Buckingham Palace Conference lasted for only three days. It was opened on 21st July in the Forty-Four Room (so named because of its occupation in 1844 by the Emperor Nicholas I of Russia) with a speech by the king. Redmond and Dillon, Carson and Craig, Asquith and Lloyd George, Bonar Law and Lansdowne were the participants, with Mr Speaker Lowther in the chair. The discussion centred on provisions for the exclusion of various Ulster counties, principally Fermanagh and Tyrone. Lowther proposed that the two latter should be included either in the North or the South, and that their inhabitants should be asked to make a final decision by plebiscite in three to five years. Lord MacDonnell made a similar proposal by letter; but Carson, according to Lowther's account, immediately became suspicious and rejected it. The conference broke up without agreement. On 24th July, while waiting in an anteroom to say farewell to the king, Lowther picked up a copy of *The Times*, to read "with astonishment and horror" the terms of the Austrian ultimatum to Serbia.[67]

On 30th July Asquith announced the postponement of the second reading of the Amendment Bill, which was to have come before the Commons on the following day. Nonetheless on 18th September 1914 the third Home Rule Bill (The Government of Ireland Act 1914) became law.[68] A suspensory Act, however, had already postponed its operation for the duration of the war or for one year, whichever might be the sooner (people were still saying that the war might be over by Christmas).[69]

On 24th June, *The Covenanter*, a short-lived magazine produced by supporters of the British covenant, appeared with a drawing by Briton Rivière showing a British lion asleep while its Ulster cub faced a horde of wolves. "Will the old lion still sleep and forget its cub?" was the caption. Sir Bartle Frere's poem "One Flag" took up the same theme, to which the imminence of European War gave added emphasis:

> Britons of old their shuttles flung across the texture of the
> world
> And wove the pattern of a Flag that traitors cry must now be
> furled.
> Oh weavers, sitting at your loom, draw tighter still the threads
> that bind,
> Think not you easily may change the pattern that you once
> designed.
> Full close together, pledge afresh the Union that has made you
> one
> Again unanimously prove you will not have your work
> undone.
> Accurst is he who turns aside from children calling for his
> help;
> Watchful, amid the circling foes, the Lion guards the Lion's
> whelp.[70]

Nationalists regarded the matter differently. Nevertheless what became a world struggle took nationalist and Unionist together to the trenches and gave their conflict and its resolution a lower place in British minds and on the agenda of British ministers.

CHAPTER FIFTEEN

The First World War

Redmond's declaration at the outbreak of war had given hope to some Catholic Unionists. To the House of Commons (3rd August 1914) he recalled that when in 1778

> the shores of Ireland were threatened with . . . invasion, a body of 100,000 Irish volunteers sprang into existence. Catholics from the first had subscribed money and sent it towards the arming of their Protestant fellow countrymen . . . May history repeat itself . . . I say to the Government that they may tomorrow withdraw every one of their troops from Ireland. I say that the coast of Ireland will be defended from foreign invasion by her armed sons, and for this purpose armed nationalist Catholics in the South will be only too glad to join arms with the armed Protestant Ulstermen in the North.

"An Irish Catholic" in *The Times* (14th September 1914) quoted a speech of Richard Lalor Sheil in 1857 who, in response to a description of Lord Lyndhurst in the House of Lords of Irish Catholics as "aliens", had expressed surprise that Wellington had not started up to recount how those "aliens" had served England at Vimeira, Badajoz, Salamanca and Waterloo. If they had so served her then, stated an "Irish Catholic", "while the Penal Laws yet hung about their necks, how shall we not fight for her now, as full sharers in all the rights and all the privileges her citizenship can give?"[1]

Wellington had been frequently credited with the saying that "it is mainly due to the Irish Catholics that we all owe our proud pre-eminence in the military career". John Shipp, a lieutenant in the 87th Regiment of Foot from 1815 to 1825 wrote in his memoirs:

> I must confess I do love to be on duty on any kind of service with the Irish. There is a promptness to obey, a hilarity, a cheerful obedience, and a willingness to act, which I have rarely met with in any other body of men; but whether, in this

particular case, those qualifications had been instilled into them by the rigid discipline of their corps. I know not, or whether these are characteristics of the Irish nation; but I have also observed in that corps (I mean the 87th or Prince's Own Irish) a degree of liberality amongst the men I have never seen in any other corps — a willingness to share their crust and drop on service with their comrades, an indescribable cheerfulness in obliging and accommodating each other, and an anxiety to serve each other, and to hide each other's faults. In that corps there was a unity I have never seen in any other; and as for fighting they were very devils!"[2]

The second battalion of the 87th Foot enrolled in 1804. They were mostly Kilkenny lads and at Barrosa took the first of Napoleon's Eagles won by the British Army (5th March 1811). Ensign Keogh was killed in the act of grasping it. For this exploit, the 87th became known as the Prince of Wales's Own Irish Regiment, since abbreviated and altered to Royal Irish Fusiliers.

There were other Irish Regiments who distinguished themselves in the wars against Napoleon. None was so severely drilled as the Connaught Rangers. George Napier, afterwards General, when wounded was visited by an Irish private of his company who, after having his arm amputated, walked seven miles to assure himself of his captain's safety. "By Heavens!", wrote Napier for his children in 1828,

it makes my anger rise and my blood boil to hear people talk of soldiers as if they were a different race of beings from themselves. Here was a poor fellow, an Irishman and a Catholic, who, out of pure affection for his officer, having seen his brother killed by his side in action, and suffered the amputation of his own arm, walks near seven miles, without meat or drink, to see his captain, who he knew was severely wounded! Could a brother have done more?

Of a later generation, Sir Stephen Tallents, Private Secretary to Lord Edmund Talbot, last Viceroy, would write:

If I had the power to call back to life and muster for a day one only of the many companies in which at different times I have lived, I should choose the body of Irishmen — officers and

men, Southerners and Northerners, Catholics and Protestants —
with whom I spent that late winter and early spring.

He was referring to the Irish Guards of 1915–16.[3]

When partition came, the colours of the regiments associated
principally with southern Ireland (The Royal Irish Regiment, the
Connaught Rangers, the Prince of Wales's Leinster Regiment, the Royal
Munster Fusiliers and the Royal Dublin Fusiliers) were received by the
king at Windsor Castle, and on 31st July 1922 the regiments were
disbanded. King George V pledged his word that "within these . . .
walls your Colours will be treasured, honoured, and protected as
hallowed memorials of the glorious deeds of brave and loyal regiments".[4]

A correspondent of the duke of Norfolk wrote him on 14th
November 1914 from Castle Bellingham that "recruiting is going well
in this county & with the exception of a small but noisy set of Sinn
Feiners, people are getting quite loyal!" Redmond was flying the Union
Flag at his house, and the National Volunteers were singing God Save
the King. Redmond had urged the British government to leave the
defence of Ireland to her "armed sons". His brother, Major Willie, died
of wounds received at the front, to be succeeded by Eamon de Valera as
M.P. for East Clare. Another nationalist member, T. M. Kettle (East
Tyrone), died on the Somme in September 1916. One of the first to join
the Irish Volunteers, the outbreak of conflict overtook him in Belgium
where he was buying them arms. What he saw there of "Prussian
frightfulness" took him into the Dublin Fusiliers in November 1914. At
recruiting meetings in Ireland he declared that "Britain, Russia, France
enter this war purged of their sins of past domination".[5]

Recruiting was thus, to begin with, fairly brisk. By late 1915 there
were about 80,000 Irish Catholics in H. M. Forces and 53,000 Irish
Protestants. Redmond Stephen wrote to the Church of Ireland Archbishop
of Dublin, J. H. Bernard, in September 1915 that it was most important
that Orangemen and all who sent recruits to the Ulster Volunteer Force
should be "constantly told in very plain language how loyally the
Roman Catholics are supporting the Army". Roman Catholic districts in
Belfast had sent as many recruits in proportion to their numbers as
Protestant districts.[6] In 1915 the National Volunteers were also furnishing
recruits, to the tune of about 11,000 by the middle of December; even
so over 150,000 were left, many of them of military age, whilst the
Ulster Volunteers had sunk to 56,000, most of them too old to fight in
the Great War.[7] Sir Morgan O'Connell's evidence to the Royal

Commission on the 1916 rebellion confirms that in August 1914 the then National Volunteers did not oppose army recruiting in County Kerry. Many of them, in fact, enlisted. But the tide was turned by a Sinn Fein demonstration planned for 23rd May 1915. Sir Morgan, a descendant of "Hunting Cap", the "Liberator's" uncle, and a staunch Catholic Unionist, telegraphed to the Lord Lieutenant on the previous day:

> A meeting under the auspices of the Sinn Fein Party is to be held here tomorrow calling itself a football match, but with the . . . open and avowed intention of being turned into an anti-recruiting meeting. Will your Government do nothing to stop this?[8]

The reply was negative, whereupon O'Connell wired again suggesting that at least all special trains into the area should be cancelled. But nothing was done and on 23rd May five of them ran into Killarney bringing with them amongst other combustibles some five hundred armed Sinn Feiners. From then on the situation steadily worsened until on 6th February 1916 a mob led by a local Justice of the Peace attempted to break up the last recruiting meeting it proved possible to hold.

The magistracy had clearly become corrupted by the appointment of unreliable people, particularly since the time of Morley, and the provision in the Defence of the Realm (Amendment) Act, passed in March 1915, for suspected persons to be tried by jury[9], was in Ireland disastrous. Except in Dublin and Belfast, neither juries nor magistrates could thenceforward be relied upon to give decisions in accordance with the evidence; whilst even there the Resident Magistrates (the breed of "R.M." popularized by Somerville and Ross) could impose no more than six months' hard labour.[10]

The report of the Royal Commission pointed out the numerous attempts made, by the Royal Irish Constabulary and by the Dublin Metropolitan Police, to impress the facts upon the Liberal Chief Secretary. "Lord Midleton in November 1915 had an interview with the Chief Secretary in which he strongly urged that the Irish Volunteers should be disarmed", and not permitted to parade, and prosecuted for seditious speeches. "His warnings were entirely neglected".[11] Plunkett afterwards wrote of Birrell: "more than any living man, he fomented this rebellion".[12] For an account of how he did so, we again turn to Sir Morgan O'Connell:

Mr Birrell in his evidence before the Commission has stated that long-established dislike, hatred and disloyalty to England has been the cause of the present deplorable condition of affairs in Ireland. As an Irishman, living entirely in Ireland, I wish to enter the strongest possible protest against this statement. I have tried to show that at all events in the South of Ireland in August 1914, the vast majority of Irishmen were in sympathy with England.

Birrell had stated that trial by jury in Ireland was a farce, but a "far greater farce" was the trial at ordinary Petty Sessions. The Government had appointed to the Commission of the Peace in the south of Ireland scores of wholly unsuitable men, who attended "solely for the purpose of carrying out the more open and flagrant jobbery".[13] The Roman Catholic Bishop of Kerry had repeatedly protested against this, and in reply to a question from Mr Justice Shearman, Sir Morgan added that in his own county at least the influence of the clergy generally was good. "I do not think there [is] a single Sinn Fein parish priest in the whole of Kerry". He paid tribute to the "unswerving loyalty and devotion to duty" of the R.I.C. "They knew the country, they knew the people, they are themselves of the people". They were "the one bright spot in this deplorable chapter of Irish history".

In September 1914 the National Volunteers split on Redmond's patriotic support of the war effort. John McNeill and other nationalists formed a new force called the Irish Volunteers. These numbered over 13,000 by the end of October and by April 1916 about 15,000 mustered with more than 1,800 rifles.[14] Connolly's "citizen army", separate at first, joined them in November 1915 to form a formidable rebel force, albeit inadequately armed.[15]

In the face of this danger to the state, a feeble government vacillated. The Under-Secretary dismissed one warning: "I look upon it as vague talk", to which Birrell added: "the whole letter is rubbish".[16] Such men were incapable of being advised. The Germans did not neglect "Ireland's opportunity" and fished in troubled waters. On 18th April 1916 it was reported to the government in Dublin that a ship had left Germany for Ireland on the twelfth, loaded with arms and escorted by two U-boats, and was due to arrive on Good Friday for a rising planned for Easter Eve. But on the twenty-second the ship in question, the *Aud*, was captured by British destroyers and blown up by her crew. Sir Roger Casement, who had landed from an accompanying German submarine, was arrested at Banna on the coast of Kerry. By six a.m. on Easter Sunday he had been brought to London.[17]

Which, on the face of it, was reassuring. Action had indeed been contemplated over Easter, and was called off by the official rebel leaders when they heard of the fate of the *Aud*. Birrell for his part assumed that all was well and settled down to a normal weekend. *Dis aliter visum.* A more militant rebel element, in which the Irish Republican Brotherhood predominated — the Easter Rising was not a Sinn Fein insurrection — received funds raised through the *Clan-na-Gael* in the United States, where Joseph McGarrity called for "a vigorous attack on English submarine bases and shipping all along the coast towns". Both the viceroy, Lord Wimborne, and the Under-Secretary, Sir Matthew Nathan, were alarmed by a report at 10.30 on Sunday morning of the forcible seizure of gelignite from the Tullagh quarry and its conveyance to Liberty Hall. Wimborne wrote to the Chief Secretary that in their view Liberty Hall and other "'Sinn Fein' arsenals should be raided tonight", but Nathan's cipher telegram did not reach London until Monday. Wimborne correctly surmised that the ringleaders, "having counter-manded their Easter day parade, are probably sitting in conclave conspiring against us . . . I have never made much of their movements, or have been or am now an alarmist, but if you don't take your chances they do not recur". At conferences held during Sunday evening Wimborne urged the arrest of sixty to a hundred leaders as well as the seizure of the gelignite, but Nathan demurred and Wimborne was unable to overrule him.[18] On Easter Monday the General Post Office in Dublin, together with St Stephen's Green, Jacob's Biscuit Factory and the Four Courts were seized. An Irish Republic was proclaimed from the steps of the Post Office.[19] Troops were promptly concentrated and not all the volunteers mustered. Within five days the rebel leader, Pearse, surrendered unconditionally to General Sir John Maxwell. Substantial damage had been done. Much of the centre of Dublin, the second city in the British Isles, was a smoking ruin. Small outbursts elsewhere were suppressed without difficulty.

There is no doubt of the initial unpopularity of a rising backed by Germany against a government pledged to Home Rule. Dr Garret FitzGerald's father recalled that those who broke with Redmond in 1914 in the hope that English defeat would bring Irish independence, had their "dream castles toppled about us with a crash". By their support of the king's war the Irish "had recognised themselves as a part of England".[20] At the outbreak the rising was largely contained by Irish units. Father Francis Shaw, SJ, writing for its fiftieth anniversary reminds us:

> Clarke, Pearse, MacDermott, MacDonagh, Colbert, Connolly, these names are known to all. Less well known is the fact that these same names are those also of men who in Easter Week of 1916 were decorated, wounded or killed, fighting on the side of the British Crown forces in Ireland.[21]

The Dublin populace, many of whom had dear ones in the trenches or their war dead to mourn and much Irish valour in which to take proper pride, jeered the beaten rebels as they passed between their captors. "It is not an Irish Rebellion", the Chief Secretary wrote to the Prime Minister on 30th April.[22] The Post Office proclamation cited the sustenance given by "our exiled children in America and by gallant allies in Europe". Lord Craigmyle recorded how in Nassau Street people were giving the king's soldiers apples, biscuits and bananas. According to P. S. Hegarty, the Easter Rising was "universally and explosively unpopular" and "if Ireland as a whole could have got hold of Tom Clarke and his comrades during that week it would have torn them to pieces".[23] Clarke was a verteran Fenian who had done time for dynamiting.

Not that the rebels were without their sympathizers. Catholic bishops condemned them; some of the lower clergy were on their side. What turned the scale of opinion, according to Plunkett and many other observers, was the shooting, after court martial, of thirteen ringleaders besides the crippled Connolly. Not that many of the prisoners suffered death — de Valera was reprieved — or even lengthy terms of imprisonment. Nevertheless, as Churchill wrote; "Well was it said, 'The grass soon grows over a battlefield, but never over a scaffold'."[24] The shootings were too long delayed.[25] Carson tried to stop them. Redmond told Asquith to stop the military executions and end martial law, "in the interests of the Empire, as well as of Ireland".[26] It was as though they watched a stream of blood coming from beneath a closed door. Tim Healy, the nationalist parliamentarian who became first Governor-general of the Irish Free State, deeply regretted the executions while deploring a rebellion "entirely done in concert with Germany".[27] Dillon cried out to a hostile House of Commons on 11th May:

> "I say I am proud of their courage, and if you were not so dense and stupid, as some of you English people are, you could

have had these men fighting for you . . . it is not murderers who are being executed; it is insurgents who have fought a clean fight, however misguided".[28]

Asquith blundered on. In deciding to visit Dublin in person he declared his conviction that the civil executive in Ireland "for the time being almost ceased to exist", and on his return he referred to the "breakdown of the existing machinery of Irish Government", a phrase which caused great offence.[29] A new system had to be instituted, "responsible to the Irish people". In other words, rebellion paid. Respectable people began to look on the republicans with less hostility when a statesman like Asquith seemed to be lending them his support, and their view was confirmed when he visited some of the rebels in prison, finding them "very fine-looking fellows: an extraordinary number had beautiful eyes".[30] An official eye-witness told Professor Alison Phillips that the prisoners, "who had been depressed and in some cases penitent and in tears, saw that they had not fought in vain, and Mr Asquith had scarce left the prison before they were insulting their guards, throwing up their caps and shouting victory".[31] Dr O'Dwyer, Catholic Bishop of Limerick, publicly protested against the execution of these "poor boys", though many Irishmen and women continued to repudiate their "canonization". Myth mastered truth. The blood of the Easter "martyrs" sowed the seed of the revolution. The rising also reinvigorated northern resistance to Home Rule and dashed the hopes of some who dreamed that an autonomous, single Ireland connected with Great Britain and the empire could bury the differences of Orange and Green in the graves of France and Flanders.

Ross-of-Bladensburg wrote to the Duke of Norfolk on 4th June that the "Irish can be kept in order, if there only be the will to do so", but there was no such will, and everything pointed to further trouble. "God knows", he added, "it was bad enough in the past, when a Govt was allowed to remain in Ireland, which fomented dissensions, & brought about the catastrophe by inconceivable weakness & folly, if not by conduct that was far worse than folly. But what is happening since the rising is amazing". Dillon was allowed to shout something akin to treason; and there was so called conciliation by yielding to rebellion. Good Catholics who were "ready to accept Home Rule when it comes", were asking for an expression and definition of Christian doctrine on the issues at stake. Ross advocated an approach to Cardinal Logue, the Primate of All Ireland, who was a less unambiguous supporter of Sinn

Fein than was Archbishop Walsh of Dublin, and also to the Vatican through Sir Henry Howard.[32] Why should the radical tail of the Government wag the dog? "This radical tail have already played a disgraceful game in this miserable country: & their game has led to disaster and disgrace." [33]

Lord Midleton, a former Secretary of State for War and for India, and by this time effectively leader of the southern Unionists, led a deputation to the prime minister and Lloyd George on 27th June. Claiming to represent some 400,000 people from the south and west of Ireland, including Unionists from almost every county and the City of Dublin, they expressed their apprehension that proposals had been formulated to exclude certain counties in Ulster and hand over the rest of Ireland to the nationalists "during the period of the war". This would not assist the empire, and the proposal had been denounced by Cardinal Logue and the Catholic bishops of the North of Ireland as it had been by the bishops of the Church of Ireland. Herein lay the seeds of disunion among Unionists, for before this meeting took place, Lloyd George had persuaded Carson that a settlement was necessary on the basis of separation, and had even persuaded Redmond to consider partition favourably.[34]

On 27th July 1916 the Government issued a White Paper "Headings of a Settlement as to the Government of Ireland" (Cd. 8310). This envisaged an "excluded area" composed of the Six Counties, to be administered by a Secretary of State, on lines not vastly dissimilar from the current scheme of "direct rule" for Northern Ireland. The Irish House of Commons was to consist of the Westminster M.P.s for the non-excluded area and the possibility of a new High Court at Belfast was adumbrated.

On 7th March 1917 Lloyd George affirmed that the government would not enforce Home Rule on Ulster, and an Irish convention was summoned to devise a scheme for self-government. Sinn Fein were not represented at the convention. Lloyd George had intimated to Midleton that he would like him to have a southern Catholic Unionist in the convention, and had asked him to arrange it.[35] John Blake Powell was the choice.

He was a King's Counsel, formerly a solicitor in Sligo. Called to the Bar in Michaelmas 1894, he took silk in 1905 and in 1918, after serving in the convention, was for a short period Solicitor-General for Ireland before being appointed a Judge of the High Court.[36] This was a judge, according to Sir Thomas Molony, last Lord Chief Justice of

(Southern) Ireland, speaking after Powell's death in 1923, who showed "great knowledge, unwearied industry, innate courtesy, and genuine kindliness of heart".[37] Not that his activities during the course of the convention had not alarmed some southern Unionists. Indeed, coupled with the attitude of Lord Midleton, they split their ranks. Ulster Unionists too, were suspicious, and H. M. Pollock later asserted in *The Times* on their behalf that they had had good ground for suspecting the loyalty of southern Unionists at the convention "when we discovered that one of their number had drafted a Home Rule measure to be submitted anonymously to the convention, and that Lord Midleton was privy to this transaction". Midleton admitted that at some time between 1914 and 1917 Powell had "sketched a modification of the Home Rule Act of 1914 in order to meet some of the main Unionist objections". The chairman of the convention, Horace Plunkett, had at some point invited him to put in his clauses. Midleton himself "had not even a copy of them, nor had they ever been submitted to our party". On hearing Midleton's disclaimer, Powell withdrew his paper.[38]

Nonetheless there is little doubt that he was active behind the scenes in assisting Midleton to try and bring the Convention to some agreement. On 1st December he wrote that the Ulster Unionists were in a "hopelessly illogical position". They had provisionally agreed to the constitution of the two Houses of a future Irish parliament; "they *must approve* of the suggestion for purifying public affairs" (this was a reference to the proposed abolition of unpaid magistrates, "whose administration of justice had become a positive scandal" and to "civil service examinations — which would put an end to jobbery which at present is sapping the integrity & *decency* of the country"); "they have us with them on Imperial Control of Customs: they now admit that Ireland must have *some* powers of taxation". But because of difficulties over the separation of customs and excise the task could not be performed. Powell thought that this "pretext" was "wholly unsustainable" and that

> it places those who rely upon it, in a wholly indefensible position in the eyes of the British public . . . The more I think over these matters, the more clouded and overcast the future seems to be for England, and recent events have not I am sure you will agree, improved matters in this respect . . . I feel that it is our duty to relieve the Government or any British Government of the difficulties of the Irish question, to say nothing of the enormous advantage to this country of doing so.

Powell had heard "from many reliable sources that Sinn Fein is on the *decline*, and that if the convention agrees to a Constitution 75 to 80 per cent of Sinn Feiners will acquiesce. It is in my opinion the one & only chance to save this country. I am having a Mem[o] prepared for you dealing, I hope *scientifically*, with the question of *Excise* and showing the erroneous views put forward by Mr Pollock". Powell looked to Midleton to settle the question & so obtain "the undying gratitude of the Empire & of all *sane* Irishmen".[39]

But Ulster objections could not be overcome. On 11th October 1917 one of Midleton's correspondents, probably Ross-of-Bladensburg, put his finger on the reason. The writer had

> told the Cabinet at the beginning of July that the release of the Sinn Fein prisoners would be a heavy blow to the Convention. It has I fear destroyed its slight chance of success. The released prisoners have had an orgy in every direction; converts to the 'winning side' have come in by thousands & the sentences since given to the ringleaders for the most open breaches of the law are being rapidly rescinded. Within the last few days all the Cabinet rules . . . announced to us, as to the wearing of rebel uniforms . . . etc have been openly violated . . . and further releases are said to be in prospect. The first result of this was shown at the Convention today. A strong Committee to whom the framing of a scheme of Govt. had been committed after weeks of debate, adjourned for a fortnight on specious grounds. The real reason is that in Ulster the masses will not listen to the madness as they consider it of giving Ireland over to Sinn Fein.[40]

Ulster then, "would not yield", as Midleton had said at a meeting held at Downing Street on 3rd December 1917 at which Archbishop Bernard and Lord Curzon were also present.[41] There was a forlorn hope that she might "acquiesce" if administrative independence were secured to her; but Midleton, Bernard and Powell had gone too far in their fight to maintain the unity of Ireland. In March 1918, while the convention was still sitting, a "Call to Unionists" was published in the newspapers. They declared that the power of Redmond's party had gone, and that there were "two distinct nationalities in Ireland . . . The tragedy of it all is that the demand for Home Rule finds no echo in the hearts of those who have a real stake in the country. The leaders of all the Churches, the farmers, especially those who have purchased their farms; commerce, industry, in fact all the stable elements which are the life-blood of any country, realises its dangers". The call was for the "enforcement of the ordinary law with firmness, justice and impartiality; for the development of the natural resources of Ireland, and the promotion of commerce, industry, and agriculture; and for the completion of land purchase. Further, the "obligations and burdens of the war" should be shared by Ireland. This presumably meant that compulsory military service should extend to Ireland, contrary to the opinion of a sub-Committee of the Irish convention on defence and the police, which predicted in an interim report of 19th November 1917 that to impose conscription against the opposition of an Irish parliament would be impossible. Powell was a member of this sub-committee.[42] Those who agreed with the call and opposed any form of local autonomy not shared with other parts of the United Kingdom, were invited to communicate with John E. Walsh at 36 Molesworth Street, Dublin.

The *Irish Times*, in a thoughtful editorial (4th March 1918) agreed with the signatories that the revolutionaries would not bring peace and prosperity to Ireland. On the other hand, a system resisted by three-quarters of the Irish people was unlikely to be satisfactory. It was true that Ireland had been contented and prosperous under Walter Long (Chief Secretary for Ireland in 1905 and a leading southern Unionist). But could the signatories "promise a procession of Longs in the future and guarantee us against a procession of Birrells?" The leader writer correctly prophesied a Labour government in London within the next ten years. "Is a Labour Executive likely to enforce the law impartially in Ireland and to complete land purchase?" This feeling of insecurity was one reason why Midleton and his colleagues had decided to enter the convention. Another was the government's assurance that a settlement would help materially in waging war. "In such a cause Southern Unionists refused to hold their political convictions dearer than their sons". The editorial concluded by expressing its confidence in the Unionist delegates to the convention.

But the "callers", or "call-boys" as they were sometimes ambiguously termed[43], saw the situation differently. To them, the Midletonites were seen as selling the pass to the nationalists, especially on the right of the Ulster Unionists to self-determination. In general, the callers represented the stouter elements of Unionism in southern Ireland; their principal organ, the Dublin *Daily Express*, fought, and fought to the end, a strong rearguard action against the coming betrayal. Winners write history. Losers are half forgotten. Nevertheless, let honour be done to those, not all of them rich, professional or landed, who were ambushed, shot or burnt out of the land they loved as dearly as any Fenian, and who suffered the still crueller fate of abandonment by those whose flag of Union they had kept flying against the southern odds. They were the first great offering upon the altar of imperial abdication. "John Bull's Other Island", the nursery of England's commanders from Wellington to "Bobs" and Kitchener, Alexander and "Monty" — as in Alsace-Lorraine frontiers breed fighters — was the first to experience the onset of imperial decline. In Robert Kee's words, it was "a rupture at the very heart of the Empire itself. The British Empire never recovered from it. Some would say that Ireland has never recovered either."[44]

Subsequent research has not altered Midleton's conclusion that it was Redmond's retirement from the scene and replacement by Bishop O'Donnell in January 1918 as leader of the nationalist delegation which finally destroyed what hope still existed of an all-Ireland solution.[45] Indeed, writing to Denis Gwynn, Redmond's biographer, in 1931, Midleton went so far as to say that O'Donnell was "determined to wreck the Convention". At a private meeting arranged by Powell, "he absolutely declined to give us any indication of the terms which (would enable him to) support a settlement" and did all he could to draw away from Redmond's followers, hinting that Lloyd George would not agree. "I fear it cannot be questioned", added Midleton, "that by wrecking an agreement which would have brought Redmond's party, Ulster and the Southern Unionists into a common Government, Bishop O'Donnell and those of his colleagues who supported him, were largely responsible for the terrible troubles which broke out within a few months and devastated Ireland".[46]

This is a shocking indictment, and other Catholic bishops were more conciliatory. Nonetheless, when the convention reassembled on 12th March 1918 after Redmond's death, it was clear that compromise resolutions drafted by the Catholic Lord MacDonnell of Swinford were unacceptable both to a substantial majority of nationalists and to the Ulster Unionists.[47] Plunkett's report was supported only by the moderate group, and opposed both by the ultra-nationalist and Ulster groups, who presented separate reports. Sinn Fein, as such, was not represented at the convention.[48]

In April a Military Service Bill, providing that conscription might be extended to Ireland by Order in Council, received the Royal Assent.[49]

This led to a declaration both by a Dublin Mansion House conference and by the Roman Catholic bishops at Maynooth. The latter, with Cardinal Logue presiding, stated that they considered "conscription forced upon Ireland as an oppressive and inhuman law, which the Irish people have a right to resist by all means consonant with the law of God".[50] Cardinal Logue made it clear, however, that he did not favour "organized physical resistance" to conscription, and the Roman Catholic Bishop of Cork, the Rt Revd T. O'Callaghan, had a letter read in his city churches calling on young men "to avoid playing into the hands of their enemies by a formal military rising".[51] The anti-conscription agitation speeded the resurgence of Sinn Fein, despite Cardinal Logue's instructions of June 1917, issued to priests with the Bishops of Cloyne and Ross and exhorting them to urge people to "beware of all dangerous Associations and sedulously shun movements that plot against the Church or lawfully constituted authority".[52] On 25th November he had gone considerably further in a pastoral read out in the churches of his archdiocese which deplored an agitation which

> has sprung up and is spreading among our people which, ill-considered and Utopian, cannot fail, if persevered in, to entail present suffering, disorganisation and danger, and is sure to end in future disaster, defeat and collapse. And all this in pursuit of a dream which no man in his sober senses can see realised: the establishment of an Irish Republic, either by an appeal to the Potentates of Europe seated at a Peace Conference, or an appeal to force by hurling an unarmed people against an Empire which has five millions of men under arms . . . The thing would be ludicrous if it were not so mischievous and fraught with such danger."[53]

Now, however, the Catholic Church in Ireland concerted opposition to conscription, which for the nonce united nationalists and Sinn Feiners, Dillon, Healy, O'Brien and de Valera. Cardinal Logue supported the priests who established a "solemn League and Covenant" at Armagh on 15th April. This called for "passive resistance".[54] Nevertheless, *The Times* reported that the voluntary recruiting in Dublin and other centres remained good.

There was a change in leadership at the Castle: Duke was replaced by Shortt as Chief Secretary, and Field-Marshal French became Lord Lieutenant. Powell was considered for the former post, but Midleton, when sounded as to his suitability, had "some doubts of his strength" and the proposal was dropped.[55] On 4th May 1918, Midleton wrote:

> Conceive the folly of a Prime Minister who desires to press Conscription to the last shred of shooting, and appoints a Chief Secretary . . . to justify Conscription who voted against it a fortnight ago.[56]

Slowly, since Gladstone's day, the viceroy's standing had been diminished, until he was no longer the effective head of the Irish administration, but rather a figurehead not even entitled, it seemed, to receive a daily police report.[57] The Chief Secretary's position had become correspondingly enhanced; he now had a seat in cabinet in London, but since the Chief Secretary sat in the House of Commons, he was less in touch with the day-to-day situation than a viceroy in the House of Lords able to give more time to Irish administration and spend more time in the country. We have seen how this caused difficulties at the time of the Howth gun-running in 1914; a more fundamental weakness was the lack of a clear chain of command. Moreover, governments in London continued to wobble, reacting with varying degrees of resolution to events as they occurred, without clear policies consistently applied. Before Lord French was appointed, Midleton had been approached and offered the post. He began by proposing to the Government that it should be split into three in the style of the old "Lords Justices"; in other words, that he and two others, such as the Lord Chief Justice of Ireland and the General Officer Commanding-in-Chief should be charged with the administration.[58] The explanation of this proposal was, he subsequently wrote to Lord Stamfordham, the king's private secretary, that the cabinet were more likely to show deference to the views of such a triumvirate than to those of a single individual, "and the state of Ireland is one which does not admit of every matter being re-discussed in Downing Street; the responsibility must rest in Dublin".[59]

This the government were prepared to accept, but, as Midleton wrote to Bernard on 4th May 1918,

> two Irish judges successively refused to co-operate with Lord French and myself as Lords Justices on the ground that it was wholly impossible to carry out the Government policy. In the course of the week I convinced three Cabinet Ministers of this but the Prime Minister came back from France, put his foot

down and said all or nothing, that Ireland might run in blood, it was nothing to what was going on in France etc. and he thought that after all this bloodshed they would take Home Rule like lambs generally.[60]

There was, after all, a war on, and ministers had other preoccupations. Nonetheless, Midleton pointed out to ministers that the government were trying to do too many things in Ireland at once. They were thinking of imposing conscription; they were meditating a new Home Rule Bill; and they were attempting to combat Sinn Fein. Effort was being dissipated in three different directions and a new viceroy would not know which of these policies he should work on at any given time. Moreover, the chances of success in any one of them were at best limited; if all three were pursued at once, the task would be hopeless. The cabinet, while sympathetic to these views, could not see their way to tie their hands for the future, and so Lord French alone was appointed.[61]

Lord Desart wrote to Bernard from Kilkenny that a "level-headed R.I.C. man" had told him that if an attempt was made to enforce conscription, "they would hardly get anyone here". Catholic and Protestant farmers were equally determined and would "simply disappear temporarily" on receipt of any notice.[62] "An Irish Officer", writing in *The Times*, took a more robust view, arguing that if conscription had been applied earlier on there would have been no "Sinn Fein rebellion". As it was, only the landlords' sons and the "scamps" (landless labourers) had enlisted; ordinary farmers' sons would not do so for fear of losing their inheritance. In a second letter he asserted roundly that "anti-conscription in Ireland is one big bluff". Not all Catholic priests were against their parishioners joining up and one to his knowledge had spoken with effect at a recruiting meeting.[63]

On 30th April 1918 Lord Edmund Talbot and others dissociated themselves, at a meeting of the Catholic Union of Great Britain, from the stand taken by the Catholic bishops of Ireland. Resistance to compulsory service implied "organized disobedience to the law". They viewed with misgivings the ecclesiastical authorities' interference in "questions which are purely temporal and political and in no way connected with faith and morals". Hampering the development of the military forces of the allies would "endanger the cause of humanity".[64] The resolutions of the Union were forwarded to the Vatican, but no comment was forthcoming. The government, too, attempted to exert pressure. At a cabinet meeting on 6th May the Foreign Secretary, Balfour, undertook to inform the British minister to the Vatican, Count de Salis, of "any cases that might come to light of the improper interference of the Irish priesthood in secular affairs and more particularly the recent promise of absolution to persons engaged in resistance to the Military Service Act"[65]; and he duly forwarded a number of police notes containing reports of such improper remarks by priests. The Cardinal Secretary of State forwarded the extracts to Cardinal Logue for his comments, and replied ultimately to the government on 9th July that whilst Cardinal Logue had agreed that there were a few priests who had exceeded the bounds of prudence and moderation, the extracts in general were unreliable because they were based solely on police officers' recollections, "qui ignorent les principes elementaires de la doctrine catholique".[66]

What then *was* Catholic doctrine on the subject of conscription? Serjeant Sullivan, in the *Irish Times* (26th April 1918) argued that it was what the Church called "a 'penal law', which the good citizen may obey, but is justified, so far as the Church goes, in disobeying"; and the Roman Catholic Bishop of Kildare, Dr Foley, described the bishops' resolution as meaning that the conscription law was no law at all, *ultra vires*. It was not until the following year that a sustained Catholic defence of conscription, by Dr Walter McDonald, was published.[67]

None of this prevented English Catholic Unionists protesting. Lord Denbigh wrote in *The Times* (29th April 1918) that "it almost makes me ashamed of the word Catholic to see the action now taken by the Irish hierarchy to combat and resist the law". However, he was as certain that the Vatican had no more to do with their action as he had been thirty years previously when the Holy See had inquired into and subsequently condemned the support given to the Plan of Campaign, at a time when he had been himself in Ireland. The Irish Catholic hierarchy's act had been deplorable and hasty, but also blameworthy was "the *régime* of Mr Birrell. There had been an orgy of stupid mishandling".[68]

Randall Davidson, Archbishop of Canterbury, thereupon wrote to Bernard, who was still Church of Ireland Archbishop of Dublin, drawing his attention to Denbigh's letter. What, Davidson asked Bernard, did the Irish hierarchy's attitude portend? Bernard replied that he thought "very badly" of the Catholic bishops. They were all bred in the Home Rule tradition and surrounded at Maynooth and elsewhere by Home Rulers. Nonetheless, they were not in general liars, and really did believe in it.

"Ulster's view" that they supported Home Rule because they wished to be popular was incorrect. Neither did Bernard believe that the Vatican was giving the bishops pro-German orders. Two or three of them had, at least at one stage, spoken up in favour of recruiting, and Redmond had been told that when the Catholic Bishop of Killaloe had spoken disloyally, "he . . . had been sharply reprimanded by the Vatican authorities". Nonetheless, Dr Walsh, the Catholic Archbishop of Dublin, "is, I am convinced pro-German".[69]

Bernard's own view was that the Catholic hierarchy's dominant motive was the desire to keep control over their own people, but it was a view accepted only by "a few of my loyalist Roman Catholic friends (such people really exist, *pace* Ulster)". The bishops would, in his view, have forfeited this control years previously had they not condoned the Plan of Campaign, and similarly had they not opposed the Home Rule scheme which the southern Unionists had accepted at the Convention. Secondly, the hierarchy wanted to avoid bloodshed and the imposition of compulsory military service would cause this in Ireland. Two years before it could have been imposed "quite easily"; even a year before it could have been done, and the Roman Catholic hierarchy had not denounced it then. "They denounce it now, because they are afraid of losing control of their people . . . Not all Irish rebels or Irish sentimentalists are pro-German. They are only playing with treason, because they want to hurt England".[70]

Archbishop Bernard's diagnosis was certainly accurate, so far as it went; but the question still has to be asked: if the Roman hierarchy's desire was to keep control of their flock, in which direction were they hoping to lead it? De Valera had already been on a deputation to Archbishops Logue and Walsh at Maynooth, and secured their concurrence to a pledge to be taken by people in every parish which read; "Denying the right of the British Government to enforce compulsory service in this country, we pledge ourselves solemnly to one another to resist conscription by the most effective means at our disposal."[71]

This could only mean that violence was not ruled out, and, as David Miller has written,

> clerical forces were at least as significant as lay forces in launching the new movement . . . When the hierarchy granted de Valera an audience at Maynooth and urged co-operation between all parties, they gave to Sinn Fein the moral sanction

of a legitimate political party and removed it from the realm of theological and moral suspicion in which it had operated for the preceding year. But for its own internal differences, the hierarchy probably possessed the power, up until this point, if not to crush Sinn Fein, to forestall the overwhelming mandate which it received eight months later. The political power of the Irish Church in this period, however, could only be exercised in such a sweeping, nationwide fashion when the fundamental issue could be depicted as a religious, moral or theological one within the framework in which those terms were understood in Ireland. A generation earlier, Parnell's moral indiscretion had provided such an issue. During the period before the conscription crisis the flirtations of Sinn Fein with armed rebellion and secret societies had offered another such issue upon which the Church might have chosen to mobilise her political power. In April 1918 she deliberately forfeited that option.[72]

Of course it may be argued in extenuation of the bishops' attitude that their primary task was to lead their flock towards their salvation and that to that extent they had to bend and yield to public opinion, even if important subsidiary theological positions were thereby compromised. Nonetheless, Archbishop Walsh's attitude in particular seems inexplicable unless Bernard were right.

The new Irish government took firm measures; on 17th May 1918 a number of important Sinn Fein leaders were arrested on grounds of association with the enemy, and on 3rd July the entire organization, as well as the volunteers, were proclaimed as dangerous associations. Meetings and even fairs were prohibited except by permit; but the only result was that republican meetings were forced to take place in secret, and public hostility to the police became more widespread.[73] Then came the armistice. On Armistice Night loyalists attacked both Sinn Fein headquarters and "Liberty Hall", and crown forces were placed in the peculiar position of sharing the defence of the latter with the "Citizen Army".[74]

Dr Walter McDonald's defence of conscription received a mixed reception. The Irish Catholic laity "of the business and better classes, who are still in favour . . . of Imperial union with Great Britain", he wrote in 1925, "were pleased; and no small number of the senior clergy shared in the sentiment". Some of them assured him that "they had read the book with delight and agreed with every word". Nonetheless, "the great body of the clergy were, undoubtedly, hurt and hostile". There was a short review in *The Month*; but the *Irish Ecclesiastical Review* ignored it, as did the *Irish Theological Quarterly* and *Studies*. "How, indeed", wrote McDonald in his *Reminiscences of a Maynooth Professor*, "could Bishops, Canonists, Theologians, argue that the Imperial Parliament had no authority to enact conscription for Ireland, seeing that the Holy See had decided officially that the *de facto* government of this country is legitimate? To get at me, they must hit at Rome; and no one who knows the higher ecclesiastics of Ireland would ever deem them capable of such folly as that".

What disturbed McDonald most of all was the general trend of Irish ecclesiastical life. "I saw with disgust", he wrote,

> Irish Bishops . . . use claptrap phrases — about self-determination, rights of nations, government by consent, and other such catch-words . . . Our Bishops were . . . becoming demagogues . . . You could not get them to write even the shortest article in ecclesiastical science for the *Irish Ecclesiastical Record*, for which they had no time, while they had time, and taste, to turn out letters and speeches on almost any aspect of the Irish Question . . . I hated, and hate, all this kind of thing . . . I thought I should do one man's part to withstand the rot; and I did.[75]

CHAPTER SIXTEEN

The Treaty

In December 1918 there was a "Khaki Election".[1] In Ireland it was very green. Seventy-three Sinn Fein members were returned, who now styled themselves the Irish Republican Party. Gone was the old mention of the constitution of 1782. The nationalists retained only six seats; but Unionists improved their position from eighteen to twenty-six, of whom twenty-three were Ulster members. Of the three Unionist members returned in the south of Ireland, two sat for Trinity College and one (Sir Maurice Dockrell) for the Rathmines division of Dublin. Triumphant Sinn Feiners refused to attend Westminster. They assembled in their own Dail Eireann, a Declaration of Independence was read in divers tongues, and de Valera was elected president. British authority did not interfere. Indeed, the Dublin Metropolitan Police provided the Dail with a guard.

French had accepted office on condition that he was to be *de facto* as well as *de jure* governor of Ireland[2], and there were clashes in this regard between him and the Chief Secretary, Edward Shortt. These had come to a head in October 1918 and in January 1919 Shortt was replaced by Ian Macpherson. At the same time, Denis Henry became Solicitor-General for Ireland in succession to John Blake Powell who was elevated to the Bench. Henry had been elected for South Derry in 1916.[3] Serjeant Sullivan wrote of him that he was

> the best man that the Irish Bar produced in my time. He had a clear deep mind comparable to that of the Lord Chief Baron Palles. His features were handsome, his carriage dignified, and he was meant, with his splendid genius and delightful humour, to be the leader of the profession.[4]

Henry was a stickler for due process. After, later in the year, he had become Attorney-General for Ireland, Sullivan relates how he refused the former's advice to abolish trials by public process, substituting in their place a submissory process which might have resulted in the execution of ten or twenty known murderers a week until crime was stopped. "Henry was appalled at my scheme", Sullivan wrote; and he refused the serjeancy which Sullivan accepted.

On 16th February 1920, Henry explained in the House of Commons[5] why it was necessary for the government to continue the war emergency laws in Ireland for twelve months. Trial by jury was suspended only in respect of offences under D.O.R.A. (Defence of the Realm Act), not for ordinary crimes. In a speech three days later[6], he pointed out that intimidation had gone to such an extent "that a very eminent counsel, who certainly does not hide — neither did his father before him — his sympathy for Ireland, has had his life attempted twice for merely making a speech in a court of justice in the discharge of his duty". "Hardly a morning passes", he added later in the debate,

> that you do not read of police barracks being bombed and blown up. Why? It is because they represent the British Government in Ireland. It is not an attack on one party . . . it is an attack on your nation. It is an attempt to drive your nation out of Ireland. Hon. Members may be willing to go, but, if they are not willing to go, there must be some force used.

The year 1919 had indeed seen a worsening of the troubles. The historian of the "Irish Citizen Army" dates the "resumption of hostilities" following the 1916 rising to an ambush at Soloheadbeag on 21st January of that year. This was also the day of the first meeting of the Dail in Dublin. Although the Citizen Army remained a separate organization, it co-operated closely with the volunteers, or "Irish Republican Army" as they were now coming to be called.[7] On 31st January 1919 the I.R.A. journal, *An tOglach*, reaffirmed the Dail's declaration that England and Ireland were at war, and asserted that the Volunteers were justified in "treating the armed forces of the enemy — whether soldiers or policemen — exactly as a National Army would treat members of an invading army".[8] A campaign of arms seizures began, and on 23rd June 1919 an R.I.C. District Inspector was murdered in the centre of Thurles, County Tipperary, in broad daylight; his assassins vanished, and the crowds of witnesses refused to give any information.

There was nothing new about this kind of terrorism. What was new and dangerous was its scale and the evidence of a sustained campaign. Cattle driving, illegal drilling, the disarming of isolated policemen, the blocking of roads and the cutting of telephone wires became normal events. In September Dail Eireann was proclaimed as a dangerous association, but continued to meet secretly. Sinn Fein newspapers were suppressed and Sinn Fein centres raided in search of arms.[9] This did not end the violence, and on 20th December 1919 there was an attempt to assassinate Lord French.[10] Early in the year *The Times* newspaper had dismissed the troubles and Sinn Fein itself, despite its success at the elections, as yet another of the customary manifestations of Irish disorder; but by the end of the year a new note was beginning to creep in. A new demeanour was being recognized in the people: "sullen — and dangerous".[11]

Conscription had been abandoned, but Home Rule, it was decided, must go ahead. The Better Government for Ireland Bill introduced in December proposed to set up in Ireland two parliaments, one for the six counties of North-East Ulster, the other for the rest of the island. A Council of Ireland was to administer those services which the two parliaments agreed to operate in common, and to prepare the way for an ultimate parliament of all Ireland. Foreign affairs and defence, customs and income tax would remain with the imperial parliament. Control of the police and magistracy would also be reserved until that all-Ireland parliament were constituted. But if either northern or southern parliament failed to function, Ireland would be governed like a crown colony, albeit retaining forty-six M.P.s at Westminster.

The Bill's reception ranged from lukewarm acceptance to outright rejection. Opposition to partition was voiced not only by Sinn Fein and nationalists but by the Unionists in the south and especially those of the three Ulster counties excluded from Northern Ireland under the Bill. The Ulster Unionists acquiesced in what they considered a "supreme sacrifice". For them it was preferable to the bringing into force of the Act of 1914. The Roman Catholic bishops denounced the 1919 legislation as an "impossible scheme". T. J. Campbell wrote that "no Irish vote was cast for or against" the measure, and it is certainly true that the three Ulster members of Lloyd George's administration (Denis Henry, D. M. Wilson and James Craig) abstained on second and third readings.[12]

The attitude of the hierarchy had deteriorated since Dr Walsh became Archbishop of Dublin in 1885. This prelate had been denied the Cardinal's hat conferred on the Primate of All Ireland, Archbishop Logue of Armagh; but Dr Walsh's influence remained considerable and unhelpful. True, in December 1919 he denounced the attempt on Lord French's life; but as Serjeant Sullivan, a fellow-Catholic and nationalist, wrote to him at the time:

As far as I can ascertain from enquiry no instruction to fortify your flock has been given from any pulpit during the three years in which the agents of the secret society have publicly represented murder as a sort of religious function. The result is that now a Catholic who will not be silent about the articles of his Faith is exposed to assassination. For my part I will not purchase peace by cowardice. By instituting a course of moral instruction . . . Your Grace may rescue hundreds of our boys and save many lives.[13]

No response whatever was made to this appeal.

The year 1919 also saw a split developing in southern Unionist ranks. The call to Unionists, of March 1918 had been a protest against a possible "sell-out" by Lord Midleton and others at the convention, and its momentum did not die away with the fiasco of the convention's demise. In January 1919 Lord Midleton's supporters at a meeting of the Irish Unionist Alliance proposed the exclusion of Ulster members if partition were under discussion. They held that "the fate of Southern Unionism must be decided by Southern Unionists alone". The majority however disagreed. They contended that Ulster members should not be kept out just because their views were unacceptable; and the charge that if it were not for the Ulster members Midleton's views would be acceptable to the majority of southern Unionists was also refuted.[14] Thereupon the Midletonites resigned and formed their new League. Some Catholics, like Kenmare and John Blake Powell, supported Midleton; others like Lord Bellew, held by the principles of the call.

The latter, who was one of the vice-chairmen of the new alliance, came from an old and distinguished Catholic family of Anglo-Norman descent.[15] The Bellews had been baronets since 1688, and a Sir John Bellew had been M.P. for County Louth in 1639.[16] The first peer and seventh baronet was Sir Patrick Bellew (1798–1866), who was Lord Lieutenant of Louth from 1831 and Whig M.P. for the county from 1831 to 1832 and from 1834 to 1837. In 1838 he was sworn a member of the Irish Privy Council, and served as a Commissioner for National Education until his death. In July 1848 he was created Lord Bellew of Barmeath.

The Bellews had held property both in Louth and in County Galway since the mid-seventeenth century, and as landlords were held in high esteem. Of the first Lord Bellew it was written:

His retiring habits and love of home prevented him from going much into society or seeking a leading position in public life, which his talents would have commanded. His greatest ambition was to advance the interests of Ireland, and to promote the social happiness of the people . . . We believe a bailiff never earned a shilling on his estate, and as for the crowbar brigade, they never set foot on Barmeath . . . He was one of the class who wished to do acts of charity and who would "blush to find them fame".[17]

His descendant George, the fourth Baron, was equally retiring. An Irish representative peer like his brother Charles (1855–1911), who sat as a Liberal Unionist from 1904, he saw service in the Afghan war of 1878–9, in the Nile expedition of 1884–5, and in the Boer War. He spoke but once in the House of Lords during the debate on the Better Government for Ireland Bill, when he repeatedly contradicted Lord Haldane's assertion that southern Ireland might work the Bill. He had lived for sixty-four years in Ireland, he said, and he knew that the people there would not. In a third intervention, Bellew challenged the government to name one single safeguard provided for the southern minority in the Bill. So did Midleton. Lord Stuart of Wortley was unable to satisfy either.[18] In one night 250 police barracks (as police stations were known) had been destroyed, mostly by explosives. This must have meant "a total of 25,000 men practically under arms in that one night".[20] Contrast this with police numbers of only 10,000, and the need for vigorous reinforcement was at once apparent.

John Blake Powell, another Catholic Unionist holding high office, took a less robust view. On 24th April 1920 he wrote to Midleton of the possibility of a treaty with the I.R.A. "There is evidently some intention", he wrote,

to change the general policy of Government here in the direction of conciliation — I think the vast majority of people here are glad . . . Undoubtedly there is no government here in the ordinarily accepted sense of the word. The present Home Rule Bill will not be worked or even tried, it has no friend in Ireland & putting it *in force* will make matters worse.[21]

The constituencies would return Sinn Fein members *exclusively*, in the south and west. The moderates among them would accept Colonial

Home Rule and County option for Ulster, "and would make a Treaty of Peace with England, and the country would be given a fair chance".

Powell's views were not shared by other Unionists. Walter Long wrote to Midleton on 26th July 1920; "We have no intention of entering into negotiations with S.F. . . . we would not bargain with men who have been guilty of those awful murders. The thing is unthinkable".[22]

But he had thought of it. Six days earlier Cardinal Gasquet had a long discussion on the condition of Ireland and the position of the Roman Catholic Church with Lord Edmund Talbot, soon to become viceroy, another Catholic, Lord Kenmare, and Lord Midleton. The cardinal informed them "that at Rome the Irish Bishops had been spoken to very strongly as to their attitude towards crime, but some of them had said they had lost the power of controlling their people".[23]

Guerilla warfare was now highly organized. Assassinations took place in broad daylight. Sixteen occupied, and four hundred and twenty-four abandoned, R.I.C. barracks were destroyed during the first six months of 1920. Forty-seven court houses were burnt out.[24] The legal system of the Crown was being superseded by "National Arbitration Courts". On 20th May a transport embargo was instituted by dockers and later by railwaymen so that communications could only be maintained by the army, whose task was made doubly difficult by the sabotage of bridges and the disruption of the railways. Many loyalists were abandoned to face their attackers undefended as Crown forces were obliged to concentrate on defending themselves and their quarters; and although in time the military learnt to combat the rebels by fighting them on their own ground and in their own style, many fine houses were destroyed in the process and many people were murdered or maimed, despoiled or left homeless.

From June 1920 sectarian passions were inflamed and violence caught fire in the north, as elsewhere. Rioting in Derry was repeated in Belfast. On 12th July Carson promised that Ulster would tolerate no Sinn Fein. On the 21st began three days of bloodshed and destruction. Protestant shipyard workers drove out Roman Catholics, some of whom had come from the south to replace serving soldiers. Tumult also gripped Lisburn and Bangor. By the end of September more than eighty had been killed in the disturbances. A "Belfast Boycott" was decreed in the Dail cabinet.[25]

At Mountjoy, eighty-nine out of 151 prisoners went on hunger-strike from 5th April. Their object was to extend "ameliorative treatment", i.e. special privileges, to all prisoners, including those convicted of the possession of firearms and explosives. As Henry pointed out in the House of Commons on 13th April, such hunger-strikes were, in effect, attempted suicides, crimes which were then condemned both by secular and ecclesiastical laws; but sympathy was nonetheless aroused in high places, especially in the case of Terence MacSwiney, Lord Mayor of Cork and Commandant of the local I.R.A. The king's private secretary, Lord Stamfordham, wrote to Midleton from Balmoral (8th September 1920) that Ireland would "never be pacified by repression. Personally, I think the Govt. made an egregious mistake in the Coercion Act; and they might have known that it would produce Hunger Strikes & Martyrs". He disclosed that of the many who wrote to the king on the subject, the great majority was against letting MacSwiney die. MacSwiney should have been let out into a private home, but under police surveillance.

Midleton cited in reply the salutary effects of severe measures in 1882 and 1887, whereupon Stamfordham rejoined that these results were only "*temporary*, whereas what we ought to strive for is *lasting* peace. You say that those who appeal to the King . . . have not thought out the problem — but surely Dunraven who has lived his life in Ireland, Horace Plunkett, the Macdermot, the members of the Irish Peace Conference think before they act?"[26]

The government, despite these appeals, held firm, and MacSwiney died on 25th October. His death in Cork was followed by two others. The stratagem was then suspended on the orders of the Sinn Fein leader, the monarchist Arthur Griffith.[27] Powell continued to advocate a settlement, writing to Midleton on 1st October that "things are going from bad to worse here. I know of course the terrible difficulties of the situation but is there no hope that the intervention of real statesmanship and diplomacy might bring about some treaty of peace"? A bridge had to be built over the chasm — "otherwise it will be all chasm here in a short time".[28]

Six days later Archbishop Bernard (Church of Ireland) wrote to Denis Kelly, Catholic Archbishop of Ross, proposing a joint appeal for peace on the basis of a modified Dominion status with county option. Kelly replied from Skibbereen on 11th October that he shared Bernard's views but there was no hope of bringing them into effect. The passing of the Partition Bill would, he felt, upset Catholics and Protestants, and indeed "Ulsterites"; nonetheless he would raise the matter at Maynooth, where the Catholic bishops were due to meet. On 23rd October, after the meeting, he wrote that "the Orange pogrom in the north, and

Government destruction in other parts have filled with indignation the minds of many of my colleagues — some of whom had been most sober and moderate".[29]

On 10th December 1920 martial law was proclaimed in the four counties of Cork, Kerry, Limerick and Tipperary. The following night part of Patrick Street, Cork, together with the City Hall and the Carnegie Library, went up in flames. The "Black and Tans" were blamed for this reprisal. More official reprisals under the martial law system included the destruction of six houses in Midleton, near Cork on 29th December, after an I.R.A. ambush in which three policemen died. Lord Midleton was embarrassed, for he owned many of the houses in the town.[30] These rough measures, which many, including Loyalists, thought brutal and outrageous, had some effect. In 1921, only two R.I.C. barracks were destroyed. But although terrorism was answered by execution, the total number of incidents continued to rise, and the task of law enforcement was hampered, especially in the martial law areas, by the lack of a single authority and command to co-ordinate the crown forces and civil power.

At the beginning of April 1921 Lord French's retirement from the lord lieutenancy, much against his will, was announced, and Lord Edmund Talbot, created Viscount FitzAlan of Derwent, became the first Catholic viceroy since Tyrconnell — and the last. The *Freeman's Journal* dismissed him as a "die-hard" and coercionist; others wished him well, though forecasting a bleak outlook. *The Times* concluded (4th April 1921): "If Lord Edmund Talbot's appointment means a truce, it means everything. If it does not mean a truce, it means nothing at all". He was "not only a great noble but a gentleman".[31]

FitzAlan, like many Midletonite Unionists (and indeed Field Marshal Sir Henry Wilson, who deplored reprisals) was worried by the violence of the government's policy[32], which was however beginning to weaken just at the time when it was beginning to show results and the crown forces had "murder by the throat".[33] In Dublin, in March, considerable rebel arms dumps were unearthed. Michael Collins's office was flushed out on two separate occasions, and an I.R.A. provincial distribution centre in Baggot Lane was discovered on 27th April.[34] The rebels were reeling, though still not broken, but the government did not hit back with no holds barred; the Better Government for Ireland Bill had come into force as the Government of Ireland Act in December 1920, and under it they were committed to hold elections in mid-May, the cabinet having rejected their postponement on 21st April. Winston Churchill,

Henry, 15th Duke of Norfolk as Lord Mayor of Sheffield by E. Moore.
Arundel Castle. By permission of His Grace the Duke of Norfolk.

Sir Denis Henry, Bt. By permission of Sir James Henry, Bt.

Edmund, 1st Viscount FitzAlan of Derwent by Oswald Birley.
Arundel Castle. By permission of His Grace the Duke of Norfolk.

C. E. McGloughlin 1866–1932 taken in 1930. By permission of Dr. Mary Belton.

then Colonial Secretary, favoured a truce. He did not believe that it would hamper the military, for if necessary "we can break up this Irish parliament and revert to coercion"; but the Irish military and police authorities, not surprisingly, did not agree with him that a truce would make no difference to them.[35]

On 12th May there was further Cabinet discussion of a truce. Both FitzAlan and Denis Henry were against it, FitzAlan asserting that "you can't make a truce without meeting with Michael Collins. We can't have that. We can't take the initiative and must hope that they will". Henry agreed. Five, including Churchill and Montagu, supported a truce; Lloyd George, Balfour, Chamberlain and seven others were against.[36]

The election results, declared on 25th May, surprised no one. There was a substantial Unionist majority in the north, but in the south, republicans won every constituency except the four University seats. That very day the Custom House, perhaps the finest building in Dublin, was destroyed by the I.R.A. Over five hundred outrages a week were recorded by the end of the month compared with three hundred in April. The Thompson sub-machine gun, then a new weapon, was being imported through the efforts of anti-British sympathizers in the United States.[37]

From a constitutional point of view, the government's dilemma now was that if the southern parliament failed to assemble some form of "crown colony" government would have to be imposed. This would mean full martial law and worse violence. Dominion Home Rule, seen by Carson as a *de facto* republic, was a solution from which many Cabinet Ministers still shrank. Why should southern Ireland be rewarded for its disloyalty with a constitutional status superior to that of Northern Ireland which had agreed, albeit reluctantly, to work the Act? This was an argument favoured by some Unionists both in and out of Ireland; but there were others, in the Midletonite Anti-Partition League especially, who by the end of 1920 were favouring Dominion status provided that it applied to the whole of Ireland.[38] Dominion Home Rule had been proposed, to Ulster Unionist horror, in the Irish convention of 1917. Plunkett, its chairman, presided over the Irish Dominion League until its demise in 1921. An all-Ireland Dominion had been the purpose of John Blake Powell's negotiations with the hierarchy in the autumn of 1920.

In the summer of 1921 the Army would make no firm prediction of success; and Macready, the General Officer Commanding-in-Chief, could make no optimistic forecast if the conflict were to be prolonged beyond October.[39] The Irish Situation Committee of the cabinet thereupon decided that martial law would be extended to all twenty-six southern counties on 12th July if the southern parliament refused to function. On 3rd June, all official reprisals were ordered to cease, and when General Macready presented his draft proclamation of martial law to the cabinet, he warned that it might involve as many as a hundred shootings a week.[40] He made no secret of his own belief that a policy of coercion would not succeed. Yet Michael Collins later told the tough last Chief Secretary, Hamar Greenwood, that in June "you had us dead-beat. We could not have lasted another three weeks. When we were told of the offer of a truce we were astounded. We thought you must have gone mad".[41]

The first sign that the government were beginning to despair of coercion came on 7th June 1921, when the new parliament of Northern Ireland held its first sitting in Belfast. In a speech after luncheon, Lord FitzAlan said that the Government of Ireland Act was not perfect. "He believed it wanted amending already, and would not be surprised if it were amended in the not too distant future".[42] On 22nd June, King George V and Queen Mary visited Belfast to open the session. The King's speech, which owed something to a reconciled rebel, General Smuts, made a profound impression. "This is a great and critical occasion in the history of the Six Counties", His Majesty said,

> but not for the Six Counties alone, for everything which interests them touches Ireland, and everything which touches Ireland finds an echo in the remotest parts of the Empire . . . I appeal to all Irishmen to pause, to stretch out the hand of forbearance and conciliation, to forgive and forget, and to join in making for the land they love a new era of peace, contentment, and good will.[43]

The effect on the cabinet in London was immediate. Two days later, Lloyd George invited de Valera and Sir James Craig, the new prime minister of Northern Ireland, to Downing Street for unconditional talks. There was also sadness and tragedy. A troop train carrying a detachment of 10th Hussars, who had formed part of the king's escort in Belfast was blown up by a land mine near Dundalk. Three soldiers and a number of horses died. Lord Midleton's paper of 22nd June on the "State of Ireland" was direly pessimistic. "Within a mile of the town of Midleton", he wrote, "close to Cork, there begins a district of 100 square miles in which there is not a single police barracks or a single magistrate, & in which no process of judgment for any offence has taken place for six months".

Within the last month the two largest houses in Cork had been burnt, the lieutenant for the county kidnapped, and three other magistrates similarly treated. If present conditions continued

> of military operations so insufficient that every landlord can be kidnapped, every house can be burned, every business ruined . . . there will not be by the end of the autumn a single supporter of British policy in the South outside the province of Leinster. Nor, when order is restored, will there be any adherent of the British connection to attempt to stem the demand for a Republic.[44]

It was in these circumstances that the cabinet decided to negotiate. There seems little doubt that their hand was forced by the wave of public support on both sides of St George's Channel for the tone of the monarch's speech. Cardinal Bourne had already, in April, pressed for the withdrawal of the Black and Tans, for an end to reprisals, and for a permanent reconciliation.[45] The ever-soft-hearted British public expects conduct of the very highest standard from the forces of law and order, and will not tolerate any derogation, while outrages by rebels are often the subject of misplaced sympathy. The king was expressing the wishes of his people, or of those vociferous enough to write to His Majesty, just as the Catholic bishops were expressing the wish of theirs. The tragedy was that a universal desire for peace and reconciliation, untempered by firm and resolute statesmanship, led to worse excesses than those which had gone before. As in so many countries where British rule had led to peace and justice, its withdrawal led to unimaginable excesses of violence.

Craig accepted Lloyd George's invitation at once; de Valera agreed only to "consult". Then, on 28th June, the parliament of southern Ireland was formally opened in the Council Chamber of the Department of Agriculture. Only the four Trinity College Members, together with fifteen out of the sixty-four senators were present. The M.P.s elected their Speaker, adjourned and went their way.

De Valera's difficulty was that he regarded himself as the president of an all-Ireland republic; and in a purported effort to secure all-Ireland agreement he summoned Craig, Midleton, Sir Maurice Dockrell, who remained a City of Dublin Unionist member of the imperial parliament,

Sir Robert Woods, Andrew Jameson, all Unionists, to confer with him beforehand as representatives of the "political minority".[46] Sir James Craig at once refused, on the grounds that he had already been summoned to Downing Street, whereupon de Valera declared Lloyd George's proposal "impossible of acceptance in its present form".[47] General Smuts then visited Dublin to mediate, and on 8th July de Valera wrote to accept Lloyd George's invitation. On the same day General Macready visited the Republicans at the Dublin Mansion House in order to discuss the cessation of hostilities, and on 10th July he signed a truce with Richard Mulcahy, "Chief of Staff of the Irish Republican Army".

De Valera, in inviting the Unionists to confer, had been careful to leave out the Irish Unionist Alliance. Midleton however was persuaded to attend by Lloyd George, but in the preliminary negotiations he failed to seek assurances from the republicans for the future status of southern Unionists in the new Ireland. This error was particularly serious because later in the negotiations it became apparent that Lloyd George was not prepared to insist on any such safeguards. Moreover, the Midletonites' participation in negotiations deepened the rift with the "callers" of the I.U.A. When H. A. Gwynne of the London *Morning Post* wrote to Austen Chamberlain on 23rd July that he was determined to oppose negotiations and argued for the imposition of martial law in the twenty-six counties, Chamberlain was able to reply that this was not the unanimous view of the southern Unionists.[48]

Negotiations with de Valera dragged on for two months. The king, through Stamfordham, expressed his delight that Midleton had "consented to meet de Valera in Dublin, as His Majesty feels sure that nothing but good can come out of the conversations which will take place and so pave the way for the London Conference. Indeed, the King hopes that you may be able to persuade de Valera that it is time that murder and outrage should cease".[49] In August the cabinet were perturbed by the impertinence of one of de Valera's letters, and FitzAlan went over to consult. He expressed the view that it was worth putting up with it, because if fighting did begin again it meant "on the very first night the murder of hosts of our friends & loyalists & the burning of their homes, & I am convinced a peaceful settlement could be & wd be reached by patience".[50] In a meeting of the cabinet held at Inverness on 7th September FitzAlan was in favour of an unconditional invitation to the republicans, as were Baldwin, Montagu, and Chamberlain; Winston Churchill, Birkenhead and Greenwood were for conditions.[51]

The conference planned by Lloyd George finally met at Downing

Street on 10th October. The Unionists of Ireland were, as such, unrepresented. FitzAlan thought it unwise for them to be present.[52] Lord Oranmore stated in a letter to Midleton that "the I.U.A. will not touch the unclean thing, therefore we need not consider the question of their having a representative".[53] Archbishop Bernard, now Provost of Trinity College Dublin, agreed, adding that the I.U.A. would wreck the conference if they could. Lloyd George proposed that three southern Unionists should remain in London during the conference to be available for consultation.[54]

On the government side were the Lord Chancellor (F. E. Smith, Earl of Birkenhead), Winston Churchill (Colonial Secretary), Austen Chamberlain (Leader of the House of Commons), Sir Hamar Greenwood (Irish Secretary) and the Secretary of State for War, Sir Laming Worthington-Evans. The rebel delegation consisted of Arthur Griffith, Michael Collins, Eamon Duggan and George Gavan Duffy.

The absence of de Valera was to have dire consequences. It has been stated that his colleagues thought that his presence would not conduce to peace and this may well have been the case.[55] The Pope sent an innocuous telegram to King George V praying that God might grant to His Majesty "the great joy and imperishable glory of bringing to an end the age-long dissension". The "President of the Irish Republic" took umbrage and sent His Holiness a long rejoinder asserting that the people of Ireland owed no allegiance to His Majesty.

On 15th November the three southern Unionists in London, Midleton, Jameson and Bernard, were summoned to Downing Street. There Lloyd George, with four of his colleagues informed them "that the negotiations had little useful result, until Mr de Valera's telegram to the Pope had been published. Upon this, the Prime Minister informed the Sinn Fein delegates that the Conference must be broken up, unless they agreed explicitly to accept (a) allegiance to the Crown. (b) association *within* the Empire and (c) British control of harbours &c in Ireland".[56] The conference resumed only after Michael Collins had hurried over to Dublin to pacify the prickly potentate. In the early hours of 6th December 1921, after His Majesty's government had threatened to break off negotiations and renew operations against rebellion were a conclusion not speedily reached, an unprecedented document entitled "articles of agreement for a treaty between Great Britain and Ireland" was signed between ministers of the crown and subjects.

A letter in the *Morning Post* (13th December 1921) drew attention to the plight of southern Unionists. Many had fled to England; others, "though not yet actually driven out of Ireland, have been reduced to beggary by the action of Sinn Fein, and are now living from hand to mouth, in extreme want and penury, and in daily and nightly fear of murder or brutal outrage". In the House of Lords on 15th December, the Duke of Northumberland argued that had the soldiers in Ireland been given a free hand, "the insurrection would have been put down in a few weeks".[57] W. M. Jellett, M.P. for Dublin University, denied in the *Morning Post* of 17th December that southern Unionists were in favour of accepting the treaty. The great body of them, he said, "were determinedly opposed to any such acceptance". Neither the two Irish Members who had addressed the House of Commons nor Lords Midleton and Donoughmore represented southern Irish opinion.

CHAPTER SEVENTEEN

Between the Wars

When a resurgent Sinn Fein, carried on the crest of the anti-conscription wave, was denounced by Cardinal Logue in a letter read throughout the Archdiocese of Armagh for "an ill-considered and Utopian" agitation, "in pursuit of a dream which no man in his sober senses can hope to see realized: the establishment of an Irish Republic"[1], His Eminence did not foresee the unprecedented "Articles of Agreement for a Treaty between Great Britain and Ireland", which were signed on 6th December 1921. The Dail approved that agreement by sixty-four votes to fifty-seven. Michael Collins was persuasive with his assessment of it as the bringer of "freedom, not the ultimate freedom that all nations desire and develop to, but the freedom to achieve it".[2] As Carson, for one, had predicted, Dominion Home Rule would not be the final destination.

An impatient, dissatisfied and remorseless de Valera resigned the presidency of the pro-treaty Dail to be succeeded by the "dual monarchist" Arthur Griffith. Collins was appointed chairman of the provisional government for which the treaty provided as an interim measure pending the constitution of the "Parliament and Government of the Irish Free State", and in the ensuing elections the republicans *a outrance* were decisively defeated throughout the twenty-six counties of Ireland. The I.R.A. split, and the anti-treaty faction broke with the Dail and began raiding the loyal North.

Precisely a year after the signing of the treaty the Irish Free State was born. The north, having opted out, had been under its own government since May 1922. The Irish version of "Irish Free State", *Saorstat Eireann*, was the title adopted by the revolutionaries in 1919. It symbolized the ambivalence of the relationship with crown and commonwealth. The Free State was something less than a dominion in outward form and considerably less than a dominion in spirit. Dr D. W. Harkness called his classic study of the Irish Free State and the British Commonwealth of Nations from 1921 to 1931, *The Restless Dominion*.[3] No other commonwealth realm had been the product of a treaty. Ireland was in any event herself a mother country of the commonwealth. The Free State was a Catholic and a European power which early on mounted the international stage at Geneva, using the League of Nations as an alternative world forum to that of the empire. At the same time, statesmen such as Kevin O'Higgins were to the fore, often with South African counterparts whose history too was one of conflict with Britain, in the assertion of complete sovereignty, a process that reached its culmination in the Statute of Westminster of 1931. In the Free State the senator or deputy taking the parliamentary Oath of Allegiance pledged his "true faith and allegiance" to the "Constitution of the Irish Free State as by law established", rather than to the crown. To the king, he promised only to be "faithful . . . in virtue of the common citizenship of Ireland with Great Britain and her adherence to and membership of the group of nations forming the British Commonwealth of Nations".[4] Even so, the Oath constituted a stumbling-block for de Valera's republicans. That prescribed for the defence forces and for the *Garda Siochana* (the new civil police force) made no mention of the monarch.

FitzAlan continued to represent the king as Lord Lieutenant (Viceroy) until December 1922, when the Free State was established with an Irishman, Tim Healy as Governor-general, and Northern Ireland acquired a Governor, the Duke of Abercorn. On 27th January 1922, the last viceroy wrote to Churchill of a "swollen head atmosphere" in the youthful provisional government. On the previous day Churchill had met Irish ministers after a cabinet meeting and "impressed upon them strongly the fact that we regarded the adequate recognition and honourable and respectful treatment of the position and status of the Governor General as a fundamental element of the Treaty to be carried out in a gentleman-like spirit on both sides".[5] However in February Midleton asked to "see the King about the position of FitzAlan and the way the Government and the Irish Ministry are ignoring him and the attempts that are anticipated to replace him by some 'novus homo'". His Majesty referred Midleton to Churchill. Midleton saw him and also Arthur Griffith.

Now on the friendliest terms with Michael Collins, Churchill was optimistic. He thought that the provisional government was doing "its best, and I still believe they will win through if they are helped in the right way".[7]

For FitzAlan however the viceregal path was not all red carpets. On 17th April he was writing of government fears that he might be kidnapped. Ministers wanted him to find a pretext to prolong a stay in London. The viceroy was given more protection. "When you come here next week", he wrote to Midleton, "you will find 2 officers and a

Co[mpany] and will be in imminent danger of yr life from a chance rifle going off."[8]

The Free State was born in blood. The fratricide of Free Stater and republican excelled the previous horrors. Irish Ministers resorted with effect to methods of repression harsher than those Asquith had condemned when practised by forces of the British crown.[9] In April 1922 republican irregulars seized the Four Courts in Dublin. The Free State borrowed guns of the Royal Artillery for their reduction. Friends of FitzAlan and General Macready prevailed on the viceroy not to attend Holy Week services in the Pro-Cathedral and other Catholic churches but to content himself with worshipping in the viceregal chapel in Dublin Castle. FitzAlan regretted this. He remarked to "Irish friends here that if 40 Communists had occupied the Law Courts in London they would not have been allowed to remain". He had attended race meetings in Phoenix Park and at the Curragh. "In this so-called Christian country it appears to me to be safe to go to the races and not to church".[10] But how many Catholic Unionists have been struck down in Irish troubles coming out of mass!

During 1922 Midleton received both bouquets and brickbats. The position of the abandoned southern Irish Unionists was indeed unenviable. On 16th March John Blake Powell wrote effusively from 41 Fitzwilliam Place:

> If the work I was privileged to do was strenuous, and the time a trying one, it was on you our leader rather than on the Rank & File that the heaviest burthen fell. None of us can ever forget your zeal, the sacrifices you made, your wisdom and your courage . . . It is sad to think that if others had been guided by you and had co-operated with you, at a time which was a turning-point in the history of this unfortunate country, the saddest of all its chapters would never have been written.[11]

But the die-hard *Morning Post* of 24th June levelled the extravagant charge that "Southern Irishmen from the Midletonian anti-Partitionists to the Rory O'Connor Republicans" regarded killing as "no murder when the victim is an Orangeman or a loyalist". Midleton demanded an apology by the following Monday and on 26th June raised the matter in the House of Lords, Lady Bathurst, proprietor of the *Morning Post*, having refused to retract. Donoughmore told their Lordships that murder had been universally condemned.[12]

As well as the *Morning Post*, *Blackwood's Magazine* tenaciously championed the lost cause of the southern Irish Unionists. The issue of December 1922 commented on the demise of that largely Catholic force, the Royal Irish Constabulary:

> Every Roman Catholic member of the R.I.C. received threatening letter after letter — their wives were also subjected to this cowardly form of terrorism — to the effect that, if they did not resign, or if they joined the R.U.C., they would be assassinated. These unfortunate men appealed to their priests to denounce this savage vendetta. The priests made no sign, and many resigned and were forced to fly the country.[13]

The Ulster correspondent of *Notes from Ireland* wrote in the May issue that there had been many loyal Roman Catholic victims of Republican terror both in southern Ireland and in the north.[14]

The civil war in the Free State added to the estrangement of north from south. As Kevin O'Higgins put it:

> We had an opportunity of building up a worthy State that would attract, and, in time, absorb and assimilate those elements. We preferred the patriotic way. We preferred to burn our own houses, blow up our own bridges, rob our own banks, saddle ourselves with millions of debt for the maintenance of an Army and for the payment of compensation for the recreations of our youth. Generally, we preferred to practise upon ourselves worse indignities than the British had practised upon us since Cromwell and Mountjoy and now we wonder why the Orangemen are not hopping like so many fleas across the Border in their anxiety to come within our fold and jurisdiction.[15]

Again: "it is useless to seek to abolish the boundary by law until we have abolished it in our hearts".[16]

The northern premier, Sir James Craig, bitterly complained that the Anglo-Irish Agreement had been signed without consultation with Ulster. Particularly obnoxious was the provision that if Northern Ireland chose to remain outside the Irish Free State (as she had) a Boundary Commission should be set up, to be composed of one Free State and one Northern Ireland appointee sitting under a chairman to be chosen by the British government. This, according to Craig, was a breach of the

Government of Ireland Act of 1920.

After a post-war boom Ulster sank into a slump after 1921. Over-dependence on linen and clothing and shipping did not help. The border severed Derry from its economic hinterland in Donegal. By 1923 eighteen per cent of insured workers were unemployed.

Churchill, as Colonial Secretary, brought Collins and Craig together. He has recorded his impression of the Irish leaders:

> In Arthur Griffith and Michael Collins . . . Richard Mulcahy and Kevin O'Higgins were found realists of the first order; men who feared God, who loved their country and who kept their word. In Ulster Sir James Craig stood solid as a rock. Imperturbable, sagacious, above hate or anger yet not without a lively sentiment; steady, true and untiring, he brought his own people out from the midst of indescribable miseries and difficulties back to daylight and civilisation.[17]

The miseries and difficulties included the Belfast boycott, kidnapping, trans-border forays, and the driving of Catholics from shipyard and other jobs. More Catholics than Protestants died and, as recently, the I.R.A. claimed to be the champion of the minority, against Protestant pogrom and bigotry. Terrorists blocked the Glenshane Pass on the trunk road from Belfast to Derry.[18]

On 30th March 1922 Craig and Collins met to declare "peace". In return for a complete cessation of IRA hostilities in the Six Counties, Roman Catholics, particularly in nationalist areas, were to be recruited to the Ulster Special Constabulary. The northern government went so far as to agree to the selection of these Catholics by an advisory committee nominated by the provisional government in Dublin and presided over by the Bishop of Connor and Down, Dr McRory. But the agreement remained on paper. It took heroism to enlist in the face of IRA intimidation and few Catholics felt able to join the B Specials. There were more of their faith, mostly ex-servicemen, in the A Specials.[19]

Craig returned to Belfast on 1st April to find it in "terrible turmoil". He held a Cabinet meeting, and afterwards, "looking exhausted", had an interview with a leading Catholic, Raymond Burke, son of Sir John Burke and a shipbroker. On 8th April he spoke to 2,000 businessmen, who immediately formed an Ulster Association for Peace. Burke and another influential and highly-respected Catholic, Hugh Dougal, came to Stormont again to talk to Craig, and Burke surprised Lady Craig by asking her to distribute the prizes at a Roman Catholic school. He wanted them to see, he explained, "that you're not the devil you're painted".[20] Craig and the Cabinet Secretary, Spender, also consulted with Burke about co-operation with the minority generally especially on education.[21]

On 2nd June 1922 Winston Churchill received a deputation at the Colonial Office. It consisted of Raymond Burke, together with Hugh Dougal and W. M. Hughes, all Catholic businessmen. The truce had been ineffective, and life in Belfast was becoming intolerable. Burke's chauffeur had been murdered.

Churchill asked "why the Catholic community could not produce 2,000 good men to act as Specials". Dougal replied that "not a single Catholic would now join the Specials, who had come to be regarded as a sectarian force. If they joined they would be in danger of their lives' from Catholic extremists. They urged a meeting between Churchill, Collins, Craig and Devlin in order to secure a further truce until the election in southern Ireland. Churchill deplored the brushing aside of Devlin which had been "one of the worst disasters of the situation". He added that failure to carry out the agreement of 30th March rested partly on the northern government but partly also on Collins, who had failed to secure the cessation of IRA activity in the Six Counties.

In reply to further questions, the deputation said that

> The Catholic business men in Belfast excluding the Republicans and the professional men, would be ready to recognise the Northern Government, but for the rest of the Catholic population the idea of religious persecution dominated their political preferences. Following upon the expulsion from the shipyards and the persecutions of the Catholics, a ghetto was being formed in Belfast. They mentioned in particular the bitterness of fathers of apprentices who had been turned out . . . They had heard of 300 such cases.[22]

The private secretary to the Lord Lieutenant, S. G. Tallents, was instructed by Churchill to proceed to Belfast and report on the implementation of the agreement of 30th March. He found that the pact had been broken down at almost every point. In less than three months to 17th June, sixty-eight Protestants and ninety-three Roman Catholics had been killed in the province as a whole; 118 out of a total of 164 deaths had occurred in Belfast. Only eight persons had been prosecuted for murder since the previous November.

On 12th July Churchill wrote to Craig referring to "grave allegations against the Loyalists in Northern Ireland". They had been accused of conducting a "pogrom against defenceless Catholic workers" and it was alleged that tens of thousands of Catholics had escaped to England and Scotland. Craig replied by saying that he had only heard of twelve cases, of whom the majority were Protestants threatened by the IRA; some Catholics had also been threatened. There was no single established case, he asserted, of a Roman Catholic fleeing from "Protestant Hooliganism" to Great Britain.

This did not entirely square with information supplied earlier to Churchill by Samuel Hoare, who drew attention amongst others to two cases: one Catholic aged twenty-five who had served in the Army during the war had been "threatened by Sinn Feiners", and another, an ex-sergeant of the Cheshire Regiment, had been similarly threatened. Craig thought both these cases were "bogus".[23] D. W. Miller has quoted evidence of the Unionist organization in Belfast helping a Catholic ex-serviceman to recover his job in the shipyard.

The October 1922 issue of *Blackwood's Magazine* divided the Ulster Catholics into "Sinn Fein, rebels, neutral Nationalists, and a small number of Loyalists. In Belfast, roughly a quarter of the population is Roman Catholic, the great majority of whom are only too anxious to be respectable and law-abiding citizens". But gunmen had been brought in and

> for many months the Roman Catholics lived a life of terror, never knowing the day or hour when two or more strange gunmen might suddenly appear in their houses and demand board and lodging for an indefinite time; nor when the I.R.A. might establish the Headquarters of an I.R.A. battalion or company with them, or make use of their houses as snipers' posts or arsenals.

They might be ordered to leave their front doors ajar and their back doors open at a certain hour on a certain day. This meant that an outrage was to be attempted. "Disobedience of this order, if found out, meant certain death".

Bombs were hidden in dispatch cases and the inside of trams. One was heard ticking and carried down by the conductor.

A kerb flower-seller (an ex-soldier and a Roman Catholic) happened to be standing close by, and had the presence of mind to throw the water he kept for his flowers over the bomb, and so saved a critical situation . . . The Corporation voted a grant of £50 to that gallant flower-seller, but when they came to look for him he had completely disappeared.

In the shipyards, the article denied that there "was any question of religion; and the proof is that there are still *loyal* Roman Catholic workers in the Belfast shipyards".[24] Other reports however told of murderous attacks upon Catholic employees and their expulsion. As assurance Craig gave Collins in London in January 1922 was that Catholics would be protected and those driven from their employment would be re-instated.[25]

In December 1922 *The Times* regarded it as a hopeful sign that "residents in a Catholic district of Belfast" had protested against the removal of a body of Special Constabulary from their midst.[26]

Griffith died; Collins fell, like many of his enemies, to the gun in ambush. The treaty was indeed his death warrant. Thereafter W. T. Cosgrave's presidency of the Executive Council of the Irish Free State was a period of some stability and moderation.

The Times Special Correspondent wrote in the issue of 11th September 1923 that

the influence of the Free State is waning among the Roman Catholics of Belfast and other northern areas . . . They are beginning to realise that they have been used as political pawns by the Republicans . . . and, to some extent, by the Free Staters. They accuse the latter of exerting pressure to continue the boycott of the Northern Parliament; they certainly paid the Roman Catholic teachers who refused any grant from the Northern Ministry of Education, but were eventually compelled by the sudden drying up of the Southern Pactolus, to make their peace with Lord Londonderry . . . they have no cause to regret their surrender.

Many Northern Roman Catholics, too, are irritated to find that every atrocity committed by the Republicans or by their allies in the Irish civil war is glibly ascribed to "refugees from Ulster" by Sinn Fein apologists. In spite of all that has happened, the Northern Roman Catholic has a distinct respect for his Protestant neighbour — often enough his racial kinsman — whom he considers more trustworthy and more constructive than his Southern co-religionist — though he may not openly admit it.

In April 1925, Craig called a general election. The Unionists made gains in the menaced counties of Fermanagh and Tyrone where nationalists of the older tradition split the opposition vote with Sinn Fein. Craig's friendly enemy, the nationalist Joseph Devlin, led his hitherto abstentionist party into the Northern Ireland parliament. In 1928 Devlin would declare that "there is not, and there is not going to be, any attempt of any kind, much less a conspiracy, to force the people of Northern Ireland into a Dublin or any other Parliament".[27]

Craig spoke in the Northern Ireland House of Commons of the Government's firm intention to see justice done to all. He thus echoed Carson's plea:

> From the outset let us see that the Catholic minority have nothing to fear from the Protestant majority. Let us take care to win all that is best among those who have been opposed to us in the past. While maintaining intact our own religion, let us give the same rights to the religions of our neighbours.[28]

Carson, the southerner, was without bigotry. He had sided with the Irish nationalists against the erection of Cromwell's statue outside the imperial House of Commons. He extolled the virtues of the Irish Catholic clergy. But there were those in Ulster less tolerant, forgiving and forbearing. It would however be a mistake to identify these with the Orange Order as a body. At their Annual Gathering in 1922 the Orangemen resolved in favour of "equal rights, equal liberties, and equal opportunities for all men, no matter what their religious outlook and no matter what their political bias", and in 1969 the Grand Orange Lodge of Ireland was quick to spring to the defence of its Catholic counterpart, the Ancient Order of Hibernians, when the integrity of its members was impugned, as was that of the Orange Order, in remarks by Sir Arthur Young, the Inspector-General of Police. Nationalist abstentionism in the early years of the statelet fed and was used to excuse Protestant bigotry. It contrasted with the co-operation given the Free State by its loyalist remnant, some of whom accepted appointment to the Senate in the generous spirit in which it was offered.

In the imperial general election of 1924 there was a nationalist-Sinn

Fein split in Tyrone and Fermanagh which the Unionists won. "It was said that many Roman Catholics voted for the Unionists so that they might not suffer inclusion in the Free State; an assertion that is strongly supported by the fact that Sir Charles Falls and J. A. Pringle received, respectively, 44,716 and 44,711 votes against 6,812 and 6,685 cast respectively for the Republicans, M. McCarten and T. Corrigan".[30]

In February 1922 Roman Catholic teachers in County Tyrone met at Omagh to deplore the control of education by the Six County regime. They called on the provisional government in Dublin to administer and finance the Catholic schools in the north and pledged themselves to take no salaries from its government. They asked Dublin to make them up. The Ulster authorities merely set the salaries aside until the teachers were ready to draw them. In the same way nationalist-dominated local authorities would send their minutes not to Belfast but to Dublin. As mentioned in *The Times'* correspondent's report quoted above, the teachers made their peace with the Minister of Education, Lord Londonderry. The department's Permanent Secretary from 1927, A. N. Bonaparte-Wyse, was a Catholic. In 1921 Londonderry persuaded him to serve on a committee planning the reform of Northern Ireland's education and he was then placed in charge of the province's elementary schools network. His knowledge in this field was unrivalled, and his ancestry was distinguished. A Sir Andrew Wyse had come over with Strongbow. During the Geraldine rebellion, Sir William Wyse, Mayor of Waterford in 1533, received three royal letters of thanks and in 1536 was knighted during or after a visit to England. He returned to Ireland with a cap of maintenance and a gilt sword, the gift of Henry VIII, to be borne before the mayor on state occasions. "Bonaparte" was added to "Wyse" as the result of a marriage between Sir Thomas Wyse, whose contributions to Catholic Unionism and to Irish education we have explored in a previous chapter, and Lucien Bonaparte's daughter. They had two sons, Napoleon Alfred Bonaparte, born in 1822, and William Charles Bonaparte who held a captaincy in the Waterford Militia, sat as a Justice of the Peace and served as High Sheriff of County Waterford in 1855. William was the author of numerous poetical works in French and English, and of *Vox Clamantis*, a work based on his efforts to combat Parnellism in Waterford and throughout Ireland from a Catholic Unionist standpoint.[31] William Wyse had two sons, Lucien William Bonaparte and Andrew Nicholas Bonaparte, born in 1870.

An M.A. of London University and an Inspector of National Schools, A. N. Bonaparte Wyse married in 1896 Marie, daughter of the

Russian Count de Chripounoff. Because of his linguistic ability he was sent to France and Germany for the Belmore Commission on manual and practical instruction in Irish primary schools. Later he became Secretary to another Catholic, William Starkie, who was resident commissioner for education in Ireland from 1899 until his death in 1920. It was Starkie who carried through the reforms recommended by the Belmore Commission, amid some controversy. Towards the end of his life he became a target for the IRA, as indeed did many other loyal servants of the crown in Ireland. But he was not to die at the hand of the gunman but on holiday at Cushenden, from natural causes. His daughter Enid, later to become a distinguished teacher of French at Oxford, wrote of him that he had been acceptable in north and south "because he was singularly free from religious bigotry; indeed, he believed that religious bigotry had ruined the country. He thought that Catholic children should be educated in Protestant schools and vice versa. His own children were educated in Protestant schools." As for his secretary, Wyse, St John Ervine described him as the best man Craig knew in Ireland.[32] Another important Catholic public servant in the early days of Stormont was Samuel Sloan, Principal Establishment Officer of the Northern Ireland Civil Service and Secretary of the Civil Service Commission. Patrick Shea recalls his friendliness to impoverished clerks in the 1920s.[33]

In the Free State another Catholic Unionist deeply respected by his employees and the larger community was Charles E. McGloughlin. He was born in 1865 and both in the Union and the Dominion served his city and country as an enlightened employer successful in business and as a civic dignitary. His family firm, of which he was chairman and managing director, was J. & C. McGloughlin, structural engineers, cast iron and brass-founders. His father started the iron and brass foundry in Brunswick (now Pearse) Street. His daughter remembers the impressive wrought iron gates and railings made by the firm which are still widely to be seen in Dublin and elsewhere.[34] He became chairman of the Irish Employers' Association and he was an influence for industrial peace from the turbulent days of the strikes organized by Jim Larkin in 1913. McGloughlin represented Irish employers at an International Labour Organization conference at Geneva in 1931. He was selected from the commercial register for the Dublin City Council, was a Peace Commissioner of the city and also Chairman of the Dublin Port and Docks Board. He was a founder member of the Dublin Rotary Club, the oldest such club in Europe, and became president. As a leading

Catholic layman, he served on the Eucharistic Congress Committee. On his death in 1932 Dr Wall, Bishop of Thasos and a number of Catholic clergy, attended McGloughlin's funeral. Workers of J. & C. McGloughlin walked nearly two miles in procession. The ceremony was attended by the Lord Mayor of Dublin, Alderman A. Byrne, T. D. and other Deputies, including General Mulcahy and President Cosgrave himself.[35]

The latter's dealings with Craig in the north were cordial. In 1925 the Tripartite Agreement and the subsequent legislation passed in Dublin and at Westminster after the abortive Boundary Commission constituted recognition by the Irish Free State of the land frontier of the United Kingdom of Great Britain and Northern Ireland. The agreement was solemnly registered with the League of Nations. The preamble expressed the desire of the three governments to "aid one another in a spirit of neighbourly comradeship".[36] Cosgrave praised the agreement in the Dail. In answer to Craig's Christmas greetings he wrote:

> You will be interested to know that the Agreement was, and is, regarded by a very large number of people here, including the professional and business classes, as the best contribution made so far by its signatories and their Governments.[37]

President Cosgrave reciprocated Craig's hope that they might "get into closer touch in future for the common good".

But they never met again. Cosgrave lost office in 1932 (O'Higgins had been assassinated in 1927 on his way to mass). De Valera and his anti-Treaty party Fianna Fáil now embarked upon the repudiation of many engagements entered into by his old enemies of the civil war. He chiselled at the crown and chipped away the symbols of dominion status. He discarded the Tripartite Agreement; and Article 2 of the Eire Constitution of 1937, which was endorsed in referendum by a small majority of the electorate of the Irish Free State, laid claim to "the whole island of Ireland, its islands and the territorial seas". Eire, like other Commonwealth countries, needed a tariff structure; but Fianna Fáil's protectionism affected Northern Ireland. Thus were the Ulster loyalists further repelled and strengthened in their determination not to quit the United Kingdom for a veiled republic whose relations with Britain and the other Commonwealth members was little more than that "external association" for which de Valera had long and consistently stood.

For southern Unionists, Protestant and Catholic, the Free State had been bitter enough. The sugar of crown connexion and Commonwealth adherence coated the pill but thinly. The smaller people, in particular, suffered in heart and substance. In 1926 the Dunedin Committee, informed by such bodies as the Southern Irish Loyalists' Relief Association and the Irish Claims Compensation Association issued a report which prompted the appointment by the Dominions Office in London of an Irish Grants Committee. Yet the loyalists felt the sting of abandonment.

Not that royalism, if not loyalism, was lacking even in southern Ireland. Indeed in June 1928 *The Freeman* discussing the possibility of a royal visit, feared that there might be too much popular enthusiasm. "A section of the community take advantage of the occasion of a Royal visit to indulge in an exhibition of 'West Britonism'."[38] At a garden party given by Healy at the Viceregal Lodge "some of the guests who had taken off their hats when at the end the band struck up 'The Soldiers' Song' [the Sinn Fein anthem] had the bad manners to replace them as soon as they realised what was being played" and "in various picture houses when King George or the Prince of Wales appears on the screen there are outbursts of applause" which, added the *Freeman*, "make the ordinary citizen feel inclined to hiss". A royal visit, it pompously concluded, "would be undesirable until we have reached the position that such proceedings would be out of the question".

In 1927 there were estimated to be upwards of 180,000 ex-servicemen of the British forces living in the Free State, at least a third of whom were unemployed. These and others continued to attend Armistice Day services regularly, and poppies were sold in the streets. In November 1924, Archbishop Bernard, who had succeeded Mahaffy as Provost of Trinity in 1919, described how 70,000 people had been present in College Green with only a few police present. The silence during the two minutes had been "almost painful in its intensity" and there had been no discordant voice. "God Save the King" had been sung by the assembly, and the Free State government had laid its wreath at the Celtic Cross. The title "Irish Legion" for Old Comrades was soon abandoned in favour of incorporation as an area of the British Legion following a questionnaire sent to branches. "The spirit of Imperialism is undoubtedly alive in Southern Ireland to a degree which has not been appreciated in England" wrote Bernard.[39]

But hostility was aroused. In 1928 it was reported that poppy sellers and men wearing medals had been molested, and an attempt had been made to set the poppy depot on fire. The activities of "poppy-snatchers" were countered by placing a razor blade also in the lapel, so that the miscreant might well be rewarded with a cut finger.[40] Some thought it was cowardice to abstain from showing the Union Flag on Haig memorial emblems; others replied that it was merely prudent. At Trinity College, the Union flag continued to be flown, together with the Free State tricolour and the college flag, until the jubilee of King George V in 1935.[41] The king's health continued to be drunk at college banquets up to 1945; and God Save the King at college races and the like was sung up to 1939. In 1929 there was an awkward incident when the Governor-general, James MacNeill, refused to attend if he was to be greeted with it. "The Board said they would defer to His Excellency's wishes, but made it so clear in the same letter that they thought His Excellency to be wrongly advised that MacNeill decided it would be better not to attend. As there was nobody to greet, 'God Save the King' was triumphantly played".[41]

On 21st January 1926, Archbishop Bernard, declared that "it had been the invariable habit of British Governments to treat Irish loyalists who live in Ireland with contempt and indifference". He praised Midleton's efforts to have the landlords' problems raised in the House of Lords; the Irish peers ought to speak up more for themselves. "If Kenmare, who has been notable, as a Roman Catholic, for his courage and loyalty, would speak out it might be a good thing".[42] On 21st May Midleton referred to the Free State pledge that the rights of the minority would be respected.[43] Arthur Griffith said he would do all he could. In her *Ireland — A Catspaw* (1928) Elizabeth Lazenby made the neglected point that "some of the best-known and wealthiest Catholic families were the most bitter opponents of the Republican cause. I think of one devout Catholic, particularly, who heatedly declared, 'I cannot understand how any member of my Church can uphold murder, political or otherwise, without divorcing himself from his faith'". Many Catholic loyalists had been the target of extremists.[44]

In 1931 the House of Lords debated an amendment of Lord Danesfort to the Statute of Westminster intended to prevent the Free State exercising its option to abolish the legal right of appeal to the Privy Council. Midleton asserted that loyalists in southern Ireland did not feel strongly on the point and paid tribute to Cosgrave's statesmanship. Danesfort was unyielding. He had been asked "by a great many of the minority in Southern Ireland to put forward their views in this matter".[45] Two complaints Midleton received are preserved. One was from a Robert E. Weir, writing from St Matthew's Rectory, Irishtown, Dublin. The second, from one Richard Carter, the Lodge,

Mountrath, Queen's County (as he still loyally called County Laois [Leix]), stated:

> it is difficult for your Lordship living as you do in England, to have any conception of the difficulties which confront loyalists in the South of Ireland, but that being so, it would perhaps be more fitting if you would refrain from giving vent publicly to utterances which must be harmful to them.

Weir was even sharper:

> It is just as well that people like your Lordship should know that you have already done enough injury to your former Unionist supporters, without adding to their hardships, now that you yourself are high & dry on the right side of St George's Channel.[46]

The Irish Grants Committee in London having heard claims, the imperial parliament voted a million for Irish residents who had lost through the British connexion. However, the contributor to the *English Review* of February 1930 who wrote under the pen-name "Pat" alleged that whilst the "Irish refugees" in London were more numerous than ever, there were still "outcast survivors" from the "reign of terror at 'home'" who had not yet been able to escape from the Free State. "They are the best citizens Southern Ireland has. The King has no truer subjects. Loyalty in England is a cheap thing compared with theirs." Most of them were Protestants, "but the Catholic among them is hated even more. The Protestants 'know no better', but by some common consent the loyal Catholic remains a dangerous freak".[47]

In 1934 an Irish Loyalist Imperial Federation was formed to guard against a possible secession of Eire from the empire. The president was Carson, its vice-presidents the Duchess of Atholl and Lord Lloyd of Dolobran.[48] On 25th July Lord Danesfort spoke in the House of Lords on the dangers facing southern Irish loyalists, including that of becoming aliens. Lord Hailsham replied that there was "no justification for saying that those whom we describe as Irish loyalists are being penalized for their loyalty in Southern Ireland".[49] Sir John Keane, Bt, writing in the *Quarterly Review* also painted a less gloomy picture. There remained in the south "a substantial section of all classes and denominations who . . . prefer in their hearts 'God Save the King' to the 'Soldier's Song'

. . . They comprise . . . a preponderance of the well-to-do section of the community", not merely (he wrote earlier in the article) a "remnant of impoverished ex-landlords existing within their demesne walls after compulsory expropriation". Sir John said that far from "surviving loyalists" being "necessarily unhappy or discontented, in many ways they were better off than in former days when Nationalists saw them as agents of foreign rule". Nevertheless in 1936 it was necessary for the Catholic Bishop of Ross to denounce the murder of Admiral Somerville simply because he had advised lads who came to him how to join the Royal Navy. "The gospel of the present-day patriot seems to be hate", said the bishop, "and his works murder". On 11th November 1935 a Union Flag was burnt at College Green and poppies were snatched.

Circumstances differed, and the ability to make material and moral adjustments. In 1925 Horace Plunkett visited his cousin, the veteran Catholic Unionist, Lord Fingall at Killeen. He found him alone with twelve cats. Plunkett's biographer, M. Digby, contrasted the two cousins. Fingall was absorbed in horses and hounds or with the innumerable cats he kept in a tower of the castle.[51]

In 1934 Lord Craigavon (Sir James Craig was created a Viscount in 1926) was mourning the death of Joe Devlin, his loved opponent. Devlin became first president of the Ancient Order of Hibernians (founded in the United States in 1838), revivified it, and for the first time made it a political force in Ireland. This was in 1904. Although at first supported by some Catholic bishops, the order, also known as the Molly Maguires, was censured by Bishop Clancy at Sligo in 1907, and Fr. O'Kane of Clogher, Co. Tyrone, denounced it as a secret society. In 1908 at a meeting in Armagh, the Ulster bishops forbade the wearing of A.O.H. regalia in Catholic churches; and in May 1909 Cardinal Logue of Armagh denounced it as "a pest, a cruel tyranny, an organized system of blackguardism". It was a Roman Catholic fraternity, as the Apprentice Boys of Derry, the Black Institution and the Orange Order were Protestant. The A.O.H. sustained the nationalists.[53] The Orangemen, for their part, were officially affiliated to the ruling Ulster Unionist Party and officially represented in the Ulster Unionist Council and on constituency delegate conferences that chose candidates for elections. Although professed to charity towards their Roman Catholic neighbours they did not make it easy for them to be active Unionists, still less to stand for election. Many however voted for Unionist candidates. Too often Catholic was equated with separatist and Craigavon spoke of "a Protestant Parliament and a Protestant State"[54], despite the presence of

Catholics in the parliament now worthily housed at Stormont. The northern prime minister's words are more often quoted than de Valera's "Ireland . . . remains a Catholic nation"[55]; and, although the Church was not established in Eire, his constitution was Catholic in character and inspiration and, many conservative-minded people would say, none the worse for that!

On 24th April 1934, Craigavon replied at Stormont to charges of unfairness to Catholics. He spoke of the reservation of 1,000 out of 3,000 places in the RUC for Roman Catholics and of their boycott of the force.[56] In 1936 however, Craigavon's most recent biographer records, seventeen per cent of the police were Catholics. Patrick Buckland also notes that at the time of Craigavon's death in 1940 the minority provided only some ten per cent of the lower, and six per cent of the higher ranks of the Northern Ireland Civil Service.[57] It must be added that the Catholic community included many, though not so many as is commonly believed, who opposed the Northern Ireland state, and that in departments such as the Post Office, which continued to be run by the U.K. Government, the proportion of Catholics employed was higher.

Craig pointed out that the first Lord Chief Justice of Northern Ireland was the Catholic Sir Denis Henry,

> a man whom everyone respected . . . if there was another man like him, there would be nothing to prevent him reaching the same high and distinguished position as was occupied by my good old friend . . . I have never yet known a country prosper where appointments to the judiciary were made on religious grounds . . . As long as I have anything to do with it . . . that aspect will never enter into my mind.[58]

When Henry died in October 1925 his widow wrote to Lady Craig that she knew no man "for whom Denis had a greater regard, a more true affection, and a more profound admiration than your husband". "Here was another example", wrote St John Ervine, "of many that might be given", of Craig's "amiable relations with his Roman Catholic countrymen. Henry, who had incurred harsh criticism from some of his co-religionists on accepting the office of Lord Chief Justice, was a faithful friend who worked for the Six Counties, as Craig wished all Ulstermen to work, in the belief that it was only by co-operation there that they could hope eventually for co-operation elsewhere".[59] In 1922

Henry had been made a baronet, and he had also served both as Solicitor-General and as Attorney-General for all Ireland during the violence of the post-war period. The latter post was of particular importance since the Chief Secretary for Ireland had no deputy to speak for him in the House of Commons other than one of the Irish Law Officers, and Henry was therefore, like many of his predecessors in the post, in effect Under-Secretary for Ireland. "His life", wrote the nationalist T. P. O'Connor, "was for years seriously and almost hourly in danger. He had to make it a rule never to leave his house at night, and even during the day he kept to the open and broad streets". O'Connor and others "hated his politics, but they did not — nobody could — hate the man".[60] The *Belfast News-Letter* wrote of him as possessing qualities of head and heart "which are given to few men, and he inspired trust and affection by his intellectual greatness and his personal humility". His legal colleagues were equally ecstatic.

T. J. Campbell paid tribute to his humour, describing him as one of the "wittiest and readiest raconteurs in the Law Library". One of the tenderest hearted of judges was William Johnson, disrespectfully called "Wooden-headed Billy". One day he came into court with his hand bandaged. The Chief Baron sympathized. "Nothing serious", replied Johnson, "but very painful. Just a splinter under my finger nail". "He must have been scratching his head", murmured Henry to Tim Healy. "Called to office in dark and troublous times", said Herbert Thompson, "to preside over the justice of a State still in the making, and threatened by enemies within and without, he guided the Court with unfailing courage, steadiness, sympathy, and impartiality".[61] There were resolutions of sympathy from Antrim and Ligoniel Unionists, and the *Irish Times* testified that he had "rendered great service to Unionists on many platforms at elections in Great Britain". "No man in the Ulster Party", it added, was more honoured by his colleagues, and he was liked and respected even by his opponents.[62]

Challenged on his education policy, Craig retorted that "after the fifty per cent grant by this House to Roman Catholic schools in Ulster I went across to the other side and a leading Roman Catholic there told me that if England would only treat the case as generously as the Ulster Government had done they would be perfectly satisfied".

This is not the book in which to rehearse the "economic war" brought on by the Fianna Fáil Government after default on the land annuities due to compensate landlords expropriated under the Land Purchase Acts; or the settlement which involved the surrender to de

Valera by Neville Chamberlain in the year of Munich, of Britain's Treaty rights in Irish bases; or the renewal of terrorism by the IRA whom de Valera hammered mercilessly with his Offences against the State Act. In his victory broadcast of 13 May 1945, the erstwhile Home Ruler who in Belfast in 1918 needed military as well as police protection and had his car lifted off its wheels by outraged Ulstermen contrasted the two Governments in Ireland:

> Owing to the action of Mr de Valera, so much at variance with the temper and instinct of thousands of Southern Irishmen who hastened to the battle-front to prove their ancient valour, the approaches which the Southern Irish ports and airfields could so easily have guarded were closed by the hostile aircraft and U-boats . . . If it had not been for the loyalty and friendship of Northern Ireland we would have been forced to come to close quarters with Mr de Valera or perish for ever from the earth.[64]

Craigavon was as obstinate as de Valera, yet warmer and less inflexible. The Catholic loyalist was his friend, unlike the Catholic who opposed or sulked against Northern Ireland and the Union. Stephen Gwynn, a political opponent, wrote to Craigavon

> on behalf of a Belfast Catholic who had joined my Company in the Connaught Rangers as a private, and rose to be a Captain and Adjutant in another battalion. My friend was given a well-paid post in the Civil Service in Belfast. It was certainly Lord Craigavon's intention that the Government of Northern Ireland should remain in Protestant control, but I believe that he was disposed to give fair play to all men, no matter what creed.

At the same time, he "did not succeed in preventing, and was probably not really aware of, discrimination in some areas of social and political life".[65]

In the Northern Ireland House of Commons, T. J. Campbell complained in May 1939 of the treatment of Ulster Catholics. In four of the six counties, he said, Catholic Clerks of the Crown had been replaced by Protestants on their retirement; Wyse's successor at the Education Department was also a Protestant. Craigavon replied more or less on the lines of his speech of five years earlier; and then G. C. Young, a Privy Councillor, in what was to be his last speech in the

House, spoke about County Antrim, where he sat for Bann Side. The County Inspector there, he said, was himself a Catholic, and the reason why there were not enough Catholics in the RUC was that they would not come forward. Whether that was "due to their own free will or whether they are not allowed to come forward" was another matter.[66] In 1938 Lord Chief Justice Richard Best addressed the Grand Jury at the Winter Assizes in Londonderry. "There are Loyalists", he said, "among every religion".[67]

Mrs Patrick O'Neill was the widow of a nationalist M.P. In 1940 she wrote to Lady Craigavon that "any little thing I did or could do, would never approach the edge of the deep gratitude owing the Prime Minister and yourself by my husband and myself, and, in fact, by the Catholic people generally, which they will some day realize".[68]

CHAPTER EIGHTEEN

War and Troubles

In heroic paradox southern Irishmen won their glory and their medals in the Second as in the First World War. Indeed it has been repeatedly claimed that Eire's contribution per head of her population was much greater than that of the North. No attempt was made during the war to counter these claims officially, for it was felt that it would encourage friendly relations between Britain and Eire if southern Ireland was allowed to claim the credit. But after the war it became a question, from Northern Ireland's point of view, not of avoiding controversy, "but of defending herself against a malignant, mendacious and dangerous attack, or allowing her case, and incidentally that of the truth, to go by default at the bar of world opinion".[1] By 1946, argued R. B. Pugh in a Dominions Office minute, "the advantage which we gain from this Eire Propaganda is trivial compared with the injury which it inflicts upon Northern Ireland".

Figures were first collected in January 1942 after a letter by Sir Hubert Gough in *The Times* (29th September 1941) had drawn attention to the contribution from southern Ireland and suggested that existing Irish units be "regrouped as an Irish brigade or division". Winston Churchill's cousin Shane Leslie wrote to him on the same day in support of the idea, stating that he had been in Eire in July "and obtained a very favourable though private acceptance from the vice president and the cardinal of an Irish Brigade". On 8th October Churchill replied that "the time seems ripe" and asked the service departments for their views. The Secretaries of State for War and Air replied on 22nd October that "were we to blazon abroad the part which the citizens of neutral Eire are taking in the war . . . the Irish Government might well feel bound to take action to prevent the departure of any further volunteers". Existing recruits might fear reprisals at home, and the IRA might attempt to subvert any purely Irish brigade. The departments were in favour of a less obvious plan, that of "brigading together" battalions of existing Irish regiments, for example the Royal Inniskillings, the Royal Irish Fusiliers and the London Irish Rifles, as a pure military measure. These regiments were not exclusively Irish (30%, 70% and 45% respectively including Ulstermen) and would not therefore so easily become recruiting grounds for the IRA. This was duly done, and 38 Brigade of 78 Div was always known as the Irish Brigade.

The possibility of recruiting an RAF Shamrock squadron of Irish-blooded men was also considered. The consensus view was that this would serve no operational purpose and might react unfavourably against individuals. Publicity for individual Irishmen's deeds of heroism was the best course. "As proposed. It is a half way house." minuted Churchill.[2]

Meanwhile the Northern Ireland government had got wind of the proposal. The prime minister (now Andrews) wrote from Stormont that the three regiments mentioned were "Ulster" regiments, the London Irish being part of the Royal Ulster Rifles. General Gough and Maurice Healy, who had first mooted the idea in public, were not speaking for the majority of Irishmen, and the name "Irish Brigade" was associated in people's minds with those who fought against England so recently as the Boer War. In Churchill's absence in the United States, Attlee replied first that no "Irish Brigade" as such, was proposed; and, secondly that even if that were the case there might be a publicity advantage in "finding, for the first time in history, an Irish Brigade fighting on the British side". Andrews rejoined that he was not satisfied that Ulster regiments should be used for recognizing the contribution of Eire citizens to the war effort and there the matter rested. Of 2,662 officers and men in the three battalions which it was proposed to brigade together, 627 or 23.5% were Northern Irish and 274 (12.5%) Southern Irish. It remained true that, as Meredith wrote in *Diana of the Crossways* "Ireland gives England her soldiers, her generals too". But when, in 1946, the South Tipperary County Council passed a resolution of sympathy with the relatives of people in Southern Ireland who died in the Second World War, an extremist organ denounced the resolution as "an exhibition of the slave mentality".

In January 1942 it was found that in the whole of the British Army 23,549 men were born in Eire and 28,287 in Northern Ireland. The figures were not published at the time, and it was even denied that they existed.[3] In 1944 the Eire figure had increased to 27,840 and that for Northern Ireland had reduced to 26,579. As the population of Eire was three million and that of Northern Ireland one and a quarter million, these figures speak for themselves.

Conscription was not imposed in Northern Ireland. Eire citizens resident in Great Britain were liable to call-up if they had been on the mainland for two years, but were given the option of returning to Eire within a fortnight if they received their papers. In 1944 the War Office estimated that there were upwards of 5,000 deserters from the British Army in Eire.[4]

The war brought prosperity as well as bombs to Belfast. Her yards turned out 140 warships and ten per cent of the total merchant shipping output of the United Kingdom. Since Eire's ports were not, but Ulster's ports were, at the disposal of Britain, Churchill did not exaggerate when he wrote to Craigavon's successor in office, J. M. Andrews:

> But for the loyalty of Northern Ireland and its devotion to what has now become the cause of thirty governments or nations, we should have been confronted with slavery and death, and the light which now shines so strongly throughout the world would have been quenched.[5]

As well as volunteering for service in the armed forces, Catholics took part in all the Civil Defence services in Northern Ireland. This did not prevent the Catholic Archbishop of Westminster saying, at a meeting of the Council of Christians and Jews held in London on 7th October 1944, that Catholics were "even in the present day being persecuted in Northern Ireland". His remarks caused great offence in Ulster, at a time when the Nazi persecution of Jews and others oppressed men's minds with its almost unbelievable horrors. The Minister of Home Affairs, Brian Maginness, responded on behalf of Sir Basil Brooke, who had succeeded Andrews as prime minister in 1943. A large number of Roman Catholics had left Eire to come and live in Northern Ireland; since January 1940, 30,000 Eire citizens had applied for permits. And, if the archbishop had internment in mind, internment that was necessary to protect the public from the IRA, then he would point out that in "Catholic Eire" the government had acted far more rigorously. In 1946, indeed, there was a complaint of employment discrimination in favour of citizens of Eire as against local ex-servicemen at Strabane.[6]

In May 1950 the subject of alleged discrimination against Catholics in the police was raised again at Stormont. The nationalist M.P., T. J. Campbell had in the course of questions in 1941 and 1944 established that there were some sixteen per cent of Catholics in the Royal Ulster Constabulary; that there had been more Catholic promotions than this percentage warranted; and that in the latter year Catholics were proportionately more numerous in higher than in lower ranks in the force, apart from the two topmost positions. As the RUC could not reasonably be criticized, Eddie McAteer in 1950 turned to the Ulster Special Constabulary. Brian Maginness, Minister for Home Affairs, repeated that there was no discrimination used either by the Specials or by the RUC; but McAteer continued to ride his hobby-horse. The historian of the "B" Specials, Sir Arthur Hezlet, confirms that Catholics were never barred from joining and a very few did so; more would have liked to apply, but for fear of "a rebuff or intimidation by their own people".[7] In 1920 and 1922, efforts were made to recruit Catholics for the Ulster Special Constabulary.

In March 1951, there were St Patrick's Day disturbances in Derry and the police again came in for criticism. Serious accusations were made and the debate ranged widely. In reply to a charge of personation at elections, the Minister of Education, Harry Midgley, said that it had been largely stamped out by the introduction of identity cards for voting at Northern Ireland elections. In his own field of responsibility, if it were really true that Catholics had been discriminated against in the educational field since 1923, as had been alleged, there was a remedy in section 5 of the Government of Ireland Act, which prohibited religious discrimination.[8]

On 6th June 1951 Maginness boasted that the anti-partition movement was dying, and that "the people of Ulster of every section and every religion are gradually coming to glory in the name of Ulster and in the name of Ulstermen and are coming to take a pride in our free institutions", as well as in the prosperity that was being created, which people in the south and elsewhere were "envying".[9]

It fell to the prime minister, Sir Basil Brooke, to answer the old charge that he had said he would not employ a Catholic. In Co. Fermanagh "Forty Unionist men", he said, "were kidnapped from around the Border". As commandant of the Ulster Special Constabulary in Co. Fermanagh, he was told his son would be kidnapped. "Therefore I told an audience — this was twenty years ago — that in view of the fact that Roman Catholics were being used to kidnap loyalists along the Border, it was just as well that loyalists who employed Roman Catholics should watch what they were doing". His son, who had been killed in the Second World War, could never be allowed outside the house, and afterwards he had to be accompanied by a man with a gun.[10]

On 13th January 1953 Henry Diamond, who sat for the Falls division of Belfast returned to the charge. Brooke's statement at Newtownbutler on 12th July 1933 had, he said, been repeated in August and again in the following year. The prime minister replied again in similar vein.[11]

Diamond went on to assert that of the six senior officials at Stormont all were Protestant, as were the three members of the Civil Service Commission and the four members of the Land Purchase Commission; similarly, of forty senior posts in the Ministries of Finance, Home Affairs, Labour, Education, Agriculture, and Commerce, none were held by Catholics. There was but one Catholic High Court Judge out of forty judges, registrars and officials of the superior courts, and only one Catholic out of twenty-two holding such positions as Recorder of Belfast, County Court judge, Resident Magistrate and Law Officer. In local government, he argued, the position was worse.

Thomas Bailie, M.P. for North Down, said in reply that if conditions were so bad for Catholics why did so many of them wish to come and work in Northern Ireland? There were omissions in the statistics given, for example many Catholic nurses were employed in hospitals. Discrimination in local government had been referred to. Yet in Strabane there were nine Roman Catholics on the local authority and only three Protestants. The council, he said, refused to employ Protestants except to sweep the streets.[12]

C. Hewitt, of the University of Maryland, in an article published in the *British Journal of Sociology* (September 1981), has examined very carefully the accusations of discrimination which were freely bandied about in the period preceding the "Troubles" of the late 1960's and which have formed the bedrock of most anti-Unionist propaganda ever since. He shows that the discrimination undoubtedly practised against Catholics prior to 1968 has been considerably exaggerated. For example, the business electorate (great play with which was made by Socialist critics, because the business vote in local elections persisted in Northern Ireland for some years after it had been abolished in Great Britain) was of "trivial significance". It numbered only 8,370, which was less than 1.3% of the local government electorate and included a number of Catholics. Some writers have claimed that it was necessary to own property to vote, but in fact it was lodgers, servants, and children of voting age living at home, not people renting accommodation as such, who were disenfranchised. Moreover, between twenty-two and twenty-eight per cent of Catholics and nineteen per cent of Protestants were unable to vote at local elections; thus Protestants with their predominance could make up about sixty per cent of the disfranchised, there being a total of 270,000 adult Catholics and 591,390 Protestants in Northern Ireland in 1961.[13]

As for gerrymandering electoral boundaries, this is an old Irish, not just an Ulster custom. Nor does the evidence when carefully examined indicate that local elections were frequently subject to such interference. Some areas have been incorrectly described as containing more Catholics than Protestants of voting age when it was the Catholic population as a whole with its preponderance of non-voting minors that outnumbered the Protestants with their smaller birth-rate. But there were more blatant errors. Thus the *Sunday Times*'s "Insight" team alleged[14] that Kilkeel was sixty per cent Catholic when in fact it was eighty-three per cent Protestant; it was the surrounding district that was sixty per cent Catholic (and nationalist controlled). Hewitt found of particular interest the Ballycastle Rural District and the Limvady Rural District, "in which Protestant majorities were governed by nationalist councils. If the Unionists had a 'carefully organized plan' to prevent Catholic control such a situation could not have existed".

Discrimination there was, both ways. In Newry, later, ironically enough, to be the scene of a civil rights march, out of 765 council houses in 1958, 743 were occupied by Catholics and 22 by Protestants; no Protestants at all were employed by the council in the early 1960s. Supposed gerrymandering at Londonderry has been much written about, yet for all the Protestant dominance of the council, more than two houses had been built for Catholic occupation to every one for Protestants as far back as 1951. In Northern Ireland as a whole, Hugh Shearman has shown that in proportion to their numbers, Catholic households had in 1971 been twenty-five per cent more generously provided with public authority housing than Protestants.[15] The Loyalty Survey carried out by Professor Richard Rose, and his co-workers in 1968 showed two things very clearly, stated Hewitt: first, that discrimination by Protestant councils was insignificant in its impact, and secondly that the greatest bias appeared to be the treatment of Protestants by Catholic councils. When Catholics were asked if they expected to be treated fairly in their dealings with local councils, only ten per cent of those living in Unionist-held areas said that they expected unfair treatment. The figure was little higher than that in areas where nationalists dominated the local authority. Hewitt's findings have been criticized by Denis O'Hearn in the September 1983 issue of the *British Journal of Sociology*, but Hewitt's rejoinder shows that his main conclusions remain unshaken.[16]

In January 1953 R. W. McConnell, who sat for South Antrim, continued the debate in the Northern Ireland House of Commons by pointing out that when T. J. Campbell had been appointed to a County

Court judgeship, certain of his Nationalist colleagues "turned upon him and branded him as a Judas Iscariot". McConnell categorically denied that there were no Roman Catholics in senior posts in the Northern Ireland Civil Service. Three out of the thirteen crown counsel were Catholics and a number had refused judicial and other posts. He might have added that in 1949 Mr Justice Sheil had become the second Catholic after Chief Justice Denis Henry to hold a senior judicial post in Northern Ireland. The Ulster constitution prohibited discrimination, said McConnell, whilst in Eire the Roman Catholic Church was declared to have a special position. In Strabane he had seen a sign outside a cafe — "No Protestant need apply". Diamond retorted that in the *Belfast Telegraph* there were advertisements stating "No Catholic required"; but McConnell was ready with his answer; there were also advertisements in that paper reading "R.C. wanted".

On education committees, although the schools belonging to the Catholics had not been handed over, and were not controlled by the Ministry of Education, Catholics were represented on school committees making appointments to other schools. Here was another example of what seemed remarkably like reversed discrimination. The treatment of Catholics in the educational field, indeed, is one area in which it is difficult to fault the Unionists of Northern Ireland. In 1947 the government defied its more extreme supporters by opening the way to the possibility of Catholics being appointed to teach Protestant children in state schools, and it increased from fifty to sixty-five per cent its grant to voluntary schools, of which Catholic schools were the main beneficiaries. In 1968 this grant was further increased to eighty per cent, in addition to which the government paid the salaries of all teachers.[17]

Unemployment was ever higher in Northern Ireland than in most regions of the United Kingdom. More Catholics than Protestants were out of work; but unlike their co-religionists in the republic, they enjoyed the same benefits of the welfare state as their fellow-subjects across the channel. Possible reasons for the higher rate of unemployment among Catholics in Northern Ireland compared to Protestants have been much discussed, and in the absence of full figures from the 1981 census being available they must, at the time of writing, be only tentative; but a very thorough analysis by P. A. Compton published in 1981 concluded that other factors than discrimination must be looked to to explain the discrepancy. The arguments are highly abstruse, and in a high degree theoretical, since unemployment statistics in Northern Ireland are not recorded by religious denomination. The Fair Employment Agency set up in 1976 to counter supposed discrimination against Catholics found evidence of such discrimination in only eight of the 130 written complaints received in the three and a half years up to January 1980.

National insurance was organized on British lines with a subsidy from the exchequer. In 1956 the Conservative government raised family allowances. A larger sum was to be paid for each child after the second. The Unionist Government at Stormont, in introducing parallel legislation, modified the increase in favour of second and third as opposed to subsequent children. In June the Presbyterian General Assembly supported the Catholics' complaint that this was discriminatory against their large families, and the government gave way to pressure from this and other sources, including some of its own supporters in the Ulster parliament.[18]

Catholics could now aspire in considerable numbers to higher education. Under the Irish Universities Act 1908 the Queen's College in Belfast, which was founded in 1845, became a separate University, those of Cork and Galway becoming Colleges of the National University of Ireland.

There were few Catholics at Queen's at its foundation; only five, or two and half per cent of the total. Thereafter up to 1909, when statistics ceased to be kept, the proportion hovered around five per cent, though by the last year absolute numbers were higher (39 out of 456). In the early days, there were much larger numbers in the other two "Godless Colleges" of Cork and Galway — 100 in 1849/50 rising to 212 in 1863/4.

Two of the first professors at Queen's, John O'Donovan (Celtic Languages) and Frederick McCoy (Mineralogy and Geology) were Catholics, but the latter moved to the infant University of Melbourne, Australia, in 1854 and the former's chair was suppressed in 1861. A third Catholic on the staff was James Cuming, Professor of Medicine from 1865 to 1899. He was also the first former student of the college to become a professor of any denomination and was the only Catholic on the staff throughout his thirty-five years of office. Chief Baron Pigot (himself a Catholic), wrote of him in 1865 that

He belongs to a class whom it is most important to encourage and extend, especially among educated and reflecting men, and . . . in Belfast. *He is a Roman Catholic of moderate opinions,* holding a considerable place in a community distracted by the wildest extremes of dissenting opinions.

Cuming combined "wide learning with a gift for research". "Cuming's powder" had in its day a widespread vogue for the relief of indigestion. But Cuming was more than a teacher and researcher. In his later years he was pre-eminent among the medical profession in Belfast. "He reigned with undisputed sway", wrote W. Whitla, "over a loyal kingdom, whose subjects were nearly all his old pupils and friends whose respect and esteem for him deepened with his advancing years".

The commissioners of the new Queen's University of Belfast set out deliberately to attract Catholic students. Five Catholic members were included in the charter senate. In 1909 a Catholic Dean of Residences was appointed and for a number of years Catholic students were more numerous than those of the Church of Ireland. In 1960 Catholics provided nearly a quarter of the total student body.

A lectureship in scholastic philosophy was established to the annoyance of some Belfast Protestants, who argued that it amounted to an endowment on denominational lines. But their appeal to the Irish privy council was unsuccessful, and the Mater Infirmorum Hospital, the principal Catholic hospital in Belfast, became associated with the University as one of its teaching hospitals. In 1922 proposals were made for a faculty of theology. Despite opposition, they were enacted in 1926. Cardinal MacRory nonetheless ruled in 1923 that no teacher trained at the University could be appointed to any school under Catholic control. Other Northern Catholic bishops ruled likewise. Nonetheless Queen's graduates were appointed to Catholic secondary schools; and students for the priesthood from the dioceses of Down and Connor often graduated in Arts at Queen's before going on to Maynooth. In 1929 Cardinal MacRory condescended to accept the honorary degree of D.Litt., though he was careful to stipulate that it should not be a theological degree! Over the years Catholics at Queen's University have provided considerable support for the idea of Catholic Unionism.[19]

1953 was coronation year, and on 20th May T. G. Henderson, who sat for the Shankhill, Belfast, said that the people he represented were rejoicing 100% at the coronation, "and among them are a large percentage of Roman Catholics who think differently from what I do".[20] However, on 7th July there was an adjournment debate on an "anti-partition proclamation" which had appeared in the *Derry Journal* repudiating the queen's jurisdiction over "any portion of the land of Ireland or of her territorial seas". The sixteen signatories included James McSparran, Q.C., Edward McAteer, Senator Cathal Bradley, Cahir Healy and other Northern Ireland senators and M.P.s. How, asked

Edward Jones, Q.C. (Londonderry City) could they reconcile this with their parliamentary oath? Diamond counter-attacked by asking why the police had pulled down posters bearing the "proclamation" and Healy invoked the memory of 1912.

Viscount Brookeborough (Sir Basil Brooke had been raised to the peerage in July 1952) was characteristically belligerent. The attitude of the sixteen signatories was "one of rebellion against the Crown and Empire" and their proclamation was "traitorous".[21] Healy argued that the majority in Fermanagh at least were against the Northern Ireland government; Brookeborough denied this. Many people from the county had come up in hundreds to see the queen in the course of her recent visit, but Healy had come up here "and repudiates the loyalty of these people". A railway explosion the day before Her Majesty arrived had been designed "to prevent the loyal men of the British Legion in the south coming up to join with their colleagues in the Balmoral showgrounds in the parade before Her Majesty".[22]

In the way of Irish things, it fell to a Taoiseach of the Redmondite rather than the Republican stamp to declare in 1948 Mr de Valera's shrewdly calculated anomaly of a state to be the Republic of Ireland. John A. Costello headed Fine Gael, a party that upheld the commonwealth connexion, but it was in coalition with Clann na Poblachta which, led by Séan Macbride, son of the martyr of the 1916, deplored Fianna Fáil's tardiness in pressing "on to the Republic". But then, as Mr de Valera told the Dáil in June 1937, "the Northern problem" stood in the way of a "flat, downright proclamation of a republic".[23]

Indeed, the political divergence between the thirty-two counties and the six was now further accentuated. J. M. Andrews was able to say that "a Unionist Government must always" rule Northern Ireland. Additional safeguards were obtained from the Labour administration at Westminster. The Ireland Act 1949 "recognized and declared" that "Eire" was no longer "part of His Majesty's dominions" whereas

> Northern Ireland remains part of His Majesty's dominions and of the United Kingdom and it is hereby affirmed that in no event will Northern Ireland or any part thereof cease to be part of His Majesty's dominions and of the United Kingdom without the consent of the parliament of Northern Ireland.

There followed something which only a conspiracy of British compromise with Irish logic would have enacted:

It is hereby declared that, notwithstanding that the Republic of Ireland is not part of His Majesty's dominions, the Republic of Ireland is not a foreign country for the purposes of any law in force in any part of the United Kingdom or in any colony, protectorate or United Kingdom trust territory".[24]

The Irish Ambassador (High Commissioner no longer) appeared in the Court Circular and on occasions of state with the Commonwealth High Commissioners and not with the heads of foreign missions in London; and the United Kingdom's relations with Dublin were handled by the Commonwealth Relations Office until it was merged with the Foreign Office. Reciprocal rights were given by the republic to citizens of the United Kingdom and Colonies resident in Eire under an order of 1949.

But for the north the declaration of the republic came as a further element of discord when forces were at work which could soften old asperities. Republic of Ireland attitudes towards the British connexion were examined in Micheál Mac Gréil's *Prejudice and Tolerance In Ireland.*[25] He describes such anti-British prejudice as exists in the republic as "quite unique" in showing what statisticians call a "negative correlation" between the "low esteem" and "hostility" subscales. In other words, the southern Irish hold the British in high esteem, but are also rather hostile to them. "An adequate explanation for this 'attitudinal schizophrenia'", he writes, "is difficult to find. It may be due to a post-colonial ambivalence towards our former masters whom we tend to admire and hate at the same time".

The resurgence of the IRA in the mid-1950s led to stern warnings by the archbishops and bishops of Catholic Ireland. Cardinal D'Alton, a classical scholar of eminence and a former president of Maynooth, became Archbishop of Armagh in 1946. In 1953, over seventy years of age, he was made a cardinal. On Christmas Day 1955, following an appeal by the Taoiseach, he called upon his flock to refrain from joining such subversive organizations, and this was followed, on 18th January 1956, by a statement by the archbishops and bishops of Ireland read at all public masses on 29th January. War, they declared, was "not lawful, unless it be declared and waged by the supreme authority of the State. No private citizen or group or organization of citizens has the right to bear arms or to use them against another State, its soldiers or citizens".

We declare that it is a moral sin for a Catholic to become or remain a member of an organization or society which arrogates to itself the right to bear arms and use them against its own or another State; that it is also sinful for a Catholic to co-operate with, express approval of, or otherwise assist, any such organization or society, and that, if the co-operation or assistance be notable, the sin committed is mortal.[26]

Lord Brookeborough welcomed the statement, though he said it was a pity it had not been made "long ago", and the *Belfast News-Letter* commended Cardinal D'Alton's "consistent opposition to violence" as "much to his credit".[27]

RUC men who remember the troubles of this period recall an attempt by three IRA terrorists to blow up the Irish Street police barracks in Armagh. They failed and fled up the 150 steps of the Catholic cathedral. A Catholic sergeant was cycling to work. Struck by this piety on a Monday he followed up the steps. As he walked down the nave the curtains of the confessional box parted, a revolver appeared, pointed at him, and there was a click. Inside the RUC man found three cowering youths, disarmed them, and brought them with a superior to Cardinal D'Alton. His Eminence heard the sergeant's story and for the first time the breech of the revolver was opened. A round had been struck but had failed to go off. In the face of cries of "sanctuary" and "police desecration of the cathedral", the cardinal issued an immediate statement condemning the abuse of sacred premises, thanking God that murder had not been done there and calling on the faithful to keep holy the Lord's House. A few hours later, acting on information provided by Catholic citizens, the RUC uncovered an underground cell, the entrance of which was a few yards from the place where the archbishop was photographed. A tunnel led to a room where food, clothing, bedding, literature and explosives were stored. The cell was a disused Victorian heating plant. There was no suggestion of clerical connivance. Rather had a great Irish churchman by his timely statement contributed to the ending of a guerilla campaign which had little Catholic support on either side of the border.[28]

By December 1956 the campaign was at its height. At Londonderry the BBC radio station was wrecked by an explosion and at Magherafelt the Quarter Sessions Court was severely damaged. Police barracks were attacked in Fermanagh. Brookeborough appealed to Unionists not to descend to the level of the terrorists by committing counter-outrages.[29]

In June 1957 a Mrs Sheila Cloney with her two children disappeared from Fethard-on-Sea, County Wexford. She was Church of Ireland, her husband a Catholic. Catholics in the parish boycotted their Protestant neighbours, and the Bishop of Galway, as well as the parish priest, appeared to be supporting them. Fourteen Catholic laymen in Northern Ireland, including G. B. Newe, C. A. Nicholson, Q.C., Angela, Countess of Antrim, Alex Dempsey F.R.C.O.G., Bradley M'Call, Q.C. and Frederick C. Towers, condemned the boycotting which, they said, must "be deplored by all right-thinking people of every creed". "The current murderous campaign", they went on,

> has increased the tensions in our country to an alarming degree. No one can tell what further calamities are at hand, but enough has already happened to demand a determined leadership on both sides directed to create a mutual confidence in which Protestants and Roman Catholics can live together in neighbourly respect and friendship.
>
> This is the outcome which the country sorely needs, and without which there can be no hope for the future.
>
> We would, therefore, earnestly appeal to our Protestant neighbours to resist any tendency to identify the Roman Catholic community with the evil tide of events. If they can do so it will accord with the admirable restraint they have shown in recent months, to which we would like to pay tribute.[30]

The Cameron Commission, which reported in September 1969 to the Northern Ireland Government, together with other authorities have taken the view that during the 1960s in Northern Ireland there was a trend away from "Nationalism", i.e., "United Irelandism" and towards agitation inspired by socialist ideals and aimed at an improvement in living standards, etc.[31] But there is not much evidence for this proposition. A more sustainable thesis is that the cause of a United Ireland rises and falls. A wave of political support precedes an IRA campaign, which then declines as the forces of law and order begin to bring the campaign under control. It then begins to rise again as the danger of violence is seen to have passed. Thus at the 1955 general election there were 168,360 votes for United Ireland candidates, representing fifty-one per cent of Catholics of voting age and twenty-eight per cent of the total Northern Ireland vote. This was, proportionately, the highest anti-partitionist vote ever recorded and it was followed by the 1956 campaign of terrorism. By the 1959 election, held after it had been crushed, support for a United Ireland had dropped to 83,497, or 14.5% of the total. In 1964 the anti-partitionist vote rose to 18.2%, and in 1966 to 21.1%. In Stormont elections, the United Ireland parties did best in 1953. In 1962 and 1965 there were slight rises following the defeat of the IRA.

In twelve Stormont constituencies Catholics were in a majority. In 1945, eleven of these seats were represented by United Irelanders. Nine of them, which were outside Belfast, invariably returned nationalists, whereas the Belfast constituencies were won by Socialist Republicans or Republican Labour. If it were true, as Cameron and others have suggested, that nationalism was being superseded by socialism during the 1960s, one would expect the Belfast pattern to be repeated in other Catholic-majority areas; but in fact the reverse was true, for in 1965 *every* Catholic-majority constituency was represented by a nationalist.

In 1968 a question was put to civil rights supporters intended to test opposition to supposed religious discrimination. They revealed themselves as significantly more intransigent over the question of the border than other Catholics, thus giving some credence to the Loyalist view that "CRA equals IRA", but not to the opinion expressed in some English papers that such a slogan monstrously misrepresented the Civil Rights movement. Cameron, whilst conceding that there were IRA sympathisers and members within the CRA, concluded that there was no sign that the IRA were "in any sense dominant or in a position to control or direct policy of the Civil Rights Association". He and his colleagues seem not to have known of a meeting, attended according to Hewitt, by the IRA Chief of Staff at Maghera, where the idea of the Northern Ireland Civil Rights Association was born. This may have been because both the former Minister of Home Affairs, William Craig, and Dr Ian Paisley, refused to give evidence before him.

Professor Rose's survey of 1968 found that fifteen per cent of Catholics in Northern Ireland thought of themselves as British rather than Irish, and T. J. Campbell, in his discussion of the Belfast Corporation Bill of 1896, mentions how a Catholic elected to the Belfast City Council before that date "spoke of the Conservatives as 'my party', and was returned by them".[32]

Dr G. B. Newe was not so much a party man as a great humanitarian. Educated at St Malachy's College, Belfast, he began his working life as a free-lance journalist, spending thirty years as editor of the *Ulster Farmer*. During the Second World War he became an instructor in air raid precautions and was later an area organizer in County Antrim, where he was responsible for the care of thousands of evacuees. For many years a member of the Northern Ireland Council of Social Service, he resigned in 1948 to become a full-time organizer of its activities. Even earlier, he had been a co-worker with Canon John Hayes in the all-Ireland, multi-denominational community organization Muintir na Tire, and we have already met Newe as a signatory to the protest against boycotting in 1957.

In 1958, in an historic speech on "The Catholic in the Northern Ireland Community" delivered at the Garron Tower Social Study Conference, Newe proclaimed that regardless of grievances, real or imagined, Catholics were obliged to co-operate with Northern Ireland non-Catholics to the full, without reservations, for the common good, and that they were giving scandal through non co-operation. Such serving ought not to be conditional on the institution of reforms, for although it might be alleged that the Northern Ireland government failed to live up to Pope Leo XIII's dictum that the civil authority should not, under any pretext, serve to the advantage of one or a few, because it was constituted for the common good, that did not excuse any failure to practise Christian virtue.

Moreover the evidence did not support the allegation against Stormont:

> One way or another I have had pretty close contact with Ministers and government departments for over thirty years and I can say, in all sincerity, that the climate has, in that period, changed greatly. Many of the Ministers and senior civil servants I have known, and know today, are men of goodwill, of the highest character and integrity, most of whom are really guided by Christian ethics. If their attitudes towards the Catholic community still leave something to be desired, we must remember two things: (a) the pressures of our historical background which affects *their* outlook as much as it does *ours*, and (b) the fact that we Catholics don't always appear to practise what we — or our Church — preach . . . It would appear to me that we have a need to examine our consciences in regard to the suggestion that we do not behave as our faith dictates — for, if it be true, then we are guilty of giving grave scandal.

Although Newe was "not quite satisfied that government at local level is completely above criticism in that it seems, too often, to 'serve to the advantage of one or few"', he would still argue that Catholics were morally obliged to work for improvements within the system:

> It may be said that it is all very well talking about being charitable and co-operative and of being tolerant, but what if "the other side" fails to respond? The fact that our willingness to co-operate in charity, in all the ways in which co-operation is possible, may be rebuffed does not relieve us of the obligation to persist in the practice of that virtue.[33]

At the 1959 general election, the dashing Miss Sheelagh Murnaghan was Liberal candidate for South Belfast. The grand-daughter of a nationalist M.P., she was the first Liberal to stand at an imperial general election in Northern Ireland since 1929, and was one of only two women candidates in the province. An international hockey-player, barrister, and former president of the Queen's University Literary and Scientific Debating Society, she refused to base her campaign "on the ancient grievances of the Irish", and boldly pledged herself "not to do anything which will alter the constitutional position of Northern Ireland unless I am required to do so by the majority of the people of the Province".[34] Ulster Liberals, she said, were "unionists with a small 'u'", and she was utterly opposed to Sinn Fein, because it was "the political wing of the I.R.A., 'which has plagued us for so long'".[35]

Miss Murnaghan lost her deposit; but she had shown Unionists that there was a vocal, as well as a silent, element among the Catholics which was prepared to support the Union; and the resounding defeat of Sinn Fein at this Westminster general election also gave them pause for thought. Sir Clarence Graham, chairman of the Standing Committee of the Ulster Unionist Council, was asked soon after the election at a Young Unionist weekend school whether it might be possible for a Catholic to stand as a Unionist for parliament. He replied that it was entirely a matter for the constituency concerned, recalling that during a recent Northern Ireland election there had been a Catholic speaker on a Unionist platform. If the Nationalist Party broke up, many of its members might wish to join the Unionists. Whether the Unionist party would accept them or not would depend on whether proof were available of their sincerity of purpose.[36]

A few days later Senator Sir George Clark, Grand Master of the Grand Orange Lodge of Ireland, in a speech at Scarva was at pains to scotch the idea. It was "difficult to see", he said, "how a Roman

Catholic, with the vast difference in our religious outlook, could be either acceptable . . . as a member or bring himself unconditionally to support its ideals". Almost as an afterthought he generously conceded that Catholics might vote Unionist if they wished! Lord Brookeborough too, was dismissive. All this talk of Catholic Unionist candidates was, he said, "charging at windmills and beating their heads against a wall about an issue which did not exist and which probably will not arise".[37]

In 1963 G. B. Newe developed his ideas further in a lecture delivered at the Conference of Catholic organizations in Belfast. "Civil authority calls for respect", he said, "*because* of its divine origin, *even* when those elected . . . may come from a political party or group to whose views, as individuals, we do not subscribe". He had chosen to emphasize the divine nature of authority, he said, "because we Irish . . . seem to suffer a proneness to be 'agin the government' . . . We need to remind ourselves", he added, "that, in the world as we know it today, the men who rule at Stormont may well be as true patriots as the men who rule at Leinster House" (the seat of the Republic of Ireland's legislature in Dublin). After repeating part of what he said at Garron House five years previously, he added that the practice of charity was the great need. "For far too long Catholic criticism of the Government has not always been dignified; it has very often been emotional, ill-informed and even childish; rarely has it been constructive". Catholics must, he said, be prepared to co-operate for the "common good", a phrase defined by Pope Leo XIII in *Rerum Novarum*.

They must moreover be prepared to take public office and to serve on committees. "That cheap, ignorant sneer: 'West Briton', 'Castle Catholic', is so often made — made against men who are not serving Britain, or 'the Establishment', but who are performing duties enjoined upon them by God. I wonder how often does it happen that many men of the highest moral and technical integrity just don't come forward because they fear such criticism".

After discussing the problems of education and juvenile deliquency, Newe went on to consider Catholic unemployment. Might not some of the problems be in part the fault of Catholics themselves? From sitting on interview boards and from discussions with others, he had found that in the great majority of instances a Catholic boy "appears for an interview with, not a chip on his shoulder but a blinking log".[38]

Sir George Clark's rejection of Catholics as Unionist candidates in 1959 was not allowed to pass without criticism. John Perceval Maxwell, writing from Finnebrogue, Downpatrick, pointed out that it was repugnant to the Bill of Rights. William of Orange "never refused the support of any Catholic who would support him. Most of his life he was in alliance with the Pope".[39] Nearly all Ulster Catholics, said F. A. Reid on 17th November, were "too proud to want to join a party in which many of the rank and file and some of the leaders would object to them because of their religion". After referring to Catholic loyalism, as shown in two world wars by many volunteers, to the Catholic Church's opposition to communism and to political violence, he went on to say that there must be many Ulster Protestants who could not bring themselves to join a political party from which their loyal Roman Catholic friends were excluded. On the other hand, there were no doubt some who were so " 'staunch' that they would not want to be associated in the Unionist Party even with a Roman Catholic ex-Serviceman who had been decorated by the King himself for valour". How long, he concluded by asking, "can the Unionist Party afford to keep the support of that kind of Protestant?"

Lt. Col. F. G. Holbrook was equally outspoken. "There must be many loyal Roman Catholic subjects of the Queen in Ulster, but I can well believe that the intolerance of Sir George Clark . . . could well result in the withholding of their votes, if not to a transfer of them to the Nationalists".[40] And "A Presbyterian" wrote on 12th November that if Sir George's views were Unionist policy, he would refrain from voting Unionist at Stormont elections, while remaining loyal to the Conservatives at Westminster. "When the safety of the country was at stake no bar was placed on Roman Catholics joining the armed forces of the Crown. They did so, and as a result many of them sacrificed their lives".

In 1963 Lord Brookeborough retired. His successor, Lord O'Neill of the Maine, has written in his autobiography that it was the tragedy of his twenty-year premiership that "he did not use his tremendous charm, and his deep Orange roots, to try and persuade his devoted followers to accept some reform".[41] The I.R.A. fought in 1956–62 almost unaided by northern Catholics and reforms might thereafter have been introduced in a spirit of *noblesse oblige* and from strength. Lord Brookeborough did give encouragement and promotion to individual Catholics, but it fell to Lord O'Neill, whose charms were less "tremendous" and whose Orange roots were shallower to essay what had long been left undone.[42]

As has been mentioned, in 1959 Miss Sheelagh Murnaghan stood for the imperial parliament on a platform which included Unionism "with a small 'u'", and in 1961, much to her own surprise, she became the first Liberal to sit in the Northern Ireland House of Commons since 1924, winning her seat as one of the Queen's University representatives by 2,622 votes against the Unionist's 2,370.[43] She was to continue to sit at Stormont until 1969, when after the abolition of the Queen's University seats, she lost North Down. In one of her last speeches to Stormont she said: "Let us try to get to the stage of accepting people as they are, respecting their views and insisting only . . . that the majority opinion of the people is to be the deciding factor . . . on . . . the Border".

By that date there was another Catholic Unionist in the field, Louis Boyle. Boyle joined the Conservative and Unionist Association of Queen's University, Belfast in 1965. He was not the first Catholic to do so, but in 1967 he came to prominence because he was the first Catholic to become president. In the same year he helped to form the South Down Branch of the Young Unionist Association, and became its first Vice-Chairman.[45]

Boyle's short period in the party was, on his own account, "controversial". Inevitably, he says, "I attracted considerable media attention, without having to look for it", and he did take an independent stand on a number of issues which increased the suspicion and antagonism which his position inevitably attracted from some within the Party. Nonetheless he had "valuable encouragement and support" from the then prime minister of Northern Ireland, Captain O'Neill, and from such as Stratton Mills, Dafton Pounder, Richard Ferguson and Robin Baillie. This sustained him through times of great pressure and discouragement, and without it he feels sure that he would have resigned much earlier.

Matters came to a head in 1969, when elections were called for the Stormont legislature. Although a prominent Young Unionist in his home town of Newry, and, as we have seen, one of its founders, he was, he states, unable to obtain membership of the corresponding adult Newry Unionist Association. This may have been because his brother Kevin was a prominent activist in the Civil Rights movement.

None of this prevented Louis Boyle putting his name forward as a candidate. The South Down constituency in which Newry lay was a safe nationalist seat, which the Unionists had no hope of winning. But on Friday 7th February the South Down Unionist Association decided not to contest the election. Taking this as a clear rebuff, Boyle then approached the party secretary, Jim Bailie, at Glengall Street (Unionist Party headquarters in Belfast), telling him that he was prepared to stand as an independent Unionist. Bailie told him that he would have the matter considered.

Then there was a further development. Nearly 250 voters in South Down (about half of them Catholics) signed an open letter pleading for a pro-O'Neill Unionist candidate. They included both the Roman Catholic parish priest, Monsignor Timothy Boyle, and the Church of Ireland Vicar in Rostrevor.[46] By the following day (12th February) it became clear that the Unionist Association had changed its mind and was approaching James Kerr, a company director and former local politician, to persuade him to stand in the Unionist interest. Kerr had no previous connexion with the constituency. Boyle, in a public statement of protest, was careful to go no further than to say that it was "Conservative fear" that had excluded him; it was not an "anti-Catholic decision".[47] Then on 13th February it was reported that the South Down Unionists had decided not to make an official nomination after all. The Unionist Party secretary at Glengall Street, when challenged to explain his attitude, said it was entirely a matter for decision at local level. Glengall Street had no machinery for approving candidates, as had the mainland Conservative Party.[48]

There were other Catholics who were prepared to support O'Neill's brand of Unionism. Sheelagh Murnaghan as prospective Liberal candidate for Larne, believed that Catholic support for Unionist candidates would be forthcoming. But Protestants must reciprocate in supporting Catholics where appropriate.[49] This they had conspicuously failed to do in South Down, and she herself was not given a free hand in opposing William Craig at Larne. However, it is not clear that she would have won against Craig, who had a narrow victory over the official O'Neill Unionist. Miss Murnaghan stood at North Down, where she was defeated by 9,013 votes to 1,567.[50]

At Clifton, Major R. L. Hall-Thompson had an easy win, with the support amongst others of Joe Burns, a life-long Labour voter and a Catholic. He was a plasterer from Clanchatten Street. Hall-Thompson declared that he would be "very happy" to see a Catholic Unionist going forward for a seat, and he hoped that there might ultimately be one or two at Stormont.[51] Meanwhile at Newry, three Young Unionists decided to resign in protest at the decision not to contest. They included two councillors.[52]

After the election, O'Neill himself was obliged to resign his position as prime minister of Northern Ireland, and in July 1969 Boyle resigned from the Unionist Party. In a resignation statement issued, perhaps significantly, just before "The Twelfth", he asserted that the Unionist Party arose out of, "and is still essentially based on sectarian foundations, and only a reconstitution of the Party away from its sectarian foundations could make Catholic membership a real possibility". The most important way of doing this was to break the link with the Orange Order. Unionist meetings were held in Orange Halls which, he said, "no Catholic could in conscience attend even if allowed" and he went on to recall how once he was due to address a Young Unionist meeting but it did not materialize because they held their meetings in the local Orange Hall, and were told that they could not use it if he were to attend. The Unionist Party could not, in his view, maintain its supremacy if it failed to attract the active support of a "considerable number" of Catholics. "In a straight vote for or against partition today", he believed that about 80% of the Catholic population would vote in favour of maintaining the then constitution. But since the election no attempt had been made to mobilize this support. "In the eyes of many Catholics, the overthrow of O'Neill even though followed by a regime pursuing similar policies, was a victory for reaction".

During the past few years, he added, he had been subjected to various pressures from both sides. There had been many difficulties and disappointments. There were people in the party who had gone out of their way to make him feel at home, but there were many others whose attitude had been quite the opposite. He knew that

> the suspicions and antagonism I have met in the Party is a result of the political attitudes and activities of many co-religionists. I have tried to break out of this, but many rank and file Unionists will not accept my "loyalty" . . . It came as a considerable surprise and shock to me recently when a leading Unionist spokesman, in discussing the link between the Party and the Orange Order said, that they may have to consider the link sometime, because it might be a bar to Catholics joining, Catholics who came from England or were in H.M. Armed Services, whose loyalty cannot be questioned. This to me can only back up my realization that the average Northern Irish Catholic is not a person who could be "loyal" enough to join the Unionist Party.

O'Neill's successor Captain Chichester-Clark (now Lord Moyola), nonetheless went out of his way to welcome Catholics into the Unionist

Party. Speaking at Stormont on 19th November 1969 he asserted his belief that the minority

> contain many men who are loyal to Northern Ireland as an integral part of the United Kingdom; who do seek to serve it; who can take an Oath of Allegiance in truth and conscience; who need fear no security check. I say to people such as this — Be in no doubt at all that you are welcome and wanted . . . decent loyal men from the majority section will be happy to work with you.[53]

In March 1971 Chichester-Clark was replaced as prime minister by Brian Faulkner, who had for a long time been an advocate of the internment of suspected terrorists. Troops were now on the streets of Belfast, and violence by the Provisional IRA now far outweighed anything that had previously been experienced in the history of Northern Ireland, or indeed of Ireland as a whole.[54] On 9th August some 350 suspected terrorists were arrested. Leaders, both of the newly-formed Social Democratic and Labour Party and of the Nationalists and of the Republican Labour Party were urging a campaign of civil disobedience and boycotting in opposition to the new policy. Newe, then Secretary of the Northern Ireland Council of Social Service, spoke out bravely. "Withdrawal from community structures", he said,

> means that true dialogue becomes impossible . . . a breeding ground for suspicion and mistrust is created . . . Bombing turns people off; so does a rhetoric of exclusion . . . We desperately need a great dose of social charity, without which it will be impossible to achieve social justice.[55]

In 1971, Brian Faulkner brought Newe into the Northern Ireland government as Minister of State in the Prime Minister's Office to advise on minority matters, the previous Minister for Community Relations, David Bleakley, having resigned because of his opposition to internment. There were the usual ritual denunciations by nationalists, though on his appointment Newe said that he would have opposed internment if in the cabinet when it was first mooted. Now it was in operation, however, the task was to see that it was administered with fairness and humanity and ended as rapidly as possible.[56] But Newe was only in office for a few months, for in March 1972 the whole Stormont system was suspended and Northern Ireland became ruled for the first time directly from Westminster, with its own Secretary of State.

On 21st February 1973 Newe proposed a form of government for the province to include a shared executive. The Secretary of State for Northern Ireland would replace the prime minister. The scheme was for a limited period only, so as to enable people to come to greater "political maturity".[57] The Westminster government did not wish direct rule to continue indefinitely, and in July 1973 passed its controversial Northern Ireland Constitution Act providing for a power-sharing executive and an elected assembly. The fly in the ointment was the insistence of the Social Democratic and Labour Party, as the price for its participation in the new assembly, on the reconstitution of a Council for Ireland which was now seen by many Unionists as the forerunner of a United Ireland.

The assembly was duly elected and constituted on 31st July 1973 and after a great deal of hard work a power-sharing executive came into being in November of that year. But it was ill-starred. A tripartite conference at Sunningdale between the new executive, the Westminster government, and the southern government produced a two-tier Council of Ireland, to consist of a council of ministers, seven from each side, and a consultative assembly, to be elected in equal proportions by the DaAil and by the Northern Ireland assembly. Not all the assurances to the contrary could make so elaborate a council appear other than an all-Ireland government in embryo. In early January 1974 the Ulster Unionist Council rejected the proposals by 427 votes to 374. Faulkner resigned as Unionist Party leader, to be succeeded by Harry West, and in February 1974, at the Westminster general election, pro-Sunningdale candidates were heavily defeated in Northern Ireland. It seemed that the electorate could accept a power-sharing executive, such as Newe had proposed, but were not prepared for a Council of Ireland as proposed at Sunningdale. Dr Paisley's Democratic Unionist Party, the Ulster Unionist Council, and the Vanguard Unionist Progressive Party of Mr William Craig, joined forces as the United Ulster Unionist Council, and called for fresh elections to the Assembly.[58]

This call went unheeded and on 14th May 1974 the assembly approved the Sunningdale agreement by forty-four votes to twenty-eight. The same evening an Ulster loyalist "strike" began in support of the demand for fresh elections. By 19th May there was a state of emergency. The Westminster government refused to talk to the strikers and the prime minister, Harold Wilson, caused offence on 26th May by describing them as "sponging on Westminster and the British democracy".

On 28th May the Unionists members of the executive resigned, and the next day the assembly was prorogued. It was never to meet again.[59]

Westminster's response was to publish a White Paper (4th July 1974) entitled "The Northern Ireland Constitution". In a further Westminster election in October the UUUC won ten out of twelve seats with fifty-eight per cent of the votes. On 1st May 1975 elections were held for a proposed constitutional convention. The UUUC manifesto proclaimed that Northern Ireland should remain part of the United Kingdom indefinitely and that there could be no power-sharing with republicans, though there was no objection to sharing power with Catholics as such. Once again, Unionists won over fifty per cent of the votes in the third Northern Ireland election within fifteen months. As the historian of that election has stated; "The result of the election suggests again that the majority of voters in Northern Ireland will not have an institutional Irish dimension".[60]

What form of government, then, do the Northern Ireland people prefer? A study published by Professor Rose and others in 1978 asked the question: "Is there a concurring majority about Northern Ireland?". They drew their net widely, asking people in Great Britain and in the republic as well as Catholics and Protestants in Northern Ireland separately for their preferred solutions. Not unexpectedly, they found that there was "no preferred constitutional formula about which a majority of the four publics concurred". However, there was a concurring majority, at least within Northern Ireland, "about the acceptability of direct rule as a second best or 'least worst' alternative".[61] A survey by E. P. Moxon-Browne of Queen's University, Belfast, carried out in 1978, confirms this. Of 1,277 Northern Ireland people asked (825 Protestants and 402 Catholics), almost half the Catholics (48 per cent) thought that "ideals apart, the most workable and acceptable solution to the Northern Irish problem was for Northern Ireland to remain part of the United Kingdom".[62] And well over ninety per cent of both communities wanted laws in Northern Ireland to be, as far as possible, the same as the laws in the rest of the U.K. An opinion poll jointly commissioned by the BBC and the *Belfast Telegraph* in 1976 found direct rule to be "acceptable" to seventy-two per cent of Protestants in Northern Ireland, and seventy-nine per cent of Catholics. It was one of the "most comprehensive" ever undertaken in the province, said *The Times*. Over 1,000 adults were interviewed in fifty different polling districts.

Even so, its results need to be viewed with caution. E. E. Davis and R. Sinnott, in a paper published by the Economic and Social

Institute of Dublin in 1979 pointed out that a differently-worded question in the Moxon-Browne survey found only nine per cent of Catholics and fifteen and a half per cent of Protestants *preferred* direct rule as the "most workable and acceptable" of a number of alternatives. The solution most favoured by Catholics (thirty-nine per cent) was for Northern Ireland to remain part of the U.K. with a devolved government based on power-sharing. Some thirty-five per cent of Protestants in Northern Ireland also favoured this solution, with a slightly greater number of Protestants (thirty-seven per cent) favouring majority rule on the Stormont model. Nearly thirty per cent of Catholics in Northern Ireland favoured a unitary United Ireland. Thus there was no absolute majority in favour of a United Ireland among Catholics in Northern Ireland, unless the eight per cent are added who favoured joint control "by the British Government and the Government of the Republic with a devolved Government of Northern Ireland".[63]

Such a welter of statistics does not necessarily provide a clear guide to action. However, such as they are the figures do suggest, first that a high percentage both of Protestants and of Catholics favour a devolved government based on power-sharing, and, secondly, that direct rule is "acceptable" to a much higher proportion both of Catholics and Protestants. The reality of the present situation being that a devolved government based on power-sharing is unattainable, it seems to us to make more sense to go for integration. T. E. Utley has written (*Daily Telegraph*, 31st October 1983) that such a policy is the "only practical method" of unequivocally recognizing the right of the people of Ulster to remain within the United Kingdom.

During his lifetime G. B. Newe received many honours. In 1966 the Queen's University of Belfast conferred upon him an honorary M.A. degree and he was subsequently awarded the degree of Doctor of Letters by the New University of Ulster at Coleraine. He was a founder-member of PACE (Protestant and Catholic Encounter), in which the last governor of Northern Ireland, Lord Grey, took helpful interest, and had served as chairman of the Northern Ireland Health and Social Services Board. Awarded the O.B.E. in 1961, Newe became a Commander of the Order in 1977.[64] Faulkner wrote of him that "his daily concern for the welfare and interests of all the Ulster people, Protestant and Catholic, was an inspiration to those who came into contact with him"[65], and Joseph Foyle that

It may be tht G.B.'s membership of the Northern Ireland cabinet, so fitting though it was that he was the only Northern

Ireland Catholic so honoured, was an example of "too little too late". But those Catholics, north and south, who kept ignoring the Newe stance for the past forty years are not in a position to throw stones.

All have a chance now to show that they are capable of learning, of continuing the Newe tradition of doing "what is extremely unpopular, very difficult and even dangerous."[66]

For, as Newe himself wrote:

In this search for unity within Northern Ireland all must participate, whether they be Protestant or Catholic, orange or green, or whatever else.

In the last analysis, it is the way of Christian brotherhood resulting in a just society.[67]

CHAPTER NINETEEN

Catholics for the Crown

Another Catholic servant of the Union was Patrick Shea, whose delightful autobiography, *Voices and the Sound of Drums*, appeared in 1981. Born in 1908, Patrick's father was a sergeant in the Royal Irish Constabulary (which in 1921 was ninety-nine per cent Irish and eighty-two per cent Roman Catholic). The family occupied one of two flats in the police barracks at Athlone. His parent were moderate Home Rulers, Redmondites in fact, but above all loyal to the force in which they were proud to serve. During Easter Week, 1916, their son recalls lorries carrying armed soldiers and police being cheered on their way to Dublin. When a lorry stopped for a few minutes, refreshments were brought. In that year, he writes,

> Yeats's "terrible beauty" was born but its birth was not celebrated by the people of Ireland. There was only anger at the wild, foolhardy men who had been responsible for many deaths and the destruction of much property in Dublin.[1]

In January 1919 Patrick Shea was eleven years old, and after the killing of two policemen between Tipperary and Soloheadbeg he was "filled with a fierce anger towards everyone associated with the new patriotism".[2] Nonetheless, his father was no West Briton[3], and condemned the British refusal to coerce Ulster in 1914.

By June 1920 when the Sheas were moved to Rathfriland, County Down, young Patrick had become confirmed in his dislike of nationalist violence and terror. Although a good many Catholics in Athlone had supported the Union, at Rathfriland "a Catholic claiming to be for King and Empire, as I indeed did, met with disbelief from both sides". All the same, the Rathfrilanders were hospitable, especially when they found that Patrick could read.

After a few months, his father was posted to Templemore in County Tipperary, where terrorism was rife. The family stayed behind in Ulster. At Templemore, Shea would accompany the District Inspector, D. T. Wilson, from his home to the barrack. One day he was diverted by an urgent message and returned to Templemore only to find his D.I. dead on the footpath.[4]

It was hardly surprising then that on the formation of the Irish Free State the Sheas decided to move to Newry. There Shea became clerk of the petty sessions court, and was at the same mass in June 1922 when J. G. Woulfe Flanagan, Resident Magistrate, was shot dead on leaving Newry Cathedral. Flanagan had written the previous September to H. E. D. Blakiston enclosing a list of ten murders or attempted murders occurring in Newry in one week in July 1921, adding, "If I get a sentence of death by tomorrow's post, I should not know whether I was sentenced for being a Catholic or a loyal subject of H.M."[5]

Patrick Shea's brother Jack was accepted for the RUC, and Patrick overcame stiff competition to obtain a post as a clerk in the Northern Ireland Civil Service, in which Catholics were few. He had heard that the bishop had advised them against seeking such employment and looked with suspicion upon such as himself. The work became in time less humdrum, and in 1935 Shea was transferred from Belfast to Enniskillen, Co. Fermanagh. Here he was able to lead a more outdoor life calling on applicants for old age pensions and so forth, but he was refused promotion.

In 1938 he returned to Belfast. He felt indignantly that he was being continually passed over. A "trawl" was held by the permanent secretary of his department and its assistant secretaries for candidates worthy of selection to the assistant principal grade normally reserved for graduates. Everyone in the clerical and executive grades was being called in for interview. Shea assumed that, as only one or two people were likely to be chosen for promotion, it would not be worth him competing seriously, and so he spoke his mind quite freely to the interviewing officials and did not hesitate to contradict them where necessary. He was promoted, not to assistant principal, but to the lower executive grade. Shortly afterwards, the establishment officer of his department informed him that he had after all been selected for an assistant principalship, but in the Ministry of Finance.

The permanent secretary in the Ministry of Finance was Sir Wilfred Spender, who in 1913 had resigned his army commission and offered his services to Carson and the Ulster Unionists. Although he had formerly commanded it, Spender, according to Shea, disliked the Ulster Special Constabulary almost as much as he disliked the IRA, and he had no use for certain politicians. These included Sir Dawson Bates.[6]

Although well aware of the prejudice which existed, Shea did not really expect "anti-Catholic prejudice to be a barrier to any rewards which I might earn".[7] Neither did he regard his new appointment as a "Catholic victory in a Protestant world". He was treated, he relates, with understanding and kindness. Nonetheless, it shortly emerged that a new financial secretary to the Ministry of Finance had refused to have this Roman Catholic as his private secretary, and he was also told that he had been transferred from Labour to Finance because the Ministry of Labour had refused to approve the appointment of a Roman Catholic to his ministry in an administrative grade.

In the early 1940s, Shea became secretary to the Joint Exchequer Board. The post took him periodically to London. In 1947 he was appointed to the Ministry of Education as a principal. The permanent secretary, who had succeeded Wyse in 1939, was Reginald Brownell. Shea pays tribute both to him and to the Minister of Education, S. H. Hall-Thompson[8], for the Northern Ireland Education Act of 1947, including as it did, in defiance of many protests, provision for increases in grants to voluntary schools, most of them under Catholic management.

Shea occupied the post of establishment officer in the Education Ministry. Despite the allegations of discriminatory practices in the government service he testifies that he heard no conversation and witnessed no decision that would justify any of them.

Hall-Thompson resigned as Minister of Education in 1949 and was succeeded by Harry Midgely, a convert from socialism. As a socialist Midgely had backed the Spanish republicans and thereby offended some Catholics; it was even rumoured that the parish priest in his then constituency of Dock (Belfast) had once threatened to fight him. Certainly his election meetings in 1938 were stormy, even by Ulster standards. He is recorded by the *Irish News* (a Catholic paper) as describing France as a "monstrosity" and "a killer of babies" and on several occasions .meetings had to be called off because of threatening mobs.[9] In 1936 he had a notable exchange with the Very Revd Dr A. H. Ryan, a leading Catholic of Queen's University on the subject of atrocities in Spain. Ryan asserted that Catholics were suffering a barrage of abuse from the "'unholy alliance' of Socialists and Orangemen". Midgley replied that "on the Spanish issue the Catholic church is wrong and the attitude I take up would be the same if any other Church followed the example". There were, he added, atrocities on both sides; and that being the case, those who had begun the conflict must bear the heaviest responsibility. Ryan, he said, was more concerned to re-secure the privileges of which the Catholic Church in Spain had been deprived in 1931 than with the "ethics of Christianity". Ryan replied that he had found Midgley's mind closed when he had attended a meeting which the latter had held at the York Street Labour Hall; and he accused him of using language against the Catholic church which amounted to "sublimated Billingsgate".[10]

The rumour of attempted clerical pugilistics appears to have been unfounded. Indeed, far from having threatened to fight Midgley, Ryan at least made a point of shaking him by the hand, thereby incurring the wrath of Captain Herbert Dixon, Unionist chief whip, who asserted that the handshake had amounted to a conjuncture of Catholicism with communism.[11] To this charge Ryan retorted that he had merely shaken Midgley's hand as a matter of courtesy. What did the Chief Whip expect him to do with opponents? "Does he suggest that I should prove my Christianity in the picturesque words of Mr P. G. Wodehouse, 'by poking my opponents in the snoot?' " One thing which Captain Dixon had quoted him as saying was correct; the only political speech he had ever made was from a Labour platform. Fr Ryan had, however, no political party.

Midgley had complained of "theological dictation" and that he had been threatened with the forfeiture of Catholic votes. But unless he displayed "some of the elementary rules of fair play, Catholics should ignore him".[12]

In the 1938 Northern Ireland election Midgley's vote dropped from 4,983 to 1,923, and he lost to the Unionist, G. A. Clark. No doubt his views on the Spanish question were decisive; but he may well also have lost votes because at a conference of the Northern Ireland Labour Party in 1937 he said that he would "rather be governed by a Socialist Government from Westminster than by a capitalist Government from Dublin".[13] There were accusations that he had become a Unionist, and indeed after his re-election for Dock in 1941 he joined the Northern Ireland government, first as Minister of Public Security (1943–44) and then as Minister of Labour (1944–45). By then he had established a Commonwealth Labour Party, pro-British, working-class, and Protestant, and in 1947 he became a Unionist.[14] In 1949, therefore, Midgley's advent as Minister of Education was viewed by Catholics with trepidation, for he had opposed the Education Act of 1947, and was expected to reduce subventions to voluntary, mainly Catholic schools. In the event, this did not happen. Brownell valiantly resisted the minister's schemes, which were effectively neutralized. Nonetheless, Midgley's bigoted utterances became more and more of an embarrassment and Shea asked for a transfer, which was refused.

In 1957 Midgley died. He was succeeded by Maurice May, a talented accountant. In the following year Brownell retired as permanent secretary. He had told Shea that because of his religion he might never succeed him. Shea for his part was beginning to make a secondary career as a writer. Several of his plays were performed, and age had mellowed him: nonetheless he prepared to ask Brownell's successor, A. C. Williams, for a transfer. Shea was not then even an assistant secretary although Brownell had told him nearly ten years earlier that he would soon be promoted to that grade. Shea knew of one Catholic who had become an assistant secretary but the failure of reputedly able principals to rise in the service had been generally attributed to their religion. It was taken for granted that Catholics were not appointed to the police division in the Ministry of Home Affairs nor to the Cabinet Office. Shea bitterly resented hearing from a colleague in the course of casual conversation that it was obviously not worth him applying for a certain appointment because he was a Catholic. What upset him was that his colleague seemed to accept this as part of the natural order of things. A Protestant colleague, J. A. Oliver, has his own answer: "Perhaps we ought to have been more obstructive: but was that our job? Perhaps one of us ought even to have resigned, but what good would that have done?"[15]

In 1959 Shea asked for a transfer and after an interview with Sir Douglas Harkness, head of the Northern Ireland Civil Service, was moved to the Public Building and Works Department of the Ministry of Finance. In 1963, he took the place of retiring assistant secretary in charge of the department. Terence O'Neill was then Minister of Finance. In December 1969 Shea was made permanent secretary of the Ministry of Education, a post which a previous holder of that office had told him he would never achieve. He was thrown almost immediately into the drafting of a new Education Bill. The Unionist government was then already paying eighty per cent of the capital cost of voluntary, mainly Catholic, schools, compared with the previous sixty-five per cent.[16]

With the indefinite prorogation of the Northern Ireland parliament in 1972 Shea, though sorry to lose his minister, Bill Long, found William Whitelaw, Paul Channon and William van Straubenzee friendly and helpful. The high standards of the Northern Ireland Civil Service, he states, never faltered.

Shea believes that after 1945 there was an opportunity for the Northern Ireland government and the Unionist Party to win the Catholic community's trust. Catholics became more co-operative in the 1930s and some voting habits had altered. But no move was made. The events surrounding the formation of the new state were seared too deeply into the minds of those who held the reins of power.

Shea like G. B. Newe sees faults on both sides: on the one hand there have been "serious discriminatory practices operating to the disadvantage of Catholics"; on the other, "Catholics failed to make full use of the opportunities which were there". J. A. Oliver confirms this second point, referring to the "tragic disregard which Catholic families and Catholic schools showed for the Northern Ireland civil service as a career" during the twenties and thirties.[17]

Shea distrusts the influence of the Orange Order on Ulster affairs. He wondered how Northern Ireland cabinet ministers with whom he came in contact, "for whom one could feel genuine respect could have acquiesced, even participated in, illiberal practices which, in the end, brought discredit on fifty years of government".[18] Unionist Members of the Northern Ireland parliament who were not Orangemen were rare exceptions.

Yet his epilogue places some Orangemen in a more agreeable setting. One Twelfth of July, Shea had been invited by friends for a drink. The bar, where he was well-known, was unusually full of Orangemen in their regalia. Ordering a round, he noticed that the Orangemen began to form a tight-knit circle around him. He began to feel apprehensive. "Is your name Paddy?" one of them asked him. He answered "Yes", but felt that they knew very well who he was. "Are you a Roman Catholic?", he continued, and it was only after some trepidation that he found himself answering "I am". Then, "What'll you have?". After much well-lubricated "crack" it was concluded by the Worshipful Master present that there was nothing much to choose between nationalist and Unionist; it was the civil servants up at Stormont who were drawing £20 a week (a large sum in those days) and laughing at both sides. It was time to go and Shea left with alacrity.

In a previous chapter we have referred to evidence for Catholic support for unionism in the general election of 1959 and to the reaction of the Unionist Party, and of the Orange Order, to such evidence. No formal resolutions were arrived at.[19]

A Catholic Englishman settled in County Down, the late Major Eric Beaumont, an architect and second-in-command of the County's Ulster Defence Regiment battalion, sought election as Unionist parliamentary candidate for Mid-Ulster. The delegates chose otherwise for the by-election of 1969 and the seat was won from the Unionists by Miss Bernadette Devlin (now Mrs McAliskey) who then described herself as the Independent Unity (i.e. anti-partionist) candidate.[20]

Another Catholic Unionist, or Union supporter, Bill O'Hara, business man and hotelier, now of Bangor, County Down, explains that, having been educated in the republic and having non-political parents, he found himself becoming "an English rather than an Irish Catholic". He has a brother-in-law and several friends who are Catholic priests in Liverpool. In 1964 O'Hara won a council seat as an independent by twelve votes in a Protestant ward. In his simplicity he had not realized that the sitting councillor was the local Unionist chairman. A friend of O'Hara who belonged to the Northern Ireland Labour Party advised him that he could find no comfort either in the Unionist Party of that time or in the abstentionist (now defunct) Nationalist Party. O'Hara then joined the Labour Party but resigned from it five years later.

> Not wishing to be in no party and finding the economic policies of the Conservative party closer to my own I joined a Lancashire branch (Chorley). I had never considered joining the Ulster Unionist Party. It had always been a party in practice of Protestant ascendancy . . . In 1922 Catholics did not believe in the permanency of the State and refused to participate fully in the early years but the generation coming up after the war showed every sign of accepting the position and a desire to play their part. Under Brookeborough they were rejected. With the increasing number of educated Catholics following the 1947 Education Act the seeds were being sown for our present troubles.[21]

Mr O'Hara then reflects on Terence O'Neill's attempt "to change the political outlook of the Ulster Protestants". In this brief hopeful moment he "was received into the Unionist Society based in Glengall Street and became a delegate to the Unionist Council". He addressed several branches on "the reforms needed within the party" and spoke at a number of Catholic debating societies "to the proposal that there was a place within Unionism for Catholics". O'Hara's party membership lasted but a year. He and O'Neill went out together. In 1974 O'Hara did not stand again under the reformed system of local government. He was made National (Northern Ireland) Governor of the BBC and could not be active in politics. "Like many people in Northern Ireland my politics are dominated by a desire to see this community united".

In 1925, by no means the worst year in the history of the Irish Free State, John Dillon said, "When we look back on the days when we were oppressed by England it would look like paradise if we could get the same sort of oppression now".[22] In like manner do many Catholics and nationalists in Ulster today compare the oppression of republican terror and "loyalist" counter terror with the "oppression" of half a century of Unionist rule in Northern Ireland. The abolition of Stormont was the first demand of the provisionals. They may claim it as a victory for terrorism. But the effect of the direct rule that replaced "Stormont" has been to make many Catholics and nationalists into supporters of the British connexion. It has converted Gerard Fitt (now Lord Fitt) from a provincial separatist into a United Kingdom politician.

The Northern Ireland attitude survey already referred to found in 1978 that ninety-two per cent of Northern Ireland Catholics wanted "laws in Northern Ireland to be as far as possible . . . the same laws as in the rest of the United Kingdom".[23] "Support for unilateral British withdrawal is greater in Britain (56 per cent) than it is among Northern Ireland Catholics". On 12th February 1982 Ulster Television showed the results of a survey carried out by National Opinion Polls earlier that month. "Full integration" with Great Britain was found to be "acceptable" to eighty-eight per cent of Protestants and forty-five per cent of Catholics.[24]

Even the anti-Unionist minority — is it the majority of the minority? — is best protected by a Union with Great Britain that provides under one sovereign parliament at Westminster as much diversity of local institutions as it affords Scotland, Wales and England. Some might call that the lesson of Stormont; as earlier it was the lesson of that Protestant parliament for the Protestants of Ireland which sat in Dublin and was described by Dean Warburton as "the object of political contention" which "moderate men" wanted removed so that "we may have peace and security."[25]

Whether it be the separatists of the north or that pro-British remnant in the south which never gave trouble to Free State or republic, there is still, in several senses, one Ireland. For the bonds that join the United Kingdom of Great Britain and Northern Ireland with the Irish Republic are multifarious. They are closer than with other countries of the commonwealth, to which the republic no longer belongs, or with other countries of the European Community, of which both states are members. They arise from history and geography and they include ecclesiastical, ethnic, economic, cultural and sporting links.

The Anglican, Roman Catholic and other communions transcend the Irish border, which is the land frontier of the United Kingdom. Until recently not only was there similar coinage but both currencies were at parity.[26] The separation of the Irish pound from the pound sterling was mutually inconvenient and detrimental to business in both countries. A number of learned societies, some of them still styled "Royal", function on both sides of the border. The British Isles (including the Channel Islands and the Isle of Man) form a common travel area. The Commissioners of Irish Lights constitute a "Trinity House" for the whole island; and parliamentary questions to the Secretary of State for Trade have shown that they are anomalously accountable to parliament as well as to the *Oeireachtas Eireann*.[27]

Much has changed constitutionally in the British Isles since 1912; yet the geo-political facts set out by L. S. Amery in his contribution to a symposium entitled *Against Home Rule: The Case for the Union* remain constant:

> Geographically the United Kingdom is a single compact island group, of which Ireland is by no means the most outlying portion. No part of Ireland is to-day, or ever was, as inaccessible from the political centre of British power as the remoter parts of the Highlands, not to speak of the Shetlands or Hebrides. Racially, no less than physically, Ireland is an integral part of the United Kingdom, peopled as it is with the same mixture of racial elements as the main island of the group. The blend of Celt with Dane, with Normans and English of the Pale, with English citizens of the seaports and Cromwellian settlers, which constitutes Celtic Ireland, so-called, is less Celtic both in speech and in blood than either Wales or the Highlands.[28]

It should be the common policy of the parties in our state to put the Union beyond a peradventure. The battle against terrorism will then be more than half won. Put the Union beyond shadow of doubt and what Mrs Thatcher styled the "unique relationship"[29] between the kingdom and the republic may then bring Irishmen into ever closer partnership without feeding loyalist fears and separatist hopes. United Ireland is a non-starter unless, which is unlikely, the south were to end its secession from the United Kingdom. United Islands makes sense.

A "Benelux" or "Nordic Union" of our islands — if "*Islands Of the North Atlantic*" be preferred to "British Isles", the acronym is hallowed — and the wider European system of sovereignties can give Ulstermen and Irishmen scope for creative work and lift their eyes to further horizons. Irish statesmen and public servants played a leading part in the evolution of the British commonwealth: they are already busy in the European communities. Given that the starting point for co-operation in Ireland is the partnership of the two sovereign nations, European as well as national resources can suitably be applied to the rational advancement of such Irish regions as that round Londonderry whose natural hinterland straddles the Foyle and reaches into Donegal.

The Irish, North and South, have so much to give these islands and to Europe. Their forbears gave much. An Irish Church that felt its debt to Britain, whence Patrick came perforce, redeemed that debt when it Christianized much of Britain and much of Europe. Columba and Columbanus, Catalud of Taranto, Killian of Franconia, Colman of Austria [29] are among the saints who are the true heroes of Ireland; and those who died for the Catholic faith were martyrs not to death but to life.

Addressing the High Tory 1900 Club on 2nd July 1973, the former Taoiseach, Mr Liam Cosgrave, spoke of the religious bonds across the border. There is no frontier to faith. Armagh is the Catholic and the Anglican metropolis for all Ireland. Mr Cosgrave cited also the Irish Council of Trade Unions, the single banking system organized by the Irish Banks Standing Committee, the Irish Republic Football Union and the Gaelic Athletic Association. Loyal Ulsterfolk are blithe to play or ride for "Ireland", preferring the Cross of St Patrick to the tricolour. One of the authors heard of a tweeded Ulster lady heard to expostulate at a reception in military circles at Lisburn, "The trouble with you English is that you don't want us Irish to remain British".[30]

NOTES

1. Introduction
1. Eoin MacNeill, *Celtic Ireland* (1921), p. 1
2. John Mitchel, *Life and Times of Aodh O'Neill* (Dublin, 1846), p. 15
3. The term *Old English* has a special sense in Irish history. It denoted people of Irish birth but of English ancestry who had become assimilated to Irish ways, and were thus distinct, as a group, from the Anglo-Normans proper. Fr. Walsh, in 1682, distinguished the "Ancient Irish" on the one hand, from the "*Old English, or English Irish*" on the other (*Prospect State of Ireland*, p. 5).
4. S. Rosenbaum (ed.) *Against Home Rule. The Case for the Union* (1912), p. 270
5. See Wallace Clark, *Rathlin — Disputed Island* (Portlaw, Co. Waterford, 1971).
6. W. F. Monypenny, *The Two Irish Nations* (1913), p. 13; Nassau Senior, "Ireland in 1843" in *Journals . . . relating to Ireland* (1868) i, 22
7. *Hansard*, 1 Jan. 1913, col. 385
8. *An Claidheamh Soluis*, 1 Nov. 1913, reprinted in F. X. Martin & Byrne, *Scholar Revolutionary* (Shannon, 1973), p. 381
9. Horace Plunkett, *Ireland in the New Century* (1905 ed.), p. 86
10. On the congested districts, see chapter 14. They included all Connemara plus Counties Donegal and Kerry and part of County Cork.
11. *Freeman's Journal*, 2 July 1915, p. 5
12. 31 Mar. 1920. Ian Colvin *Life of Lord Carson* (1936), iii, 384
13. Fr Francis Shaw, S.J., "The Canon of Irish history — a challenge", *Studies*, Summer 1972, p. 145

2. Before 1700
1. Four of the "nine hostages" of Nial Noigiallach (d. c. 427 A.D.) one of the earliest historical Kings of Tara, have been variously explained as taken from Britain, from Scotland, from the Saxons, and from the Franks. See F. J. Byrne, *Irish Kings and High Kings* (1973), p. 76; T. F. O'Rahilly, *Early Irish History & Mythology* (1946), p. 233.
2. W. L. Warren, *Henry II* (1973), p. 196

3. J. O'Connor, *History of Ireland 1798–1924* (1925), i, 150

4. The word 'merus" (mere) originally meant "pure", i.e. with no admixture of English blood; it was only later that the pejorative sense crept in. See E. Curtis, *History of Mediaeval Ireland* (1923), p. 225, and the *Oxford English Dictionary*.

5. H. Richardson and G. O. Sayles, *Irish Parliament in the Middle Ages*, (1952), p. 57

6. *Calendar of the Close Rolls*, 50 Edward III, part II, p. 373. Some of the men of Cork proving recalcitrant in this respect; a direct message was sent to that city on 27 August, ordering them to pay up (ibid., p. 384). See also R. Frame, *English Lordship in Ireland 1318–61* (1982), p. 289 for a similar summons in 1348.

7. Hoveden, *Chronica* (Rolls series, ed. Stubbs, 1869) ii, 30

8. 33 Hen. VIII, c. 1 (Irish) (Crown of Ireland Act, 1542)

9. R. King, *Primer of the History of the Holy Catholic Church in Ireland* (1846), ii, p. 706

10. 3 & 4 Philip & Mary, c. 4 (Irish)

11. 3 & 4 Philip & Mary, c. 2 (Irish)

12. ibid., c. 1

13. ibid., c. 15

14. *Calendar of the State Papers (Ireland)* (CSPI) *1629*, p. 499

15. This was in August 1566. *Nineteenth Century & After*, Dec. 1921, p. 1082. See also James Stuart, *Historical Memoirs of the City of Armagh* (1900 ed.), pp. 162–3

16. King's *Primer* (note 9 above), p. 713; H. O'Grady, *Strafford and Ireland* (1923), i, p. 403

17. King, op. cit., p. 721. For Sir Thomas More and King Henry, see J. J. Scarisbrick, *Henry VIII* (1968), p. 270; chapter 12 for Henry's later views.

18. *CSPI 1599,* pp. 293–4. Although Ormonde had been brought up as a Protestant, it is clear from this exchange that he nonetheless regarded himself as a Catholic, at least in the broad sense.

19. 1 Eliz. 1, c. 1, s.9 (English); *Statutes of the Realm*, Record edn., iv, 352 (spelling slightly modernized)

20. E. Curtis, *History of Ireland* (1950 ed.), p. 166; M. V. Ronan, *Reformation in Dublin* (1926), pp. 117–8

21. See chapter 10, note 87. A legendary (c. 1st century A.D.) King of Ulster; his home fort was near Dundalk

22. A. Clarke, *The Old English in Ireland 1625–42* (1966)

23. *CPSI 1509–73*, pp. 151–4; Thomas Russell's *Relation of the fitzGeralds of Ireland* 1638 in *Geraldine Documents* ed. Hayman & Graves (1870), i, 20
24. *CPSI*, loc. cit., 181–95, 392
25. ibid., 363–4
26. Sir John Perrot (1527?–1592) took up office as first President of Munster in 1571. He acted under the control of the lord deputy and council but had justices, his own provincial council, and a military force. Sir Edward Fitton had already been appointed to a similar post in Connaught (1569). The presidencies of the two provinces were abolished in 1672 (T. W. Moody and others, *New History of Ireland* iii (1976), 91–2, 449)
27. It was one of Theobald Burke's musketeers who killed FitzMaurice. Burke's father, Sir William Burke, was granted the title of Baron of Castle Connell when the loyal Munster Lords assembled at Limerick, 10th May 1580 (R. Bagwell, *Ireland under the Tudors*, 1890, iii, 23)
28. Unless otherwise indicated, L'Estrange is our authority for the story of Sir Thomas FitzGerald (Desmond). The *New History of Ireland* (vol. iii) mentions him only once, implying that he was in rebellion in 1569, but our sources fail to confirm this; and whilst L'Estrange may have glossed over certain points there is no reason to doubt that Sir Thomas was, for most of his active life, loyal to the crown.
29. T. D. Ingram, *Critical Examination of Irish History* (1900), i, 207
30. J. Otway-Ruthven in *Irish Historical Studies* (IHS), v (1940), 1–28
31. B. Bradshaw, *Irish Constitutional Revolution of the Sixteenth Century* (1979), p. 15
32. translated by J. G. Smyly in *Hermathena* (Dublin), no. 40 (1914), p. 14
33. Bradshaw, op. cit. chapter 2; D. B. Quinn in *IHS* i, pp. 354–81; William Parnell, *Historical Apology for the Irish Catholics* (Dublin, 1807)
34. James I & VI, *An Apologie for the Oath of Allegiance* in *Works* (1616), p. 248 (spelling modernized)
35. e.g. Naturalization Bills. See *The Table*, xlii (1973), 17
36. C. H. McIlwain's edition of King James's *Political Works* (1918), p. 85
37. Ingram, op. cit., i, 62; B. and M. Pawley, *Rome and Canterbury Through Four Centuries* (1974)
38. H. Kearney in B. Farrell (ed.) *Irish Parliamentary Tradition* (1973), p. 92

39. Ingram, op. cit., i, 82 *et seqq*; *CSPI* 1611–14, pp. 398–9

40. Kearney in Farrell, op. cit

41. *CSPI* 1611–14, pp. 514–7. See also p. 536

42. Ingram, op. cit., i, 79

43. *Commons Journals* (Ireland), i, 138

44. See *Folklore*, lxxxv (1974), 276–78. Henry VIII had been careful to describe himself as "Supreme Head of the Church under Christ"; and the substitution of "Governor" for "Head" is treated by some authorities as of little technical moment. The Appendix to Burnet's *History of the Reformation* (1829 edn., ii, pt. II, 559) states that Queen Mary held two Parliaments in whose writs of summons she was styled as Supreme Head of the Church, before laying aside the title a year after her accession. See also *Statutes of the Realm* (Record edn., 1819, iv, 197, 199). For Queen Elizabeth's *Injunctions*, see Burnet, op. cit., (1829), ii, 797–8.

45. Clarke, op. cit., pp. 48, 121

46. Ingram, op. cit., i, pp. 70–1

47. ibid., p. 71. The Catholic Lord Deputy was Ulick de Burgh, fifth Earl and Marquess of Clanricarde (1604–57; see below).

48. J. Lynch, *Cambrensis Eversus* (1662; trans. M. Kelly, Celtic Soc., Dublin, 1851–2), iii, 117. Lynch's book is dedicated to Charles II, and defends throughout the conduct of Ormonde.

49. E. A. D'Alton, *History of Ireland* (1906), ii, 233–59

50. Lodge & Archdale's *Peerage of Ireland* (1789), i, 240; G. E. C., *Complete Peerage,* vol. xii, pt II, 527.

51. *State Papers of John Thurloe* (1742), v, pp. 238–40

52. Mary Hickson, *Ireland in the Seventeenth Century* (1884), i, 156

53. Seals illustrated in J. T. Gilbert's *History of the Irish Confederation* (1882), ii, 84 vary in their spellings of *Hibernia* (*Hiberni*) and *unanimis* (*unanimes*). Ormonde (12th Earl, Marquess 1642, Duke 1661) was appointed Lieutenant-General of the Army in Ireland in 1641 and succeeded Leicester as Lord Lieutenant in January 1644 (*DNB*).

54. Ingram, op. cit., i, 109, 111; M. J. Hynes, *Mission of Rinuccini 1645–9* (Université de Louvain, Recueil des Travaux, Conferences d'Histoire et Philologie, ser. 2, fasc. 24, 1932)

55. Ingram, op. cit., i, 117.

56. J. G. Simms, *Jacobite Ireland* (1969), p. 4 gives the figures for Catholic landholding as 60% in 1641, 8–9% in 1660 and 20% in 1685. By 1703 the percentage had been reduced to fourteen (D. W. Miller, *Queen's Rebels*, 1978, p. 26).

57. P. Walsh, *Ample Accompt* (1662)
58. Ingram, op. cit., i, 214–5.
59. One reason for its rejection may have been that a "Catholic Declaration" found in the pocket of one Nangle after a raid on Longford by 200 "Tories" concluded with the words "We . . . do . . . unanimously declare that the Pope's Holiness is the Supreme Head of Christ's Church Militant; and with our swords drawn we will stand against and oppose all that believe the contrary and to unjustly rob any of our due liberties of conscience and rights". (*CSPI* 1666–9, p. 159).
60. Ingram, op. cit., i, 135–46.
61. On the subject of the etymology of "Tory" much might be said. Authorities however seem agreed that it is derived from an Irish word meaning "pursuer" and implying pursuit with hostile intent. In an Irish context the word is recorded from 1646 with reference to outlaws, generally Catholic and sometimes Royalist, and from 1679 was applied in England to those opposed to the exclusion of James, Duke of York (afterwards James II, and a Roman Catholic) from succession to the Crown. From 1689 it began to acquire its modern political meaning, although right up until the accession of George II there was a tendency for "Tories" to recognize only the House of Stuart. A statute of William and Mary, repealed in 1776, put a reward of £20 on any Tory head and assessed Papist inhabitants of the barony for any loss caused by these raiders. See John Biggs-Davison, *Tory Lives* (1952); *OED* s.v. 'Tory"; and R. Willman in *Historical Journal* xvii (1974), 247–64.
62. W. Harris, *History of the Life and Reign of William-Henry* (1749), p. 157.
63. Ingram, op. cit., i, 160–9; also his *Two Chapters of Irish History* (1888).
64. C. O'Kelly, *Excidium Macariae* (1692) (Camden Soc. , ed. T. C. Croker, 1841, p. 93). See also T. Witherow, *Boyne & Aghrim* (1879), pp. 62–3.

3. The Penal Laws
  1. 2 Eliz. I. c. 2, ss. 2, 3. (Irish)
  2. 27 Eliz. I, c. 2 (English)
  3. T. D. Ingram, *Two Chapters of Irish History* (1888) p. 105.

4. *Journals of the House of Lords* (Dublin) 12 June 1780 (vol. V., p. 181). (Lord Cahir). See also vol. I, p. 466 (Viscount Mountgarrett, 29 Oct. 1692), and 31 March 1740 (Lord Kingsland).

5. 7 & 8 William III, c. 27. (English); F. G. James, *Ireland in the Empire* (1973) p. 97

6. W. H. Lecky, *History of Ireland in the Eighteenth Century* (Cabinet ed.)., i, 156. For the background of the legislation of 1703–4 see also F. G. James, *(Ireland in the Empire 1688–1770* (Cambridge, Mass. 1973) pp. 56–7 (Harvard Historical Monographs, no. 68).

7. W. P. Burke, *Irish Priests in Penal Times* (1914), pp. 464–7

8. *Dublin Gazette*, 29 July 1712; *Archivium Hibernicum*, vol xvii (1953), Appendix, pp. 13–14, 24

9. I Geo. II, c. 9, s. 7 (Irish). Evidence for Catholics voting in 1710 may be found in the Talbot-Crosbie Papers, Trinity College Dublin MS3821, Q.9.6/124.

10. *London Gazette*, 2–6 April 1728

11. 7 Geo. II, c. 5, 6 (Irish); Commons Journals (Ireland), v., 290

12. 9 Geo. II, c. 16 (Irish). Quakers were first allowed to affirm by an Act of 1724. (*Journals of the House of Lords*, Dublin, vol. II, p. 803).

13. 6 Geo. I., c. 5 (Irish)

14. *Journals of the House of Lords* (Dublin) 29 Oct. 1692, i, 466.

15. ibid., ii, 71.

16. ibid., ii, 298, 300, 675

17. ibid., p. 680

18. ibid., p. 739

19. Commons Journals (Ireland), v, 153

20. *D.N.B.* s.v. "Nary"

21. The earliest copy in the British Library is bound up with Reilly's *Impartial History of Ireland* (1754 reprint, pp. 102–22). See also *An Examination of the Case of the Roman-Catholics of Ireland Lately Published*.

22. *House of Lords Journals*, Dublin, ii, 830

23. *Commons Journals* (Ireland), v, 171–2.

24. op. cit., (note 6, *supra*) i, 164–6

25. *Journals of the House of Lords* (Dublin), iii, 257, 259, 282

26. ibid., ii, 837

27. Lord E. Fitzmaurice, *Life of Petty* (1895), pp. 40–41

28. Quoted in T. D. Ingram, *History Legislative Union* (1887), p. 11; see also Fitzmaurice, *Life of Petty* (op. cit.), pp. 148–9, 277

29. Bonnell to Harley, 3 Nov. 1691 Hist MSS Commission, *Portland Mss* (1891–1931) iii, 481; *The Case of Ireland's being bound by Acts of Parliament in England Stated* (1698)

30. *Journals*, ii, p. 29

31. *Commons Journals* (Ireland) vol. iii, p. 368. The Queen's reply, tactful and evasive, is at p. 420.

32. ibid., 20 Oct. 1703, p. 342

33. T. D. Ingram, *Critical Examination of Irish History* (1900), i, 255–6

34. ibid., p. 258. See also C. T. Clay in *Thoresby Society Publications* (1924), pp. 155–60.

35. Ingram, *Critical Examination*, i, 272. The Whiteboys were so called because they went about with white shirts over their other clothes. (*Annual Register* 1762, quoted *OED*).

36. Art O'Leary was made an outlaw for striking a Protestant who offered him such a sum for his horse. See F. O'Connor (transl.), *Lament for Art O'Leary* (Cuala Press, Dublin, 1940.)

37. Lecky, op. cit., i, 277–8; *Studies*, Sept. 1939, p. 489; Maureen Wall, *The Penal Laws* (Irish Historical Association, 1976); Henry Brooke, *The Farmer's Second Letter to the Protestants of Ireland* (1745), p. 8; *Tour Through Ireland* (1748), p. 199

38. Public Record Office of Northern Ireland, Education facsimile no. 105; *Archivium Hibernicum*, xvii (1953), Appendix, pp. 46–7; *Letters by Hugh Boulter* (1769), pp. 188–9

39. Arthur Young's Tour in Ireland 1776–79 (1892), i, 114. This was at Cullen House, Co. Meath.

40. Lecky, op. cit., ii, 188

41. 2 Anne c. 6 cited by M. Wall in *Irish Historical Studies*, vol xi (1958), pp. 95 *et seqq.*

42. M. MacGeehin, "The Catholics of the towns and the Qurterage dispute in eighteenth century Ireland", *Irish Historical Studies*, viii (1952), 91–114

43. *The Querist*, no. 96, p 20. Likewise Josiah Tucker, Dean of Gloucester, in 1775.

44. *Essay on the Causes of the Decline of the Foreign Trade* (1744), p. 93

45. Adam Smith, *Wealth of Nations* (1776), bk. 5, ch. iii

46. *Dublin Gazette*, 11–15 Dec. 1759 (no. 968), pp. 2–3

47. R. L. Sheil, "Catholic leaders and Associations" in *Sketches Legal and Political*, 1855), ii, 160.

48. *Abstract of Letters & Papers of State Relating to . . . Ireland* (1798), ii, in B.L. Add MSS 24,138, fo. 28. For the Galway Address, see *Dublin*

Gazette, 18–22 Dec. 1759 (no. 970, p. 2). According to Frances Plowden's *History of Ireland* (1809), ii, 129 there was a strand among Catholic opinion which held that as they were not subjects in the eyes of the law, "it would be presumptuous to address; and they could only express their obedience by letter". These "anti-addressers", as they were called, were over-ruled on this occasion.

49. Nicholas, Viscount Taafe, *Observations on Affairs in Ireland 1691 to the Present* (1766); Samuel Derrick, *Letters Written from Leverpoole, Chester etc* (Dublin 1767); *London Gazette*, no. 10076, 3–7 Feb. 1761

50. ibid., no. 10075, 31 Jan.–3 Feb. 1761

51. ibid. T. Wyse in his *Historical Sketch of the Late Catholic Association of Ireland* (1829), i, 71–2, stated that Kildare also adopted a separate form, and that the Catholic Bishops refused their concurrence to either.

52. R. E. Burns in *Church History*, vol. xxxii (1963), p. 182

53. A. P. Levack in *Catholic Historical Review* xxxvii (1952), 385–414

54. 15 Aug. 1765 (Public Record Office of Northern Ireland, D 562/1/757)

55. 13 & 14 Geo. III, c. 36 (Ireland) of 1773–4

56. M. O'Connell, *Daniel O'Connell and the Irish Eighteenth Century* (1976); see also M. Wall, "Catholic Loyalty to King and Pope in Eighteenth Century Ireland" *Proceedings of the Irish Catholic Historical Committee* (Dublin, 1961); D. W. Miller, *Queen's Rebels* (1978), p. 38. The Oath, slightly modified, formed the basis of the English Roman Catholic Relief Act of 1791, which according to Bernard and Margaret Pawley, (*Rome & Canterbury Through Four Centuries*, 1981 ed., p. 67) enabled the Roman Mass to be said for the first time openly for 232 years. In Ireland, according to Constantia Maxwell (*Country & Town in Ireland under the Georges*, 1940, p. 356) it was in 1744, after the floor of a house in which Mass was being celebrated in Dublin collapsed, killing the priest and nine people, that permission was obtained to open the chapels of Dublin; and Chesterfield later extended this to the whole of the Kingdom.

57. *Church History*, xxxii (1963)

58. *Harcourt Papers*, (ed. E. Harcourt, privately printed, n.d.), vol. xxix, pp. 357–8. Besides Fingall, the signatories were: Trimblestone, Joseph and Bartholomew Barnwell, Robert Caddell, John Johnstone, Anthony Dermot, James Reynolds, Myles Keon and John Curry.

59. *Magee's Weekly Packet*, 23 Feb. 1782, p. 1. On Catholic participation in the Volunteers, see also Patrick Rogers, *Irish Volunteers & Catholic Emancipation 1778–93* (1934).

60. Here used to mean non-Catholics and not, as once, members of the Church of Ireland.

61. *Dublin Evening Post*, 10 July 1784, p. 4

62. Keogh's speech to the Catholic meeting of Dublin in *Magee's Weekly Packet*, 10 Nov. 1792, p. 3. The rejected Address was from the Catholics of Cork.

63. *Dublin Evening Post*, 10 Jan. 1792, p. 2. See Appendix no. LXXXVI to Plowden's *Historical Review of the State of Ireland* (1803), ii, part II, 173–5 for a full list of the seceders and the text of the Address which they presented to Westmoreland on 27 Dec. 1791 and which was received "with great satisfaction". Besides Fingall, Gormanston and Kenmare, the signatories included Archbishop Troy, Valentine Browne of Killarney, and Sir Patrick Bellew.

64. *Dublin Evening Post*, ibid. See also ibid., 19 Jan., p. 1.

65. ibid., 10 Jan. What seems to have been a pro-Kenmare Address from Co. Mayo was published on 21 Jan., and another, signed *inter alios* by the Roman Catholic pastors of Carlow and Dunleekry and the Bishop of Leighlin and Kildare, David Delany, took a similar line (ibid. 7 Feb.).

66. ibid. 4 Feb. 1792, p. 1; also published separately.

67. Lecky, op. cit., iii, 29

68. n.e.i.

69. *Letters, Speeches and Tracts on Irish Affairs* ed. M. Arnold (1881)

70. *Catholic Historical Review*, xxxvii (1952) 385–414

71. Wentworth Papers in ibid., p. 412

72. Lecky, op. cit., iii, 35–6

73. Ingram, *Critical Examination*, ii, (1900), 87–8; Patrick Rogers, *Irish Volunteers and Catholic Emancipation* (1934), pp. 232 *et seqq*; Henry Joy, *Belfast Politics* (1794); John Lawless, *Belfast Politics* (1818)

74. 32 Geo. III c. 22 (Irish)

75. *Magee's Weekly Packet*, 10 Nov. 1792, p. 4; Plowden, *Historical Review*, op. cit. (1803), ii, part I, 387; ii, part II, 215–224

76. *Thoughts on Ireland*

77. The expression "wild geese" is said to have taken its origin from French smugglers entering the emigrants as such in ships' books, especially from the coast of Clare. *O.E.D.* s.v. Wild Goose

78. Castlereagh, *Memoirs and Correspondence* i (1848), 161–2

79. ibid., p. 175
80. ibid., p. 211
81. T. Wyse, op. cit., ii (1829), p. xvii
82. Castlereagh, op. cit., iii (1849), 96–7
83. Plowden, *Historical Review* (op. cit.), ii, 680.

4. Enfranchisement
 1. Lecky, op. cit., iii, 134
 2. ibid., p. 148
 3. Ponsonby was a supporter of Catholic claims who after the Union was Lord Chancellor of Ireland for a year.
 4. *Parliamentary Register* (Ireland), xiii (1793), 216 (18 Feb. 1793)
 5. William Bennett
 6. Quoted in K. McAnally, *Irish Militia 1793–1816* (1949), pp. 16–17
 7. See the Attorney-General's speech in *Parl. Reg.* (Ireland), xiii (1793), 535.
 8. McAnally, op. cit., p. 204
 9. T. MacKenna, *Essay on Parliamentary Reform* (1793), p. 2
10. Anthologia Hibernica, July–Dec. 1793, pp. 74, 75, 316
11. W. J. McNeven, *Pieces of Irish History*, (1807), p. 61
12. Westmorland Papers, 18 Nov., cited Lecky, op. cit., iii, 74
13. Fingall to Portland, 15 Jan. 1795, cited Lecky, id., p. 265
14. J. Beresford, *Correspondence* (1854), vol. II, p. 51
15. Letter of 6 Feb. 1795 in Stanhope's *Pitt* (1861), ii, p. 304; appendix, pp. xxiii–xxv. A more correct, but shortened, version is in Aspinall & Smith, *English Historical Documents*, xi (1959) pp. 158–9.
16. *DNB* s.v. Hussey
17. W. W. Seward, *Collectanea Politica* (1804), iii, 133–35
18. *Parliamentary Register of Ireland* (1795), xv, 208–361
19. Lecky, op. cit., p. 458. On Maynooth, see Fergus O'Ferrall in *Studies* (Winter 1981) pp. 308–24.
20. Grattan, *Speeches* (1822), iii, 263 (17 Oct. 1796)
21. D. A. Chart, *Ireland from the Union to Catholic Emancipation* (1910), p. 240
22. Lecky, op. cit., p. 474; R. B. McDowell, *Ireland in the Age of Imperialism & Revolution* (1979) p. 559
23. The Brigade had been formally dissolved in 1791 (J. C. O'Callaghan, *History of the Irish Brigades in the Service of France*, 1870, p. 633)
24. Grattan, *Speeches* (1822), iii, 254–5

25. Wolfe Tone, Journal, March 1796 in W. T. W. Tone, (ed.), *Life* (Washington, 1826), ii, 70–71
26. M. R. O'Connell in *Studies in Eighteenth Century Culture*, v (1976) 480, 482–3; M. MacDonagh, *Daniel O'Connell* (1903), pp. 3, 29
27. Lecky, op. cit., (1892 ed.) iii, 541
28. See Grotius, *De Jure Belli et Pacis* (W. Whewell's translation, I, ii. 7). "Those not yet born have not yet acquired any right, and therefore their rights may be cut off by the will of the people".
29. Reference is made to Gregorio Leti's *Cromwell*, a work first published in 1692 in Italian.
30. He later met Wesley and made friends with him. Wesley wrote in his *Journal* (12 May 1787) that "he is not the stiff, queer man that I expected, but of an easy, genteel carriage, and seems not to be wanting either in sense or learning".
31. Although Kenmare, in a declaration from Killarney dated 20 November 1783, denied that he had sent any such statement, those were nonetheless known to be his views. Sir Boyle Roche, upon whom many an Irish "bull" had been fathered, is thought to have been at the bottom of this "hoax".
32. Rutland MSS; H.M.C. 14th Report, App. I, iii (1894), 140–2
33. ibid., p. 135.
34. Cited R. E. Burns, "Parsons, priests, & the people; the Rise of Irish anti-clericalism 1785–89". *Church History*, June 1962, pp. 151–63. See also J. A. Murphy in *Christus Rex* xxiii (1969, 235–59.
35. *Dublin Evening Post*, 25 July 1786, cited in *Archivium Hibernicum*, vol. XIX (1956), p. 239
36. 18, 21 Feb., 19 Nov., 1786
37. *Finn's Leinster Journal*, 19 July 1786, cited *Archivium Hibernicum*, xix (1956), Appendix, 238.
38. R. E. Burns in *Church History*, June 1962, loc. cit.
39. H. M. C. Rutland MSS (1894), iii, 345–6.
40. Lecky, op. cit., p. 547. In *The Tablet* of 28 Feb. 1891 (p. 355) O'Leary's remains were said to be in the Catholic cemetery at Kensal Green, in a grave close to that of Cardinal Wiseman.

5. The Rebellion of 1798

1. Lecky, op. cit., iv, 4
2. Thomas Pakenham, *The Year of Liberty* (1969)

3. *Reports of Debates in the House of Commons of Ireland* (1797), 114, 146
4. Camden to Portland, 21 Mar. 1797, quoted Lecky, op. cit., p. 25
5. Loftus to Pelham, 2 June 1797
6. Lecky, op. cit., iv, 55
7. Grattan's *Speeches* (1822), iii, 337
8. Also spelt McNevin. He was arrested in 1798 and subsequently went to America. See the *DNB*.
9. (Feb. 1797). *Correspondence* ix (1970), p. 257. Burke had not approved of the legislative independence of 1782.
10. Sir Thomas succeeded his mother in 1805. In 1814 he committed suicide after a bank which he had founded in 1804 came to grief (Debrett; G. E. C., *Complete Peerage*, v (1926), 370).
11. Quoted in Lecky, op. cit., pp. 188–9
12. *Memoirs of Grattan* (1842), v, 345
13. ibid., p. 346
14. 26 Mar. 1798 (Lecky, op. cit., p. 211)
15. ibid., p. 216
16. ibid., p. 232 (Auckland, *Correspondence*, iii, 401). In the same letter (Lecky, p. 239) he states: "I must say the Roman Catholics of property who have been on the juries have done their duty".
17. ibid., pp. 242–3
18. In 1796 he was made a baronet. (*DNB*. See B. and M. Pawley, *Rome and Canterbury Through Four Centuries* (1981 edn.), pp. 76–9.
19. Letter of 22 Sept. 1802 in Lecky, op. cit., iv, 247. The Catholic Unionist Theobald MacKenna was another who argued for a State provision for Roman Catholic clergy.
20. F. Plowden, *Historical Review State of Ireland* (1803), ii, pt I, 679–80
21. See below, note 25. The date of the Tara Hill engagement was 25 May.
22. See *Trial for Libel in the Anti-Jacobin Review*, Troy v Symonds (1805).
23. R. Musgrave, *Rebellion in Ireland* (1801), pp. 251–8
24. For the office of Chief Secretary, see the *Handbook of British Chronology* (2nd ed., p. 169). Castlereagh, who succeeded Pelham, was the first Irishman to hold the office, which in the eighteenth century was more of a personal assistantship to the Lord Lieutenant than the Cabinet post which it afterwards became. The office of *Secretary of State for Ireland*, technically superior but in practice a sinecure, was held concurrently by Pelham to give him greater status; but most of its duties had been absorbed by the (English)

Home Secretary in the early part of the century. See also H. Wood in *Proceedings of the Royal Irish Academy*, vol. xxxviii (1928–9), 51–68.

25. Lecky, op. cit., p. 378; *The History of the Irish Rebellion in the Year 1798* (Alston, Cumberland, 1814) i, 305–6; *History of the Rebellion in Ireland in the Year 1798* (Workington, 1805) pp. 34–7; Elizabeth, Countess of Fingall, *Seventy Years Young* (1937), pp. 108–9

26. Lecky, op. cit., p. 390

27. 28–29 May 1798; op. cit., p. 415

28. P. Harwood, *History of the Irish Rebellion of 1798* (1844), p. 185

29. R. Musgrave, *Memoirs of the Rebellions in Ireland* (1802), i, 533

30. 6 June 1798; Lecky, op. cit., p. 435.

31. 22 March 1798; 18 March 1801 (Lecky, op. cit., v, 3.).

32. *Correspondence* (1859), ii, 355

33. i, p. 407

34. "I met with Napper Tandy and he took me by the hand. And he said 'How's poor old Ireland, and how does she stand?' 'Tis the most distressful country, for it's plainly to be seen. They are hanging men and women for the wearing of the green" (quoted in Harold Nicolson, *The Desire to Please*, 1943, p. 94).

35. *Reply of the Rt. Revd Dr Caulfield R.C. Bishop and of the R.C. Clergy of Wexford to . . . Sir Richard Musgrave* (Dublin, 1801)

36. *Observations on the Reply of the Rt Rd Doctor Caulfield . . . to the Misrepresentations of Sir Richard Musgrave*, Dublin, 1802; Dr Coppinger's *Remonstrance* was published at Cork, 1798, and Dr Moylan's at Dublin.

37. Charles Dixon, *The Wexford Rising in 1798* (Tralee, 1956) pp. 15–20

38. Myles Byrne *Memoirs* (1863; revised ed. 1907), i, 39

6. The Union

1. *Mémoires*, (1823 ed.) ii, 335, cited in Lecky, op. cit., v, 39

2. 31 July 1798, quoted in G. C. Bolton *Passing of the Act of Union*, (1966), p. 62

3. See Hansard, *Parl. Hist.* (1819) xxxiv, cols, 229–30, (23 Jan 1799)

4. 1798, n.d. Auckland, *Correspondence*, iv, (1862)

5. Cornwallis, *Correspondence* (1859), ii, 414–5

6. Auckland *Correspondence*, (1862), iv, 52 (30 Aug. 1798).

7. That he had, earlier, been favourable to Emancipation, is shown by a note in the Pelham Mss quoted in Lecky (op. cit. p. 202), where

he commented on a "plan of Union" containing the passage: "Catholics to be eligible to all offices, civil and military, taking the present oath. Such as shall take the Oath of Supremacy in the Bill of Rights, may sit in Parliament without subscribing the Abjuration. Corporation offices to be Protestant". Pitt commented: "the first part seems unexceptionable, and is exactly what I wish . . . but if this oath is sufficient for office, why require a different one for Parliament? and why are Corporation offices to be exclusively Protestant, when those of the State may be Catholic?"

8. Cornwallis, op. cit., ii, 439–41
9. 9 November 1798 (Pelham Mss cited Lecky, op. cit., p. 161)
10. Lecky, op. cit., v, 204
11. p. 14
12. Mackenna was referred to as a lawyer in Molyneux's pamphlet, though R. B. McDowell (*Irish Public Opinion 1750–1800*) refers to him as a physician (1944, p. 164).
13. The right of inflicting capital punishment
14. p. 38
15. See P. Sheehy, *Union a Plague* (1799) for a further tribute to MacKenna.
16. Dr Troy in Castlereagh, *Memoirs & Correspondence* (1848), ii, 61
17. Lecky, op. cit., v, 216. The position in Canada was that in 1763 the Catholics of newly-conquered Quebec were required to take the Oath of Supremacy as well as of Allegiance. In 1774 the Supremacy requirement was abandoned. (*Annual Register* for 1827, p. 44).
18. Charles Butler, *Historical Memoirs Respecting the English, Irish & Scottish Catholics*, ii (1819), 159–61.
19. Charles Coote's *History of the Union* (1802), pp. 47–63
20. The modern equivalent of the procedure by Resolution is the Debate on the "White Paper" containing the Government's proposals for legislation; although Resolutions could theoretically still be used for especially important legislation and a shadow of them remains in the shape of the Budget Resolutions moved annually and which have the force of law prior to the passing of the Finance Act, they are not now considered appropriate. The legality of imposts raised under the Budget Resolutions was indeed successfully challenged in a Court of Law in 1913, and a special Act of Parliament had to be passed to clarify the position.
21. Lecky, op. cit., v, 248
22. Matthew Lennan in Castlereagh, op. cit., ii, 168

23. Lecky, op. cit., v, p. 296

24. see the *Nineteenth Century*, October 1887, pp. 445–59; and for Ingram's reply, pp. 766–90. Mr Gladstone's rejoinder of 9 December 1887 appeared in the *Westminster Review* (1888), cxxix, pp. 77–81.

25. *Critical Examination of Irish History*, vol ii, (1900), 299

26. Cornwallis, op. cit., iii, 105, 151, 153; FitzGerald Papers 10/18, p. 38.

27. Lord Donoughmore, who presented both this Address and that from Waterford, afterwards stated that this was the first favourable turn which the Union question experienced after its rejection, in 1799. (Cobbett's *Parl Deb* xvii, 1810, col 435).

28. *Belfast News-Letter*, (*BNL*) 13 September 1799, p. 1; W. Carrigan, *History and Antiquities of the Diocese of Ossory* (1905), i, 213–4

29. *BNL*, 19 Nov. 1799.

30. ibid., 29 Oct., p. 4

31. ibid., 15 Oct., p. 1

32. ibid., 1 Oct., p. 1 (meeting held on 31 August 1799)

33. ibid., 23 August, p. 1 (meeting held on 28 July)

34. ibid.

35. ibid., 10 January 1800, p. 4

36. These addresses are discussed in T. D. Ingram's *History of the Union* (1887) at pp. 113 *et seq.*, but we have gone to original sources for our account.

37. Figures calculated from table in *Irish Committee of Historical Sciences Bulletin*, no. 33 (May 1944).

38. *Belfast News-Letter*, 4 March 1800, p. 4; 11 March, p. 4

39. Cornwallis, op. cit., iii, 143

40. ibid., 105; Castlereagh, op. cit., iii, 26, 27, 353

41. Colchester MSS, 13 Oct. 1801, cited Lecky, op. cit., v, 313

42. Lecky, op. cit., v, 328

43. "Address to the Parliament of Great Britain" in *Collected Works* (Boston, 1868), p. 541

44. M. R. O'Connell in *Studies in Eighteenth Century Culture*, v (1976), 480

45. ibid., pp. 485–6

46. ibid., pp. 484–5

47. The soubriquet was derived from his having, when a tax was imposed on beaver hats (then a favourite with the Irish gentry) taken to wearing a small velvet cap. See M. MacDonagh, *Daniel O'Connell* (1903), p. 3

48. *A Letter to Sir Robert Peel on the Endowment of the Roman Catholic Church of Ireland* (1845), p. 10. Daunt, in his *Personal Recollections of the late Daniel O'Connell* (1848) reproduced what purports to be a conversation with Daniel in which the latter is made to say that his uncle did not really approve of the Union. Nevertheless, "Hunting Cap" was firm in his denunciations of his nephew's proposing anti-Union resolutions at the Catholic Meeting held in Dublin in January 1800 referred to in the next note (M. R. O'Connell, op. cit., [1976], pp. 484–5). See also FitzGerald Papers 2/3/9, 14, 17 (pp. 28, 38, 44).

49. Cited by Ingram in *Nineteenth Century* (1887), p. 778 (see note 24 above). A satirical *"Anti-Union"* (27 Dec. 1798 to 9 Mar. 1799 — 32 numbers) seems to be a different work. The meeting addressed by O'Connell and referred to in the preceding note was held at the Royal Exchange, Dublin, and was chaired by Ambrose Moore. Among the resolutions passed was one stating that "even if there were advantages in the giving up of an independent legislature they would be only the bounty of the master to the slave". (*The Constitution: or Anti-Union Evening Post*, 14 Jan. 1800).

50. Lecky, op. cit., v, 330. We have been unable to trace the work referred to as "Barnes on the Union" which Lecky gives as his authority for the existence of Catholic anti-Union petitions. George Cooper in his *Letters on the Irish Nation* (1800), pp. 197 *et seqq.* emphasized that opposition to the Union, centred in Dublin, was confined to "a few discontented individuals who assume the voice of the whole Catholic body". No reference was found to such petitions in George Barnes's *Rights of the Imperial Crown of England* (1799), a reply to Edward Cooke's *Arguments for and Against an Union*

51. Lecky, op. cit., p. 350

52. Grattan's *Life, v (1846), 71, cited ibid., p. 351*

53. His father, to his death in 1793, was an ardent supporter of the Union, and in 1751 published *A Proposal for Uniting the Kingdoms of Great Britain and Ireland*. Both he and an earlier pamphleteer (*Some Thoughts Humbly Offer'd Towards an Union between Great Britain and Ireland*, 1708–9) thought that a Union might have the result not only of increasing the prosperity and population of Ireland, but of gradually turning its Catholic inhabitants' minds towards a more favourable view of Protestantism.

7. Emancipation

1. The term *emancipation* originally had to do with the freeing of slaves, or, in the case of Roman Law, of releasing children from the power of their parents. It was used by Jefferson in the former sense in a letter written in 1785 (see the New Supplement to *OED*, 1972), and was soon taken up in Ireland. It seems to have been first applied in print to the removal of Catholic disabilities by Theobald Mackenna, who in the preface to his *Political Essays*, published in 1794, wrote of the then recent grant of the vote to Catholics, "I use this familiar word *emancipation* to avoid a paraphrase, although I do not consider it as perfectly applicable" (p. lii). The *OED* records that by 1797 the word "emancipation" was being applied by Burke to further schemes of reform. There still lingered however a flavour of novelty and even of slang and the word tended to be avoided in official circles. A present-day analogy might be "Women's Lib".

2. Castlereagh's letter to Pitt 1 Jan. 1801 in Castlereagh, *Correspondence*, iv, 8–12

3. *Life of William Wilberforce by his Sons* (1838), iii, 7; G. Pellew's *Sidmouth* (1847) i, 285–6

4. Stanhope's *Pitt*, iii, Appendix, pp. xxiii, xxviii, xxx; Cornwallis, *Correspondence*, iii, 333; Lecky, op. cit., p. 440

5. John Brooke, *King George III* (1972), p. 367. "I had rather beg my bread from door to door throughout Europe than consent to any such measure", the King is reported as saying (Pellew, op. cit., p. 286).

6. The phrase "Prime Minister" was not then regarded as quite respectable, importing as it did a degree of dominance over colleagues from which Walpole, to whom it was first applied, resiled.

7. George Canning, *Oracle* (1803–4)

8. Lecky, op. cit., pp. 447–8

9. See the summary of the evidence on the King's illness by H.R.H. the present Prince of Wales in John Brooke, op. cit., pp. vii–ix.

10. Colchester's *Diary & Correspondence* (1861), i, 441

11. This is no doubt a reference to the crime of misprision of treason.

12. The reference is to Emmet's rebellion (see later in this chapter).

13. Napoleon Bonaparte

14. This correspondence was published both in the newspapers of the time, and as a pamphlet in 1804 with the title *The Catholic Question*.

15. Plowden's *History of Ireland 1801–1810* (1811), i, 177

16. ibid., p. 183

17. ibid., p. 198

18. M. Macdonagh, *Viceroy's Post-Bag* (1905), p. 235
19. Plowden, op. cit., i, 270, 272–5
20. Kenmare to FitzGerald, 13 Feb. 1805. FitzGerald Papers, 9/51 p. 106. We are indebted for these references to Mr Adrian FitzGerald.
21. Kenmare to FitzGerald, 24 Feb. 1805. FitzGerald Papers, 9/56, p. 116; D. J. McDougall in *Catholic Historical Review*, xxxi (1945), 255–81; Plowden, op. cit., ii, pp. 24, 82–9. The petition was signed by 93 other gentlemen besides the six peers mentioned.
22. Plowden, op. cit., ii, 42
23. *Transactions of the Royal Historical Society* 3rd s. (1908), ii, p. 14
24. See *Trial for a Libel in the Anti-Jacobin Review, Troy v Symonds* (1805).
25. *Dublin Evening Post*, 5 Apr. 1808, p. 3; 7 Apr., p. 3
26. Letter of 18 Feb. 1806 in Plowden, op. cit., ii, 304–7.
27. Plowden, op. cit., p. 488
28. ibid., p. 507
29. ibid., p. 554
30. FitzGerald Papers 10/15, p. 32; 10/38
31. British Library Add. MSS 38,359, fos. 203–8; FitzGerald Papers, 10/10/15, p. 32
32. Plowden, op. cit., iii, 563; Militia (Ireland) Act, 1807 47 Geo. III, st. II, c. 55, s. 13; B. Ward, *The Eve of Catholic Emancipation* (1911), ii, 246–7
33. T. Wyse, *Historical Sketch of the Late Catholic Association of Ireland*, i, 166 *et seqq.*; FitzGerald Papers, 10/53, (25 March 1810), 9/61, p. 126 (26 May 1810)
34. Wyse, op. cit., p. 172
35. *Annual Register* (*A.R.*), p. 17
36. J. J. Dillon, *A Letter on the Apprehension of the Earl of Fingall* (1812)
37. Moira, subsequently Governor of Bengal and Marquess of Hastings, had been an opponent of the Union (*DNB*). His letter is in the Fingall papers (National Library of Ireland, MS 8023/11).
38. *A.R.* 1812, part I, p. 66; part II, pp. 342–6 for text of Catholic petition.
39. *A.R.*, 120. On 5 June Kenmare and five others presented an Address of appreciation to the Duke (*Correspondence of Daniel O'Connell*, ed. M. R. O'Connell, 1972, i, 301, citing *Freeman's Journal*, 9 June 1812).
40. O'Connell, op. cit., i, 295
41. *A.R.*, Part I, pp. 100–1; *Waterford Mirror*, 29 May 1813

42. C. S. Parker, *Sir Robert Peel* (1891), i, 123.
43. O'Connell, op. cit., ii, 3
44. N. Gash, *Mr Secretary Peel* (1961), p. 170.
45. British Library Add. MSS 40216, fos. 98, 181 (July–Dec. 1813).
46. C. Forster, *Life of Jebb* (1836), i, 247–8, 323; I. Murphy in *Irish Ecclesiastical Record*, 5th ser. (1966), p. 96.
47. *A.R.*, 1814, pt. I., p. 216.
48. O'Connell, op. cit., i, 370. The General had had a distinguished career in the service of Royalist France. After 1792 he was appointed to command an Irish regiment in British service (Webb, *Compendium*, 1878).
49. *Dublin Evening Post*, 30 Aug. 1814 cited ibid., p. 377; see also pp. 379–82.
50. Lord Fingall had refused to attend an earlier meeting on 26 Nov., despite a personal appearance by O'Connell (op. cit., i, 388).
51. *Dublin Evening Post (DEP)*, 24 Jan. 1815, 2nd ed., p. 2
52. *A.R. 1815, pt. I, p. 143; Dublin Evening Post*, 16 Feb. 1815, p. 3
53. Parker, op. cit., i, 225
54. O'Connell, op. cit., ii, 22, 28–30, 59
55. ibid., p. 94; *DEP*, 17 Feb. 1816, p. 3; 20 Feb., p.2
56. *A.R.* 1816, pt I, pp. 49–54
57. *DEP*, 17 Dec. 1816, p. 3; 6 Feb. 1817, p. 3; 8 Feb., p. 2
58. O'Connell, op. cit., ii, 126, 146
59. *DEP*, 5 July 1817, p. 3; 10 July, p. 2; 22 July, p. 3; 24 July, p. 2; O'Connell, op. cit., ii, p. 101
60. O'Connell, op. cit., ii, p. 184
61. T. Wyse, op. cit., (1829), i, 148
62. *Encyclopaedia Britannica*, 11th edition, s.v. Grattan, Henry; *Dublin Journal*, 31 May, 7 June, 14 July 1820; *Annual Register* 1821 for Plunket's speech (28 Feb. 1821), a slightly different version of which is in *Hansard* (n.s. iv. 966).
63. 22 Mar. 1821, cited O'Connell, *Correspondence* (1972) ii.312. Text of Bills is in *Dublin Journal* 14 Mar. 1821, p. 2; for O'Connell's denunciation see ibid., 21 Mar. pp. 3–4.
64. Parker, *Peel*, i, 302
65. *A.R.* 1822, part I, p. 7
66. 3 Geo. IV., c. 103
67. *A.R.* 1822, part I, pp. 30 *et seqq.*
68. *A.R.* 1822; *A.R.* 1823, pp. 203–5, 209 for the bottle-throwing incident and its *sequelae*.

69. J. A. Reynolds, *Catholic Emancipation Crisis in Ireland 1823–9* (1954), pp. 31–2.

70. Letter to Thomas Drummond of 25th Sept. 1837 in Reynolds, op. cit., p. 32

71. *A.R.* 1823, p. 238. The speaker was Tierney. Cf. *Hansar* n.s. viii (1823), 1070–1123.

72. Parker, *Peel*, (1899), iii, 53–4, 183. In a letter to Sir James Graham (16 June 1843) he wrote: "we must *look out for respectable Roman Catholics for office. There are many grounds for not rigidly acting in Ireland on that specious principle, that, if Protestants are better qualified for appointments that fall vacant, Protestants ought to be preferred to Catholics*".

73. *A.R.* 1824, part I, p. 150

74. Reynolds, op. cit., p. 65

75. *A.R.– 1824, part I, p. 162*

76. *Dublin Morning Register*, 21 Mar. 1825, cited O'Connell, *Correspondence* (1974), ii, 190; *A.R.* 1825, part I, p. 43

77. On 26 Jan. 1826 a "Catholic Association for 1826" was established for a period of 14 days only and dissolved on 29 Jan. (*Dublin Evening Post* cited O'Connell, op. cit., p. 218). This body was quite separate from the New Catholic Association founded on 13 July 1825.

78. These, the so-called "wings" were accepted by O'Connell; and many Catholics opposed him for doing so.

79. Peel had replied in the House of Commons (*A.R.* 1827, i, 14) that the law was not enforced for reasons of administrative discretion rather than because of legal difficulties.

80. *A.R.* 1827, pt I, p. 46

81. "J.K.L.", "The Conciliation of Ireland" quoted in W. J. Fitzpatrick, *Life of Doyle* (1861) i, 338 *et seqq.*

82. Peel to Foster, 16 July 1826, in B. L. Add. MSS 40335, fos. 224–5.

83. *Dublin Evening Post*, 21 April 1827

84. See *OED* and *A.R.* 1828, i, 122

85. *A.R.* 1828, i, 127

86. Reynolds, op. cit., pp. 149, 152

87. "A Roman Catholic Barrister", *Letter to the Duke of Wellington . . . on . . . Catholic Emancipation* (1828). On Blake, see Donal A. Kerr, *Peel, Priests and Politics* (1982), pp. 136–9.

88. FitzGerald Papers, 18/29, p. 29; *Notes on Conversations with the Duke of Wellington* by Philip Henry, 5th Earl Stanhope (1938 ed.) p. 45; B. Ward, *The Eve of Catholic Emancipation* (1912), iii, 259

8. The Repeal Agitation

1. *Dublin Evening Post (DEP)*, 15 Dec. 1829, p. 3
2. O'Connell in *DEP*, 2 Jan. 1830
3. ibid., 12 Jan., p. 4
4. ibid., 30 Mar. 1830
5. ibid., 16 Dec. 1830; *Hansard*, 14 Dec., cols. 1132–3.
6. Fagan, *O'Connell* (1848), ii, 63–5; A. Macintyre, *The Liberator* (1965), p. 16n
7. *DEP*, 18 Jan., 14 June 1831
8. FitzGerald Papers, 13/99, p. 162
9. *DEP*, 10, 17 Feb., 5 Apr. 1831
10. *Wexford Herald*, 18 Aug. 1830. See also ibid., 10, 31 July, 4 Aug. For the family background, H. A. Lambert in *The Past* (Ui Ceinnsealaigh Hist. Soc., Wexford), Dec. 1921, pp. 129–38.
11. *New Monthly Magazine*, xxxii, p. 287
12. *Hansard*, 25 May 1832, col. 161; "A Roman Catholic", *The Liberal Party in Ireland* (1862)
13. *Wexford Independent*, 8 Dec. 1832
14. quoted ibid., p. 2
15. ibid., 19 Dec.
16. ibid., 29 Dec.
17. Fagan's *O'Connell* (1848), ii, 298
18. *Hansard*, 12 Mar. 1834, col. 83
19. ibid., 25 Apr. 1834, cols. 29–41
20. ibid., col. 40
21. "He valued popular opinion as much as any man", Killeen had stated, "but . . . he did not think he ought to profess any opinions but those he really held". (*Hansard*, 14 Dec. 1830, cols. 1132–3)
22. At the election of 1835, Lambert stood down. (B. M. Walker, *Parliamentary Election Results in Ireland*, 1978).
23. See *History of The Times*, i (1935), 334–5 and, for O'Crolly, *The Revd David O'Crolly's Farewell Address to the Roman Catholics of the Diocese of Cork* (Dublin, 1836).
24. FitzGerald Papers 15/5, 15/14, 15/45
25. ibid., 15/18 (p. 19)
26. ibid., 15/23 (p. 50), 15/42
27. ibid., 15/36, (p. 78)

28. ibid., 15/39. In the same letter, Catherine FitzGerald mentions an English Catholic reporter having been sent over by *The Times* to cover the election.

29. R. B. McDowell, *Public Opinion & Government Policy in Ireland 1801–46* (1952), pp. 134 *et seqq*. The academic writers are not always in agreement as to the number of Irish M.P.s at this period who should properly be classed as "Repealers".

30. See the *OED* s.v. "inside" sb. 3. The original poem is dated 1798. Stanley and his fellow-seceders did not join the Conservatives until 1841.

31. 5 May 1835. This was in reply to a speech by O'Connell in which the latter asserted that Disraeli had "just the qualities of the impenitent thief".

32. Fagan, *O'Connell*, ii, 631

33. The Irish Association

34. Fagan, *O'Connell*, ii, 659

35. 1920 ed., p. 113

36. Fagan, op. cit., ii, 662

37. *Ireland and its Rulers since 1829*, ii (1844) 294

38. J. F. M'Lennan, *Drummond* (1867), pp. 337–8. Woulfe was in London at the time.

39. Madden, op. cit., p. 304. See also *Report of a Speech Delivered by Stephen Woulfe* (Dublin, 1816).

40. W. J. O'Neill Daunt, *A Life Spent for Ireland* (1896), p. 156; J. R. O'Flanagan, *Irish Bar* (1879), p. 317; W. H. Curran, *Sketches of the Irish Bar* (1855), i, 3–76; *DNB*

41. O'Flanagan, op. cit., p. 317

42. M. A. G. Ó'Tuathaigh, *Thomas Drummond & the Government of Ireland* (O'Donnell Lecture, 1977)

43. ibid., p. 10

44. *Hansard*, 7 Mar. 1839, cols. 44–5, 82

45. E. Lucas, *Life of Frederick Lucas* (1886), i, 61–2

46. F. P. Carey, *Archbishop Murray of Dublin* (1951), p. 24

47. B. O'Reilly, *John MacHale* (1890), i, 413–76

48. McDowell, loc. cit.; C. G. Duffy, *Young Ireland* (1896 ed.), i, 27. K. B. Nowlan in his *Politics of Repeal* (1965), p. 24, puts the figure at between 15 and 22. Crolly's letter is cited in D. A. Kerr, *Peel, Priests & Politics* (1982), p. 88.

49. Letter of 29th May 1843 in Irish College Archives at Rome quoted in Broderick, op. cit., p. 136.

50. Angus Macintyre, *The Liberator* (1965), p. 275. The O'Conor Don was one of the signatories. In form it was an "Address of Irish M.P.s to the English people".

51. Macintyre, op. cit., pp. 274–5.

52. S. Walpole, *History of England* (1886), iv, 235

53. L. J. McCaffrey, *Daniel O'Connell & the Repeal Year* (1966), p. 199, shows the delay to be due to "inefficiency or stupidity rather than a sinister plot".

54. McCaffrey, op. cit., p. 206

55. The title of a poem by James Clarence Mangan. "Rosaleen" (1846) is said to personify Ireland's nationhood as addressed by Red Hugh O'Donnell at the time of Elizabeth I.

56. *The Repealer Repulsed* (Belfast, 1841), pp. 134–5

57. *Dublin Evening Post*, 11 Nov. 1830, p. 3

58. 7 & 8 Vict., c. 97

59. W. J. Walsh, *O'Connell, Archbishop Murray & the Board of Charitable Bequests* (Dublin, 1916), pp. 3–4. Donal A. Kerr, *Peel, Priests & Politics* (1982), p. 122, states that one member of the Bequests Board was a Catholic, but gives no authority.

60. Walsh, op. cit., p. 1. Kerr (op. cit., pp. 178–9, 352) suggests that Walsh's criticisms of O'Connell were overdrawn, and that he was not the Act's chief opponent. Nonetheless, he does not dispute its beneficial effects.

61. Words used in an Act of 1763 (3 Geo. III, c. 18 (I))

62. Walsh, op. cit., p. 33

63. E. R. Norman in *Irish Historical Studies*, Sept. 1967, p. 412

64. *Hansard*, 3rd series, lxxix, col. 559. See also McDowell, op. cit., p. 219, Kerr, op. cit., pp. 224–89.

65. The O'Conor Don, for example, deferred to the opinion of a County Roscommon meeting on 14 Jan. 1831 and decided to support O'Connell; see note 10 above, also Macintyre, op. cit., p. 54 for an account of pressure on another candidate in 1832.

66. see *Hansard*, 9 May 1845, col. 378. "It was a gigantic scheme of Godless education" said Inglis. Wyse's role in the genesis of the scheme for National Education is regarded as only a small one in D. H. Akenson's *Irish Education Experiment* (1970), where it is pointed out that Anthony Blake and others also contributed.

67. In 1880 the Queen's University became the Royal University, and in 1908 Queen's College, Belfast became Queen's University, whilst

the other two became constituent colleges of the National University of Ireland.

68. J. J. Auchmuty, *Sir Thomas Wyse* (1939), p. 186. On the Wyse family, see also Olga Bonaparte-Wyse, *The Spurious Brood* (1969).
69. Fr Philip Fitzgerald, *Narrative of the Confederates of 1848*, cited D. Gwynn in *Irish Ecclesiastical Record* (1948), lxx, 590–609

9. Famine and Fenianism

1. W. P. O'Brien, *Great Famine in Ireland* (1896)
2. quoted in O'Brien, op. cit., p. 36
3. see Disraeli's *Lord George Bentinck* (1852) chapter 2.
4. *Encyclopaedia Britannica*, eleventh edition, s.v. PEEL, Sir Robert
5. *A.R.*, 1846, i, 199
6. ibid., p. 203
7. ibid., 1847, i, p. 4
8. ibid., p. 23
9. Thackeray (M. A. Titmarsh), *Irish Sketch-Book 1842* (1863), i, 74
10. *DNB*
11. J. F. Maguire, *Father Mathew* (1863), pp. 376–7
12. *Dublin University Magazine*, February 1852, pp. 268–9
13. *Annual Register, 1849, History*, pp. 71–2
14. *Annual Register 1849, Chronicle*, p. 86. The Prince of Wales was afterwards created Earl of Dublin in honour of the visit (*London Gazette*, 11 Sept. 1849).
15. *Dublin Gazette*, 8, 9 August 1849.
16. ibid., 11 August 1849, p. 762
17. ibid., 16 August 1849, p. 778
18. ibid., p. 781
19. See alsò B. O'Reilly, *John MacHale* (1890).
20. Whyte in P. J. Corish (ed.) *History of Irish Catholicism* v., (1967) 3–4
21. *Dublin Evening Post,* 14 Jan. 1845, p. 1
22. by Johnstone Stoney. See E. R. Norman, *The Catholic Church and Ireland* (1965) p. 18.
23. Quoted by T. H. Whyte in Corish, op. cit., p. 5
24. Quoted in T. H. Whyte, *The Independent Irish Party* (1958), p. 20. See also B. and M. Pawley, *Rome and Canterbury Through Four Centuries* (1981 ed.), pp. 147 *et seqq.*
25. *The Government of Lord Aberdeen and the Government of Lord Derby.* by an Irish Catholic (Dublin, 1853), p. 25

26. Somerville to Russell, 4 Mar. 1851. P.R.O. 30/22, 9, quoted by Whyte in Corish, op. cit., p. 11

27. Cullen to Propaganda 25 May 1854 in Corish, op. cit., p. 12. On Cullen generally, see now Desmond Bowen, *Paul Cardinal Cullen* (1983).

28. Newman, *My Campaign in Ireland* (1896), pt. I, p. xiv

29. Newman, *Autobiographical Writings* (1956), pp. 324–6

30. e.g. Letter to Bishop Ullathorne, 27 Feb. 1857 (C. S. Dessain, *Letters & Diaries of Cardinal Newman* (1967), xvii, 533

31. *The Liberal Party in Ireland . . . Its Present Condition & Prospects* by a Roman Catholic. Dublin, 1862

32. ibid., p. 17

33. T. H. Whyte, *Independent Irish Party* (1958), pp. 28, 88. By October 1852 it had apparently ceased to exist, for reasons which are still obscure.

34. Whyte, op. cit., p. 14 (figures approximated)

35. ibid., p. 7

36. *London Gazette*, 15 June 1852

37. Whyte, op. cit. (1958), p. 61

38. Sligo Election petition, pp. 12–13, quoted ibid., p. 72

39. *Daily Express* (Dublin), 17 Aug. 1852, quoted ibid., p. 71

40. "An ex-M.P.", *A Memoir of Ireland in 1850* (James McGlashan, Dublin; Ridgway, London, 1851), p. 31. T. P. O'Neill argued in *The Great Famine* (ed. R. D. Edwards & Williams, 1956) that if the ports had been closed, there could have been an increase in the daily rations of the three million destitute of one and a third ounces of wheat and nine ounces of oats.

41. ibid., p. 33

42. In an earlier *Letter on the Currency to . . . Viscount Althorp*, Lambert had argued for a National Bank issuing notes which would be legal tender and exchangeable for silver.

43. Arguments against the Bank Charter Act continue to be heard, and have been especially associated with the name of Henry Meulen (d. 1978), editor of *The Individualist*.

44. See Boswell's *Life, A.D. 1773 Aetat. 64 (Everyman ed., 1949, i, 483–4). After a discourse on toleration, Johnson, "bursting forth with a generous indignation" said that "the Irish are in a most unnatural state; for we see there the minority prevailing over the majority. There is no instance, even in the ten persecutions, of such severity as that which the protestants of Ireland have exercised against the Catholicks. Did we tell them we have*

conquered them, it would be above board; to punish them by confiscation and other penalties, as rebels, was monstrous injustice".

45. *Memoir of Ireland*, pp. 108–9
46. *Dublin University Magazine*, June 1852, pp. 773 *et seqq.*
47. C. G. Duffy, *League of North & South* (1886), pp. 197 *et seqq.*; *Wexford Independent*, 5 Feb. 1834; *Constitution* (Cork), 4 Dec. 1834.
48. Whyte (1958) (figures calculated from Appendices B and C)
49. *The Government of Lord Aberdeen & the Government of Lord Derby* (op. cit., 1853), p. 32
50. British Library Add. MSS 43250, fo. 141b
51. ibid., fo. 148. This was not the end of Monsell's pro-Catholic activities. He objected to the promise of allegiance only to the heirs of the Electress Sophia, as set out in the Oath provided for Catholics under the Emancipation Act, as a slur on Catholic loyalty, and when sworn as a Privy Counsellor on 13 Aug. 1855 he was, it appears, allowed to omit references to the Royal Supremacy. In 1865 he introduced a Private Member's Bill for altering the Catholic oaths; and this was followed the next year by a Government Bill which became the Parliamentary Oaths Act of 1866 (Dessain, op. cit. (1965), xvi, 457).
52. *The Government of Lord Aberdeen & the Government of Lord Derby* (op. cit.)
53. *The Tablet*, 21 Oct., 11 Nov. 1854
54. Cullen to Moriarty, 20 Jan. 1855; Nat. Library of Ireland MSS 8319 cited Whyte (1958), pp. 115–6
55. *The Nation*, 10 Nov. 1855; see also 18 Aug., pp. 776–7.
56. Sir William Gregory, *Autobiography* (1894), pp. 161–3.
57. Gregory, letter to *The Times* (23 Sept. 1890)
58. S. Low & L. C. Sanders, *History of England during the Reign of Victoria* (1907), p. 131
59. Royal Commission on Historical Manuscripts. Report on the papers of Sir John Pope Hennessy (1974) (Bodleian Library, Oxford; cyclostyled)
60. Bodleian Library, British Empire MSS, S 409/1, fo. 189
61. *Saturday Review*, 21 May 1859, pp. 621–2. The reference is to Sir George Bowyer, who sat for Dundalk from 1852 to 1868. From 1874 to 1880 he sat for Wexford as a Home Ruler and was expelled from the Reform Club in 1876.
62. *Oxford English Dictionary*.
63. E. R. Norman, *History of Modern Ireland* (1971), pp. 155–6

64. R. Kee, *The Green Flag* (1972), pp. 300–1
65. Kee, op. cit., p. 309
66. H.M. Queen Victoria, *Tours in England & Ireland & Yachting Excursions* in *Leaves from the Journal of our Life in the Highlands* (1868), p. 181
67. L. Ó Broin "The Phoenix Conspiracy", *The Irish Sword*, Winter 1980, p. 169
68. 1 Sept. 1853
69. *Annual Register 1867*, Chronicle, p. 23
70. *The Tablet*, 23 Feb. 1867, p. 124
71. *Cork Examiner*, 20 Feb. 1867
72. see Brendan Behan, *Borstal Boy* (1961 ed.), p. 254
73. *Hansard*, 7 May 1867, col. 176
74. See *Irish Sword*, Winter 1980, p. 170. In his early years he had been a friend of Young Irelanders. See C. S. Dessain, op. cit., xvi, (1965), p. 619, and J. H. Newman *Autobiographical Writings*, (1956), p. 328.
75. E. R. Norman, *The Catholic Church and Ireland* (1965), pp. 131, 133
76. *The Times*, 7 Feb. 1872, p. 12
77. Speech at Repeal Association meeting, 29 May 1843, reprinted in *Occasional Papers & Addresses* (1884)
78. O'Hagan, *Occasional Papers & Addresses* (1884), pp. 319–39
79. *DNB*
80. B.L. Add. MSS 44416, fos. 347–8
81. ibid., Add. MSS 44473, fos. 187–9

10. The First Home Rule Bill

1. A. M. Sullivan, *New Ireland* (10th edn. n.d.), p. 344
2. Sullivan, op. cit., p.345
3. ibid., pp. 349–353. Some of Moriarty's clergy however supported Blennerhassett; Monsell MSS N.L.I. 8319, cited *Irish Historical Studies* (*IHS*), vol. XI (1958), p. 216.
4. *The Times*, 4 Jan. 1871, p. 11
5. ibid., 7 Jan. 1871, p. 10
6. ibid., 13 Jan. 1872, p. 12
7. ibid., 27 Jan. 1872, p. 6
8. ibid., 13 Feb. 1872, p. 12; T. de Vere White, *Road of Excess* (1946), p. 243
9. W. Ward, *Aubrey de Vere*, (1904), p. 283

10. ibid., p. 339

11. *Essays* (1889, p. 156

12. ibid., p. 158

13. Disraeli, *Speeches on Parliamentary Reform*, ed. M. Corry (1867)

14. *The Times*, 11 Nov. 1904, p. 4

15. Quoted in de Vere, *Recollections* (1897), p. 348. This was perhaps the same denunciation attributed to Cullen in *The Tablet* which Walsh repudiated in the *Dublin Evening Mail* of 15 Sept. 1887. There is independent evidence, however, of Cullen's opposition. E. D. Steele (*IHS*, xix, 1974–5) has argued that Cullen was much more of a Nationalist than such writers as Dr Norman have made him out to be; but even Steele is obliged to concede that in 1874 he did try to help Gladstone's former Irish Secretary, Chichester Fortescue, in County Louth (see also David Thornley, *Isaac Butt and Home Rule*, 1964, pp. 180–1). Earlier, Cullen had held aloof even from the Home Government Association (*IHS* ix, 1954–5, p. 191).

16. quoted in de Vere, *Recollections* (op. cit.)

17. *Mediaeval Records & Sonnets*, pp. 262–3

18. Sullivan, op. cit., p. 353

19. W. J. Fitzpatrick, *Memories of Father Healy* (1896), chapter 7

20. (*IHS*), xi (1958), 217

21. 2 March 1873 (Monsell MSS, N.L.I. 8317). We are indebted for this reference to Mr Adrian FitzGerald.

22. *IHS* vol. ix (1954–5), p. 206

23. J. Altholz in *Catholic Historical Review*, lvii (1971), 593–605; J. P. Rossi in ibid., lxiii (1977).

24. H. Jenkins in *Journal of Ecclesiastical History*, xxx (1979), 353–77

25. "Scrutator", *Ultramontanism versus Education in Ireland* (1875); see also H. Jenkins (1979, note 24 *supra*); E. Norman, *Catholic Church in Ireland* (1965), pp. 431–6.

26. J. P. Rossi in *Catholic Historical Review*, lxiii (1977), p. 414; Victoria Hicks Beach, *Life of Sir Michael Hicks Beach* (1932), i, 37–62. R. F. Foster, *Lord Randolph Churchill* (1981) treats the intermediate education policy in some detail, but he errs in stating that Sir William Gregory was a Catholic.

27. *Catholic Directory*, 1881, p. 44, cited Rossi, op. cit., p. 425. The *Irish Catholic Directory* for 1881, however (pp. 20–1) lists only The O'Donoghue and Edward J. Synan (Limerick) as uncommitted Catholic Liberals.

28. 23 Feb. 1880. See T. W. Moody *Davitt* (1981), p. 357.

29. B.L. Add. MSS 44473, fos. 185–7
30. ibid., fos. 208–9
31. B.L. Add. MSS 43625, fos. 179 *et seqq.* See also A. F. Denholm in *Recusant History*, x (1969), 111–8.
32. *IHS* xviii (1972–3), 29–60. See also Anthony Rhodes in *The Tablet*, 22 May 1982, pp. 510–3. The Duke of Norfolk led a delegation of English Catholics to the Vatican in 1875.
33. *Freeman's Journal*, 10 Jan. 1881, p. 6.
34. T. W. Reid, *Life of Forster*, (1970 reissue), ii, 327
35. See also J. Enoch Powell, "Kilmainham — the Treaty that never was". *Historical Journal*, xxi (1978), 949–59
36. R. C. K. Ensor, *England 1870–1914* (1936), p. 76; T. Corfe, *The Phoenix Park Murders* (1968)
37. *The Times*, 12 Feb. 1885, p. 7
38. *Cork Constitution*, 28 Apr. 1880, p. 2; T. W. Moody, *Davitt* (1981), p. 421
39. Errington to Ampthill, 5 Mar. 1883, quoted in *IHS*, xviii (1972–3), 43.
40. *Freeman's Journal*, 1 Jan. 1883, p. 3
41. ibid., 11 Jan. 1883; 19 Jan., p. 4
42. *Cork Constitution*, 24 Jan. 1883, p. 2
43. *Irish Law Times*, 23 August 1890, p. 44
44. *IHS*, xviii (1972–3), 44
45. *Freeman's Journal*, 11 Dec. 1883, p. 6; see also W. O'Brien, *Evening Memories* (1920), pp. 50–2.
46. Granville to Spencer, 17 Mar. 1885 (Spencer Papers); Errington to Granville 26 Mar. 1885 (P.R.O. F.O. 800/239 no. 195); quoted *IHS*, vol. xviii, p. 58
47. P. J. Walsh, *W. J. Walsh* (1928), p. 151
48. Gwynn & Tuckwell, *Life of Dilke* (1917), ii, 151
49. Sir Sydney Lee, *Edward VII* (1925), i, 222 *et seqq.*
50. Lee, loc. cit., p. 227
51. 25 April 1868
52. Lee, loc. cit., p. 231
53. ibid., p. 238
54. *The Times*, 19 Oct. 1901, p. 6
55. ibid., 18 Apr. 1885, p. 9
56. ibid., 14 Apr. 1885, p. 10
57. ibid., 16 April, p. 6

58. A different interpretation is offered by some writers, for example A. B. Cooke and John Vincent, *The Governing Passion* (1974), pp. 52–3, who suggested that Gladstone's conversion to Home Rule came later. Nevertheless their book contains no detailed refutation of the arguments in Appendix A of R. C. K. Ensor's contribution to the Oxford History of England, and in the absence of such refutation his account has been accepted here. For Carnarvon's account of his conversation with Parnell see Carnarvon Papers (B.L. Add. MSS 60829).

59. The so-called "Hawarden Kite"

60. P. J. Walsh, op. cit., p. 203

61. D. C. Heron, *Constitutional History of the University of Dublin* (1847), p. 82.

62. Heron, op. cit., pp. 83–5, citing *Report of the Proceedings in the Case of the Borough of Trinity College*, Dublin, 1791.

63. *Irish Parliamentary Debates*, xv, 203 in W. M. Dixon, *Trinity College Dublin* (1902), p. 124.

64. Heron, op. cit., pl 192; McDowell & Webb, *Trinity College Dublin* (1982), pp. 213–4.

65. Dixon, op. cit.

66. Maguire, *Reasons* etc., p. 8

67. *History of The Times: The Twentieth Century Test* (1947), pp. 43–4, 64 *et seqq*; R. Barry O'Brien, *The Life of Lord Russell of Killowen* (1901); R. B. McDowell & Webb, op. cit., p. 282; *The Times*, 27 Feb. 1889, p. 5

68. *DNB*; *The Times*, 23 Mar. 1909

69. L. McKenna in Society of Jesus, *A Page of Irish History: the Story of University College Dublin* (1930).

70. A reference to the fourteen principal families of Galway, who traditionally were very exclusive and tended to marry only among themselves.

71. *Irish Times*, 9 Sept. 1901, p. 5

72. *Galway Vindicator*, 1, 15 July 1865. The figures were: Morris, 883; Blennerhassett, 672; Lever, 291; Stubber, 22.

73. *Galway Vindicator*, 6, 13 Feb., 1867

74. ibid., 3 Apr. 1876

75. ibid., 17 Mar. 1880

76. ibid., 9 Sept., 1868

77. ibid., 19 Sept., 30 Sept. 1868

78. ibid., 10 Oct. 1868

79. ibid., 31 Jan. 1874

80. ibid., 13, 17 Mar. 1880

81. *Galway Express*, 14 Sept. 1912

82. M. Wynne, *An Irishman and His Family* (1937), p. 41

83. ibid., p. 45

84. ibid.

85. ibid., pp. 46–7

86. S. M. Hussey, *Reminiscences of an Irish Land Agent* (1904), p. 170

87. John Biggs-Davison, *The Hand is Red* (1973), pp. 10–11, gives the following account of Chuchullain: "Pre-historic Ireland knew perhaps a hundred kingdoms, each occupied by a *tuath* or tribe, headed by a *rí* or king. The *Táin Bó Cualgne* tells of an island divided between four main peoples, of which one was the Ulaid in the north with Conchobar mac Nessa as their King. The River Erne and its lakes barred traffic overland. There and to the east, the bogs and forests cut Ulaid off from Southern Ireland. *Táin Bó Cualgne* means the '*Cattle Raid of Cooley*'. King Conchobar's previous bull was made off with by Medb (Maeve), Queen of Connachta (Connaught). The prowess of the outraged Ulaid was sapped by a mysterious *cess*; but Cú Chulainn, a champion from elsewhere, and a skilled hurler too, was immune to the disease and came to the resue of the Ulstermen. This defender of the Ulaid against the four Southern realms died, we are told, standing upright, strapped to a pillar, 'facing his enemies, the men of Ireland'. So we trace a thread in the tapestry of history from Cú Chulainn to James Craig. Notwithstanding Cú Chulainn's statue stands in the General Post Office in Dublin to commemorate the Easter Rising of 1916. Perhaps the statue of this Ulster separatist should be removed to the City Hall in Belfast!" Michael Morris, like Cú Chulainn, was immune to a weakening disease. In his time, it was called nationalism.

88. Wynne, op. cit., p. 98

89. *Galway Observer*, 29 Sept. 1900. Father Dooley had alleged that Lord Morris had "got £300,000 from the British Government and . . . never did anything for Galway". An anonymous correspondent, "Veritas", replied in the *Galway Observer* of 15 Sept. that during the time that Lord Morris and his brother had represented the city "they jointly succeeded in getting a debt of something like £40,000 wiped off the harbour of Galway and also got the present military barracks in Renmore built, by which many a person in Galway benefited largely".

90. W. J. Fitzpatrick, *Memories of Father Healy of Little Bray* (1896), chapter 12

91. ibid., pp. 147–8.

92. ibid., chapter 6; Henry Neville, *A Few Remarks on Mr Gladstone's Expostulation With Some Remarks on "Vaticanism"* (1875); *Cork Examiner*, 16 Dec. 1889, p. 2; *The Tablet*, 21 Dec. 1889, p. 999.

11. The Pope and the Plan of Campaign

1. *Annual Register 1886* (1887), Hist., p. 310

2. A. M. Sullivan, *Old Ireland* (1927), pp. 38–9

3. P. J. Walsh, *Archbishop Walsh*, p. 235; L. P. Curtis, *Coercion & Conciliation in Ireland* (1963), p. 258

4. D. E. Fitzpatrick, *New Guide to Killarney* (ed. 3, 1837) pp. 30–31. An annotation (ca. 1845) in the British Library copy points out that "the Earl of Fingall is the head of the Irish Catholic Aristocracy".

5. G.E.C., *Complete Peerage*, vii

6. *Killarney Echo*, 18 Feb. 1905

7. Dr McSweeney and James Egan, ibid.; the *Echo* of 25 Feb. records a tribute from the Gaelic League.

8. Gladstone Papers, B.L. Add. MSS. 44510, fos. 71–76

9. cited in Walsh, op. cit., p. 237

10. Walsh, op. cit., p. 245; *The Tablet*, 11 Dec. 1886, pp. 921–22; Arundel MSS., C 767

11. A. T. Q. Stewart, *Edward Carson* (1981), p. 25

12. Arundel MSS, C 764, 767; *The Times*, 22 Feb. 1886, p. 8

13. *The Tablet*, 27 Mar. 1886, pp. 483–4. Bury had become a Catholic in 1879, Ashburnham in 1872 (*Complete Peerage*).

14. *The Tablet*, 22 Mar. 1886, pp. 184–5

15. ibid., 17 Oct.˙ 1868, pp. 664–5

16. Walsh, op. cit., pp. 250–1

17. *Freeman's Journal*, 8 Feb. 1887; M. Tierney *Croke of Cashel* (1976), pp. 206 et seqq.

18. Cardinal Edward Henry Howard (1829–1892) was a grandson of the youngest brother of the twelfth Duke of Norfolk. After serving in the Life Guards, he spent most of his life at Rome, where he was made a Cardinal in 1877.

19. John Ross-of-Bladensburg to 15th Duke of Norfolk, 15 Sept. 1885. Arundel Castle MSS

20. "I hate Persico". A Latin pun based on a passage in the *Odes* of Horace, I, 38.
21. Edmund Dease to 15th Duke of Norfolk, 14 Oct. 1887. Arundel MSS
22. *Pall Mall Gazette*, 16 Dec. 1887, p. 7
23. J. S. Crone, *Concise Dictionary of Irish Biography* (1937)
24. A. M. Sullivan, op. cit., pp. 38–9
25. *Irish Times, Northern Whig* and *Belfast Newsletter*, 12 July 1926. For McGettigan, see James Stuart, *Historical Memoirs of the City of Armagh* (1900 ed.), pp. 316–7.
26. Ross-of-Bladensburg papers, Northern Ireland Public Record Office, D/2004/4/9 refers to his wife's conversion in 1876. For letters written by Ross to Carnarvon during a visit to Rome in 1886 see Carnarvon papers, Brit. Library Add. MSS 60830. He had found the Pope's private secretary, Mgr Boccali, "strongly imbued" with the idea that "although there might be evil events attending upon the present movements in Ireland yet that result would not be in anyway bad for the Church". The Vatican's only source of information being the Bishops, he wrote on 6 Apr. 1886, it was "blindness and folly" not to have a British official representative to give information. The Duke of Norfolk's letters of credence in 1887 made no direct reference to the Pope's jubilee; the congratulations were not omitted, but they took the form of a personal letter from Queen Victoria to His Holiness (*Letters of Queen Victoria*, 3rd ser. i, 364, cited in *Law Quarterly Review*, July 1932, pp. 389–90).
27. Papers of the 15th Duke of Norfolk, Dec. 1887. Arundel Castle MSS
28. Walsh, op. cit., pp. 329–32; *The Tablet*, 5 May 1888, p. 719; 12 May, pp. 753–4
29. Norfolk to Salisbury, 22 June 1892 cited Curtis, op. cit., pp. 265, 272; Tierney, op. cit., p. 221
30. Quoted by Anthony Rhodes in *Encounter* (Feb. 1980), pp. 17–18
31. Ross-of-Bladensburg papers, Northern Ireland Public Record Office, D2004/4/45
32. Brit. Library Add. MSS 49828, fos. 552–3, 565–6, 797. Ross's letters to Balfour during this mission are in Add. MSS 49821, fos. 33–52. He returned in April 1890.
33. Add. MSS 49821, fos. 33 *et seqq.*
34. ibid., fo. 43v.
35. Curtis, op. cit.

36. P. J. Joyce, *John Healy* (1931)

37. ibid., pp. 68–69.

38. *United Ireland*, 12 Dec. 1885, p. 1

39. Joyce, op. cit., pp. 88–9

40. W. Ward, *Aubrey de Vere* (1904), p. 374

41. Healy, *Papers and Addresses* (1909), pp. 35–6

42. Joyce, op. cit., p. 149

43. *The Times*, 30 Jan. 1891, p. 10

44. *A.R. 1889*, i, 269

45. *A.R. 1890*, pt. II, p. 271

46. ibid., p. 272

47. Gladstone Papers, British Library Add. MSS 44510, fos. 71–76

48. B. L. Solow, *Land Question & Irish Economy* (Cambridge, Mass., 1971, p. 13).

49. ibid., p. 202. See also B. L. Solow, "A new look at the Irish land question", *Economic & Social Review* (Dublin) xii (July 1981), 301–14.

50. S. M. Hussey, *Reminiscences of an Irish Land Agent* (1904)

51. A. M. Sullivan, op. cit., p. 45

52. David Thornley, *Isaac Butt & Home Rule* (1964), pp. 178–9; *Hansard*, 30 June 1876, cols. 821–2

53. *The Times, 29 Sept. 1894, p. 10; F. Boase, Modern English Biography* (1908), iv

54. Arundel MSS, July 1886. (C 766)

55. B. Sykes, letter to Arnold Power, 22 April 1885, in B.L. Add. MSS., 58069–70. These papers also contain evidence (baptismal and interment certificates) of Power's father being a Catholic.

56. Frank Power, *Letters from Khartoum* (1885). B.L. Add. MSS 58069 contains the original manuscripts of these letters; the omissions in the printed text seem to have been relatively few, but they have not been systematically collated.

57. The authorship of the epitaph is unknown but it is subscribed "M.A. of Kings' College, Cambridge, Sept. 20, 1886".

58. Chapter 2 of *The History of* The Times: *The Twentieth Century Test* (1947) (vol. III) contains a full account of Power's activities in the Sudan.

59. Gordon, *Journals* (1885), pp. 286, 310

60. Frank Power, *Letters from Khartoum* (1885), pp. 39, 57, 73–4

12. The Second Home Rule Bill

1. *Hansard*, 11 March 1890, col. 516
2. C. J. Woods in Lyons & Hawkins (eds.) *Ireland under the Union* (1980), p. 289
3. *Irish Times*, 22 Jan. 1891, p. 5
4. Marjoribanks & Colvin, *Life of Lord Carson* (1932), i, 19 *et seqq.*
5. *Irish Times*, 8 June 1887, pp. 4–5
6. *Irish Times*, 30 Nov. 1887, p. 6
7. These were Edmund Dease (1829–1904) and Col. Gerald Dease (1831–1903). Along with many others, they signed the Irish Catholic petition against Home Rule.
8. *Irish Times*, 30 Nov. 1887, p. 6
9. ibid., 1 Dec. 1887, p.5.
10. *Dublin Review*, 3rd ser. April 1888, pp. 374 *et seqq.*
11. Quoted in *Irish Times*, 1 Dec. 1887, p. 6
12. *Irish Times*, 5 Feb. 1921, p. 7. At a meeting of the Liberal Union of Ireland held on 1 February 1889 (*Irish Times*, 2 Feb., p. 5) it was disclosed that membership had more than trebled since 1887. The Executive Committee included Sir Rowland Blennerhassett, W. F. Cogan, P.C., Sir Richard Martin, Peter O'Brien (Attorney-General for Ireland) James Talbot Power and Piers Whyte, Q.C., all Catholics. Together they comprised, with Kenny, nearly a quarter of the committee with its officers.
13. P. Buckland, *Irish Unionism*, i (1972), 1; *Kerry Evening Post*, 21 Oct. 1885.
14. An I.L.P.U. leaflet in the British Library collection claimed that the organisation had arranged for forty-eight contests. In the event, the nationalists were opposed in fifty-two constituencies in the south.
15. J. F. Harbinson, *The Ulster Unionist Party* (Belfast, 1974), p. 7
16. ibid., p. 10
17. ibid., p. 12
18. *Ulster Unionist Convention Belfast, 17 June 1892; Report of the Great Meeting of 12,000 Delegates from all the Counties of Ulster and of the Open-Air Meeting in the Royal Botanical Gardens, Belfast*, p. 108.
19. ibid., p. 36
20. ibid., p. 110
21. *Unionist Convention for Provinces of Leinster, Munster & Connaught (June 1892). Report of Proceedings, Lists of Committees, Delegates, etc.*, p. 90
22. *Irish Times*, 24 June 1892, p. 5

23. *Irish Times*, 25 June 1892, p. 6
24. ibid.
25. Horace Plunkett (1854–1932). At first a moderate Unionist, he later became converted to Home Rule. There is a vivid portrait of him in St. John Ervine's *Craigavon* (1949), pp. 342–5.
26. *Irish Times*, 27 June 1892, p. 6
27. The "Balfour banquet" was held on 2 February 1889 when Balfour was the guest of the Liberal Union of Ireland (*Irish Times*, 4 Feb. 1889).
28. *Irish Times*, 1 July 1892, p. 6
29. *The Times* (London), 13 July 1892, p. 6
30. *Irish Times*, 4 July 1892; 9 July, pp. 4, 5. See also "M", *An Election Journal* (1894), esp. pp. 153–156.
31. Timothy Harrington (1851–1910), Parnellite Member for the Dublin Harbour division.
32. *Irish Daily Independent*, 5 July 1892, p. 6. This was founded in Dec. 1891 as a Parnellite organ, becoming the *Irish Independent* after 1905. It referred to the *Freeman's Journal*, which had turned against Parnell, as the "Fallen Journal" (see, e.g. the issue of 30 Aug. 1895, p. 5).
33. ibid., 9 July 1892.
34. ibid., 7 July, p. 2
35. *Irish Times*, 9 July 1892, p. 5. On 4 July (*Irish Daily Independent*, 5 July, p. 6) the Lord Mayor had admitted that he admired Kenny as a lawyer.
36. B. M. Walker, *Parliamentary Election Results in Ireland, 1801–1922* (1978)
37. Marjoribanks & Colvin, op. cit., pp. 142 *et seqq.*; *Oxford Dictionary of Quotations* (3rd ed.); *D.N.B.*
38. *The Times*, 8 Nov. 1892, p.9
39. ibid., 12 Nov., p.8
40. *Hansard*, 13 Mar. 1893, cols. 1916–27
41. ibid., 19 July 1894, cols. 443–54; 14 Aug., cols. 893–979, also called the Tenants Arbitration (Ireland) Bill.
42. 4 Mar. 1895
43. *Hansard*, 4 Mar. 1895, cols. 343–8
44. Buckland, op. cit., p. 16
45. R. C. K. Ensor, *England 1870–1914* (1936), pp. 211–2
46. Irish Unionist Alliance, Leaflet no. 23 (6th series, 1891–2; British Library collection)
47. *Fortnightly Review*, 1 May 1893, pp. 606–7

48. I.U.A. Leaflets, 7th series, ii, 519 *et seqq.*

49. *Daily Express* (Dublin), 23 March 1893, p.4

50. ibid., 7 March 1893, p.7

51. *Sligo Independent*, 25 Mar. 1893, p.3; 15 July 1893, p.3; I.U.A. leaflets, nos. 47 and 102 (7th series)

52. *Irish Times*, 13 Apr. 1893, quoted in I.U.A. leaflet no. 96 (7th series, iii, 224)

53. I.U.A. leaflet no. 95 (7th series, iii, pp. 219–21). Emly had also presided over the meeting at Limerick on 22 March, at which Fingall spoke as well as Dunraven.

54. I.U.A. leaflets, ii, pp. 441–55

55. ibid., iii, p. 226.

56. I.U.A. leaflet no. 142 (iii, p. 386)

57. *A Duke of Norfolk Notebook*, (n.d. ca. 1917), p. 45. See also Lord Fingall's speech at Limerick on 22 March 1893. "In the present crisis and for the future, we are confident that the real union of hearts which is being established between us now can only be firmly cemented by the avoidance of all possible causes of friction between all different denominations in Ireland." (*Dublin Daily Express*, 23 Mar., p. 6).

58. Col. Saunderson to Duke of Norfolk, 18 Mar. 1893 (Arundel Papers). On 29 Mar. the editor of the Sheffield *Daily Telegraph* (Sir William Long) wrote to apologize for a "rather vicious and decidedly vulgar letter attacking the Catholics" which had appeared in the paper (ibid.).

59. St John Ervine, *Craigavon* (1949), p. 221. Lord FitzAlan (created 28 Apr. 1921) assumed the surname and arms of Talbot in 1876, resuming his paternal surname of Fitzalan-Howard in June 1921.

60. Quoted in an unpublished memoir of the 15th Duke of Norfolk by Bernard Holland (Arundel papers). A Religious Disabilities Removal Bill to open the Lord Chancellorship of Great Britain and the Lord Lieutenancy of Ireland to Catholics was introduced into the House of Commons in 1890 and again in 1891 (Commons Journals, 1890, cxlv, cxlvi (indexes); Rule 3 of the *Laws & Ordinances of the Orange Institution of Ireland* (Belfast, 1872), provided for the exceptional admittance of Catholics into the Orange Order by unanimous vote of the Grand Lodge, but it is not known if this rule has ever been implemented (M. MacDonagh in *Contemporary Review*, Aug. 1896, p. 227).

61. Marjoribanks, op. cit., p. 165

62. *Hansard*, 16 Feb., 1893, cols. 1648–56

63. ibid., 21 June 1893, cols. 1609–12

64. ibid., 12 July 1893, cols. 1413 *et seqq.*

65. This was because of his views on Irish Church disestablishment. See, e.g., G. W. E. Russell, *Gladstone* (1891), chapter 7.

66. *Hansard*, 29 May 1895, cols. 580–2; 12 June 1895, cols. 1014–6.

67. *Irish Times*, 18 July 1895, p. 6

68. *Irish Daily Independent*, 13 July 1895, p. 5

69. *Freeman's Journal*, 12 July 1895, p. 3

70. *Irish Times*, 18 July 1895, p. 6

71. *Freeman's Journal*, 18 July 1895 (editorial). "Coercionist" was its word for "Unionist".

72. *Irish Daily Independent*, 18 July 1895, p. 4

73. The history of the laws regarding the re-election of Ministers of the Crown is set out in W. R. Anson's *Law & Custom of the Constitution* (1922 ed.) i, 84–89. The Act of Settlement of 1700 disqualified all office-holders from Membership of the House of Commons. This was repealed by 4 Anne c. 8 s. 28, and the Succession to the Crown Act of 1707 (6 Anne c. 41 (c. 7 in Ruffhead)) provided merely for the re-election of office-holders, with certain exceptions like the Chiltern Hundreds. These re-election provisions were construed to apply only to "old" offices, i.e. those created before 1705; for offices created subsequent to that date, unless special provision was made, subsequent re-election could not validate or reverse the disqualification. In 1919 the re-election provisions were abolished by the Re-election of Ministers Act (9 Geo. 5 c. 2).

74. *Irish Times*, 22nd August 1895, p. 5. There had been rumours of other appointments, e.g. that of Dunbar Barton (*Freeman's Journal*, 31 July, p. 4; 13 Aug., p. 5). The *Irish Times* on 29 Aug. quoted from *The Times* (London) in approbation of Kenny's appointment.

75. *Irish Daily Independent*, 30 Aug. 1895, p. 5

76. ibid., 31 Aug. 1895, p. 5. On anti-semitism in Ireland, see G. Moore in *Economic & Social Review*, (Dublin) xii (1981), 187–201.

77. *Irish Times*, 31 Aug. 1895, p. 8

78. T. M. Healy, *Letters & Leaders of My Day* (1928), ii, 407–8

79. *Irish Times*, 5 Feb. 1921, p. 7; *Who Was Who 1916–28*; *Irish Law Times*, 12 Feb. 1921, pp. 44–5.

13. Land and Education
 1. *Final Report* of the Royal Commission on Financial Relations between Great Britain and Ireland (C. 8262) p. 2 (*Parliamentary Papers* (Commons) (1896), xxxiii
 2. Cork Constitution, 14 Dec. 1896
 3. *Annual Register* (*A.R.*) 1896, i, 225.
 4. *The Times*, 29 Dec. 1896, p. 4
 5. *A.R.* 1896, i, 226
 6. Sir David Barbour (1841–1928) had been financial member of the Viceroy's Council in India and was an authority on bimetallism.
 7. *A.R.* 1896, i, 223–7. A Mr Brown, who presumed to mention imperial expenditure in Ireland in the Dublin Corporation on 14 Dec., was asked whether he was holding a "Castle brief" (*Cork Constitution*, 15 Dec., p. 8).
 8. *A.R.* 1897, i, 237
 9. 9 Sept. 1897, quoted in Harold Nicolson's *King George V* (1952), p. 57
10. *The Times*, 19 Aug. 1897, p. 6; 30 Aug., p. 7
11. *The Times*, 4 Sept. 1897, p. 6; *Dublin Gazette*, 24 Aug., p. 946
12. *The Times*, 4 Sept. 1897, p. 6
13. *A.R.* 1898, i, 206; *Parliamentary Papers* (Commons), 1898, xxxv (C. 8734, 8859)
14. D. W. Miller, *Church, State & Nation in Ireland 1898–1921* (1973), p. 19
15. Miller, op. cit., pp. 20–22
16. ibid., pp. 44–57
17. *A.R.* 1898, i, 210
18. *A.R.* (1899, i, 242
19. *A.R.* 1900, i, 251–2
20. *Dublin Gazette*, 13 Apr. 1900
21. *Letters of Queen Victoria*, 3rd series (1932), iii, 521
22. *The Universe*, 4 Dec. 1931, quoted ibid., p. 531
23. Sir Shane Leslie, *The Film of Memory* (1938), p. 365
24. *Irish Times*, 25 Apr. 1900, p. 5
25. *Letters of Queen Victoria*, op. cit., iii (1932), 544
26. *Irish Times*, 19 Apr. 1900, p. 5
27. *A.R.* 1900, i, 254
28. B. M. Walker, *Parliamentary Election Results in Ireland, 1801–1922* (1978). In 1895 the seat was won by an anti-Parnellite Nationalist with a Parnellite, Edmund Leamy, coming second. In 1900 Leamy stood as sole nationalist candidate, giving Morris a straight fight.

29. Walker, op. cit., p. xvi.; St. John Ervine, *Craigavon* (1949), pp. 101– et seqq.

30. *A.R.* 1902, i, 231–4

31. *A.R.* 1902, i, 245–50

32. Lord Rosebery's speech in *The Times*, 11 Mar. 1892, p. 11; Sir Sydney Lee, *King Edward VII* (1927), ii, 164–5

33. W. L. Micks, *Congested Districts Board* (Dublin, 1925), pp. 104–5; Royal Commission on Congestion in Ireland, *First Report, Minutes of Evidence* (1906, Cd. 3267), p. 1; Appendix 26 to *Twelfth Report Congested Districts Board* (1903, Cd. 1622, *Parl. Papers* vol. LV). The expression "congested districts", has been traced back to 1882 (Cd. 3267, supra., p. 1) and refers to an area of land "of which the resources are inadequate to support its population" (New Supplement to the Oxford English Dictionary, 1972 edition).

34. *A.R.* 1902, i, 247

35. ibid., p. 248

36. For the Land Bill, see John Biggs-Davison, *George Wyndham* (1951), chapter 9

37. 22 Apr. 1901; *Hansard*, cols. 955–66

38. ibid., col 961

39. ibid., 20 June 1901, cols. 925–6; 16 Jan. 1902, col. 4

40. ibid., 27 July 1908, cols. 745–6

41. P. J. Joyce, *John Healy* (1931), pp. 179–80; E. Dease in *Freeman's Journal*, 2 June 1899

42. *Hansard*, 27 July 1908, cols 779–87

43. *Dublin Review*, Jan. 1890, pp. 1–32

44. Joyce, op. cit., p. 242. On MacEvilly, see D'Alton, *History of the Archdiocese of Tuam* (1928) vol II, pp. 109–12.

45. Joyce, op. cit., pp. 248–9

46. Miller, op. cit., p. 246

47. Joyce, op. cit., pp. 247–5.

14. The Third Home Rule Bill

1. Sir Sydney Lee, *King Edward VII* (1927), vol. II, p. 165; *Hansard*, 25 June 1823, cols. 1212–41; Lady Clarendon's Journal, 6 Mar. 1850; Sir Herbert Maxwell's Life of Clarendon, vol. I; *Hansard*, 17 May 1850, col. 219, 27 June 1850, cols. 468–71. Cadogan had been Lord Lieutenant of Ireland from 1895.

2. *Irish Times*, 22 July 1903, p. 5; J. Biggs-Davison, *George Wyndham* (1951), pp. 135–6

3. *Irish Times*, 23 July 1903, p. 5

4. ibid., p. 6; Biggs-Davison, op. cit., p. 137

5. *Irish Times*, 1 Aug. 1903, p. 5

6. ibid., 31 July, p. 5

7. J. W. Good, *Irish Unionism* (1920), pp. 215–6

8. W. A. Phillips, *Revolution in Ireland* (1923), p. 48; Good, op. cit.

9. Lee, op. cit., p. 172

10. Biggs-Davison, op. cit., p. 151

11. ibid., p. 155

12. Lee, op. cit., p. 472; R. F. Brooke, *The Brimming River* (1961), pp. 99 *et seqq.*; P. Jalland in *Historical Journal* (1976) on the relations between the Aberdeens and Birrell; see also F. F. Moore, *The Truth About Ulster* (1914), p. 55.

13. On the state jewels, see Peter Galloway, *The Most Illustrious Order of St. Patrick* (1983). Vicars was shot by a gang of armed raiders at Kilmorna House, Co. Kerry, in 1921 (ibid., pp. 41–6).

14. *The Times*, 11 July 1907, p. 8

15. J. F. Harbinson, *The Ulster Unionist Party* (Belfast, 1974), p. 23

16. ibid., pp. 26–7

17. *Northern Whig*, 10 Apr. 1912, p. 12

18. Phillips, op. cit., p. 63. The word "Parliament" had not been used in previous Home Rule Bills.

19. ibid., p. 64. William O'Brien had split with Redmond in 1903. See J. V. O'Brien, *William O'Brien* (1976).

20. Robert Blake, *The Unknown Prime Minister* (1955), p. 130.

21. *Cork Constitution*, 22 Apr. 1912, pp. 5–7

22. *Galway Express*, 1 June 1912, p. 6

23. *Irish Times*, 2 Oct. 1925, p. 9

24. *Strabane Chronicle*, 13 Jan. 1906

25. ibid., 20 Jan. 1906, p. 4

26. ibid., 13, 20 Jan. 1906

27. ibid., 27 Jan. 1906

28. Ulster Herald, 2 Mar. 1907, p. 5

29. *Strabane Chronicle*, 9 Mar. 1907

30. *Ulster Herald*, 16 Mar. 1907, p. 2; 27 Jan. 1906, p. 7

31. *Strabane Chronicle*, 30 Mar. 1907

32. ibid., 20 Apr. 1907

33. *Daily Express (Dublin), 30 Nov. 1912, p. 6*

34. A. T. Q. Stewart, *Edward Carson (1981), pp. 77–78. See also D. W. Miller, Queen's Rebels* (1978), pp. 96–97.
35. Stewart, op. cit., p. 78.
36. *The Times*, 27 Mar. 1913; 23 Nov., p. 10; A. T. Q. Stewart, *Ulster Crisis* (1967) p. 137. By 7 Aug. 1914 the League had enrolled over 16,000 vounteers (Dublin *Daily Express*, 7 Aug. 1914, p. 4).
37. *Hansard*, (Lords), 29 Jan. 1913, cols. 682–98
38. A. T. Q. Stewart, *Edward Carson* (1981), pp. 81–2
39. Phillips, op. cit., pp. 46–7
40. Arundel MSS.
41. ibid.
42. Phillips, op. cit., pp. 68–70; *Daily Express* (Dublin), 26 Nov. 1913, p. 5 for the inaugural meeting of the Irish National Volunteers. The words "citizen army" were also used in its manifesto, but the fact that it had no support from the Larkinites, at least in its inception, is shown by this report of their attempts to break it up. On "Bloody Sunday" see E. Larkin, *James Larkin* (1965), pp. 123–6. Larkin had publicly looked forward to the formation of a "citizen army" as early as 1908 (id., p. 58).
43. Arundel MSS.
44. *Annual Register 1913*, p. 204.
45. For text of proclamations, see Dublin *Daily Express*, 6 Dec. 1913, p. 5. A Barrister-at Law's article was printed on 8 Dec., p. 6 and the Divisional Court's judgment on appeal on 16 June 1914, p. 7. The proclamation under the Customs Consoidation Act was withdrawn on 5 Aug. 1914 (*London Gazette*, Suppl., p. 6169) and replaced by an amendment under D.O.R.A. on 5 Dec. 1914.
46. A. T. Q. Stewart, *Carson* (1981), p. 84.
47. P. M. Young, *Elgar, O. M.* (1955), p. 169
48. A. T. Q. Stewart, *Carson* (1981), p. 85
49. Young, op. cit.
50. Stewart, op. cit., p. 87
51. *Manchester Guardian*, 4 Feb. 1919, p. 4
52. St John Ervine, *Craigavon* (1949), p. 263. Estimates of the number of rifles landed varied from 50,000 to 70,000 in the Dublin *Daily Express* of 27 Apr 1914.
53. Ervine, op. cit., pp. 265–7. See also P. Jalland in *Hist. Jrnl.* (1976) vol. XIX, p. 444. Jalland, drawing on the Asquith papers, states that the King also influenced the decision, as did Carson's pacific tone in

Parliament. Aberdeen seems to have been much more strongly in favour of arresting all the Larne gun-runners than was Birrell.

54. *The Times*, 29 Nov. 1913, p. 9; *Irish Times*, 29 Nov. p. 11
55. Arundel MSS.
56. ibid.
57. P. Buckland, *Irish Unionism* (1972), i, 23
58. Ross-of-Bladenburg's letter of 12 Jan. 1915 in Midleton Papers (Public Record Office) PRO 30/67/29, fo. 1513. The Royal Irish Constabulary (a separate force) were armed, but could not be contacted at Phoenix Park. Harrel's authority to call on them, and indeed his power to act at Howth, arose from the fact that he and Ross were magistrates for the County of Dublin, not merely for the city.
59. The literature on Howth and Bachelor's Walk is enormous. The account in the preceding paragraphs is based mainly on Phillips, op. cit., pp. 77–81, supplemented by reference to the *Report of the Royal Commission on the Howth (Landing of Arms) Incident* with its Minutes of Evidence in Parl. Papers 1914–16 (Cd. 7631 and 7649 in xxiv, 805, 821).
60. Ross to Birrell, 19 Aug. 1914 in Balfour Papers (British Library Add MSS. 49821, fos. 70–86)
61. Hansard (Lords) 2 July 1914, cols. 692–7
62. ibid., 6 July 1914, cols. 734–6
63. ibid., 8 July, cols. 858–60
64. ibid., cols. 928–9
65. ibid., 14 July, cols. 1166–9
66. Harold Nicolson, *King George V* (1952), pp. 241–2
67. Viscount Ullswater, *A Speaker's Commentaries* 1925, ii, 163–4; J. Harris & others, *Buckingham Palace* (1968), p. 81
68. 4 & 5 Geo. V. c. 90
69. 4 & 5 Geo. V., c. 88
70. *The Covenanter*, 24 June 1914

15. The First World War

1. *Hansard* (Commons), 3 Aug. 1914, cols. 1828–9; *The Times*, 14 Sept., p. 9
2. Ian Adamson, *Cruthin* (1974), p. 88; J. G. Swift MacNeill in *Freeman's Journal*, 1 July 1915, p. 7; *Memoirs of John Shipp* (1843 ed), p. 152

3. Edward Fraser, *The Soldiers whom Wellington Led* (1913) chapter 9; Sir Arthur Bryant, *The Great Duke* (1971), pp. 300–1; *Passages in the early Military Life of General Sir George Napier* (1884), pp. 191–3; Marcus Cunliffe, *Royal Irish Fusiliers* (1952), p. 96; S. G. Tallents, *Man and Boy* (1943), p. 220

4. H. F. N. Jourdain and Fraser, *The Connaught Rangers* (1926), ii, 466

5. Arundel MSS; *Clare Champion*, 7 July 1917

6. Jack White, *Minority Report* (1975) p. 75; Bernard Papers, B.L. Add. MSS 52782, fos. 39–40

7. W. A. Phillips, *Revolution in Ireland* (1923), pp. 86–7

8. Cd. 8311 (Parl. Papers, 1916, xi), 97.

9. 5 Geo. V, c. 34. Before this for some months British subjects and aliens were triable only by Court Martial for certain offences (O. Hood Phillips, *Constitutional & Administrative Law*, 1978 ed., pp. 367–8).

10. Resident magistrates in the countryside could be outvoted by the unpaid magistracy; Sir Christopher Lynch-Robinson, *Last of the Irish R.M.s* (1951), pp. 95, 104–5.

11. Cd. 8279 (Parl. Papers, 1916), p.9

12. Quoted by M. Digby, *Horace Plunkett* (1949), p. 212

13. Cd. 8311 (Parl. Papers, 1916), pp. 97–8

14. Cd. 8279 (1916), p.10

15. See Ruth Dudley Edwards, *James Connolly* (1981), pp. 114, 134–5. The "citizen army" was small — only about 200 strong; but 120 of them turned out on Easter Monday, forming over ten per cent of the rebel forces (id., p. 137). R. M. Fox, in his *History of the Irish Citizen Army* (1943), pp. 120–1 put the turn-out figure as high as 220 (cf. p. 144).

16. Phillips, op. cit., p. 94.

17. B. L. Reid, *Lives of Roger Casement* (1976), p. 358

18. Sean Cronin, *The McGarrity Papers* (1972); Royal Commission, Minutes of Evidence, pp. 36–7; L. O'Broin, *Dublin Castle & the 1916 Rising* (1966), pp. 85–6

19. Phillips, op. cit., pp. 99–100

20. *Memoirs of Desmond FitzGerald* (1968), p. 47

21. *Studies*, Summer 1972, p. 117

22. Quoted by J. Biggs-Davison, *The Hand is Red* (1973), p. 91

23. Lord Craigmyle (Shaw of Dunfermline), *Letters to Isabel* (1936), p. 290; P. S. O'Hegarty, *Victory of Sinn Fein* (1924), p. 3

24. W. S. Churchill, *The World Crisis: the Aftermath* (1929), p. 281

25. M. Digby, op. cit., p. 214
26. J. Biggs-Davison, op. cit., p. 91
27. ibid.
28. *Hansard* (Commons), 11 May 1916, cols. 945, 951
29. *The Times*, 12 May 1916, p. 12; Hansard (Commons), 25 May, col. 2309
30. Asquith to his wife, 14 May 1916 in Spender & Asquith, *Life* (1932), ii, 216
31. Phillips, op. cit., p. 108
32. Sir Henry Howard (1843–1921) was Minister Plenipotentiary to the Pope from 1914 to 1916.
33. Arundel MSS.
34. P. Buckland, *Irish Unionism*, i, (1972), 55
35. Midleton Papers, P.R.O. reference PRO 30/67/33, fos. 1690–1; Fox, op. cit., p. 189 for the release of the unexecuted men.
36. *Belfast News-Letter*, 14 Sept. 1923, p. 5; *Irish Times*, 14 Sept., p. 4; *Tablet*, 22 Sept., p. 372
37. *Irish Law Times*, 22 Sept. 1923, pp. 236–7. Molony was appointed in 1918 as Lord Chief Justice of Ireland, and remained in post until 1924 when the Free State's Reorganization Act came into force. After 1921, however, his jurisdiction did not extend to Northern Ireland and he is described by some authorities (though not by the *Irish Law Times* of the period) as "Lord Chief Justice of Southern Ireland".
38. *The Times*, 5 Nov. 1919. Midleton's reply was published on 6 Nov. A possible draft of Powell's Bill is in the Midleton Papers (PRO/30/67/35, fos. 1941–58). See also R. B. McDowell, *The Irish Convention* (1970), p. 114. According to this author, Powell's scheme provided for two provincial legislatures, each with an executive, plus an all-Ireland senate, also with an executive.
39. Midleton Papers, loc. cit., PRO 30/67/33, fos. 1772–5.
40. ibid., fos. 1739–40. A number of the rebel rank and file were released, as we have seen, in Dec. 1916; others on 17 June 1917 (Fox, op. cit., p. 195).
41. Bernard Papers, Brit. Library Add. MSS 52781, fos. 19 *et seq*.
42. *Irish Times*, 4 Mar. 1918; Midleton Papers, loc. cit., PRO 30/67/34 fo. 1821; also PRO 30/67/35, fos. 1993–2012 (28 Feb. 1918) for the final report of this sub-committee.
43. Midleton Papers, loc. cit., PRO 30/67/40, fo. 2368 (30 Jan. 1919)
44. Robert Kee, *The Green Flag* (1972), p. 5

45. Midleton's *Ireland: Dupe or Heroine* (1932), pp. 118, 121; D. W. Miller, *Church, State & Nation in Ireland 1898–1921* (1973), pp. 372–80

46. Midleton Papers, loc. cit., PRO 30/67/56, fo. 3272 (28 Nov. 1931)

47. Miller, op. cit., p. 387

48. ibid., p. 388

49. *Hansard* (Commons), 9 Apr. 1918, cols. 1357–62

50. *The Times*, 19 Apr. 1918, p. 7

51. ibid., 15 Apr. 1918, p. 9

52. *Irish Times*, 29 June 1917

53. *Irish Catholic*, 1 Dec. 1917, cited Miller, op. cit., p. 399

54. *The Times*, 16 Apr. 1918, p. 7

55. Bernard Papers, B.L. Add. MSS 52781, fo. 74

56. ibid., fo. 77

57. Lord Wimborne's statement in Cd. 8311 (*Parl. Papers*, 1916, xi); R. B. McDowell, *Irish Administration 1801–1914* (1964), pp. 56–62

58. Midleton Papers, loc. cit., PRO 30/67/38, fo. 2282

59. loc. cit., fo. 2292 (Midleton to Stamfordham, 4 May 1918)

60. Bernard Papers, loc. cit., Add. MSS 52781, fos. 77 *et seq.*

61. Midleton, *Records & Reactions (1939), pp. 247–57*

62. Bernard Papers, loc. cit., Add MSS 52781, fo. 179

63. *The Times*, 5 Apr. 1918, p. 8

64. *The Times*, 1 May 1918, p. 6

65. Cabinet Minute 23 Apr. 1918, quoted in Miller, op. cit., p. 406

66. Cardinal Gasparri to de Salis, 9 July 1918, quoted in Miller, op. cit., pp. 406–7

67. *Some Ethical Questions of Peace and War*, Part 2; *The Tablet*, 27 Apr. 1918, pp. 536–7

68. *The Times*, 29 Apr. 1918, p. 10

69. Bernard Papers, loc. cit., Add. MSS 52783, fo. 17

70. ibid., fo. 20

71. Quoted in Miller, op. cit., p. 405

72. ibid., pp. 405, 413–4

73. Charles Townshend, *British Campaign in Ireland 1919–21* (1975), pp. 10–11

74. Fox, op. cit., p. 201

75. Walter McDonald, *Reminiscences of a Maynooth Professor* (1925), pp. 388–98

16. The Treaty

1. Sometimes also referred to as the "coupon" election.
2. Richard Holmes, *The Little Field Marshal* (1981), chapter 11
3. *Irish Daily Telegraph*, 24 May 1916, p. 2. He obtained 3,808 votes against his opponent's 214.
4. A. M. Sullivan, *Old Ireland* (1927), p. 283
5. *Hansard* (Commons), 16 February 1920, cols. 601–3
6. ibid., 19 Feb. 1920, cols. 1147–8
7. R. M. Fox, *History of the Irish Citizen Army* (1943), p. 202
8. Charles Townshend, *British Campaign in Ireland 1919–21* (1975), p. 19
9. ibid., p. 31; W. A. Phillips, *Revolution in Ireland 1906–23* (1923), p. 169
10. Townshend, op. cit., pp. 48–49. On hearing the news, Lloyd George is said to have remarked: 'they are bad shots".
11. *The Times*, 10 Dec. 1919
12. Phillips, op. cit., p. 172; T. J. Campbell, *Fifty Years of Ulster* (1941) p. 103. *Hansard* (Commons) 21 Mar. 1920, cols. 1335–9; 11 Nov. 1920, cols. 1463–6
13. A. M. Sullivan, *Old Ireland* (1927), p. 263
14. *The Times*, 25 Jan. 1919, p. 9; *Daily Express & Irish Daily Mail* (Dublin), 25 Jan. William Jellett pointed out that if the Midleton resolution were passed, excluding the Ulster members, "it would admit the very principle of Partition which it was their joint interest to defeat".
15. *The Times*, 17 July 1911, p. 11
16. *Complete Peerage*
17. *Dundalk Express*, 22 Dec. 1866
18. *Hansard* (Lords), 23 Nov. 1920, cols. 492–3, 497
19. *The Times*, 26 Mar. 1920, p. 8; *Hansard*, cols. 722–4
20. *Hansard* (Commons), 13 Apr. 1920, col. 1560
21. Midleton Papers (Public Record Office, Kew) PRO/30/67/42 (Powell to Midleton, 24 Apr. 1920
22. ibid., PRO 30/67/43, fo. 2474
23. ibid., PRO 30/67/43
24. Townshend, op. cit., p. 65; *The Times*, 6 Apr. 1920, p. 10
25. (Sir) John Biggs-Davison, *The Hand is Red* (1973), p. 99
26. Midleton Papers, loc. cit., PRO 30/67/43
27. Townshend, op. cit., p. 122
28. Midleton Papers, loc. cit., PRO 30/67/43

29. Bernard Papers, British Library Add. MSS 52783, fos. 65–73

30. Townshend, op. cit., pp. 138, 149–50

31. *The Times*, 2 Apr. 1921, p. 9

32. Townshend, op. cit., pp. 173–4; Midleton Papers, loc. cit., PRO 30/67/44, fo. 2614

33. Lloyd George had used this phrase at the Lord Mayor's Banquet, 9 Nov. 1920; "unless I am mistaken, by the steps we have taken [in Ireland] we have murder by the throat" (Frank Owen, *Tempestuous Journey*, 1954, pp. 569–70

34. Townshend, op. cit., pp. 175–6

35. ibid., p. 178

36. Thomas Jones, *Whitehall Diary*, ed. K. Middlemas, iii (1971), 63–70

37. Townshend, op. cit., pp. 180–1

38. P. Buckland, *Irish Unionism* (1972), i, 227–8

39. Townshend, op. cit., p. 182

40. ibid., pp. 184–5, 189

41. L. S. Amery, *My Political Life* (1953), ii, 230. Greenwood was Amery's brother-in-law.

42. *The Times*, 8 June 1921, p. 14

43. Phillips, op. cit., pp. 210–11; Sir Harold Nicolson, *King George V* (1952), p. 353

44. Midleton Papers, loc. cit., PRO 30/67/45

45. *The Times*, 7 Apr. 1921, p. 10

46. Phillips, op. cit., p. 214

47. ibid.

48. Buckland, op. cit., p. 247

49. Midleton Papers, loc. cit., PRO 30/67/45, fo. 2642

50. ibid., fo. 2702

51. Jones, op. cit., p. 108

52. Midleton Papers, loc. cit., PRO 30/67/45, fos. 2750–2

53. ibid., fo. 2755

54. ibid., fo. 2767

55. Phillips, op. cit., p. 229; Robert Kee, *Green Flag* (1972), p. 723

56. Bernard Papers, loc. cit., Add. MSS 52781, fo. 33

57. *Morning Post*, 16 December 1921, p. 11

17. Between the Wars
 1. D. W. Miller, *Church, State & Nation in Ireland 1898–1921* (1973), p. 399

2. Dail Eireann, *Treaty Debates*, p. 32. For a discussion of the legal status of the agreement, see *University of Toronto Law Journal*, xii (1957–8), pp. 3–5. The Irish Free State Constitution Act (U.K. 13 Geo. V c. 3) described it as an "Agreement"; the Constituent Act in Eire (no. 1 of 1922, s. 2) described it as a "Treaty". That Act itself was described as a "measure" in the U.K. Act.

3. Macmillan, 1969.

4. Frank Pakenham (Lord Longford), *Peace by Ordeal* (1972 ed.), p. 288; M. Moynihan, *Speeches & Statements by Eamon de Valera* (1980), p. 196

5. Martin Gilbert, *Winston S. Churchill* (1977), iv, companion III, 1737

6. Bernard Papers, B.L., Add. MSS 52781, fo. 105

7. 5 April 1922. Midleton Papers, Public Record Office, PRO 30/67/50, fos. 2924–5

8. Midleton Papers, loc. cit., fo. 2930

9. In a speech on 19 Feb. 1921 Asquith referred to "an orgy of reprisals which confuse the innocent and guilty in a common tumult of lawless violence." Great Britain, he said, had never in "the lifetime of the oldest among us" "sunk so low in the moral scale of nations" (*Speeches*, 1927, pp. 286–9).

10. Midleton Papers, loc. cit., fo. 2930. Collins made no secret, in conversation with Hamar Greenwood, that for his part he was not dissatisfied with the behaviour of the Black and Tans. "We are not going to be as gentle as you were with those who are up against us" (L. S. Amery, *Political Life* (1953), ii, 228).

11. Midleton Papers, loc. cit., PRO 30/67/49

12. ibid., PRO 30/67/50

13. *Blackwood's Magazine*, Dec. 1922, p. 747

14. Notes from Ireland, May 1922, p. 79

15. Quoted in J. Biggs-Davison, *The Hand is Red* (1973), pp. 104–5

16. ibid.

17. Winston S. Churchill, *The World Crisis: the Aftermath* (1929, p. 313

18. Biggs-Davison, op. cit., pp. 99–110

19. The "A" Specials were a full-time and paid force; the "B" Specials an occasional force with an allowance; and the "C" Specials were unpaid. P. Buckland, *Factory of Grievances* (1979), p. 181; Sir A. Hezlet, *"B Specials"* (1972). For the background to and text of the Craig-Collins Pact see Kevin Boyle in *Irish Jurist*, xii (1977), 148–75.

20. St John Ervine, *Craigavon* (1949), p. 476

21. Craig to Spender, 3 May 1922. (Public Record Office, Northern Ireland, PM 9/2, cited Patrick Buckland, *James Craig* (1980), pp. 81–2)

22. Public Record Office, Kew, CO 906/25. cf. M. Gilbert, *Winston S. Churchill*, iv, companion III (1977), p. 1909

23. loc. cit., HO45/11992 (Public Record Office, Kew). Public Record Office (Northern Ireland), Cab. 6. Box 1, nos. 958, 1005, 1033 cited P. W. Miller, *Queen's Rebels* (1978) p. 127

24. *Blackwood's Magazine*, Oct. 1922, pp. 434, 451

25. Biggs-Davison, op. cit., p. 109

26. *The Times*, 5 Dec. 1922 (Northern Ireland Supplement, p. ix)

27. Quoted in Biggs-Davison, op. cit., p. 113. See also *Northern Ireland Parliamentary Debates* (Commons), 9 Oct. 1928, col. 2254

28. Speech on relinquishing Ulster leadership, 4 Feb. 1921 (H. M. Hyde, *Carson*, 1953, p. 449)

29. Biggs-Davison, op. cit., p. 113; *Belfast Telegraph*, 13 Nov. 1969, p. 1

30. St John Ervine, op. cit., p. 493

31. See chapter 7 for Sir Thomas Wyse, and chapter 12 for William Bonaparte Wyse. Also P. Higgins, "The Wyses of the Manor of St. John's Waterford", in *Journal of the Waterford & South-East of Ireland Archaeological Society* (1899), v, 199–206; Olga Bonaparte-Wyse, *Spurious Brood* (Gollancz, 1969).

32. Belmore Commission, Final Report, C-8925, Parl. Papers, 1898, xliv, Appendix B; Enid Starkie, *A Lady's Child* (1941), p. 97; Joanna Richardson, *Enid Starkie* (1973); Starkie Papers, Box 1, file 3, and W. J. M. Starkie's Diary, Bodleian Library, Oxford; St John Ervine, op. cit., p. 124; D. H. Akenson, *Education & Enmity (1973), p. 97. We are indebted for access to the Starkie Papers to Professor Robert Shackleton, F. B. A. Wyse underwent a serious operation in 1938 and retired in 1939 (Akenson, op. cit., p. 146).*

33. St John Ervine, op. cit., p. 124; P. Shea, *Voices & the Sound of Drums* (1981), pp. 110, 115, 159

34. Letter from his daughter to G. C.-B.

35. Accounts of his funeral from press cuttings by courtesy of his daughter.

36. 16 Geo V, c. 77 (Schedule) for text of Agreement; Kevin Kelley, *Longest War* (1982) for background. File HO45/12296 (Public Record Office, Kew) gives details of the Boundary Commission negotiations.

See also *The Times*, 2 Mar. 1926 for the registration of the Agreement.

37. Biggs-Davison, op. cit., p. 117
38. *The Freeman (sic)*, 30 June 1928, p. 4. For the Dunedin Committee, see *Notes from Ireland*, 1926, p. 31
39. *Notes from Ireland*, Feb. 1927, p. 37; Bernard Papers, British Library, Add. MSS 52781, fos. 134–7
40. *Notes from Ireland*, Nov. 1928, pp. 92–3; L. Fleming, *Head or Harp* (1965), p. 97
41. McDowell & Webb, *Trinity College Dublin* (1982), p. 433
42. Bernard Papers, British Library Add. MSS 52781, fo. 139
43. ibid., fo. 142
44. E. Lazenby, *Ireland — a Catspaw* (1928), pp. 68, 70
45. *Hansard* (Lords), 1 Dec. 1931, cols. 243–5
46. Midleton Papers, loc. cit., PRO 30/67/56
47. *English Review*, Feb. 1930, pp. 173–82
48. *Notes from Ireland*, May 1934, p. 1
49. ibid., Nov. 1934, p. 13
50. *Quarterly Review*, Jan. 1934, pp. 159 *et seqq*; *Notes from Ireland*, May 1936, pp. 54, 58
51. M. Digby, *Horace Plunkett* (1949), pp. 44, 277. See also pp. 60–1, 74, 81, for other references to Fingall.
52. D. W. Miller, op. cit., pp. 209–17; *Irish Independent*, 14 May 1909
53. Biggs-Davison, op. cit., pp. 118–9
54. ibid., p. 118. See also Northern Ireland Parl. Deb. (Commons) (*NIPD*), 24 Apr. 1934, col. 1095 and Nicholas Mansergh, *Government of Northern Ireland*, p. 240.
55. *Catholic Bulletin*, Apr. 1935, quoted in J. H. Whyte, *Church & State in Modern Ireland* (1980 ed.), p. 48
56. *NIPD*, 24 Apr. 1934, cols. 1093–4
57. Buckland, *James Craig* (1980); Public Record Office of Northern Ireland (PRONI) file CAB 9A/90/ 1,2
58. *NIPD*, 24 Apr. 1934, col. 1094
59. St John Ervine, op. cit., p. 498
60. *Belfast News-Letter*, 2 Oct. 1925, pp. 7, 9; 3 Oct., p. 8; T. J. Campbell, *Fifty Years of Ulster* (1941), p. 143
61. Thompson was the Recorder of Belfast. T. J. Campbell, loc. cit., (p. 143), for "Wooden-headed Billy" story. The *mot* is also attributed to Healy. (Sir James Henry, private information).
62. *Irish Times*, 2 Oct. 1925, p. 9.

63. *NIPD*, 24 Apr. 1934, col. 1113
64. W. S. Churchill, *Victory* (1946), p. 133
65. Stephen Gwynn in *Time & Tide* (1940) quoted from St John Ervine, op. cit., p. 563; Calton Young, *A State of Disunion* (1972), p. 217
66. *NIPD*, 31 May 1939, cols. 1785–97
67. *Belfast Telegraph*, 23 Feb. 1938, p. 12
68. St John Ervine, op. cit., p. 543

18. War and Troubles
1. R. B. Pugh, Minute of 25 Feb. 1946 in DO 35/1230/WX 132/1/124 (Public Record Office). When the figures were eventually given, there was an inevitable outcry that they were understated (*The Times*, 3 Apr. 1946).
2. PREM 3/129/5 (Public Record Office). See also Robert Fisk, *In Time of War* (1983), pp. 452–3.
3. *Irish Times*, 23 Jan. 1946, p. 2
4. DO 35/1230/WX132/1/124, HO45/24212 Part I (Public Record Office). The Northern Ireland government was consistently in favour of conscription being applied as in the rest of the U.K., but was as consistently over-ruled by the imperial government. After the bombing of Belfast, Andrews visited London and a Bill was drafted, though not proceeded with. In 1946 Brooke, accompanied by three cabinet colleagues, met the Home Secretary in London but failed to persuade him to extend peace-time National Service to the Province. An Ulster Unionist amendment to the National Service Bill failed. London believed that conscription would be so widely resisted in Ulster that the prisons would not be able to contain all the recalcitrants, which would provide material for "hostile propaganda" (Minute by C. T. H. Morris in HO45/24213, loc. cit., 8 Apr. 1947). It was stated in the House of Commons on 8 Apr. 1946 that at least 780 decorations had been awarded to Eire-born persons during the war, including eight V.C.s and one G.C. One V.C., Leading Seaman J. J. Magennis, came from Belfast (*Irish Times*, 21 Jan. 1946, p. 1, John Winton, *Victoria Cross at Sea*, 1978, pp. 239–44).
5. PREM 4/53/1 (Public Record Office). It is clear from the file that the letter to Andrews was entirely W.S.C.'s work. Almost none of the official draft was used.
6. J. A. Oliver, *Working at Stormont* (1978), p. 68; *Northern Ireland Parliamentary Debates* (NIPD), 14 Nov. 1944, col. 2240; 10 Dec.

1946, col. 3324. Brooke explained to Ministers during a visit to London in May 1946 that the permit system had been introduced partly so as to enable employment to be found for demobilized ex-servicemen from Northern Ireland. In October 1945 the Eire government objected when it was rumoured that the system might be terminated, and when it was extended until December 1947 de Valera again objected, stating in the Dáil "that its object was to maintain a majority for Partition by mass expulsions from Northern Ireland" on its ultimate expiry. (DO35/1228/WX101/146 Public Record Office, Kew).

7. *NIPD*, 23 Sept. 1941, cols. 1588–90; 28 Nov. 1944, cols. 2459–60; T. J. Campbell, *Fifty Years of Ulster* (1941), chapter 23; *NIPD*, 16 May 1950, cols. 960–2; 6 June, 1283–4; Sir A. Hezlet, *The "B" Specials* (1973 ed.), p. 240; J. Whyte in Gallagher & O'Connell (eds.) *Contemporary Irish Studies* (1983), pp. 1–35.

8. *NIPD*, 20 Mar. 1951, cols. 552–71

9. ibid., 6 June 1951, col. 1505

10. ibid., col. 1515; cf. *NIPD*, 24 Apr. 1934, cols. 1116–7

11. ibid., 13 Jan. 1953, cols. 2057–103

12. ibid., col. 2084. E. A. Aunger in *Economic & Social Review* (Dublin), Oct. 1975, p. 8, stated that Catholics comprised 43% of nurses in Northern Ireland.

13. The proportion of Catholics has risen only slightly in Northern Ireland since 1922. Forecasts such as that of Elizabeth Downe in *Time & Tide* (21 Aug. 1948) that within a very short time Catholics would "vote Northern Ireland into a United Ireland by sheer weight of numbers" have been repeatedly falsified.

14. Sunday Times, *Ulster* (1972), p. 35

15. D. P. Barritt & C. F. Carter, *The Northern Ireland Problem* p. 67; Hugh Shearman in *Yearbook of World Affairs* (1982), p. 191

16. C. R. Rose, *Governing Without Consensus* (1971), pp. 474–510; O'Hearn and Hewitt in *British Journal of Sociology*, Sept. 1983, pp. 438–51

17. NIPD, 13 Jan. 1953, col. 2091; John Whyte (1983), loc. cit. Oliver, op. cit., pp. 37–8; *Economic & Social Review*, Jan. 1977, p. 80; P. Buckland, *A History of Northern Ireland* (1981), pp. 77–8, 90, 115; R. J. Lawrence, *Government of Northern Ireland* (1965), chapter 6.

18. P. A. Compton, *The Contemporary Population of Northern Ireland and Population-related issues*, Institute of Irish Studies, QUB, 1981, pp.

127–42; John Whyte (1983) loc. cit. Biggs-Davison, op. cit., p. 128; *NIPD*, 12 June 1956, cols. 1906–7; 6 June, cols. 1788–9

19. T. W. Moody and J. C. Beckett, *Queen's, Belfast* (1959); Biggs-Davison, loc. cit.

20. *NIPD*, 20 May 1953, col. 1272

21. ibid., 7 July 1953, cols. 1317–8

22. ibid.

23. Dáil Eireann Debates, 14 June 1937, col. 430.

24. Ireland Act 1949 (12 & 13 Geo. VI, c. 41.) A statutory instrument of 1923 (no. 405) had already provided that references to Ireland in British legislation were to be construed as exclusive of Southern Ireland.

25. Dublin, 1977, p. 375

26. Henry Boylan, *Dictionary of Irish Biography* (1978); *Belfast News-Letter*, 27 Dec. 1955, p. 4; 19 Jan. 1956, p. 5

27. *Belfast News-Letter*, 21 Jan. 1956

28. private information

29. *Belfast News-Letter*, 12, 14 Dec. 1956

30. ibid., 11 July 1957, p. 5

31. *Disturbances in Northern Ireland* (Cmd. 532, Northern Ireland), pp. 15, 77–9. The members of the Cameron Commission were the Hon. Lord Cameron, Professor Sir John Biggart and James Joseph Campbell. See also R. Deutsch & V. Magowan, *Northern Ireland Chronology of Events* (1973), i, 154.

32. Rose, op. cit., p. 208; Campbell, op. cit

33. Joseph Foyle in *This Week*, 19 May 1972; Biggs-Davison, op. cit., p. 129; I. McAllister, *The Northern Ireland Social Democratic & Labour Party* (1977), p. 10

34. *Belfast News-Letter*, 2 Oct. 1959, p. 4

35. ibid., 7 Oct. 1959, p. 10

36. *Belfast Telegraph*, 2 Nov. 1959, p. 10

37. ibid., 10 Nov. 1959, p. 3; Biggs-Davison, op. cit., p. 132

38. *Christus Rex*, xviii (1964), 22–36. In 1983 the Unionist M.P. Harold McCusker complained that almost two-thirds of the staff in the DHSS offices serving the Armagh region were Roman Catholic (*Belfast News-Letter*, 23 Feb. 1983, p. 1.)

39. *Belfast News-Letter*, 18 Nov. 1959

40. ibid., 13 Nov., p. 6. One letter in this correspondence (11 Nov., p. 4), was signed "Unionist-Catholic". "When will Ulster Protestants

realize", it asserted, "that all Roman Catholics are not necessarily Nationalists and anti-British, neither are all Protestants Unionists".

41. *Autobiography of Terence O'Neill* (1972), p. 47
42. Biggs-Davison, op. cit., p. 140
43. *Belfast News-Letter*, 25 Nov. 1961, p. 1
44. She was elected unopposed for Queen's University in 1965 (ibid., 5 Feb. 1969, p. 6).
45. *Newry Reporter*, 15 June 1967, p. 1
46. *Belfast Telegraph*, 11 Feb. 1969, p. 8
47. ibid., 12 Feb., p. 8
48. ibid., 13 Feb., pp. 8–9
49. ibid., 6 Feb., p. 1
50. see Belfast *News-Letter* 17 Feb. 1969 for her views, especially on education.
51. *Belfast Telegraph*, 21 Feb. 1969, p. 15; 25 Feb., p. 1
52. *Newry Telegraph*, 15 Feb. 1969, p. 1. We are indebted for what follows and for some of what precedes this note to correspondence and interviews with Louis Boyle. In an editorial on 9 July 1969 the *Belfast Telegraph* said that he had "shown courage" in trying to establish a place for Catholics in the Unionist Party.
53. *Belfast News-Letter*, 20 Nov. 1969, p. 5; *NIPD*, 19 Nov., col. 1498
54. A. T. Q. Stewart, *Narrow Ground* (1977), p. 153. The author points out, however, that it may be a mistake to distinguish too sharply between "traditional" violence and that motivated by contemporary politics. The distinction may be more apparent than real, as far more deadly weapons are now available to the terrorist and are being used.
55. *Irish News*, 31 Aug. 1971, p. 7
56. Buckland, op. cit., p. 139; Bleakley, op. cit., p. 104; *The Times*, 28 Oct. 1971, p. 3
57. Deutsch & Magowan, op. cit., (n. 31, *supra*) ii (1974), 274b
58. The Democratic Unionist (DUP) was formed in Sept. 1971, but had earlier roots. The distinguishing feature has been described as a "strident anti-republicanism". The Vanguard Unionist Progressive Party (afterwards called the Vanguard Unionist Party) was founded at the time of the suspension of Stormont in March 1973 and was at one time said to have flirted with the idea of a Unilateral Declaration of Independence (Buckland, op. cit., pp. 168–70).
59. ibid., pp. 170–2
60. J. Knight, *Election Constitutional Convention* (1975), p. 12

61. Rose and others, *Is there a Concurring Majority about Northern Ireland?* (Centre for the Study of Public Policy, University of Strathclyde, no. 22. Glasgow, 1978).

62. K. Heskin, *Northern Ireland: a Psychological Analysis* (1980), p. 45 and E. Moxon-Browne, *Nation, Class and Creed in Northern Ireland* (1983), p. 103

63. *The Times*, 20 Mar. 1976, p. 2

64. *Who's Who*, 1982

65. *Memoirs of a Statesman* (1978), p. 132

66. Joseph Foyle in *This Week*, 19 May 1972.

67. Preface to J. Biggs-Davison, *Catholics & the Union* (Unionist Research & Publicity Department, 1972)

19. Catholics for the Crown

1. P. Shea, *Voices & The Sound of Drums* (Belfast 1981), p. 20

2. ibid., p. 27

3. A phrase probably coined by John Giffard, ancestor of the first Earl of Halsbury. See Brian Inglis, *West Briton* (1962), pp. 143–4.

4. Shea, op. cit.; *The Times*, 17 Aug. 1920, p. 14

5. Shea, op. cit., p. 93; *The Times*, 5 June 1922, p. 6; 7 June, p. 15. Flanagan's sister, who was also at mass, tried to capture one of the murderers.

6. Sir Wilfred Spender (1876–1960) was permanent secretary to the Ministry of Finance and head of the Northern Ireland Civil Service from 1925 to 1944. Sir Dawson Bates (1876–1949) was Home Secretary under the government of Northern Ireland from 1921 to 1943.

7. Shea, op. cit., p. 141

8. Lt. Col. The Rt. Hon. S. H. Hall-Thompson (1885–1954). See D. M. Akenson, *Education and Enmity* (1973) chapter 8 for a full account of Northern Ireland educational policy developments up to 1950.

9. *Irish News* (Belfast), 3, 4 Feb. 1938.

10. ibid., 11 Nov. 1936, p. 5; 14 Nov., p. 7; 17 Nov., p. 2

11. ibid., 10 November 1936. In an editorial, this Catholic paper drew attention to a 13 July Orange Resolution calling for the brethren to "close ranks . . . against the propaganda of Communism and Romanism". But, for its part, the paper had never supported Communism and never would.

12. ibid., 11 Nov. 1936, p. 5

13. ibid., 5 Feb. 1938, p. 5; 11 Feb., p. 7

14. Shea, op. cit.; P. A. Buckland, *History of Northern Ireland* (1981), pp. 68–9

15. J. A. Oliver, *Working at Stormont* (1978), p. 79

16. Buckland, op. cit., p. 115. This was under the 1968 Education Act.

17. Oliver, op. cit., p. 60

18. Nonetheless, they had enabled him to rise to the post of assistant secretary without a degree, a rise which many a Civil Servant on the other side of the water might envy.

19. John Darby, *Conflict in Northern Ireland* (1977), pp. 87–88

20. Major Beaumont was not among those listed as having formally sought the nomination (*Tyrone Constitution*, 14 Feb. 1969, p. 5). Mrs Anne Forrest, widow of the former M.P., was selected. The Catholic majority was estimated to be about 3,500 (*The Times*, 19 Apr. 1969, p. 4).

21. Letter to Sir John Biggs-Davison, 5 Aug. 1982.

22. Speech at National Liberal Club, 9 Jan. 1925 (F. S. L. Lyons, *John Dillon*, 1968, p. 477)

23. E. Moxon-Browne, "The Northern Ireland Attitude Survey". MS Report, Queen's University, Belfast, May 1979, cited E. E. Davis & R. Sinnott, Economic & Social Research Institute (Dublin), Paper no. 97, Sept. 1979, p. 147

24. Letter by Boyd Black (*The Times*, 29 Mar. 1982)

25. 31 July, 1798; see chapter 6, note 2.

26. Until March 1979 the republic's punt (pound) was at par with the pound sterling (*Europa Yearbook*, 1982, i, 822).

27. See *Hansard* (Written Answers, House of Commons), 11 Jan. 1978, cols 771–2. The subject of Irish Lights was discussed at a meeting between Brooke and Attlee in 1948. (Public Record Office File PREM 8/1222, Part II).

28. S. Rosenbaum (ed.) *Against Home Rule* (1912), p. 135

29. See the communiqué issued after talks between Mrs Thatcher and the Taoiseach, 8 Dec. 1980 (*Annual Register*, pp. 510–511).

30. J. Biggs-Davison, *The Hand is Red* (1973), p. 152

BIBLIOGRAPHY AND LIST OF SOURCES

For ease of reference, all the sources listed, whether manuscript, typewritten, cyclostyled, or printed, have been incorporated in a single alphabetical list, with cross-references which it is hoped will be sufficient to identify individual items. Only sources actually cited in footnotes or text are listed. Place of publication, and full titles, are given only where it is thought that there may be some difficulty in tracking down the item in a research library.

Adamson, Ian, *Cruthin: the Ancient Kindred* (Newtownards, Co. Down, 1974)

Akenson, D. H., *Irish Education Experiment* (1970), *Education and Enmity* (1973)

Altholz, J., "The Vatican Decrees Controversy, 1874–1880", *Catholic Historical Review*, lvii (Jan. 1971), pp. 593–605

Amery, L. S., *My Political Life* (1953)

Analecta Gregoriana — See Broderick.

Annual Register (London, 1758–) abbreviated: *A.R.* (year to which volume relates, not date of publication, is given).

Anson, W. R. *Law and Custom of the Constitution* (1922)

Anthologia Hibernica (Dublin, 1793–4)

The Anti-Protestantism of the Irish Government Exposed (1850)

A.R. see *Annual Register*.

Archdall, M. — see Lodge.

Archivium Hibernicum (Dublin, Catholic Record Society of Ireland)

Arundel MSS. By courtesy of His Grace the Duke of Norfolk, K.G.

Aspinall, A. and Smith, E. A., *English Historical Documents 1783–1832* (1959)

Asquith, H. H. (Earl of Oxford & Asquith), *Speeches* (1927)

Auchmuty, J. J., *Sir Thomas Wyse* (1939).

Auckland, William Eden, Lord, *Journal and Correspondence* (1860–2)

Aunger, E. A., "Religion and Occupational class in Northern Ireland", *Economic & Social Review*, (vii, Oct. 1975, no. 1, pp. 1–18)

Bacon, Francis, *Letters* (1702).

Bagwell, R., *Ireland Under the Tudors*, iii (1890)

Barnes, G. *Rights of the Imperial Crown of England*, Dublin, 1799

Barritt, D. P. & Carter, C. F., *The Northern Ireland Problem* (1962)

Behan, Brendan, *Borstal Boy* (1961)

Belfast News-Letter, ca. 1738–1962, afterwards called *News Letter*, abbreviated: BNL.

Belfast Politics [by William Bruce & Henry Joy] (Belfast, 1794)

Belfast Telegraph (Belfast) formerly (1871–1918) *Belfast Evening Telegraph*

Beresford, J., *Correspondence* (1854)

Berkeley, Bishop George, *The Querist* (no. 96, 1737)

Biggs-Davison, Sir John, *Catholics & The Union* (Unionist Research & Publicity Department, Belfast, August 1972) — , *George Wyndham* (1951) — , *The Hand is Red* (1973) — , *Tory Lives* (1952)

Blackwood's Magazine.

Blake, Anthony, *Thoughts Upon the Catholic Question* (1828)

Blake, Robert (Lord), *The Unknown Prime Minister* (1955)

BNL (abbreviation) — see *Belfast News-Letter*

Bodleian Library, Oxford: Pope-Hennessy papers. By permission of Sir John Pope-Hennessy. — :Starkie Papers. By permission of Professor Robert Shackleton, F.B.A.

Bolton, G. C., *The Passing of the Act of Union* (1966)

Bonaparte-Wyse, Olga, *Spurious Blood* (1969)

Bonaparte-Wyse, W. C., *Vox Clamantis* (1880)

Boulter, Hugh, *Letters* (1769)

Bowen, Desmond, *Paul Cardinal Cullen and the Shaping of Modern Irish Catholicism* (1983)

Boyce, D. G., *Nationalism in Ireland* (1982)

Boylan, H., *Dictionary of Irish Biography* (1978)

Boyle, Kevin, "The Tallents Report on the Craig-Collins Pact of 30 March 1922", *Irish Jurist* (new series xii, 1977, 148–75)

Bradshaw, B., *Irish Constitutional Revolution of the Sixteenth Century* (1979)

British Journal of Sociology

British Library: Balfour papers — : Bernard papers — : Carnarvon papers — : Gladstone papers — : Peel papers

Broderick, J. F., *The Holy See and the Irish Movement for . . . Repeal 1829–1847, Analecta Gregoriana*, lv (Rome , 1951)

Brooke, Henry, *The Farmer's Second Letter to the Protestants of Ireland* (1745)

Brooke, John, *King George III* (1972)

Bruce, William — see *Belfast Politics*

Bryant, Sir Arthur, *The Great Duke* (1971)

Buckland, P., *The Factory of Grievances* (1979) — , *A History of Northern Ireland* (1981) — , *Irish Unionism* 2 vols. (Dublin, 1972–3) —, *Irish*

Unionism 1885–1923; a Documentary History (Belfast, 1973) — , *James Craig*, (1980)

[Bullen, William], *Memoir of the Union and the Agitation for its Repeal By an Irish Catholic* (1843)

Burke, Sir Bernard, *Burke's Irish Family Records* (1976) — , *History of the Commoners* (1838) — , *Landed Gentry of Ireland* (1912)

Burke, Edmund, *The Correspondence of Edmund Burke*. Edited by T. W. Copeland and others (Cambridge & Chicago, 1958–78) — , *Letter to a Member of the National Assembly* (1791) , *Letters, Speeches & Tracts on Irish Affairs*. Edited by M. Arnold (1881)

Burke, T. A., "Irish Catholics and the legislative union, 1800", *Irish Committee of Historical Sciences Bulletin* (no. 33, May 1944, pp. 3–6)

Burke, W. P., *Irish Priests in the Penal Times* (1914)

Burnet, G., *The History of the Reformation of the Church of England* (1679–1715)

Burns, R. E., "The Catholic Relief Act in Ireland, 1778". *Church History*, (June 1963, pp. 181–206) — , "Parsons, priests and the people: the rise of Irish anti-clericalism 1785–89", *Church History* (June 1962, pp. 151–63)

Butler, Charles, *Historical Memoirs Respecting the English, Irish and Scottish Catholics* (1819)

Byrne, F. J., *Irish Kings and high-kings* (1973)

Byrne, F. J., — see also Martin, F. X.

Byrne, Miles, *Memoirs* (1906)

Calendar of the Close Rolls

Calendar of the State Papers (Ireland)

Campbell, T. J., *Fifty Years of Ulster* (1941)

Canning, George, *The Oracle* (1803–4)

Carey, F. P., *Archbishop Murray of Dublin* (1951)

Carnarvon papers. British Library.

Carrigan, W., *History and Antiquities of the Diocese of Ossory* (Dublin 1905)

Castlereagh, Lord (2nd Marquess of Londonderry), *Memoirs and Correspondence* (1848)

Catholic Bulletin

Catholic Directory

Catholic Historical Review (Washington, D.C.)

Caulfield, Dr. James — See *Reply* . . .

Cavour, Count C., *Thoughts on Ireland*, translated by W. P. Hodgson (1868).

Chart, D. A., *Ireland from the Union to Catholic Emancipation* (1910)

Chieregato, Francesco, Bishop of Teramo, Translation in *Hermathena* (Dublin), no. 40 (1914), p. 14; see Mahaffy, J. P.

Chowdharay-Best, G., "Peeresses at the Opening of Parliament". *The Table*, (xlii 1973), pp. 10–27. "Royalty and Prayer", *Folklore*, (lxxxv 1974), 276–8.

Christus Rex (Cork, Naas and Maynooth, 1947–71), continued as *Social Studies.*

Church History (New York)

Churchill, W. L. S., *Victory* (war speeches) (1946) — *The World Crisis: the Aftermath* (1929)

The Clare Champion (Ennis, Co. Clare)

Clark, Wallace, *Rathlin: Disputed Island* (Portlaw Co. Waterford 1971)

Clarke, A., *The Old English in Ireland 1625–42* (1966)

Clay, C. T., "Notes on the Importation of English wool into Ireland as Affected by the Union". *Publications of the Thoresby Society* (Leeds, xxvi, 1924, 155–60)

Cobbett, W. & Hansard, T. C., *The Parliamentary History of England* (1806–20)

Cockayne, G. E. and others, *Complete Peerage* (new ed., 1910–59)

Colvin, Ian, *Life of Lord Carson* (ii, 1936). See also Marjoribanks.

Commons Journals (Ireland)

Commons Journals (Westminster)

Commons Debates. See: *Hansard*; *Report*; *Parliamentary Register* (Dublin).

Complete Peerage — see Cockayne.

Compton, P. A., *The Contemporary Population of Northern Ireland* (Institute of Irish Studies, Queen's University, Belfast 1981)

Constitution (Cork, 1823–1924) — also called *Cork Constitution.*

The Constitution: or Anti-Union Evening Post (Dublin, 1799–1800)

Contemporary Review

Cooke, A. B. and Vincent J., *The Governing Passion* (1974)

Cooke, Edward, *Arguments for and against an Union between Great Britain and Ireland Considered* (1798)

Coote, Charles, *History of the Union* (1802)

Coppinger, William, *A Remonstrance . . . to the Lower Orders of Roman Catholics in the diocese of Cloyne and Ross* (Cork, 1798)

Corfe, T., *The Phoenix Park Murders* (1968)

Corish, P. J. (ed.) *History of Irish Catholicism* (1967–)

Cork Constitution — see *Constitution.*

The Cork Examiner (Cork, 1841–)

Cornwallis, 1st Marquess, *Correspondence* (1859)

The Covenanter (London, 20 May–5 Aug. 1914)

Craigmyle, Lord, *Letters to Isabel* (1936)

Crone, J. S., *Concise Dictionary of Irish Biography* (1937)

Cronin, S., *The McGarrity Papers* (1972)

Cunliffe, Marcus, *The Royal Irish Fusiliers* (1952)

Curran, W. H., *Sketches of the Irish Bar* (1855)

Curtis, E., *History of Ireland* (1950) — , *History of Mediaeval Ireland* (1923)

Curtis, L. P., *Coercion and Conciliation in Ireland* (1963)

Dáil Eireann, *Parliamentary Debates* (1922–) — , *Treaty Debates* (1922)

Daily Express (Dublin, 1851–1921, called *Daily Express and Irish Daily Mail*, 1917–21)

Daily Telegraph (London)

D'Alton, E. A., *History of Ireland* (1906)., *History of the Archdiocese of Tuam* (1928)

Darby, John, *Conflict in Northern Ireland* (1977)

Daunt, W. J. O'Neill, *A Life Spent for Ireland* (1896) — *Personal Recollections of the Late Daniel O'Connell* (1848)

Davis, E. E. and Sinnott, R., "Attitudes in the Republic of Ireland relevant to the Northern Ireland problem: i. Descriptive analysis and some comparisons with attitudes in Northern Ireland and Great Britain." *Economic & Social Research Institute paper* no. 97, (Dublin, 1979)

Debrett's Peerage

Decker, Sir M., *Essay on the Causes of the Decline of the Foreign Trade* (1744)

Denholm, A. F., "The conversion of Lord Ripon in 1874", *Recusant History*, (x, 1969, 111–8)

Derrick, Samuel, *Letters Written from Leverpoole, Chester* [etc] (Dublin 1767)

Deutsch, R. & Magowan, V., *Northern Ireland Chronology of Events* (1973)

de Valera, E., *Speeches & Statements*, ed. M. Moynihan (1980)

de Vere, Aubrey (1814–1902), *Constitutional and Unconstitutional Political Action* (1882) — , *English Misrule and Irish Misdeeds* (1848) — , *Essays* (1889) — , *Ireland and Proportional Representation* (1885) — , *Mediaeval Records and Sonnets* (1893) — , *Recollections* (1897) — , — see also Reilly, S. M. P.

Dickson, Charles, *The Wexford Rising in 1798* (Tralee, 1956)

Dictionary of National Biography

Digby, M., *Horace Plunkett* (1949)

Dillon, J. J., *A Letter on the Apprehension of the Earl of Fingall* (1812)

Disraeli, Benjamin, Earl of Beaconsfield, *Coningsby* (1844) — , *Lord George Bentinck* (1852) — , *Speeches on Parliamentary Reform*, ed. M. Corry (1867)

Dixon, W. M., *Trinity College, Dublin* (1902)

Downshire, Wills Hill, Marquess of, *A Proposal for Uniting the Kingdom of Great Britain and Ireland* (1751)

(Dublin) *Daily Express* — see *Daily Express*

Dublin Evening Mail (1823–1928, continued as *Evening Mail* 1928–62)

Dublin Evening Post (ca. 1778– 1875).

Dublin Gazette (ca. 1706–1922)

Dublin Journal (1726–1824)

Dublin Review (London)

The Dublin University Magazine (1833–77)

Duffy, Sir C. G., *League of North and South 1850–4* (1886) — , *Young Ireland* (1896)

A Duke of Norfolk Notebook (London, 1917)

Dundalk Express (newspaper, varying titles, Dundalk, Co. Louth, 1860–70)

Economic and Social Review (Dublin)

Edwards, R. Dudley, *James Connolly* (1981)

Encylopaedia Britannica (11th edn, 1910)

English Review

Ensor, R. C. K., *England 1870–1914* (1936)

Ervine, St. John, *Craigavon* (1949)

Europa Yearbook

An Examination of the Case of the Roman-Catholics of Ireland Lately Published (Dublin, 1755)

Fagan, W., *The Life and Times of Daniel O'Connell* (Cork, 1847–8)

Farrell, B. (ed.), *The Irish Parliamentary Tradition* (1973)

Fingall, Arthur James Plunkett, 8th Earl of — see Redesdale

Fingall, Elizabeth Plunkett, Countess of, *Seventy Years Young* (1937)

Fisk, Robert, *In Time of War* (1983)

FitzGerald, D., *Memoirs of Desmond FitzGerald* (1968)

FitzGerald, M., *A Letter to Sir Robert Peel on the endowment of the Roman Catholic Church of Ireland* (1845)

Fitzpatrick, D. E., *New Guide to Killarney* (3rd edn, 1837)

Fitzmaurice, E., (Lord Fitzmaurice), *Life of Sir William Petty* (1895)

Fitzpatrick, W. J., *Memories of Father Healy of Little Bray* (1896)

Fleming, L., *Head or Harp* (1965)

Forster, C., *Life of J. Jebb* (1836)

The Fortnightly

Foster, R. F., *Lord Randolph Churchill* (1981)

Fox, R. W., *History of the Irish Citizen Army* (1943)

Frame, R., *English Lordship in Ireland 1318–61* (1982)

Franklin, Benjamin, *Works*, (edited by J. Sparks, Chicago, 1882) — *Writings*, (Edited by A. H. Smyth, New York, 1906)

Fraser, Edward, *The Soldiers Whom Wellington Led* (1913)

The Freeman (Dublin, 1927–28)

Freeman's Journal, (Dublin, 1763–1924, Begun as *The Public Register*)

Gallagher and O'Connell (eds), *Contemporary Irish Studies* (1983. See Whyte, John)

Galloway, P., *The Most Illustrious Order of St Patrick* (1983)

Galway Express (1853–1920)

The Galway Observer (ca. 1882– 1966)

The Galway Vindicator and Connaught Advertiser (1841–1899)

Gash, N., *Mr Secretary Peel* (1961)

Gilbert, J. T., *History of the Irish Confederation* (1882)

Gilbert, J. T. (ed.), *Jacobite Narrative* (1892)

Gilbert, M. and Churchill, R., *Winston S. Churchill* (In progress)

Gladstone, Rt. Hon. W. E., Review of Ingram on the Union, *Nineteenth Century* (xxii, Oct., 1887, 445–69) — , Reply to Ingram, *Westminster Review*, (cxxix 1888, 77–81)

Godwin, W., *History of the Commonwealth of England* (1828)

Good, J. W., *Irish Unionism* (1920)

Gordon, Gen. C. G., *Journals* (1885)

Grattan, Henry, *Speeches* (1822)

Grattan, Henry (the Younger), *Memoirs of the Life and Times of the Rt Hon. Henry Grattan* (1839–46)

Gregory, Sir William, *Autobiography* (1894)

Grotius, Hugo, *De Jure Belli et Pacis* abridged translation by W. Whewell (1853)

Gwynn, A., "John Lynch's 'De Praesulibus Hiberniae'", *Studies* (xxxiv, 1945, 37–52)

Gwynn, D., "The Priests and Young Ireland in 1848", *Irish Ecclesiastical Record* (lxx, 1948, 590–609)

Gwynn, S. L. and Tuckwell, G. M., *The Life of the Rt. Hon. Sir Charles Dilke* (1917)

Hamilton, John, *Letter to Theobald M'Kenna Esq . . .* (James Moore, Dublin, 1799)

Handbook of British Chronology (2nd edn., 1961)

Hansard, T. C. and others, *Parliamentary Debates* — , — see also Cobbett, W.; Dáil Eireann; Northern Ireland Parliamentary Debates; Parliamentary Register.

Harbinson, J. F., *The Ulster Unionist Party* (Belfast, 1974)

Harcourt, E. W. (ed.), *Harcourt Papers* (Privately printed, Oxford, 1880–1905)

Harkness, D. W., *The Restless Dominion* (1969)

Harris, J. and others, *Buckingham Palace* (1968)

Harris, W., *History of the Life and Reign of William-Henry* (1749)

Harwood, P., *History of the Irish Rebellion of 1798* (1844)

Hawkins, R. A. J. — see Lyons

Hayman, S. and Graves, *Unpublished Geraldine Documents* (1870–81)

Healy, T. M., *Letters and Leaders of My Day* (1928)

Hermathena (Dublin)

Heron, D. C., *Constitutional History of the University of Dublin* (1847)

Hewitt, C., "Catholic grievances, Catholic nationalism and violence in Northern Ireland during the civil rights period: a reconsideration", *British Journal of Sociology* xxxii (1981), 362–80. "Discrimination in Northern Ireland: a rejoinder", ibid., xxxiv (1983), 446–51

Hezlet, Sir A., *The "B" Specials* (1972)

Hibernian Magazine

Hickson, Mary, *Ireland in the Seventeenth Century* (1884)

Higgins, P., "The Wyses of the Manor of St John's Waterford". *Journal of the Waterford & South East Ireland Archaeological Society*, v (1899), 199–206.

History of the Irish Rebellion in the Year 1798 (Alston, Cumberland, 1814)

History of the Rebellion in Ireland in the Year 1798(Workington, 1805)

History of The Times, iii (1947)

Holland, Bernard, Unpublished memoir of the 15th Duke of Norfolk, Arundel papers, quoted by permission of His Grace the Duke of Norfolk.

Holmes, R., *The Little Field Marshal* (1981)

Hoveden, Roger of, *Chronica* (Rolls series, ed. W. Stubbs, 1869)

Hull, Eleanor, "Ireland's Allegiance to the Crown", *Nineteenth Century and After* (Dec. 1921, pp. 1076–86)

Hussey, S. M., *Reminiscences of an Irish Land Agent* (1904)

Hynes, M. J., *Mission of Rinuccini 1645–9* (Université de Louvain, Recueil des Travaux, Conferences d'Histoire et Philologie, sér. 2, fasc. 24, 1932)

Inglis, B., *West Briton* (1962)

Ingram, T. D., *Critical Examination of Irish History* (1900) — *History of the Legislative Union* (1887) — *Two Chapters of Irish History* (1888) — Reply to W. E. Gladstone, *Nineteenth Century*, xxii (1887), 766–90 — see also Gladstone, Rt. Hon. W. E.

An Irish Catholic, *The Government of Lord Aberdeen and the Government of Lord Derby* (Dublin, 1853)

Irish Catholic Directory

Irish Committee of Historical Sciences, *Bulletin*

Irish Daily Independent (Dublin, 1891–1904, continued under different titles)

Irish Ecclesiastical Record

Irish Historical Studies

Irish Independent (Dublin, continuation of *Irish Daily Independent*)

The Irish Law Times and Solicitors' Journal (Dublin)

Irish News (Belfast)

Irish Sword

Irish Times(Dublin)

Irish Unionist Alliance, *Publications* (5 vols, Dublin, 1893–1913)

Jacobite Narrative, edited by J. T. Gilbert (Dublin, 1892)

Jalland, P., "A Liberal Chief Secretary and the Irish Question: Augustine Birrell 1907–1914". *Historical Journal* (xix, 1976, 421–51)

James I and VI, King, *An apologie for the Oath of Allegiance* in *Works* (1616). *Political Works*, edited by C. H. McIlwain (1918)

James, F. G., *Ireland in the Empire 1668–1770* (Harvard Historical Monographs no. 68, Cambridge, Mass., 1973)

Jenkins, H., "The Irish dimension of the British *Kulturkampf*: Vaticanism and civil allegiance 1870–1875", *Journal of Ecclesiastical History* (xxx, 1979), 353–77

Jones, Thomas, (*C. H.*) *Whitehall Diary*, ed. K. Middlemas (1969 —)

Jourdain, H. F. N. and Fraser, *The Connaught Rangers* (1926)

Journal of the Cork Historical and Archaeological Society

Journals of the House of Commons (19 vols, Dublin, 1796–1800)

Journals of the House of Lords (8 vols, Dublin, 1779–1800)

Joy, Henry — See *Belfast Politics*.

Joyce, P. J., *John Healy* (1931)

Keane, Sir John, "Ireland: Comonwealth or Republic?" *Quarterly Review* (Jan. 1934, pp. 154–170)

Kearney, H., "The Irish Parliament in the early seventeenth century," in B. Farrell (ed.), *The Irish Parliamentary Tradition* (1973), pp. 88–101

Kee, Robert, *The Green Flag* (1972)

Kelley, K., *The Longest War* (1982)

Kerr, D. A., *Peel, Priests and Politics* (1982)

Kerry Evening Post

Killarney Echo

King, R., *Primer of History of the Holy Catholic Church in Ireland* (1846)

Lambert, H. A., "Lambert of Wexford." *The Past* (Wexford, Dec. 1921, pp. 129–38)

Lambert, Henry, *Letter on the Currency to . . . Viscount Althorp* (1832)

[Lambert, Henry], *A Memoir of Ireland in 1850 By an ex-M.P.* (Dublin and London, 1851)

Larkin, E., *James Larkin* (1965)

Lawless, John, *Belfast Politics* (1818)

Law Quarterly Review (July 1932)

Lawrence, R. J., *Government of Northern Ireland* (1965)

Laws and Ordinances of the Orange Institution of Ireland (Belfast, 1872)

A Lay Roman Catholic, *A Letter to the Most Reverend Doctor Murray* (1844)

Lazenby, E., *Ireland — a Catspaw* (1928)

Lecky, W. H., *History of Ireland in the Eighteenth Century* (Cabinet edn., 1892)

Lee, Sir Sydney, *King Edward VII* (1925)

Leslie, Sir Shane, *The Film of Memory* (1938)

Leti, Gregorio, *Cromwell* (1692)

Levack, A. P., "Edmund Burke, his friends, and the dawn of Irish Catholic Emancipation", *Catholic Historical Review*, xxxvii (1952), 385–414

Lodge, J., and Archdall, M., *Peerage of Ireland* (1789)

London Gazette (1665 —)

Longford, Earl of, — see Pakenham

Lords Journals (Dublin, 1779–1800)

Lew, S. and Sanders, L. C., *History of England in the Reign of Victoria* (1907)

Lucas, E., *Life of Frederick Lucas* (1886)

Lynch, J., *Cambrensis Eversus* [1662], translated by M. Kelly (Celtic Society, Dublin, 1851–2)

Lynch-Robinson, Sir C., *Last of the Irish R.M.s.* (1951)

Lyons, F. S. L., *John Dillon* (1968)

Lyons, F. S. L. and Hawkins (eds.), *Ireland Under the Union* (1980)

McAllister, I., *The Northern Ireland Social Democratic and Labour Party* (1977)

McAnally, H., *Irish Militia 1793–1816* (1949)

McCaffrey, L. J., *Daniel O'Connell and the Repeal Year* (1966) — "Home Rule and the General Election of 1874 in Ireland", *Irish Historical Studies*, ix (1955), 190–212

MacDonagh, M., *Daniel O'Connell* (1903) — *Viceroy's Post-Bag* (1905) — "The Orange Society", *Contemporary Review*, lxx (August 1896) 215–31

McDonald, W., *Some Ethical Questions of Peace and War* (1919) — , *Reminiscences of a Maynooth Professor* (1925)

McDougall, D. J., "George III, Pitt and the Irish Catholics", *Catholic Historical Review*, xxxi (1945), 255–81

McDowell, R. B., *Ireland in the Age of Imperialism & Revolution 1760–1801 (1979)* — , *Irish Administration 1801–1914* (1964) — , *The Irish Convention* (1970) — , *Public Opinion and Government Policy in Ireland, 1801–46* (1952) — , *Irish Public Opinion 1750–1800* (1944)

McDowell, R. B., and Webb., *Trinity College Dublin* (1982)

MacGeehin, M., "The Catholics of the towns and the quarterage dispute in eighteenth century Ireland". *Irish Historical Studies*, viii (1952), 91–114

Mac Gréil, M., *Prejudice and Tolerance in Ireland* (Dublin, 1977)

Macintyre, A., *The Liberator* (1965)

McKenna, L., Section in Society of Jesus, *A Page of Irish History* (1930)

Mackenna, Theobald, *Constitutional Objections to the Government of Ireland by a Separate Legislature* (Dublin, 1799) — , *A Memoire on some Questions respecting the Projected Union of Great Britain and Ireland* (Dublin, 1799) — , *Political Essays* (1794) — , — see also C. Molyneux, Hamilton.

M'Lennan, J. F., *Life of Drummond* (1867)

MacNeill, Eoin, *Celtic Ireland* (1921) — , *An Claidheamh Soluis* (1 Nov. 1913) — see Martin, F. X.

McNeven, W. J., *Pieces of Irish History* (1807)

Madden, D. O., *Ireland and its Rulers since 1829* (1844)

Magee's Weekly Packet (1777–93)

Magowan, V. — see Deutsch.

Maguire, J. F., *Father Mathew* (1863)

Magurie, Thomas, *The Effects of Home Rule on Higher Education* (1886) — , *England's Duty to Ireland* (1886) — , *Reasons Why Britons should oppose Home Rule* (1886)

Mahaffy, J. P., "Two Early Tours in Ireland", *Hermathena* (Dublin) xviii (1919, 1–16

The Manchester Guardian (1821–1959). Now called *The Guardian*)

Mangan, J. C., "Rosaleen" (1846) in *Poems* (1850)

Mansergh, N., *The Government of Northern Ireland. A Study in Devolution* (1936)

Marjoribanks, E., *The Life of Lord Carson*, i, (1932) — see also Colvin, Ian.

Martin, F. X. and Byrne, F. J., *The Scholar Revolutionary* (1973)

Mathew, Fr. Theobald, — see Rogers, Patrick.

Maxwell, Constantia, *Country and Town in Ireland Under the Georges* (1940)

Micks, W. L., *The Congested Districts Board* (Dublin, 1925)

Midleton, 1st Earl of (St John Brodrick), *Ireland: Dupe or Heroine?* (1932) — , *Records and Reactions* (1939)

Miller, D. W., *Church, State and Nation in Ireland 1898–1921* (1973) — *The Queen's Rebels* (1978)

Mitchel, John, *Life and Times of Aodh O'Neill* (Dublin, 1846)

Mitford, John — see Redesdale

Mokyr, Joel, *Why Ireland Starved* (1983)

Molyneux, C., *A Reply to the Memoire of T. McKenna Esq.* (1799)

Molyneux, William, *The Case of Ireland's being bound by Acts of Parliament in England Stated* (1698)

The Month

Monypenny, W. F., *The Two Irish Nations* (1913)

Moody, T. W., *Davitt* (1981)

Moody, T. W. and Beckett, J. C., *Queen's, Belfast* (1959)

Moody, T. W. and others, *New History of Ireland* iii, 1976)

Moore, F. F., *The Truth about Ulster* (1914)

Moore, G., "Socio-economic aspects of anti-semitism in Ireland, 1880–1905", *Economic & Social Review* (Dublin), xii (1981), 187–201

The Morning Post (London, 1801–1937)

Moxon-Browne, E., *Nation, Class and Creed in Northern Ireland* (1983).

Moylan, Francis, *Pastoral Instructions to the Roman Catholics of the Diocese of Cork* (Dublin, 1798)

Murphy, I., "Some attitudes to religious freedom and ecumenism in pre-Emancipation Ireland." *Irish Ecclesiastical Record*, cv (1966), 93–104

Murphy, J. A., "Priests and people in modern Irish history" *Christus Rex*, xxiii (1969), 235–59

Musgrave, Sir R., *Memoirs of the Different Rebellions in Ireland* (Dublin, 1801)

Napier, Sir George, *Passages in the early military life of General Sir George Napier* (1884)

Nary, Cornelius, *Case of the Roman Catholics of Ireland* — see Reily

The Nation (Dublin, 1842–1900) (title varies)

National Library of Ireland, Dublin: Fingall papers — : Monsell papers

Neville, Henry, *A few remarks on Mr Gladstone's Expostulation with some remarks on "Vaticanism" (1875)*

Newman, John Henry, Cardinal, Autobiographical Writings (1956) — , *Letters and Diaries*, ed. C. S. Dessain (1961 —)

— , *My Campaign in Ireland* (1896)

Newry Reporter (Newry, Co. Down)

Newry Telegraph (1877–1970)

News Letter (Belfast, 1962–) (Formerly called *Belfast News-Letter*)

The New Witness

Nicolson, Sir Harold, *The Desire to Please* (1943) — , *King George V* (1952)

Norman, E. R., *The Catholic Church and Ireland* (1965) — , "The Maynooth Question of 1845', *Irish Historical Studies*, xv (Sept. 1967), 407–37

Northern Ireland Parliamentary Debates (Commons)

Northern Ireland Public Record Office: Ross-of-Bladensburg papers

Northern Whig

Notes from Ireland (Dublin, 1886–1938)

Nowlan, K. B., *The Politics of Repeal* (1965)

O'Brien, J. V., *William O'Brien* (1976)

O'Brien, R. Barry, *The Life of Lord Russell of Killowen* (1901)

O'Brien, W., *Evening Memories* (1920)

O'Brien, W. P., *Great Famine in Ireland* (1896)

Ó Broin, I., *Dublin Castle and the 1916 Rising* (1966), "The Phoenix Conspiracy", *The Irish Sword* (Winter 1980)

O'Callaghan, J. C., *History of the Irish Brigades in the Service of France* (1870)

Observations on the Reply of the Rt Rd Doctor Caulfield . . . to the Misrepresentations of Sir Richard Musgrave (Dublin, 1802)

O'Connell, Daniel, *Correspondence*, edited by M. R. O'Connell (Shannon, 1972–)

O'Connell, M., "Daniel O'Connell and the Irish Eighteenth Century". *Studies in Eighteenth Century Culture*, v (University of Wisconsin Press, 1976)

O'Connor, F. (translator), *Lament for Art O'Leary* (Cuala Press, Dublin, 1940)

O'Connor, Sir James, *History of Ireland 1798–1924* (1925)

O'Crolly, David, *Farewell Address to the Roman Catholics of the Diocese of Cork* (Dublin, 1836)

O'Donovan J., "The Anatomy of the Volunteers in Cork, 1775–1782", *Journal of the Cork Historical and Archaeological Society*, lxxxvii (1982), part II, 118–27

O'Ferrall, F., " 'The only lever . . .?' The Catholic Priest in Irish politics 1823–29", *Studies* (Winter, 1981) pp. 308–324

O'Flanagan, J. R., *The Irish Bar* (1879)

O'Grady, H., *Strafford and Ireland* (1923)

O'Hagan, Thomas (Lord), *Occasional Papers and Addresses* (1884)

O'Hegarty, P. S., *The Victory of Sinn Fein* (1924)

O'Kelly, C., *Excidium Macariae* [1692] ed. T. C. Croker (Camden Society, 1841)

O'Leary, Arthur, *Collected Works* (Boston, 1868)

Oliver, J. A., *Working at Stormont* (1978)

O'Neill, Terence, Lord O'Neill of the Maine, *Autobiography* (1972)

Orange Institution of Ireland, *Laws and Ordinances* (Belfast, 1872)

O'Rahilly, T. F., *Early Irish History and Mythology* (1946)

Ordnance Survey of Ireland (1837)

O'Reilly, B., *John MacHale* (1890)

Ó'Tuathaigh, M. A. G., *Thomas Drummond and the Government of Ireland* (O'Donnell Lecture, 1977)

Otway-Ruthven, J., "Anglo-Irish shire government in the thirteenth century" *Irish Historical Studies*, v (1940), 1–28

Owen, Frank, *Tempestuous Journey* (1954)

Oxford Dictionary of Quotations (3rd edn., 1979)

The Oxford English Dictionary (1933); *A Supplement to the Oxford English Dictionary* (1972—)

Pakenham, Frank (Earl of Longford), *Peace by Ordeal* (1972)

Pakenham, Thomas, *The Year of Liberty* (1969)

Pall Mall Gazette

Parker, C. S., *Sir Robert Peel* (1891)

Parliamentary Command Papers (Westminster): C. 8262 (1896); C. 8734, 8859, 8925 (1898); Cd. 1622 (1903); Cd. 3267 (1906); Cd. 7631, 7649 (1914–16); Cd. 8311 (1916); Cd. 8279 (1916).

Parliamentary Command Paper (Belfast): Cmd. 532.

The Parliamentary Register; or, History of the Proceedings and Debates of the House of Commons of Ireland (1781–1795, 15 vols (Dublin, 1784–95)

Parnell, William, *Historical Apology for the Irish Catholics* (Dublin, 1807)

Pawley, B. and M., *Rome and Canterbury Through Four Centuries* (Revised and abridged edn., 1981)

Pellow, G., *Life of Sidmouth* (1847)

Phillips, O. Hood, *Constitutional and Administrative Law* (1978)

Phillips, W. A., *Revolution in Ireland* (1923)

Plowden, Francis, *History of Ireland* (1809) — , *History of Ireland 1801–1810* (1811) — , *Historical Review of the State of Ireland* (1803)

Plunkett, A. J. — see Fingall

Plunkett, Elizabeth — see Fingall

Plunkett, Horace, *Ireland in the New Century* (1905)

Portland MSS (Historical Manuscripts Commission, 1891–1931)

Powicke, Sir M. and Fryde, E. B., *Handbook of British Chronology* (1961)

Powell, J. Enoch, "Kilmainham — The Treaty that Never Was", *Historical Journal* xxi (1978), 949–59

Power, Frank, *Letters from Khartoum* (1885)

Public Record Office (London, Kew): Dominions Office Files; Home Office Files; Midleton Papers; Prime Minister's papers

Public Record Office of Northern Ireland. Educational facsimile no. 105. Ross-of-Bladensburg Papers.

Quarterly Review

Quinn, D. B., "Anglo-Irish local government, 1485–1534" *Irish Historical Studies*, (1939), 354–81

Redesdale, Lord (John Mitford, afterwards Freeman) and Fingall, 8th Earl of, *The Catholic Question: Correspondence between Lord Redesdale . . . and . . . The Earl of Fingall* (1804)

Reid, B. L., *The Lives of Roger Casement* (1976)

Reid, T. W., *Life of Forster* (1970)

Reilly, S. M. P., *Aubrey de Vere* (University of Nebraska Press, 1953)

Reily, S., *Impartial History of Ireland . . . to which is annexed . . . the Case of the Roman Catholicks of Ireland . . . by Doctor Nary* (1754)

The Repealer Repulsed (Belfast, 1841)

Reply of the Rt. Revd Dr Caulfield R.C. Bishop and of the R.C. Clergy of Wexford to . . . Sir Richard Musgrave (Dublin, 1801)

Reports of Debates in the House of Commons of Ireland (Dublin, 1797)

Reynolds, J. A., *The Catholic Emancipation Crisis in Ireland 1823–9* (1954)

Rhodes, A., article in *The Tablet*, 22 May 1982, pp. 510–3.

Richardson, H. G. and Sayles, G. O., *The Irish Parliament in the Middle Ages* (1952)

Richardson, Joanna, *Enid Starkie* (1973)

Rogers, Patrick, *Father Theobald Mathew: Apostle of Temperance* (Dublin, 1943) — , *Irish Volunteers and Catholic Emancipation 1778–93* (1934)

A Roman Catholic, *The Liberal Party in Ireland . . . Its Present Condition and Prospects* (Dublin, 1862)

A Roman Catholic Barrister, *Letter to the Duke of Wellington . . . on the Justice and Expediency of Catholic Emancipation* (1828)

Ronan, M. V., *Reformation in Dublin* (1926)

Rose, C. Richard, *Governing Without Consensus* (1971)

Rosenbaum, S., *Against Home Rule: The Case for the Union* (1912)

Rossi, J. P. "English Catholics, the Liberal Party and the General Election of 1880", *Catholic Historical Review* lxiii (1977), pp. 411–27

Royal Commission on Historical Manuscripts: *Report on the Papers of Sir John Pope Hennessy* (Cyclostyled, Bodleian Library, 1974)

Russell, G. W. E., *Gladstone* (1891)

Russell, Thomas, *Relation of the FitzGerald's of Ireland* [1638] — see Hayman, S., & Graves (vol. i)

Rutland MSS (Historical Manuscripts Commission)

Sanders, L. C., see Low.

Saturday Review (London, 1855–1938)

Sayles, G. O. — see Richardson

"Scrutator", *Ultramontanism versus Education in Ireland* (1875)

Senior, Nassau, "Ireland in 1843" in *Journals . . . relating to Ireland* (1868)

Seward, W. W., *Collectanea Politica* (1804)

Shaw of Dunfermline, Lord, — see Craigmyle

Shaw, Francis, "The canon of Irish history: a challenge", *Studies* (Summer 1972)

Shea, P., *Voices and the Sound of Drums* (1981)

Shearman, Hugh, in *Yearbook of World Affairs* (1982)

Sheehy, P., *Union and Plague* (1799)

Sheil, R. L., "Catholic Leaders and Associations", in *Sketches Legal and Political* (1855)

Shipp, John, *Memoirs of John Shipp* (1843)

Simms, J. G., *Jacobite Ireland* (1969)

Sinnott, R. — see Davis

Sligo Independent (1855–1927)

Smith, Adam, *Wealth of Nations* (1776)

Society of Jesus, *A Page of Irish History: the Story of University College Dublin* (1930)

Solow, B. L., *The Land Question and the Irish Economy*, Cambridge, Mass., 1981. "A new look at the Irish land question". *Economic & Social Review* (Dublin) vol. XII (July 1981) pp. 301–14.

Some Thoughts Humbly Offer'd Towards an Union between Great-Britain and Ireland (J. Morphew, London, 1708)

Spender, J. A., *Life of Herbert Henry Asquith* (1932)

Stanhope, P. H., 5th Earl, *Life of the Rt. Hon. William Pitt* (1861–2)

Starkie, Enid, *A Lady's Child* (1941)

State Papers, Calendar of the (Ireland)

State Papers of John Thurloe (1742)

The Statutes at large, passed in the Parliaments held in Ireland (20 vols., Dublin, 1786–1801)

The Statutes of the Realm (1101–1713) (Record Commission, London, 1810–28)

Stewart, A. T. Q., *Edward Carson* (1981) — , *The Narrow Ground* (1977) — , *Ulster Crisis* (1967)

The Strabane Chronicle [etc] (Strabane, Co. Tyrone)

Stuart, James, *Historical Memoirs of the City of Armagh* (1900)

Studies (Dublin)

Studies in Eighteenth-Century Culture

Sullivan, A. M. (1830–1884), *New Ireland* (1877)

Sullivan, A. M. (1871–1959), *Old Ireland* (1927)

Sunday Times "Insight" team, *Ulster* (1972)

A Supplement to the Oxford English Dictionary (1972–)

Taafe, Nicholas, Viscount, *Observations on Affairs in Ireland . . . 1691 to the Present* (1766)

The Tablet

Talbot-Crosbie Papers: Trinity College, Dublin

Tallents, Sir Stephen, *Man and Boy* (1943)

[Thackeray, W. M.], *Irish Sketch-Book 1842* (1863)

This Week

Thoresby Society — see Clay

Thornley, D., "The Irish Conservatives and Home Rule, 1869–73", *Irish Historical Studies*, xi (1958), 200–22

Thurloe, John, *State Papers* (1742)

Tierney, M., *Croke of Cashel* (1976)

Time and Tide

The Times — see also *History of* The Times

Tipperary Constitution

Titmarsh, M. A. [pseudonym] — see Thackeray.

Tone, W. T. W. (ed.), *Life of Wolfe Tone* (Washington, 1826)

A Tour Through Ireland In Several Entertaining Letters . . . By two English Gentlemen (J. Roberts, London, 1748)

Townshend, C., *British Campaign in Ireland 1919–21* (1975)

Transactions of the Royal Historical Society

Trial for Libel in the Anti-Jacobin Review (1805)

Trinity College Dublin: Talbot-Crosbie papers

Trollope, Anthony, *The Land Leaguers* (1883)

Troy v. Symonds — see *Trial* . . .

Tuckwell, G. M., see Gwynn, S. L.

Tyrone Constitution (Omagh, Co. Tyrone)

Ullswater, Viscount, *A Speaker's Commentaries* (1925)

Ulster Herald (Omagh, Co. Tyrone)

Ulster Unionist Convention Belfast 17 June 1892, *Report* . . . (Belfast)

Unionist Convention for Provinces of Leinster, Munster and Connaught, *Report of Proceedings* (Dublin, 1892)

The Universe

University of Toronto Law Journal

Victoria, H.M. Queen, *The Letters of Queen Victoria*, edited by A. C. Benson and others (1907–32); *Tours in England and Ireland* and *Yachting Excursions* in *Leaves from the Journal of Our Life in the Highlands* (1868)

Walker, B. M., *Parliamentary Election Results in Ireland 1801–1922* (Royal Irish Academy, 1978)

Wall, Maureen, "Catholic Loyalty to King and Pope in Eighteenth Century Ireland", *Proceedings of the Irish Catholic Historical Committee* (Dublin, 1961); *The Penal Laws* (Irish Historical Association, 1976)

Walpole, S., *History of England from . . . 1815* (1878–1886)

Walsh, P., *The More Ample Accompt. The answers to the exceptions, the inducements, and invitation, promised in the Advertisement annexed to the late printed Remonstrance, Protestation &c of the Clergy of Ireland* (1662); *A Prospect of the State of Ireland, from the Year of the World, 1756, to . . . the Year of Christ, 1652* (London, 1682)

Walsh, P. J., *W. J. Walsh* (1928)

Walsh, W. J., *O'Connell, Archbishop Murray and the Board of Charitable Bequests* (Dublin, 1916)

Ward, B., *The Eve of Catholic Emancipation* (1912)

Ward, W., *Aubrey de Vere* (1904)

Warren, W. L., *Henry II* (1973)

Waterford Mirror

Webb, Alfred, *Compendium of Irish Biography* (1878)

Webb, D. A. — see McDowell and Webb

Webb, S. J. and Beatrice (Lord and Lady Passfield), *History of Trade Unionism* (1920)

Wesley, John, *Journals*

The Wexford Herald (Wexford)

The Wexford Independent (1830–1906)

White, T. de Vere, *Road of Excess* (1946)

Who was Who

Whyte, J. H., *Church and State in Modern Ireland* (1980) — , *The Independent Irish Party* (1958)

Whyte, John, "How much discrimination was there under the Unionist regime 1921–68?", in T. Gallagher and J. O'Connell (eds) *Contemporary Irish Studies* (Manchester University Press, 1983), pp. 1–35

Wilberforce, William. *Life*. By his sons. (1838)

Willman, R., "The Origins of 'Whig' and 'Tory' in English political language". *Historical Journal*, vol. XVII (1974), pp. 267–64.

Winton, John. *The Victoria Cross at Sea* (1978)

Witherow, T., *Boyne and Aghrim* (1879)

Wood, H., Paper in *Proceedings of the Royal Irish Academy*, vol. XXXVIII (1928–9), pp. 51–68

Woods, C. J., "Ireland and Anglo-Papal relations 1880–85". *Irish Historical Studies*, vol. XVIII (1972), pp. 29–60. See also in Lyons, F. S. L. and Hawkins, *Ireland Under the Union* (1980)

Woulfe, Stephen, *Report of a Speech Delivered by Stephen Woulfe* (Dublin, 1816)

Wynne, M., *An Irishman and his Family* (1937)

Wyse, T., *Education Reform* (1836) — , *Historical Sketch of the Late Catholic Association of Ireland* (1829)

Yearbook of World Affairs (New Commonwealth Institute of World Affairs, London)

Young, Arthur, *Tour in Ireland 1776–9* (1892)

Young, C., *A State of Disunion* (1972)

Young, P. M., *Elgar O. M.* (1955)

Index